PIMLICO

621

THE WORST JOURNEY IN THE WORLD

Apsley Cherry-Garrard (1886-1959) was one of the youngest members of Captain Scott's final expedition to the Antarctic. He was away for almost three years. During his first winter down South, he was chosen as one of the three-man team which trekked to Cape Crozier to collect the eggs of the Emperor penguin, and he later served in the First World War. With the zealous encouragement of his neighbour, George Bernard Shaw, Cherry-Garrard wrote *The Worst Journey in the World* (1922), universally acknowledged as the finest work of literature ever to emerge from the Antarctic.

Sara Wheeler is the author of *Terra Incognita*, of which Geoffrey Moorhouse said, 'I cannot believe anything better will ever be written about Antarctica' and the critically acclaimed *Cherry: A Life of Apsley Cherry-Garrard*.

THE WORST JOURNEY
IN THE WORLD

Antarctica 1910–13

———

APSLEY
CHERRY-GARRARD

With an introduction by
Sara Wheeler

PIMLICO

Published by Pimlico 2003

4 6 8 10 9 7 5

Copyright © Angela Mathias 1922, 1965

Introduction © Sara Wheeler 2003

Maps redrawn by E. J. Hatch from the author's original design

First published in Great Britain by Constable and Co., 1922
Pimlico edition 2003

Pimlico
Random House, 20 Vauxhall Bridge Road,
London SW1V 2SA

Random House Australia (Pty) Limited
20 Alfred Street, Milsons Point, Sydney,
New South Wales 2061, Australia

Random House New Zealand Limited
18 Poland Road, Glenfield,
Auckland 10, New Zealand

Random House South Africa (Pty) Limited
Endulini, 5A Jubilee Road, Parktown 2193, South Africa

Random House UK Limited Reg. No. 954009

A CIP catalogue record for this book
is available from the British Library

ISBN 1-8441-3103-3

Papers used by Random House UK Limited are natural,
recyclable products made from wood grown in sustainable forests.
The manufacturing processes conform to the environmental
regulations of the country of origin

Printed and bound in Great Britain by
Bookmarque Ltd, Croydon, Surrey

Contents

List of Maps

Introduction to the Pimlico edition

The Worst Journey in the World is a masterpiece and its author is a hero — a true hero, I mean, not one of those tinpot adventurers who crowd the front pages in our own gruesomely unheroic age. He was a vital protagonist in an epic feat of exploration, survived against what seemed like insuperable odds in the middle of heartbreaking beauty and crucifying hardship, lost his two best friends, his health and his peace of mind to boot — then he went and redeemed those losses by transforming them, on the page, into an allegory of hope that will uplift the human spirit till the next ice age. What more can you ask of a hero?

He was born Apsley Cherry in 1886, still a sunlit era for the English landed classes. The roar of the now fabled technological progress of nineteenth-century Britain could barely be heard in genteel Bedford: the streets were lit by gas, the cabs were drawn by horses, the swollen tribes of domestic servants had not yet shrunk, even in the red-brick street where baby Apsley mewled. His father, another Apsley, was a solid and upstanding member of the officer class, but in fact he was not yet landed: all that was to come.

Fifty-three-year-old Colonel Cherry had recently returned from more than twenty years soldiering in India and Africa*. The walrus-whiskered veteran was enjoying a peacetime post in command of Kempston Barracks on the outskirts of Bedford, and there he had met and married Evelyn Sharpin, the young daughter of an eminent local doctor. Apsley senior was descended from a prosperous line of lawyers and colonial civil servants who had lately settled in Berkshire. When, in 1887, his elder brother died unexpectedly without issue, the startled colonel found himself the owner of Denford Manor, near Newbury, and other properties besides. He promptly retired from the regiment

---

*   More detailed biographical information follows in George
      Seaver's Foreword to the 1965 edition.

with the rank of honorary major-general and shifted his family – Apsley junior already had a sister – down to leafy Berkshire. Five years later, when the general's aunt, Honora Drake Garrard, also died without issue, he inherited a much bigger estate up in Hertfordshire, and a minor fortune to go with it. As a condition of the inheritance he was obliged to take his aunt's name in addition to his own. And so, in 1892, the name Cherry-Garrard came into existence.

The burgeoning family – two more girls had arrived – duly installed themselves in their new home, Lamer Park, just outside Wheathampstead. The house was a model of eighteenth-century architectural chastity (it was always said, in the family, that Robert Adam had been employed there), with well-stocked parkland landscaped by Humphry Repton in the golden age of the English country house estate. Apsley junior shortly submitted to the rigours of prep school in the bracing air of Folkestone, and after that seven modestly unhappy years at Winchester College were followed by a slightly more satisfactory stint as an undergraduate at Christ Church, Oxford, where his father and grandfather had preceded him. His eyesight was very poor, and the difficulties this caused him were compounded by his shyness, and by his paralysing anxiety. He read Classics at first, but soon switched to Modern History. He was not an especially gifted scholar, and was awarded a third-class degree.

Sisters persisted, and Cherry, as he came to be known, was finally outnumbered by five to one. When his father died in 1907 he became a substantial landowner and head of the family, a responsibility he took seriously, but did not enjoy. After graduating, he went off round the world on a cargo ship. He was five feet ten, slim and handsome, with glossy dark brown hair, chocolate-brown eyes and well-proportioned features. The trouble was, he didn't know what to do with himself. When he travelled up to Scotland in the early autumn of 1908 for a spot of shooting at a lodge owned by his cousin Reginald Smith, he was at a loose end. But there he met Edward 'Bill' Wilson, the doctor and naturalist who had accompanied Scott to the Antarctic on his first journey, in 1901. A committed Christian with marble-blue eyes and a raking stride, Wilson walked with his new friend through the purple mists of the grouse moors and told him stories about long marches and lonely camps in the bloodless snowfields of the south. Cherry had grown up with his father's tales of bivvying on the veldt, and, like all schoolboys, he had pored over images of little wooden ships in the pincers of ice floes inching their way up the north-west passage, or of stout-hearted Britons battling their way through the broiling, malarial heart of Africa. He determined to apply for a position on Scott's second expedition.

Here *The Worst Journey in the World* takes up the baton. Cherry explains how he came to be appointed zoological assistant, and how the *Terra Nova* steamed out of Cardiff in June 1910 among a flotilla of flag-bedecked tugs. He was twenty-four when he sailed south, and, two-and-a-half years later, he came back a different man. England was different too. Those years – 1910 to 1913 – turned out to be the most tumultuous of the twentieth century for Britain. The comfy certainties of Cherry's youth ('God in his heaven,' as his exact contemporary Siegfried Sassoon put it, 'and sausages for breakfast') had vanished as if in, it seemed to the young polar explorer in his bewilderment, a single national gulp.

In the first weeks of 1914 the doughty denizens of the Committee in charge of Scott's expedition, busily ensuring that its reputation was moulded by their hands alone, asked Cherry if he would write the official narrative, setting down for posterity the story of the whole show (as Scott's deputy, Teddy Evans was first in line for the job, but he was too busy). Cherry was delighted, and with characteristic diligence began interviewing scientists and seamen, writing to firms which had supplied equipment and amassing piles of paper listing exactly what had gone south with the *Terra Nova*. Essentially, he was at that stage planning to compile a guide for future explorers. Then the war came, and he hurried off to command a battalion of armoured cars in Flanders. After a few months, having seen little action, Cherry was invalided home with ulcerative colitis, a debilitating condition often associated with anxiety and one for which there was no sure cure. His convalescence was long, and painful, but through it, his thoughts on his book matured. In his attitude to writing he was influenced in no small measure by a friendly neighbour whose land abutted his own – George Bernard Shaw, the most famous author in the world.

A fugleman for those out of step with the times, Shaw was an ideal companion and mentor for Cherry. I do not think *The Worst Journey* would be so wonderful had the two men never met. Shaw helped Cherry realise that he did not want to write the standard expedition narrative, some wooden affair lacking any psychological light and shade. By the start of 1920, Cherry had severed his links with the expedition committee and turned himself into an independent author. His working title was now 'Never Again: Scott, Some Penguins and the Pole' (he had briefly considered calling the book, 'To Hell: With Scott'). Although 'Never Again' survived at the top of his powerful final chapter, Cherry realised that the title was a weak one for a whole book. In a letter drafted (but never sent) to the Arctic explorer Vilhjalmur Steffansson, Cherry later revealed, 'it was objected that it [the title] was too much like, "Christ, Some Coppers and the Cross".' This last has a Shavian ring.

In December 1922 *The Worst Journey in the World* appeared in a two-volume edition financed by the author and distributed by the publishing firm Constable. Together the books tell the story of the expedition from beginning to end: but Cherry draws a landscape, not a map. The Winter Journey to Cape Crozier lies at the heart of the narrative, both literally and emotionally; this is the journey that was the worst in the world. In the tar blackness of a polar winter Cherry and his friends Bill Wilson and Henry 'Birdie' Bowers trekked across Ross Island to the Cape Crozier rookery to collect the eggs of the Emperor penguin. At that time it was thought that Emperor embryos, if examined at a sufficiently early stage of development, would provide a vital link in the evolutionary chain (a theory subsequently disproved). The three men did not take dogs: they pulled their own sledges for five weeks, often over ice ridges that were six feet high. The temperature fell to minus seventy-six degrees Fahrenheit, their teeth shattered in the cold and the tent blew away. But they were still friends when they staggered back to the hut. 'In civilisation', Cherry wrote, 'men are taken at their own valuation because there are so many ways of concealment, and there is so little time, perhaps even so little understanding. Not so down South. These two men … were gold, pure, shining, unalloyed.'

The following February, after marching more than half way to the Pole earlier in the season, Cherry took a team of dogs out from the hut as winter shouldered in across the polar plateau. He drove them 130 miles south to a food depôt in order to wait for Captain Scott and his four companions, expected home from the Pole any day. Cherry tells the story, in *The Worst Journey*, of the decisions he made on this abortive trip, and why he made them. But he could have made other decisions, and they might have led to other outcomes. He could never forget it. In November of that same year he pushed back the cambric flap of a small tent buried in drift fewer than thirteen miles from where he had made his last camp on that dog journey – the last camp, that is, before turning back. In the stygian gloom he made out Birdie and Bill, frozen solid, like wood, and lying on either side of Scott. All three had perished on the return march from the Pole. 'That scene,' Cherry wrote, 'can never leave my memory.' Many years later he said that his book – this book – was in fact a memorial to Bill and Birdie. 'It is hard', Cherry wrote, 'that often such men must go first when others far less worthy remain.'

So what about the book? It is a graceful blend of narrative, reflection and anecdote threaded with literary reference and allusion and the occasional historical digression. Cherry is a very English writer, his prose characterised by quizzical detachment, a fine sense of irony and an infinite capacity for gloom tempered with elegiac melancholy. The bitter brilliance of his sentences glimmers with dignified scepticism. As a stylist he is Mozart rather than Wagner, eschewing sonorous tempests in favour of harmonious quadrilles and sonatas. No writer is a more faithful adherent to Flaubert's dictum prescribing clarity, clarity, clarity: the words of *The Worst Journey* are as plain as crotchets on a stave.

It was instantly recognised as a modern classic, a few dissenting voices notwithstanding. The London *Evening Standard* reviewer called it 'the most wonderful story in the world', and Shaw announced that its success, 'has exceeded all expectations'. As the double-decker cost three guineas, the price of a weekend at the seaside, the books hardly raced off the shelves; but to Cherry, the thought that he had put the record straight was more important. 'It has done what I specifically wanted it to do', he wrote to his printer, '– get the business into some kind of perspective and proportion'. But he did want the book read, and to his unending delight, throughout his lifetime many other editions followed the Constable original, both overseas and in Britain. (The work first appeared as a single volume in 1937.) After a hesitant start in the United States, a country Cherry profoundly mistrusted, in the spring of 1930 the Dial Press finally brought out a successful edition. 'Where shall the likes of it', asked the *New York Times* reviewer, 'be read for sheer strength, clarity and beauty of phrase in the literature of polar exploration?' Dial's timing was flawless: Antarctica had not been off the front pages for months, as the young Virginian naval pilot Richard Byrd had just claimed to have flown over the South Pole in an aluminium aeroplane – the first man there since Scott. But the *Bookman* was far more impressed with Cherry's story. 'It makes Byrd's journey', the review read, ' . . . seem no more harassing than a train trip from Albany to Troy.' 'He [Cherry] is plainly far more intelligent than most explorers', wrote H. L. Mencken in the *American Mercury*, though this was not a hotly contested field. Back at home, in June 1937, two smart sixpenny volumes appeared as numbers 99 and 100 in Allen Lane's revolutionary Penguin series. A poster was printed depicting a penguin with a cricket bat tucked under one flipper bowing to a distant crowd. 'We celebrate our centenary', read the caption, 'with Mr Cherry-Garrard's *Worst Journey in the World*'.

Many officers and scientists on Scott's team also wrote books about the expedition. None has lasted: all take a factual approach that ignores a whole layer of emotional and imaginative experience. The Antarctic committee rushed out an edited version of Scott's diary in 1913, and it is rightly recognised as a significant contribution to the literature of exploration. But Scott has lost his mythic status, and the diary reads now more like a historical document than a work of art. (In our own tawdry times, Scott has come in for the usual wallop of historical revisionism – it is, for heroes, after all, as unavoidable as the grave. Shackleton has risen up to challenge the hegemony of Scott as the Antarctic explorer par excellence. Sir Ernest was a showman. He drank too much, smoked too much and slept with other men's wives: that's why we like him. He's like we'd like to be. Poor old Scott, on the other hand, was shy, and discreet, and prone to depression – like we are.) And of course, the world has shrunk: even young women writers find their way to the South Pole these days, and the bookshelves are jammed with tales of contemporary polar derring-do. But *The Worst Journey in the World* has endured. Why? Because, like all great writers (and he is a great writer), Cherry frees his story from the shackles of time and place and ushers it into the immortal zone. Yes, he conjures a specific landscape (who can forget his descriptions of the pleated, blue-shadowed cliffs of a glacier, the patter of dogs whooshing across the snowcrust and the friendly smell of tobacco at the end of a long day on the trail?) Yes, he writes about crampons and snowgoggles. But his description and detail are a means to an end. The book is a parable, which is what he most wanted it to be. It is about not the winning or the losing (or being the fastest or the first without oxygen or any other superlative); it is about 'the response of the spirit': a notion as valid today as it was in 1922 or in 1322. 'We did not forget the please and the thank you', Cherry noted in his account of the trek to Cape Crozier. 'And we kept our tempers, even with God.' And so the book is not just about what happened at the South Pole in 1912. It is about me and you and here and now; it is about leaky taps and finding the money to pay the gas bill and discovering that perhaps one isn't quite the person one thought one was. You could say the same about the *Iliad*, or the *Nun's Priest's Tale*. After all, as Cherry acknowledged, we all have our winter journeys, sooner or later. And if you march them, he concluded (you see there really is hope there, at the bottom of it all), 'you will have your reward, so long as all you want is a penguin's egg.'

The book was published in the same year as *The Waste Land* and *Ulysses*, works that epitomised the new wave of literary modernism. Both Cherry and *The Worst Journey* are at first glance deeply traditional. Yet a central preoccupation of each, the notion of the sterility and fragmentation of post-war western culture, is also a vital modernist theme – as in Eliot's 'heap of broken images'. So Cherry wasn't entirely out of step.

Cherry married Angela Turner in September 1939 (it was a popular time to get married). She was a land agent's daughter from Ipswich, and thirty years his junior. Theirs was a happy union, though there were desperately bleak periods when Cherry submitted to catastrophic nervous breakdowns and what would today be diagnosed as clinical depression. As Cherry's biographer I am often asked whether his experiences in the south, above all his loss of his most loved friends and the vague sense that he might have been able to save them, 'caused' his mental collapse. Of course, I do not know. I think Cherry was genetically predisposed to depression, and he might well have entered his dark tunnels if he had never been south of Brighton. After all, many do. But events in the Antarctic did not help him cope with his anxiety. In short, a toxic combination of genes and events set off a dysfunctional reaction in his neurotransmittors that brought him down.

He died in 1959 at the age of seventy-three, of congestive heart failure and bronchopneumonia.

Who was Cherry? He was a cynic, and a committed pessimist. He responded deeply to literature, and was not very interested in God. Like many authors, he found writing easier than speaking. He liked ice cream and strong coffee, enjoyed birdwatching and book collecting. In middle age he was, in many ways, a curmudgeonly reactionary: he complained a lot, he had an obsessive hatred of vicars and income tax, and he was convinced that the world was going – had gone, rather – to the dogs ('This post-war business is inartistic', he wrote in the little-read preface to the second edition of *The Worst Journey*, 'for it is seldom that anyone does anything well for the sake of doing it well.') But in his heart he was a romantic: he believed in the redemptive powers of both nature and art. How can you resist a man who wrote of the Antarctic photographs taken by Scott's 'camera artist' Herbert Ponting, 'Here in these pictures is beauty linked to tragedy – one of the great tragedies – and the beauty is inconceivable for it is endless and runs through eternity.' Somewhere in the deeper recesses of his consciousness, Cherry believed (I believe) in the perfectibility of the human spirit. In an introduction to George Seaver's 1938 biography of Bowers, Cherry wrote of Birdie's 'spirit without boundaries.' He went on to say that Birdie and his companions 'have left something behind in men's minds; it is shadowy and intangible and perhaps a little fanciful, but it is something greater than all the pyramids in the world, and much more important.' Indeed.

Cherry was thirty-six when *The Worst Journey* was published. In many places his book – he only wrote one, as he had nothing further to say – reads like a restless threnody for lost youth; the disquiet of a man approaching middle-age sings through the clear prose. There are moments of pure Chekhovian longing as he contemplates the good gone days ('And the good times were such as the Gods might have envied us') and mourns the grubby superficiality of the present ('For we are a nation of shopkeepers'). It is this strand of lyricism that gives the book its poetry – and it is profoundly poetic. As a writer Cherry had flawless instincts, however, and he recognised that the tone of wistful recollection and sorrow had to be leavened with humour. 'Polar exploration', he began robustly, 'is at once the cleanest and most isolated way of having a bad time which has been devised.' He smuggled in a lot of jokes.

The greatest adventure book of all time? I think so. None other combines such a thrillingly gripping story with such heartbreaking prose: no, I cannot think of a single one that comes close. *Seven Pillars of Wisdom*? As a writer, Lawrence is a lightweight next to Cherry. Maurice Herzog's *Annapurna*? Fabulous, but in the end, it's just about mountains. *Arabian Sands*? A classic, but it lacks the Homeric touch. From the crucible of suffering, Cherry fashioned a great work of art. Like all writers, he goes on talking after his death – and we should listen. *The Worst Journey*, as its author wrote, 'is a story about human minds with all kinds of ideas and questions involved, which stretch beyond the furthest horizons.'

Notes

Introduction

POLAR EXPLORATION is at once the cleanest and most
isolated way of having a bad time which has been
devised. It is the only form of adventure in which you put on
your clothes at Michaelmas and keep them on until
Christmas, and, save for a layer of the natural grease of the
body, find them as clean as though they were new. It is more
lonely than London, more secluded than any monastery, and
the post comes but once a year. As men will compare the
hardships of France, Palestine, or Mesopotamia, so it would
be interesting to contrast the rival claims of the Antarctic as a
medium of discomfort. A member of Campbell's party tells
me that the trenches at Ypres were a comparative picnic. But
until somebody can evolve a standard of endurance I am
unable to see how it can be done. Take it all in all, I do not
believe anybody on earth has a worse time than an Emperor
penguin.

Even now the Antarctic is to the rest of the earth as the
Abode of the Gods was to the ancient Chaldees, a precipitous
and mammoth land lying far beyond the seas which encircled
man's habitation, and nothing is more striking about the
exploration of the Southern Polar regions than its absence,
for when King Alfred reigned in England the Vikings were
navigating the ice-fields of the North; yet when Wellington
fought the battle of Waterloo there was still an undiscovered
continent in the South.

For those who wish to read an account of the history of
Antarctic exploration there is an excellent chapter in Scott's
Voyage of the Discovery and elsewhere. I do not propose to
give any general survey of this kind here but complaints have
been made to me that *Scott's Last Expedition* plunges the
general reader into a neighbourhood which he is supposed to
know all about, while actually he is lost, having no idea what
the *Discovery* was, or where Castle Rock or Hut Point stand.
For the better understanding of the references to particular

expeditions to the lands discovered by them and the traces left by them, which must occur in this book I give the following brief introduction.

From the earliest days of the making of maps of the Southern Hemisphere it was supposed that there was a great continent called Terra Australis. As explorers penetrated round the Cape of Good Hope and Cape Horn, and found nothing but stormy oceans beyond, and as, later, they discovered Australia and New Zealand, the belief in this continent weakened, but was not abandoned. During the latter half of the eighteenth century eagerness for scientific knowledge was added to the former striving after individual or State aggrandizement.

Cook, Ross and Scott; these are the aristocrats of the South.

It was the great English navigator James Cook who laid the foundations of our knowledge. In 1772 he sailed from Deptford in the *Resolution*, 462 tons, and the *Adventure*, 336 tons, ships which had been built at Whitby for the coal trade. He was, like Nansen, a believer in a varied diet as one of the preventives of scurvy, and mentions that he had among his provisions 'besides Saur Krout, Portable Broth, Marmalade of Carrots and Suspissated Juice of Wort and Beer.' Medals were struck 'to be given to the natives of new discovered countries, and left there as testimonies of our being the first discoverers.'[1] It would be interesting to know whether any exist now.

After calling at the Cape of Good Hope Cook started to make his Easting down to New Zealand, purposing to sail as far south as possible in search of a southern continent. He sighted his first 'ice island' or iceberg in latitude 50° 40' S., longitude 2° 0' E., on December 10, 1772. The next day he 'saw some white birds about the size of pigeons with blackish bills and feet. I never saw any such before.'[2] These must have been Snowy petrel. Passing through many bergs, where he notices how the albatross left them and penguins appeared, he was brought up by thick pack ice along which he coasted. Under the supposition that this ice was formed in bays and rivers Cook was led to believe that land was not far distant. Incidentally he remarks that in order to enable his men to support the colder weather he 'caused the sleeves of their jackets (which were so short as to expose their arms) to be lengthened with baize; and had a cap made for each man of the same stuff, together with canvas; which proved of great service to them.'[3]

For more than a month Cook sailed the Southern Ocean, always among bergs and often among pack. The weather was consistently bad and generally thick; he mentions that he had only seen the moon once since leaving the Cape.

It was on Sunday, January 17, 1773, that the Antarctic Circle was crossed for the first time, in longitude 39° 35′ E. After proceeding to latitude 67° 15′ S. he was stopped by an immense field of pack. From this point he turned back and made his way to New Zealand.

Leaving New Zealand at the end of 1773 without his second ship, the *Adventure*, from which he had been parted, he judged from the great swell that 'there can be no land to the southward, under the meridian of New Zealand, but what must lie very far to the south.' In latitude 62° 10′ S. he sighted the first ice island on December 12, and was stopped by thick pack ice three days later. On the 20th he again crossed the Antarctic Circle in longitude 147° 46′ W. and penetrated in this neighbourhood to a latitude of 67° 31′ S. Here he found a drift towards the north-east.

On January 26, 1774, in longitude 109° 31′ W., he crossed the Antarctic Circle for the third time, after meeting no pack and only a few icebergs. In latitude 71° 10′ S. he was finally turned back by an immense field of pack, and wrote:

'I will not say it was impossible anywhere to get farther to the south; but the attempting it would have been a dangerous and rash enterprise, and what, I believe, no man in my situation would have thought of. It was indeed, my opinion, as well as the opinion of most on board that this ice extended quite to the Pole, or perhaps joined to some land, to which it had been fixed from the earliest time; and that it is here, that is to the south of this parallel, where all the ice we find scattered up and down to the north is first formed, and afterwards broken off by gales of wind, or other causes, and brought to the north by the currents, which are always found to set in that direction in the high latitudes. As we drew near this ice some penguins were heard, but none seen; and but a few other birds, or any other thing that could induce us to think any land was near. And yet I think there must be some to the south beyond this ice, but if there is it can afford no better retreat for birds, or any other animals, than the ice itself, with which it must be wholly covered. I, who had ambition not only to go farther than any one had been before, but as far as it was possible for man to go, was not sorry at meeting with this interruption, as it, in some measure, relieved us; at least, shortened the dangers and hardships inseparable from the navigation of the Southern Polar regions.'[4]

And so he turned northwards, when, being 'taken ill of the bilious colic,' a favourite dog belonging to one of the officers (Mr Forster, after whom *Aptenodytes forsteri*, the Emperor penguin, is named) 'fell a sacrifice to my tender stomach. . . . Thus I received nourishment and strength, from food which would have made most people in Europe sick; so true it is that necessity is governed by no law.'[5]

'Once and for all the idea of a populous fertile southern continent was proved to be a myth, and it was clearly shown that whatever land might exist to the South must be a region of desolation hidden beneath a mantle of ice and snow. The vast extent of the tempestuous southern seas was revealed, and the limits of the habitable globe were made known. Incidentally it may be remarked that Cook was the first to describe the pecularities of the Antarctic icebergs and floe-ice.'[6]

A Russian expedition under Bellingshausen discovered the first certain land in the Antarctic in 1819, and called it Alexander land, which lies nearly due south of Cape Horn.

Whatever may have been the rule in other parts of the world, the flag followed trade in the southern seas during the first part of the nineteenth century. The discovery of large numbers of seals and whales attracted many hundreds of ships, and it is to the enlightened instructions of such firms as Messrs Enderby, and the pluck and enterprise of such commanders as Weddell, Biscoe and Balleny, that we owe much of our small knowledge of the outline of the Antarctic continent.

'In the smallest and craziest ships they plunged boldly into stormy ice-strewn seas; again and again they narrowly missed disaster; their vessels were racked and strained and leaked badly, their crews were worn out with unceasing toil and decimated with scurvy. Yet in spite of inconceivable discomforts they struggled on, and it does not appear that any one of them ever turned his course until he was driven to do so by hard necessity. One cannot read the simple, unaffected narratives of these voyages without being assured of their veracity, and without being struck by the wonderful pertinacity and courage which they displayed.'[7]

The position in 1840 was that the Antarctic land had been sighted at a few points all round its coasts. On the whole the boundaries which had been seen lay on or close to the Antarctic Circle, and it appeared probable that the continent, if continent it was, consisted of a great circular mass of land with the South Pole at its centre, and its coasts more or less equidistant from this point.

Two exceptions only to this had been found. Cook and Bellingshausen had indicated a dip towards the Pole south of the Pacific; Weddell a still more pronounced dip to the south of the Atlantic, having sailed to a latitude of 74° 15' S. longitude 34° 16' W.

Had there been a Tetrahedronal Theory in those days, someone might have suggested the probability of a third indentation beneath the Indian Ocean, probably to be laughed at for his pains. When James Clark Ross started from England in 1839 there was no particular reason for him to suppose that the Antarctic coast-line in the region of the magnetic Pole, which he was to try to reach, did not continue to follow the Antarctic Circle.

Ross left England in September 1839 under instructions

from the Admiralty. He had under his command two of Her Majesty's sailing ships, the *Erebus*, 370 tons, and the *Terror*, 340 tons. Arriving in Hobart, Tasmania, in August 1840, he was met by news of discoveries made during the previous summer by the French Expedition under Dumont D'Urville and the United States Expedition under Charles Wilkes. The former had coasted along Adélie Land, and sixty miles of ice cliff to the west of it. He brought back an egg now at Drayton which Scott's Discovery Expedition definitely proved to be that of an Emperor penguin.

All these discoveries were somewhere about the latitude of the Antarctic Circle (66° 32′ S.) and roughly in that part of the world which lies to the south of Australia. Ross, 'impressed with the feeling that England had ever *led* the way of discovery in the southern as well as in the northern region, . . . resolved at once to avoid all interference with their discoveries, and selected a much more easterly meridian (170° E.), on which to penetrate to the southward, and if possible reach the magnetic Pole.'[8]

The outlines of the expedition in which an unknown and unexpected sea was found, stretching 500 miles southwards towards the Pole, are well known to students of Antarctic history. After passing through the pack he stood towards the supposed position of the magnetic Pole, 'steering as nearly south by the compass as the wind admitted,' and on January 11, 1841, in latitude 71° 15′ S., he sighted the white peaks of Mount Sabine and shortly afterwards Cape Adare. Foiled by the presence of land from gaining the magnetic Pole, he turned southwards (true) into what is now called the Ross Sea, and, after spending many days in travelling down this coast-line with the mountains on his right hand, the Ross Sea on his left, he discovered and named the great line of mountains which here for some five hundred miles divides the sea from the Antarctic plateau. On January 27, 'with a favourable breeze and very clear weather, we stood to the southward, close to some land which had been in sight since the preceding noon, and which we then called the High Island; it proved to be a mountain twelve thousand four hundred feet of elevation above the level of the sea, emitting flame and smoke in great profusion; at first the smoke appeared like snowdrift, but as we drew nearer its true character became manifest. . . . I named it Mount Erebus and an extinct volcano to the eastward, little inferior in height, being by measurement ten thousand nine hundred feet high, was called Mount Terror.' That is the first we hear of our two old friends, and Ross Island is the land upon which they stand.

'As we approached the land under all studding-sails we perceived a low white line extending from its eastern extreme point as far as the eye could discern to the eastward. It presented an extraordinary appearance, gradually increasing in height as we got nearer to it, and proving at length to be a perpendicular cliff of ice, between one hundred and fifty and two hundred feet above the level of the sea, perfectly flat and level at the top, and without any fissures or promontories on its even seaward face.'⁹

Ross coasted along the Barrier for some 250 miles from Cape Crozier, as he called the eastern extremity of Ross Island, after the commander of the *Terror*. This point where land, sea and moving Barrier meet will be constantly mentioned in this narrative. Returning, he looked into the South which divides Ross Island from the western mountains. On February 16 'Mount Erebus was seen at 2.30 A.M., and the weather becoming very clear, we had splendid view of the whole line of coast, to all appearance connecting it with the mainland, which we had not before suspected to be the case.' The reader will understand that Ross makes a mistake here, since Mounts Erebus and Terror are upon an island connected to the mainland only by a sheet of ice. He continues: 'A very deep bight was observed to extend far to the south-west from Cape Bird (Bird was the senior lieutenant of the *Erebus*), in which a line of low land might be seen; but its determination was too uncertain to be left unexplored; and as the wind blowing feebly from the west prevented our making any way in that direction through the young ice that now covered the surface of the ocean in every part, as far as we could see from the mast-head, I determined to steer towards the bight to give it a closer examination, and to learn with more certainty its continuity or otherwise. At noon we were in latitude 87° 32' S., longitude 166° 12' E., dip 88° 24' and variation 107° 18' E.

'During the afternoon we were nearly becalmed, and witnessed some magnificent eruptions of Mount Erebus, the flame and smoke being projected to a great height; but we could not, as on a former occasion, discover any lava issuing from the crater, although the exhibitions of to-day were upon a much grander scale. . . .

'Soon after midnight (February 16–17) a breeze sprang up from the eastward and we made all sail to the southward until 4 A.M., although we had an hour before distinctly traced the land entirely round the bay connecting Mount Erebus with the mainland. I named it McMurdo Bay, after the senior lieutenant of the *Terror*, a compliment that his zeal and skill well merited.'[10] It is now called McMurdo Sound.

In making the mistake of connecting Erebus with the mainland Ross was looking at a distance upon the Hut Point Peninsula running out from the S.W. corner of Erebus towards the west. He probably saw Minna Bluff, which juts out from the mainland towards the east. Between them and in front of the Bluff, lie White Island, Black Island and Brown Island. To suppose them to be part of a line of continous land was a very natural mis⁺ake.

Ross broke through the pack ice into an unknown sea; he laid down many hundreds of miles of mountainous coastline, and (with further work completed in 1842) some 400 miles of the Great Ice Barrier; he penetrated in his ships to the extraordinarily high latitude of 78° 11' S., four degrees farther than Weddell. The scientific work of the expedition was no less worthy of praise. The South Magnetic Pole was fixed with comparative accuracy, though Ross was disappointed in his natural but 'perhaps too ambitious hope I had so long cherished of being permitted to plant the flag of my country on both the magnetic Poles of our globe.'

Before all things he was at great pains to be accurate, both in his geographical and scientific observations, and his records of meteorology, water temperatures, soundings, as also those concerning the life in the oceans through which he passed, were not only frequent but trustworthy.

When Ross returned to England in 1843 it was impossible not to believe that the case of those who advocated the existence of a South Pole continent was considerably strengthened. At the same time there was no proof that the various blocks of land which had been discovered were connected with one another. Even now in 1921, after twenty years of determined exploration aided by the most modern appliances, the interior of this supposed continent is entirely unknown and uncharted except in the Ross Sea area, while the fringes of the land are only discovered in perhaps a dozen places on a circumference of about eleven thousand miles.

In his *Life of Sir Joseph Hooker*, Dr Leonard Huxley has given us some interesting sidelights on this expedition under Ross. Hooker was the botanist of the expedition and assistant surgeon to the *Erebus*, being twenty-two years old when he left England in 1839. Natural history came off very badly in the matter of equipment from the Government, who provided twenty-five reams of paper, two botanizing vascula and two cases for bringing home live plants; that was all, not an instrument, nor a book, nor a bottle, and rum from the ship's stores was the only preservative. And when they returned, the rich collections which they brought back were never fully worked out. Ross's special branch of science was terrestrial magnetism, but he was greatly interested in natural history, and gave up part of his cabin for Hooker to work in. 'Almost every day I draw, sometimes all day long and till two and three in the morning, the Captain directing me; he sits on one side of the table, writing and figuring at night, and I on the other, drawing. Every now and then he breaks off and comes to my side to see what I am after . . .' and, 'as you may suppose, we have had one or two little tiffs, neither of us perhaps being helped by the best of tempers, but nothing can exceed the liberality with which he has thrown open his cabin to me and made it my workroom at no little inconvenience to himself.'

Another extract from Hooker's letters after the first voyage runs as follows:

'The success of the Expedition in Geographical discovery is really wonderful, and only shows what a little perseverance will do, for we have been in no dangerous predicaments, and have suffered no hardships whatever; there has been a sort of freemasonry among Polar voyagers to keep up the credit they have acquired as having done wonders, and accordingly, such of us as were new to the ice made up our minds for frost-bites, and attached a most undue importance to the simple operation of boring packs, etc., which have now vanished, though I am not going to tell everybody so; I do not here refer to travellers, who do indeed undergo unheard-of hardships, but to voyagers who have a snug ship, a little knowledge of the Ice, and due caution is all that is required.'

In the light of Scott's leading of the expedition of which I am about to tell, and the extraordinary scientific activity of Pennell in command of the *Terra Nova* after Scott was landed, Hooker would have to qualify a later extract, 'nor is it probable that any future collector will have a Captain so devoted to the cause of Marine Zoology and so constantly on the alert to snatch the most trifling opportunities of adding to the collection. . . .'

Finally, we have a picture of the secrecy which was imposed upon all with regard to the news they should write home and the precautions against any leakage of scientific results. And we see Hooker jumping down the main hatch with a penguin skin in his hand which he was preparing for himself, when Ross came up the after hatch unexpectedly. That *has* happened on the *Terra Nova*!

Ross had a cold reception upon his return, and Scott wrote to Hooker in 1905:

'At first it seems inexplicable when one considers how highly his work is now appreciated. From the point of view of the general public, however, I have always thought that Ross was neglected, and as you once said he is very far from doing himself justice in his book. I did not known that Barrow was the *bête noire* who did so much to discount Ross's results. It is an interesting sidelight on such a venture.'[11]

In discussing and urging the importance of the Antarctic Expedition which was finally sent under Scott in the *Discovery*, Hooker urged the importance of work in the South Polar Ocean, which swarms with animal and vegetable life. Commenting upon the fact that the large collections made chiefly by himself had never been worked out, except the diatoms, he writes:

'A better fate, I trust, awaits the treasures that the hoped-for Expedition will bring back, for so prolific is the ocean that the naturalist need never be idle, no, not even for one of the twenty-four hours of daylight during a whole Antarctic summer, and I look to the results of a comparison of the oceanic life of the Arctic and Antarctic regions as the heralding of an epoch in the history of biology.'[12]

When Ross went to the Antarctic it was generally thought that there was neither food nor oxygen nor light in the depths of the ocean, and that therefore there was no life. Among other things the investigations of Ross gave ground for thinking this was not the case. Later still, in 1873, the possibility of laying submarine cables made it necessary to investigate the nature of the abyssal depths, and the *Challenger* proved that not only does life, and in quite high forms, exist there, but that there are fish which can see. It is now almost certain that there is a great oxidized northward-creeping current which flows out of the Antarctic Ocean and under the waters of the other great oceans of the world.

It was the good fortune of Ross, at a time when the fringes of the great Antarctic continent were being discovered in comparatively low latitudes of 66° and thereabouts, sometimes not even within the Antarctic Circle, to find to the south of New Zealand a deep inlet in which he could sail to the high latitude of 78°. This inlet, which is now known as the Ross Sea, has formed the starting-place of all sledging parties which have approached the South Pole. I have dwelt upon this description of the lands he discovered because they will come very intimately into this history. I have also emphasized his importance in the history of Antarctic exploration because Ross having done what it was possible to do by sea, penetrating so far south and making such memorable discoveries, the next necessary step in Antarctic exploration was that another traveller should follow up his work on land. It is an amazing thing that sixty years were allowed to elapse before that traveller appeared. When he appeared he was Scott. In the sixty years which elapsed between Ross and Scott the map of the Antarctic remained practically unaltered. Scott tackled the land, and Scott is the Father of Antarctic sledge travelling.

This period of time saw a great increase in the interest taken in science both pure and applied, and it had been pointed out in 1893 that 'we knew more about the planet Mars than about a large area of our own globe.' The Challenger Expedition of 1874 had spent three weeks within the Antarctic Circle, and the specimens brought home by her from the depths of those cold seas aroused curiosity. Meanwhile Borchgrevink (1897) landed at Cape Adare, and built a hut which still stands and which afforded our Cape Adare party valuable assistance. Here he lived during the first winter which men spent in the Antarctic.

Meanwhile in the Arctic, brave work was being done. The names of Parry, M'Clintock, Franklin, Markham, Nares, Greely and De Long are but a few of the many which suggest themselves of those who have fought their way mile by mile over rough ice and open leads with appliances which now seem to be primitive and with an addition to knowledge which often seemed hardly commensurate with the hardships suffered and the disasters which sometimes overtook them. To those whose fortune it has been to serve under Scott the Franklin Expedition has more than ordinary interest, for it was the same ships, the *Erebus* and *Terror*, which discovered Ross Island, that were crushed in the northern ice after Franklin himself had died, and it was Captain Crozier (the same Crozier who was Ross's captain in the South and after whom Cape Crozier is named) who then took command and led that most ghastly journey in all the history of exploration; more we shall never know, for none survived to tell the tale. Now, with the noise and racket of London all around them, a statue of Scott looks across to one of Franklin and his men of the *Erebus* and *Terror*, and surely they have some thoughts in common.

Englishmen had led the way in the North, but it must be admitted that the finest journey of all was made by the Norwegian Nansen in 1893–1896. Believing in a drift from the neighbourhood of the new Siberian Islands westwards over the Pole, a theory which obtained confirmation, by the discovery off the coast of Greenland of certain remains of a ship called the *Jeannette* which had been crushed in the ice off these islands, his bold project was to be frozen in with his ship and allow the current to take him over, or as near as possible to, the Pole. For this purpose the most famous of Arctic ships was built, called the *Fram*. She was designed by Colin Archer, and was saucer-shaped, with a breadth one-third of her total length. With most of the expert Arctic opinion against him, Nansen believed that this ship would rise and sit on the top of the ice when pressed, instead of being crushed. Of her wonderful voyage with her thirteen men, of how she was frozen into the ice in September 1893 in the north of Siberia (79° N.) and of the heaving and trembling of the ship amidst the roar of the ice pressure, of how the *Fram* rose to the occasion as she was built to do, the story has still, after twenty-eight years, the thrill of novelty. She drifted over the eightieth degree on February 2, 1894. During the first winter Nansen was already getting restive; the drift was so slow, and sometimes it was backwards; it was not until the second autumn that the eighty-second degree arrived. So he decided that he would make an attempt to penetrate northwards by sledging during the following spring. As Nansen has told me, he felt that the ship would do her job in any case. Could not something more be done also?

This was one of the bravest decisions a polar explorer has

ever taken. It meant leaving a drifting ship which could not be regained; it meant a return journey over drifting ice to land; the nearest known land was nearly five hundred miles south of the point from which he started northwards; and the journey would include travelling both by sea and by ice.

Undoubtedly there was more risk in leaving the *Fram* than in remaining in her. It is a laughable absurdity to say, as Greely did after Nansen's almost miraculous return, that he had deserted his men in an ice-beset ship, and deserved to be censured for doing so.[13] The ship was left in the command of Sverdrup. Johansen was chosen to be Nansen's one companion, and we shall hear of him again in the *Fram*, this time with Amundsen in his voyage to the South.

The polar traveller is so interested in the adventure and hardships of Nansen's sledge journey that his equipment, which is the most important side of his expedition to us who have gone South, is liable to be overlooked. The modern side of polar travel begins with Nansen. It was Nansen who first used a light sledge based upon the ski sledge of Norway in place of the old heavy English sledge which was based upon the Eskimo type. Cooking apparatus, food, tents, clothing and the thousand and one details of equipment without which no journey nowadays stands much chance of success, all date back to Nansen in the immediate past, though beyond him of course is the experience of centuries of travellers. As Nansen himself wrote of the English polar men: 'How well was their equipment thought out and arranged with the means they had at their disposal! Truly, there is nothing new under the sun. Most of what I prided myself upon and what I thought to be new, I find they had anticipated. M'Clintock used the same things forty years ago. It was not their fault that they were born in a country where the use of snowshoes is unknown. . . .'[14]

All the more honour to the men who dared so much and travelled so far with the limited equipment of the past. The real point for us is that, just as Scott is the Father of Antarctic sledge travelling, so Nansen may be considered the modern Father of it all.

Nansen and Johansen started on March 14, when the *Fram* was in latitude 84° 4' N., and the sun had only returned a few days before, with three sledges (two of which carried kayaks) and twenty-eight dogs. They reached their northern-most camp on April 8, which Nansen has given in his book as being in latitude 86° 13.6' N. But Nansen tells me that Professor Geelmuyden, who had his astronomical results and his diary, reckoned that owing to refraction the horizon was lifted, and if so the observation had to be reduced accord-ingly. Nansen therefore gave the reduced latitude in his book, but he considers that his horizon was very clear when he took that observation, and believes that his latitude was higher than that given. He used a sextant and the natural horizon.

They turned, and travelling back round pressed-up ice and open leads they failed to find the land they had been led to expect in latitude 83°, which indeed was proved to be non-existent. At the end of June they started using the kayaks, which needed many repairs after their rough passage, to cross the open leads. They waited long in camp, that the travelling conditions might improve, and all the time Nansen saw a white spot he thought was a cloud. At last, on July 24, land was in sight, which proved to be that white spot. Fourteen days later they reached it to find that it consisted of a series of islands. These they left behind them and, unable to say what land they had reached, for their watches had run down, they coasted on westwards and southwards until winter approached. They built a hut of moss and stones and snow, and roofed it with walrus skins cut from the animals while they lay in the sea, for they were too heavy for two men to drag on to the ice. When I met Nansen he had forgotten all about this, and would not believe that it had happened until he saw it in his own book. They lay in their old clothes that winter, so soaked with blubber that the only way to clean their shirts was to scrape them. They made themselves new clothes from blankets, and sleeping-bags from the skins of the bears which they ate, and started again in May of the following year to make Spitzbergen. They had been travel-ling a long month, during which time they had at least two very narrow escapes – the first due to their kayaks floating away, when Nansen swam out into the icy sea and reached them just before he sank, and Johansen passed the worst moments of his life watching from the shore; the second caused by the attack of a walrus which went for Nansen's kayak with tusks and flippers. And then one morning, as he looked around at the cold glaciers and naked cliffs, not knowing where he was, he heard a dog bark. Intensely excited, he started towards the sound, to be met by the leader of the English Jackson–Harmsworth Expedition whose party was wintering there, and who first gave him the definite news that he was on Franz Josef Land. Nansen and Johansen were finally landed at Vardo in the north of Norway, to learn that no tidings had yet been heard of the *Fram*. That very day she cleared the ice which had imprisoned her for nearly three years.

I cannot go into the *Fram*'s journey save to say that she had drifted as far north as 85° 55′ N., only eighteen geographical miles south of Nansen's farthest south. But the sledge journey and the winter spent by the two men has many points in common with the experience of our own Northern Party, and often and often during the long winter of 1912 our thoughts turned with hope to Nansen's winter, for we said if it had been done once why should it not be done again, and Campbell and his men survive.

Before Nansen started, the spirit of adventure, which has always led men into the unknown, combined with the increased interest in knowledge for its own sake to turn the thoughts of the civilized world southwards. It was becoming plain that a continent of the extent and climate which this polar land probably possessed might have an overwhelming influence upon the weather conditions of the whole Southern Hemisphere. The importance of magnetism was only rivalled by the mystery in which the whole subject was shrouded; and the region which surrounded the Southern Magnetic Pole of the earth offered a promising field of experiment and observation. The past history, through the ages, of this land was of obvious importance to the geological story of the earth, whilst the survey of land formations and ice action in the Antarctic was more useful perhaps to the physiographer than that of any other country in the world, seeing that he found here in daily and even hourly operation the conditions which he knew had existed in the ice ages of the past over the whole world, but which he could only infer from vestigial remains. The biological importance of the Antarctic might be of the first magnitude in view of the significance which attaches to the life of the sea in the evolutionary problem.

And it was with these objects and ideals that Scott's first expedition, known officially as the British Antarctic Expedition of 1901–1904, but more familiarly as 'The Discovery Expedition' from the name of the ship which carried it, was organized by the Royal Society and the Royal Geographical Society, backed by the active support of the British Government. The executive officers and crew were Royal Navy almost without exception, whilst the scientifc purposes of the expedition were served in addition by five scientists. These latter were not naval officers.

The *Discovery* left New Zealand on Christmas Eve 1901, and entered the belt of pack ice which always has to be penetrated in order to reach the comparitively open sea beyond, when just past the Antarctic Circle. But a little more than four days saw her through, in which she was lucky, as we now know. Scott landed at Cape Adare and then coasted down the western coast of Victoria Land just as Ross had done sixty years before. As he voyaged south he began to look for safe winter quarters for the ship, and when he pushed into McMurdo Sound on January 21, 1902, it seemed that here he might find both a sheltered bay into which the ship could be frozen, and a road to the southland beyond.

The open season which still remained before the freezing of the sea made progress impossible was spent in surveying the 500 miles of cliff which marks the northern limit of the Great Ice Barrier. Passing the extreme eastward position reached by Ross in 1842, they sailed on into an unknown world, and discovered a deep bay, called Balloon Bight, where the rounded snow-covered slopes undoubtedly were land and not, as heretofore, floating ice. Farther east, as they sailed, shallow soundings and gentle snow slopes gave place to steeper and more broken ridges, until at last small black patches in the snow gave undoubted evidence of rock; and an undiscovered land, now known as King Edward VII's Land, rose to a height of several thousand feet. The presence of thick pack ahead, and the advance of the season, led Scott to return to McMurdo sound, where he anchored the *Discovery* in a little bay at the end of the tongue of land now known as the Hut Point Peninsula, and built the hut which, though little used in the *Discovery* days, was to figure so largely in the story of this his last expedition.

The first autumn was spent in various short journeys of discovery – discovery not only of the surrounding land, but of many mistakes in sledging equipment and routine. It is amazing to one who looks back upon these first efforts of the Discovery Expedition that the results were not more disastrous than was actually the case. When one reads of dog-teams which refused to start, of pemmican which was considered to be too rich to eat, of two officers discussing the ascent of Erebus and back in one day, and of sledging parties which knew neither how to use their cookers or lamps, nor how to put up their tents, nor even how to put on their clothes, then one begins to wonder that the process of education was gained at so small a price. 'Not a single article of the outfit had been tested; and amid the general ignorance that prevailed the lack of system was painfully apparent in everything.'[15]

This led to a tragedy. A returning sledge party of men was overtaken by a blizzard on the top of the Peninsula near Castle Rock. They quite properly camped, and should have been perfectly comfortable lying in their sleeping-bags after a hot meal. But the primus lamps could not be lighted, and as they sat in leather boots and inadequate clothing being continually frost-bitten they decided to leave the tent and make their way to the ship – sheer madness as we now know. As they groped their way in the howling snowdrift the majority of the party either slipped or rolled down a steep slippery snow slope some thousand feet high ending in a precipitous ice-cliff, below which lay the open sea. It is a nasty place on a calm summer day; in a blizzard it must be ghastly. Yet only one man, named Vince, shot down the slope and over the precipice into the sea below. How the others got back heaven knows. One seaman called Hare, who separated from the others and lay down under a rock, awoke after thirty-six hours, covered with snow but in full possession of his faculties and free from frost-bites. The little cross as Hut Point commemorates the death of Vince.

One of this party was a seaman called Wild, who came to the front and took the lead of five of the survivors after the death of Vince. He was to take the lead often in future expeditions under Shackleton and Mawson, and there are few men living who have so proved themselves as polar travellers.

I have dwelt upon this side of the early sledging deficiencies of the *Discovery* to show the importance of experience in Antarctic land travelling, whether it be at first or second hand. Scott and his men in 1902 were pioneers. They bought their experience at a price which might easily have been higher; and each expedition which has followed has added to the fund. The really important thing is that nothing of what is gained should be lost. It is one of the main objects of this book to hand on as complete a record as possible of the methods, equipment, food and weights used by Scott's Last Expedition for the use of future explorers. 'The first object of writing an account of a Polar voyage is the guidance of future voyages; the first duty of the writer is to his successors.'[16]

The adaptability, invention and resource of the men of the *Discovery* when they set to work after the failures of the autumn to prepare for the successes of the two following summers showed that they could rise to their difficulties. Scott admitted that 'food, clothing, everything was wrong, the whole system was bad.'[17] In determining to profit by his mistakes, and working out a complete system of Antarctic travel, he was at his best; and it was after a winter of drastic reorganization that he started on November 2, 1903, on his first southern journey with two companions, Wilson and Shackleton.

It is no part of my job to give an account of his journey. The dogs failed badly; probably the Norwegian stockfish which had been brought through the tropics to feed them was tainted; at any rate they sickened; and before the journey was done all the dogs had to be killed or had died. A fortnight after starting, the party was relaying – that is, taking on part of their load and returning for the rest; and this had to be continued for thirty-one days.

The ration of food was inadequate and they became very hungry as time went on; but it is not until December 21 that Wilson disclosed to Scott that Shackleton had signs of scurvy which had been present for some time. On December 30, in latitude 82° 16' S., they decided to return. By the middle of January the scurvy signs were largely increased and Shackleton was seriously ill and spitting blood. His condition became more and more alarming, and he collapsed on January 18, but revived afterwards. Sometimes walking by the sledge, sometimes being carried upon it, Shackleton survived; Scott and Wilson saved his life. The three men reached the ship on February 3, after covering 960 statute miles in 93 days. Scott and Wilson were both extremely exhausted and seriously affected by scurvy. It was a fine journey, the geographical results of which comprised the survey of some three hundred miles of new coast-line, and a further knowledge of the Barrier upon which they travelled.

While Scott was away southwards an organized attempt was made to discover the nature of the mountains and glaciers which lay across the Sound to the west. This party actually reached the plateau which lay beyond, and attained a height of 8,900 feet, when 'as far as they could see in every direction to the westward of them there extended a level plateau, to the south and north could be seen isolated nunataks and behind them showed the high mountains which they had passed;' a practicable road to the west had been found.

I need note no more than these two most important of the many journeys carried out this season; nor is it necessary for me to give any account of the continous and fertile scientific work which was accomplished in this virgin land. In the meantime a relief ship, the *Morning*, had arrived. It was intended that the *Discovery* should return this year as soon as the sea-ice in which she was imprisoned should break up and set her free. As February passed, however, it became increasingly plain that the ice conditions were altogether different from those of the previous year. On the 8th the *Morning* was still separated from the *Discovery* by eight miles of fast ice. March 2 was fully late for a low-powered ship to remain in the Sound, and on this date the *Morning* left. By March 13 all hope of the *Discovery* being freed that year was abandoned.

The second winter passed much as the first, and as soon as spring arrived sledging was continued. These spring journeys on the Barrier, with sunlight only by day and low temperatures at all times, entailed great discomfort and, perhaps worse, want of sleep, frost-bites, and a fast accumulation of moisture in all one's clothing and in the sleeping-bags, which resulted in masses of ice which had to be thawed out by the heat of one's body before any degree of comfort could be gained. A fortnight was considered about the extreme limit of such a journey, and generally parties were not absent so long; for at this time a spring journey was considered a dreadful experience. 'Wait till you've had a spring journey' was the threat of the old stagers to us. A winter journey lasting nearly three times as long as a spring journey was not imagined. I advise explorers to be content with imagining it in the future.

The hardest journey of this year was carried out by Scott with two seamen of whom much will be written in this history. Their names are Edgar Evans and Lashly. The object of the journey was to explore westwards into the interior of the plateau. By way of the Ferrar Glacier they reached the ice-cap after considerable troubles, not the least of which was the loss of the data necessary for navigation contained in an excellent publication called *Hints to Travellers*, which was blown away. Then for the first time it was seen what additional difficulties are created by the climate and position of this lofty plateau, which we now know extends over the Pole and probably reaches over the greater part of the Antarctic continent. It was the beginning of November; that is, the beginning of summer; but the conditions of work were much the same as those found during the spring journeys on the Barrier. The temperature dropped into the minus forties; but the worst feature of all was a continous head-wind blowing from the west to east which combined with the low temperature and rarefied air to make the conditions of sledging extremely laborious. The supporting party returned, and the three men continued alone, pulling out westwards into an unknown waste of snow with no land-marks to vary the rough monotony. They turned homewards on December 1, but found the pulling very heavy; and their difficulties were increased by their ignorance of their exact position. The few glimpses of land which they obtained as they approached it in the thick weather which prevailed only left them in horrible uncertainty as to their whereabouts. Owing to want of food it was impossible to wait for the weather to clear; there was nothing to be done but to continue their eastward march. Threading their way amidst the ice disturbances which mark the head of the glaciers, the party pushed blindly forward in air which was becoming thick with snowdrift. Suddenly Lashly slipped; in a moment the whole party was flying downwards with increasing speed. They ceased to slide smoothly; they were hurled into the air and descended with great force on to a gradual snow incline. Rising they looked round them to find above them an ice fall 300 feet high down which they had fallen; above it the snow was still drifting, but where they stood there was peace and blue sky. They recognized now for the first time their own glacier and the well remembered landmark, and far away in the distance was the smoking summit of Mount Erebus. It was a miracle.

Excellent subsidiary journeys were also made of which space allows no mention here; nor do they bear directly upon his last expedition. But in view of the Winter Journey undertaken by us, if not for the interest of the subject iself, some account must be given of those most aristocratic inhabitants of the Antarctic, the Emperor penguins, with whom Wilson and his companions in the *Discovery* now became familiar.

There are two kinds of Antarctic penguins – the little Adélie with his blue-black coat and his white shirt-front, weighing 16 lbs., an object of endless pleasure and amusement, and the great dignified Emperor with long curved beak, bright orange headwear and powerful flippers, a personality of 6½ stones. Science singles out the Emperor as being the more interesting bird because he is more primitive, possibly the most primitive of all birds. Previous to the Discovery Expedition nothing was known of him save that he existed in the pack and on the fringes of the continent.

We have heard of Cape Crozier as being the eastern extremity of Ross Island, discovered by Ross and named after the captain of the *Terror*. It is here with immense pressures and rendings the moving sheet of the Barrier piles itself up against the mountain. It is here also that the ice-cliff which runs for hundreds of miles to the east, with the Barrier behind it and the Ross Sea beating into its crevasses and caves joins the basalt precipice which bounds the Knoll, as the two-knobbed saddle which forms Cape Crozier is called. Altogether it is the kind of place where giants have had a good time in their childhood, playing with ice instead of mud – so much cleaner too!

But the slopes of Mount Terror do not all end in precipices. Farther to the west they slope quietly into the sea, and the Adélie penguins have taken advantage of this to found here one of their largest and most smelly rookeries. When the *Discovery* arrived off this rookery she sent a boat ashore and set up a post with a record upon it to guide the relief ship in the following year. The post still stands. Later it became desirable to bring the record left here more up to date, and so one of the first sledging parties went to try and find a way by the Barrier to this spot.

They were prevented from reaching the record by a series of most violent blizzards, and indeed Cape Crozier is one of the windiest places on earth, but they proved beyond doubt that a back-door to the Adélie penguin's rookery existed by way of the slopes of Mount Terror behind the Knoll. Early the next year another party reached the record all right, and while exploring the neighbourhood looked down over the 800-feet precipice which forms the snout of Cape Crozier. The sea was frozen over, and in a small bay of ice formed by the cliffs of the Barrier below were numerous little dots which resolved themselves into Emperor penguins. Could this be the breeding-place of these wonderful birds? If so, they must nurse their eggs in mid-winter, in unimagined cold and darkness.

Five days more elapsed before further investigaiton could be made, for a violent blizzard kept the party in their tents. On October 18 they set out to climb the high pressure ridges which lie between the level barrier and the sea. They found that their conjectures were right; there was the colony of Emperors. Several were nursing chicks, but all the ice in the Ross Sea was gone; only the small bay of ice remained. The number of adult birds was estimated at four hundred, the number of living chicks was thirty, and there were some eighty dead ones. No eggs were found.[18]

Several more journeys were made to this spot while the *Discovery* was in the south, generally in the spring: and the sum total of the information gained came to something like this. The Emperor is a bird which cannot fly, lives on fish which it catches in the sea, and never steps on land even to breed. For a reason which was not then understood it lays its eggs upon the bare ice, sometime during the winter, and carries out the whole process of incubation on the sea ice, resting the egg upon its feet pressed closely to a patch of bare skin in the lower abdomen, and protected from the intense cold by a loose falling lappet of skin and feathers. By September 12, the earliest date upon which a party arrived, all the eggs which were not broken or addled were hatched, and there were then about a thousand adult Emperors in the rookery. Arriving again on October 19, a party experienced a ten days' blizzard which confined them during seven days to their tents, but during their windy visit they saw one of the most interesting scenes in natural history. The story must be told by Wilson, who was there:

'The day before the storm broke we were on an old outlying cone of Mount Terror, about 1,300 feet above the sea. Below us lay the Emperor penguin rookery on the bay ice, and Ross Sea, completely frozen over, was a plain of firm white ice to the horizon. There was not even the lane of open water which usually runs along the Barrier cliff stretching away as it does like a winding thread to the east and out of sight. No space or crack could be seen with open water. Nevertheless the Emperors were unsettled owing, there can be no doubt, to the knowledge that bad weather was impending. The mere fact that the usual canal of open water was not to be seen along the face of the Barrier meant that the ice in Ross Sea had a southerly drift. This in itself was unusual, and was caused by a northerly wind with snow, the precursor here of a storm from the south-west. The sky looked black and threatening, the barometer began to fall, and before long down came snowflakes on the upper heights of Mount Terror.

'All these warnings were an open book to the Emperor penguins, and if one knew the truth there probably were many others too. They were in consequence unsettled, and although the ice had not yet started moving the Emperor penguins had; a long file was moving out from the bay to the open ice, where a pack of some one or two hundred had already collected about two miles out at the edge of a refrozen crack. For an hour or more that afternoon we watched this exodus proceeding and returned to camp, more than ever convinced that bad weather might be expected. Nor were we disappointed, for on the next day we woke to a southerly gale and smother of snow and drift, which effectually prevented any one of us from leaving our camp at all. This continued without intermission all day and night till the following morning, when the weather cleared sufficiently to allow us to reach the edge of the cliff which overlooked the rookery.

'The change here weas immense. Ross Sea was open water
for nearly thirty miles; a long line of white pack ice was just
visible on the horizon fromwhere we stood, some 800 to 900
feet above the sea. Large sheets of ice were still going out and
drifting to the north, and the migration of the Emperors was
in full swing. There were again two companies waiting on
the ice at the actual water's edge, with some hundred more
tailing out in single file to join them. The birds were waiting
far out at the edge of the open water, as far as it was possible
for them to walk, on a projecting piece of ice, the very next
piece that would break away and drift to the north. The line
of tracks in the snow along which the birds had gone the day
before was now cut off short at the edge of the open water,
showing that they had gone, and under the ice-cliffs there
was an appreciable diminution in the number of Emperors
left, hardly more than half remaining of all that we had seen
there six days before.'[19]

Two days later the emigration was in full swing, but only
the unemployed seemed to have gone as yet. Those who
were nursing chicks were still huddled under the ice-cliffs,
sheltered as much as possible from the storm. Three days
later (October 28) no ice was to be seen in the Ross Sea; the
little bay of ice was gradually being eaten away; the same
exodus was in progress and only a remnant of penguins was
still left.

Of the conditions under which the Emperor lays her eggs,
the darkness and cold and blighting winds, of the excessive
mothering instinct implanted in the heart of every bird, male
and female, of the mortality and gallant struggles against
almost inconceivable odds, and the final survival of some 26
per cent of the eggs, I hope to tell in the account of our
Winter Journey, the object of which was to throw light upon
the development of the embryo of this remarkable bird, and
through it upon the history of their ancestors. As Wilson
wrote:

'The possibility that we have in the Emperor penguin the
nearest approach to a primitive form not only of a penguin
but of a bird makes the future working out of its embryology

a matter of the greatest possible importance. It was a great disappointment to us that although we discovered their breeding-ground, and although we were able to bring home a number of deserted eggs and chicks, we were not able to procure a series of early embryos by which alone the points of particular interest can be worked out. To have done this in a proper manner from the spot at which the *Discovery* wintered in McMurdo Sound would have involved us in endless difficulties, for it would have entailed the risks of sledge travelling in mid-winter with an almost total absence of light. It would at any time require that a party of three at least, with full camp equipment, should traverse about a hundred miles of the Barrier surface in the dark and should, by moonlight, cross over with rope and axe the immense pressure ridges which form a chaos of crevasses at Cape Crozier. These ridges moreover, which have taken a party as much as two hours of careful work to cross by daylight, must be crossed and recrossed at every visit to the breeding site in the bay. There is no possibility even by daylight of conveying over them the sledge or camping kit, and in the darkness of mid-winter the impracticability is still more obvious. Cape Crozier is a focus for wind and storm, where every breath is converted, by the configuration of Mounts Erebus and Terror, into a regular drifting blizzard full of snow. It is here, as I have already stated, that on one journey or another we have had to lie patiently in sodden sleeping-bags for as many as five and seven days on end, waiting for the weather to change and make it possible for us to leave our tents at all. If, however, these dangers were overcome there would still be the difficulty of making the needful preparations from the eggs. The party would have to be on the scene at any rate early in July. Supposing that no eggs were found upon arrival, it would be well to spend the time in labelling the most likely birds, those, for example, that have taken up their stations close underneath the ice-cliffs. And if this were done it would be easier then to examine them daily by moonlight, if it and the weather generally were suitable; conditions, I must confess, not always easily obtained at Cape Crozier. But if by good luck things happened to go well, it would by this time be useful to have a shelter built of snow blocks on the sea-ice in which to work with the cooking lamp to prevent the freezing of the egg before the embryo was cut out, and in order that fluid solutions might be handy for the various stages of its preparation; for it must be borne in mind that the temperature all the while may be anything between zero and −50° F. The whole work no doubt would be full of difficulty, but it would not be quite impossible, and it is with a view to helping those to whom the opportunity may occur in future that this outline has been added to the difficulties that would surely beset their path.'[20]

We shall meet the Emperor penguins again, but now we must go back to the *Discovery*, lying off Hut Point, with the season advancing and twenty miles of ice between her and the open sea. The prospects of getting out this year seeming almost less promising than those of the last year, an abortive attempt was made to saw a channel from a half-way point. Still, life to Scott and Wilson in a tent at Cape Royds was very pleasant after sledging, and the view of the blue sea framed in the tent door was very beautiful on a morning in January when two ships sailed into the frame. Why two? One was of course the *Morning*; the second proved to be the *Terra Nova*.

It seemed that the authorities at home had been alarmed at the reports brought back the previous year by the relief ship of the detention of the *Discovery* and certain outbreaks of scurvy which had occurred both on the ship and on sledge journeys. To make sure of relief two ships had been sent. That was nothing to worry about, but the orders they brought were staggering to sailors who had come to love their ship 'with a depth of sentiment which cannot be surprising when it is remembered what we had been through in her and what a comfortable home she had proved.'[21] Scott was ordered to abandon the *Discovery* if she could not be freed in time to accompany the relief ships to the north. For weeks there was little or no daily change. They started to transport the specimens and make the other necessary preparations. They almost despaired of freedom. Explosions in the ice were started in the beginning of February with little effect. But suddenly there came a change, and on the 11th, amidst intense excitement, the ice was breaking up fast. The next day the relief ships were but four miles away. On the 14th a shout of 'The ships are coming, sir!' brought out all the men racing to the slopes above Arrival Bay. Scott wrote:

'The ice was breaking up right across the Strait, and with a rapidity which we had not thought possible. No sooner was one great floe borne away than a dark streak cut its way into the solid sheet that remained, and carved out another, to feed the broad stream of pack which was hurrying away to the north-west.

'I have never witnessed a more impressive sight; the sun was low behind us, the surface of the ice-sheet in front was intensely white, and in contrast the distant sea and its leads looked almost black. The wind had fallen to a calm, and not a sound disturbed the stillness about us.

'Yet in the midst of this peaceful silence was an awful unseen agency rending that great ice-sheet as though it had been naught but the thinnest paper. We knew well by this time the nature of our prison bars; we had not plodded again and again over those long dreary miles of snow without realizing the formidable strength of the great barrier which held us bound; we knew that the heaviest battleship would have shattered itself ineffectually against it, and we had seen a million-ton iceberg brought to rest at its edge. For weeks we had been struggling with this mighty obstacle . . . but now, without a word, without an effort on our part, it was all melting away, and we knew that in an hour or two not a vestige of it would be left, and that the open sea would be lapping on the black rocks of Hut Point.'[22]

Almost more dramatic was the grounding of the *Discovery* off the shoal at Hut Point owing to the rise of a blizzard immediately after her release from the ice. Hour after hour she lay pounding in the shore, and when it seemed most certain that she had been freed only to be destroyed, and when all hope was nearly gone, the wind lulled, and the waters of the Sound, driven out by the force of the wind, returned and the *Discovery* floated off with little damage. The whole story of the release from the ice and subsequent grounding of the *Discovery* is wonderfully told by Scott in his book.

Some years after this I met Wilson in a shooting lodge in Scotland. He was working upon grouse disease for the Royal Commission which had been appointed, and I saw then for the first time something of his magnetic personality and glimpses also of his methods of work. He and Scott both meant to go back and finish the job, and I then settled that when they went I would go too if wishing could do anything. Meanwhile Shackleton was either in the South or making his preparations to go there.

He left England in 1908, and in the following Antarctic summer two wonderful journeys were made. The first, led by Shackleton himself, consisted of four men and four ponies. Leaving Cape Royds, where the expedition wintered in a hut, in November, they marched due south on the Barrier outside Scott's track until they were stopped by the eastward trend of the range of mountains, and by the chaotic pressure caused by the discharge of a Brobdingnagian glacier.

But away from the main stream of the glacier, and separated from it by land now known as Hope Island, was a narrow and steep snow slope forming a gateway which opened on to the main glacier stream. Boldly plunging through this, the party made its way up the Beardmore Glacier, a giant of its kind, being more than twice as large as any other known. The history of their adventures will make anybody's flesh creep. From the top they travelled due south toward the Pole under the trying conditions of the plateau and reached the high latitude of 88° 23′ S. before they were forced to turn by lack of food.

While Shackleton was essaying the geographical Pole another party of three men under Professor David reached the magnetic Pole, travelling a distance of 1,260 miles, of which 740 miles were relay work, relying entirely on man-haulage, and with no additional help. This was a very wonderful journey, and when Shackleton returned in 1909 he and his expedition had made good. During the same year the North Pole was reached by Peary after some twelve years of travelling in Arctic regions.

Scott published the plans of his second expedition in 1909. This expedition is the subject of the present history.

The *Terra Nova* sailed from the West India Dock, London, on June 1, 1910, and from Cardiff on June 15. She made her way to New Zealand, refitted and restowed her cargo, took on board ponies, dogs, motor sledges, certain further provisions and equipment, as well as such members of her executive officers and scientists as had not travelled out in her, and left finally for the South on November 29, 1910. She arrived in McMurdo Sound on January 4, 1911, and our hut had been built on Cape Evans and all stores landed in less than an fortnight. Shortly afterwards the ship sailed. The party which was left at Cape Evans under Scott is known as the Main Party.

But the scientific objects of the expedition included the landing of a second but much smaller party under Campbell on King Edward VII's Land. While returning from an abortive attempt to land here they found a Norwegian expedition under Captain Roald Amundsen in Nansen's old ship the *Fram* in the Bay of Whales; reference to this expedition will be found elsewhere.[23] One member of Amundsen's party was Johansen, the only companion of Nansen on his famous Arctic sledge journey, of which a brief outline has been given above.[24] Campbell and his five companions were finally landed at Cape Adare, and built their hut close to Borchgrevinck's old winter quarters.[25] The ship returned to New Zealand under Pennell; came back to the Antarctic a year later with further equipment and provisions, and again two years later to bring back to civilization the survivors of the expedition.

The adventures and journeyings of the various members of the Main Party are so numerous and simultaneous that I believe it will help the reader who approaches this book without previous knowledge of the history of the expedition to give here a brief summary of the course of events. Those who are familiar already with these facts can easily skip a page or two.

Two parties were sent out during the first autumn: the one under Scott to lay a large depôt on the Barrier for the Polar Journey, and this is called the Depôt Journey; the other to carry out geological work among the Western Mountains, so called because they form the western side of McMurdo Sound; this is called the First Geological Journey, and another similar journey during the following summer is called the Second Geological Journey.

Both parties joined up at the Old Discovery Hut at Hut Point in March, 1911, and here waited for the sea to freeze a passage northwards to Cape Evans. Meanwhile the men left at Cape Evans were continuing the complex scientific work of the station. All the members of the Main Party were not gathered together at Cape Evans for the winter until May 12. During the latter half of the winter a journey was made by three men led by Wilson to Cape Crozier to investigate the embryology of the Emperor penguin; this is called the Winter Journey.

The journey to the South Pole absorbed the energies of most of the sledging members during the following summer of 1911–12. The motor party turned back on the Barrier; the dog party at the bottom of the Beardmore Glacier. From this point twelve men went forward. Four of these men under Atkinson returned from the top of the glacier in latitude 85° 3′ S.; they are known as the First Return Party. A fortnight later in latitude 87° 32′ S. three more men returned under Lieutenant Evans; these are the Second Return Party. Five men went forward, Scott, Wilson, Bowers, oates and Seaman Evans. They reached the Pole on January 17 to find that Amundsen had reached it thirty-four days earlier. They returned 721 statute miles and perished 177 miles from their winter quarters.

The supporting parties got back safely, but Lieutenant Evans was very seriously ill with scurvy. The food necessary for the return of the Polar party from One Ton Camp had not been taken out at the end of February, 1912. Evans' illness caused a hurried reorganization of plans, and I was ordered to take out this food with one lad and two dog-teams. This was done, and the journey may be called the Dog Journey to One Ton Camp.

We must now go back to the six men led by Campbell who were landed at Cape Adare in the beginning of 1911. They were much disappointed by the small mount of sledge work which they were able to do in the summer of 1911–1912, for the sea-ice in front of them was blown out early in the year, and they were unable to find a way up through the mountains behind them on to the plateau. Therefore, when the *Terra Nova* appeared on January 4, it was decided that she should land them with six weeks' sledging rations and some extra biscuits, pemmican and general food near Mount Melbourne at Evans Coves, some 250 geographical miles south of Cape Adare, and some 200 geographical miles from our Winter Quarters at Cape Evans. Late on the night of January 8, 1912, they were camped in this spot and saw the last of the ship steaming out of the bay. They had arranged to be picked up again on February 18.

Let us return to McMurdo Sound. My two dog-teams arrived at Hut Point from One Ton Depot on March 16 exhausted. The sea-ice was still in from the Barrier to Hut Point, but from there onwards was open water, and therefore no communication was possible with Cape Evans. Atkinson, with one seaman, was at Hut Point and the situation which he outlined to me on arrival was something as follows:

The ship had left and there was now no possibility of her returning owing to the lateness of the season, and she carried in her Lieut. Evans, sick with scurvy, and five other officers and three men who were returning home this year. This left only four officers and four men at Cape Evans, in addition to the four of us at Hut Point.

The serious part of the news was that owing to a heavy pack the ship had been absolutely unable to reach Campbell's party at Evans Coves. Attempt after attempt had been made without success. Would Campbell winter where he was? Would he try to sledge down the coast?

In the absence of Scott the command of the expedition under the extraordinarily difficult circumstances which arose, both now and during the coming year, would naturally have devolved upon Lieutenant Evans. But Evans, very sick, was on his way to England. The task fell to Atkinson, and I hope that these pages will show how difficult it was, and how well he tackled it.

There were now, that is since the arrival of the dog-teams, four of us at Hut Point; and no help could be got from Cape Evans owing to the open water which intervened. Two of us were useless for further sledging and the dogs were absolutely done. As time went on anxiety concerning the non-arrival of the Polar Party was added to the alarm we already felt about Campbell and his men; winter was fast closing down, and the weather was bad. So little could be done by two men. What was to be done? When was it to be done with the greatest possible chance of success? Added to all his greater anxieties Atkinson had me on his hands – and I was pretty ill.

In the end he made two attempts.

The first with one seaman, Keohane, to sledge out on to the Barrier, leaving on March 26. They found the conditions very bad, but reached a point a few miles south of Corner Camp and returned. Soon after we knew the Southern Party must be dead.

Nothing more could be done until communication was effected with Winter Quarters at Cape Evans. This was done by a sledge journey over the newly frozen ice in the bays on April 10. Help arrived at Hut Point on April 14.

The second attempt was then made, and this consisted of a party of four men who tried to sledge up the Western Coast in order to meet and help Campbell if he was trying to sledge to us. This plucky attempt failed, as indeed it was practically certain it would.

The story of the winter that followed will be told, and of

1

the decision which had to be taken to abandon either the search for the Polar Party (who must be dead) and their records, or Campbell and his men (who might be alive). There were not enough men left to do both. We believed that the Polar Party had come to grief through scurvy, or through falling into a crevasse – the true solution never occurred to us for we felt sure that except for accident or disease they could find their way home without difficulty. We decided to leave Campbell to find his way unaided down the coast, and to try and find the Polar Party's records. To our amazement we found their snowed-up tent some 140 geographical miles from Hut Point, only 11 geographical miles from One Ton Camp. They had arrived there on March 19. Inside the tent were the bodies of Scott, Wilson and Bowers. Oates had willingly walked out to his death some eighteen miles before in a blizzard. Seaman Evans lay dead at the bottom of the Beardmore Glacier.

Having found the bodies and the records the Search-party returned, proposing to make their way up the Western Coast in search of Campbell. On arrival at Hut Point with the dog-teams, I must have gone to open the hut door and found pinned on to it a note in Campbell's handwriting; but my recollection of this apparently memorable incident is extra-ordinarily vague. It was many long months since we had had good news. This was their story.

When Campbell originally landed at Evans Coves he brought with him sledging provisions for six weeks, in addition to two weeks' provisions for six men, 56 lb. sugar, 24 lb. cocoa, 36 lb. chocolate and 210 lb. of biscuit, some Oxo and spare clothing. In short, after the sledge work which they proposed, and actually carried out, the men were left with skeleton rations for four weeks. They had also a spare tent and an extra sleeping bag. It was not seriously anticipated that the ship would have great difficulty in picking them up in the latter half of February.

Campbell's party had carried out successful sledging and

useful geological work in the region of Evans Coves. They had then camped on the beach and looked for the ship to relieve them. There was open water lashed to fury by the wind so far as they could see, and yet she did not come. They concluded that she must have been wrecked. The actual fact was that thick pack ice lay beyond their vision through which Pennell was trying to drive his ship time after time, until he had either to go or to be frozen in. He never succeeded in approaching nearer than 27 miles.

It was now that the blizzard wind started to blow down from the plateau behind them out into the continually open sea in front. The situation was bad enough already, but of course such weather conditions made it infinitely worse. Evans Coves is paved with boulders over which all journeys had to be fought leaning against the wind as it blew; when a lull came the luckless traveller fell forward on to his face. Under these circumstances it was decided that preparations must be made to winter where they were, and to sledge down the coast to Cape Evans in the following spring. The alternative of sledging down the coast in March and April never seems to have been seriously considered. At Hut Point, of course, we were entirely in the dark as to what the party would do, hence Atkinson's journey over to the western side in April, 1912.

Meanwhile, the stranded men divided into two parties of three men each. The first under Campbell sank a shaft 6 feet down into a large snow-drift and thence, with pick and shovel, excavated a passage and at the end of it a cave, 12 feet by 9 feet, and 5 feet 6 inches high. The second under Levick sought out and killed all the seal and penguin they could find, but their supply was pitifully small, and the men never had a full meal until mid-winter night. One man always had to be left to look after the tents, which were already so worn and damaged that it was unsafe to leave them in the wind.

By March 17 the cave was sufficiently advanced for three men to move in. Priestley must tell how this was done, but it should not be supposed that the weather conditions were in any way abnormal on what they afterwards called Inexpressible Island:

'March 17. 7 P.M. Strong south-west breeze all day, freshening to a full gale at night. We have had an awful day but have managed to shift enough gear into the cave to live there temporarily. Our tempers have never been so tried during the whole of our life together, but they have stood the strain pretty successfully. . . . May I never have such another three trips as were those to-day. Every time the wind lulled a little I fell over to windward, and at every gust I was pitched to leeward, while a dozen times or more I was taken off my feet and dashed against the ground or against unfriendly boulders. The other two had equally bad times. Dickason hurt his knee and ankle and lost his sheath-knife, and Campbell lost a compass and some revolver cartridges in the two trips they made. Altogether it was lucky we got across at all.'[26]

It was a fortunate thing that this wind often blew quite clear without snowfall or drift. Two days later in the same gale the tent of the other three men collapsed on top of them at 8 A.M. At 4 A.M. the sun was going down and they settled to make their way across to their comrades. Gevick tells the story as follows:

'Having done this (securing the remains of the tent, etc.), we started on our journey. This lay, first of all, across half a mile of clear blue ice, swept by the unbroken wind, which met us almost straight in the face. We could never stand up, so had to scramble the whole distance on "all fours," lying flat on our bellies in the gusts. By the time we had reached the other side we had had enough. Our faces had been rather badly bitten, and I have a very strong recollection of the men's countenances, which were a leaden blue, streaked with white patches of frost-bite. Once across, however, we reached the shelter of some large boulders on the shore of the island, and waited here long enough to thaw out our noses, ears, and cheeks. A scramble of another six hundred yards brought us to the half-finished igloo, into which we found that the rest of the party had barricaded themselves, and, after a little shouting, they came and let us in, giving us a warm welcome, and about the most welcome hot meal that I think any of us had ever eaten.'

Priestley continued:

'After the arrival of the evicted party we made hoosh, and, as we warmed up from the meal, we cheered up and had one of the most successful sing-songs we had ever had, forgetting all our troubles for an hour or two. It is a pleasing picture to look back upon now, and, if I close my eyes, I can see again the little cave cut out in snow and ice with the tent flapping in the doorway, barely secured by ice-axe and shovel arranged cross-wise against the side of the shaft. The cave is lighted up with three or four small blubber lamps, which give a soft yellow light. At one end lie Campbell, Dickason and myself in our sleeping bags, resting after the day's work, and, opposite to us, a raised dais formed by a portion of the floor not yet levelled, Levick, Browning and Abbott sit discussing their seal hoosh, while the primus hums cheerily under the cooker containing the coloured water which served with us instead of cocoa. As the diners warm up jests begin to fly between the rival tents and the interchange is brisk, though we have the upper hand to-day, having an inexhaustible subject in the recent disaster to their tent, and their forced abandonment of their household goods. Suddenly someone starts a song with a chorus, and the noise from the primus is dwarfed immediately. One by one we go through our favourites, and the concert lasts for a couple of hours. By this time the lamps are getting low, and gradually the cold begins to overcome the effects of the hoosh and the cocoa. One after another the singers begin to shiver, and all thoughts of song disappear as we realize what we are in for. A night with one one-man bag between two men! There is a whole world of discomfort in the very thought, and no one feels inclined to jest about that for the moment. Those jests will come all right to-morrow when the night is safely past, but this evening it is anything but a cheery subject of contemplation.

There is no help for it, however, and each of us prepares to take another man in so far as he can.'[27]

In such spirit and under very similar conditions this dauntless party set about passing through one of the most horrible winters which God has invented. They were very hungry, for the wind which kept the sea open also made the shore almost impossible for seals. There were red-letter days, however, such as when Browning found and killed a seal, and in its stomach, 'not too far digested to be still eatable,' were thirty-six fish. And what visions of joy for the future. 'We never again found a seal with an eatable meal inside him, but we were always hoping to do so, and a kill was, therefore, always a gamble. Whenever a seal was sighted in future, someone said "Fish!" and there was always a scramble to search the beast first.'[28]

They ate blubber, cooked with blubber, had blubber lamps. Their clothes and gear were soaked with blubber, and the soot blackened them, their sleeping bags, cookers, walls and roof, choked their throats and inflamed their eyes. Blubbery clothes are cold, and theirs were soon so torn as to afford little protection against the wind, and so stiff with blubber that they would stand up by themselves, in spite of frequent scrapings with knives and rubbings with penguin skins, and always there were underfoot the great granite boulders, which made walking difficult even in daylight and calm weather. As Levick said: 'The road to hell might be paved with good intentions, but it seemed probable that hell itself would be paved something after the style of Inexpressible Island.'

But there were consolations; the long-waited-for lump of sugar: the sing-songs – and about these there hangs a story. When Campbell's Party and the remains of the Main Party foregathered at Cape Evans in November, 1912, Campbell would give out the hymns for Church. The first Sunday we had 'Praise the Lord, ye heavens adore Him,' and the second, and the third. We suggested a change, to which Campbell asked: 'Why?' We said it got a bit monotonous. 'Oh, no,' said Campbell, 'we always sang it on Inexpressible Island.' It was also about the only one he knew. Apart from this I do not know whether 'Old King Cole' or the *Te Deum* was more popular. For reading they had *David Copperfield*, the *Decameron*, the *Life of Stevenson* and a New Testament. And they did Swedish drill, and they gave lectures.

Their worst difficulties were scurvy[29] and ptomaine poisoning, for which the enforced diet was responsible. From the first they decided to keep nearly all their unused rations for sledging down the coast in the following spring, and this meant that they must live till then on the seal and penguin which they could kill. The first dysentery was early in the winter, and was caused by using the salt from the sea-water. They had some Cerebos salt, however, in their sledging rations, and used it for a week, which stopped the disorder and they gradually got used to the sea-ice salt. Browning, however, who had had enteric fever in the past, had dysentery almost continually right through the winter. Had he not been the plucky, cheerful man he is, he would have died.

In June again there was another bad attack of dysentery. Another thing which worried them somewhat was the 'igloo back,' a semi-permanent kink caused by seldom being able to stand upright.

Then, in the beginning of September, they had ptomaine poisoning from meat which had been too long in what they called the oven, which was a biscuit box, hung over the blubber stove, into which they placed the frozen meat to thaw it out. This oven was found to be not quite level, and in a corner a pool of old blood, water and scraps of meat had collected. This and a tainted hoosh which they did not have he strength of mind to throw away in their hungry condition, seems to have caused the outbreak, which was severe. Browning and Dickason were especially bad.

They had their bad days: those first days of realization that they would not be relieved; days of depression, disease and hunger, all at once; when the seal seemed as if they would give out and they were thinking they would have to travel down the coast in the winter – but Abbott killed two seals with a greasy knife, losing the use of three fingers in the process, and saved the situation.

But they also had their good, or less-bad days; such was mid-winter night when they held food in their hands and did not want to eat it, for they were full; or when they got through the *Te Deum* without a hitch; or when they killed some penguins; or got a ration of mustard plaster from the medical stores.

Never was a more cheerful or good-tempered party. They set out to see the humorous side of everything, and, if they could not do so one day, at any rate they determined to see to it the next. What is more, they succeeded, and have I never seen a company of better welded men than that which joined us for those last two months in McMurdo Sound.

On September 30 they started home – so they called it. This meant a sledge journey of some two hundred miles along the coast, and its possibility depended upon the presence of sea-ice, which we have seen to have been absent at Evans Coves. It also meant crossing the Drygalski Ice Tongue, an obstacle which bulked very formidably in their imaginations during the winter. They reached the last rise of this glacier in the evening of October 10, and then saw Erebus, one hundred and fifty miles off. The igloo and the past were behind; Cape Evans and the future were in front – and the sea-ice was in as far as they could see.

Dickason was half crippled with dysentery when they started, but improved. Browning, however, was still very ill, but now they were able to eat a ration of four biscuits a day and a small amount of pemmican and cocoa which gave him a better chance than the continual meat. As they neared Granite Harbour, a month after starting, his condition was so serious that they discussed leaving him there with Levick until they could get medicine and suitable food from Cape Evans.

But their troubles were nearly over, for on reaching Cape Roberts they suddenly sighted the depot left by Taylor in the previous year. They searched round, like dogs, scratching in the drifts, and found – a whole case of biscuits; and there were butter and raisins and lard. Day and night merged into one long lingering feast, and when they started on again their mouths were sore[30] with eating biscuits. More, there is little doubt that the change of diet saved Browning's life. As they moved down the coast they found another depôt, and yet another. They reached Hut Point on November 5.

The story of this, our Northern Party, has been told in full by the two men most able to tell it: by Campbell in the second volume of Scott's book, by Priestley in a separate volume called *Antarctic Adventure*.[31] I have added only these few pages because, save in so far as their adventures touch the Main Party or the Ship, it is better that I should refer the reader ot these two accounts than that I should try and write at second hand what has been already twice told. I will only say that the history of what these men did and suffered has been overshadowed by the more tragic tale of the Polar Party. They are not men who wish for public applause, but that is no reason why the story of a great adventure should not be known; indeed, it is all the more reason why it should be known. To those who have not read it I recommend Priestley's book mentioned above, or Campbell's equally modest account in *Scott's Last Expedition*.[32]

The *Terra Nova* arrived at Cape Evans on January 18, 1913, just as we had started to prepare for another year. and so the remains of the expedition came home that spring. Scott's book was published in the autumn.

The story of Scott's Last Expedition of 1910–13 is a book of two volumes, the first volume of which is Scott's personal diary of the expedition, written from day to day before he turned into his sleeping-bag for the night when sledging, or in the intervals of the many details of organization and preparation in the hut, when at Winter Quarters. The readers of this book will probably have read that diary and the accounts of the Winter Journey, the last year, the adventures of Campbell's Party and the travels of the *Terra Nova* which follow. With an object which I will explain presently I quote a review of Scott's book from the pen of one of Mr Punch's staff:[33]

'There is courage and strength and loyalty and love shining out of the second volume no less than out of the first: there were gallant gentlemen who lived as well as gallant gentlemen who died; but it is the story of Scott, told by himself, which will give the book a place among the great books of the world. That story beings in November, 1910, and ends on March 29, 1912, and it is because when you come to the end you will have lived with Scott for sixteen months, that you will not be able to read the last pages without tears. That message to the public was heartrending enough when it came first to us, but it was as the story of how a great hero fell that we read it; now it is just the tale of how a dear friend died. To have read this book is to have known Scott; and if I were asked to describe him, I think I should use some such words as those which, six months before he died, he used of the gallant gentleman who went with him, "Bill" Wilson. "Words must always fail when I talk of him," he wrote; "I believe he is the finest character I ever met – the closer one gets to him the more there is to admire. Every quality is so solid and dependable. Whatever the matter, one knows Bill will be sound, shrewdly practical, intensely loyal, and quite unselfish." That is true of Wilson, if Scott says so, for he knew men; but most of it is also true of Scott himself. I have never met a more beautiful character than that which is revealed unconsciously in these journals. His humanity, his courage, his faith, his steadfastness, above all, his simplicity, mark him as a man among men. It is because of his simplicity that his last message, the last entries in his diary, his last letters, are of such undying beauty. The letter of consolation (and almost of apology) which, in the verge of death, he wrote to Mrs Wilson, wife of the man dying by his side, may well be Scott's monument. He could have no finer. And he has raised a monument for those other gallant gentlemen who died – Wilson, Oates, Bowers, Evans. They are all drawn for us clearly by him in these pages; they stand out unmistakably. They, too, come to be friends of ours, their death is as noble and as heartbreaking. And there were gallant gentlemen, I said, who lived – you may read amazing stories of them. Indeed, it is a wonderful tale of manliness that these two volumes tell us. I put them down now; but I have been for a few days in the company of the brave . . . and every hour with them has made me more proud for those that died and more humble for myself.'

I have quoted this review at length, because it gives the atmosphere of hero-worship into which we were plunged on our return. That atmosphere was very agreeable; but it was a refracting medium through which the expedition could not be seen with scientific accuracy – and the expedition was nothing if not scientific. Whilst we knew what we had suffered and risked better than anyone else, we also knew that science takes no account of such things; that a man is no better for having made the worst journey in the world; and that whether he returns alive or drops by the way will be all the same a hundred years hence if his records and specimens come safely to hand.

In addition to *Scott's Last Expedition* and Priestley's *Antarctic Adventures*, Griffith Taylor, who was physiographer to the Main Party, has written an account of the two geological journeys of which he was the leader, and of the domestic life of the expedition at Hut Point and at Cape Evans, up to February, 1912, in a book called *With Scott: The Silver Lining*. This book gives a true glimpse into the more boisterous side of our life, with much useful information about the scientific part.

Though it bears little upon this book I cannot refrain from drawing the reader's attention to, and earning some of his thanks for, a little book called *Antarctic Penguins*, written by Levick, the Surgeon of Campbell's Party. It is almost entirely about Adélie penguins. The author spent the greater part of a summer living as it were upon sufferance, in the middle of one of the largest penguin rookeries in the world. He has described the story of their crowded life with a humour with which perhaps we hardly credited him, and with a simplicity which many writers of children's stories might envy. If you think your own life hard, and would like to leave it for a short hour I recommend you to beg, borrow or steal this tale, and read and see how the penguins live. It is all quite true.

So there is always a considerable literature about the expedition, but no connected account of it as a whole. Scott's diary, had he lived, would merely have formed the basis of the book he would have written. As his personal diary it has an interest which no other book could have had. But a diary in this life is one of the only ways in which a man can blow off steam, and so it is that Scott's book accentuates the depression which used to come over him sometimes.

We have seen the importance which must attach to the proper record of improvements, weights and methods of each and every expedition. We have seen how Scott took the system developed by the Arctic Explorers at the point of development to which it had been brought by Nansen, and applied it for the first time to Antarctic sledge travelling. *Scott's Voyage of the Discovery* gives a vivid picture of mistakes rectified and of improvements of every kind. Shackleton applied the knowledge they gained in his first expedition, Scott in this, his second and last. On the whole I believe this expedition was the best equipped there has ever been, when the double purpose, exploratory and scientific, for which it was organized, is taken into consideration. It is comparatively easy to put all your eggs into one basket, to organize your material and to equip and choose your men entirely for one object, whether it be the attainment of the Pole, or the running of a perfect series of scientific observations. Your difficulties increase manifold directly you combine the one with the other, as was done in this case. Neither Scott nor the men with him would have gone for the Pole alone. Yet they considered the Pole to be an achievement worthy of a great attempt, and 'We took risks, we knew we took them; things have come out against us, and therefore we have no cause for complaint. . . .'

It is, it must be, of the first importance that a system, I will not say perfected, but developed, to a pitch of high excellence at such a cost should be handed down as completely as possible to those who are to follow. I want to so tell this story that the leader of some future Antarctic expedition, perhaps more than one, will be able to take it up and say: 'I have here the material from which I can order the articles and quantities which will be wanted for so many men for such and such a time; I have also a record of how this material was used by Scott, of the plans of his journeys, and how his plans worked out, and of the improvements which his parties were able to make on the spot or suggest for the future. I don't agree with such and such, but this is a foundation and will save me many months of work in preparation, and give me useful knowledge for the actual work of my expedition.' If this book can guide the future explorer by the light of the past, it will not have been written in vain.

But this was not my main object in writing this book. When I undertook in 1913 to write, for the Antarctic Committee, an Official Narrative on condition that I was given a free hand, what I wanted to do above all things was to show what work was done; who did it; to whom the credit of the work was due; who took the responsibility; who did the hard sledgingp; and who pulled us through that last and most ghastly year when two parties were adrift, and God only knew what was best to be done; when, hd things gone on much longer, men would undoubtedly have gone mad. There is no record of these things, though perhaps the world thinks there is. Generally as a mere follower, without much responsibility, and often scared out of my wits, I was in the thick of it all, and I know.

Unfortunately I could not reconcile a sincere personal confession with the decorous obliquity of an Official Narrative; and I found that I had put the Antarctic Committee in a difficulty from which I could rescue them only by taking the book off their hands; for it was clear that what I had written was not what is expected from a Committee, even though no member may disapprove of a word of it. A proper Official Narrative presented itself to our imaginings and sense of propriety as a quarto volume, uniform with the scientific reports dustily invisible on Museum shelves, and replete with

– in the words of my Commission – 'times of starting, hours of march, ground and weather conditions,' not very useful as material for future Antarcticists, and in no wise effecting any catharsis of the writer's conscience. I could not pretend that I had fulfilled these conditions; and so I decided to take the undivided responsibility on my own shoulders. None the less the Committee, having given me access to its information, is entitled to all the credit of a formal Official Narrative, without the least responsibility for the passages which I have studied to make as personal in style as possible, so that no greater authority may be attached to them than I deserve.

I need hardly add that the nine years' delay in the appearance of my book was caused by the war. Before I had recovered from the heavy overdraft made on my strength by the expedition I found myself in Flanders looking after a fleet of armoured cars. A war is like the Antarctic in one respect. There is no getting out of it with honour as long as you can put one foot before the other. I came back badly invalided; and the book had to wait accordingly.

Notes

1 Cook, *A Voyage Towards the South Pole*, Introduction.
2 *Ibid.*, vol. i, p. 23.
3 *Ibid.*, p. 28.
4 *Ibid.*, p. 268.
5 *Ibid*, p. 275.
6 Scott, *Voyage of the Discovery*, vol. i, p. 9.
7 *Ibid.*, p. 14.
8 Ross, *Voyage to the Southern Seas*, vol. i, p. 117.
9 *Ibid.*, pp. 216–18.
10 *Ibid.*, pp. 244, 245.
11 Leonard Huxley, *Life of Sir J. D. Hooker*, vol. ii, p. 443.
12 *Ibid.*, p. 441.
13 Nansen, *Farthest North*, vol. i, p. 52.
14 *Ibid.*, vol. ii, pp. 19, 20.
15 Scott, *Voyage of the Discovery*, vol. i, p. 229.
16 *Ibid.*, p. vii.

17 *Ibid.*, p. 273.
18 See Scott, *Voyage of the Discovery*, vol. ii, pp. 5, 6, 490.
19 Wilson, *Nat. Ant. Exp.*, 1901–1904, 'Zoology,' Part ii, pp. 8, 9.
20 *Ibid.*, p. 31.
21 Scott, *Voyage of the Discovery*, vol. ii, p. 327.
22 *Ibid.*, pp. 347, 348.
23 See p. xix.
24 See p. xix.
25 See p. xviii.
26 Priestley, *Antarctic Adventure*, pp. 232, 233.
27 *Ibid.*, pp. 236, 237.
28 *Ibid.*, p. 243.
29 Atkinson has no doubt that the symptoms of the Northern Party were those of early scurvy. Conditions of temperature in the igloo allowed of decomposition occurring in seal meat. Fresh seal meat brought in from outside reduced the scurvy symptoms.
30 This tenderness of gums and tongue is additional evidence of scurvy.
31 Published by Fisher Unwin, 1914.
32 Vol. ii, Narrative of the Northern Party.
33 A. A. Milne.

Foreword

APSLEY GEORGE BENET CHERRY-GARRARD, only son of
Major-General Apsley Cherry-Garrard, C.B., was
born at Bedford on 2 January 1886.

The Cherry family – properly De Chéries – is of old
French origin. The English branch of it settled in Northamp-
tonshire in the beginning of the fifteenth century, at the
village of Plumpton. Here for several generations the elder
sons farmed their paternal acres and the younger sons served
the State at home or abroad. With the rise of the British
Government in India they found important posts in the
judiciary and civil administration in the Bengal province.
Major-General Cherry-Garrard's great-grandfather, George
Cherry, at the age of sixteen lost a leg when in action at the
Battle of Finisterre in 1747 on board H.M.S. *Neptune*, commanded by his uncle Captain Breton, R.N. In later life he was
Chairman to the Board of Commissioners for victualling the
Navy. His eldest son, George Frederick Cherry, born 1761,
of the Bengal Civil Service, was on Lord Cornwallis's staff
and became Resident at Benares. In 1798 he was assassinated
with two junior officers at a public breakfast at the Residency
by the Vizier Ali, formerly Nabob of Oude, who accused
him unjustly of being the cause of his deposition by the new
Governor-General, the Marquis of Wellesley. His young
widow returned to England with their little son George
Henry, and lived in the Cherry family's London house, in
Gloucester Place. George Henry Cherry, a brilliant classical
scholar, took a double first at Oxford. He married Charlotte,
daughter of Charles Drake-Garrard of Lamer Park, Wheathampstead, Herts, and himself bought Denford Park near
Hungerford, Berks. Their fifth child Emily became the wife
of John Smith of Britwell, Oxon, whose son Reginald Smith,
K.C., married Isabel, daughter of George Smith, the famous
publisher, and succeeded his father-in-law as head of the firm

of Smith and Elder. George and Charlotte's youngest child
was Apsley, the future general.

As a young officer in the 90th Light Infantry – later to
become the Cameronians – Apsley Cherry served with
gallantry in the Indian Mutiny and in the Kaffir and Zulu
Wars: he was described by F. M. Lord Wolseley as 'the
bravest man I have ever seen'. With the rank of Major-
General he was in command of the Garrison at Bedford when
at the age of 53 he married Evelyn, daughter of Henry
Sharpin, MD, the local doctor, in whose house their eldest
child and only son, the subject of this memoir, was born. A
year later the General's elder brother George, to whom he
was greatly attached, died unmarried and he inherited the
Denford estate; and till he was seven the future Antarctic
explorer was brought up at Denford, which he loved.

The Garrards had been lords of the manor of Lamer since
the middle of the sixteenth century. Part of the house, now
demolished, dated from 1272. Members of this family also
had been prominent servants of the State: no less than three
had been Lord Mayors of London. Sir Benet Garrard, the last
of his name and title, died in 1767 and Lamer was inherited
by his distant cousin Charles Drake of Shardloes, Bucks,
who assumed his name and arms. He married Anne Barne of
Sotherly Hall in Suffolk, and it was their daughter Charlotte
who married George Henry Cherry. Their son Charles
married Honora Pauncefort-Duncombe, and on her death in
1893 – her husband having predeceased her without issue –
the Lamer estate went to his sister Charlotte's distinguished
son, on condition of his assuming the additional name and
arms of Garrard.

Major-General Cherry-Garrard thus, when comparatively
late in life the father of a growing family (one son and three
daughters; two more daughters followed), found himself the
possessor of two large estates. With great reluctance but in
duty bound he leased Denford and removed his family and
household to Lamer. But it proved an even more delectable
abode than Denford had been, and his son grew up to love
every stick and stone of it. His letters from his preparatory

school, The Grange, in Folkestone, put a good face on things, but he was always longing to be home. An excessive short-sightedness debarred him from proficiency in games, though he played them with enthusiasm; and this handicap made him no happier at Winchester where, however, he found a good friend in one of the masters, Mr Beloe. But at Oxford, where he read Classics and Modern History, he found congenial friends and interests, and also a sport in which he could literally pull his weight and to which bad eyesight was no bar: this was rowing. Though he just failed to get his blue, he rowed bow in the Christ Church first VIII in 1908 and helped the Christ Church crew to win the Grand Challenge Cup at Henley in the same year.

During Cherry's time at college his father had a long and painful illness, which terminated in his death in 1907. All his life Cherry had been thrilled by stories of his father's courage and achievements, and he always had before him the example of his father's high standard of conduct. He loved his father devotedly, though with some awe, and felt that he had left him an example that he must strive to live up to. Cherry felt that he could never equal his father, and, perhaps, without realizing it, he was looking for some way to prove himself to himself. His opportunity was to come quite soon. He was twenty-one years old when his father died. Three years later he was to be one of the youngest members of Scott's last expedition.

In September 1907 when Dr Wilson and his wife were staying with the Reginald Smiths at their bungalow in Cortachy near Kirriemuir, Captain Scott came to join them for a few days and unfolded his plans for another Antarctic expedition. In the following summer the Smiths lent their bungalow to the Wilsons (their greatest friends), and Reginald Smith's young cousin Apsley Cherry-Garrard paid them a visit. 'When I first met Wilson it was certain that he and Scott were going south again if possible: they wanted to finish the job. I do not know whether Scott would have gone again without Wilson.' But he thereupon decided, if this possibility became a fact, to volunteer. In May 1909 Cherry embarked on the S.S. *Ormuz* with Mr Woolcombe, the head of the Oxford House, who was making a lecture tour in Australia. They travelled together for a time in Western Australia and then Cherry went off on his own. Hearing of Scott's second venture south as official news, he wrote to Dr Wilson on 3 October 1909, from Brisbane applying for service. He continued the voyage on cargo-boats – visiting the Celebes, China, and Japan; and when at Calcutta on 4 January 1910, he received a reply from Wilson, dated 8 December 1909.

Your letter duly reached me and I have discussed your proposal with Captain Scott as well as with Reginald Smith. I fully sympathize with your eagerness to come, but I write now only to endorse what you already have heard from Reginald Smith – namely that no object would be gained by shortening your present programme. . . . Scott thinks that it is just possible that when we have filled up the actual scientific staff with the necessary experts in each branch, there may still be a vacancy for an adaptable helper, such as I am sure you would be; ready to lend a hand where it was wanted. Only I must frankly say that as it is a matter of real importance in these Shore parties to reduce numbers to a minimum, the reverse may be possible and there may be no room for any but the absolutely necessary Staff.

If however you are content to let the matter stand over until your return – and if, after coming into closer touch with your home ties, you are still anxious to go – I can promise that your application will not have been forgotten, and you will not have suffered by the waiting. Only at present it is quite impossible to make you any promise – I wish it were otherwise – and you must be prepared for disappointment . . .

Cherry returned home early in April and wrote immediately, this time to back his application with the offer of £1,000 to the funds of the Expedition. Among some eight thousand applicants were several who offered similar donations, but these offers carried no weight with Scott despite his lack of financial resources: Oates was in fact the only other contributor – and of a like sum – who was accepted, but he was a specialist in an indispensable branch of service. It must have given Wilson as much pain to write the following letter, dated 20 April 1910, as it gave Cherry to receive it:

> I am more sorry than I can say to have been the means of conveying to you your disappointment. . . . However, let me thank you for the kind things you have said in thanking me for my very unsuccessful mediations. I am very glad indeed that you could say them.

Two things emerge from Wilson's next and very interesting letter, dated 25 April: one, that Cherry had asked that his offer of a subscription might stand, despite his non-acceptance; the other, less evident, that Wilson had another serious talk with Scott on his behalf.

> Captain Scott wants to see you again and have a talk over things with you before giving a final answer. . . . He says he must satisfy himself by a talk with you that there is no misunderstanding on the subject before coming to a determination, otherwise he feels you might both be in something of a false position. I believe he is right, and the time has come when you and he must understand one another. I can tell you one thing however, and that is that he very *much* appreciates the motive which induced you to send your subscription independently of your chance of being taken. That is an action which appeals to him, not because of the money for which he cares very little, except impersonally, in so far as it helps the Expedition to be a success – but because he knows what to expect of a man who felt it was the right thing to do.
>
> I know Scott intimately, as you know. I have known him now for ten years, and I believe in him so firmly that I am often sorry when he lays himself open to misunderstanding. I am sure that you will come to know him and believe in him as I do, and none the less because he is sometimes difficult. However you will soon see for yourself.

Meanwhile come and see him on Wednesday – at 11 – and come prepared to be examined medically in the event of your being accepted. . . .

After such a letter the result could hardly be in doubt. But these letters show that it was only by the skin of his teeth, so to speak, that Cherry boarded the *Terra Nova* bound for the enterprise which proved to be Scott's Last Expedition. Despite excessive pressure of work during these last few weeks of preparation, Wilson and his wife contrived a special visit to Lamer that he might thank Mrs Cherry-Garrard personally for allowing her son to go, and also assure her that he would keep an eye on him.

Thus Cherry was duly enlisted as 'assistant zoologist' to Wilson who was Chief of the Scientific Staff. It was a joke at first among the officers and scientists that he was accepted for the South because he knew a lot of Latin and Greek! Yet from the outset he proved his value among the personnel of the Expedition, and before its close he had more major sledge-journeys to his credit than any other surviving member of it.

Two or three extracts from Wilson's journal on shipboard suffice to show Cherry's zeal to make himself useful as an 'adaptable helper'.

(Off Cardiff) 'Got to filthy work right off, shifting cases . . . Cherry-Garrard was invaluable, as he had kept an eye on the whereabouts of everything.' – (Off Madeira) 'I slept with Cherry-Garrard on the ice-house, where 5 hours sleep is more good than 8 below.' . . . (Off South Trinidad after a perilous re-embarkation and the difficult salvage of bird-specimens through salt water) 'Cherry-Garrard was so keen to save them that he continued skinning all night till breakfast.' And from a letter to Reginald Smith on arrival in New Zealand:

As for Cherry, he is such a success – and it is apparent to every one. I am so delighted with him. . . . He has taken most kindly to the position of taxidermist amongst many

others. Where he shines most is as Pennell's assistant. . . .
Cherry has been doing a tremendous amount of magnetic
figures and observation record-keeping for Pennell in which
his exceptional handwriting – and neatness and accuracy –
comes in most usefully. He is in excellent spirits and as strong
as a horse.

Scott joined the ship in New Zealand and also wrote to
Reginald Smith from Christchurch on 18 November:

Cherry-Garrard has won all hearts; he shows himself ready
for any sort of hard work and is always to the front when the
toughest jobs are on hand. He is the most unselfish, kind-
hearted fellow, and will be of the greatest use to the
Expedition. . . . You will be equally glad to know that he is
exceedingly happy. I haven't asked if he is, but when I see his
cheerful brown face charged with enthusiasm and wreathed
in smiles I cannot doubt it – but indeed it is a good life for
any young man who has the right stuff in him.

Early in 1911 Scott organized his pony- and dog-teams to
transport a large quantity of stores to One Ton Camp as
provision for the returning Polar Party next year. He found
time for another letter to Reginald Smith from Safety Camp
on the Great Ice Barrier on 1 February 1911:

I am reduced to sending a last greeting from this camp in
the hope that the ship will duly recover this note and post it
in New Zealand. . . . Wilson outdoes himself and is just
perfection as sledge traveller and companion. And I find it
difficult to express my satisfaction with Cherry-Garrard. He
is ready for everything – one of the best pony leaders we have
and always to the front when hard work is to be done – he
said he wouldn't mind what work he was put to and he
doesn't – but more than this, he is always ready to take on
himself other people's hard work and does it all in a genial
unostentatious way that is wholly admirable.

Some redistribution took place at various stages on the Depot journey, but on the first outward marches Scott's own tent included Oates, Bowers, and Cherry-Garrard. It was Cherry's first experience of close association with a leader who demanded thoroughness and efficiency. Scott never had occasion to revise his impressions of this young colleague. 'Cherry-Garrard is remarkable because of his eyes. He can only see through glasses and has to wrestle with all sorts of inconveniences in consequence. yet one would never guess it – for he manages somehow to do more than his share of the work.' – 'Cherry-Garrard is cook. He is excellent, and is quickly learning all the tips for looking after himself and his gear.'

This, the first major Journey, was fraught with hazards and adventures which severely tested the qualities of all concerned. There was first the disappearance down a crevasse of an entire dog-team; the difficult extrication of eleven of the thirteen, and then the rescue by Scott single-handed of the two remaining in its depths. 'My companions today were excellent: Wilson and Cherry-Garrard if anything the most intelligently and readily helpful.' Then there was the harrowing incident, graphically recounted by Bowers in this book, when he and Cherry were marooned for hours on a drifting ice-floe. 'Practical Cherry' is Bowers's tribute more than once to his companion – high praise from one possessed of such inexhaustible resource and courage as that 'undefeatable little sportsman' was himself – and the experience was another link in the chain that bound them in an unbreakable friendship. 'When you have been through as bad times with someone as I went through with Birdie you get to know him so well that you do not seem to know anyone in civilization at all.'

On return to the comparative comfort of life in the Hut, Scott penned a memorable passage in his diary:

> I do not think there can be any life quite so demonstrative of character as that which we had on these expeditions. One sees a remarkable reassortment of values. Under ordinary conditions it is so easy to carry a point with a little bounce:

self-assertion is a mask which covers many a weakness. As a rule we have neither the time nor the desire to look beneath it, and so it is that commonly we accept people on their own valuation. Here the outward show is nothing, it is the inward purpose that counts. So the 'gods' dwindle and the humble supplant them. Pretence is useless . . .

He goes on to select a few for special commendation:

. . . Cherry-Garrard is another of the open-air, self-sufficing, quiet workers; his whole heart is in the life, with profound eagerness to help everyone. One has caught glimpses of him in tight places; sound all through and pretty hard also. Indoors he is editing our Polar Journal, out of doors he is busy making trial of stone huts and blubber stoves, primarily with a view to the winter journey to Cape Crozier, but incidentally these are instructive experiments for any party which may get into difficulty by being cut off from the home station.

Cherry was not only the judicious editor of the *South Polar Times* but also the flawless and meticulous typist of its text, cleverly interspaced between Wilson's artistic productions. This obscure periodical attracted the interest of so many friends of the Expedition on its return that it was printed by Reginald Smith's firm in exact facsimile for private circulation. Its editor displayed another useful and unexpected accomplishment. 'At our morning service Cherry-Garrard, good fellow, vamped the accompaniment of two hymns; he received encouraging thanks and will cope with all three hymns next Sunday.'

Scott had been averse to Wilson's proposed Winter Journey as being altogether too dangerous an enterprise, but he had been eventually overborne by Wilson's reassurances. The purpose of this – 'the weirdest bird-nesting expedition that has been or ever will be' – was to collect as many eggs as possible of the Emperor Penguin at early stages of incubation so as to work out their embryology. Wilson had determined on it ever since the discovery of their breeding-ground at

Cape Crozier nine years before: 'but I'm not saying much about it; it might never come off' he had confided to Cherry in London. His choice of companions was simple: 'the two I like best of all our party.' He continued, in a letter to his wife:

> It is going to be a regular snorter, I can see that; but I have got the two best sledgers of the whole Expedition to come with me. Scott has allowed me to have them, and they are desperately keen to come. . . . He hopes I shall bring them back safe and sound for the Southern Journey. He told me today again that I had the pick of the sledging element and mustn't get them crocked.

Scott saw the trio off and returned to the Hut to complete a book of his diary with the words: 'This winter travel is a new and bold venture, but the right men have gone to attempt it. All good luck go with them!'

More than five weeks later, when they staggered back to the Hut looking more dead than alive, Scott spoke of their exploit as 'the hardest journey that has ever been made' and as 'one of the most gallant stories in Polar History. . . . It makes a tale for our generation which I hope may not be lost in the telling.' – It has not been.

Exactly three calendar months intervened between the return from the Winter Journey and the start for the great Southern Journey, and with the gradual return of the sun preparations for the long march proceeded with increasing tempo.

On the eve of the start Scott wrote again to Reginald Smith:

> . . . As for Cherry-Garrard, he is a perfect brick, the most unselfish good-natured fellow in the world, with plenty of intelligence and bottomless pluck. He is extremely popular and personally I could not wish for a better companion. He has already reaped a heap of experience and some startling adventures – quite enough to show the stuff he's made of. He

and Bowers were in a very tight place on the sea-ice last year [*sic*] and both behaved just as the best sort of Englishmen behave on such occasions. On this very severe Cape Crozier journey in the winter he suffered more than his companions but neither of them heard a word from him about it, and when his fingers were a mass of frost bites and blisters he had to be ordered not to do things for other people. You may well be proud of him, and I hope you will let his people know what golden opinions he has deserved and won.

A day or two later he added a postscript:

> Really Cherry is very delightful – he has just come to me with a very anxious face to say that I must not count on his navigating powers. For a moment I didn't know what he was driving at, but then remembered that some months ago I said that it would be a good thing for all the officers going South to have some knowledge of navigation so that in emergency they would know how to steer a sledge home. It appears that Cherry thereupon commenced a serious and arduous course of study of abstruse navigational problems which he found exceedingly tough and now despairs of mastering. Of course there is not one chance in a hundred that he will ever have to consider navigation on our journey, and in that one chance the problem must be of the simplest nature; but it makes matters much easier for me to have men who take the details of our work so seriously and who strive so simply and honestly to make it successful.

On 1 November 1911, Scott, Wilson, and Cherry-Garrard set forth together – the 'flying rearguard' of the pony-teams – and Ponting's cinematograph recorded their departure. From the end of the Great Ice Barrier three chosen parties man-hauled their sledges up the Beardmore Glacier. On 22 December the first of the two teams to return was sent back from a day's march beyond the Upper Glacier Depot: it comprised Atkinson, Wright, Cherry-Garrard, and Keohane the youngest seaman. Wilson in a letter to his wife sincerely expressed not only his own but everyone's estimation of Cherry.

> ... Please write to Mrs Cherry-Garrard and say how splendidly her son has worked on this sledge journey. He has been a real trump, and has made himself beloved by everyone – a regular brick to work and a splendid tentmate. I am simply proud of having had something to do with getting him on to this Expedition. He is very disappointed at having to go back with the first four; but this is right, because he is the youngest. He is not worn out in the least, though he has worked his utmost all the way. I am very fond of him.

Nearly a year was to elapse before he saw his friends again – Scott, Wilson, Bowers – dead in their tent on the Great Ice Barrier, within only eleven miles of One Ton Camp: so much nearer than anyone had guessed. He does not say, though Atkinson did, that his was the suggestion of the last line from Tennyson's *Ulysses* inscribed on the cross, erected on Observation Hill to the memory of the Polar Party;[1] as well as of the epitaph commemorating Oates.[2]

And it is worth noticing that in the shock of this discovery, at the very moment when the thought of 'what might have been if only' might be supposed to have struck him hardest, it did not, for there is no trace of it in his diary; nor certainly did it for one moment cross the minds of any of his comrades. Nor do any self-reproaches appear ten years later when he wrote *The Worst Journey*: it is only mentioned as one among other remote hypotheses on page 610. There were indeed a few arm-chair critics who, when the Ship reached New Zealand again early in 1913, wondered why a strenuous effort had not been made to rescue the Polar Party; but this carried no weight with him or with any other member of the Expedition. It was not till long afterwards that the thought of what he might have done – and the fantasy of what others were thinking and saying about him – became a little cloud

---

1. *The Worst Journey*, p. 630.   2. ibid., pp. 546–7.

on the margin of his mind that grew till it covered his whole sky.

The Antarctic – two-and-a-half brief years of youth – was the highlight of his life's experience; the long remainder was anticlimax. Whatever subsequent activities engaged his interest, they were incidental to his real interest which was his memories. Early in 1914 he was invited by Atkinson to join him unofficially in an expedition to China led by Robert Leiper, C.M.G., D.S.C., M.D. (the same helminthologist to whom Wilson had divulged his discovery of the cause of grouse disease in 1909). Its purpose was to investigate a sheep liver fluke disease which affected British seamen in China waters. It found that the infection was water-borne and entered the feet of sailors when swabbing the decks. In later years Professor Leiper came to live at Leasy Bridge Farm near Wheathampstead and was a frequent and welcome guest at Lamer.

With the outbreak of war in August of this year Cherry tried first for a job as an orderly in the R.A.M.C. and Sir Frederick Treves offered him a motor-car for the transport of wounded men, but he was no mechanic. However, he bought a Douglas motor-cycle and applied for service as a dispatch rider, was accepted, and sent to Aldershot on 20 September for training in 8th Signalling Company, R.E. After a month in barracks with 150 men, among whom on his first night he had to fight for a bed, he was 'about to be made a corporal' when he was sent for to the orderly room. His Captain informed him that a wire had arrived from a Commander in the Admiralty asking whether he would accept an appointment with armoured cars. Within a few days he was commissioned Lieut. Commander R.N.V.R. As this rank was equivalent to that of Major in the army he thought it would not be impertinent to bestow his motor-cycle upon his late Captain as a parting gift! He was posted to the command of no. 5 squadron, which served in Flanders from April to August 1915 when it was disbanded. By this time Cherry was himself a sick man and was invalided out with chronic colitis. During a long convalescence he began writing *The Worst Journey* which he finished in 1922. In his Introduction he clearly shows how little he esteemed comradeship in arms beside comradeship in exploration: 'Talk of ex-soldiers: give me ex-antarcticists, unsoured and with their ideals intact: they could sweep the world.'

In 1916 he brought to the attention of the Tasmanian Government an iniquity which Wilson had exposed to the Zoological Society in 1904. This was the hunting of King Penguins on Macquarie Island into cauldrons of boiling water for their oil. As a result the practice was suppressed and the island declared a bird and seal sanctuary. In 1917 he 'obtained certain reforms in the treatment of invalided men'. This was an effort prompted by the case of G. P. Abbott, a seaman in Scott's Last Expedition, who had been removed from a military to a civilian hospital with consequent loss of pension. He paid for this man's treatment, and secured his rights.

During the 1920s he made acquaintance with certain men of action whose exploits and characters he admired. One was Mallory of Everest: 'burning with a kind of fire, an ardent impatient soul, winding himself up to a passion the higher he got.' Another was Lawrence of Arabia, of whom he contributed a personal memoir in the Symposium by his Friends. This shows acute psychological insight. The book was edited by Lawrence's younger brother, A. W., who wrote to him: 'I have read your article several times and it seems to me perfectly true.'

All his life he retained the keenest interest in exploration everywhere, but especially in its development with modern equipment in the Antarctic; and was delighted when the French explorers Barré, Cendron, and Imbert telegraphed to him on their return in 1951 the offer of an Emperor Penguin's egg, which he was quite thrilled to accept. And when the trans-Antarctic Expedition of 1957–8 under Fuchs and Hillary was launched he received regularly its Newsletter bulletin. During this expedition, the Journey to Cape Crozier was re-enacted, though in the autumn instead of winter. A party consisting of Sir Edmund Hillary, Murray Ellis, Jim Bates, and Peter Mulgrew, with a copy of *The Worst Journey* as a guide book, set off to follow the route taken by Wilson, Bowers, and Cherry, and made, to quote from their News-letter, 'the most spectacular discovery of an historical nature to be made in the Antarctic for many years'. For after searching in an area of two square miles, in high winds, and minus 20° temperatures, they found the stone igloo erected by Doctor Wilson's party in 1911. Only eighteen inches to two feet remained, but still securely fixed between the rocks were the remains of the green Willesden canvas used as a roof. Inside, they found, amongst other things, a nine-foot man-hauling sledge, Doctor Wilson's scientific case, a ther-mos flask, thermometers, all in perfect working order, and a packet of salt, which after a lapse of 46 years poured as if it were just out of the desiccator. The Trans-Antarctic Expedition Committee consulted with Cherry as to the most suitable home for these relics, and he was very happy to agree that they should be placed in museums in New Zealand; these are the Dominion, Canterbury, and the Gisborne Museums. But perhaps he valued even more than these associations the memory of a visit to Lamer soon after his return of the first and greatest pioneer of polar travel, who had befriended and counselled Scott before his *Discovery* days, and who in the old age stood before the world – 'just, brave, and compassionate' – as the representative of enlight-ened humanity, Fridtjof Nansen.

Cherry was well read in the humanities, especially in religious philosophy and psychology, he had the instincts of the scholar. Always an idealist, he was also a critically minded thinker: a sceptic in the best sense of a word that has lost its true meaning. A lover of classical literature and art, ancient and modern, from his soul he loathed those post-war produc-tions that masquerade as works of art and reflect the malaise of a diseased sensibility. Of modern English writers none, I think, ever displaced Kipling as his first choice. Conrad was another favourite. Galsworthy, whom he liked and whose work he admired, paid a graceful tribute to *The Worst Journey* in one of the Forsyte novels. H. G. Wells, the most justly popular novelist of his times, proved a most helpful supporter of his campaign for the abolition of the cruel slaughter of penguins, and gave the matter publicity in *The Undying Fire*. Arnold Bennett was another acquaintance. Scott's dearest friend, the sad, shy Barrie, came several times to stay with Cherry.

But his own closest friends in the literary world were his nearest neighbours Mr and Mrs Bernard Shaw, whose home at Ayot St Lawrence was within easy walking distance of Lamer. Of them he says modestly that 'they taught me to write'. Despite disparity in age they had much in common. Cherry gave Shaw full marks as a writer of faultless English prose and as an exposer of popular fallacies, but he had little faith in him as a genuinely constructive thinker. Shaw's skill in debate was so scintillating and elusive that it was difficult to detect him in an inconsistency. But Cherry, who preferred truth to victory in argument, was determined to catch him out, and during one of Shaw's brilliant monologues he lay low waiting his chance. At last it came: a clear contradiction to some previous assertion. 'But you said such-and-such just now,' protested Cherry. 'Ah yes,' replied the sage, quite unabashed, 'but that was half an hour ago!' Shaw and Cherry had many an argument over politics, but they remained the best of friends. The Shaws opened up new worlds for him, and gave him stimulating companionship and fun, and it was the Shaws also who gave him the same constant companionship, kindness, and help during his long years of illness. In Cherry's copy of *The Black Girl in Search of God*, Shaw wrote in February 1948,

> For Cherry and Angela
> Greatest of my friends.

It was appropriately enough in the hard winter of February of 1929 that I first went to Lamer – from the Scott Polar

Research Institute in Cambridge when English weather came as near Antarctic as Debenham remembered. Though I had read both volumes of *Scott's Last Expedition* – often, I had not as yet read *The Worst Journey in the World*. The failure of an electric heater in the garage where Cherry's car (a Vauxhall sporting racer) was iced up, kept him busy for some time whilst I waited in a pleasant room before a comfortable hearth. Suddenly entering – a dark, compact figure of middle height with sloping shoulders and wearing thick-lensed glasses – he stood tense and rigidly still, apologizing for the delay. This attitude was in fact characteristic on occasion. The impression was that of a highly strung individual habituated to the practice of deliberate self-control. Over lunch he relaxed completely and allowed himself to reminisce. I had come by favour of an introduction from Mrs Wilson to learn something of his experiences and those of his companions in the South, and, no doubt because she had been Bill's wife and was also his good friend, he was generous in sharing his memories with a stranger. He spoke of the routine and technique of sledging; of Scott's reorganization of the Polar team while actually on the march, five men instead of four – a mistake; of Oates gallantly concealing the effects of an old Boer War leg-wound ('If it hadn't been him for the Pole it would have been me'); of the lack of vitamins that finally starved the Polar Party – and much else. This led him to speak of the Dog Journey which he had undertaken alone, save for Dimitri the boy Russian driver, with provisions for their return. 'I often wonder whether, if I had plugged on after that blizzard from One Ton killing dogs for food as necessary, I might have reached them.' A rough computation of dates and distances, pointing to the impossibility, left him unconvinced. Too often he had worked them out himself. I did not realize then to what a disastrous extent this sense of having failed his friends was already preying on his mind. He went on to speak of the wreck that long spells of illness had made of him. To a remonstrance – 'But surely you are the same man that went on the Winter Journey' – he answered,

'Am I? I wonder.' But it was worth it, wasn't it? whatever the price of physical prostration. 'Yes,' he replied: 'I'm all in favour of getting ragged out.'

What are the essential prerequisites for a Polar traveller? A good blood-circulation, sound constitution, tough physique? –

> No, not necessarily so at all. It is a matter of mind rather than of body. Look at Wilson: poor circulation, once a consumptive, not strong above the waist. Compare him with Taff Evans, the giant of the whole lot of us. Yet it was Evans who succumbed long before the others. Wilson stuck it out to the last, but he had them as well as himself to look after. It was the sensitive men, the men with nerves, with a background of education – 'good blood' – who went farthest, pulled hardest, stayed longest. Bowers, of course, was exceptional by any standards. Scott, Wilson, Oates, Bowers were not unduly depressed to find that Amundsen had forestalled them at the Pole, though naturally they were disappointed (Wilson perhaps not even that). But Evans was really disheartened: he began to go downhill from then on.

If Oates had taken the course that he took ten days or even a week earlier than he did, when the others knew that he was already beyond hope, might they have got in? – 'They would almost certainly have reached One Ton before the blizzard hit them. But it is natural that Oates should not give up hope, and natural that they should urge him to slog on as long as he could.' What do you think actually happened? – 'I think that, the night before he walked out, he asked Wilson for an opium pill, and that Bill gave him one which would be enough to ease his pain and put him to sleep for a few hours. "He slept through the night, hoping not to wake; but he woke in the morning." Then he went out.' – Do you think that the decision of the others not to finish themselves but to fight it out to the last biscuit and die naturally in the track, was due to Wilson's refusal of Scott's first request to hand over the contents of the medicine case, and that, when Scott made it an order, Wilson's objections were so strong that the idea was abandoned – abandoned for good? – 'Yes, that is how I read it. When we found them and Atkinson examined them, their skin was clear. There were no dark traces under their eyes as there would have been if they had taken an overdose of opium or morphia.'

Arising from this conversation are two points that require elucidation.

First: 'If it hadn't been Oates for the Pole it would have been me.' Compare page 378: 'Wilson told me it was a toss-up whether Titus or I should go on. . . .' And: 'Oates was limping slightly from an old wound on the top of the Glacier, and Atkinson, who knew him best, told me that he did not want to go on.' Scott was of course not told this: if he had been, Oates would certainly have returned with Atkinson's party. If Cherry had been substituted, he would have been added as fifth man. He was aware of his own limitations and his considered opinion was that had Scott adhered to his original plan of a four-man party, and had it comprised Scott and Wilson, Bowers and Lashly, they might have got through despite every misfortune.

Second: 'I often wonder whether, if I had plugged on after that blizzard from One Ton killing dogs for food as necessary, I might have reached them.' Compare page 565: 'If the dogs had not been taken so far and the One Ton Depot [of dog-food] had been laid. . . . If I had disobeyed my instructions and gone on from One Ton, killing dogs as necessary. . . .' He had previously shown (p. 427) that it had proved impossible to make a depot of dog-food. – He started from Hut Point with Dimitri and the dog-teams late at night on 26 February and reached One Ton on the night of 3 March – six days. Next day a blizzard blew up and prevented movement for four days. During this time it was found necessary to give the dogs extra food because they were weak and their coats were moulting. On 8 March, when the blizzard cleared, the Polar Party were still the other side of Mt Hooper, more than 70 miles away, but Cherry had every reason to suppose that they were nearing One Ton.

The situation as it presented itself to him then and there was one that hardly admitted of doubt. He had enough dogfood left for two more days before returning. He could either run a day – perhaps 25 miles' distance – farther south and back, and chance missing the Polar Party on the way; or he could remain at One Ton where they were certain to meet. Or, a third alternative: he could, disobeying explicit orders, go on blindly southwards killing dogs to feed the dwindling remainder. He chose to remain and wait as long as possible. His companion was not well, but this fact did not affect his decision.

But now consider the situation as it presented itself to him *post eventum*. His friends were fighting a losing battle for their lives more than 70 miles away. He would have gone to any lengths to reach them: he would have adopted the third alternative. And he never afterwards forgave himself that he did not.

On my next visit he was writing an Introduction for my book on Wilson, as he did later for that on Bowers. Apart from those two very special friends, and from Scott himself, the men of the Expedition who most won his admiration were Atkinson and Oates ('the Inseparables'), Priestley and Campbell, and seaman Lashly; and chiefly Pennell who was in charge of the ship and not among any of the Shore Parties, but whom for character and capacity he ranked with Wilson. He had it in mind at one time to follow *The Worst Journey* with a tribute to the six men of the Northern Party who endured seven months of a Polar winter in an ice-cave; but what after all could be added to Priestley's own graphic and restrained account in *Antarctic Adventure*?

Cherry's method of writing was peculiar to himself. He did not write consecutively in pages, but in separate paragraphs dealing with such matters as came to mind; these he then pieced together in appropriate sequence. His writing has thus sometimes a certain abruptness which sharpens interest. His use of short simple sentences and of monosyllables is also effective. For example, on page 497 of this book: 'Wright came across to us. "It is the tent." I do not know how he knew. Just a waste of snow: to our right the remains of one of last year's cairns, a mere mound. . . .' Though he confessed 'My writing is my own despair,' as descriptive narrative *The Worst Journey* is without doubt a literary achievement that will always stand high in the annals of exploration. He also essayed another form of expression. He had caught something of the inspiration of water-colour painting from watching Wilson at work. But his own productions show conscious effort rather than native aptitude; he tried 'stippling' for effects of shade, a device of which Wilson would have disapproved. When showing me his sketches of Mount Erebus and other features of Antarctic scenery he asked for a definition of Art. When I hesitated, he said, 'Mine is: Reality touched with Emotion.' Walking in the garden he commented on his loneliness which advancing years did not lessen. To a suggestion that the remedy was in his own hands he smiled pensively but said nothing. Indeed he seemed the personification of a confirmed bachelor.

In 1932 an exhibition of Polar relics was held privately in London under the auspices of Frank Debenham. Gino Watkins was there, a modest and inconspicuous young fellow with a charming manner, on the very eve of his embarkation upon his last and fatal expedition to the Arctic. Cherry had turned up to arrange his corner of Antarctic treasures. He was in a rare mood of positive hilarity, bubbling over with gaiety and good cheer. It was as though the presences of his old sledging comrades were there beside him invisibly. And one realized how it was that he, almost the babe of the Expedition, had been dubbed at once 'The Cheery One'.

It was about this time that he became engaged in a private war with the local fox-hunting gentry and brought an action against them for trespass and damage. The defendants' Counsel tried in vain with professional facetiousness to elicit from the appellant a motive for bringing this action, and was disconcerted by his studiously laconic replies. Was it personal pique? Hurt pride? A taste for litigation? A crank's distaste for good old British blood-sports? Mr Cherry-Garrard was a famous explorer, as all knew; he was also a man of considerable property. Why make a mountain out of a mole-hill? – Counsel little knew that the quiet man whom he was thus interrogating was seething inwardly with suppressed fury. To all these questions the reply was simply and stonily: 'I have brought this case as a test-case. I am here for a decision.' He won it, but this did not make for his popularity among the sporting country folk.

In 1939 he did the best day's work for himself that he ever did, when near the middle fifties, by marrying Angela, daughter of the late Kenneth Turner of Ipswich, whose name was her nature and who gave him the best years of her life in selfless devotion. She brought a brightness into his life which shone through many 'a dark tremendous sea of cloud' that threatened to engulf him increasingly as the years went on. 'For a time,' wrote Frank Debenham,

> he recovered some of his flair for conversation and some interests in a wider prospect than the past. The war years were hardly such as to help him regain full mental balance and he became more withdrawn, more introspective than ever, and ceaselessly worried about his health. To his friends of earlier days this was a tragedy; they felt it was a case of a once noble mind now overthrown and disordered by dwelling on a far-off past of glorious friendship and perhaps a needlessly uneasy conscience about the part he played.

In 1947 Lamer, which like many another stately home had been for generations the grace and glory of the English countryside, was no more. The fiscal exactions of shortsighted politicians had rendered it uninhabitable as a private residence; demolition gangs of rapacious building contractors did the rest. But the estate is still beautiful and well farmed; other houses built and lived in, as well as the original tenants' cottages; and the 300 acres which Cherry planted after the first World War – three larch to one beech – have become fine and beautiful woods. He perforce exchanged the freehold of a landed proprietor for the exiguous tenancy of a London flat. By a singular coincidence, of which he was unaware till much later, this flat in Dorset House, Gloucester Place, overlooked the site of the former home, now demolished, of some of his Cherry ancestors two centuries before.

In October 1950 I received a (to me cryptic) letter from Cherry to the effect that he had 'never really managed to accept (1) that no mention was or is made that Scott took on his dog-teams further than he originally intended and (2) that it should be admitted that a depot was not laid.' (By 'no mention' he must have meant 'insufficient mention'; by 'depot' he meant the depot of dog-food that should have been laid at One Ton Camp.) He evidently intended to rectify this. The result, a year later, was *Postscript to The Worst Journey in the World*, printed for the author, a copy of which I received from him in September 1951. It is a somewhat tortuous document, and adds little of importance to the story, and has been omitted from the present text, but an attempt must be made to simplify what he intended to put on record.

Before starting south Scott had instructed Meares (on 20 October) that the dog-teams must be back at Hut Point in time, after sufficient rest, to transport to One Ton Camp five XS (extra Summit) rations, or at all hazards three, for the two returning Support Parties and Polar Party; and as much dog-food as they could carry. (One XS ration was a weekly supply of food per man.) The dog-teams were scheduled to return from 81° 15' and would thus have ample time to recuperate. (See Evans: *South with Scott*, pp. 161–3.) These orders were repeated to Simpson, who remained at the base, on 31 October. Scott's words were 'In case the dog-teams are unable to perform this work it will be necessary to organize a man-hauling party to undertake it. . . . The party should start about December 26th at latest.' The depot should be laid at One Ton not later than 10 January.

Enforced delays on the march obliged Scott to take the dogs more than 120 geographical miles further, in fact to the Lower Glacier Depot. Accordingly before pushing on from 81° 15' he sent back on 24 November a re-direction to Simpson that 'I am carrying the dog-teams further than I intended at first – the teams may be late returning, unfit for further work or non-existent' (page 347 *n*.: first part of message only quoted). The second part of the message ran '*so don't forget that the 3 XS ration units must be got to One Ton Camp Lat. 79½ S. somehow. Owing to delays the latest date can be extended to January 15th. . . .*' This was done. The dog-teams did not return till 4 January but a man-hauling party, leaving the base on 26 December, duly delivered three of the XS rations well before the appointed time (p. 397). 'The weights of the man-hauling party did not allow for the transport of the remaining two XS rations, nor for any of the dog-food' (pp. 426–7). The remaining two XS rations were in fact taken and depoted by Cherry on his lone Dog Journey early in March; but – and this omission was to prove crucial – no dog-food was ever taken to One Ton. For the purpose which the dog-food would have served was already long past. The dog-teams had been intended – never in any sense as a relief to the Polar Party – but as a reserve in case dog-teams should be available to speed Scott's return, by proceeding southwards as far as possible, and enable him (and possibly Wilson and Oates) to catch the ship home before the freezing of the sea. Hence his verbal instruction to Atkinson on the Summit: 'with the depot [of dog-food] which has been laid [at One Ton] come as far as you can' (p. 426).

This explains Scott's disappointment in finding that the dogs never came back along the southern route at all: they had never reached Mt Hooper, the next big depot south of One Ton. 7 March: 'We hope against hope that the dogs will have been to Mt Hooper; then we might pull through.' 8 March: 'The great question is: What shall we find at the depot? If the dogs have visited it we may get along a good distance, but if there is another short allowance of fuel, God help us indeed.' 10 March: 'Yesterday we marched up the depot, Mt Hooper. Cold comfort. Shortage on our allowance all round. I don't know that anyone is to blame. The dogs which would have been our salvation have evidently failed. Meares had a bad trip home I suppose.' (This surmise was in fact correct.)

These diary entries and those that follow have an almost unbearable poignancy. To continue from *The Worst Journey*:

> Thus it was that when Atkinson came to make his plans to go South with the dogs he found that there was no dog-food south of Corner Camp, and that the rations for the return of the Polar Party from One Ton Depot had still to be taken out. That is to say, the depot of dog-food spoken of by Scott did not exist.[3]

But Scott had also left instructions, never changed, that, in the event of the dogs returning fit with Meares, they should not be risked since they would be needed for scientific journeys in the following year. The teams would be augmented by the arrival of a fresh batch of dogs (and mules) in February (p. 424).

The situation with which Atkinson was faced at the end of February was this. The arrival of fresh animals and fresh equipment (though the dogs proved of little use); and of Crean with bad news of the collapse of Lieut. Evans, but good news of the prospects of the Polar Party; his own immediate duty to rescue Lieut. Evans and get him to Hut Point; the necessity of transporting the extra two XS rations to One Ton in time for the Polar Party, and the choice of an officer for this purpose. There were only two available; one was Wright but he, a scientist, was required for another duty; the other was Cherry-Garrard. Cherry was not a navigator, but this did not matter since the route from Hut Point to One Ton was well marked with cairns and it was confidently

3. *The Worst Journey*, p. 427.

expected that the Polar Party would be nearing One Ton when he reached it. He was given 24 days' food for himself and Dimitri and 21 days' food for the two dog-teams, together with the two XS rations for the Polar Party. He was to remember that Scott was not now dependent on the dogs for his return, and that he had given particular instructions that the dogs were not to be risked. If Scott had not reached One Ton before him, he must judge what to do.

Reasons for the near-impossibility of his deciding otherwise than he did have been adduced above; and reflection upon the whole sequence of events serves but to confirm one's belief in the inevitability of the final tragedy.

But if the first part of the 'Postscript' does little to add to our knowledge of the circumstances that wrought disaster to a heroic enterprise, the second part of it is sheer inspiration. For it is the expression of his ultimate faith. He writes as though the words were wrung from him. The short, rather jerky sentences, the poetic feeling, the patriotic sense, the touches of philosophy – they show that despite all his experience of and reflection upon life's disillusionment, he kept to the end his early ideals – his Christian ideals – intact and untarnished: his conviction that in spite of all appearances to the contrary nothing is too good to be true: that the best is the truest and the truest best; that through all frustrated purposes and apparently defeated endeavours there shines a light, reflecting the light that no darkness can overwhelm. He sees this truth exemplified in the fortitude of such men as Giordano Bruno, of Galileo, of Tyndale; in the thoughts of men like Sir Thomas Browne and George Herbert; in the nature-mysticism of St Francis; in the heroism of parachutists and fighters in the Resistance during the war. He sees it triumphantly vindicated in the characters of the men he knew and loved down South.

> . . . In such a world, violent, angry and tired, Wilson sets a standard of faith and work. In a world which destroys itself and beauty, desperately and impotently desiring peace, he helps . . .

We have missed him ever since he died. But you must find him: his voice, it is a quiet voice, is for those who listen. . . . Wilson's idea was forgetfulness of self. By putting that idea into action as well as in contemplation, and in suffering, by the time he started on our Winter Journey he had reached another plateau which is round no earthly Pole, where he was beyond ambition and beyond fear. He had the quiet mind. That feeling he could communicate to others. Such men do occur in history, but they are very rare, and when they do happen they are among the great ones of our race.

Glory? He knew it for a bubble: he had proved himself to himself. He was not worrying about glory. Power? He had power.

And again:

We cannot stop knowledge: we must use it well or perish. And we must do our tiny scrap to see that those who do use it are sound in mind and body, especially in mind, of good education, with a background of tradition, a knowledge of human nature and of history: with a certain standard of decency which inspires trust: with disinterestedness and self-control. Plato said the good ruler is a reluctant man. The really wise man knows what an awful thing it is to govern, and keeps away from it. Our problems are not new: they are as old as the men who hunted the prehistoric hills. When *they* hit one another on the head with stones the matter was confined to a few caves: now it shakes a crowded world more complicated than any watch. Human nature does not change: it becomes more dangerous. Those who guide the world now may think they are doing quite well: so perhaps did the dodo.

Man, having destroyed the whales, may end by destroying himself. The penguins may end like the prehistoric reptiles from which they sprang. All may follow the mammoths and dinosaurs into fossilized oblivion, like the ferns which grew at the South Pole two hundred million years ago, found by the Polar Party on the Beardmore, and carried on their sledge to the end at Wilson's special request: museum pieces of life in time.

Any age, new or old, wants courage and faith. To me, and perhaps to you, the interest of this story is the men, and it is the spirit of the men, 'the response of the spirit', which is interesting rather than what they did or failed to do: except in a superficial sense they never failed. That is how I see it, and I knew them pretty well. It is a story about human minds with all kinds of ideas and questions involved, which stretch beyond the furthest horizons.

Does it really matter, in the long run, whether Amundsen or Scott was first, by four weeks, at the Pole? Wilson did not think so, and we did not think so when we found them dead. Their story, Depot Journey and Polar Journey combined, has in it the elements of great tragedy, where each step follows the step before, probably, if not inevitably, with Fate not far away: a human story (not just a tale of adventure) told magnificently by Scott. Their England has been with us in two wars, by land, and sea, and in the air. 'Must fight it out to the last biscuit.'[4] Dunkirk to Pearl Harbour, no less. England took her risks, she knew she took them. Things came out for her that time: a winter journey indeed. Men who have faith; a Wilson who believed – in God: a Churchill who believed – in himself and in the essential guts of England. And men and women who, in appalling crisis, knew they were not beaten yet. . . .

Wilson was convinced he would come home: that he had more work to do. And indeed he had. Is it not remarkable what such a man can do not only when he is alive but also after his death? That is the power which lasts for good. Like Petrarch and St Francis he loved nature, and his love of nature went with his love of God. He interpreted all experience in the light of Christ. Surely 'the earth *is* the Lord's and all that therein is.' The flowers and the birds, the sea and sky, the ice and snow, the blizzards and hunger and pain were from the eternal God. 'Those which others call crosses, afflictions,

4. *Scott's Last Expedition*, vol. i, p. 591.

judgements, misfortunes, to me, who inquire further into them than their visible effects, they both appear, and in event have ever produced, the secret and dissembled favours of his affection' – is Sir Thomas Browne, but it might have been Bill, who had no doubt that it was good; even to the end when he wrote that he loved God with all his heart. Such a man is followed willingly, and quite literally, to the uttermost ends of the earth.

> But there are left delights as high as these,
> And I shall ever bless my destiny,
> That in a time, when under pleasant trees
> Pan is no longer sought, I feel a free,
> A leafy luxury, seeing I could please
> With these poor offerings, a man like thee.[5]

It is not in *my* power to put him into that stream of thought which runs like a thread of gold through the more hopeful side of history and religion, and leads through happiness, sorrow and much pain to beauty – beauty without any bitterness at all.

Why do some human beings desire with such urgency to do such things: regardless of consequences, voluntarily, conscripted by no one but themselves? No one knows. There is a strong urge to conquer the dreadful forces of nature, and perhaps to get consciousness of ourselves, of life, and of the shadowy workings of our human minds. Physical capacity is the only limit. I have tired to tell how, and when, and where. But why? That is a mystery.

When he wrote those words the clouds were lifting, his sky was clear. How this happened is best told by the one who has the best right to tell it. Angela writes:

Two wise and skilled psychiatrists looked after him from 1947. The first, Rupert Reynell, had literally got him on his

5. Keats, 1817.

feet again after a cataleptic stroke in the summer of 1946 which had left him bedridden for nearly a year. To our great sorrow that good friend died suddenly in 1948, but he gave Cherry in many ways the happiest six years of his life. He used these years to the very best advantage. He became very interested in book-collecting, and in a remarkably short time he made himself something of an expert on early books of travel, illustrated manuscripts, and the English classics. He was a regular visitor at Sotheby's and Hodgson's book sales, as well as the London book shops, and was surprised and delighted by the help, kindness and encouragement of all these people. He was the guest of honour at the Antiquarian Booksellers' Association dinner on 22 May 1952, the best attended meeting in the memory of anyone present. His speech on that occasion, printed in 'The Clique' on 7 June, was described by the Secretary as 'unforgettable and moving.' He also renewed his old pleasure of cruising in the Mediterranean. He loved being on the sea, watching the sea-birds, sketching the sunsets, and delighted in showing his wife the treasures of Venice, Athens, Rhodes and other ancient cities. After the long years of recurrent illness and immobility he rejoiced in walking, and made long stays at Eastbourne just for the pleasure of whole-day walks over the springy downland turf to the little villages of Jevington, Wilmington and Alfriston. He rejoiced to renew old friendships and show his friends how well he was! – and to make new ones through his book collecting, particularly with Mr and Mrs John Hodgson.

Then with devastating and inexplicable suddenness in the autumn of 1953 he broke down again. In 1955 the specialist who attended him was Doctor Gordon Mathias, who, by a strange coincidence, had as a young medical student met Mrs Wilson, and Mr Reginald Smith, and had become a friend and constant visitor to both their homes. So, though he had never met Cherry, he already knew a great deal about the Expedition and Cherry's part in it, when he came to look after him. This, of course, made an immediate bond between them. Gordon cared for him with great skill, patience, and gentleness, and it was he who succeeded in dispelling the last shreds of unjustified remorse that had haunted him, so that long before he reached journey's end as he did with quiet serenity on 18 May 1959 – Whitmonday – he could truly have affirmed with Bunyan's Pilgrim:

> Then fancies flee away,
> I'll care not what men say,
> I'll labour night and day
> To be a pilgrim.

Newman's 'Lead, kindly Light' and Bunyan's 'He who would valiant be' were in fact the two hymns most fitly chosen by his wife to be sung at his funeral service, and every line of both of them 'spoke to his condition'. He was buried in the Parish Church of Wheathampstead in the family grave; and in September 1962 a small statue of him by the sculptor Ivor Roberts-Jones was unveiled and dedicated in the presence of his closest friends. The figure, in polar clothing, stands in a small niche in the north transept of the church among many other Garrard memorials. He was the last of the Cherrys of Denford and the last of the Garrards of Lamer.

GEORGE SEAVER
1965

Chapter One
FROM ENGLAND TO
SOUTH AFRICA

Take a bowsy short leave of your nymphs on the shore,
And silence their mourning with vows of returning,
Though never intending to visit them more.

Dido and Aeneas

SCOTT USED TO say that the worst part of an expedition was over when the preparation was finished. So no doubt it was with a sigh of relief that he saw the *Terra Nova* out from Cardiff into the Atlantic on 15 June 1910. Cardiff had given the expedition a most generous and enthusiastic send-off, and Scott announced that it should be his first port on returning to England. Just three years more and the *Terra Nova*, worked back from New Zealand by Pennell, reached Cardiff again on 14 June 1913, and paid off there.

From the first everything was informal and most pleasant, and those who had the good fortune to help in working the ship out to New Zealand, under steam or sail, must, in spite of five months of considerable discomfort and very hard work, look back upon the voyage as one of the very happiest times of the expedition. To some of us perhaps the voyage out, the three weeks in the pack ice going South, and the Robinson Crusoe life at Hut Point are the pleasantest of many happy memories.

Scott made a great point that so far as was possible the personnel of the expedition must go out with the *Terra Nova*. Possibly he gave instructions that they were to be worked hard, and no doubt it was a good opportunity of testing our mettle. We had been chosen out of 8000 volunteers, executive officers, scientific staff, crew, and all.

We differed entirely from the crew of an ordinary merchant ship both in our personnel and in our methods of working. The executive officers were drawn from the Navy, as were also the crew. In addition there was the scientific staff, including one doctor who was not a naval surgeon, but who was also a scientist, and two others called by Scott 'adaptable helpers', namely Oates and myself. The scientific staff of the expedition numbered twelve members all told, but only six were on board: the remainder were to join the ship at Lyttelton, New Zealand, when we made our final embarcation for the South. Of those on the ship Wilson was chief of the scientific staff, and united in himself the various functions of vertebral zoologist, doctor, artist, and, as this book will soon show, the unfailing friend-in-need of all on board. Lieutenant Evans was in command, with Campbell as first officer. Watches were of course assigned immediately to the executive officers. The crew was divided into a port and starboard watch, and the ordinary routine of a sailing ship with auxiliary steam was followed. Beyond this no work was definitely assigned to any individual on board. How the custom of the ship arose I do not know, but in effect most things were done by volunteer labour. It was recognized that every one whose work allowed turned to immediately on any job which was wanted, but it was an absolutely voluntary duty – Volunteers to shorten sail? To coal? To shift cargo? To pump? To paint or wash down paintwork? They were constant calls – some of them almost hourly calls, day and night – and there was never any failure to respond fully. This applied not only to the scientific staff but also, whenever their regular duties allowed, to the executive officers. There wasn't an officer on the ship who did not shift coal till he was sick of the sight of it, but I heard no complaints. Such a system soon singles out the real willing workers, but it is apt to put an undue strain upon them. Meanwhile most of the executive officers as well as the scientific staff had their own work to do, which they were left to fit in as most convenient.

The first days out from England were spent in such hard and crowded work that we shook down very quickly. I then noticed for the first time Wilson's great gift of tact, and how quick he was to see the small things which make so much difference. At the same time his passion for work set a high standard. Pennell was another glutton.

We dropped anchor in Funchal Harbour, Madeira, about 4 p.m. on 23 June, eight days out. The ship had already been running under sail and steam, the decks were as clear as possible, there was some paintwork to show, and with a good harbour stow she looked thoroughly workmanlike and neat. Some scientific work, in particular tow netting and magnetic observations, had already been done. But even as early as this we had spent hours on the pumps, and it was evident that these pumps were going to be a constant nightmare.

In Madeira, as everywhere, we were given freely of such things as we required. We left in the early morning of 26 June, after Pennell had done some hours' magnetic work with the Lloyd Creak and Barrow Dip Circle.

On 29 June (noon position lat. 27° 10' N., long. 20° 21' W.) it was possible to write: 'A fortnight out today, and from the general appearance of the wardroom we might have been out a year.'

We were to a great extent strangers to one another when we left England, but officers and crew settled down to their jobs quickly, and when men live as close as we did they settle down or quarrel before very long. Let us walk into the cabins which surround the small wardroom aft. The first on the left is that of Scott and Lieutenant Evans, but Scott is not on board, and Wilson has taken his place. In the next cabin to them is Drake, the secretary. On the starboard side of the screw are Oates, Atkinson and Levick, the two latter being doctors, and on the port side Campbell and Pennell, who is navigator. Then Rennick and Bowers, the latter just home from the Persian Gulf – both of these are watchkeepers. In the next cabin are Simpson, meteorologist, back from Simla, with Nelson and Lillie, marine biologists. In the last cabin, the Nursery, are the youngest, and necessarily the best behaved, of this community, Wright, the physicist and chemist, Gran the Norwegian ski-expert, and myself, Wilson's helper and assistant zoologist. It is difficult to put a man down as performing any special job where each did so many, but that is roughly what we were.

Certain men already began to stand out. Wilson, with an apparently inexhaustible stock of knowledge on little things and big; always ready to give help, and always ready with sympathy and insight, a tremendous worker, and as unselfish as possible; a universal adviser. Pennell, as happy as the day was long, working out sights, taking his watch on the bridge, or if not on watch full of energy aloft, trimming coal, or any other job that came along; withal spending hours a day on magnetic work, which he did as a hobby, and not in any way as his job. Bowers was proving himself the best seaman on board, with an exact knowledge of the whereabouts and contents of every case, box and bale, and with a supreme contempt for heat or cold. Simpson was obviously a first-class scientist, devoted to his work, in which Wright gave him very great and unselfish help, while at the same time doing much of the ship's work. Oates and Atkinson generally worked together in a solid, dependable and somewhat humorous way.

Evans, who will always be called Lieutenant Evans in this book to distinguish him from Seaman Evans, was in charge of the ship, and did much to cement together the rough material into a nucleus which was capable of standing without any friction the strains of nearly three years of crowded, isolated and difficult life, ably seconded by Victor Campbell, first officer, commonly called The Mate, in whose hands the routine and discipline of the ship was most efficiently maintained. I was very frightened of Campbell.

Scott himself was unable to travel all the way out to New Zealand in the *Terra Nova* owing to the business affairs of the expedition, but he joined the ship from Simon's Bay to Melbourne.

The voyage itself on the sailing track from Madeira to the Cape was at first uneventful. We soon got into hot weather, and at night every available bit of deck space was used on which to sleep. The more particular slung hammocks, but

4

generally men used such deck space as they could find, such as the top of the icehouse, where they were free from the running tackle, and rolled themselves into their blankets. So long as we had a wind we ran under sail alone, and on those days men would bathe over the side in the morning, but when the engines were going we could get the hose in the morning, which was preferred, especially after a shark was seen making for Bowers's red breast as he swam.

The scene on deck in the early morning was always interesting. All hands were roused before six and turned on to the pumps, for the ship was leaking considerably. Normally, the well showed about ten inches of water when the ship was dry. Before pumping, the sinker would show anything over two feet. The ship was generally dry after an hour to an hour and a half's pumping, and by that time we had had quite enough of it. As soon as the officer of the watch had given the order, 'Vast pumping', the first thing to do was to strip, and the deck was dotted with men trying to get the maximum amount of water from the sea in a small bucket let down on a line from the moving ship. First efforts in this direction would have been amusing had it not been for the caustic eye of the 'Mate' on the bridge. If the reader ever gets the chance to try the experiment, especially in a swell, he will soon find himself with neither bucket nor water. The poor Mate was annoyed by the loss of his buckets.

Everybody was working very hard during these days; shifting coal, reefing and furling sail aloft, hauling on the ropes on deck, together with magnetic and meteorological observations, tow-netting, collecting and making skins and so forth. During the first weeks there was more cargo stowing and paintwork than at other times, otherwise the work ran in very much the same lines all the way out – a period of nearly five months. On 1 July we were overhauled by the only ship we ever saw, so far as I can remember, during all that time, the *Inverclyde*, a barque out from Glasgow to Buenos Aires. It was an oily, calm day with a sea like glass, and she looked, as Wilson quoted, 'like a painted ship upon a painted ocean', as she lay with all sail set.

We picked up the N.E. Trade two days later, being then north of the Cape Verde Islands (lat. 22° 28' N., long. 23° 5' W. at noon). It was a Sunday, and there was a general 'make and mend' throughout the ship, the first since we sailed. During the day we ran from deep clear blue water into a darkish and thick green sea. This remarkable change of colour, which was observed by the Discovery Expedition in much the same place, was supposed to be due to a large mass of pelagic fauna called plankton. The plankton, which drifts upon the surface of the sea, is distinct from the nekton, which swims submerged. The *Terra Nova* was fitted with tow nets with very fine meshes for collecting these inhabitants of the open sea, together with the algae, or minute plant organisms, which afford them an abundant food supply.

The plankton nets can be lowered when the ship is running at full speed, and a great many such hauls were made during the expedition.

July 5 had an unpleasant surprise in store. At 10.30 a.m. the ship's bell rang and there was a sudden cry of 'Fire quarters'. Two Minimax fire extinguishers finished the fire, which was in the lazarette, and was caused by a lighted lamp which was upset by the roll of the ship. The result was a good deal of smoke, a certain amount of water below and some singed paper, but we realized that a fire on such an old wooden ship would be a very serious matter, and greater care was taken after this.

Such a voyage shows Nature in her most attractive form, and always there was a man close by whose special knowledge was in the whales, porpoises, dolphins, fish, birds, parasites, plankton, radium and other things which we watched through microscopes or field-glasses. Nelson caught a Portuguese man-of-war (Arethusa) as it sailed past us close under the counter. These animals are common, but few can realize how beautiful they are until they see them, fresh-coloured from the deep sea, floating and sailing in a big glass bowl. It vainly tried to sail out, and vigorously tried to sting all who touched it. Wilson painted it.

From first to last the study of life of all kinds was of

absorbing interest to all on board, and when we landed in the Antarctic, as well as on the ship, everybody worked and was genuinely interested in all that lived and had its being on the fringe of that great sterile continent. Not only did officers who had no direct interest in anything but their own particular work or scientific subject spend a large part of their time in helping, making notes and keeping observations, but the seamen also had a large share in the specimens and data of all descriptions which have been brought back. Several of them became good pupils for skinning birds.

Meanwhile, perhaps the constant cries of 'Whale, whale!' or 'New bird!' or 'Dolphins!' sometimes found the biologist concerned less eager to leave his meal than the observers were to call him forth. Good opportunities of studying the life of sea birds, whales, dolphins and other forms of life in the sea, even those comparatively few forms which are visible from the surface, are not too common. A modern liner moves so quickly that it does not attract life to it in the same way as a slow-moving ship like the *Terra Nova*, and when specimens are seen they are gone almost as soon as they are observed. Those who wish to study sea life – and there is much to be done in this field – should travel by tramp steamers, or, better still, sailing vessels.

Dolphins were constantly playing under the bows of the ship, giving a very good chance for identification, and whales were also frequently sighted, and would sometimes follow the ship, as did also hundreds of sea birds, petrels, shearwaters and albatross. It says much for the interest and keenness of the officers on board that a complete hourly log was kept from beginning to end of the numbers and species which were seen, generally with the most complete notes as to any peculiarity or habit which was noticed. It is to be hoped that full use will be made, by those in charge of the working out of the results, of these logs which were kept so thoroughly and sometimes under such difficult circumstances and conditions of weather and sea. Though many helped, this log was largely the work of Pennell, who was an untiring and exact observer.

We lost the N.E. Trade about 7 July, and ran into the Doldrums. On the whole we could not complain of the weather. We never had a gale or big sea until after leaving South Trinidad, and though an old ship with no modern ventilation is bound to be stuffy in the tropics, we lived and slept on deck so long as it was not raining. If it rained at night, as it frequently does in this part of the world, a number of rolled-up forms could be heard discussing as to whether it was best to stick it above or face the heat below; and if the rain persisted, sleepy and somewhat snappy individuals were to be seen trying to force themselves and a maximum amount of damp bedding down the wardroom gangway. At the same time a thick wooden ship will keep fairly cool in the not severe heat through which we passed.

One want which was unavoidable was the lack of fresh water. There was none to wash in, though a glass of water was allowed for shaving! With an unlimited amount of sea water this may not seem much of a hardship; nor is it unless you have very dirty work to do. But inasmuch as some of the officers were coaling almost daily, they found that any amount of cold sea water, even with a euphemistically named 'sea-water soap', had no very great effect in removing the coal dust. The alternative was to make friends with the engine-room authorities and draw some water from the boilers.

Perhaps therefore it was not with purely disinterested motives that some of us undertook to do the stoking during the morning watch, and also later in the day during our passage through the tropics, since the engine-room staff was reduced by sickness. A very short time will convince any-body that the ease with which men accustomed to this work get through their watch is mainly due to custom and method. The ship had no forced draught nor modern ventilating apparatus. Four hours in the boiling fiery furnace which the *Terra Nova*'s stokehold formed in the tropics, unless there was a good wind to blow down the one canvas shaft, was a real test of staying power, and the actual shovelling of the coal into the furnaces, one after the other, was as child's play to handling the 'devil', as the weighty instrument used for breaking up the clinker and shaping the fire was called. The boilers were cylindrical marine or return tube boilers, the furnaces being six feet long by three feet wide, slightly lower at the back than at the front. The fire on the bars was kept wedge-shape, that is, some nine inches high at the back, tapering to about six inches in front against the furnace doors. The furnaces were corrugated for strength. We were supposed to keep the pressure on the gauge between 70 and 80, but it wanted some doing. For the most part it was done.

We did, however, get uncomfortable days with the rain sluicing down and a high temperature – everything wet on deck and below. But it had its advantages in the fresh water it produced. Every bucket was on duty, and the ship's company stripped naked and ran about the decks or sat in the stream between the laboratories and wardroom skylight and washed their very dirty clothes. The stream came through into our bunks, and no amount of caulking ever stopped it. To sleep with a constant drip of water falling upon you is a real trial. These hot, wet days were more trying to the nerves than the months of wet, rough but cooler weather to come, and it says much for the good spirit which prevailed that there was no friction, though we were crowded together like sardines in a tin.

July 12 was a typical day (lat. 4° 57′ N., long. 22° 4′ W.). A very hot, rainy night, followed by a squall which struck us while we were having breakfast, so we went up and set all sail, which took until about 9.30 a.m. We then sat in the water on the deck and washed clothes until just before midday, when the wind dropped, though the rain continued. So we went up and furled all sail, a tedious business when the sails are wet and heavy. Then work on cargo or coal till 7 p.m., supper and glad to get to sleep.

On 15 July (lat. 0° 40′ N., long. 21° 56′ W.) we crossed the Line with all pomp and ceremony. At 1.15 p.m. Neptune in the person of Seaman Evans hailed and stopped the ship. He came on board with his motley company, who solemnly paced aft to the break of the poop, where he was met by

Lieutenant Evans. His wife (Browning), a doctor (Paton), barber (Cheetham), two policemen and four bears, of whom Atkinson and Oates were two, grouped themselves round him while the barrister (Abbott) read an address to the captain, and then the procession moved round to the bath, a sail full of water slung in the break of the poop on the starboard side.

Nelson was the first victim. He was examined, then overhauled by the doctor, given a pill and a dose, and handed over to the barber, who lathered him with a black mixture consisting of soot, flour and water, was shaved by Cheetham with a great wooden razor, and then the policemen tipped him backward into the bath where the bears were waiting. As he was being pushed in he seized the barber and took him with him.

Wright, Lillie, Simpson and Levick followed, with about six of the crew. Finally Gran, the Norwegian, was caught as an extra – never having been across the Line in a British ship. But he threw the pill-distributing doctor over his head into the bath, after which he was lathered very gingerly, and Cheetham having been in once, refused to shave him at all, so they tipped him in and wished they had never caught him.

The procession re-formed, and Neptune presented certificates to those who had been initiated. The proceedings closed with a sing-song in the evening.

These sing-songs were of very frequent occurrence. The expedition was very fond of singing, though there was hardly anybody in it who could sing. The usual custom at this time was that everyone had to contribute a song in turn all round the table after supper. If he could not sing he had to compose a limerick. If he could not compose a limerick he had to contribute a fine towards the wine fund, which was to make much-discussed purchases when we reached Cape Town. At other times we played the most childish games – there was one called 'The Priest of the Parish has lost his Cap', over which we laughed till we cried, and much money was added to the wine fund.

As always happens, certain songs became conspicuous for a time. One of these I am sure that Campbell, who was always at work and upon whom the routine of the ship depended, will never forget. I do not know who it was that started singing

> Everybody works but Father,
> That poor old man,

but Campbell, who was the only father on board and whose hair was popularly supposed to be getting thin on the top of his head, may remember.

We began to make preparations for a run ashore – a real adventure on an uninhabited and unknown island. The sailing track of ships from England round the Cape of Good Hope lies out towards the coast of Brazil, and not far from the mysterious island of South Trinidad, 680 miles east of Brazil, in 20° 30′ S. and 29° 30′ W.

This island is difficult of access, owing to its steep rocky coast and the big Atlantic swell which seldom ceases. It has therefore been little visited, and as it is infested with land crabs the stay of the few parties which have been there has been short. But scientifically it is of interest, not only for the number of new species which may be obtained there, but also for the extraordinary attitude of wild sea birds towards human beings whom they have never learnt to fear. Before we left England it had been decided to attempt a landing and spend a day there if we should pass sufficiently near to it.

Those who have visited it in the past include the astronomer Halley, who occupied it, in 1700. Sir James Ross, outward bound for the Antarctic in 1839, spent a day there, landing 'in a small cove a short distance to the northward of the Nine Pin Rock of Halley, the surf on all other parts being too great to admit of it without hazarding the destruction of our boats'. Ross also writes that

Horsburgh mentions . . . 'that the island abounds with wild pig and goats; one of the latter was seen. With the view to add somewhat to the stock of useful creatures, a cock and two hens were put on shore; they seemed to enjoy the change, and, I have no doubt, in so unfrequented a situation, and so delightful a climate, will quickly increase in numbers.' I am afraid we did not find any of their descendants, nor those of the pig and goats.[1]

I doubt whether fowls would survive the land crabs very long. There are many wild birds on the island, however, which may feed the shipwrecked, and also a depot left by the Government for that purpose. Another visitor was Knight, who wrote a book called *The Cruise of the Alerte*, concerning his efforts to discover the treasure which is said to have been left there. Scott also visited it in the *Discovery* in 1901, when a new petrel was found which was afterwards called *Oestrelata wilsoni*, after the same 'Uncle Bill' who was zoologist of both Scott's Expeditions.

And so it came about that on the evening of 25 July we furled sail and lay five miles from South Trinidad with all our preparations made for a very thorough search of this island of treasure. Everything was to be captured, alive or dead, animal, vegetable or mineral.

At half-past five the next morning we were steaming slowly towards what looked like a quite impregnable face of rock, with bare cliffs standing straight out of the water, which, luckily for us, was comparatively smooth. As we coasted to try and find a landing-place the sun was rising behind the island, which reaches to a height of two thousand feet, and the jagged cliffs stood up finely against the rosy sky.

We dropped our anchor to the south of the island and a boat's crew left to prospect for a landing-place, whilst Wilson seized the opportunity to shoot some birds as specimens, including two species of frigate bird, and the seamen caught some of the multitudinous fish. We also fired shots at the sharks which soon thronged round the ship, and about which we were to think more before the day was done.

The boat came back with the news that a possible landing-place had been found, and the landing parties got off about

1. Ross, *Voyage to the Southern Seas*, vol. i, pp. 22–4.

8.30. The landing was very bad – a ledge of rock weathered out of the cliff to our right formed, as it were, a staging along which it was possible to pass on to a steeply shelving talus slope in front of us. The sea being comparatively smooth, everybody was landed dry, with their guns and collecting gear.

The best account of South Trinidad is contained in a letter written by Bowers to his mother, which is printed here. But some brief notes which I jotted down at the time may also be of interest, since they give an account of a different part of the island:

Having made a small depot of cartridges, together with a little fluffy tern and a tern's egg, which Wilson found on the rocks, we climbed westward, round and up, to a point from which we could see into the East Bay. This was our first stand, and we shot several white-breasted petrel (*Oestrelata trinitatis*), and also black-breasted petrel (*Oestrelata arminjoniana*). Later on we got over the brow of a cliff where the petrel were nesting. We took two nests, on each of which a white-breasted and a black-breasted petrel were paired. Wilson caught one in his hands and I caught another on its nest; it really did not know whether it ought to fly away or not. This gives rise to an interesting problem, since these two birds have been classified as different species, and it now looks as though they are the same.

The gannets and terns were quite extraordinary, like all the living things there. If you stay still enough the terns perch on your head. In any case they will not fly off the rocks till you are two or three feet away. Several gannets were caught in the men's hands. All the fish which the biologist collected today can travel quite fast on land. When the *Discovery* was here Wilson saw a fish come out of the sea, seize a land crab about eighteen inches away and take it back into the water.

The land crabs were all over the place in thousands; it seems probable that their chief enemies are themselves. They are regular cannibals.

Then we did a real long climb northwards, over rocks and tufty grass till 1.30 p.m. From the point we had reached we could see both sides of the island, and the little Martin Vas islands in the distance.

We found lots of little terns and terns' eggs, lying out on the bare rock with no nest at all. Hooper also brought us two little gannets – all fluffy, but even at this age larger than a rook. As we got further up we began to come across the fossilized trees for which the island is well known.

Four or five Captain biscuits made an excellent lunch, and afterwards we started to the real top of the island, a hill rising to the west of us. It was covered with a high scrubby bush and rocks, and was quite thick; in fact there was more vegetation here than on all the rest we had seen, and in making our way through it we had to keep calling in order to keep in touch with one another.

The tree ferns were numerous, but stunted. The gannets were sleeping on the tops of the bushes, and some of the crabs had climbed up the bushes and were sunning themselves on the top. These crabs were round us in thousands – I counted seven watching me out of one crack between two rocks.

We sat down under the lee of the summit, and thought it would not be bad to be thrown away on a desert island, little thinking how near we were to being stranded, for a time at any rate.

The crabs gathered round us in a circle, with their eyes turning towards us – as if they were waiting for us to die to come and eat us. One big fellow left his place in the circle and waddled up to my feet and examined my boots. First with one claw and then with the other he took a taste of my boot. He went away obviously disgusted: one could almost see him shake his head.

We collected, as well as our birds and eggs, some spiders, very large grasshoppers, wood-lice, cockchafers, with big and small centipedes. In fact, the place teemed with insect life. I should add that their names are given rather from the general appearance of the animals than from their true scientific classes.

We had a big and fast scramble down, and about half-way, when we could watch the sea breaking on the rocks far below, we saw that there was a bigger swell running. It was getting late, and we made our way down as fast as we could – denting our guns as we slipped on the rocks.

The lower we got the bigger the sea which had risen in our absence appeared to be. No doubt it was the swell of a big disturbance far away, and when we reached the débris slope where we had landed, flanked by big cliffs, we found everybody gathered there and the boats lying off – it being quite impossible for them to get near the shore.

They had just got a life-line ashore on a buoy. Bowers went out on to the rocks and secured it. We put our guns and specimens into a pile, out of reach, as we thought, of any possible sea. But just afterwards two very large waves took us – we were hauling in the rope, and must have been a good thirty feet above the base of the wave. It hit us hard and knocked us all over the place, and wetted the guns and specimens above us through and through.

We then stowed all gear and specimens well out of the reach of the seas, and then went out through the surf one by one, passing ourselves out on the line. It was ticklish work, but Hooper was the only one who really had a bad time. He did not get far enough out among the rocks which fringed the steep slope from which he started as a wave began to roll back. The next wave caught him and crashed him back, and he let go of the line. He was under quite a long time, and as the waves washed back all that we could do was to try and get the line to him. Luckily he succeeded in finding the slack of the line and got out.

When we first got down to the shore and things were looking nasty, Wilson sat down on the top of a rock and ate a biscuit in the coolest possible manner. It was an example to avoid all panicking, for he did not want the biscuit.

He remarked afterwards to me, apropos to Hooper, that it was a curious thing that a number of men, knowing that there was nothing they could do, could quietly watch a man fighting for his life, and he did not think that any but the British temperament could do so. I also found out later that he and I had both a touch of cramp while waiting for our turn to swim out through the surf.

The following is Bowers's letter:

Sunday, 31st July

The past week has been so crowded with incident, really, that I don't know where to start. Getting to land made me long for the mails from you, which are such a feature of getting to port. However, the strange uninhabited island which we visited will have to make up for my disappointment till we get to Cape Town – or rather Simon's Town. Campbell and I sighted S. Trinidad from the fore yardarm on 25th, and on 26th, at first thing in the morning, we crept up to an anchorage in a sea of glass. The S.E. Trades, making a considerable sea, were beating on the eastern sides, while the western was like a mill-pond. The great rocks and hills to over 2000 feet towered above us as we went in very close in order to get our anchor down, as the water is very deep to quite a short distance from the shore. West Bay was our selection, and so clear was the water that we could see the anchor at the bottom in 15 fathoms. A number of sharks and other fish appeared at once and several birds. Evans wanted to explore, so Oates, Rennick, Atkinson and myself went away with him – pulling the boat. We examined the various landings and found them all rocky and dangerous. There was a slight surf although the sea looked like a mill-pond. We finally decided on a previously unused place, which was a little inlet among the rocks.

There was nothing but rock, but there was a little nook where we decided to try and land. We returned to breakfast and found that Wilson and Cherry-Garrard had shot several Frigate and other birds from the ship, the little Norwegian boat – called a Pram – being used to pick them up. By way of explanation I may say that Wilson is a specialist in birds and is making a collection for the British Museum.

We all landed as soon as possible. Wilson and Garrard with their guns for birds: Oates with the dogs, and Atkinson with a small rifle: Lillie after plants and geological specimens: Nelson and Simpson along the shore after sea beasts, etc.: and last but not least came the entomological party, under yours truly, with Wright and, later, Evans, as assistants. Pennell joined up with Wilson, so altogether we were ready to 'do' the island. I have taken over the collection of insects for the expedition, as the other scientists all have so much to do that they were only too glad to shove the small beasts on me. Atkinson is a specialist in parasites: it is called 'Helminthology'. I never heard that name before. He turns out the interior of every beast that is killed, and also being a surgeon I suppose the subject must be interesting. White terns abounded on the island. They were ghost-like and so tame that they would sit on one's hat. They laid their eggs on pinnacles of rock without a vestige of nest, and singly. They looked just like stones. I suppose this was a protection from the land-crabs, about which you will have heard. The land-crabs of Trinidad are a byword and they certainly deserve the name, as they abound from sea-level to the top of the island. The higher up the bigger they were. The surface of the hills and valleys was covered with loose boulders, and the whole island being of volcanic origin, coarse grass is everywhere, and at about 1500 feet is an area of tree ferns and subtropical vegetation, extending up to nearly the highest parts. The withered trees of a former forest are everywhere and their existence unexplained, though Lillie had many ingenious theories. The island has been in our hands, the Germans', and is now Brazilian. Nobody has been able to settle there permanently, owing to the land-crabs. These also exclude mammal life. Captain Kidd made a treasure depot there, and some five years ago a chap named Knight lived on the island for six months with a party of Newcastle miners – trying to get at it. He had the place all right, but a huge landslide has covered up three-quarters of a million of the pirate's gold. The land-crabs are little short of a nightmare. They peep out at you from every nook and boulder. Their dead staring eyes follow your every step as if to say, 'If only you will drop down we will do the rest.' To lie down and sleep on any part of the island would be suicidal. Of course, Knight had a specially cleared place with all sorts of precautions, otherwise he would never have survived these beasts, which even tried to nibble your boots as you stood –

staring hard at you the whole time. One feature that would soon send a lonely man off his chump is that no matter how many are in sight they are all looking at you, and they follow step by step with a sickly deliberation. They are all yellow and pink, and next to spiders seem the most loathsome creatures on God's earth. Talking about spiders [Bowers always had the greatest horror of spiders] – I have to collect them as well as insects. Needless to say I caught them with a butterfly net, and never touched one. Only five species were known before, and I found fifteen or more – at any rate I have fifteen for certain. Others helped me to catch them, of course. Another interesting item to science is the fact that I caught a moth hitherto unknown to exist on the island, also various flies, ants, etc. Altogether it was a most successful day. Wilson got dozens of birds, and Lillie plants, etc. On our return to the landing-place we found to our horror that a southerly swell was rolling in, and great breakers were bursting on the beach. About five p.m. we all collected and looked at the whaler and pram on one side of the rollers and ourselves on the other. First it was impossible to take off the guns and specimens, so we made them all up to leave for the morrow. Second, a sick man had come ashore for exercise, and he could not be got off: finally, Atkinson stayed ashore with him. The breakers made the most awe-inspiring cauldron in our little nook, and it meant a tough swim for all of us. Three of us swam out first and took a line to the pram, and finally we got a good rope from the whaler, which had anchored well out, to the shore. I then manoeuvred the pram, and everybody plunged into the surf and hauled himself out with the rope. All well, but minus our belongings, and got back to the ship; very wet and ravenous was a mild way to put it. During my 12 to 4 watch that night the surf roared like thunder, and the ship herself was rolling like anything, and looked horribly close to the shore. Of course she was quite safe really. It transpired that Atkinson and the seaman had a horrible night with salt water soaked food, and the crabs and white terns which sat and watched them all night, squawking in chorus whenever they moved. It must have been horrible, though I would like to have stayed, and had I known anybody was staying would have volunteered. This with the noise of the surf and the cold made it pretty rotten for them. In the morning, Evans, Rennick, Oates and I, with two seamen and Gran, took the whaler and pram in to rescue the maroons. At first we thought we would do it by a rocket line to the end of the sheer cliff. The impossibility of such an idea was at once evident, so Gran and I went in close in the pram, and hove them lines to get off the gear first. I found the spoon-shaped pram a wonderful boat to handle. You could go in to the very edge of the breaking surf, lifted like a cork on top of the waves, and as long as you kept head to sea and kept your own head, you need never have got on the rocks, as the tremendous back-swish took you out like a shot every time. It was quite exciting, however, as we would slip in close in a lull, and the chaps in the whaler would yell, 'Look out!' if a big wave passed them, in which case you would pull out for dear life. Our first lines carried away, and then, with others, Rennick and I this time took the pram while Atkinson got as near the edge as safe to throw us the gear. I was pulling, and by watching our chances we rescued the cameras and glasses, once being carried over 12 feet above the rocks and only escaping by the back-swish. Then the luckiest incident of the day occurred, when in a lull we got our sick man down, and I jumped out, and he in, as I steadied the boat's stern. The next minute, the boat flew out on the back-wash with the seaman absolutely dry, and I was of course enveloped in foam and blackness two seconds later by a following wave. Twice the day before this had happened, but this time for a moment I thought, 'Where will my head strike?' as I was like a feather in a breeze in that swirl. When I banked it was about 15 feet above, and, very scratched and winded, I clung on with my nails and scrambled up higher. The next wave, a bigger one, nearly had me, but I was just too high to be sucked back. Atkinson and I then started getting the gear down, Evans having taken my place in the pram. By running down between waves we hove some items into the boat, including the guns and rifles, which I went right down to throw. These were caught and put into the boat, but Evans was too keen to save a bunch of boots that Atkinson threw down, and the next minute the pram passed over my head and landed high and dry, like a bridge, over the rocks between which I was wedged. I then scrambled out as the next wave washed her still higher, right over and over, with Evans and Rennick just out in time. The next wave – a huge one – picked her up, and out she bumped over the rocks and out to sea she went, water-logged, with the guns, fortunately, jammed under the thwarts. She was rescued by the whaler, baled out, and then Gran and one of the seamen manned her battered remains again, and we, unable to save the gear otherwise, lashed it to life-buoys, threw it into the sea and let it drift out with the back-wash to be picked up by the pram.

Clothes, watches and ancient guns, rifles, ammunition, birds (dead) and all specimens were, with the basket of crockery and food, soaked with salt water. However, the choice was between that or leaving them altogether, as anybody would have said had they seen the huge rollers breaking among the rocks and washing 30 to 40 feet up with the spray; in fact, we were often knocked over and submerged for a time, clinging hard to some rock or one of the ropes for dear life. Evans swam off first. Then I was about half an hour trying to rescue a hawser and some lines entangled among the rocks. It was an amusing job. I would wait for a lull, run down and haul away, staying under for smaller waves and running up the rocks like a hare when the warning came from the boat that a series of big ones were coming in. I finally rescued most of it – had to cut off some and got it to the place opposite the boat, and with Rennick secured it and sent it out to sea to be picked up. My pair of brown tennis shoes (old ones) had been washed off my feet in one of the scrambles, so I was wearing a pair of sea-boots – Nelson's, I found – which, fortunately for him, was one of the few pairs saved. The pram came in, and waiting for a back-wash Rennick swam off. I ran down after the following wave, and securing my green hat, which by the by is a most useful asset, struck out through the boiling, and grabbed the pram safely as we were lifted on the crest of an immense roller. However, we were just beyond its breaking-point, so all was well, and we arrived aboard after eight hours' wash and wetness, and none the worse, except for a few scratches, and yours truly in high spirits. We stayed there that night, and the following, Thursday, morning left. Winds are not too favourable so far, as we dropped the S.E. Trades almost immediately, and these are the variables between the Trades and the Westerlies. Still 2500 miles off our destination. Evans has therefore decided to steer straight for Simon's Town and miss out the other islands. It is a pity, but as it is winter down here, and the worst month of the year for storms at Tristan Da Cunha, it is perhaps just as well. I am longing to get to the Cape to have your letters and hear all about you. Except for the absence of news, life aboard is much to be desired. I simply love it, and enjoy every day of my existence here. Time flies like anything, and though it must have been long to you, to us it goes like the wind – so different to that fortnight on the passage home from India.[2]

After the return of the boat's crew we left South Trinidad, and the zoologists had a busy time trying to save as many as possible of the bird skins which had been procured. They skinned on all through the following night, and, considering that the birds had been lying out in the tropics for twenty-four hours soaked with sea-water and had been finally capsized in the overturned boat, the result was not so disappointing as was expected. But the eggs and many other articles were lost. Since the black-breasted and white-breasted petrels were seen flying and nesting paired together, it is reasonable to suppose that their former classification as two separate species will have to be revised.

Soon after leaving South Trinidad we picked up our first big long swell, logged at 8, and began to learn that the *Terra Nova* can roll as few ships can. This was followed by a stiff gale on our port beam, and we took over our first green seas. Bowers wrote home as follows:

2. Bowers's letter.

August 7th, Sunday

All chances of going to Tristan are over, and we are at last booming along with strong Westerlies with the enormous Southern rollers lifting us like a cork on their crests. We have had a stiff gale and a very high sea, which is now over, though it is still blowing a moderate gale, and the usual crowd of Albatross, Mollymawks, Cape Hens, Cape Pigeons, etc., are following us. These will be our companions down to the South. Wilson's idea is that, as the prevailing winds round the forties are Westerlies, these birds simply fly round and round the world – via Cape Horn, New Zealand and the Cape of Good Hope. We have had a really good opportunity now of testing the ship's behaviour, having been becalmed with a huge beam swell rolling 35° each way, and having stood out a heavy gale with a high sea. In both she has turned up trumps, and really I think a better little sea boat never floated. Compared to the Loch Torridon – which was always awash in bad weather – we are as dry as a cork, and never once shipped a really heavy sea. Of course a wooden ship has some buoyancy of herself, and we are no exception. We are certainly an exception for general seaworthiness – if not for speed – and a safer, sounder ship there could not be. The weather is now cool too – cold, some people call it. I am still comfortable in cotton shirts and whites, while some are wearing Shetland gear. Nearly everybody is provided with Shetland things. I am glad you have marked mine, as they are all so much alike. I am certainly as well provided with private gear as anybody, and far better than most, so, being as well a generator of heat in myself, I should be O.K. in any temperature. By the by Evans and Wilson are very keen on my being in the Western Party, while Campbell wants me with him in the Eastern Party. I have not asked to go ashore, but am keen on anything and am ready to do anything. In fact there is so much going on that I feel I should like to be in all three places at once – East, West and Ship.

Chapter Two
MAKING OUR EASTING DOWN

'TEN MINUTES to four, sir!'

It is an oilskinned and dripping seaman, and the officer of the watch, or his so-called snotty, as the case may be, wakes sufficiently to ask: 'What's it like?'

'Two hoops, sir!' answers the seaman, and makes his way out.

The sleepy man who has been wakened wedges himself more securely into his six foot by two – which is all his private room on the ship – and collects his thoughts, amid the general hubbub of engines, screw and the roll of articles which have worked loose, to consider how he will best prevent being hurled out of his bunk in climbing down, and just where he left his oilskins and sea-boots.

If, as is possible, he sleeps in the Nursery, his task may not be so simple as it may seem, for this cabin, which proclaims on one of the beams that it is designed to accommodate four seamen, will house six scientists or pseudo-scientists, in addition to a pianola. Since these scientists are the youngest in the expedition their cabin is named the Nursery.

Incidentally it forms also the gangway from the ward-room to the engine-room, from which it is divided only by a wooden door, which has a bad habit of swinging open and shutting with the roll of the ship and the weight of the oilskins hung upon it, and as it does so, wave upon wave, the clatter of the engines advances and recedes.

If, however, it is the officer of the watch he will be in a smaller cabin farther aft which he shares with one other man only, and his troubles are simplified.

Owing to the fact that the seams in the deck above have travelled many voyages, and have been strained in addition by the boat davits and deck-houses built on the poop, a good deal of water from this part of the deck, which is always awash in bad weather, finds its way below, that is into the upper bunks of our cabins. In order that only a minimum of this may find its way into our blankets a series of shoots, invented and carefully tended by the occupants of these bunks, are arranged to catch this water as it falls and carry it over our heads on to the deck of the cabin.

Thus it is that when this sleepy officer or scientist clambers down on to the deck he will, if he is lucky, find the water there, instead of leaving it in his bunk. He searches round for his sea-boots, gets into his oilskins, curses if the strings of his sou'wester break as he tries to tie them extra firmly round his neck, and pushes along to the open door into the wardroom. It is still quite dark, for the sun does not rise for another hour and a half, but the diminished light from the swinging oil-lamp which hangs there shows him a desolate early morning scene which he comes to hate – especially if he is inclined to be sick.

As likely as not more than one sea has partially found its way down during the night, and a small stream runs over the floor each time the ship rolls. The white oilcloth has slipped off the table, and various oddments, dirty cocoa cups, ash-trays and other litter from the night are rolling about too. The tin cups and plates and crockery in the pantry forrard of the wardroom come together with a sickening crash.

The screw keeps up a ceaseless chonk-chonk-chonk (pause), chonk-chonk-chonk (pause), chonk-chonk-chonk.

Watching his opportunity he slides down across the wet linoleum to the starboard side, whence the gangway runs up to the chart-house and so out on to the deck. Having glanced at the barograph slung up in the chart-room, and using all his strength to force the door out enough to squeeze through, he scrambles out into blackness.

The wind is howling through the rigging, the decks are awash. It is hard to say whether it is raining, for the spray cut off by the wind makes rain a somewhat insignificant event. As he makes his way up on to the bridge, not a very lofty climb, he looks to see what sail is set, and judges so far as he can the force of the wind.

Campbell, for he is the officer of the morning watch (4 a.m.–8 a.m.) has a talk with the officer he is relieving, Bowers. He is given the course, the last hour's reading on the Cherub patent log trailing out over the stern, and the experiences of the middle watch of the wind, whether rising or falling or squalling, and its effect on the sails and the ship. 'If you keep her on her present course, she's all right, but if you try and bring her up any more she begins to shake. And, by the way, Penelope wants to be called at 4.30.' Bowers's 'snotty', who is Oates, probably makes some ribald remarks, such as no midshipman should to a full lieutenant, and they both disappear below. Campbell's snotty, myself, appears about five minutes afterwards trying to look as though some important duty and not bed had kept him from making an earlier appearance. Meanwhile the leading hand musters the watch on deck and reports them all present.

'How about that cocoa?' says Campbell. Cocoa is a useful thing in the morning watch, and Gran, who used to be Campbell's snotty, and whose English was not then perfect, said he was glad of a change because he 'did not like being turned into a drumstick' (he meant a domestic).

So cocoa is the word and the snotty starts on an adventurous voyage over the deck to the galley which is forrard; if he is unlucky he gets a sea over him on the way. Here he finds the hands of the watch, smoking and keeping warm, and he forages round for some hot water, which he gets safely back to the pantry down in the wardroom. Here he mixes the cocoa and collects sufficient clean mugs (if he can find them), spoons, sugar and biscuits to go round. These he carefully 'chocks off' while he goes and calls Wilson and gives him his share – for Wilson gets up at 4.30 every morning to sketch the sunrise, work at his scientific paintings and watch the seabirds flying round the ship. Then back to the bridge, and woe betide him if he falls on the way, for then it all has to be done over again.

Pennell, who sleeps under the chart table on the bridge, is also fed and inquires anxiously whether there are any stars showing. If there are he is up immediately to get an observation, and then retires below to work it out and to tabulate the endless masses of figures which go to make up the results of his magnetic observations – dip, horizontal force and total force of the magnetic needle.

A squall strikes the ship. Two blasts of the whistle fetches the watch out, and 'Stand by topsail halyards', 'In inner jib', sends one hand to one halyard, the midshipman of the watch to the other, and the rest on to foc'stle and to the jib down-haul. Down comes the jib and the man standing by the fore topsail halyard, which is on the weather side of the galley, is drenched by the crests of two big seas which come over the rail.

But he has little time to worry about things like this, for the wind is increasing and 'Let go topsail halyards' comes through the megaphone from the bridge, and he wants all his wits to let go the halyard from the belaying-pins and jump clear of the rope tearing through the block as the topsail yard comes sliding down the mast.

'Clew up,' is the next order, and then 'All hands furl fore and main upper topsails', and up we go out on to the yard. Luckily the dawn is just turning the sea grey and the ratlines begin to show up in relief. It is far harder for the first and middle watches, who have to go aloft in complete darkness. Once on the yard you are flattened against it by the wind. The order to take in sail always fetches Pennell out of his chart-house to come and take a hand.

The two sodden sails safely furled – luckily they are small ones – the men reach the deck to find that the wind has shifted a little farther aft and they are to brace round. This finished, it is broad daylight, and the men set to work to coil up preparatory to washing decks – not that this would seem very necessary. Certainly there is no hose wanted this morn-ing, and a general kind of tidying up and coiling down ropes is more what is done.

The two stewards, Hooper, who is to land with the Main Party, and Neale, who will remain with the Ship's Party, turn out at six and rouse the afterguard for the pumps, a daily evolution, and soon an unholy din may be heard coming up from the wardroom. 'Rouse and shine, rouse and shine: show a leg, show a leg' (a relic of the old days when seamen took their wives to sea). 'Come on, Mr Nelson, it's seven o'clock. All hands on the pumps!'

From first to last these pumps were a source of much exercise and hearty curse. A wooden ship always leaks a little, but the amount of water taken in by the *Terra Nova* even in calm weather was extraordinary, and could not be traced until the ship was dry-docked in Lyttelton, New Zealand, and the forepart was flooded.

In the meantime the ship had to be kept as dry as possible, a process which was not facilitated by forty gallons of oil which got loose during the rough weather after leaving South Trinidad, and found its way into the bilges. As we found later, some never-to-be-sufficiently-cursed stevedore had left one of the bottom boards only half-fitted into its neighbours. In consequence the coal dust and small pieces of coal, which was stowed in this hold, found their way into the bilges. Forty gallons of oil completed the havoc and the pumps would gradually get more and more blocked until it was necessary to send for Davies, the carpenter, to take parts of them to pieces and clear out the oily coal balls which had stopped them. This pumping would sometimes take till nearly eight, and then would always have to be repeated again in the evening, and sometimes every watch had to take a turn. At any rate it was good for our muscles.

The pumps were placed amidships, just abaft the main mast, and ran down a shaft adjoining the after hatch, which led into the holds which were generally used for coal and patent fuel. The spout of the pump opened about a foot above the deck, and the plungers were worked by means of two horizontal handles, much as a bucket is wound up on the drum of a cottage well. Unfortunately, this part of the main deck, which is just forward of the break of the poop, is more subject to seas breaking inboard than any other part of the ship, so when the ship was labouring the task of those on the pump was not an enviable one. During the big gale going South the water was up to the men's waists as they tried to turn the handles, and the pumps themselves were feet under water.

From England to Cape Town these small handles were a great inconvenience. There was very much pumping to be done and there were plenty of men to do it, but the handles were not long enough to allow more than four men to each handle. Also they gave no secure purchase when the ship was rolling heavily, and when a big roll came there was nothing to do but practically stop pumping and hold on, or you found yourself in the scuppers.

At Cape Town a great improvement was made by extending the crank handles right across the decks, the outside end turning in a socket under the rail. Fourteen men could then get a good purchase on the handles and pumping became a more pleasant exercise and less of a nuisance.

Periodically the well was sounded by an iron rod being lowered on the end of a rope, by which the part that came up wet showed the depth of water left in the bilge. When this had been reduced to about a foot in the well, the ship was practically dry, and the afterguard free to bathe and go to breakfast.

Meanwhile the hands of the watch had been employed on the ropes and sails as the wind made necessary, and, when running under steam as well as sail, hoisting ashes up the two shoots from the ash-pits of the furnaces to the deck, whence they went into the ditch.

It is eight bells (8 o'clock) and the two stewards are hurrying along the decks, hoping to get the breakfast safely from galley to wardroom. A few naked officers are pouring seawater over their heads on deck, for we are under sail alone and there is no steam to work the hose. The watch keepers and their snotties of the night before are tumbling out of their bunks, and a great noise of conversation is coming from the wardroom, among which some such remarks as: 'Give the jam a wind, Marie'; 'After you with the coffee'; 'Push along the butter' are frequent. There are few cobwebs that have not been blown away by breakfast-time.

Rennick is busy breakfasting preparatory to relieving

Campbell on the bridge. Meanwhile, the hourly and four-hourly ship's log is being made up – force of the wind, state of the sea, height of the barometer, and all the details which a log has to carry – including a reading of the distance run as shown by the patent log line – (many is the time I have forgotten to take it just at the hour and have put down what I thought it ought to be, and not what it was).

The morning watch is finished.

Suddenly there is a yell from somewhere amidships – 'STEADY' – a stranger might have thought there was something wrong, but it is a familiar sound, answered by a 'STEADY IT IS, SIR', from the man at the wheel, and an anything but respectful, 'One – two – three – STEADY' from everybody having breakfast. It is Pennell who has caused this uproar. And the origin is as follows:

Pennell is the navigator, and the standard compass, owing to its remoteness from iron in this position, is placed on the top of the ice-house. The steersman, however, steers by a binnacle compass placed aft in front of his wheel. But these two compasses for various reasons do not read alike at a given moment, while the standard is the truer of the two.

At intervals, then, Pennell or the officer of the watch orders the steersman to 'Stand by for a steady', and goes up to the standard compass, and watches the needle. Suppose the course laid down is S. 40 E. A liner would steer almost true to this course unless there was a big wind or sea. But not so the old *Terra Nova*. Even with a good steersman the needle swings a good many degrees either side of the S. 40 E. But as it steadies momentarily on the exact course Pennell shouts his 'Steady', the steersman reads just where the needle is pointing on the compass card before him, say S. 47 E., and knows that this is the course which is to be steered by the binnacle compass.

Pennell's yells were so frequent and ear-piercing that he became famous for them, and many times in working on the ropes in rough seas and big winds, we have been cheered by this unmusical noise over our heads.

We left Simon's Bay on Friday, 2 September, 'to make

our Easting down' from the Cape of Good Hope to New Zealand, that famous passage in the Roaring Forties which can give so much discomfort or worse to sailing ships on their way.

South Africa had been hospitable. The Admiral Commanding the Station, the Naval Dockyard, and H.M.S. *Mutine* and H.M.S. *Pandora*, had been more than kind. They had done many repairs and fittings for us and had sent fatigue parties to do it, thus releasing men for a certain amount of freedom on shore, which was appreciated after some nine weeks at sea. I can remember my first long bath now.

Scott, who was up country when we arrived, joined the ship here, and Wilson travelled ahead of us to Melbourne to carry out some expedition work, chiefly dealing with the Australian members who were to join us in New Zealand.

One or two of us went out to Wynberg, which Oates knew well, having been invalided there in the South African War with a broken leg, the result of a fight against big odds when, his whole party wounded, he refused to surrender. He told me later how he had thought he would bleed to death, and the man who lay next to him was convinced he had a bullet in the middle of his brain – he could feel it wobbling about there! Just now his recollections only went so far as to tell of a badly wounded Boer who lay in the next bed to him when he was convalescent, and how the Boer insisted on getting up to open the door for him every time he left the ward, much to his own discomfort.

Otherwise the recollections which survive of South Africa are an excellent speech made on the expedition by John Xavier Merriman, and the remark of a seaman who came out to dinner concerning one John, the waiter, that 'he moved about as quick as a piece of sticking-plaster!'

Leaving Simon's Town at daybreak we did magnetic work all day, sailing out from False Bay with a biggish swell in the evening. We ran southerly in good weather until Sunday morning, when the swell was logged at 8 and the glass was falling fast. By the middle watch it was blowing a full gale and for some thirty hours we ran under reefed foresail, lower topsails and occasionally reefed upper topsails, and many of us were sick.

Then after two days of comparative calm we had a most extraordinary gale from the east, a thing almost unheard of in these latitudes (38° S. to 39° S.). All that we could do was to put the engines at dead slow and sail northerly as close to the wind as possible. Friday night, 9 September it blew force 10 in the night, and the morning watch was very lively with the lee rail under water.

Directly after breakfast on Saturday, 10 September, we wore ship, and directly afterwards the gale broke and it was raining, with little wind, during the day.

The morning watch had a merry time on Tuesday, 13 September when a fresh gale struck them while they were squaring yards. So unexpected was it that the main yards were squared and the fore were still round, but it did not last long and was followed by two splendid days – fine weather with sun, a good fair wind and the swell astern.

The big swell which so often prevails in these latitudes is a most inspiring sight, and must be seen from a comparatively small ship like the *Terra Nova* for its magnitude to be truly appreciated. As the ship rose on the crest of one great hill of water the next big ridge was nearly a mile away, with a sloping valley between. At times these seas are rounded in giant slopes as smooth as glass; at others they curl over, leaving a milk-white foam, and their slopes are marbled with a beautiful spumy tracery. Very wonderful are these mottled waves: with a following sea, at one moment it seemed impossible that the great mountain which is overtaking the ship will not overwhelm her, at another it appears inevitable that the ship will fall into the space over which she seems to be suspended and crash into the gulf which lies below.

But the seas are so long that they are neither dangerous nor uncomfortable – though the *Terra Nova* rolled to an extraordinary extent, quite constantly over 50° each way, and sometimes 55°.

The cooks, however, had a bad time trying to cook for some fifty hands in the little galley on the open deck. Poor

Archer's efforts to make bread sometimes ended in the scuppers, and the occasional jangle of the ship's bell gave rise to the saying that 'a moderate roll rings the bell and a big roll brings out the cook'.

Noon on Sunday, 18 September found us in latitude 39° 20' S. and longitude 66° 9' E., after a very good run, for the *Terra Nova*, of 200 miles in the last twenty-four hours. This made us about two days' run from St Paul, an uninhabited island formed by the remains of an old volcano, the crater of which, surrounded as it were by a horseshoe of land, forms an almost landlocked harbour. It was hoped to make a landing here for scientific work, but it is a difficult harbour to make. We ran another 200 miles on Monday, and on Tuesday all preparations were made for the landing, with suitable equipment, and we were not a little excited at the opportunity.

At 4.30 a.m. the next morning all hands were turned out to take in sail preparatory to rounding St Paul which was just visible. The weather was squally, but not bad. By 5 a.m., however, it was blowing a moderate gale, and by the time we had taken in all sail we had to give up hopes of a landing. We were thoroughly sick of sails by the time we finally reefed the foresail and ran before the wind under this and lower topsails.

We passed quite close to the island and could see into the crater, and the cliffs beyond which rose from it, covered with greenish grass. There were no trees, and of birds we only saw those which frequent these seas. We had hoped to find penguins and albatross nesting on the island at this time of the year, and this failure to land was most disappointing. The island is 860 feet high, and, for its size, precipitous. It extends some two miles in length and one mile in breadth.

The following day all the afterguard were turned on to shift coal. It should be explained that up to this time the bunkers, which lay one on the port and the other on the starboard side of the furnaces, had been entirely filled as required by two or more officers who volunteered from day to day.

We took on board 450 tons of Crown Patent Fuel at Cardiff in June 1910. This coal is in the form of bricks, and is most handy since it can be thrown by hand from the holds through the bunker doors in the boiler-room bulkhead which after a time was left higher than the sinking level of the coal. The coal to be landed was this patent fuel, and it was now decided to shift farther aft all the patent fuel which was left, and stack it against the boiler-room bulkhead, the coal which was originally there having been fed to the furnaces. Thus the dust which was finding its way through the floorboards, and choking the pumps, could be swept up, and a good stow could be made preparatory to the final fit-out in New Zealand, while the coal which was to be taken on board at Lyttelton could be loaded through the main hatch.

In the meantime the gale which had sprung up six days before and prevented us landing had died down. After leaving St Paul we had let the fires out and run under sail alone, and the following two days we ran 119 and 141 miles respectively, being practically becalmed at times on the following day, and only running 66 miles.

By Tuesday night, 27 September, we had finished the coaling, and we celebrated the occasion by a champagne dinner. At the same time we raised steam. Scott was anxious to push on, and so indeed was everybody else. But the wind was not disposed to help us, and headed us a good deal during the next few days, and it was not until 2 October that we were able to set all plain sail in the morning watch.

This absence of westerly winds in a region in which they are usually too strong for comfort was explained by Pennell by a theory that we were travelling in an anti-cyclone, which itelf was travelling in front of a cyclone behind us. We were probably moving under steam about the same pace as the disturbance, which would average some 150 miles a day.

From this may be explained many of the reports of continual bad weather met by sailing ships and steamers in these latitudes. If we had been a sailing ship without auxiliary steam the cyclone would have caught us up, and we should have been travelling with it, and consequently in continual bad weather. On the other hand, a steamer pure and simple would have steamed through good and bad alike. But we, with our auxiliary steam, only made much the same headway as the disturbance travelling in our wake, and so remained in the anticyclone.

Physical observations were made on the outward voyage by Simpson and Wright[1] into the atmospheric electricity over the ocean, one set of which consisted of an inquiry into the potential gradient, and observations were undertaken at Melbourne for the determination of the absolute value of the potential gradient over the sea.[2] Numerous observations were also made on the radium content of the atmosphere over the ocean, to be compared afterwards with observations in the Antarctic air. The variations in radium content were not large. Results were also obtained on the voyage of the *Terra Nova* to New Zealand upon the subject of natural ionization in closed vessels.

In addition to the work of the ship and the physical work above mentioned, work in vertebrate zoology, marine biology and magnetism, together with four-hourly observations of the salinity and temperature of the sea, was carried out during the whole voyage.

In vertebrate zoology Wilson kept an accurate record of birds, and he and Lillie another record of whales and dolphins. All the birds which could be caught, both at sea and on South Trinidad Island, were skinned and made up into museum specimens. They were also examined for external and internal parasites by Wilson, Atkinson and myself, as were also such fish and other animals as could be caught, including flying fish, a shark, and last but not least, whales in New Zealand.

The method of catching these birds may be worth describing. A bent nail was tied to a line, the other end of which was made fast to the halyards over the stern. Sufficient length

1. Vide *Scott's Last Expedition*, vol. ii, pp. 454–6.
2. 'Atmospheric Electricity over the Ocean', by G. C. Simpson and C. S. Wright, *Pro. Royal Soc.* A, vol. 85, 1911.

of line was allowed either to cause the nail to just trail in the sea in the wake of the ship or for the line to just clear the sea. Thus when the halyard was hoisted to some thirty or forty feet above the deck, the line would be covering a considerable distance of sea.

The birds flying round the ship congregate for the main part in the wake, for here they find the scraps thrown overboard on which they feed. I have seen six albatross all together trying to eat up an empty treacle tin.

As they fly to and fro their wings are liable to touch the line which is spread out over the sea. Sometimes they will hit the line with the tips of their wings, and then there is no resulting capture, but sooner or later a bird will touch the line with the part of the wing above the elbow-joint (humerus). It seems that on feeling the contact the bird suddenly wheels in the air, thereby causing a loop in the line which tightens round the bone. At any rate the next thing that happens is that the bird is struggling on the line and may be hauled on board.

The difficulty is to get a line which is light enough to fly in the air, but yet strong enough to hold the large birds, such as albatross, without breaking. We tried fishing line with no success, but eventually managed to buy some 5-ply extra strong cobbler's thread, which is excellent for the purpose. But we wanted not only specimens, but also observations of the species, the numbers which appeared, and their habits, for little is known as yet of these sea birds. And so we enlisted the help of all who were interested, and it may be said that all the officers and many of the seamen had a hand in producing the log of sea birds, to which additions were made almost hourly throughout the daylight hours. Most officers and men knew the more common sea birds in the open ocean, and certainly of those in the pack and fringes of the Antarctic continent, which, with rare exceptions, is the southern limit of bird life.

A number of observations of whales, illustrated by Wilson, were made, but the results so far as the seas from England to the Cape and New Zealand are concerned, are not of great importance, partly because close views were seldom obtained, and partly because the whales inhabiting these seas are fairly well known. On 3 October 1910, in latitude 42° 17′ S. and longitude 111° 18′ E., two adults of *Balaenoptera borealis* (Northern Rorqual) were following the ship close under the counter, length 50 feet, with a light-coloured calf some 18–20 feet long swimming with them. It was established by this and by a later observation in New Zealand, when Lillie helped to cut up a similar whale at the Norwegian Whaling Station at the Bay of Islands, that this Rorqual which frequents the sub-Antarctic seas is identical with our Northern Rorqual;[3] but this was the only close observation of any whales obtained before we left New Zealand.

General information with regard to such animals is useful, however, as showing the relative abundance of plankton on which the whales feed in the ocean. There are, for instance, more whales in the Antarctic than in warmer seas; and some whales at any rate (e.g. Humpback whales) probably come north into warmer waters in the winter rather for breeding purposes than to get food.[4]

With regard to dolphins four species were observed beyond question. The rarest dolphin seen was *Tersio peronii*, the peculiarity of which is that it has no dorsal fin. This was seen on 20 October 1910, in latitude 42° 51′ S. and longitude 153° 56′ E.

Reports of whales and dolphins which are not based upon carcasses and skeletons must be accepted with caution. It is most difficult to place species with scientific accuracy which can only be observed swimming in the water, and of which more often than not only blows and the dorsal fins can be observed. The nomenclature of dolphins especially leaves much to be desired, and it is to be hoped that some expedition in the future will carry a Norwegian harpooner, who could

3. *See* B.A.E., 1910, Nat. Hist. Report, vol. i, No. 3, p. 117.
4. ibid., p. 111.

do other work as well since they are very good sailors. Wilson was strongly of this opinion and tried hard to get a harpooner, but they are expensive people so long as the present boom in whaling lasts, and perhaps it was on the score of expense that the idea was regretfully abandoned. We carried whaling gear formerly taken on the Discovery Expedition, and kindly lent for this expedition by the Royal Geographical Society of London. A few shots were tried, but an unskilled harpooner stands very little chance. If you go whaling you must have had experience.

The ship was not slowed down to enable marine biological observations to be taken on this part of the expedition, but something like forty samples of plankton were taken with a full-speed net. We were unable to trawl on the bottom until we reached Melbourne, when a trawl was made in Port Phillip Harbour to try the gear and accustom men to its use. It was not a purpose of the expedition to spend time in deep-sea work until it reached Antarctic seas.

For four days the wind, such as there was of it, was dead ahead; it is not very often in the Forties that a ship cannot make progress for want of wind. But having set all plain sail on 2 October with a falling glass we got a certain amount of wind on the port beam, and did 158 miles in the next twenty-four hours. Sunday being quiet Scott read service while the officers and men grouped round the wheel. We seldom had service on deck; for Sundays became proverbial days for a blow on the way out, and service, if held at all, was generally in the ward-room. On one famous occasion we tried to play the pianola to accompany the hymns, but, since the rolls were scored rather for musical effect than for church services, the pianola was suddenly found to be playing something quite different from what was being sung. All through the expedition the want of someone who could play the piano was felt, and such a man is certainly a great asset in a life so far removed from all the pleasures of civilization. As Scott wrote in *The Voyage of the Discovery*, where one of the officers used to play each evening:

37

This hour of music has become an institution which none of us would willingly forgo. I don't know what thoughts it brings to others, though I can readily guess; but of such things one does not care to write. I can well believe, however, that our music smooths over many a ruffle and brings us to dinner each night in that excellent humour, where all seem good-tempered, though 'cleared for action' and ready for fresh argument.

The wind freshened to our joy; Scott was impatient; there was much to be done and the time for doing it was not too long, for it had been decided to leave New Zealand at an earlier date than had been attempted by any previous expedition, in order to penetrate the pack sooner and make an early start on the depot journey. The faintest glow of the Aurora Australis which was to become so familiar to us was seen at this time, but what aroused still more interest was the capture of several albatross on the lines flowing out over the stern.

The first was a 'sooty' (cornicoides). We put him down on the deck, where he strutted about in the proudest way, his feet going flop – flop – flop as he walked. He was a most beautiful bird, sooty black body, a great black head with a line of white over each eye and a gorgeous violet line running along his black beak. He treated us with the greatest con-tempt, which, from such a beautiful creature, we had every appearance of deserving. Another day a little later we caught a wandering albatross, a black-browed albatross, and a sooty albatross all together, and set them on the deck tethered to the ventilators while their photographs were taken. They were such beautiful birds that we were loath to kill them, but their value as scientific specimens outweighed the wish to set them free, and we gave them ether so that they did not suffer.

The Southern Ocean is the home of these and many species of birds, but among them the albatross is pre-eminent. It has been mentioned that Wilson believed that the albatross, at any rate, fly round and round the world over these stormy seas before the westerly winds, landing but once a year on such islands as Kerguelen, St Paul, the Auckland Islands and others to breed. If so, the rest that they can obtain upon the big breaking rollers which prevail in these latitudes must be unsatisfactory judged by the standard of more civilized birds. I have watched sea birds elsewhere of which the same individuals appeared to follow the ship day after day for many thousands of miles, but on this voyage I came to the conclusion that a different set of birds appeared each morning, and that they were hungry when they arrived. Certainly they flew astern and nearer to the ship in the morning, feeding on the scraps thrown overboard. As the day went on and the birds' hunger was satisfied, they scattered, and such of them as continued to fly astern of the ship were a long way off. Hence we caught the birds in the early morning, and only one bird was caught after midday.

The wind continued favourable and was soon blowing quite hard. On Friday, 7 October, we were doing 7·8 knots under sail alone, which was very good for the old Terra Push, as she was familiarly called: and we were then just 1000 miles from Melbourne. By Saturday night we were standing by topgallant halyards. Campbell took over the watch at 4 a.m. on Sunday morning. It was blowing hard and squally, but the ship still carried topgallants. There was a big following sea.

At 6.30 a.m. there occurred one of those incidents of sea life which are interesting though not important. Quite suddenly the first really big squall we had experienced on the voyage struck us. Topgallant halyards were let go, and the fore topgallant yard came down, but the main topgallant yard jammed when only half down. It transpired afterwards that a gasket which had been blown over the yard had fouled the block of the sheet of the main upper topsail. The topgallant yard was all tilted to starboard and swaying from side to side, the sail seemed as though it might blow out at any moment, and was making a noise like big guns, and the mast was shaking badly.

It was expected that the topgallant mast would go, but

nothing could be done while the full fury of the wind lasted. Campbell paced quietly up and down the bridge with a smile on his face. The watch was grouped round the ratlines ready to go aloft, and Crean volunteered to go up alone and try and free the yard, but permission was refused. It was touch and go with the mast and there was nothing to be done.

The squall passed, the sail was freed and furled, and the next big squall found us ready to lower upper topsails and all was well. Finally the damage was a split sail and a strained mast.

The next morning a new topgallant sail was bent, but quite the biggest hailstorm I have ever seen came on in the middle of the operation. Much of the hail must have been inches in circumference, and hurt even through thick clothes and oilskins. At the same time there were several waterspouts formed. The men on the topgallant yard had a beastly time. Below on deck men made hail-balls and pretended they were snow.

From now onwards we ran on our course before a gale. By the early morning of 12 October Cape Otway light was in sight. Working double tides in the engine-room, and with every stitch of sail set, we just failed to reach Port Phillip Heads by midday, when the tide turned, and it was impossible to get through. We went up Melbourne Harbour that evening, very dark and blowing hard.

A telegram was waiting for Scott:

Madeira. Am going South, AMUNDSEN.

This telegram was dramatically important, as will appear when we come to the last act of the tragedy. Captain Roald Amundsen was one of the most notable of living explorers, and was in the prime of life – forty-one, two years younger than Scott. He had been in the Antarctic before Scott, with the Belgica Expedition in 1897–9, and therefore did not consider the South Pole in any sense our property. Since then he had realized the dream of centuries of exploration by passing through the North-West Passage, and actually doing so in a 60-ton schooner in 1905. The last we had heard of him was that he had equipped Nansen's old ship, the *Fram*, for further exploration in the Arctic. This was only a feint. Once at sea, he had told his men that he was going south instead of north; and when he reached Madeira he sent this brief telegram, which meant, 'I shall be at the South Pole before you.' It also meant, though we did not appreciate it at the time, that we were up against a very big man.

The Admiral Commanding the Australian Station came on board. The event of the inspection was Nigger, the black ship's cat, distinguished by a white whisker on the port side of his face, who made one adventurous voyage to the Antarctic and came to an untimely end during the second. The seamen made a hammock for him with blanket and pillow, and slung it forward among their own bedding. Nigger had turned in, not feeling very well, owing to the number of moths he had eaten, the ship being full of them. When awakened by the Admiral, Nigger had no idea of the importance of the occasion, but stretched himself, yawned in the most natural manner, turned over and went to sleep again.

This cat became a well-known and much photographed member of the crew of the *Terra Nova*. He is said to have imitated the Romans of old, being a greedy beast, by having eaten as much seal blubber as he could hold, made himself sick, and gone back and resumed his meal. He had most beautiful fur. When the ship was returning from the Antarctic in 1911 Nigger was frightened by something on deck and jumped into the sea, which was running fairly rough. However, the ship was hove to, a boat lowered, and Nigger was rescued. He spent another happy year on board, but disappeared one dark night when the ship was returning from her second journey to the South in 1912, during a big gale. He often went aloft with the men, of his own accord. This night he was seen on the main lower topsail yard, higher than which he never would go. He disappeared in a big squall, probably because the yard was covered with ice.

Wilson rejoined the ship at Melbourne; and Scott left her,

to arrange further business matters, and to rejoin in New Zealand. When he landed I think he had seen enough of the personnel of the expedition to be able to pass a fair judgement upon them. I cannot but think that he was pleased. Such enthusiasm and comradeship as prevailed on board could bear only good fruit. It would certainly have been possible to find a body of men who could work a sailing ship with greater skill, but not men who were more willing, and that in the midst of considerable discomfort, to work hard at distasteful jobs and be always cheerful. And it must have been clear that with all the energy which was being freely expended, the expedition came first, and the individual nowhere. It is to the honour of all concerned that from the time it left London to the time it returned to New Zealand after three years, this spirit always prevailed.

Among the executive officers Scott was putting more and more trust in Campbell, who was to lead the Northern Party. He was showing those characteristics which enabled him to bring his small party safely through one of the hardest winters that men have ever survived. Bowers also had shown sea-manlike qualities which are an excellent test by which to judge the Antarctic traveller; a good seaman in sail will probably make a useful sledger: but at this time Scott can hardly have foreseen that Bowers was to prove 'the hardest traveller that ever undertook a Polar journey, as well as one of the most undaunted'. But he had already proved himself a first-rate sailor. Among the junior scientific staff too, several were showing qualities as seamen which were a good sign for the future. Altogether I think it must have been with a cheerful mind that Scott landed in Australia.

When we left Melbourne for New Zealand we were all a bit stale, which was not altogether surprising, and a run ashore was to do us a world of good after five months of solid grind, crowded up in a ship which thought nothing of rolling 50° each way. Also, though everything had been done that could be done to provide them, the want of fresh meat and vegetables was being felt, and it was an excellent thing that a body of men, for whom every precaution against scurvy that modern science could suggest was being taken, should have a good course of antiscorbutic food and an equally beneficial change of life before leaving civilization.

And so it was with some anticipation that on Monday morning, 24 October, we could smell the land – New Zealand, that home of so many Antarctic expeditions, where we knew that we should be welcomed. Scott's *Discovery*, Shackleton's *Nimrod*, and now again Scott's *Terra Nova* have all in turn been berthed at the same quay in Lyttelton, for aught I know at the same No. 5 Shed, into which they have spilled out their holds, and from which they have been restowed with the addition of all that New Zealand, scorning payment, could give. And from there they have sailed, and thither their relief ships have returned year after year. Scott's words of the *Discovery* apply just as much to the *Terra Nova*. Not only did New Zealand do all in her power to help the expedition in an official capacity, but the New Zealanders welcomed both officers and men with open arms, and 'gave them to understand that although already separated by many thousands of miles from their native land, here in this new land they would find a second home, and those who would equally think of them in their absence, and welcome them on their return'.

But we had to sail round the southern coast of New Zealand and northwards up the eastern coast before we could arrive at our last port of call. The wind went ahead, and it was not until the morning of 28 October that we sailed through Lyttelton Heads. The word had gone forth that we should sail away on 27 November, and there was much to be done in the brief month that lay ahead.

There followed four weeks of strenuous work into which was sandwiched a considerable amount of play. The ship was unloaded, when, as usual, men and officers acted alike as stevedores, and she was docked, that an examination for the source of the leak might be made by Mr H. J. Miller of Lyttelton, who has performed a like service for more than one Antarctic ship. But the different layers of sheathing protecting a ship which is destined to fight against ice are so complicated that it is a very difficult matter to find the origin of a leak. All that can be said with any certainty is that the point where the water appears inside the skin of the ship is almost certainly not the locality in which it has penetrated the outside sheathing. 'Our good friend Miller,' wrote Scott, 'attacked the leak and traced it to the stern. We found the false stern split, and in one case a hole bored for a long-stern through-bolt which was much too large for the bolt. . . . The ship still leaks but the water can now be kept under with the hand pump by two daily efforts of a quarter of an hour to twenty minutes.' This in Lyttelton; but in a not far distant future every pump was choked, and we were baling with three buckets, literally for our lives.

Bowers' feat of sorting and restowing not only the stores we had but the cheese, butter, tinned foods, bacon, hams and numerous other products which are grown in New Zealand, and which any expedition leaving that country should always buy there in preference to carrying them through the tropics, was a masterstroke of clear-headedness and organization. These stores were all relisted before stowing and the green-banded or Northern Party and red-banded or Main Party stores were not only easily distinguishable, but also stowed in such a way that they were forthcoming without difficulty at the right time and in their due order.

The two huts which were to form the homes of our two parties down South had been brought out in the ship and were now erected on a piece of waste ground near, by the same men who would be given the work to do in the South.

The gear peculiar to the various kinds of scientific work which it was the object of the expedition to carry out was also stowed with great care. The more bulky objects included a petrol engine and small dynamo, a very delicate instrument for making pendulum observations to test the gravity of the earth, meteorological screens, and a Dines anemometer. There was also a special hut for magnetic observations, of which only the framework was finally taken, with the necessary but bulky magnetic instruments. The biological and photographic gear was also of considerable size.

For the interior of the huts there were beds with spring mattresses – a real luxury but one well worth the space and money – tables, chairs, cooking ranges and piping, and a complete acetylene gas plant for both parties. There were also extensive ventilators which were not a great success. The problem of ventilation in polar regions still remains to be solved.

Food can be packed into a comparatively small space, but not so fuel, and this is one of the greatest difficulties which confront the polar traveller. It must be conceded that in this respect Norway, with her wonderful petrol-driven *Fram*, is far ahead of us. The *Terra Nova* depended on coal, and the length of the ship's stay in the South, and the amount of exploration she could do after landing the shore parties, depended almost entirely upon how much coal she could be persuaded to hold after all the necessaries of modern scientific exploration had been wedged tightly into her.

The *Terra Nova* sailed from New Zealand with 425 tons of coal in her holds and bunkers, and 30 tons on deck in sacks. We were to hear more of those sacks.

Meanwhile stalls were being built under the forecastle for fifteen ponies, and, since room could not be found below for the remaining four, stalls were built on the port side of the fore hatch. The decks were caulked, and deck houses and other fittings which might carry away in the stormy seas of the South were further secured.

As the time of departure drew near, and each day of civilization appeared to be more and more desirable, the scene in Lyttelton became animated and congested. Here is a scientist trying to force just one more case into his small laboratory, or decanting a mass of clothing, just issued, into the bottom of his bunk, to be slept on since there was no room for it on the deck of his cabin. On the main deck Bowers is trying to get one more frozen sheep into the ice-house, in the rigging working parties are overhauling the running gear. The engine-room staff are busy on the engine, and though the ship is crowded there is order everywhere, and it is clean.

But the scene on the morning of Saturday, 26 November, baffles description. There is no deck visible: in addition to 30 tons of coal in sacks on deck there are 2½ tons of petrol, stowed in drums which in turn are cased in wood. On the top of sacks and cases, and on the roof of the ice-house are thirty-three dogs, chained far enough apart to keep them from following their first instinct – to fight the nearest animal they can see: the ship is a hubbub of howls. In the forecastle and in the four stalls on deck are the nineteen ponies, wedged tightly in their wooden stalls, and dwarfing everything are the three motor sledges in their huge crates, 16'×5'×4', two of them on either side of the main hatch, the third across the break of the poop. They are covered with tarpaulins and secured in every possible way, but it is clear that in a big sea their weight will throw a great strain upon the deck. It is not altogether a cheerful sight. But all that care and skill can do has been done to ensure that the deck cargo will not shift, and that the animals may be as sheltered as possible from wind and seas. And it's no good worrying about what can't be helped.

Chapter Three
SOUTHWARD

Open the bones, and you shall nothing find
In the best face but filth; when, Lord, in Thee
The beauty lies in the discovery.

GEORGE HERBERT

TELEGRAMS from all parts of the world, special trains, all
ships dressed, crowds and waving hands, steamers out
to the Heads and a general hullabaloo – these were the
incidents of Saturday, 26 November 1910, when we slipped
from the wharf at Lyttelton at 3 p.m. We were to call at
Dunedin before leaving civilization, and arrived there on
Sunday night. Here we took on the remainder of our coal.
On Monday night we danced, in fantastic clothing for we
had left our grand clothes behind, and sailed finally for the
South the following afternoon amidst the greatest enthusiasm. The wives remained with us until we reached the open
sea.

Amongst those who only left us at the last minute was Mr
Kinsey of Christchurch. He acted for Scott in New Zealand
during the Discovery days, and for Shackleton in 1907. We
all owe him a deep debt of gratitude for his help.

His interest in the expedition is wonderful, and such
interest on the part of a thoroughly shrewd business man is
an asset of which I have taken full advantage. Kinsey will act
as my agent in Christchurch during my absence; I have given
him an ordinary power of attorney, and I think have left him
in possession of all the facts. His kindness to us was beyond
words.[1]

1. *Scott's Last Expedition*, vol. i, p. 6.

Evening. – Loom of land and Cape Saunders Light blinking.[2]

The ponies and dogs were the first consideration. Even in quite ordinary weather the dogs had a wretched time.

> The seas continually break on the weather bulwarks and scatter clouds of heavy spray over the backs of all who must venture into the waist of the ship. The dogs sit with their tails to this invading water, their coats wet and dripping. It is a pathetic attitude deeply significant of cold and misery; occasionally some poor beast emits a long pathetic whine. The group forms a picture of wretched dejection; such a life is truly hard for these poor creatures.[3]

The ponies were better off. Four of them were on deck amidships and they were well boarded round. It is significant that these ponies had a much easier time in rough weather than those in the bows of the ship.

> Under the forecastle fifteen ponies close side by side, seven one side, eight the other, heads together, and groom between – swaying, swaying continually to the plunging, irregular motion.
> One takes a look through a hole in the bulkhead and sees a row of heads with sad, patient eyes come swinging up together from the starboard side, whilst those on the port swing back; then up come the port heads, while the starboard recede. It seems a terrible ordeal for these poor beasts to stand this day after day for weeks together, and indeed though they continue to feed well the strain quickly drags down their weight and condition; but nevertheless the trial cannot be gauged from human standards.[4]

The seas through which we had to pass to reach the pack-ice must be the most stormy in the world. Dante tells us that

2. ibid., p. 7.   3. ibid., p. 9.   4. ibid., p. 8.

those who have committed carnal sin are tossed about ceaselessly by the most furious winds in the second circle of Hell. The corresponding hell on earth is found in the southern oceans, which encircle the world without break, tempest-tossed by the gales which follow one another round and round the world from West to East. You will find albatross there – great Wanderers, and Sooties, and Mollymawks – sailing as lightly before these furious winds as ever do Paolo and Francesca. Round the world they go. I doubt whether they land more than once a year, and then they come to the islands of these seas to breed.

There are many other beautiful sea-birds, but most beautiful of all are the Snowy petrels, which approach nearer to the fairies than anything else on earth. They are quite white, and seemingly transparent. They are the familiar spirits of the pack, which, except to nest, they seldom if ever leave, flying 'here and there independently in a mazy fashion, glittering against the blue sky like so many white moths, or shining snowflakes'.[5] And then there are the Giant petrels, whose coloration is a puzzle. Some are nearly white, others brown, and they exhibit every variation between the one and the other. And, on the whole, the white forms become more general the farther south you go. But the usual theory of protective coloration will not fit in, for there are no enemies against which this bird must protect itself. Is it something to do with radiation of heat from the body?

A ship which sets out upon this journey generally has a bad time, and for this reason the overladen state of the *Terra Nova* was a cause of anxiety. The Australasian meteorologists had done their best to forecast the weather we must expect. Everything which was not absolutely necessary had been ruthlessly scrapped. Yet there was not a square inch of the hold and between-decks which was not crammed almost to bursting, and there was as much on the deck as could be expected to stay there. Officers and men could hardly move in their living quarters when standing up, and certainly they

5. Wilson in the *Discovery Natural History Reports*.

could not all sit down. To say that we were heavy laden is a very moderate statement of the facts.

Thursday, 1 December, we ran into a gale. We shortened sail in the afternoon to lower topsails, jib and staysail. Both wind and sea rose with great rapidity, and before the night came our deck cargo had begun to work loose.

> You know how carefully everything had been lashed, but no lashings could have withstood the onslaught of these coal sacks for long. There was nothing for it but to grapple with the evil, and nearly all hands were labouring for hours in the waist of the ship, heaving coal sacks overboard and re-lashing the petrol cases, etc., in the best manner possible under such difficult and dangerous circumstances. The seas were continually breaking over these people and now and again they would be completely submerged. At such times they had to cling for dear life to some fixture to prevent themselves being washed overboard, and with coal bags and loose cases washing about, there was every risk of such hold being torn away.
>
> No sooner was some semblance of order restored than some exceptionally heavy wave would tear away the lashing, and the work had to be done all over again.[6]

The conditions became much worse during the night and things were complicated for some of us by sea-sickness. I have lively recollections of being aloft for two hours in the morning watch on Friday and being sick at intervals all the time. For sheer downright misery give me a hurricane, not too warm, the yard of a sailing ship, a wet sail and a bout of sea-sickness.

It must have been about this time that orders were given to clew up the jib and then to furl it. Bowers and four others went out on the bowsprit, being buried deep in the enormous seas every time the ship plunged her nose into them with great force. It was an education to see him lead those men out into that roaring inferno. He has left his own vivid

6. *Scott's Last Expedition*, vol i, pp. 11–12.

impression of this gale in a letter home. His tendency was always to underestimate difficulties, whether the force of wind in a blizzard, or the troubles of a polar traveller. This should be remembered when reading the vivid accounts which his mother has so kindly given me permission to use:

We got through the forties with splendid speed and were just over the fifties when one of those tremendous gales got us. Our Lat. was about 52° S., a part of the world absolutely unfrequented by shipping of any sort, and as we had already been blown off Campbell Island we had nothing but a clear sweep to Cape Horn to leeward. One realized then how in the *Nimrod* – in spite of the weather – they always had the security of a big steamer to look to if things came to the worst. We were indeed alone, by many hundreds of miles, and never having felt anxious about a ship before, the old whaler was to give me a new experience.

In the afternoon of the beginning of the gale I helped make fast the T.G. sails, upper topsails and foresail, and was horrified on arrival on deck to find that the heavy water we continued to ship, was starting the coal bags floating in places. These, acting as battering-rams, tore adrift some of my carefully stowed petrol cases and endangered the lot. I had started to make sail fast at 3 p.m. and it was 9.30 p.m. when I had finished putting on additional lashings to everything I could. So rapidly did the sea get up that one was continually afloat and swimming about. I turned in for 2 hours and lay awake hearing the crash of the seas and thinking how long those cases would stand it, till my watch came at midnight as a relief. We were under 2 lower topsails and hove to, the engines going dead slow to assist keeping head to wind. At another time I should have been easy in my mind; now the water that came aboard was simply fearful, and the wrenching on the old ship was enough to worry any sailor called upon to fill his decks with garbage fore and aft. Still 'Risk nothing and do nothing', if funds could not supply another ship, we simply had to overload the one we had, or suffer worse things down south. The watch was eventful as the shaking up got the fine coal into the bilges, and this mixing with the oil from the engines formed balls of coal and grease which, ordinarily, went up the pumps easily; now however with the great strains, and hundreds of tons on deck, as she continually filled, the water started to come in too fast for the half-clogged pumps to cope with. An alternative was offered to me in going faster so as to shake up the big pump on the main engines, and this I did – in spite of myself – and in defiance of the first principles of seamanship. Of course, we shipped water more and more, and only to save a clean breach of the decks did I slow down again and let the water gain. My next card was to get the watch on the hand-pumps as well, and these were choked, too, or nearly so.

Anyhow with every pump, – hand and steam, – going, the water continued to rise in the stokehold. At 4 a.m. all hands took in the fore lower topsail, leaving us under a minimum of sail. The gale increased to storm force (force 11 out of 12) and such a sea got up as only the Southern Fifties can produce. All the afterguard turned out and the pumps were vigorously shaken up, – sickening work as only a dribble came out. We had to throw some coal overboard to clear the after deck round the pumps, and I set to work to rescue cases of petrol which were smashed adrift. I broke away a plank or two of the lee bulwarks to give the seas some outlet as they were right over the level of the rail, and one was constantly on the verge of floating clean over the side with the cataract force of the backwash. I had all the swimming I wanted that day. Every case I rescued was put on the weather side of the poop to help get us on a more even keel. She sagged horribly and the unfortunate ponies, – though under cover, – were so jerked about that the weather ones could not keep their feet in their stalls, so great was the slope and strain on their forelegs. Oates and Atkinson worked among them like Trojans, but morning saw the death of one, and the loss of one dog overboard. The dogs, made fast on deck, were washed to and fro, chained by the neck, and often submerged for a consider-able time. Though we did everything in our power to get them up as high as possible, the sea went everywhere. The wardroom was a swamp and so were our bunks with all our nice clothing, books, etc. However, of this we cared little, when the water had crept up to the furnaces and put the fires out, and we realized for the first time that the ship had met her match and was slowly filling. Without a pump to suck we started the forlorn hope of buckets and began to bale her out. Had we been able to open a hatch we could have cleared the main pump well at once, but with those appalling seas literally covering her, it would have meant less than 10 minutes to float, had we uncovered a hatch.

The Chief Engineer (Williams) and carpenter (Davies), after we had all put our heads together, started cutting a hole in the engine room bulkhead, to enable us to get into the pump-well from the engine room; it was iron and, therefore, at least a 12 hours job. Captain Scott was simply splendid, he might have been at Cowes, and to do him and Teddy Evans credit, at our worst strait none of our landsmen who were working so hard knew how serious things were. Capt. Scott said to me quietly – 'I am afraid it's a bad business for us – What do you think?' I said we were by no means dead yet, though at that moment, Oates, at peril of his life, got aft to report another horse dead; and more down. And then an awful sea swept away our lee bulwarks clean, between the fore and main riggings, – only our chain lashings saved the lee motor sledge then, and I was soon diving after petrol cases. Captain Scott calmly told me that they 'did not matter' – This was our great project for getting to the Pole – the much advertised motors that 'did not matter'; our dogs looked finished, and horses were finishing, and I went to bale with a strenuous prayer in my heart, and 'Yip-i-addy' on my lips, and so we pulled through that day. We sang and resang every silly song we ever knew, and then everybody in the ship later on was put on 2-hour reliefs to bale, as it was impossible for flesh to keep heart with no food or rest. Even the fresh-water pump had gone wrong so we drank neat lime juice, or anything that came along, and sat in our saturated state awaiting our next spell. My dressing gown was my great comfort as it was not very wet, and it is a lovely warm thing.

To make a long yarn short, we found later in the day that the terrible storm was easing a bit and that though there was a terrible lot of water in the ship, which, try as we could, we could not reduce, it certainly had ceased to rise to any great extent. We had reason to hope then that we might keep her afloat till the pump wells could be cleared. Had the storm lasted another day, God knows what our state would have been, if we had been above water at all. You cannot imagine how utterly helpless we felt in such a sea with a tiny ship, – the great expedition with all its hopes thrown aside for its life. God had shown us the weakness of man's hand and it was enough for the best of us, – the people who had been made such a lot of lately – the whole scene was one of pathos really. However, at 11 p.m. Evans and I with the carpenter were able to crawl through a tiny hole in the bulkhead, burrow over the coal to the pump-well cofferdam, where, another hole having been easily made in the wood, we got down below with Davy lamps and set to work. The water was so deep that you had to continually dive to get your hand on to the suction. After 2 hours or so it was cleared for the time being and the pumps worked merrily. I went in again at 4.30 a.m. and had another lap at clearing it. Not till the afternoon of the following day, though, did we see the last of the water and the last of the great gale. During the time the pumps were working, we continued the baling till the water got below the furnaces. As soon as we could light up, we did, and got the other pumps under weigh, and, once the ship was empty, clearing away the suction was a simple matter. I was pleased to find that after all I had only lost about 100 gallons of the petrol and bad as things had been they might have been worse . . .

You will ask where all the water came from seeing our forward leak had been stopped. Thank God we did not have that to cope with as well. The water came chiefly through the deck where the tremendous strain, – not only of the deck load, but of the smashing seas, – was beyond conception. She was caught at a tremendous disadvantage and we were dependent for our lives on each plank standing its own strain.

Had one gone we would all have gone, and the great anxiety was not so much the existing water as what was going to open up if the storm continued. We might have dumped the deck cargo, a difficult job at best, but were too busy baling to do anything else . . .

That Captain Scott's account will be moderate you may be sure. Still, take my word for it, he is one of the best, and behaved up to our best traditions at a time when his own outlook must have been the blackness of darkness . . .

Characteristically Bowers ends his account:

Under its worst conditions this earth is a good place to live in.

Priestley wrote in his diary:

If Dante had seen our ship as she was at her worst, I fancy he would have got a good idea for another Circle of Hell, though he would have been at a loss to account for such a cheerful and ribald lot of Souls.

The situation narrowed down to a fight between the incoming water and the men who were trying to keep it in check by baling her out. The *Terra Nova* will never be more full of water, nearly up to the furnaces, than she was that Friday morning, when we were told to go and do our damndest with three iron buckets. The constructors had not allowed for baling, only for the passage of one man at a time up and down the two iron ladders which connected the engine-room floor plates with the deck. If we used more than three buckets the business of passing them rapidly up, emptying them out of the hatchway, and returning them empty, became unprofitable. We were divided into two gangs, and all Friday and Friday night we workd two hours on and two hours off, like fiends.

Wilson's Journal describes the scene:

It was a weird night's work with the howling gale and the darkness and the immense seas running over the ship every few minutes and no engines and no sail, and we all in the engine-room oil and bilge water, singing chanties as we passed up slopping buckets full of bilge, each man above slopping a little over the heads of all below him; wet through to the skin, so much so that some of the party worked altogether naked like Chinese coolies; and the rush of the wave backwards and forwards at the bottom grew hourly less in the dim light of a couple of engine-room oil lamps whose light just made the darkness visible, the ship all the time rolling like a sodden lifeless log, her lee gunwale under water every time.

There was one thrilling moment in the midst of the worst hour on Friday when we were realizing that the fire must be drawn, and when every pump had failed to act, and when the bulwarks began to go to pieces and the petrol cases were all afloat and going overboard, and the word was suddenly passed in a shout from the hands at work in the waist of the ship trying to save petrol cases that smoke was coming up through the seams in the afterhold. As this was full of coal and patent fuel and was next the engine-room, and as it had not been opened for the airing it required to get rid of gas, on account of the flood water on deck making it impossible to open the hatchway, the possibility of a fire there was patent to every one, and it could not possibly have been dealt with in any way short of opening the hatches and flooding the ship, when she must have foundered. It was therefore a thrilling moment or two until it was discovered that the smoke was really steam, arising from the bilge at the bottom having risen to the heated coal.[7]

Meanwhile men were working for all our lives to cut through two bulkheads which cut off all communication with the suction of the hand-pumps. One bulkhead was iron, the other wood.

Scott wrote at this time:

7. Wilson's Journal.

We are not out of the wood, but hope dawns, as indeed it should for me, when I find myself so wonderfully served. Officers and men are singing chanties over their arduous work. Williams is working in sweltering heat behind the boiler to get the door made in the bulkhead. Not a single one has lost his good spirits. A dog was drowned last night, one pony is dead and two others in a bad condition – probably they too will go. Occasionally a heavy sea would bear one of them away, and he was only saved by his chain. Meares with some helpers had constantly to be rescuing these wretched creatures from hanging, and trying to find them better shelter, an almost hopeless task. One poor beast was found hanging when dead; one was washed away with such force that his chain broke and he disappeared overboard; the next wave miraculously washed him on board again and he is fit and well. [I believe the dog was Osman.] The gale has exacted heavy toll, but I feel all will be well if we can only cope with the water. Another dog has just been washed overboard – alas! Thank God the gale is abating. The sea is still mountainously high but the ship is not labouring so heavily as she was.[8]

The highest waves of which I can find any record were thirty-six feet high. These were observed by Sir James C. Ross in the North Atlantic.[9]

On 2 December the waves were logged, probably by Pennell, who was extremely careful in his measurements, as being 'thirty-five feet high (estimated)'. At one time I saw Scott, standing on the weather rail of the poop, buried to his waist in green sea. The reader can then imagine the condition of things in the waist of the ship, 'over and over again the rail, from the fore-rigging to the main, was covered by a solid sheet of curling water which swept aft and high on the poop'.[10] At another time Bowers and Campbell were standing upon the bridge, and the ship rolled sluggishly over until

8. *Scott's Last Expedition*, vol. i, pp. 14–15.
9. Raper, *Practice of Navigation*, article 547.
10. *Scott's Last Expedition*, vol. i, p. 13.

the lee combings of the main hatch were under the sea. They watched anxiously, and slowly she righted herself, but 'she won't do that often,' said Bowers. As a rule if a ship gets that far over she goes down.

Our journey was uneventful for a time, but of course it was not by any means smooth.

> I was much disturbed last night by the motion; the ship was pitching and twisting with short sharp movements on a confused sea, and with every plunge my thoughts flew to our poor ponies. This afternoon they are fairly well, but one knows that they must be getting weaker as time goes on, and one longs to give them a good sound rest with a ship on an even keel. Poor patient beasts! One wonders how far the memory of such fearful discomfort will remain with them – animals so often remember places and conditions where they have encountered difficulties or hurt. Do they only recollect circumstances which are deeply impressed by some shock of fear or sudden pain, and does the remembrance of prolonged strain pass away? Who can tell? But it would seem strangely merciful if nature should blot out these weeks of slow but inevitable torture.[11]

On 7 December, noon position 61° 22' S., 179° 56' W., one berg was sighted far away to the west, as it gleamed every now and then in the sun. Two more were seen the next day, and at 6.22 a.m. on 9 December, noon position 65° 8' S., 177° 41' W., the pack was sighted ahead by Rennick. All that day we passed bergs and streams of ice. The air became dry and bracing, the sea was calm, and the sun shining on the islands of ice was more than beautiful. And then Bump! We had just charged the first big floe, and we were in the pack.

11. ibid., pp. 21–2.

The sky has been wonderful, with every form of cloud in every condition of light and shade; the sun has continually appeared through breaks in the cloudy heavens from time to time, brilliantly illuminating some field of pack, some steep-walled berg, or some patch of bluest sea. So sunlight and shadow have chased each other across our scene. Tonight there is little or no swell – the ship is on an even keel, steady, save for the occasional shocks on striking ice.

It is difficult to express the sense of relief this steadiness gives after our storm-tossed passage. One can only imagine the relief and comfort afforded to the ponies, but the dogs are visibly cheered and the human element is full of gaiety. The voyage seems full of promise in spite of the imminence of delay.[12]

We had met the pack farther north than any other ship.

What is pack? Speaking very generally indeed, in this region it is the sea-ice which forms over the Ross Sea area during the winter, and is blown northwards by the southerly blizzards. But as we shall see, the ice which forms over this area is of infinite variety. As a rule great sheets spread over the seas which fringe the Antarctic continent in the autumn, grow thicker and thicker during the winter and spring, and break up when the temperatures of sea and air rise in summer. Such is the ice which forms in normal seasons round the shores of McMurdo Sound, and up the coast of the western mountains of Victoria Land. In sheltered bays this ice will sometimes remain in for two years or even more, growing all the time, until some phenomenal break-up releases it. We found an example of this in the sea-ice which formed between Hut Point and the Barrier. But there are great waters which can never freeze for very long. Cape Crozier, for instance, where the Emperor penguins nest in winter, is one of the windiest places in the world. In July it was completely frozen over as far as we could see in the darkness from a height of

12. ibid., pp. 24–5.

900 feet. Within a few days a hurricane had blown it all away, and the sea was black.

I believe, and we had experiences to prove me right, that there is a critical period early in winter, and that if sea-ice has not frozen thick enough to remain fast by that time, it is probable that the sea will remain open for the rest of the year. But this does not mean that no ice will form. So great is the wish of the sea to freeze, and so cold is the air, that the wind has only to lull for one instant and the surface is covered with a thin film of ice, as though by magic. But the next blizzard tears it out by force or a spring tide coaxes it out by stealth, whether it be a foot thick or only a fraction of an inch. Such an example we had at our very doors during our last winter, and the untamed winds which blew as a result were atrocious.

Thus it is that floes from a few inches to twenty feet thick go voyaging out to join the belt of ice which is known as the pack. Scott seems to have thought that the whole Ross Sea freezes over.[13] I myself think this doubtful, and I am, I believe, the only person living who has seen the Ross Sea open in mid-winter. This was on the Winter Journey undertaken by Wilson, Bowers and myself in pursuit of Emperor penguin eggs – but of that later.

It is clear that winds and currents are, broadly speaking, the governing factors of the density of pack-ice. By experience we know that clear water may be found in the autumn where great tracts of ice barred the way in summer. The tendency of the pack is northwards, where the ice melts into the warmer waters. But the bergs remain when all traces of the pack have disappeared, and, drifting northwards still, form the menace to shipping so well known to sailors rounding the Horn. It is not hard to imagine that one monster ice island of twenty miles in length, such as do haunt these seas, drifting into navigated waters and calving into hundreds of great bergs as it goes, will in itself produce what seamen call a bad year for ice. And the last stages of these, when the bergs have degenerated into 'growlers', are even worse, for

13. *Scott's Last Expedition*, vol. i, p. 2.

then the sharpest eye can hardly distinguish them as they float nearly submerged though they have lost but little of their powers of evil.

There are two main types of Antarctic berg. The first and most common is the tabular form. Bergs of this shape cruise about in thousands and thousands. A less common form is known as the pinnacled berg, and in almost every case this is a tabular berg which has been weathered or has capsized. The number of bergs which calve direct from a mountain glacier into the sea is probably not very great. Whence then do they come?

The origin of the tabular bergs was debated until a few years ago. They have been recorded up to forty and even fifty miles in length, and they have been called floe bergs, because it was supposed that they froze first as ordinary sea-ice and increased by subsequent additions from below. But now we know that these bergs calve off from the Antarctic Barriers, the largest of which is known as the Great Ice Barrier, which forms the southern boundary of the Ross Sea. We were to become very familiar with this vast field of ice. We know that its northern face is afloat, we guess that it may all be afloat. At any rate the open sea now washes against its face at least forty miles south of where it ran in the days of Ross. Though this Barrier may be the largest in the world, it is one of many. The most modern review of this mystery, Scott's article on The Great Ice Barrier, must serve until the next firsthand examination by some further explorer.

A berg shows only about one-eighth of its total mass above water, and a berg two hundred feet high will therefore reach approximately fourteen hundred feet below the surface of the sea. Winds and currents have far more influence upon them than they have upon the pack, through which these bergs plough their way with a total disregard for such flimsy obstacles, and cause much chaos as they go. For the rest woe betide the ship which is so fixed into the pack that she cannot move if one of these monsters bears down upon her.

Words cannot tell the beauty of the scenes through which we were to pass during the next three weeks. I suppose the pack in winter must be a terrible place enough: a place of darkness and desolation hardly to be found elsewhere. But forms which under different conditions can only betoken horror now conveyed to us impressions of the utmost peace and beauty, for the sun had kissed them all.

We have had a marvellous day. The morning watch was cloudy, but it gradually cleared until the sky was a brilliant blue, fading on the horizon into green and pink. The floes were pink, floating in a deep blue sea, and all the shadows were mauve. We passed right under a monster berg, and all day have been threading lake after lake and lead after lead. 'There is Regent Street,' said somebody, and for some time we drove through great streets of perpendicular walls of ice. Many a time they were so straight that one imagined they had been cut off with a ruler some hundreds of yards in length.[14]

On another occasion:

Stayed on deck till midnight. The sun just dipped below the southern horizon. The scene was incomparable. The northern sky was gloriously rosy and reflected in the calm sea between the ice, which varied from burnished copper to salmon pink; bergs and packs to the north had a pale greenish hue with deep purple shadows, the sky shaded to saffron and pale green. We gazed long at these beautiful effects.[15]

But this was not always so. There was one day with rain, there were days of snow and hail and cold wet slush, and fog.

The position tonight is very cheerless. All hope that this easterly wind will open the pack seems to have vanished. We are surrounded with compacted floes of immense area. Openings appear between these floes and we slide crab-like from

14. My own diary.   15. *Scott's Last Expedition*, vol. i, p. 25.

one to another with long delays between. It is difficult to keep hope alive. There are streaks of water sky over open leads to the north, but everywhere to the south we have uniform white sky. The day has been overcast and the wind force 3 to 5 from the E.N.E. – snow has fallen from time to time. There could scarcely be a more dreary prospect for the eye to rest upon.[16]

With the open water we left behind the albatross and the Cape pigeon which had accompanied us lately for many months. In their place we found the Antarctic petrel, 'a richly piebald bird that appeared to be almost black and white against the ice floes',[17] and the Snowy petrel, of which I have already spoken.

No one of us whose privilege it was to be there will forget our first sight of the penguins, our first meal of seal meat, or that first big berg along which we coasted close in order that London might see it on the film. Hardly had we reached the thick pack, which prevailed after the suburbs had been passed, when we saw the little Adélie penguins hurrying to meet us. Great Scott, they seemed to say, what's this, and soon we could hear the cry which we shall never forget. 'Aark, aark,' they said, and full of wonder and curiosity, and perhaps a little out of breath, they stopped every now and then to express their feelings,

and to gaze and cry in wonder to their companions; now walking along the edge of a floe in search of a narrow spot to jump and so avoid the water, and with head down and much hesitation judging the width of the narrow gap, to give a little standing jump across as would a child, and running on the faster to make up for its delay. Again, coming to a wider lead of water necessitating a plunge, our inquisitive visitor would be lost for a moment, to reappear like a jack-in-the-box on a nearer floe, where wagging his tail, he immediately resumed his race towards the ship. Being now but a hundred yards or

16. ibid., p. 60.   17. Wilson

so from us he pokes his head constantly forward on this side and on that, to try and make out something of the new strange sight, crying aloud to his friends in his amazement, and exhibiting the most amusing indecision between his desire for further investigation and doubt as to the wisdom and propriety of closer contact with so huge a beast.[18]

They are extraordinarily like children, these little people of the Antarctic world, either like children or like old men, full of their own importance and late for dinner, in their black tail-coats and white shirt-fronts – and rather portly withal. We used to sing to them, as they to us, and you might often see 'a group of explorers on the poop, singing "She has rings on her fingers and bells on her toes, and she shall have music wherever she goes," and so on at the top of their voices to an admiring group of Adélie penguins.'[19]

Meares used to sing to them what he called 'God save', and declared that it would always send them headlong into the water. He sang flat: perhaps that was why.

Two or more penguins will combine to push a third in front of them against a skua gull, which is one of their enemies, for he eats their eggs or their young if he gets the chance. They will refuse to dive off an ice-foot until they have persuaded one of their companions to take the first jump, for fear of the sea-leopard which may be waiting in the water below, ready to seize them and play with them much as a cat will play with a mouse. As Levick describes in his book about the penguins at Cape Adare:

At the place where they most often went in, a long terrace of ice about six feet in height ran for some hundreds of yards along the edge of the water, and here, just as on the sea-ice, crowds would stand near the brink. When they had succeeded in pushing one of their numnber over, all would crane their

18. Wilson, *Discovery Natural History Report*, vol. ii, part ii, p. 38.
19. Wilson's Journal.

necks over the edge, and when they saw the pioneer safe in the water, the rest followed.[20]

It is clear then that the Adélie penguin will show a certain spirit of selfishness in tackling his hereditary enemies. But when it comes to the danger of which he is ignorant his courage betrays want of caution. Meares and Dimitri exercised the dog-teams out upon the larger floes when we were held up for any length of time. One day a team was tethered by the side of the ship, and a penguin sighted them and hurried from afar off. The dogs became frantic with excitement as he neared them: he supposed it was a greeting, and the louder they barked and the more they strained at their ropes, the faster he bustled to meet them. He was extremely angry with a man who went and saved him from a very sudden end, clinging to his trousers with his beak, and furiously beating his shins with his flippers. It was not an uncommon sight to see a little Adélie penguin standing within a few inches of the nose of a dog which was almost frantic with desire and passion.

The pack-ice is the home of the immature penguins, both Emperor and Adélie. But we did not see any large numbers of immature Emperors during this voyage.

We soon became acquainted with the sea-leopard, which waits under the ice-foot for the little penguins; he is a brute, but sinuous and graceful as the seal world goes. He preys especially upon the Adélie penguin, and Levick found no less than eighteen penguins, together with the remains of many others, in the stomach of one sea-leopard. In the water the leopard seems

a trifle faster than the Adélies, as one of them occasionally would catch up with one of the fugitives, who then, realizing that speed alone would not avail him, started dodging from side to side, and sometimes swam rapidly round and round in a circle of about twelve feet diameter for a full minute or

20. Levick, *Antarctic Penguins*, p. 83.

more, doubtless knowing that he was quicker in turning than his great heavy pursuer, but exhaustion would overtake him in the end, and we could see the head and jaws of the great sea-leopard rise to the surface as he grabbed his victim. The sight of a panic-stricken little Adélie tearing round and round in this manner was sadly common late in the season.[21]

Fish and small seal have also been found in its stomach. With long powerful head and neck and a sinuous body, it is equipped with most formidable teeth with which it tears strips out of the still living birds, and flippers which are adapted entirely for speed in the water. It is a solitary animal with a large range of distribution. It has been supposed to bring forth its young in the pack, but nothing definite is known on this subject. One day we saw a big sea-leopard swimming along with the ship. He dived under the floes and reappeared from floe to floe as we went, and for a time we thought he was interested in us. But soon we sighted another lying away on a floe, and our friend in the water began to rear his head up perpendicularly, and seemed to be trying to wind his mate, as we supposed. He was down wind from her, and appeared to find her at a distance of 150 to 200 yards, and the last we saw of him he was heading up the side of the floe where she lay.

There are four kinds of seal in the Antarctic; of one of these, the sea-leopard, I have already spoken. Another is called the Ross seal, for Sir James Ross discovered it in 1840. It seems to be a solitary beast, living in the pack, and is peculiar for its 'pug-like expression of countenance'.[22] It has always been rare, and no single specimen was seen on this expedition, though the Terra Nova must have passed through more pack than most whalers see in a lifetime. It looks as if the Ross seal of the Antarctic is the Weddell, which seldom lives in the pack but spends its life catching fish close to the

21. Levick, Antarctic Penguins, p. 85.
22. Wilson in the Discovery Natural History Report, Zoology, vol. ii, part i, p. 44.

shores of the continent, and digesting them, when caught, lying sluggishly upon the ice-foot. We came to know them later in their hundreds in McMurdo Sound, for the Weddell is a land-loving seal and is only found in large numbers near the coast. Just at this time it was the crab-eating seal which we saw very fairly often, generally several of them together, but never in large numbers.

Wilson has pointed out in his article upon seals in the *Discovery Report*[23] that the Weddell and the crab-eater seal, which are the two commoner of the Antarctic seals, have agreed to differ both in habit and in diet, and therefore they share the field successfully. He shows that 'the two penguins which share the same area have differentiated in a somewhat similar manner'. The Weddell seal and the Emperor penguin

> have the following points in common, namely, a littoral distribution, a fish diet and residential non-migratory habit, remaining as far south the whole year round as open water will allow; whereas the other two (the crab-eating seal and the Adélie penguin) have in common a more pelagic habit, a crustacean diet, and a distribution definitely migratory in the case of the penguin, and although not so definitely migratory in the case of the seal, yet checked from coming so far south as Weddell's seal in winter by a strong tendency to keep in touch with pelagic ice.[24]

Wilson considers that the advantage lies in each case with the 'non-migratory and more southern species', i.e. the Weddell seal and the Emperor penguin. I doubt whether he would confirm this now. The Emperor penguin, weighing six stones and more, seems to me to have a very much harder fight for life than the little Adélie.

Before the *Discovery* started from England in 1901 an 'Antarctic Manual' was produced by the Royal Geographical

23. *Discovery Natural History Report, Zoology*, vol. ii, part i, Wilson, pp. 32, 33.
24. ibid., p. 33.

Society, giving a summary of the information which existed up to that date about this part of the world. It is interesting reading, and to the Antarctic student it proves how little was known in some branches of science at that date, and what strides were made during the next few years. To read what was known of the birds and beasts of the Antarctic and then to read Wilson's *Zoological Report of the Discovery Expedition* is an education in what one man can still do in an out-of-the-way part of the world to elucidate the problems which await him.

The teeth of a crab-eating seal 'are surmounted by perhaps the most complicated arrangements of cusps found in any living mammal'.[25] The mouth is so arranged that the teeth of the upper jaw fit into those of the lower, and 'the cusps form a perfect sieve . . . a hitherto unparalleled function for the teeth of a mammal'.[26] The food of this seal consists mainly of Euphausiae, animals much like shrimps, which it doubtless keeps in its mouth while it expels the water through its teeth, like those whales which sift their food through their baleen plates.

This development of cusps in the teeth of the [crab-eating seal] is probably a more perfect adaptation to this purpose than in any other mammal, and has been produced at the cost of all usefulness in the teeth as grinders. The grit, however, which forms a fairly constant part of the contents of the stomach and intestines, serves, no doubt, to grind up the shells of the crustaceans, and in this way the necessity for grinders is completely obviated.[27]

The sea-leopard has a very formidable set of teeth suitable for his carnivorous diet. The Weddell, living on fish, has a more simple group, but these are liable to become very worn in old age, due to his habit of gnawing out holes in the ice

25. *Antarctic Manual: Seals*, by Barrett-Hamilton, p. 216.
26. ibid., p. 217.
27. *Discovery Natural History Report, Zoology*, vol. ii, part i, by E. A. Wilson, p. 36.

for himself, so graphically displayed on Ponting's cinematograph. When he feels death approaching, the crab-eating seal, never inclined to live in the company of more than a few of his kind, becomes still more solitary. The Weddell seal will travel far up the glaciers of South Victoria Land, and there we have found them lying dead. But the crab-eating seal will wander even farther. He leaves the pack. 'Thirty miles from the sea-shore and 3000 feet above sea-level, their carcasses were found on quite a number of occasions, and it is hard to account for such vagaries on other grounds than that a sick animal will go any distance to get away from its companions'[28] (and perhaps it should be added from its enemies).

Often the under sides of the floes were coloured a peculiar yellow. This coloration is caused by minute unicellular plants called diatoms. The floating life of the Antarctic is most dense. 'Diatoms were so abundant in parts of the Ross Sea, that a large plankton net (18 meshes to an inch) became choked in a few minutes with them and other members of the Phytoplankton. It is extremely probable that in such localities whales feed upon the plants as well as the animals of the plankton.'[29] I do not know to what extent these open waters are frequented by whales during the winter, but in the summer months they are full of them, right down to the fringe of the continent. Most common of all is the kind of sea-wolf known as the Killer Whale, who measures 30 feet long. He hunts in packs up to at least a hundred strong, and as we now know, he does not confine his attacks to seal and other whales, but will also hunt man, though perhaps he mistakes him for a seal. This whale is a toothed beast and a flesh-eater, and is more properly a dolphin. But it seems that there are at least five or six other kinds of whales, some of which do not penetrate south of the pack, while others cruise in large numbers right up to the edge of the fast ice. They

28. *Discovery Natural History Report, Zoology*, vol. ii, part i, by E. A. Wilson.
29. *Terra Nova Natural History Report, Cetacea*, vol. i, No. 3, p. 111, by Lillie.

feed upon the minute surface life of these seas, and large numbers of them were seen not only by the *Terra Nova* on her various cruises, but also by the shore parties in the waters of McMurdo Sound. In both Wilson and Lillie we had skilled whale observers, and their work has gone far to elucidate the still obscure questions of whale distribution in the South.

The pack-ice offers excellent opportunities for the identification of whales, because their movements are more restricted than in the open ocean. In order to identify, the observer generally has only the blow, and then the shape of the back and fin as the whale goes down, to guide him. In the pack he sometimes gets more, as in the case of *Balaenoptera acutorostrata* (Piked whale) on 3 March 1911. The ship

was ploughing her way through thick pack-ice, in which the water was freezing between the floes, so that the only open spaces for miles around were those made by the slow movement of the ship. We saw several of these whales during the day, making use of the holes in the ice near the ship for the purpose of blowing. There was scarcely room between the floes for the whales to come up to blow in their usual manner, which consists in rising almost horizontally, and breaking the surface of the water with their backs. On this occasion they pushed their snouts obliquely out of the water, nearly as far as the eye, and after blowing, withdrew them below the water again. Commander Pennell noted that several times one rested its head on a floe not twenty feet from the ship, with its nostrils on the water-line; raising itself a few inches, it would blow and then subside again for a few minutes to its original position with its snout resting on the floe. They took no notice of pieces of coal which were thrown at them by the men on board the ship.[30]

30. *Terra Nova Natural History Report, Zoology*, vol. i, No. 3, *Cetacea*, by D. G. Lillie, p. 114.

But no whale which we saw in the pack, and we often saw it elsewhere also, was so imposing as the great Blue whale, some of which were possibly more than 100 feet long.

We used to watch this huge whale come to the surface again and again to blow, at intervals of thirty to forty seconds, and from the fact that at each of four or five appearances no vestige of a dorsal fin was visible, we began to wonder whether we had not found the Right whale that was once reported to be so abundant in Ross Sea. Again and again the spout went up into the cold air, a white twelve-foot column of condensed moisture, followed by a smooth broad back, and yet no fin. For some time we remained uncertain as to its identity, till at last in sounding for a longer disappearance and a greater depth than usual, the hinder third of the enormous beast appeared above the surface for the first time with its little angular dorsal fin, at once dispelling any doubts we might have had.[31]

It is supposed to be the largest mammal that has ever existed.[32] As it comes up to blow,

one sees first a small dark hump appear and then immediately a jet of grey fog squirted upwards fifteen to eighteen feet, gradually spreading as it rises vertically into the frosty air. I have been nearly in these blows once or twice and had the moisture in my face with a sickening smell of shrimpy oil. Then the hump elongates and up rolls an immense blue-grey or blackish-grey round back with a faint ridge along the top, on which presently appears a small hook-like dorsal fin, and then the whole sinks and disappears.[33]

To the biologist the pack is of absorbing interest. If you want to see life, naked and unashamed, study the struggles of

31. *Discovery Natural History Report, Zoology*, vol. ii, part i, pp. 3–4, by E. A. Wilson.
32. *Scott's Last Expedition*, vol. i, p. 22.
33. Wilson's Journal, *Scott's Last Expedition*, vol. i, p. 613.

this ice-world, from the diatom in the ice-floe to the big killer whale; each stage essential to the life of the stage above, and living on the stage below:

THE PROTOPLASMIC CYCLE

Big floes have little floes all around about 'em,
 And all the yellow diatoms[34] couldn't do without 'em.
Forty million shrimplets feed upon the latter,
 And *they* make the penguin and the seals and whales
                                                    Much fatter.
Along comes the Orca[35] and kills these down below,
 While up above the Afterguard[36] attack them on the floe:
And if a sailor tumbles in and stoves the mushy pack in,
 He's crumpled up between the floes, and so they get
                                                    Their wack in.
Then there's no doubt he soon becomes a Patent Fertilizer,
 Invigorating diatoms, although they're none the wiser,
So the protoplasm passes on its never-ceasing round,
 Like a huge recurring decimal . . . to which no
                                                    End is found.[37]

We were early on the scene compared with previous expeditions, but I do not suppose this alone can explain the extremely heavy ice conditions we met. Possibly we were too far east. Our progress was very slow, and often we were hung up for days at a time, motionless and immovable, the pack all close about us. Patience and always more patience! 'From the masthead one can see a few patches of open water in different directions, but the main outlook is the same scene of desolate hummocky pack.'[38] And again: 'We have scarcely moved all day, but bergs which have become quite old

---

34. Minute plants.   35. Killer whale.
 36. Officers' mess on the *Terra Nova*.
 37. Griffith Taylor in *South Polar Times*.
 38. *Scott's Last Expedition*, vol. i, p. 35.

friends are on the move, and one has approached and almost circled us.'[39]

And then without warning and reason, as far as we could see, it would open out again, and broad black leads and lakes would appear where there had been only white snow and ice before, and we would make just a few more miles, and sometimes we would raise steam only to suffer further disappointment. Generally speaking, a dark black sky means open water, and this is known as an open-water sky; high lights in the sky mean ice, and this is known as ice-blink.

The changes were as sudden as they were unexpected. Thus early in the morning of Christmas Eve, about a fortnight after we had entered the pack, 'we have come into a region of where the open water exceeds the ice; the former lies in great irregular pools three or four miles or more across and connecting with many leads. The latter – and the fact is puzzling – still contain floes of enormous dimensions; we have just passed one which is at least two miles in diameter. . . .' And then, 'Alas! alas! at 7 a.m. this morning we were brought up with a solid sheet of pack extending in all directions, save that from which we had come.'[40]

Delay was always irksome to Scott. As time went on this waiting in the pack became almost intolerable. He began to think we might have to winter in the pack. And all the time our scanty supply of coal was being eaten up, until it was said that Campbell's party would never be taken to King Edward VII's Land. Scott found decisions to bank fires, to raise steam or to let fires out, most difficult at this time. 'If one lets fires out it means a dead loss of over two tons, when the boiler has to be heated again. But this two tons would only cover a day under banked fires, so that for anything longer than twenty-four hours it is economy to put the fires out. At each stoppage one is called upon to decide whether it is to be for more or less than twenty-four hours.'[41]

39. ibid., p. 39.   40. ibid., pp. 54, 55.
41. *Scott's Last Expedition*, vol. i, p. 56.

Certainly England should have an oil-driven ship for polar work.

The *Terra Nova* proved a wonderfully fine ice ship. Bowers's middle watch especially became famous for the way in which he put the ship at the ice, and more than once Scott was alarmed by the great shock and collisions which were the result: I have seen him hurry up from his cabin to put a stop to it! But Bowers never hurt the ship, and she gallantly responded to the calls made upon her. Sometimes it was a matter of forcing two floes apart, at others of charging and breaking one. Often we went again and again at some stubborn bit, backing and charging alternately, as well as the space behind us would allow. If sufficient momentum was gained the ship rode upon the thicker floes, rising up upon it and pressing it down beneath her, until suddenly, perhaps when its nearest edge was almost amidships, the weight became too great and the ice split beneath us. At other times a tiny crack, no larger than a vein, would run shivering from our bows, which widened and widened until the whole ship passed through without difficulty. Always when below one heard the grumbling of the ice as it passed along the side. But it was slow work, and hard on the engines. There were days when we never moved at all.

> I can imagine few things more trying to the patience than the long wasted days of waiting. Exasperating as it is to see the tons of coal melting away with the smallest mileage to our credit, one has at least the satisfaction of active fighting and the hope of better fortune. To wait idly is the worst of conditions. You can imagine how often and how restlessly we climbed to the crow's nest and studied the outlook. And strangely enough there was generally some change to note. A water lead would mysteriously open up a few miles away, or the place where it had been would as mysteriously close. Huge icebergs crept silently towards or past us, and continually we were observing these formidable objects with range finder and compass to determine the relative movement, sometimes with misgivings as to our ability to clear them.

Under steam the change of conditions was even more marked. Sometimes we would enter a lead of open water and proceed for a mile or two without hindrance; sometimes we could come to big sheets of thin ice which broke easily as our iron-shod prow struck them, and sometimes even a thin sheet would resist all our attempts to break it; sometimes we would push big floes with comparative ease and sometimes a small floe would bar our passage with such obstinacy that one would almost believe it possessed of an evil spirit; sometimes we passed through acres of sludgy sodden ice which hissed as it swept along the side, and sometimes the hissing ceased seemingly without rhyme or reason and we found our screw churning the sea without any effect.

Thus the steaming days passed away in an ever-changing environment and are remembered as an unceasing struggle.

The ship behaved splendidly – no other ship, not even the *Discovery*, would have come through so well. Certainly the *Nimrod* would never have reached the south water had she been caught in such pack. As a result I have grown strangely attached to the *Terra Nova*. As she bumped the floes with mighty shocks, crushing and grinding a way through some, twisting and turning to avoid others, she seemed like a living thing fighting a great fight. If only she had more economical engines she would be suitable in all respects.

Once or twice we got among floes which stood 7 or 8 feet above water, with hummocks and pinnacles as high as 25 feet. The ship could have stood no chance had such floes pressed against her, and at first we were a little alarmed in such situations. But familiarity breeds contempt; there never was any pressure in the heavy ice, and I'm inclined to think there never would be.

The weather changed frequently during our journey through the pack. The wind blew from the west and from the east; the sky was often darkly overcast; we had snowstorms, flaky snow, and even light rain. In all such circumstances we were better placed in the pack than outside of it. The foulest weather could do us little harm. During quite a large percentage of days, however, we had bright sunshine, which, even with the temperature well below freezing, made everything look bright and cheerful. The sun also brought us wonderful cloud effects, marvellously delicate tints of sky, cloud and ice, such effects as one might travel far to see. In spite of our impatience we would not willingly have missed many of the beautiful scenes which our sojourn in the pack afforded us. Ponting and Wilson have been busy catching these effects, but no art can reproduce such colours as the deep blue of the icebergs.[42]

As a rule the officer of the watch conned from the crow's nest, shouting his orders to the steersman direct, and to the engine-room through the midshipman of the watch, who stood upon the bridge. It is thrilling work to the officer in charge, who not only has to face the immediate problem of what floes he dare and what he dare not charge, but also to puzzle out the best course for the future, – but I expect he soon gets sick of it.

About this time Bowers made a fancy sketch of the *Terra Nova* hitting an enormous piece of ice. The masts are all whipped forward, and from the crow's nest is shot first the officer of the watch, followed by cigarette ends and empty cocoa mugs, and lastly the hay with which the floor was covered. Upon the forecastle stands Farmer Hayseed (Oates) chewing a straw with the greatest composure, and waiting until the hay shall fall at his feet, at which time he will feed it to his ponies. This crow's nest, which was a barrel lashed to the top of the mainmast, to which entrance was gained by a hinged trap-door, shielded the occupant from most of the wind. I am not sure that the steersman did not have the most uninviting job, but hot cocoa is a most comforting drink and there was always plenty to be had.

Rennick was busy sounding. The depths varied from 1804 to at least 3890 fathoms, and the bottom generally showed volcanic deposits. Our line of soundings showed the transition from the ocean depths to the continental shelf. A series

42. *Scott's Last Expedition*, vol. i, pp. 73–5.

of temperatures was gained by Nelson by means of reversible thermometers down to 3891 metres.

The winch upon which the sounding line was wound was worked by hand on this cruise. It was worked mechanically afterwards, and of course this ought always to be done if possible. Just now it was a wearisome business, especially when we lowered a water-sample bottle one day to 1800 metres, spent hours in winding it up and found it still open when it arrived at the surface! Water samples were also obtained at the various depths. Lillie and Nelson were both busy tow-netting for plankton with full-speed, Apstein, Nansen, 24- and 180-mesh nets.

I don't think many at home had a more pleasant Christmas Day than we. It was beautifully calm with the pack all round. At 10 we had church with lots of Christmas hymns, and then decorated the ward-room with all our sledging flags. These flags are carried by officers on Arctic expeditions, and are formed of the St George's Cross with a continuation ending in a swallow-tail in the heraldic colour to which the individual is entitled, and upon this is embroidered his crest. The men forrard had their Christmas dinner of fresh mutton at midday; there was plenty of penguin for them, but curiously enough they did not think it good enough for a Christmas dinner. The ward-room ate penguin in the evening, and after the toast of 'absent friends' we began to sing, and twice round the table everybody had to contribute a song. Ponting's banjo songs were a great success, also Oates's 'The Vly on the tu-urmuts'. Meares sang 'a little song about our Expedition, and many of the members that Southward would go', of his own composition. The general result was that the watches were all over the place that night. At 4 a.m. Day whispered in my ear that there was nothing to do, and Pennell promised to call me if there was – so I remembered no more until past six.

And Crean's rabbit gave birth to seventeen little ones, and it was said that Crean had already given away twenty-two.

We had stopped and banked fires against an immense composite floe on the evening of Christmas Eve. How we watched the little changes in the ice and the wind, and scanned the horizon for those black patches which meant open water ahead. But always there was that same white sky to the south of us. And then one day there came the shadow of movement of the sea, the faintest crush on the brash ice, the whisper of great disturbances afar off. It settled again: our hopes were dashed to the ground. Then came the wind. It was so thick that we could not see far; but even in our restricted field changes were in progress.

We commence to move between two floes, make 200 or 300 yards, and are then brought up bows on to a large lump. This may mean a wait of anything from ten minutes to half-an-hour, whilst the ship swings round, falls away, and drifts to leeward. When clear she forges ahead again and the operation is repeated. Occasionally when she can get a little way on she cracks the obstacle and slowly passes through it. There is a distinct swell – very long, very low. I counted the period as about nine seconds. Every one says the ice is breaking up.[43]

On 28 December the gale abated. The sky cleared, and showed signs of open water ahead. It was cold in the wind but the sun was wonderful, and we lay out on deck and basked in its warmth, a cheerful, careless crowd. After breakfast there was a consultation between Scott and Wilson in the crow's nest. It was decided to raise steam.

Meanwhile we sounded, and found a volcanic muddy bottom at 2035 fathoms. The last sounding showed 1400 fathoms; we had passed over a bank.

Steam came at 8 p.m. and we began to push forward. At first it was hard going, but slowly we elbowed our way until the spaces of open water became more frequent. Soon we found one or two large pools, several miles in extent; then

---

43. *Scott's Last Expedition*, vol. i, p. 62.

the floes became smaller. Later we could see no really big floes at all; 'the sheets of thin ice are broken into comparatively regular figures, none more than thirty yards across', and 'we are steaming amongst floes of small area evidently broken by swell, and with edges abraded by contact'.[44]

We could not be far from the southern edge of the pack. Twenty-four hours after raising steam we were still making good progress, checking sometimes to carve our way through some obstacle. At last we were getting a return for the precious coal expended. The sky was overcast, the outlook from the masthead flat and dreary, but hour by hour it became more obvious that we neared the threshold of the open sea. At 1 a.m. on Friday, 30 December (lat. about $71\frac{1}{2}°$ S., noon observation 72° 17′ S., 177° 9′ E.) Bowers steered through the last ice stream. Behind was some 400 miles of ice. Cape Crozier was 334 miles (geog.) ahead.

44. ibid., vol. i, pp. 68, 69.

Chapter Four
LAND

Beyond this flood a frozen continent
Lies dark and wilde, beat with perpetual storms
Of whirlwind and dire hail, which on firm land
Thaws not, but gathers heap, and ruin seems
Of ancient pile; all else deep snow and ice . . .

MILTON *Paradise Lost*, II

'THEY SAY it's going to blow like hell. Go and look at the glass.' Thus Titus Oates quietly to me a few hours before we left the pack.

I went and looked at the barograph and it made me feel sea-sick. Within a few hours I was sick, *very* sick; but we newcomers to the Antarctic had yet to learn that we knew nothing about its barometer. Nothing very terrible happened after all. When I got up to the bridge for the morning watch we were in open water and it was blowing fresh. It freshened all day, and by the evening it was blowing a southerly with a short choppy North Sea swell, and very warm. By 4 a.m. the next morning there was a big sea running and the dogs and ponies were having a bad time. Rennick had the morning watch these days, and I was his humble midshipman.

At 5.45 we sighted what we thought was a berg on the port bow. About three minutes later Rennick said, 'There's a bit of pack,' and I went below and reported to Evans. It was very thick with driving snow and also foggy, and before Evans got up to the bridge we were quite near the pack, and amongst bits which had floated from it, one of which must have been our berg. We took in the headsails as quickly as possible, these being the only sails set, and nosed along dead slow to leeward under steam alone. Gradually we could see either pack or the blink of it all along our port and starboard beam, while gradually we felt our way down a big patch of open water.

There was quite a meeting on the bridge, and it was decided to get well in, and lie in open water under lee of the pack till the gale blew itself out.

> Under ordinary circumstances the safe course would have been to go about and stand to the east. But in our case we must risk trouble to get smoother water for the ponies. We passed a stream of ice over which the sea was breaking heavily, and one realized the danger of being amongst loose floes in such a sea. But soon we came to a compacter body of floes, and running behind this we were agreeably surprised to find comparatively smooth water. We ran on for a bit, then stopped and lay to.[1]

All that day we lay behind that pack, steaming slowly to leeward every now and then, as the ice drifted down upon us. Towards night it began to clear. It was New Year's Eve.

I turned in, thinking to wake in 1911. But I had not been long asleep when I found Atkinson at my side. 'Have you seen the land?' he said. 'Wrap your blankets round you, and go and see.' And when I got up on deck I could see nothing for a while. Then he said: 'All the high lights are snow lit up by the sun.' And there they were: the most glorious peaks appearing, as it were like satin, above the clouds, the only white in a dark horizon. The first glimpse of Antarctic land, Sabine and the great mountains of the Admiralty Range. They were 110 miles away. But

> Icy mountains high on mountains pil'd
> Seem to the shivering sailor from afar
> Shapeless and white, an atmosphere of cloud;[2]

and, truth to tell, I went back to my warm bunk. At midnight a rowdy mob, ringing the New Year in with the dinner-bell, burst into our Nursery. I expected to be hauled out, but got off with a dig in the ribs from Birdie Bowers.

1. *Scott's Last Expedition*, vol. i, p. 77.   2. Thomson.

In brilliant sunshine we coasted down Victoria Land. 'Tonight it is absolutely calm, with glorious bright sunshine. Several people were sunning themselves at 11 o'clock! Sitting on deck and reading.'[3]

At 8.30 on Monday night, 2 January, we sighted Erebus, 115 miles away. The next morning most of us were on the yards furling sail. We were heading for Cape Crozier, the northern face of Ross Island was open to our fascinated gaze, and away to the east stretched the Barrier face until it disappeared below the horizon. Adélie penguins and Killer whales were abundant in the water through which we steamed.

I have seen Fuji, the most dainty and graceful of all mountains; and also Kinchinjunga: only Michael Angelo among men could have conceived such grandeur. But give me Erebus for my friend. Whoever made Erebus knew all the charm of horizontal lines, and the lines of Erebus are for the most part nearer the horizontal then the vertical. And so he is the most restful mountain in the world, and I was glad when I knew that our hut would lie at his feet. And always there floated from his crater the lazy banner of his cloud of steam.

Now we had reached the Barrier face some five miles east of the point at which it joins the basalt cliffs of Cape Crozier. We could see the great pressure waves which had proved such an obstacle to travellers from the *Discovery* to the Emperor penguin rookery. The Knoll was clear, but the summit of Mount Terror was in the clouds. As for the Barrier we seemed to have known it all our lives, it was so exactly like what we had imagined it to be, and seen in the pictures and photographs.

Scott had a whaler launched, and we pulled in under the cliffs. There was a considerable swell.

We were to examine the possibilities of landing, but the swell was so heavy in its break among the floating blocks of

3. *Scott's Last Expedition*, vol. i, p. 80.

ice along the actual beach and ice foot that a landing was out of the question. We should have broken up the boat and have all been in the water together. But I assure you it was tantalizing to me, for there about six feet above us on a small dirty piece of the old bay ice about ten feet square one living Emperor penguin chick was standing disconsolately stranded, and close by stood one faithful old Emperor parent asleep. This young Emperor was still in the down, a most interesting fact in the bird's life history at which we had rightly guessed, but which no one had actually observed before. It was in a stage never yet seen or collected, for the wings were already quite clean of down and feathered as in the adult, also a line down the breast was shed of down and part of the head. This bird would have been a treasure to me, but we could not risk life for it, so it had to remain where it was. It was a curious fact that with as much clean ice to live on as they could have wished for, these destitute derelicts of a flourishing colony, now gone north to sea on floating bay ice, should have preferred to remain standing on the only piece of bay ice left, a piece about ten feet square and now pressed up six feet above water level, evidently wondering why it was so long in starting north with the general exodus which must have taken place just a month ago. The whole incident was most interesting and full of suggestion as to the slow working of the brain of these queer people. Another point was most weird to see, that on the *under* side of this very dirty piece of sea-ice, which was about two feet thick and which hung over the water as a sort of cave, we could see the legs and lower halves of dead Emperor chicks hanging through, and even in one place a dead adult. I hope to make a picture of the whole quaint incident, for it was a corner crammed full of Imperial history in the light of what we already knew, and it would otherwise have been about as unintelligible as any group of animate or inanimate nature could possibly have been. As it is, it throws more light on the life history of this strangely primitive bird . . .

We were joking in the boat as we rowed under these cliffs and saying it would be a short-lived amusement to see the overhanging cliff part company and fall on us. So we were glad to find that we were rowing back to the ship and already 200 or 300 yards away from the place and in open water when there was a noise like crackling thunder and a huge plunge into the sea and a smother of rock dust like the smoke of an explosion, and we realized that the very thing had happened which we had just been talking about. Altogether it was a very exciting row, for before we got on board we had the pleasure of seeing the ship shoved in so close to these cliffs by a belt of heavy pack ice that to us it appeared a toss-up whether she got out again or got forced in against the rocks. She had no time or room to turn, and got clear by backing out through the belt of pack stern first, getting heavy bumps under the counter and on the rudder as she did so, for the ice was heavy and the swell considerable.[4]

Westward of Cape Crozier the sides of Mount Terror slope down to the sea, forming a possible landing-place in calm weather. Here there is a large Adélie penguin rookery in summer, and it was here that the *Discovery* left a record of her movements tied to a post to guide the relieving ship the following year. It was the return of a sledge party which tried to reach this record from the Barrier that led to Vince's terrible death. As we coasted along we could see this post quite plainly, looking as new as the day it was erected, and we know now that there is communication with the Barrier behind, while this rookery itself is free from the blizzards which sweep out to sea by Cape Crozier. It was therefore an excellent place to winter and it was a considerable disappointment to find that it was impossible to land.

This was the first sight we had of a rookery of the little Adélie penguin. Hundreds of thousands of birds dotted the shore, and there were many thousands in the sea round the ship. As we came to know these rookeries better we came to look upon these quaint creatures more as familiar friends than as casual acquaintances. Whatever a penguin does has individ-

4. Wilson's Journal, *Scott's Last Expedition*, vol. i, pp. 613, 614.

uality, and he lays bare his whole life for all to see. He cannot fly away. And because he is quaint in all that he does, but still more because he is fighting against bigger odds than any other bird, and fighting always with the most gallant pluck, he comes to be considered as something apart from the ordinary bird – sometimes solemn, sometimes humorous, enterprising, chivalrous, cheeky – and always (unless you are driving a dog-team) a welcome and, in some ways, an almost human friend.

The alternative landing-place to Cape Crozier was somewhere in McMurdo Sound, the essential thing being that we should have access to and from the Barrier, such communication having to be by sea-ice, since the land is for the most part impassable. As we steamed from Cape Crozier to Cape Bird, the N.W. extremity of Ross Island, we carried out a detailed running survey.

When we neared Cape Bird and Beaufort Island we could see that there was much pack in the mouth of the Strait. By keeping close in to the land we avoided the worst of the trouble, and 'as we rounded Cape Bird we came in sight of the old well-remembered landmarks – Mount Discovery and the Western Mountains – seen dimly through a hazy atmosphere. It was good to see them again, and perhaps after all we are better this side of the Island. It gives one a homely feeling to see such a familiar scene.'[5]

Right round from Cape Crozier to Cape Royds the coast is cold and forbidding, and for the most part heavily crevassed. West of Cape Bird are some small penguin rookeries, and high up on the ice slopes could be seen some grey granite boulder. These are erratics, brought by ice from the Western Mountains, and are evidence of a warmer past when the Barrier rose some two thousand feet higher than it does now, and stretched many hundreds of miles farther out to sea. But now the Antarctic is becoming colder, the deposition of snow is therefore farther north, and the formation of ice correspondingly less.

5. *Scott's Last Expedition*, vol. i, p. 87.

Many watched all night, as this new world unfolded itself, cape by cape and mountain by mountain. We pushed through some heavy floes and

at 6 a.m. (on 4 January) we came through the last of the Strait pack some three miles north of Cape Royds. We steered for the Cape, fully expecting to find the edge of the pack-ice ranging westward from it. To our astonishment we ran on past the Cape with clear water or thin sludge ice on all sides of us. Past Cape Royds, past Cape Barne, past the glacier on its south side, and finally round and past Inaccessible Island, a good two miles south of Cape Royds. The Cape itself was cut off from the south. We could have gone farther, but the last sludge ice seemed to be increasing in thickness, and there was no wintering spot to aim for but Cape Armitage.[6] I have never seen the ice of the Sound in such a condition or the land so free from snow. Taking these facts in conjunction with the exceptional warmth of the air, I came to the conclusion that it had been an exceptionally warm summer. At this point it was evident that we had a considerable choice of wintering spots. We could have gone to either of the small islands, to the mainland, the Glacier Tongue, or pretty well anywhere except Hut Point. My main wish was to choose a place that would not be easily cut off from the Barrier, and my eye fell on a cape which we used to call the Skuary, a little behind us. It was separated from the old *Discovery* quarters by two deep bays on either side of the Glacier Tongue, and I thought that these bays would remain frozen until late in the season, and that when they froze over again the ice would soon become firm. I called a council and put these propositions. To push on to the Glacier Tongue and winter there; to push west to the 'tombstone' ice and to make our way to an inviting spot to the northward of the cape we used to call 'the Skuary'. I favoured the latter course, and on discussion we found it

6. The extreme south point of the island, a dozen miles farther, on one of whose minor headlands, Hut Point, stood the *Discovery* hut.

obviously the best, so we turned back close around Inaccessible Island and steered for the fast ice off the Cape at full speed. After piercing a small fringe of thin ice at the edge of the fast floe the ship's stem struck heavily on hard bay ice about a mile and a half from the shore. Here was a road to the Cape and a solid wharf on which to land our stores. We made fast with ice anchors.[7]

Scott, Wilson and Evans walked away over the sea-ice, but were soon back. They reported an excellent site for a hut on a shelving beach on the northern side of the Cape before us, which was henceforward called Cape Evans, after our second in command. Landing was to begin forthwith.

First came the two big motor sledges which took up so much of our deck space. In spite of the hundreds of tons of sea-water which had washed over and about them they came out of their big crates looking 'as fresh and clean as if they had been packed on the previous day'.[8] They were running that same afternoon.

We had a horse-box for the ponies, which came next, but it wanted all Oates's skill and persuasion to get them into it. All seventeen of them were soon on the floe, rolling and kicking with joy, and thence they were led across to the beach where they were carefully picketed to a rope run over a snow slope where they could not eat sand. Shackleton lost four out of eight ponies within a month of his arrival. His ponies were picketed on rubbly ground at Cape Royds, and ate the sand for the salt flavour it possessed. The fourth pony died from eating shavings in which chemicals had been packed. This does not mean that they were hungry, merely that these Manchurian ponies eat the first thing that comes in their way, whether it be a bit of sugar or a bit of Erebus.

Meanwhile the dog-teams were running light loads between the ship and the shore.

7. *Scott's Last Expedition*, vol. i, pp. 88–90   8. ibid., p. 91.

The great trouble with them has been due to the fatuous conduct of the penguins. Groups of these have been constantly leaping on to our floe. From the moment of landing on their feet their whole attitude expressed devouring curiosity and a pig-headed disregard for their own safety. They waddle forward, poking their heads to and fro in their usually absurd way, in spite of a string of howling dogs straining to get at them. 'Hulloa!' they seem to say, 'here's a game – what do all you ridiculous things want?' And they come a few steps nearer. The dogs make a rush as far as their harness or leashes allow. The penguins are not daunted in the least, but their ruffs go up and they squawk with semblance of anger, for all the world as though they were rebutting a rude stranger – their attitude might be imagined to convey, 'Oh, that's the sort of animal you are; well, you've come to the wrong place – we aren't going to be bluffed and bounced by you,' and then the final fatal steps forward are taken and they come within reach. There is a spring, a squawk, a horrid red patch on the snow, and the incident is closed.[9]

Everything had to be sledged nearly a mile and a half across the sea-ice, but at midnight, after seventeen hours' continuous work, the position was most satisfactory. The large amount of timber which went to make the hut was mostly landed. The ponies and dogs were sleeping in the sun on shore. A large green tent housed the hut builders, and the site for the hut was levelled.

Such weather in such a place comes nearer to satisfying my ideal of perfection than any condition I have ever experienced. The warm glow of the sun with the keen invigorating cold of the air forms a combination which is inexpressibly health-giving and satisfying to me, whilst the golden light on this wonderful scene of mountain and ice satisfies every claim of scenic magnificence. No words of mine can convey the impressiveness of the wonderful panorama displayed to our

9. *Scott's Last Expedition*, vol. i, pp. 92–3.

eyes . . . It's splendid to see at last the effect of all the months of preparation and organization. There is much snoring about me as I write (2 a.m.) from men tired after a hard day's work and preparing for such another tomorrow. I also must sleep, for I have had none for 48 hours – but it should be to dream happily.[10]

Getting to bed about midnight and turning out at 5 a.m. we kept it up day after day. Petrol, paraffin, pony food, dog food, sledges and sledging gear, hut furniture, provisions of all kinds both for life at the hut and for sledging, coal, scientific instruments and gear, carbide, medical stores, clothing – I do not know how many times we sledged over that sea-ice, but I do know that we were landed as regards all essentials in six days. 'Nothing like it has been done before; nothing so expeditious and complete.'[11] . . . and 'Words cannot express the splendid way in which every one works.'[12]

The two motors, the two dog-teams, man-hauling parties, and, as they were passed for work by Oates, the ponies; all took part in this transport. As usual Bowers knew just where everything was, and where it was to go, and he was most ably seconded on the ship by Rennick and Bruce. Both man-hauling parties and pony-leaders commonly did ten journeys a day, a distance of over thirty miles. The ponies themselves did one to three or four journeys as they were considered fit.

Generally speaking the transport seemed satisfactory, but it soon became clear that sea-ice was very hard on the motor sledge runners.

The motor sledges are working well, but not very well; the small difficulties will be got over, but I rather fear they will never draw the loads we expect of them. Still they promise to be a help, and they are a lively and attractive feature of our present scene as they drone along over the floe.

10. ibid., pp. 92–4.   11. ibid., p. 111.   12. ibid., p. 94.

At a little distance, without silencers, they sound exactly like threshing machines.[13]

The ponies were the real problem. It was to be expected that they would be helpless and exhausted after their long and trying voyage. Not a bit of it! They were soon rolling about, biting one another, kicking one another, and any one else, with the best will in the world. After two days' rest on shore, twelve of them were thought fit to do one journey, on which they pulled loads varying from 700 to 1000 lbs. with ease on the hard sea-ice surface. But it was soon clear that these ponies were an uneven lot. There were the steady workers like Punch and Nobby; there were one or two definitely weak ponies like Blossom, Blücher and Jehu; and there were one or two strong but rather impossible beasts. One of these was soon known as Weary Willie. His outward appearance belied him, for he looked like a pony. A brief acquaintance soon convinced me that he was without doubt a cross between a pig and a mule. He was obviously a strong beast and, since he always went as slowly as possible and stopped as often as possible it was most difficult to form any opinion as to what load he was really able to draw. Consequently I am afraid there is little doubt that he was generally overloaded until that grim day on the Barrier when he was set upon by a dog-team. It was his final collapse at the end of the Depot journey which caused Scott to stay behind when we went out on the sea-ice. But of that I shall speak again.

Twice only have I ever seen Weary Willie trot. We were leading the ponies now as always with halters and without bits. Consequently our control was limited, especially on ice, but doubtless the ponies' comfort was increased, especially in cold weather when a metal bit would have been difficult if not impossible. On this occasion he and I had just arrived at the ship after a trudge in which I seemed to be pulling both Weary and the sledge. Just then a motor back-fired, and we started back across that floe at a pace which surprised Weary

13. ibid., p. 100.

even more than myself, for he fell over the sledge, himself and me, and for days I felt like a big black bruise. The second occasion on which he got a move on was during the Depot journey when Gran on ski tried to lead him.

Christopher and Hackenschmidt were impossible ponies. Christopher, as we shall see, died on the Barrier a year after this, fighting almost to the last. Hackenschmidt, so called 'from his vicious habit of using both fore and hind legs in attacking those who came near him',[14] led an even more lurid life but had a more peaceful end. Whether Oates could have tamed him I do not know: he would have done it if it were possible, for his management of horses was wonderful. But in any case Hackenschmidt sickened at the hut while we were absent on the Depot journey, for no cause which could be ascertained, gradually became too weak to stand, and was finally put out of his misery.

There was a breathless minute when Hackenschmidt, with a sledge attached to him, went galloping over the hills and boulders. Below him, all unconscious of his impending fate, was Ponting, adjusting a large camera with his usual accuracy. Both survived. There were runaways innumerable, and all kinds of falls. But these ponies could tumble about unharmed in a way which would cause an English horse to lie up for a week. 'There is no doubt that the bumping of the sledges close at the heels of the animals is the root of the evil.'[15]

There were two adventures during this first week of landing stores which might well have had a more disastrous conclusion. The first of these was the adventure of Ponting and the Killer whales.

I was a little late on the scene this morning, and thereby witnessed a most extraordinary scene. Some six or seven killer whales, old and young, were skirting the fast floe edge ahead of the ship; they seemed excited and dived rapidly, almost

14. *Scott's Last Expedition*, vol. i, p. 230.
15. ibid., pp. 113–14.

touching the floe. As we watched, they suddenly appeared astern, raising their snouts out of water. I had heard weird stories of these beasts, but had never associated serious danger with them. Close to the water's edge lay the wire stern rope of the ship, and our two Esquimaux dogs were tethered to this. I did not think of connecting the movement of the whales with this fact, and seeing them so close I shouted to Ponting, who was standing abreast of the ship. He seized his camera and ran towards the floe edge to get a close picture of the beasts, which had momentarily disappeared. The next moment the whole floe under him and the dogs heaved up and split into fragments. One could hear the booming noise as the whales rose under the ice and struck it with their backs. Whale after whale rose under the ice, setting it rocking fiercely; luckily Ponting kept his feet and was able to fly to security. By an extraordinary chance also, the splits had been made around and between the dogs, so that neither of them fell into the water. Then it was clear that the whales shared our astonishment, for one after another their huge hideous heads shot vertically into the air through the cracks which they had made. As they reared them to a height of six or eight feet it was possible to see their tawny head markings, their small glistening eyes, and their terrible array of teeth – by far the largest and most terrifying in the world. There cannot be a doubt that they looked up to see what had happened to Ponting and the dogs.

The latter were horribly frightened and strained to their chains, whining; the head of one killer must certainly have been within five feet of one of the dogs.

After this, whether they thought the game insignificant, or whether they missed Ponting is uncertain, but the terrifying creatures passed on to other hunting grounds, and we were able to rescue the dogs, and what was even more important, our petrol – five or six tons of which was waiting on a piece of ice which was not split away from the main mass.

Of course, we have known well that killer whales continually skirt the edge of the floes and that they would undoubtedly snap up any one who was unfortunate enough to fall into the water; but the facts that they could display such deliberate cunning, that they were able to break ice of such thickness (at least 2½ feet), and that they could act in unison, were a revelation to us. It is clear that they are endowed with singular intelligence, and in future we shall treat that intelligence with every respect.[16]

We were to be hunted by these Killer whales again.

The second adventure was the loss of the third motor sledge. It was Sunday morning, 8 January, and Scott had given orders that this motor was to be hoisted out of the ship.

This was done first thing and the motor placed on firm ice. Later Campbell told me one of the men had dropped a leg through crossing a sludgy patch some 200 yards from the ship. I didn't consider it very serious, as I imagined the man had only gone through the surface crust. About 7 a.m. I started for the shore with a single man load, leaving Campbell looking about for the best crossing for the motor.[17]

I find a note in my own diary as to what happened after that:

Last night the ice was getting very soft in places, and I was a little doubtful about leading ponies over a spot on the route to the hut which is about a quarter of a mile from the ship. It has been thawing very fast the last few days, and has been very hot as Antarctic weather goes. This morning was the same, and Bailey went in up to his neck.

Some half-hour after the motor was put on to the floe, we were told to tow it on to firm ice as that near the ship was breaking up. All hands started on a long tow line. We got on to the rotten piece, and somebody behind shouted 'You must run.' From that moment everything happened very quickly.

16. *Scott's Last Expedition*, vol. i, pp. 94–6.   17. Ibid., p. 106.

Williamson fell right in through the ice; immediately afterwards we were all brought up with a jerk. Then the line began to pull us backwards; the stern of the motor had sunk through the ice, and the whole car began to sink. It slowly went right through and disappeared and then the tow line followed it. Everything possible was done to hang on to the rope, but in the end we had to let it go, each man keeping his hold until he was dragged to the lip of the hole. Then we made for the fast ice, leaving the rotten bit between us and the ship.

Pennell and Priestley sounded their way back to the ship, and Day asked Priestley to bring his goggles when he returned. They came back with a life-line, Pennell leading. Suddenly the ice gave way under Priestley, who disappeared entirely and came up, so we learned afterwards, under the ice, there being a big current. In a moment Pennell was lying flat upon the floe on his chest, got his hand under Priestley's arm, and so pulled him out. All Priestley said was, 'Day, here are your goggles.' We all got back to the ship, but communication between the ship and the shore was interrupted for the rest of the day, when a solid road was found right up to the ship in another place.[18]

Meanwhile the hut was rising very quickly, and Davies, who was Chippy Chap, the carpenter, deserves much credit. He was a leading shipwright in the navy, always willing and bright, and with a very thorough knowledge of his job. I have seen him called up hour after hour, day and night, on the ship, when the pumps were choked by the coal balls which formed in the bilges, and he always arrived with a smile on his face. Altogether he was one of our most useful men. In this job of hut-building he was helped by two of our seamen, Keohane and Abbott, and others. Latterly I believe there were more people working than there were hammers!

The hut was a roomy place, 50 feet long, by 25 feet wide, and 9 feet to the eaves. The insulation, which was very satisfactory, was seaweed, sewn up in the form of a quilt.

18. My own diary.

94

The sides have double [match-] boarding inside and outside the frames, with a layer of our excellent quilted seaweed insulation between each pair of boardings. The roof has a single match-boarding inside, but on the outside is a match-boarding, then a layer of 2-ply ruberoid, then a layer of quilted seaweed, then a second match-boarding, and finally a cover of 3-ply ruberoid.[19]

The floor consisted of a wooden boarding next the frame, then a quilt of seaweed, then a layer of felt upon which was a second boarding and finally linoleum.

We thought we should be warm, and we were. In fact, during the winter, with twenty-five men living there, and the cooking range going, and perhaps also the stove at the other end, the hut not infrequently became fuggy, big though it was.

The entrance was through a door in a porch before you got to the main door. In the porch were the generators of the acetylene gas, which was fitted throughout by Day, who was also responsible for the fittings of the ventilator, cooking range, and stove, the chimney pipes from these running along through the middle of the hut before entering a common vent. Little heat was lost. The pipes were fitted with dampers, and air inlets which could be opened or shut at will to control the ventilation. Besides a big ventilator in the top of the hut there was an adjustable air inlet also at the base of the chamber which formed the junction of the two chimneys. The purpose of this was also ventilation, but it was not successful.

The bulkhead which separated the men's quarters, or mess deck, from the rest of the hut, was formed of such cases as contained goods in glass, including wine, which would have frozen and broken outside. The bulkhead did not go as high as the top of the hut. When the contents of a case were wanted, a side of the box was taken out, and the empty case then formed a shelf.

19. *Scott's Last Expedition*, vol. i, p. 111.

We started to live in the hut on 18 January, beautifully warm, the gramophone going, and everybody happy. But for a long time before this most of the landing party had been living in tents on shore. It was very comfortable, far more so than might be supposed, judging only by the popular idea of a polar life. We were now almost landed, there were just a few things more to come over from the ship.

It was blowing a mild blizzard from the south, and I took a sledge over to the ship, which was quite blotted out in blinding snow at times. It was as hard to get an empty sledge over, as generally it is to drag a full one. Tea on the ship, which was very full of welcome, but also very full of the superiority of their own comforts over those of the land. Their own comforts were not so very obvious, since they had tried to get the stove in the wardroom going for the first time. They were all coughing in the smoke, and everything inside was covered with smuts.[20]

The hut itself was some twelve feet above the sea, and situated upon what was now an almost sandy beach of black lava. It was thought that this was high enough to be protected from any swell likely to arrive in such a sheltered place, but, as we shall see, Scott was very anxious as to the fate of the hut, when, on the Depot journey, a swell removed not only miles of sea-ice and a good deal of Barrier, but also the end of Glacier Tongue. We never saw this beach again, for the autumn gales covered it with thick drifts of snow, and the thaw was never enough to remove this for the two other summers we spent here. There is no doubt this was an exceptional year for thaw. We never again saw a little waterfall such as was now tumbling down the rocks from Skua Lake into the sea.

The little hill 66 feet high behind us was soon named Wind Vane Hill and there were other meteorological instruments there besides. A snow-drift or ice-drift always forms to

20. My own diary.

leeward of any such projection, and that beneath this hill was large enough for us to drive into it two ice caves. The first of these was to contain our larder, notably the frozen mutton carcasses brought down by us from New Zealand in the ice-house on deck. These, however, showed signs of mildew, and we never ate very freely of them. Seal and penguin were our stock meat foods, and mutton was considered to be a luxury.

The second cave, 13 feet long by 5 feet wide, hollowed out by Simpson and Wright, was for the magnetic instruments. The temperature of these caves was found to be fairly constant. Unfortunately, this was the only drift into which we could tunnel, and we had no such mass of snow and ice as is afforded by the Barrier, which can be burrowed, and was burrowed extensively by Amundsen and his men.

The cases containing the bulk of our stores were placed in stacks arranged by Bowers up on the sloping ground to the west of the hut, beginning close to the entrance door. The sledges lay on the hill side above them. This arrangement was very satisfactory during the first winter, but the excessive blizzards of the second winter and the immense amount of snow which was gathering about the camp caused us to move everything up to the top of the ridge behind the hut where the wind kept them more clear. Amundsen found it advisable to put his cases in two long lines.[21]

The dogs were tethered to a long chain or rope. The ponies' stable was built against the northern side of the hut, and was thus sheltered from the blizzards which always blow here from the south. Against the south side of the hut Bowers built himself a store-room. 'Every day he conceives or carries out some plan to benefit the camp.'[22]

'Scott seems very cheery about things,' I find in my diary about this time. And well he might be. A man could hardly be better served. We slaved until we were nearly dead-beat, and then we found something else to do until we were quite dead-beat. Ship's company and landing parties alike, not only

21. *The South Pole*, vol. i, p. 278.
22. *Scott's Last Expedition*, vol. i, p. 128.

now but all through this job, did their very utmost, and their utmost was very good. The way men worked was fierce.

If you can picture our house nestling below this small hill on a long stretch of black sand, with many tons of provision cases ranged in neat blocks in front of it and the sea lapping the ice-foot below, you will have some idea of our immediate vicinity. As for our wider surroundings it would be difficult to describe their beauty in sufficiently glowing terms. Cape Evans is one of the many spurs of Erebus and the one that stands closest under the mountain, so that always towering above us we have the grand snowy peak with its smoking summit. North and south of us are deep bays, beyond which great glaciers come rippling over the lower slopes to thrust high blue-walled snouts into the sea. The sea is blue before us, dotted with shining bergs or ice floes, whilst far over the Sound, yet so bold and magnificent as to appear near, stand the beautiful Western Mountains with their numerous lofty peaks, their deep glacial valley and clear cut scarps, a vision of mountain scenery that can have few rivals.[23]

Before I left England people were always telling me the Antarctic must be dull without much life. Now we are in ourselves a perfect farmyard. There are nineteen ponies fifty yards off and thirty dogs just behind, and they howl like the wolves they are at intervals, led by Dyk. The skuas are nesting all round and fighting over the remains of the seals which we have killed, and the penguins which the dogs have killed, whenever they have got the chance. The collie bitch which we have brought down for breeding purposes wanders about the camp. A penguin is standing outside my tent, presumably because he thinks he is going to moult here. A seal has just walked up into the horse lines – there are plenty of Weddell and penguins and whales. On board we have Nigger and a blue Persian kitten, with rabbits and squirrels. The whole place teems with life.

23. *Scott's Last Expedition*, vol. i, p. 129.

> Franky Drake is employed all day wandering round for ice for watering the ship. Yesterday he had made a pile out on the floe, and the men wanted to have a flag put on it and have it photographed, and called 'Mr Drake's Furthest South'![24]

January 25 was fixed as the day upon which twelve of us, with eight ponies and the two dog-teams, were to start south to lay a depot upon the Barrier for the Polar Journey. Scott was of opinion that the bays between us and the Hut Point Peninsula would freeze over in March, probably early in March, and that we should most of us get back to Cape Evans then. At the same time the ponies could not come down over the cliffs of this tongue of land, and preparations had to be made for a lengthy stay at Hut Point for them and their keepers. For this purpose Scott meant to use the old *Discovery* hut at Hut Point.

On 15 January he took Meares and one dog-team, and started for Hut Point, which was fifteen statute miles to the south of us. They crossed Glacier Tongue, finding upon it a depot of compressed fodder and maize which had been left by Shackleton. The open water to the west nearly reached the Tongue.

On arrival at the hut Scott was shocked to find it full of snow and ice. This was serious, and, as we found afterwards, the drifted snow had thawed down into ice: the whole of the inside of this hut was a big ice block. In the middle of this ice was a pile of cases left by the *Discovery* as a depot. They were, we knew, full of biscuit.

'There was something too depressing in finding the old hut in such a desolate condition. I had had so much interest in seeing all the old landmarks and the huts apparently intact. To camp outside and feel that all the old comforts and cheer had departed was dreadfully heart-rending.'[25]

That night

---

24. My own diary.
25. *Scott's Last Expedition*, vol. i, p. 122.

we slept badly till the morning and, therefore, late. After breakfast we went up the hills; there was a keen S.E. breeze, but the sun shone and my spirits revived. There was very much less snow everywhere than I had ever seen. The ski run was completely cut through in two places, the Gap and Observation Hill almost bare, a great bare slope on the side of Arrival Heights, and on top of Crater Heights an immense bare table-land. How delighted we should have been to see it like this in the old days! The pond was thawed and the confervae green in fresh water. The hole we had dug in the mound in the pond was still there, as Meares discovered by falling into it up to his waist, and getting very wet.

On the south side we could see the pressure ridges beyond Pram Point as of old – Horseshoe Bay calm and unpressed – the sea-ice pressed on Pram Point and along the Gap ice front, and a new ridge running around C. Armitage about 2 miles off. We saw Ferrar's old thermometer tubes standing out of the snow slope as though they'd been placed yesterday. Vince's cross might have been placed yesterday – the paint was so fresh and the inscription so legible.[26]

We had two officers who had been with Shackleton in his 1908 Expedition – Priestley, who was in our Northern Party, and Day, who was in charge of our motors. Priestley with two others sledged over to Cape Royds and has left an account of the old hut there:

After pitching tent Levick and I went over to the hut to forage. On the way I visited Derrick Point and took a large seven-pound tin of butter while Levick opened up the hut. It was very dark inside but I pulled the boarding down from the windows so that we could see all right. It was very funny to see everything lying about just as we had left it, in that last rush to get off in the lull of the blizzard. On Marston's bunk was a sixpenny copy of the *Story of Bessie Costrell*, which some one had evidently read and left open. Perhaps what

26. *Scott's Last Expedition*, vol. i, pp. 122–3.

brought the old times back again more than anything else was the fact that as I came out of the larder the sleeve of my wind clothes caught the tap of the copper and turned it on. When I heard the drip of the water I turned instinctively and turned the tap off, almost expecting to hear Bobs' raucous voice cursing me for my clumsiness. Perhaps what strikes one more forcibly than anything else is the fact that nothing has been disturbed. On the table was the remains of a batch of bread that Bobs had cooked for us and that was only partially consumed before the *Nimrod* called for us. Some of the rolls showed the impression of bites given to them in 1909. All round the bread were the sauces, pickles, pepper and salt of our usual standing lunch, and a half-opened tin of ginger-breads was a witness to the dryness of the climate for they were still crisp as the day they were opened.

In the cubicle near the larder were the loose tins that poor Armytage and myself had collected from round the hut before we left.

On the shelves of my cubicle are still stacked the magazines and paper brought down by the relief ship. Nothing is changed at all except the company. It is almost dismal. I expect to see people come in through the door after a walk over the surrounding hills.

We had not much time to look round us; for Campbell was cooking in the tent, so we slung a few tins of jam, a plum-pudding, some tea, and gingerbreads into a sack, and returned to camp. By this time it was snowing heavily and continued to do so after dinner so that we turned in immediately (1.30 p.m.) and went off to sleep. One thing worth mentioning is that on several of the drifts are well-defined hoof marks, some of them looking so new that we could have sworn that they had been made this year.

The Old Sport [Levick] gave us a start by suddenly announcing that he could see a ship quite close, and for some time we were on tenterhooks, but his ship proved to be the *Terra Nova* ice-anchored off the Skuary.

The whole place is very eerie, there is such a feeling of life about it. Not only do I feel it but the others do also. Last night after I turned in I could have sworn that I heard people shouting to each other.

I thought that I had only got an attack of nerves but Campbell asked me if I had heard any shouting, for he had certainly done so. It must have been the seals calling to each other, but it certainly did sound most human. We are getting so worked up that we should not be a bit surprised to see a settlement of Japanese or some other such people some day when we stroll round towards Blacksand Beach. The Old Sport created some amusement this evening by opening a tin of Nestlé's milk at both ends instead of making the two holes at one end. He informed us that he had got so used to using two whole tins of milk for cocoa for fourteen people at night that he always opened them that way.

As a consequence we have to spend most of our spare time making bungs to keep the milk in the tin.[27]

Meanwhile, as was to be expected, the action of the, I suspect, abnormal summer sea temperature was showing its effect upon the sea-ice. Sea-ice thaws from below when the temperature of the water rises. The northern ice goes out first here, being next to the open water, but big thaw pools form at the same time wherever a current of water flows over shallows, as at the end of Cape Evans, Hut Point and Cape Armitage.

On 17 January the ice was breaking away between the point of Cape Evans and the ship, although a road still remained fast between the ship and the shore. The ship began to get up steam, but the fast ice broke away quickly that night. I believe they got steam in three hours, twelve hours being the time generally allowed: only just in time, however, for she broke adrift as it was reported. The next morning she made fast to the ice only 200 yards from the ice-foot of the Cape.

27. Priestley's diary.

For the present the position is extraordinarily comfortable. With a southerly blow she would simply bind on to the ice, receiving great shelter from the end of the Cape. With a northerly blow she might turn rather close to the shore, where the soundings run to three fathoms, but behind such a stretch of ice she could scarcely get a sea or swell without warning. It looks a wonderfully comfortable little nook, but of course one can be certain of nothing in this place; one knows from experience how deceptive the appearance of security may be.[28]

The ship's difficulties were largely due to the shortage of coal. Again on the night of 20–21 January we had an anxious time.

Fearing a little trouble I went out of the hut in the middle of the night and saw at once that she was having a bad time – the ice was breaking with a northerly swell and the wind increasing, with the ship on dead lee shore; luckily the ice anchors had been put well in on the floe and some still held. Pennell was getting up steam and his men struggling to replace the anchors.

We got out the men and gave some help. At 6 steam was up, and I was right glad to see the ship back out to windward, leaving us to recover anchors and hawsers.[29]

A big berg drove in just after the ship had got away, and grounded where she had been lying. The ship returned in the afternoon, and it seems that she was searching round for an anchorage, and trying to look behind this berg. There was a strongish northerly wind blowing. The current and soundings round Cape Evans were then unknown. The current was setting strongly from the north through the strip of sea which divides Inaccessible Island from Cape Evans, a distance of some two-thirds of a mile. The engines were going astern,

28. *Scott's Last Expedition*, vol. 1, p. 127.
29. ibid., p. 134.

103

but the current and wind were too much for her, and the ship ran aground, being fast for some considerable distance aft – some said as far as the mainmast.

Visions of the ship failing to return to New Zealand and of sixty people waiting here arose in my mind with sickening pertinacity, and the only consolation I could draw from such imaginations was the determination that the southern work should go on as before – meanwhile the least ill possible seemed to be an extensive lightening of the ship with boats as the tide was evidently high when she struck – a terribly depressing prospect.

Some three or four of us watched it gloomily from the shore whilst all was bustle on board, the men shifting cargo aft. Pennell tells me they shifted 10 tons in a very short time.

The first ray of hope came when by careful watching one could see that the ship was turning very slowly, then one saw the men running from side to side and knew that an attempt was being made to roll her off. The rolling produced a more rapid turning movement at first, and then she seemed to hang again. But only for a short time; the engines had been going astern all the time and presently a slight movement became apparent. But we only knew she was getting clear when we heard cheers on board, and more cheers from the whaler.

Then she gathered stern way and was clear. The relief was enormous.[30]

All this took some time, and Scott himself came back into the hut with us and went on bagging provisions for the Depot Journey. At such times of real disaster he was a very philosophical man. We were not yet ready to go sledging, but on 23 January the ice in North Bay all went out, and that in South Bay began to follow it. Because this was our road to the Barrier, it was suddenly decided that we must start on the Depot journey the following day or perhaps not at all. Already it was impossible to get sledges south off the Cape:

30. ibid., p. 136.

but there was a way to walk the ponies along the land until they could be scrambled down a steep rubbly slope on to sea-ice which still remained. Would it float away before we got there? It was touch and go. 'One breathes a prayer that the Road holds for the few remaining hours. It goes in one place between a berg in open water and a large pool of the Glacier face – it may be weak in that part, and at any moment the narrow isthmus may break away. We are doing it on a very narrow margin.'[31]

31. *Scott's Last Expedition*, vol. i, p. 138.

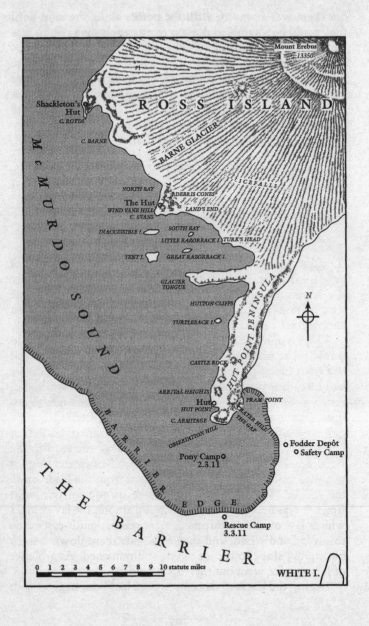

Mount Erebus
13350

ROSS ISLAND

Shackleton's
Hut
C. ROYDS

C. BARNE

BARNE GLACIER

ICEFALLS

NORTH BAY
DEBRIS CONES
The Hut
WIND VANE HILL
C. EVANS
LAND'S END

INACCESSIBLE I.
SOUTH BAY
LITTLE RAZORBACK I.
TURK'S HEAD

TENT I.
GREAT RAZORBACK I.

GLACIER
TONGUE

HUTTON CLIFFS

TURTLEBACK I.

CASTLE ROCK

N

McMURDO SOUND

HUT POINT PENINSULA

ARRIVAL HEIGHTS

Hut
HUT POINT
C. ARMITAGE

PRAM POINT

CRATER HILL

THE GAP

OBSERVATION HILL

Fodder Depôt
Safety Camp

Pony Camp
2.3.11

BARRIER
EDGE

THE BARRIER

Rescue Camp
3.3.11

0 1 2 3 4 5 6 7 8 9 10 statute miles

WHITE I.

Chapter Five
THE DEPOT JOURNEY

The dropping of the daylight in the west.

ROBERT BROWNING

January to March 1911

SCOTT	MEARES	CREAN
WILSON	ATKINSON	FORDE
LIEUT. EVANS	CHERRY-GARRARD	DIMITRI
BOWERS	GRAN	
OATES	KEOHANE	

IMAGINATIVE friends of the thirteen men who started from Cape Evans on 24 January 1911, may have thought of them as athletes, trained for some weeks or months to endure the strains which they were to face, sleeping a good nine hours a night, eating carefully regulated meals and doing an allotted task each day under scientific control.

They would be far from the mark. For weeks we had turned in at midnight too tired to take off our clothes, and had been lucky if we were allowed to sleep until 5 a.m. We had eaten our meals when we could, and we had worked in the meantime just as hard as it was physically possible to do. If we sat down on a packing-case we went to sleep.

And we finally left the camp in a state of hurry bordering upon panic. Since the ice to the south of us, the road to the Barrier, was being nibbled away by thaw, winds and tides, it was impossible to lead the ponies down from the Cape on to the sea-ice. The open sea was before us and on our right front. It was necessary to lead them up among the lava blocks which lay on the escarpment of Erebus, south-eastwards towards Land's End, and thence to slide them down a steep but rubbly slope to the ice which still remained. As a matter of fact that ice went out the very next day.

During the last two days provisions had been bagged with

the utmost dispatch; sledges packed; letters scribbled; clothing sorted and rough alterations to it made. Scott was busy, with Bowers's help, making such arrangements as could be suggested for a further year's stay, for which the ship was to order the necessaries. Oates was busy weighing out the pony food for the journey, sorting harness and generally managing a most unruly mob of ponies. Many were the arguments as to the relative value of a pair of socks or their equivalent in tobacco, for we were allowed 12 lbs of private gear apiece, to consist of everything which we did not habitually wear on our bodies. This included such things as:

Sleeping-boots
Sleeping-socks
Extra pair of day socks
A shirt
Tobacco and pipe
Notebook for diary and pencil
Extra Balaclava helmet
Extra woollen mitts
Housewife containing buttons, needles, darning needles,
    thread and wool
Extra pair of finnesko
Big safety-pins with which to hang up our socks
And perhaps one small book

My most vivid recollection of the day we started is the sight of Bowers, out of breath, very hot, and in great pain from a bad knock which he had given his knee against a rock, being led forward by his big pony Uncle Bill, over whom temporarily he had but little control. He had been left behind in the camp, giving last instructions about the storage of cases and management of provisions, and had practically lost himself in trying to follow us over what was then unknown ground. He was wearing all the clothing which was not included in his personal gear, for he did not think it fair to give the pony the extra weight. He had bruised his leg in an ugly way, and for many days he came to me to bandage it.

He was afraid that if he let the doctors see it they would forbid him to go forward. He had had no sleep for seventy-two hours.

That first night (24 January) we pitched our inexperienced camp not far from Hut Point. But our first taste of sledging was not without incident. Starting with the ponies only we walked them to Glacier Tongue, where the ice and open water joined, and as we went we watched the ship pass us out in the Strait and moor up to the end of the Tongue. Getting our ponies across the Tongue with its shallow but numerous crevasses and holes was ticklish work, but we tethered them safely off the *Terra Nova*, which meanwhile was landing dogs, sledges and gear. Then we got some lunch on board. A large lead in the sea-ice to the south of the Tongue necessitated some hours' work in man-hauling all sledges along the back of the Tongue until a way could be found down on to safe ice. We then followed with the ponies. 'If a pony falls into one of these holes I shall sit down and cry,' said Oates. Within three minutes my pony was wallowing, with only his head and forelegs visible, in a mess of brash and snow, which had concealed a crack in the sea-ice which was obviously not going to remain much longer in its present position. We got lashings round him and hauled him out. Poor Guts! He was fated to drown; but in an hour he appeared to have forgotten all about his mishap, and was pulling his first load towards Hut Point as gallantly as always.

The next day we took further stores from the ship to the camp which we had formed. Some of these loads were to be left on the edge of the Barrier when we got there, but for the present we had to relay, that is, take one load forward and come back for another.

On the 26th we sledged back to the ship for our last load, and said good-bye on the sea-ice to those men with whom we had already worked so long, to Campbell and his five companions who were to suffer so much, to cheery Pennell and his ship's company.

Before we left, Scott thanked Pennell and his men

for their splendid work. They have behaved like bricks, and a finer lot of men never sailed in a ship. . . . It was a little sad to say farewell to all these good fellows and Campbell and his men. I do most heartily trust that all will be successful in their ventures, for indeed their unselfishness and their generous high spirit deserve reward. God bless them.

Four of that Depot party were never to see these men again, and Pennell, Commander of the *Queen Mary*, went down with his ship in the battle of Jutland.

Two days later, 28 January, we sledged our first loads on to the Barrier. By that day we had done nearly ninety miles of relay work, first from the ship at Glacier Tongue to our camp off Hut Point, and then onwards. Those first days of sledging were wonderful! What memories they must have brought to Scott and Wilson when to us, who had never seen them before, these much-discussed landmarks were almost like old friends. As we made our way over the frozen sea every seal-hole was of interest, and every type of windswept snow a novelty. The peak of Terror opened out behind the crater of Erebus, and we walked under Castle Rock and Danger Slope until, rounding the promontory, we saw the little jagged Hut Point, and on it the cross placed there to Vince's memory, all unchanged. There was the old *Discovery* hut and the Bay in which the *Discovery* lay, and from which she was almost miraculously freed at the last moment, only to be flung upon the shoal which runs out from the Point, where some tins of the old *Discovery* days lie on the bottom still and glint in the evening sun. And round about the Bay were the Heights of which we had read, Observation Hill, and Crater Hill separated from it by The Gap – through which the wind was streaming; of course it was, for this must be the famous Hut Point wind.

A few hundred more blizzards had swept over it since those days, but it was all just the same, even to Ferrar's little stakes placed across the glacierets to mark their movement, more, even to the footsteps still plainly visible on the slopes.

The ponies were dragging up to 900 lbs. each these days,

and though they did not seem to be unduly distressed, two of them showed signs of lameness. This caused some anxiety, but the trouble was mended by rest. On the whole, though the surface was hard, I think we were giving them too much weight.

The sea-ice off Hut Point and Observation Hill was already very dangerous, and had we then had the experience and knowledge of sea-ice with which we can now look back, it is probable that we should not have slept so easily upon its surface. Parties travelling to Hut Point and beyond in summer must keep well out from the Point and Cape Armitage. But all haste was being made to transport the necessary stores on to the Barrier surface, where a big home depot could be made, so far as we could judge, in safety. The pressure ridges in the sea-ice between Cape Armitage and Pram Point, which are formed by the movement of the Barrier, were large, and in some of the hollows countless seals were playing in the water. Judging by the size of these ridges and by the thickness of this ice when it broke up, the ice south of Hut Point was at least two years old.

I well remember the day we took the first of our loads on to the Barrier. I expect we were all a little excited, for to walk upon the Barrier for the first time was indeed an adventure: what kind of surface was it, and how about these beastly crevasses of which we had read so much? Scott was ahead, and so far as we could see there was nothing but the same level of ice all round – when suddenly he was above us, walking up the sloping and quite invisible drift. A minute after and our ponies and sledges were up and over the tide crack, and beneath us soft and yielding snow, very different from the hard wind-swept surface of the frozen sea, which we had just left. Really it was rather prosaic and a tame entrance. But the Barrier is a tricky place, and it takes years to get to know her.

On our outward journey this day Oates did his best to kill a seal. My own tent was promised some kidneys if we were good, and our mouths watered with the prospect of the hoosh before us. The seal had been left for dead, and when on our homeward way we neared the place of his demise Titus went off to carve our dinner from him. The next thing we saw was the seal lolloping straight for his hole, while Oates did his best to stab him. The quarry made off safely not much hurt, for, as we discovered later, a clasp-knife is quite useless to kill a seal. Oates returned with a bad cut, as his hand had slipped down the knife; and it was a long time before he was allowed to forget it.

This Barrier, which we were to know so well, was soft, too soft for the ponies, and apparently flat. Only to our left, some hundreds of yards distant, there were two little snowy mounds. We got out the telescope which we carried, but could make nothing of them. While we held our ponies Scott walked towards them, and soon we saw him brushing away snow and uncovering something dark beneath. They were tents, obviously left by Shackleton or his men when the *Nimrod* was embarking his Southern party from the Barrier. They were snowed up outside, and iced up inside almost to the caps. Afterwards we dug them out, a good evening's work. The fabric was absolutely rotten, we just tore it down with our hands, but the bamboos and caps were as sound as ever. When we had dug down to the floor-cloth we found everything intact as when it was left. The cooker was there and a primus – Scott lighted it and cooked a meal; we often used it afterwards. And there were Rowntree's cocoa, Bovril, Brand's extract of beef, sheep's tongues, cheese and biscuits – all open to the snow and all quite good. We ate them for several days. There is something impressive in these first meals off food which has been exposed for years.

It was on a Saturday, 28 January, that we took our first load a short half-mile on to the Barrier and left it at a place afterwards known as the Fodder Depot. Two days later we moved our camp 1 mile 1200 yards farther on to the Barrier and here was erected the main depot, known as Safety Camp. 'Safety' because it was supposed that even if a phenomenal break-up of sea-ice should occur, and take with it part of the Barrier, this place would remain. Subsequent events proved the supposition well founded. This short bit of Barrier sledging gave all of us food for thought, for the surface was appallingly soft, and the poor ponies were sinking deep. It was obvious that no animals could last long under such conditions. But somehow Shackleton had got his four a long way.

There was now no hurry, for there was plenty of food. It was only when we went on from here that we must economize and travel fast. It was determined to give the ponies a rest while we made the depot and rearranged sledges, which we did on the following day. We had with us one pair of pony snow-shoes, a circle of wire as a foundation, hooped round with bamboo, and with beckets of the same material. The surface suggested their trial, which was completely successful. The question of snow-shoes had been long and anxiously considered, and shoes for all the ponies were at Cape Evans; but as we had so lately landed from the ship the ponies had not been trained in their use, and they had not been brought.

Scott immediately sent Wilson and Meares with a dog-team to see whether the sea-ice would allow them to reach Cape Evans and bring back shoes for the other ponies. Meanwhile the next morning saw us trying to accustom the animals to wearing snow-shoes by exercising them in the one pair we possessed. But it seemed no use continuing to do this after the dog party came in. They had found the sea-ice gone between Glacier Tongue and Winter Quarters and so were empty-handed. They reported that a crevasse at the edge of the Tongue had opened under the sledge, which had tilted back into the crevasse but had run over it. These Glacier Tongue crevasses are shallow things; Gran fell into one later and walked out of the side of the Tongue on to the sea-ice beyond!

It was determined to start on the following day with five weeks' provisions for men and animals; to go forward for about fourteen days, depot two weeks' provisions and return. Most unfortunately Atkinson would have to be left behind with Crean to look after him. He had chafed his foot, and the chafe had suppurated. To his great disappointment there was no alternative but to lie up. Luckily we had another tent, and there was the cooker and primus we had dug out of Shackleton's tent. Poor Crean was to spend his spare time in bringing up loads from the Fodder Depot to Safety Camp and, worse still from his point of view, dig a hole downwards into the Barrier for scientific observations!

We left the following morning, 2 February, and marched on a patchy surface for five miles (Camp 4). The temperature was above zero and Scott decided to see whether the surface was not better at night. On the whole, it is problematical whether this is the case – we came to the conclusion later that the ideal surface for pulling a sledge on ski was found at a temperature of about +16°. But there is no doubt whatever that ponies should do their work at night, when the temperature is colder, and rest and sleep when the sun has its greatest altitude and power. And so we camped and turned in to our sleeping bags at 4 p.m. and marched again soon after midnight, doing five miles before and five miles after lunch; lunch, if you please, being about 1 a.m., and a very good time, for just then the daylight seemed to be thin and bleak and one always felt the cold.

Our road lay eastwards through the Strait, some twenty-five miles in width, which runs between the low, rather uninteresting scarp of White Island to the south, and the beautiful slopes of Erebus and Terror to the north. This part of the Barrier is stagnant, but the main stream in front of us, unchecked by land, flows uninterruptedly northwards towards the Ross Sea. Only where the stream presses against the Bluff, White Island and, most important of all, Cape Crozier, and rubs itself against the nearly stationary ice upon which we were travelling, pressures and rendings take place, forming some nasty crevasses. It was intended to steer nearly east until this line was crossed some distance north of White Island, and then steer due south.

It is most difficult on a large snow surface to say whether it is flat. Certainly there are plenty of big crevasses for several miles in this neighbourhood, though they are generally well covered, and we found only very small ones on this outward journey. I am inclined to think there are also some considerable pressure waves. As we came up to Camp 5 we floundered into a pocket of soft snow in which one pony after another plunged deeper and deeper until they were buried up to their bellies and could move no more. I suppose it was an old crevasse filled with soft snow, or perhaps one of the pressure-ridge hollows which had been recently drifted up. My own pony somehow got through with his sledge to the other side, and every moment I expected the ground to fall below us and a chasm to swallow us up. The others had to be unharnessed and led out. The only set of snow-shoes was then put on to Bowers's big pony and he went back and drew the stranded sledges out. Beyond we pitched our camp.

On 3–4 February we marched for ten miles to Camp 6. In the last five miles we crossed several crevasses, our first; and I heard Oates ask someone what they looked like. 'Black as hell,' he said, but we saw no more just now, for this march carried us beyond the line of pressure which runs between White Island and Cape Crozier. This halt was called Corner Camp, as we turned here and marched due south. Corner Camp will be heard of again and again in this story: it is thirty miles from Hut Point.

By 4 p.m. it was blowing our first Barrier blizzard. We were to find out afterwards that a Corner Camp blizzard blows nearly as often as a Hut Point wind. The Bluff seems to be the breeding-ground for these disturbances, which pour out towards the sea by way of Cape Crozier. Corner Camp is in the direct line between the two.

One summer blizzard is much like another. The temperature, never very low, rises, and you are not cold in the tent. Sometimes a blizzard is a very welcome rest: after weeks of hard pulling, dragging yourself awake each morning, feeling as though you had only just gone to sleep, with the mental strain perhaps which work among crevasses entails, it is most pleasant to be put to bed for two or three days. You may sleep dreamlessly nearly all the time, rousing out for meals, or waking occasionally to hear from the soft warmth of your reindeer bag the deep boom of the tent flapping in the wind, or drowsily you may visit other parts of the world, while the drifting snow purrs against the green tent at your head.

But outside there is raging chaos. It is blowing a full gale: the air is full of falling snow, and the wind drives this along and adds to it the loose snow which is lying on the surface of the Barrier. Fight your way a few steps away from the tent, and it will be gone. Lose your sense of direction and there is nothing to guide you back. Expose your face and hands to the wind, and they will very soon be frostbitten. And this is midsummer. Imagine the added cold of spring and autumn: the cold and darkness of winter.

The animals suffer most, and during this first blizzard all our ponies were weakened, and two of them became practically useless. It must be remembered that they had stood for five weeks upon a heaving deck; they had been through one very bad gale: the time during which we were unloading the ship was limited, and since that time they had dragged heavy loads the greater part of 200 miles. Nothing was left undone for them which we could manage, but necessarily the Antarctic is a grim place for ponies. I think Scott felt the sufferings of the ponies more than the animals themselves. It was different for the dogs. These fairly warm blizzards were only a rest for them. Snugly curled up in a hole in the snow they allowed themselves to be drifted over. Bieleglas and Vaida, two half brothers who pulled side by side, always insisted upon sharing one hole, and for greater warmth one would lie on the top of the other. At intervals of two hours or so they fraternally changed places.

This blizzard lasted three days.

We now marched nearly due south, the open Barrier in front, Mount Terror and the sea behind, for five days, covering fifty-four miles, when, being now level with the southern extremity of the Bluff, we laid the Bluff Depot. The bearings of Bluff Depot, as well as those of Corner Camp, are given in *Scott's Last Expedition*.

The characteristics of these days were the collapse of two of the ponies, Blücher and Blossom, and the partial collapse of a third, Jimmy Pigg, although the surface hardened, becoming a marbled series of wind-swept ridges and domes in this region. For the rest the new hands were finding out how to keep warm on the Barrier, how to pitch a tent and cook a meal in twenty minutes, and the thousand and one little tips which only experience can teach. But all the care in the world could do little for the poor ponies.

It must be confessed at once that some of these ponies were very poor material, and it must be conceded that Oates who was in charge of them started with a very great handicap. From first to last it was Oates's consummate management, seconded by the care and kindness of the ponies' leaders, which obtained results which often exceeded the most sanguine hopes.

One evening we watched Scott digging crumbly blocks of snow out of the Barrier and building a rough wall, something like a grouse butt, to the south of his pony. In our inmost hearts I fear we viewed these proceedings with distrust, and saw in it but little usefulness, – one little bit of leaky wall in a great plain of snow. But a very little wind (which you must understand comes almost invariably from the south) convinced us from personal experience what a boon these walls could be. Henceforward every night on camping each pony leader built a wall behind his pony while his pemmican was cooking, and came out after supper to finish this wall before he turned in to his sleeping-bag – no small thing when you consider that the warmth of your hours of rest depends largely upon getting into your bag immediately you have eaten your hoosh and cocoa. And not seldom you might hear a voice in your dreams: 'Bill! Nobby's kicked his wall down'; and out Bill would go to build it up again.

Oates wished to take certain of the ponies as far south as possible on the Depot journey, and then to kill them and leave the meat there as a depot of dog food for the Polar journey. Scott was against this plan. Here at Bluff Depot he decided to send back the three weakest ponies (Blossom, Blücher and Jimmy Pigg, with their leaders, Lieutenant Evans, Forde and Keohane). They started back the next morning (13 February) while the remainder of the party went forward over a surface which gradually became softer as we left behind the windy region of the Bluff. We now had with us the two teams of dogs, driven by Meares and Wilson, and five ponies.

> Scott with 'Nobby'
> Oates with 'Punch'
> Bowers with 'Uncle Bill'
> Gran with 'Weary Willie'
> Cherry-Garrard with 'Guts'

Scott, Wilson, Meares and myself inhabited one tent, Bowers, Oates and Gran the other. Scott was evolving in his mind means by which ponies should follow one another in a string, the second pony with his leading rein fastened to the back of the sledge of the first and so on, the cavalcade to be managed by two or three men only, instead of one man to lead each pony.

Sunday night (12 February) we started from Bluff Depot and did seven miles before lunch against a considerable drift and wind. It was pretty cold, and ten minutes after we left our lunch camp with the ponies it was blowing a full blizzard. The dog party had not started, so we camped and slept five in the four-man tent, and it was by no means uncomfortable. Probably this was the time when Scott first thought of taking a five-man party to the Pole. By Monday evening the blizzard was over, the dogs came up, and we did 6½ miles of very heavy going. Gran's pony, Weary Willie, a sluggish and obstinate animal, was far behind, as usual, when we halted our ponies at the camping place. Farther off the dog-teams were coming up. What happened never became clear. Poor Weary, it seems, was in difficulties in a snow-drift: the dogs of one team being very hungry took charge of their sledge and in a moment were on the horse, to all purposes a pack of ravenous wolves. Gran and Weary made a good fight and the dogs were driven off, but Weary came into camp without his sledge, covered with blood and looking very sick.

We halted after doing only ¾ mile more after lunch; for the pony was done, and little wonder. The following day we did 7½ miles with difficulty, both Uncle Bill and Weary Willie going very slowly and stopping frequently. The going was very deep. The ponies were fast giving out, and it was evident that we had much to learn as to their use on the Barrier; they were thin and very hungry; their rations were unsatisfactory; and the autumn temperatures and winds were beyond their strength. We went on one more day in a minus twenty temperature and light airs, and then in latitude 79° 29′ S. it was determined to lay the depot, which was afterwards known as One Ton, and return. In view of subsequent events it should be realized that this depot was just a cairn of snow in which were buried food and oil, and over which a flag waved on a bamboo. There is no land visible from One Ton except on a very clear day and it is 130 geographical miles from Hut Point.

We spent a day making up the mound which contained about a ton of provisions, oil, compressed fodder, oats and other necessaries for the forthcoming Polar Journey. Scott was satisfied with the result, and indeed this depot ensured that we could start southwards for the Pole fully laden from this point.

Here the party was again split into two for the return. Scott was anxious to get such news about the landing of Campbell's party on King Edward VII's Land as the ship should have left at Hut Point on her return journey. He decided to take the two dog-teams, the first with himself and Meares, the second with Wilson and myself, and make a quick return, leaving Bowers with Oates and Gran to help him to bring back the five ponies, driving them one behind the other.

THE RETURN OF THE PONY PARTY FROM
ONE TON DEPOT

From a letter written by Bowers

As our loads were so light Titus thought it would be better for the ponies to do their full march in one stretch and so have a longer rest. We, therefore, decided to forgo lunch and have a good meal on camping. The recent trails were fresh enough to follow and so saved us steering by compass, which is very difficult as the needle will only come to rest after you have been standing still for about a minute. That march was extraordinary, the snowy mist hid all distant objects and made all close ones look gigantic. Although we were walking on a flat undulating plain, one could not get away from the impression that the ground was hilly – quite steep in places with deep hollows by the wayside. Suddenly a herd of apparent cattle would appear in the distance, then you would think, 'No, it's a team of dogs broken loose and rushing towards you.' In another moment one would be walking over the black dots of some old horse droppings which had been the cause of the hallucinations. Since then I have often been completely taken in by appearances under certain conditions of light, and the novelty has worn off. Sastrugi are the hard waves formed by wind on a snow surface; these are seldom more than a foot or so in height, and often so obscured as to be imperceptible irregularities. On this occasion they often appeared like immense ridges until you walked over them. After going about 10 miles we spotted a tiny black triangle in the dead white void ahead, it was over a mile away and was the lunch camp of the dogs. We were fairly close before they broke camp and hurriedly packed up. I thought they looked rather sheepish at having been caught up, like the hare and the tortoise again. Still we had been marching very quickly and Scott was delighted to see Weary Willie going so well. They then dashed off, and after completing just over 12 miles we reached Pagoda Cairn where a bale of fodder had been left.

Here we camped and threw up our walls as quickly as possible to shelter the beasts from the cold wind. Weary was the most annoying, he would deliberately back into his wall and knock the whole structure down. In the case of my own pony, I had to put the wall out of his reach as his aim in life was to eat it, generally beginning at the bottom. He would diligently dislodge a block, and bring down the whole fabric. One cannot be angry with the silly beggars – Titus says a horse has practically no reasoning power, the thing to do is simply to throw up another wall and keep on at it.

The weather cleared during the night, and the next day, 19 February, we started off under ideal conditions, the sun was already dipping pretty low, marks easy to pick up, and on this occasion we could plainly see a cairn over seven miles away, raised by the mirage; the only trouble about seeing things so far off is that they take such an awful time to reach. Mirage is a great feature down here and one of the most common of optical phenomena on the Barrier; it is often difficult to persuade oneself that open water does not lie ahead. We passed the scene of Weary Willie's fight with the dogs during the march and also had an amusing argument as to a dark object on the snow ahead. At first we thought it was the dog camp again, but it turned out to be an empty biscuit tin, such is the deceptive nature of the light. Later we sighted our old blizzard camp and decided to utilize the walls again. Weary Willie was decidedly worse and had to be literally jumped along by the pony to which he was attached. Within half a mile of the walls Weary refused to go farther, and after wasting some time in vain efforts to urge him on we had to camp where we were, having only done 10½ miles. This was very sad, but I took hope from the fact that Titus, who is usually pretty pessimistic, had not yet given up hopes of getting him back alive. He had an extra whack of oats at the expense of the other ponies, and my big beast made up for his shortage by hauling the sledge towards him with his tethered leg, and forcing his nose into our precious biscuit tank, out of which he helped himself liberally at our expense. The sledges were now too light to anchor the animals, so we had to peg them down with anything we could and bank them up with snow.

Weary was better the next day (20 February) but we decided at the outset to go no farther than the Bluff Camp where we had left some fodder. This was barely 10 miles off, yet my old animal showed signs of lassitude before the end; there was nothing alarming, however, and we saw the depot over five miles off which interested the beasts, who see these things and somehow connect them, in the backs of their silly old heads, with food and rest. Weary Willie made a decided improvement, so we camped in high spirits. Captain Scott had asked me if possible to take some theodolite observations for the determination of the position of Bluff Camp. Ours is much farther off and farther beyond the Bluff than the old Discovery Depot A, which was practically the same position Shackleton used. In both cases, Scott and Shackleton were keeping nearer the coast; now, however, that the Beardmore has been discovered we can aim straight for that, which takes one farther east by at least 15 miles off the Bluff. This is rather an advantage, I think, as close in to this remarkable headland the onward movement of the Barrier arrested by the immovable hills causes a terrific chaos of crevasses off the cliffs at the end. These extend many miles and include some chasms big enough to take the *Terra Nova* all standing. Needless to remark, one is well clear of this sort of scenery with ponies – hence our course. I was unable to get any observations, unfortunately, as it clouded over almost at once and later in the day started to snow without wind. This often happens before a bliz, and as we were anxious about the ponies to say nothing of our own shortage of biscuit we felt a trifle apprehensive. It was very gloomy when we left camp at midnight, as the midnight sun was already cartwheeling the southern horizon, the first sign of autumn, also the season had undoubtedly broken up, and the sky was covered with low stratus clouds as thick as a hedge. We lost sight of the cairn almost at once and followed the remains of old tracks for a little while till the snowy gloom made it impossible to

see them. You will remember that it was at the Bluff Camp
that Teddy Evans returned with the three weak ponies, so
there were plenty of traces of our march now. Just on four
miles from the start I saw a small mound some distance to the
west, and struck over there: it was a small cairn without the
signs of a camp and rather puzzled me at the time. As I shall
mention it later I will call it X for convenience. We then
pushed on and I found steering most difficult. In the fuzzy
nothingness ahead one could see no point on which to fix the
eye, and the compass required standing still to look at it every
time. Our sledging compasses are spirit ones, and as steady as
a small hand compass could possibly be. You will understand,
however, that owing to the proximity of the Magnetic Pole
the pull of the needle is chiefly downwards. It is forced into a
horizontal position by a balancing weight on the N. side, so
it is obvious that its direction power is greatly reduced. On
the ship, owing to the vibration of the engines and the motors,
we were absolutely unable to steer by the compass at all when
off the region of the Magnetic Pole.

On this occasion (21 February) we zig-zagged all over the
place – first I went ahead, and Oates said I zig-zagged, then
he went ahead, and I understood at once, as it was impossible
to walk straight for two consecutive minutes. However, we
plodded along with frequent stoppages till the wind came
away, and then having determined the direction of that,
steered by keeping the snow on our backs. The wind was not
strong enough to be unpleasant, and all was well. We legged
it into the void for nearly seven miles beyond X Cairn when
I suddenly found myself only a few yards away from another
cairn. This shows that somehow, without the use of tracks or
landmarks, we had marched seven miles without being able
to see thirty yards, and had yet hit off the direct track to a T;
of course, it was only coincidence, though some people might
credit themselves with superlative navigating powers on such
evidence. The wind increased, and with the knowledge I now
have of blizzards I would camp at once. Then I thought it
better to shove on, as the ponies were marching splendidly.
The danger lay in the fact that though it is easy for you to

march with the wind behind you, you can't march for ever and you will probably get tired before the wind does. Camping in a stiff breeze is always difficult, to say nothing of a gale; and for three men with five ponies to manage would be wellnigh impossible. Fortunately for us this was not really a blizzard, though it was quite near enough to one. The sky broke later and showed the Bluff and White Island, and then the scurrying clouds of drift would encircle us to break again and come on again.

After having done seventeen miles we got a lull and stopped to camp right away. We were pretty quick about it, and fortunately got the ponies picketed, and tent pitched, before the wind came down on us again. We were pretty hungry by the time the walls were erected. Still we were quite happy, ate everything we could get, except the three lumps of sugar I always kept for old Uncle Bill out of my whack. The little blow blew itself out towards evening and in perfect calm and sunshine I got a splendid set of observations. Erebus and Terror were showing up as clear as a bell and I got a large number of angles for Evans's survey. We started out as usual, and had the most pleasant, as well as the longest, of our return marches on the last day of summer, 22 February. We did eighteen miles right off the reel, the sun was brilliant from midnight onwards. He now half immersed himself below the horizon for a short interval once in 24 hours. All old cairns were visible a tremendous distance, six or seven miles at least for big ones. Mount Terror lay straight ahead and looked so clear that it seemed impossible to imagine it 70 miles away. At the end of our march we saw a small cairn beyond our 8th camp mound. Nobody would have rigged up another cairn so close without an object, so the thought of a dead horse flashed through my mind at once. Titus was so sure that Blücher would never get back, that he had bet Gran a biscuit on it. I saw the cairn had a fodder bale on the top, and later saw a note made fast to the wire. It was in Teddy Evans's handwriting and to our surprise recorded Blossom's death. Titus was so sure that Blossom would survive Blücher that we started to think back and thus the mystery of X Cairn was clear to me. I was quite certain now that both the ancient ponies had died and that Jimmy Pigg had returned alone. The following day (23 February) was a good marching day also, but a bit cloudy latterly. We did fourteen miles as this evidence of pony failure made us all the more anxious about ours, though really they were going very well. About eight miles on we came to one of Evans's camps and the solitary pony wall told its own tale of the death of the other two. He must have had a miserable return. At eleven miles there were two bales of fodder depoted, we were only 50 miles odd from our destination off Cape Armitage, and had one meal over three days' food. If, therefore, we could average 15 miles a day that would suffice. It was a silly risk in view of blizzards and other possibilities, chiefly our own inexperience. As it was I took it and left the fodder there for next year.

February 24 was another march into impenetrable gloom. Fortunately Corner Camp, though dark enough, was not shaded in mist. I examined it for notes and evidence and found some. The sun set properly now, and had we been farther from home I should have changed to day marching. I have seldom seen such a scene of utter desolation as Corner Camp presented on that gloomy day. The fog then settled down and like people of the mist, we struck off blindly to the N.W. At 3.15 a.m. a light S. breeze came away; I dreaded a blizzard with so little pony food, and already regretted my folly in leaving the fodder. After doing twelve miles we had to camp, as it was impossible even to march straight in the white haze. We made five colossal walls and turned in, hoping for the best. Fortune favours the reckless, as well as the brave, at times, and it did this time, as the blizzard still held off. The signs of one impending were unmistakable notwithstanding. Weary Willie did less well on 25 February, and as the surface became heavier, we had to camp after only doing eleven miles.

I thought best in view of the threatening appearance of the weather to have a six hours' rest, and march into Safety Camp the same day, a distance of eight miles. We found to our horror that Gran had dropped the top cap of our primus at the last camp. Cold food stared us in the face!

However, we did manage to melt some snow for a cheering drink by cutting a piece of tin as near the shape of the cap as possible. Our biscuit was finished owing to the ravages of my pony. Before turning in I saw some specks to the N. and skipping my theodolite on its tripod, looked through the telescope and saw two tents and a number of ski stuck up. [This was Scott's man-hauling party together with Jimmy Pigg, going out to Corner Camp.] This we concluded was either a man-hauling, or man and beast party bound for Corner Camp. We overslept and so did not get away till the afternoon. It was still very cloudy and threatening. I found that I had steered considerably to the southward of the right direction in the fog, and it is lucky we met with no crevasses off White Island. Safety Camp at last appeared, and the last four miles seemed interminable. We had given the animals their last feed before starting, not a particle remained, but they stuck it. The surface was very heavy. Once, however, that they had seen the camp they never stopped, I suppose they knew they were nearly home. We marched in about 9.30 p.m. I said 'Thank God' when I looked at the weather, and the empty sledges. The dogs were in camp, also the dome tent [we had some tents shaped like a dome in addition to those we used for sledging], out of which Uncle Bill (the real 'Uncle Bill Wilson') and Meares emerged. We soon had the ponies behind walls and well fed, borrowed their primus for ourselves, and had a square meal of pemmican and biscuit with fids of seal liver in it.

(End of Bowers's account)

THE RETURN OF THE DOG PARTY

The history of the dog-teams was eventful. We travelled fast, doing nearly 78 miles in the first three days, by which time we were approaching Corner Camp. The dogs were thin and hungry and we were pushing them each day just so long as they could pull, running ourselves for the most part. Scott determined to cut the corner, that is to miss Corner Camp and cut diagonally across our outward track. It was not expected that this would bring us across any badly crevassed area.

We started on the evening of 20 February in a very bad light. It was coldish, with no wind. After going about three miles I saw a drop in the level of the Barrier which the sledge was just going to run over. I shouted to Wilson to look out, but he had already jumped on to the sledge (for he was running) having seen Stareek put his paws through. It was a nasty crevasse, about twenty feet across with blue holes on both sides. The sledge ran over and immediately on the opposite side was brought up by a large 'haystack' of pressure which we had not seen owing to the light. Meares's team, on our left, never saw any signs of pressure. The light was so bad that we never saw this cairn of ice until we ran into it.

We ran level for another two miles, Meares and Scott on our left. We were evidently crossing many crevasses. Quite suddenly we saw the dogs of their team disappearing, following one another, just like dogs going down a hole after some animal.

'In a moment,' wrote Scott,

> the whole team were sinking – two by two we lost sight of them, each pair struggling for foothold. Osman the leader exerted all his strength and kept a foothold – it was wonderful to see him. The sledge stopped and we leapt aside. The situation was clear in another moment. We had been actually travelling along the bridge [or snow covering] of a crevasse, the sledge had stopped on it, whilst the dogs hung in their harness in the abyss, suspended between the sledge and the leading dog. Why the sledge and ourselves didn't follow the dogs we shall never know.

We of the other sledge stopped hurriedly, tethered our team and went to their assistance with the Alpine rope. Osman, the big leader, was in great difficulties. He crouched resisting with all his enormous strength the pull of the rope upon which the team hung in their harness in mid air. It was clear that if Osman gave way the sledge and dogs would probably all be lost down the crevasse.

First we pulled the sledge off the crevasse, and drove the tethering peg and driving stick through the cross pieces to hold it firm. Scott and Meares then tried to pull up the rope from Osman's end, while we hung on to the sledge to prevent it slipping down the crevasse. They could not move it an inch. We then put the strain as much as possible on to a peg. Meanwhile two dogs had fallen out of their harness into the crevasse and could be seen lying on a snow-ledge some 65 feet down. Later they curled up and went to sleep. Another dog as he hung managed to get some purchase for his feet on the side of the crevasse, and a free fight took place among several more of them, as they dangled, those that hung highest using the backs of those under them to get a purchase.

'It takes one a little time,' wrote Scott,

> to make plans under such sudden circumstances, and for some minutes our efforts were rather futile. We could not get an inch on the main trace of the sledge or on the leading rope, which was binding Osman to the snow with a throttling pressure. Then thought became clearer. We unloaded our sledge, putting in safety our sleeping-bags with the tent and cooker. Choking sounds from Osman made it clear that the pressure on him must soon be relieved. I seized the lashing off Meares's sleeping-bag, passed the tent poles across the crevasse, and with Meares managed to get a few inches on the leading line; this freed Osman, whose harness was immediately cut.

> Then securing the Alpine rope to the main trace we tried to haul up together. One dog came up and was unlashed, but by this time the rope had cut so far back at the edge that it was useless to attempt to get more of it. But we could now unbend the sledge, and do that for which we should have aimed from the first, namely, run the sledge across the gap and work from it. We managed to do this, our fingers

constantly numbed. Wilson held on to the anchored trace whilst the rest of us laboured at the leader end. The leading rope was very small and I was fearful of its breaking, so Meares was lowered down a foot or two to secure the Alpine rope to the leading end of the trace; this done, the work of rescue proceeded in better order. Two by two we hauled the animals up to the sledge and one by one cut them out of their harnesses. Strangely the last dogs were the most difficult, as they were close under the lip of the gap, bound in by the snow-covered rope. Finally, with a gasp we got the last poor creature on to firm snow. We had recovered eleven of the thirteen.[1]

The dogs had been dangling for over an hour, and some of them showed signs of internal injuries. Meanwhile the two remaining dogs were lying down the crevasse on a snow-ledge. Scott proposed going down on the Alpine rope to get them; all his instincts of kindness were aroused, as well as the thought of the loss of two of the team. Wilson thought it was a mad idea and very dangerous, and said so, asking however whether he might not go down instead of Scott if anybody had to go. Scott insisted, and we paid down the 90-foot Alpine rope to test the distance. The ledge was about 65 feet below. We lowered Scott, who stood on the ledge while we hauled up the two dogs in turn. They were glad to see him, and little wonder!

But the rescued dogs which were necessarily running about loose on the Barrier, in their mangled harnesses, chose this moment to start a free fight with the other team. With a hurried shout down the crevasse we had to rush off to separate them. Nougis I had been considerably mauled before this was done – also, incidentally, my heel! But at last we separated them, and hauled Scott to the surface. It was all three of us could do and our fingers were frost-bitten towards the end.

Scott's interest in the incident, apart from the recovery of

1. *Scott's Last Expedition*, vol. 1, pp. 180–81.

the dogs, was scientific. Since we were running across the line of cleavage when the dogs went down, it was to be expected that we should be crossing the crevasses at right angles, and not be travelling, as actually happened, parallel to, or along them. While we were getting him up the sixty odd feet to which we had lowered him he kept muttering: 'I wonder why this is running the way it is – you expect to find them at right angles,' and when down the crevasse he wanted to go off exploring, but we managed to persuade him that the snow-ledge upon which he was standing was utterly unsafe, and indeed we could see the nothingness below through the blue holes in the shelf. Another regret was that we had no thermometer: the temperature of the inside of the Barrier is of great interest and a fairly reliable record of the average temperature throughout the year might have been obtained when so far down into it. Altogether we could congratulate ourselves on a fortunate ending to a nasty business. We expected several more miles of crevasses, and the wind was getting up, driving the surface drift like smoke over the ground, with a very black sky to the south. We pitched the tent, had a good meal and mended the dog harness which had been ruthlessly cut in clearing the dogs. Luckily we found no more crevasses for it was now blowing hard, and rescue work would have been difficult, and we pushed on as far as possible that night, doing eleven miles after lunch, and sixteen for the day. It had been strenuous, for we had been working in or over the crevasse for $2\frac{1}{2}$ hours, and dogs and men were tired out. It cleared and became quite warm as we camped. There was a pleasant air of friendship in the tent that night, rather more than usual. That is generally the result of this kind of business.

We reached Safety Camp next day (22 February) anxious for news of the ship's doings, the landing of Campbell's party, and of the ponies which had been sent back from the Bluff Depot. Lieutenant Evans, Forde and Keohane, the pony leaders, were there, but only one pony. The other two had died of exhaustion soon after they left us and we had passed the cairns which marked their graves without knowledge.

Their story was grim, and they had had a mournful journey back. First Blossom, and then Blücher collapsed, their ends being hastened by the blizzard of 1 February.

This crevasse incident, followed by the news of the loss of the ponies, was a blow to Scott, and his mind was also uneasy about Atkinson and Crean, whom we had left here, and who had disappeared leaving no record. Nor was the report from the *Terra Nova* here, so we judged that the missing men and the report must be at Hut Point. After three or four hours' sleep, and a cup of tea and a biscuit, we started man-hauling with cooker and sleeping bags: the former because we were to have our good meal at the hut, the latter in case we were hung up. Travelling over the sea-ice as far as the Gap, from which we saw that the open sea reached to Hut Point, we made our way into the hut, and there was a mystery. The accumulations of ice which we found in it were dug away: there was a notice outside dated 8 February saying 'mail for Captain Scott is in bag inside south door'. We hunted everywhere, but there was no Atkinson nor Crean, nor mail, nor the things which the ship was to have brought. All kinds of wild theories were advanced. By the presence of a fresh onion and some bread it was clear that the ship's party had been there, but the rest was utterly vague. It was then suggested that we were expected back about this time, and that the missing men had been sledging to Safety Camp round Cape Armitage on the very shaky sea-ice while we passed them as we came through the Gap. Sledge tracks were found leading on to the sea-ice: we started back in doubt. Scott was terribly anxious, we were all tired, and the depot never seemed to come nearer. It was not until we were some two hundred yards from it that we saw the extra tent. 'Thank God!' I heard Scott mutter under his breath, and 'I believe you were even more anxious than I was, Bill.'

Atkinson had the ship's mail, signed by Campbell. 'Every incident of the day,' Scott wrote, 'pales before the startling contents of the mail-bag which Atkinson gave me – a letter from Campbell setting out his doings and the finding of Amundsen established in the Bay of Whales.'

Strongly as Scott tries to word this, it quite fails to convey how he felt, and how we all felt more or less, in spite of the warning conveyed in the telegram from Madeira to Melbourne. For an hour or so we were furiously angry, and were possessed with an insane sense that we must go straight to the Bay of Whales and have it out with Amundsen and his men in some undefined fashion or other there and then. Such a mood could not and did not bear a moment's reflection; but it was natural enough. We had just paid the first instalment of the heart-breaking labour of making a path to the Pole; and we felt, however unreasonably, that we had earned the first right of way. Our sense of cooperation and solidarity had been wrought up to an extraordinary pitch; and we had so completely forgotten the spirit of competition that its sudden intrusion jarred frightfully. I do not defend our burst of rage – for such it was – I simply record it as an integral human part of my narrative. It passed harmlessly; and Scott's account proceeds as follows:

> One thing only fixes itself definitely in my mind. The proper, as well as the wiser, course for us is to proceed exactly as though this had not happened. To go forward and do our best for the honour of the country without fear or panic. There is no doubt that Amundsen's plan is a serious menace to ours. He has a shorter distance to the Pole by 60 miles – I never thought he could have got so many dogs safely to the ice. His plan of running them seems excellent. But, above and beyond all, he can start his journey early in the season – an impossible condition with ponies.[2]

We read that on leaving McMurdo Sound the *Terra Nova* coasted eastward along the Barrier face, with Campbell and his men who were to be landed on King Edward VII's Land if possible. She surveyed the face of the Barrier as she went

2. *Scott's Last Expedition*, vol. i, pp. 187–8. Scott started for the Pole on 1 November 1911. Amundsen started on 8 September 1911, but had to turn back owing to low temperatures; he started again on 19 October.

from Cape Crozier to longitude 170° W., whence she shaped a course direct for Cape Colbeck, which Priestley states in his diary 'is only 200 feet high according to our measurements and looks uncommonly like common or garden Barrier'.

Here they met heavy pack, and were forced to return without finding any place where the cliff was low enough to allow Campbell and his five men to land. They coasted back, making for an inlet known as Balloon Bight. Priestley tells the story:

1 February 1911. Our trip has not been without outcome after all, and all our doubts about wintering here or in South Victoria Land have been settled in a startling fashion. About ten o'clock we steamed into a deep bay in the Barrier which proved to be Shackleton's Bay of Whales, and our observations in the last expedition [Shackleton's] have been wonderfully upheld. Our present sights and angles Pennell tells me are almost a duplicate of those that we got. Every one has always been doubtful about the Bay of Whales we reported, but now the matter has been set at rest finally. There is no doubt now that Balloon Bight and the neighbouring bay marked on the *Discovery*'s chart have become merged into one, and further, that since that period the resulting bight has broken back considerably more: indeed it seems to have altered a good deal on its western border since our visit to it in 1908. Otherwise it is the same, the same deceptive caves and shadows having from a distance the appearance of rock exposures, the same pressure-ridged cliffs, the same undulations behind, the same expanse of sea-ice and even the same crowds of whales. I hope that before we leave we shall find it possible to survey the bight, and that depends on the weather. It was satisfactory to find all our observations coming right and everybody backing up Shackleton, and I turned in last night feeling quite cheerful and believing that there would be a really good chance of the Eastern Party finding a home on the Barrier here – our last chance of surveying King Edward's Land.

However, man proposes but God disposes, and I was

waked up by Lillie at one o'clock this morning by the astounding news that there was a ship in the bay at anchor to the sea-ice. All was confusion on board for a few minutes, everybody rushing up on deck with cameras and clothing.

It was no false alarm, there she was within a few yards of us, and what is more, those of us who had read Nansen's books recognized the *Fram*.

She is rigged with fore and aft sails and as she has petrol engines she has no funnel. Soon afterwards the men forward declared that they sighted a hut on the Barrier, and the more excited declared that there was a party coming out to meet us. Campbell, Levisk, and myself were therefore lowered over the side of the ship while she was being made fast, and set off on ski towards the dark spot we could see. This proved to be only an abandoned depot and we returned to the ship, where Campbell, who in his anxiety to be the first to meet them had left us beginners far behind, had opened up conversation with the night watchman.

He informed us that there were only three men on board and that the remainder of them were settling Amundsen in winter quarters about as far from the depot as the depot was from the ship. Amundsen is coming to visit the *Fram* tomorrow, and we are staying long enough to allow Pennell and Campbell to interview him. They reached the pack about 6 January and were through it by the 12th, so they did not have as bad a time as we did. They inform us that Amundsen does not intend to make his descent on the Pole until next year. This is encouraging as it means a fair race for the next summer, though the news we are bringing to them will keep the Western [Main] Party on tenterhooks of excitement all the winter.

Our plans have of course been decided for us. We cannot according to etiquette trench on their winter quarters, but must return to McMurdo Sound and then go off towards Robertson Bay and settle ourselves as best we can. While we are waiting events we have not been by any means idle. Rennick got a sounding, 180 fathoms, and the crew have killed three seals, including one beautiful silver crab-eater,

Lillie has secured water samples at 50, 100, and 170 fathoms and has had a haul with the plankton net, and Williams is endeavouring to fit up the trawl for a haul tomorrow if we get time and appropriate weather. I got a roll of films and gave the roll to Drake to take home and get developed in Christchurch. There are photographs of the *Fram*, of the *Fram* and *Terra Nova* together, of their depot, and of the ice-cliffs and the sea-ice which is decidedly overcut, the thick snow having been removed in places by the swell until a ledge several yards wide is lying just submerged.

It has been calm all the night with the snow falling at intervals.

February 4, 1911. I was waked at seven o'clock this morning by Levick demanding the loan of my camera. It appears that Amundsen, Johansen and six men had arrived at the *Fram* this morning at about 6.30 a.m., and had come over to interview Campbell and Pennell. Campbell, Pennell and Levick then went back to breakfast with them and stayed until nearly noon when they returned telling us to expect Amundsen, Nilsen, the first lieutenant of the *Fram* who is taking her back after landing the party, and a young lieutenant whose name none of us caught, to lunch. After lunch a party of officers and men went to see the rest of the Norwegians, see over the ship, and say good-bye. I did not go and was able to show Lieut. Jensen over the ship in the meantime. About three o'clock we let go the ice anchor and parted from the *Fram*, steaming along the ice very slowly in order to dredge from 190 to 300 fathoms. The haul was successful, about two bucketsful of the muddy bottom being secured, and a still more valuable catch from the biological point of view were two long crinoids, about a couple of feet in length and in fairly perfect condition, which had become attached to the outside of the net.

We are now standing along the Barrier continuing our survey to the bight we first struck, after which we sail to Cape Evans, stay a day there and then make up North to try and effect a lodgement on the coast beyond Cape Adare.

During the morning Browning and I examined the ice-face

forming the eastern face of the bight. We found it to be made of clear ice of grain from a quarter to three-eighths of an inch in size and full of bubbles.

On the way there I took a couple of photographs of some of Amundsen's dogs, and when we were there I got a few of crevasses and caves in the Barrier face.

Well! we have left the Norwegians and our thoughts are full, too full, of them at present. The impression they have left with me is that of a set of men of distinctive personality, hard, and evidently inured to hardship, good goers and pleasant and good-humoured. All these qualities combine to make them very dangerous rivals, but even did one want not to, one cannot help liking them individually in spite of the rivalry.

One thing I have particularly noticed is the way in which they are refraining from getting information from us which might be useful to them. We have news which will make the Western Party as uneasy as ourselves and the world will watch with interest a race for the Pole next year, a race which may go any way, and may be decided by luck or by dogged energy and perseverance on either side.

The Norwegians are in dangerous winter quarters, for the ice is breaking out rapidly from the Bay of Whales which they believe to be in Borchgrevink's Bight, and they are camped directly in front of a distinct line of weakness. On the other hand if they get through the winter safely (and they are aware of their danger), they have unlimited dogs, the energy of a nation as northern as ourselves, and experience with snow-travelling that could be beaten by no collection of men in the world.

There remains the Beardmore Glacier. Can their dogs face it, and if so, who will get there first. One thing I feel and that is that our Southern Party will go far before they permit themselves to be beaten by any one, and I think that two parties are very likely to reach the Pole next year, but God only knows which will get there first.

A few of the things we learnt about the Norwegians are as follows:

The engines of the *Fram* occupy only half the size of our wardroom, the petrol tanks have not needed replenishment since they left Norway, and their propeller can be lifted by three men. They kept fresh potatoes from Norway to the Barrier. (Some of them must surely be renegade Irishmen.) They have each a separate cabin 'tween-decks in the *Fram*, and are very comfortable. They are using for transporting their stores to the hut, eight teams of five dogs each, working every alternate day.

They intend to use for the Polar Journey teams of ten dogs, each team working one day out of two. Their dogs stop at a whistle, and if they make a break they can be stopped by overturning the sledge, empty or full as the case may be. They are nine in the shore party and ten in the ship. Their ship is going back to Buenos Ayres with Nilsen in charge and during the winter is to encircle the world, sounding all the way.

They are not starting on the dash South this year and do not yet know whether they will lay depots this year. They have 116 dogs and ten of these are bitches, so that they can rear pups, and have done so very successfully on the way out. The *Fram* acts like a cork in the sea; she rolls tremendously but does not ship water, and during the voyage they have had the dogs running loose about the decks. There is a lot more miscellaneous information, but I may remember it more coherently a little later when the main impressions of the rencontre are a little more faint.[3]

It will be seen that Priestley missed three points. First, he was left with a conventional but very erroneous impression of Amundsen as a blunt Norwegian sailor, not in the least an intellectual. Second, he thought Amundsen had camped on the ice and not on terra firma. Third, he thought Amundsen was going to the Pole by the old route over the Beardmore. The truth was that Amundsen was an explorer of the markedly intellectual type, rather Jewish than Scandinavian,

3. Priestley's diary.

THE WORST JOURNEY IN THE WORLD

who had proved his sagacity by discovering solid footing for the winter by pure judgement. For the moment, let it be confessed, we all underrated Amundsen, and could not shake off the feeling that he had stolen a march on us.

Back to McMurdo Sound, and the news left at Hut Point. Then the two ponies which had been allotted to Campbell were swum ashore at Cape Evans, since he thought that now they would be of more use to Scott than to himself. Subsequent events proved the extreme usefulness of this unselfish act. The *Terra Nova* would steam north and try and land Campbell's party on the extreme northern shores of Queen Victoria Land. At the same time there was so little coal left that it might be necessary to go straight back to New Zealand. Campbell regretted not being able to see Scott, supposing that the altered circumstances caused Scott to wish to rearrange his parties, and also because Amundsen had asked Campbell to land his party at the Bay of Whales, giving him the area to the east to explore, and Campbell did not wish to accept before getting Scott's permission.

As we know now coal ran so short that it came to an alternative of dumping Campbell, his men and gear hastily on the beach at Cape Adare, or taking them back to New Zealand. As one member of the crew said: 'Exploring is all very well in its way, but it is a thing which can be very easily overdone.' The ship was as ready to get rid of them as they were to get rid of the ship. They were landed, working to their waists in the surf, and the ship got safely back to New Zealand.

Scott decided that the period of waiting until the pony party arrived from One Ton should be employed in sledging stores out to Corner Camp. But the dog-teams were done, 'the dogs are thin as rakes; they are ravenous and very tired. I feel this should not be, and that it is evident that they are underfed. The ration must be increased next year and we must have properly-thought-out diet. The biscuit alone is not good enough.'[4] In addition, several dogs were feeling the

4. *Scott's Last Expedition*, vol. i, p. 185.

effects of injuries due to the crevasse incident. There remained the men and the one pony which had survived out of the three sent back from Bluff Depot, namely Jimmy Pigg.

The party started on Friday, 24 February, marching by day. It consisted of Scott, Crean and myself with one sledge and tent, Lieutenant Evans, Atkinson and Forde with a second sledge and tent, and Keohane leading James Pigg. On the second night out we saw the pony party pass us in the distance on their way to Safety Camp.[5] At Corner Camp Scott decided to leave Lieutenant Evans's party to come in with the pony more slowly, and himself to push on with Crean and myself at top speed for Safety Camp. We made a forced march well into the night, doing twenty-six miles for the day, and camped some ten miles from Safety Camp, where the pony party must by this time have arrived.

The events which followed were disastrous, and the steps which led to a catastrophe which entailed the loss of much of our best transport, and only by a miracle did not lead to the loss of several lives, were complicated. At this moment, the night of 26 February, there were three parties on the Barrier. Behind Scott was Lieutenant Evans's party and the pony, James Pigg. Scott himself was camped within easy marching distance of Safety Camp with Crean and myself. At Safety Camp were the two dog-teams with Wilson and Meares, while the pony party from One Ton Depot had just arrived with five ponies which were for the most part thin, hungry and worn. Between Safety Camp and Hut Point lay the frozen sea, which might or might not break up this year, but we knew from our observations a few days before that the ice was in a shaky condition. At that time the ice sheet extended some seven miles to the north of Hut Point. The season was fast closing in: temperatures of fifty or sixty degrees of frost had been common for the last fortnight, and this was bad for the ponies. We had been unfortunate in having several severe blizzards, and it was already clear that it was these autumn blizzards more than cold temperatures

5. see p. 125.

and soft surfaces which the ponies could not endure. Scott was most anxious to get the animals into such shelter as we could make for them at Hut Point.

The next morning, 27 February, we woke to a regular cold autumn blizzard – very thick, wind force 9 and temperature about minus twenty. This was disheartening, and indeed with our six worn ponies still on the Barrier the outlook for them was discouraging. The blizzard came to an end the next morning. Scott must take up the first part of that day's story:

> Packed up at 6 a.m. and marched into Safety Camp. Found every one very cold and depressed. Wilson and Meares had had continuous bad weather since we left, Bowers and Oates since their arrival. The blizzard had raged for two days. The animals looked in a sorry condition, but all were alive. The wind blew keen and cold from the east. There could be no advantage in waiting here, and soon all arrangements were made for a general shift to Hut Point. Packing took a long time. The snowfall had been prodigious, and parts of the sledges were 3 or 4 feet under drift. About 4 o'clock the two dog-teams got safely away. Then the pony party prepared to go. As the cloths were stripped from the ponies the ravages of the blizzard became evident. The animals, without exception, were terribly emaciated, and Weary Willie was in a pitiable condition.
>
> The plan was for the ponies to follow the dog tracks, our small party to start last and get in front of the ponies on the sea-ice. I was very anxious about the sea-ice passage owing to the spread of the water holes.[6]

The two dog-teams left with Meares and Wilson some time before the ponies, and for the moment they go out of this story.

Bowers's pony, Uncle Bill, was ready first, and he started with him. We got three more ponies harnessed, Punch, Nobby and Guts, and tried to harness Weary Willie, but

6. *Scott's Last Expedition*. vol. 1, pp. 190–91.

when we attempted to lead him forward he immediately fell down.

Scott rapidly reorganized. He sent Crean and me forward with the three better ponies to join Bowers, now waiting a mile ahead. Oates and Gran he kept with himself, to try and help the sick pony. His diary tells how 'we made desperate efforts to save the poor creature, got him once more on his legs, gave him a hot oat mash. Then, after a wait of an hour, Oates led him off, and we packed the sledge and followed on ski; 500 yards from the camp the poor creature fell again and I felt it was the last effort. We camped, built a snow wall round him, and did all we possibly could to get him on his feet. Every effort was fruitless, though the poor thing made pitiful struggles. Towards midnight we propped him up as comfortably as we could and went to bed.

> Wednesday, 1 March. a.m. Our pony died in the night. It is hard to have got him back so far only for this. It is clear that these blizzards are terrible for the poor animals. Their coats are not good, but even with the best of coats it is certain they would lose condition badly if caught in one, and we cannot afford to lose condition at the beginning of a journey. It makes a late start necessary for next year.
>
> Well, we have done our best and bought our experience at a heavy cost. Now every effort must be bent on saving the remaining animals.[7]

A letter of Bowers's home, which certainly does not overstate the adventures of himself and the two men sent forward to join him, is probably the best description of the incidents which followed. It will be remembered that Crean and I with three ponies were sent from Safety Camp to join him: he was already leading one pony. Night was beginning to fall, and the light was bad, but from the edge of the Barrier the two dog-teams could still be seen as black dots in the distance towards Cape Armitage.

7. ibid., pp. 191–2.

On the night of 28 February I led off with my pony and was surprised at the delay in the others leaving – knowing nothing of Weary's collapse. Over the edge of the Barrier I went, and at the bottom of the snow incline awaited the others. To my surprise Cherry and Crean appeared with Punch, Nobby and Guts in a string, and then I heard the reason for Oates and Scott not having come on. My orders were to push on to Hut Point over the sea-ice without delay, and to follow the dogs; previously I had been told to camp on the sea-ice in case of the beasts being unable to go on. We had four pretty heavy sledges, as we were taking six weeks' man food and oil to the hut, as well as a lot of gear from the depot, and pony food, etc. Unfortunately the dogs misunderstood their orders and, instead of piloting us, dashed off on their own. We saw them like specks in the distance in the direction of the old seal crack. Having crossed this they wheeled to the right in the direction of Cape Armitage and disappeared into a black indefinite mist, which seemed to pervade everything in that direction. We heard afterwards that in a mile or two they came to some alarming signs and, turning, made for the Gap where they got up on to the land about midnight.

I plugged on in their tracks, till we came to the seal crack which was an old pressure-ridge running many miles S.W. from Pram Point. We considered the ice behind this crack – over which we had just come – fast ice; it was older ice than that beyond, as it had undoubtedly frozen over first. Having crossed the crack we streaked on for Cape Armitage. The animals were going badly, owing to the effects of the blizzard, and frequent stoppages were necessary. On coming to some shaky ice we headed farther west as there were always some bad places off the cape, and I thought it better to make a good circuit. Crean, who had been over the ice recently, told me it was all right farther round. However, about a mile farther on I began to have misgivings; the cracks became too frequent to be pleasant, and although the ice was frozen from five to ten feet thick, one does not like to see water squelching between them, as we did later. It spells motion, and motion on sea-ice means breakage. I shoved on in the hope of getting on better ice round the cape, but at last came a moving crack, and that decided me to turn back. We could see nothing owing to the black mist, everything looked solid as ever, but I knew enough to mistrust moving ice, however solid it seemed. It was a beastly march back: dark, gloomy and depressing. The beasts got more and more down in their spirits and stopped so frequently that I thought we would never reach the seal crack. I said to Cherry, however, that I would take no risks, and camp well over the other side on the old sound ice if we could get there. This we managed to do eventually. Here there was soft snow, whereas on the sea side of the crack it was hard: that is the reason we lost the dogs' tracks at once on crossing. Even over this crack I thought it best to march as far in as possible. We got well into the bay, as far as our exhausted ponies would drag, before I camped and threw up the walls, fed the beasts, and retired to feed ourselves. We had only the primus with the missing cap and it took over 1½ hours to heat up the water; however, we had a cup of pemmican. It was very dark, and I mistook a small bag of curry powder for the cocoa bag, and made cocoa with that, mixed with sugar; Crean drank his right down before discovering anything was wrong. It was 2 p.m. before we were ready to turn in. I went out and saw everything quiet: the mist still hung to the west, but you could see a good mile and all was still. The sky was very dark over the Strait though, the unmistakable sign of open water. I turned in. Two and a half hours later I awoke, hearing a noise. Both my companions were snoring, I thought it was that and was on the point of turning in again having seen that it was only 4.30, when I heard the noise again. I thought – 'my pony is at the oats!' and went out.

I cannot describe either the scene or my feelings. I must leave those to your imagination. We were in the middle of a floating pack of broken-up ice. The tops of the hills were visible, but all below was thin mist and as far as the eye could see there was nothing solid; it was all broken up, and heaving up and down with the swell. Long black tongues of water were everywhere. The floe on which we were had split right under our picketing line, and cut poor Guts's wall in half. Guts himself had gone, and a dark streak of water alone showed the place where the ice had opened under him. The two sledges securing the other end of the line were on the next floe and had been pulled right to the edge. Our camp was on a floe not more than 30 yards across. I shouted to Cherry and Crean, and rushed out in my socks to save the two sledges; the two floes were touching farther on and I dragged them to this place and got them on to our floe. At that moment our own floe split in two, but we were all together on one piece. I then got my finnesko on, remarking that we had been in a few tight places, but this was about the limit. I have been told since that I was quixotic not to leave everything and make for safety. You will understand, however, that I never for one moment considered the abandonment of anything.

We packed up camp and harnessed up our ponies in remarkably quick time. When ready to move I had to decide which way to go. Obviously towards Cape Armitage was impossible, and to the eastward also, as the wind was from that direction, and we were already floating west towards the open sound. Our only hope lay to the south, and thither I went. We found the ponies would jump the intervals well. At least Punch would and the other two would follow him. My idea was never to separate, but to get everything on to one floe at a time, and then wait till it touched or nearly touched another in the right direction, and then jump the ponies over and drag the four sledges across ourselves. In this way we made slow, but sure progress. While one was acting all was well, the waiting for a lead to close was the worst trial. Sometimes it would take 10 minutes or more, but there was so much motion in the ice that sooner or later bump you would go against another piece, and then it was up and over. Sometimes they split, sometimes they bounced back so quickly that only one horse could get over, and then we had to wait again. We had to make frequent detours and we were moving west all the time with the pack, still we were getting south, too.

Very little was said. Crean like most bluejackets behaved as if he had done this sort of thing often before. Cherry, the practical, after an hour or two dug out some chocolate and biscuit, during one of our enforced waits, and distributed it. I felt at that time that food was the last thing on earth I wanted, and put it in my pocket: in less than half an hour, though, I had eaten the lot. The ponies behaved as well as my companions, and jumped the floes in great style. After getting them on a new floe we simply left them, and there they stood chewing at each others' head ropes or harness till we were over with the sledges and ready to take them on again. Their implicit trust in us was touching to behold. A 12-feet sledge makes an excellent bridge if an opening is too wide to jump. After some hours we saw fast ice ahead, and thanked God for it. Meanwhile a further unpleasantness occurred in the arrival of a host of the terrible 'killer' whales. These were reaping a harvest of seal in the broken-up ice, and cruised among the floes with their immense black fins sticking up, and blowing with a terrific roar. The Killer is scientifically known as the Orca, and, though far smaller than the sperm and other large whales, is a much more dangerous animal. He is armed with a huge iron jaw and great blunt socket teeth. Killers act in concert, too, and, as you may remember, nearly got Ponting when we were unloading the ship, by pressing up the thin ice from beneath and splitting it in all directions.

It took us over six hours to get close to the fast ice, which proved to be the Barrier, some immense chunks of which we actually saw break off and join the pack. Close in, the motion was less owing to the jambling up of the ice somewhat farther west. We had only just cleared the Strait in time though, as all the ice in the centre, released beyond Cape Armitage, headed off into the middle of the Strait, and thence to the Ross Sea. Our spirits rose as we neared the Barrier edge, and I made for a big sloping floe which I expected would be touching; at any rate I anticipated no difficulty. We rushed up the slope towards safety, and were little prepared for the scene that met our eyes at the top. All along the Barrier face a broad lane of water from thirty to forty feet wide extended. This

was filled with smashed-up brash ice, which was heaving up
and down to the swell like the contents of a cauldron. Killers
were cruising there with fiendish activity, and the Barrier
edge was a sheer cliff of ice on the other side fifteen to twenty
feet high. It was a case of so near and yet so far. Suddenly our
great sloping floe calved in two, so we beat a hasty retreat. I
selected a sound-looking floe just clear of this turmoil, that
was at least ten feet thick, and fairly rounded, with a flat
surface. Here we collected everything and having done all that
man could do, we fed the beasts and took counsel.

Cherry and Crean both volunteered to do anything, in the
spirit they had shown right through. It appeared of first
necessity to communicate with Captain Scott. I guessed his
anxiety on our behalf, and, as we could do nothing more, we
wanted help of some sort. It occurred to me that a man
working up to windward along the Barrier face might happen
upon a floe touching [the Barrier]. It was obviously impossible
to take ponies up there anywhere, but an active man might
wait his opportunity. Going to windward, too, he could
always retreat on to our floe, as the ice was being pushed
together in our direction. The next consideration was, whom
to send. To go myself was out of the question. The problem
was whether to send one, or both, my companions. As my
object was to save the animals and gear, it appeared to me
that one man remaining would be helpless in the event of a
floe splitting up, as he would be busy saving himself. I
therefore decided to send one only. This would have to be
Crean, as Cherry, who wears glasses, could not see so well.
Both volunteered, but as I say, I thought out all the pros and
cons and sent Crean, knowing that, at the worst, he could get
back to us at any time. I sent a note to Captain Scott, and,
stuffing Crean's pockets with food, we saw him depart.

Practical Cherry suggested pitching the tent as a mark of
our whereabouts, and having done this I mounted the theodolite to watch Crean through the telescope. The rise and fall of
the floe made this difficult, especially as a number of Emperor
penguins came up and looked just like men in the distance.
Fortunately the sunlight cleared the frost smoke, and as it fell

calm our westerly motion began to decrease. The swell started
to go down. Outside us in the centre of the Strait all the ice
had gone out, and open water remained. We were one of a
line of loose floes floating near the Barrier edge. Crean was
hours moving to and fro before I had the satisfaction of seeing
him up on the Barrier. I said: 'Thank God one of us is out of
the wood, anyhow.'

It was not a pleasant day that Cherry and I spent all alone
there, knowing as we did that it only wanted a zephyr from
the south to send us irretrievably out to sea; still there is
satisfaction in knowing that one has done one's utmost, and I
felt that having been delivered so wonderfully so far, the same
Hand would not forsake us at the last.

We gave the ponies all they could eat that day. The Killers
were too interested in us to be pleasant. They had a habit of
bobbing up and down perpendicularly, so as to see over the
edge of a floe, in looking for seals. The huge black and yellow
heads with sickening pig eyes only a few yards from us at
times, and always around us, are among the most disconcerting recollections I have of that day. The immense fins were
bad enough, but when they started a perpendicular dodge
they were positively beastly. As the day wore on skua gulls,
looking upon us as certain carrion, settled down comfortably
near us to await developments. The swell, however, was
getting less and less as it resolved itself into a question of
speed, as to whether the wind or Captain Scott would reach
us first.

Crean had got up into the Barrier at great risks to himself
as I gathered afterwards from his very modest account. He
had reached Captain Scott some time after his [Scott's]
meeting with Wilson.[8] I heard that at the time Captain Scott
was very angry with me for not abandoning everything and
getting away safely myself. For my own part I must say that
the abandoning of the ponies was the one thing that had never

8. Wilson camped with the two dog-teams on the land, and in the morning
saw us floating on the ice-floes through his field-glasses. He made his way
along the peninsula until he could descend on to the Barrier, where he
joined Scott.

entered my head. It was a long way round, but at 7 p.m. he arrived at the edge of the Barrier opposite us with Oates and Crean. Everything was still, and Cherry and I could have got on safe ice at any time during the last half hour by using the sledge as a ladder. A big overturned fragment had jambed in the lane, between a high floe and the Barrier edge, and, there being no wind, it remained there. However, there was the consideration of the ponies, so we waited.

Scott, instead of blowing me up, was too relieved at our safety to be anything but pleased. I said: 'What about the ponies and the sledges?' He said: 'I don't care a damn about the ponies and sledges. It's you I want, and I am going to see you safe here up on the Barrier before I do anything else.' Cherry and I had got everything ready, so, dragging up two sledges, we dumped the gear off them, and using them as ladders, one down from the berg on to the buffer piece of ice, and the other up to the top of the Barrier, we got up without difficulty. Captain Scott was so pleased, that I realized the feeling he must have had all day. He had been blaming himself for our deaths, and here we were very much alive. He said: 'My dear chaps, you can't think how glad I am to see you safe – Cherry likewise.'

I was all for saving the beasts and sledges, however, so he let us go back and haul the sledges on to the nearest floe. We did this one by one and brought the ponies along, while Titus dug down a slope from the Barrier edge in the hope of getting the ponies up it. Scott knew more about ice than any of us, and realizing the danger we didn't, still wanted to abandon things. I fought for my point tooth and nail, and got him to concede one article and then another, and still the ice did not move till we had thrown and hauled up every article on to the Barrier except the two ladders and the ponies.

To my intense disappointment at this juncture the ice started to move again. Titus had been digging down a road in the Barrier edge, and I hoped to dig down a similar slope from the floe, the snow thus shovelled down would go over the blue ice chunk, cover up the slippery ice and level it up. It would have taken hours, but was the only chance of getting the animals up. We dug like fury until Captain Scott peremptorily ordered us up. I ran up on the floe and took the nosebags off the ponies before we got on to the Barrier, and hauled the sledges up. It was only just in time. There was the faintest south-easterly air, but, like a black snake, the lane of water stretched between the ponies and ourselves. It widened almost imperceptibly, 2 feet, 6 feet, 10 feet, 20 feet, and, sick as we were about the ponies, we were glad to be on the safe side of that.

We dragged the sledges in a little way, and, leaving them, pitched the two tents half a mile further in, for bits of the Barrier were continually calving. While supper (it was about 3 a.m.) was being cooked, Scott and I walked down again. The wind had gone to the east, and all the ice was under weigh. A lane 70 feet wide extended along the Barrier edge, and Killers were chasing up and down it like racehorses. Our three unfortunate beasts were some way out, sailing parallel to the Barrier. We returned, and if ever one could feel miserable I did then. My feelings were nothing to what poor Captain Scott had had to endure that day. I at once broached the hopeful side of the subject, remarking that, with the two Campbell had left, we had ten ponies at Winter quarters. He said however, that he had no confidence whatever in the motors after the way their rollers had become messed up unloading the ship. He had had his confidence in the dogs much shaken on the return journey, and now he had lost the most solid asset – the best of his pony transport. He said: 'Of course we shall have a run for our money next season, but as far as the Pole is concerned I have but very little hope.' We had a mournful meal, but after the others turned in I went down again, and by striking across diagonally came abreast of the ponies' floe, over a mile away. They were moving west fast, but they saw me, and remained huddled together not the least disturbed, or doubting that we would bring them their breakfast nosebags as usual in the morning. Poor trustful creatures! If I could have done it then, I would gladly have killed them rather than picture them starving on that floe out on the Ross Sea, or eaten by the exultant Killers that cruised around.

After breakfast Captain Scott sent me to bring up the sledges. It was dead calm again. Hope always springs, so I took a pair of glasses and looked west from the Barrier edge. Nearly all the ice had gone, but a medley of floes had been hurled up against a long point of Barrier much farther west. To my delight I saw three green specks on one of these – the pony rugs – and all four of us legged it back to the tent to tell Captain Scott. We were soon all over the Barrier. It was a long way, but we had a tent and some food. Crean had a bad day of snow-blindness, and could see absolutely nothing. So, on arrival at the place, we pitched the tent and left him there. The ponies were in a much worse place than the day before, but the ice was still there, and some floes actually touched the Barrier.

After our recent experience Captain Scott would only let us go on condition that as soon as he gave the order we were to drop everything and run for the Barrier. I was in a feverish hurry, and with Titus and Cherry selected a possible route over about six floes, and some low brash ice. The hardest jump was the first one, but it was nothing to what they had done the day before, so we put Punch at it. Why he hung fire I cannot think,[9] but he did, at the very edge, and the next moment was in the water. I will draw a veil over our struggle to get the plucky little pony out. We could not manage it, and Titus had at last to put an end to his struggle with a pick.

There was now my pony and Nobby. We abandoned that route, while Captain Scott looked out another and longer one by going right out on the sea-floes. This we decided on, if we could get the animals off their present floe, which necessitated a good jump on any side. Captain Scott said he would have no repetition of Punch's misfortune if he could help it. He would rather kill them on the floe. Anyhow, we rushed old Nobby at the jump, but he refused. It seemed no good, but I rushed him at it again and again. Scott was for killing them

9. I think he was stiff after standing so many hours. – A. C.-G.

[it should be remembered that this ice, with the men on it, might drift away from the Barrier at any moment, and then there might be no further chance of saving the men] but I was not, and, pretending not to hear him, I rushed the old beast again. He cleared it beautifully, and Titus, seizing the opportunity, ran my pony at it with similar success. We then returned to the Barrier and worked along westward till a suitable place for getting up was found. There Scott and Cherry started digging a road, while Titus and I went out via the sea-ice to get the ponies. We had an empty sledge as a bridge or ladder, in case of emergency, and had to negotiate about forty floes to reach the animals. It was pretty easy going, though, and we brought them along with great success as far as the two nearest floes. At this place the ice was jambed.

Nobby cleared the last jump splendidly, when suddenly in the open water pond on one side a school of over a dozen of the terrible whales arose. This must have flurried my horse just as he was jumping, as instead of going straight he jumped [sideways] and just missed the floe with his hind legs. It was another horrible situation, but Scott rushed Nobby up on the Barrier, while Titus, Cherry and I struggled with poor old Uncle Bill. Why the whales did not come under the ice and attack him I cannot say – perhaps they were full of seal, perhaps they were so engaged in looking at us on the top of the floe that they forgot to look below; anyhow, we got him safely as far as [the bottom of the Barrier cliff], pulling him through the thin ice towards a low patch of brash.

Captain Scott was afraid of something happening to us with those devilish whales so close, and was for abandoning the horse right away. I had no eyes or ears for anything but the horse just then, and getting on to the thin brash ice got the Alpine rope fast to each of the pony's forefeet. Crean was too blind to do anything but hold the rescued horse on the Barrier, but the other four of us pulled might and main till we got the old horse out and lying on his side. The brash ice was so thin that, had a 'Killer' come up then he would have scattered it, and the lot of us into the water like chaff. I was sick with disappointment when I found that my horse could not rise. Titus said: 'He's done; we shall never get him up alive.' The cold water and shock on top of all his recent troubles had been too much for the undefeated old sportsman. In vain I tried to get him to his feet; three times he tried and then fell over backwards into the water again. At that moment a new danger arose. The whole piece of Barrier itself started to subside.

It had evidently been broken before, and the tide was doing the rest. We were ordered up and it certainly was all too necessary; still Titus and I hung over the old Uncle Bill's head. I said: 'I can't leave him to be eaten alive by those whales.' There was a pick lying up on the floe. Titus said: 'I shall be sick if I have to kill another horse like I did the last.' I had no intention that anybody should kill my own horse but myself, and getting the pick I struck where Titus told me. I made sure of my job before we ran up and jumped the opening in the Barrier, carrying a blood-stained pick-axe instead of leading the pony I had almost considered safe.

We returned to our old camp that night (2 March) with Nobby, the only one saved of the five that left One Ton Depot. I was fearfully cut up about my pony and Punch, but it was better than last night; we knew they would not have to starve and that all their troubles were now at an end. Before supper I went for a walk along the Barrier with Scott, and the next day we started back. We left one tent, two sledges and a lot of gear as Nobby could only pull two light sledges, and we could not pull an excessive weight on that bad surface. As it was we had over 800 lbs on the sledge when we left. It was a glaring day with the surface soft and sandy, a combination of unpleasant circumstances. It took five hours to drag as far as the place we had originally gone down on to the sea-ice from the Barrier.

Evans and his party should now have arrived from Corner Camp, and as Captain Scott wanted to see if they had left a note at Safety Camp, I walked up there while the tea was being brewed. It was about $1\frac{1}{4}$ miles away, and I found traces of the party in the snow, but no note. It fed me up to see the walls so recently occupied by our ponies, and I was glad to leave. The afternoon march was interminable; it seemed as if we would never reach the coast. At last we came to the Pram Point Pressure Ridges where the Barrier joins the peninsula to eastward of Cape Armitage. They are waves of ice up to 20 feet in height running along parallel to each other with a valley in between each, and are only crevassed badly at the outer end as far as we have seen, though there are smaller crevasses right along. We camped in one of these valleys about 9.30 p.m.; I was thoroughly tired, so I think was everybody else. We were about a mile from the ice edge; and the problem was where to get Nobby up the precipitous slopes. This was solved by the arrival of Evans, Atkinson, Forde and Keohane about midnight. They had seen us coming in from the heights, and had come down for news. Teddy Evans had arrived the day before, and, being warned off the Barrier edge by a note left by Captain Scott, had made for the land with his party, and one horse Jimmy Pigg. He had found a good way up a mile or so farther east, almost under Castle Rock. He had walked to Hut Point with Atkinson the next day and heard of the loss of Cherry, myself and the animals from Bill Wilson and Meares who had been left there to look after their teams. I hadn't seen Atkinson for quite a while when we met this time.

The next day we relayed the sledges up the slope which was about 700 feet high rising from a small bay. It was so steep that the pony could only be led up and we had to put on crampons to grip the ice. These are merely a sole of leather with light metal plates for foot and heel containing spikes. [These were altered afterwards.] They have leather beckets and a lanyard rove off for making them fast over the finnesko. It took us all the morning to get everything up to the top and then it started to blow. The camp was wonderfully sheltered. Jimmy Pigg and Nobby were reunited after many weeks, and to show their friendliness the former bit the latter in the back of the neck as a first introduction. Atkinson had gone to Hut Point to reassure Uncle Bill as to our safety and arrived again with Gran just as we got the last load up. There was no sugar at the hut except what the dogs had brought in, so Gran, who was quite fresh, volunteered to get a couple of bags from the depot at Safety Camp, which could plainly be seen out on the Barrier. We all went to the edge of the slope to see him go down it on ski. He did it splendidly and must have been going with the speed of an express train down the incline, as he was on the Barrier in an incredibly short time compared to the hours we had dragged up the same slope with the loads. Teddy, Titus and Keohane were left at the camp to be joined by Gran later. Scott started off for Hut Point with Crean and Cherry on his sledge, while I followed with Forde and Atkinson. The others helped us up several hundred feet of slope and left us under Castle Rock.

It was here that they mistook their way in the blizzard and lost a man from the *Discovery*. Though it was fine below it was blowing like anything on the heights. I was too busily occupied to see much of the hills and snow-slopes which I got to know so well later. It was about three miles direct to the hut, but very up and down hill. At the last, however, you see the Bay in panorama with Cape Armitage on one side, and Hut Point on the other, where the *Discovery* lay two whole years. It is a magnificent view from the heights and for wild desolate grandeur would take some beating; the Western Mountains and the great dome of Mount Discovery across the black strait of water, covered with dark frost smoke, and here and there an ice-berg driving fast towards the sea. About half a mile below us was the little hut and, on the left, the 800-feet pyramid of Observation Hill. It is a perfect chaos of hills and extinct craters just here.

It was blowing like fun. We left one sledge on the top of Ski Slope and just took what was necessary on the other, such as our bags, etc. It was my first experience of steep downhill sledging. Instead of anybody pulling forward we all had to hang back and guide the sledge down the slippery incline without letting it take charge or getting upset. It is great fun. On reaching the head of the Bay, however, we had quite a dangerous little bit to cross. Here it was swept of snow and there was nothing but glassy ice and the incline ended in a low ice-cliff with the water below it. Attached as we were to the sledge we should have been at a disadvantage had it come to swimming, which a slip might easily have brought about. We scratched carefully across this and then headed down on the snow, arriving at the hut all well. The old hut had changed tremendously since I last saw it, having been dug out and cleared of snow and ice. Two unrecognizable sweeps greeted us heartily, they were Bill and Meares; the dogs howled a chorus for our benefit; it was quite like coming home. Inside the hut, the cause of the blackness was apparent, they had a blubber fire going, an open one, with no chimney or uptake for the smoke. After such a long open-air life it fairly choked me, and for once I could not eat a square meal. We all slept in a row against the west wall of the hut with our feet inboard.

The next morning Captain Scott, Bill, Cherry and I set out to walk to Castle Rock and meet the other party. It was fairly fizzing from the sea, but clear. Once up on the Heights, however, we seemed to get less wind. A couple of hours later we were at the great rock, Castle Rock, which is one of the best landmarks around here. The party in the Saddle Camp had relayed two of the sledges up the slope; these we hauled on to the top while the two ponies were harnessed and brought up. There were three sledges left to take on altogether, so the ponies took one each and we the other. Meanwhile Captain Scott walked over the shoulder under Castle Rock to see down the Strait and came back with the intelligence that he could hardly believe his eyes, but half the Glacier Tongue had broken off and disappeared. This great Tongue of ice had stood there on arrival of the *Discovery*, ten years before, and had remained ever since; it had a depot of Shackleton's on it, and Campbell had depoted his fodder on it for us. On the eventful night of the break-up of the ice at least three miles of the Tongue which had been considered practi-cally terra firma had gone, after having been there probably for centuries. We headed for the hut: Bill had looked out a route for the ponies, to avoid slippery places. It started to bliz, but was not too thick for us to see our bearings. At the top of Ski Slope the ponies were taken out of the sledges and led down a circuitous route over the rocks. The rest of us put everything we wanted on one sledge and leaving the others up there went down the slope as before. The two ponies arrived before us and were stabled in the verandah.

That night for the first time since the establishment of Safety Camp the depot party were all together again, minus six ponies. In concluding my report to Captain Scott on the 'floe' incident, which he asked me to set down long afterwards, I said, 'In reconsidering the foregoing I have come to the conclusion that I underestimated the danger signs on the sea-ice on 28 February, and on the following day might have attached more importance to the safety of my companions. As it was, however, all circumstances seemed to conspire together to make the situation unavoidable.' I did not forget to mention the splendid behaviour of Cherry and Crean, and, for my own part, I have no regrets. I took the blame for my lack of experience, but knew that having done everything I could do, it did not concern me if anybody liked to criticize my action. My own opinion is that it just had to be, the circumstances leading to it were too devious for mere coincidence. Six hours earlier we could have walked to the hut on sound sea-ice. A few hours later we should have seen open water on arrival at the Barrier edge. The blizzard that knocked out our beasts, the death of Weary, the misunderstanding of the dogs, everything, fitted in to place us on the sea-ice during the only two hours of the whole year that we could possibly have been in such a position. Let those who believe in coincidence carry on believing. Nobody will ever convince me that there was not something more. Perhaps in the light of next year we shall see what was meant by such an apparent blow to our hopes. Certainly we shall start for the Pole with less of that foolish spirit of blatant boast and ridiculous blind self-assurance, that characterized some of us on leaving Cardiff.

Poor Captain Scott had now a new anxiety thrust upon him. The Winter Station with ponies, stores and motors was all situated on a low beach not twenty yards from the water's edge, and now that the ice had gone out (and the hut was not six feet above sea-level at the floor) how had they fared in the storm? This was a problem we could not solve without going to see. Cape Evans, though dimly in sight, was as far off as New Zealand till the sea froze over. The idea of attempting the shoulder of Erebus did occur to Captain Scott, but it was so heavily crevassed as to make a journey from our side almost impossible. On the other side Professor David's party got up to the Summit without finding a crevasse. Captain Scott took his reverses like a brick. I often went out for a walk with him and sometimes he discussed his plans for next season. He took his losses very philosophically and never blamed any of us.

This is the end of that part of Bowers's letter which deals with the incident. Crean told me afterwards how he got on to the Barrier. He first made for the Gap, following the best path of the ice, but then had to retrace his steps and make for White Island jumping from floe to floe. But then 'I was pretty lively,' said he: and 'there were lots of penguins and seals and killers knocking round that day.'

Crean had one of the ski sticks and that

was a great help to me for getting over the floes. It was a sloping piece like what you were on and it was very near touching the Barrier, in one corner of it only. Well, I dug a hole with the ski stick in the side of the Barrier for a step for one foot, and when I finished the hole I straddled my legs and got one on the floe and one in the side of the Barrier. Then I got the stick and dug it in on top and I gave myself a bit of a spring and got my outside leg up top. It was a terrible place but I thought it was the only chance.

I made straight for Safety Camp and they must have spotted me: for I think it was Gran that met me on skis. Then Scott and Wilson and Oates met me a long way out: I explained how it happened. He was worried-looking a bit, but he never said anything out of the way. He told Oates to go inside and light the primus and give me a meal.

A more detailed account of the behaviour of the hundreds of whales which infested the lanes of open water between the broken floes and calved bergs is of interest. Most of them at any rate were Killer whales (*Orca gladiator*), and they were cruising about in great numbers, snorting and blowing, while occasionally they would in some extraordinary way raise themselves and look about over the ice, resting the fore part of their enormous yellow and black bodies on the edge of the floes. They were undisguisedly interested in us and the ponies, and we felt that if we once got into the water our ends would be swift and bloody.

But I have a very distinct recollection that the whales were not all Killers, and that some, at any rate, were Bottlenosed whales. This was impressed upon me by one of the most dramatic moments of that night and day.

We made our way very slowly, sometimes waiting twenty minutes for the floe on which we were to touch the next one in the direction we were trying to go, but before us in the distance was a region of sea-ice which appeared to slope gradually up on to the fast Barrier beyond. As we got nearer we saw a dark line appear at intervals between the two. This we considered was a crevasse at the edge of the Barrier which was opening and shutting with the very big swell which was running, and on which all the floes were bobbing up and down. We told one another that we could rush the ponies over this as it closed.

We approached the Barrier and began to rise up on the sloping floes which had edged the Barrier and so on to small bergs which had calved from the Barrier itself. Leaving Crean with the ponies, Bowers and I went forward to prospect, and rose on to a berg from which we hoped to reach the Barrier.

I can never forget the scene that met us. Between us and the Barrier was a lane of some fifty yards wide, a seething cauldron. Bergs were calving off as we watched: and capsizing: and hitting other bergs, splitting into two and falling apart. The Killers filled the whole place. Looking downwards into a hole between our berg and the next, a hole not bigger than a small room, we saw at least six whales. They were so crowded that they could only lie so as to get their snouts out of the water, and my memory is that their snouts were bottle-nosed. At this moment our berg split into two parts and we hastily retreated to the lower and safer floes.

Now in the *Zoological Report of the Discovery Expedition* Wilson states that the true identity of the Bottle-nosed whale (*Hyperodon rostrata*) in Antarctic Seas has not been conclusively established. But that inasmuch as it certainly frequents seas so far as 48° S. latitude it is probable that certain whales which he and other members of that expedition saw frequenting the edge of the ice were, as they appeared to be, Bottle-nosed whales. For my part, without great knowledge of whales, I am convinced that these whales which lay but twenty feet below us were whales of this species.

After our rescue by Scott we pitched our tents, as has been described, at least half a mile from the fast edge of the Barrier. All night long, or as it really was, early morning, the Killers were snorting and blowing under the Barrier, and sometimes, it seemed, under our tents. Time and again some member of the party went out of the tent to see if the Barrier had not broken farther back, but there was no visible change, and it must have been that the apparently solid ice on which we were, was split up by crevasses by the big swell which had been running, and that round us, hidden by snow bridges, were leads of water in which whales were cruising in search of seal.

The next day most of the ice had gone out to sea, and I do not think the whales were so numerous. The most noticeable thing about them that day was the organization shown by the band of whales which appeared after Bowers's pony, Uncle Bill, had fallen between two floes, and we were trying to get him towards the Barrier. 'Good God, look at the whales,' said someone, and there, in a pool of water behind the floe on which we were working, lay twelve great whales in perfect line, facing the floe. And out in front of them, like the captain of a company of soldiers, was another. As we turned they dived as one whale, led by the big fellow in front, and we certainly expected that they would attack the floe on which we stood. Whether they never did so, or whether they tried and failed, for the floes here were fifteen or sixteen feet thick, I do not know; we never saw them again.

One other incident of those days is worth recalling. 'Cherry, Crean, we're floating out to sea,' was the startling awakening from Bowers, standing in his socks outside the tent at 4.30 a.m. that Wednesday morning. And indeed at first sight on getting outside the tent it looked a quite hopeless situation. I thought it was madness to try and save the ponies and gear when, it seemed, the only chance at all of saving the men was an immediate rush for the Barrier, and I said so. 'Well, I'm going to try,' was Bowers's answer, and, quixotic or no, he largely succeeded. I never knew a man who treated difficulties with such scorn.

There must be some of my companions who look back upon Hut Point with a peculiar fondness, such as men get for places where they have experienced great joys and great trials. And Hut Point has an atmosphere of its own. I do not know what it is. Partly aesthetic, for the sea and great mountains, and the glorious colour effects which prevail in spring and autumn, would fascinate the least imaginative; partly mysterious, with the Great Barrier knocking at your door, and the smoke of Erebus by day and the curtain of Aurora by night; partly the associations of the place – the old hut, the old landmarks, so familiar to those who know the history of the *Discovery* Expedition, the stakes in the snow, the holes for which ice was dug to water the ship, Vince's Cross on the Point. Now there is another Cross, on Observation Hill.

And yet when we first arrived the hut was comfortless enough. Wilson and Meares and Gran had been there some days; they had found some old bricks and a grid, and there was an open blubber fire in the middle of the floor. There was no outlet for the smoke and smuts and it was impossible to see your neighbour, to speak without coughing, or to open your eyes long before they began to smart. Atkinson and Crean had cleared the floor of ice in our absence, but the space between the lower and upper roofs was solid with blue ice, and the lower roof sagged down in places in a dangerous way. The wind howled continuously and to say that the hut was cold is a very mild expression of the reality.

This hut was built by the *Discovery* Expedition, who themselves lived in the ship which lay off the shore frozen into the sea-ice, as a workroom and as a refuge in case of shipwreck. It was useful to them in some ways, but was too large to heat with the amount of coal available, and was rather a white elephant. Scott wrote of it that

> on the whole our large hut has been and will be of use to us, but its uses are never likely to be of such importance as to render it indispensable, nor cause it to be said that circumstances have justified the outlay made on it, or the expenditure of space and trouble in bringing it to its final home. It is here now, however, and here it will stand for many a long year with such supplies as will afford the necessaries of life to any less fortunate party who may follow in our footsteps and be forced to search for food and shelter.[10]

Well! It was to be more useful to Scott in 1910 to 1913 than he imagined in 1902. We found the place with its verandah complete, the remains of the two magnetic huts and a rubbish heap. It was wonderful what that rubbish heap yielded up. Bricks to build a blubber stove, a sheet of iron to put over the top of it, a length of stove piping to form a chimney. Somehow somebody made cement, and built the bricks together, and one of the magnetic huts gave up its asbestos sheeting to insulate the chimney from the woodwork of the roofs. An old door made a cook's table, old cases turned upside down made seats. The provisions left by the *Discovery* were biscuits contained in some forty large packing cases. These we piled up across the middle of our house as a

10. Scott, *The Voyage of the Discovery*, vol. i, p. 350.

bulkhead and the old *Discovery* winter awning was dug out of the snow outside and fixed against the wall thus made to keep the warmth in. At night we cleared the floor space and spread our bags.

The two precious survivors of the eight ponies with which we started on our journey were housed in the verandah, which was made wind-proof and snow-proof. The more truculent dogs lay tethered outside, the more docile were allowed their freedom, but even so the dog fights were not infrequent. We had one poor little dog, Makaka by name. When unloading the ship this dog had been overrun by the sledge which he was helping to pull; he suffered again when the team of dogs fell down the crevasse, and was now partially paralysed. He was a wretched object, for the hair refused to grow on his hind quarters, but he was a real sportsman and had no idea of giving in. Meares and I went out one night when it was blowing hard, attracted by the cries of a dog. It was Makaka who had ventured to climb a steep slope and was now afraid to return. When the dogs finally returned to Cape Evans, Makaka was allowed to run by the side of the team; but when Cape Evans was reached he was gone. Search failed to find him and, after some weeks, hope of him was abandoned. But a month afterwards Gran and Debenham went over to Hut Point, and here at the entrance of the hut they found Makaka, pitifully weak but able to bark to them. He must have lived on seal, but how he did so in that condition is a mystery.

The reader may ask how it was that being so near our Winter Quarters at Cape Evans we were unable to reach them immediately. Cape Evans is fifteen miles across the sea from Hut Point, and though both huts are on the same island – Hut Point being at the end of a peninsula and Cape Evans on the remains of a flow of lava which juts out into the sea – the land which joins the two has never yet been crossed by a sledge party owing to the great ice falls which cover the slopes of Erebus. A glance at the map will show that although Hut Point is surrounded with sea, or sea-ice, on every side except that of Arrival Heights, the Barrier abuts upon the

Hut Point Peninsula to the south beyond Pram Point. Thus there is always communication with the Barrier by a devious route by which indeed we had just arrived, but farther progress north is cut off until the cold temperature of the autumn and winter causes the open sea to freeze. We arrived at Hut Point on 5 March and Scott expected to be able to cross on the newly-frozen ice by about 21 March. However, it was nearly a month after that when the first party could pass to Cape Evans, and then only the Bays were frozen and the Sound was still open water, owing to the winds which swept the ice out to sea almost as soon as it was formed.

On the top of all the anxieties which had oppressed him lately Scott had a great fear that a swell so phenomenal as to break up Glacier Tongue, a landmark which had probably been there for centuries, might have swept away our hut at Cape Evans. He was so alarmed about it that he told Wilson and myself to prepare to form a sledging party with him to penetrate the Erebus icefalls and reach Cape Evans.

> Went yesterday to Castle Rock with Wilson to see what chance there might be of getting to Cape Evans. The day was bright and it was quite warm walking in the sun. There is no doubt the route to Cape Evans lies over the worst corner of Erebus. From this distance (some 7 or 8 miles at least) the whole mountain side looks a mass of crevasses, but a route might be found at a level of 3000 or 4000 feet.[11]

After some days the project was abandoned as being hopeless.

On 8 March Bowers led a party to bring in the gear and provisions which had been left at Disaster Camp, the material, that is, which had been rescued from the sea-ice. They were away three days and found the pulling very hard.

> At the corner of the bay the Barrier was buckled into round ridges which took a couple of hours to cross. We marched for some time alongside an enormous crevasse,

11. *Scott's Last Expedition*, vol. i, p. 201.

which lay like a street near us. I examined it at one point which must have been 15 feet wide, and though it was impossible to see the bottom for snow cornices it was undoubtedly open as I could hear a seal blowing below.[12]

Bowers's letter describes them dragging their heavy load up the slope to Castle Rock:

It took us all the morning to reach Saddle Camp with the loads in two journeys. I found a steady plod up a steep hill without spells is better and less exhausting than a rush and a number of rests. This theory I put into practice with great success. I don't know whether everybody saw eye to eye with me over the idea of getting to the top without a spell. After the second sledge was up Atkinson said: 'I don't mind you as a rule, but there are times when I positively hate you.'

Defoe could have written another *Robinson Crusoe* with Hut Point instead of San Juan Fernandez. Our sledging supplies were mostly exhausted and we depended upon the seals we could kill for food, fuel and light. We were smutty as sweeps from the blubber we burned; and a more black-guard-looking crew would have been hard to find. We spent our fine days killing, cutting up and carrying in seal when we could find them, or climbing the various interesting hills and craters which abound here, and our evenings in long discussions which seldom settled anything. Some looked after dogs, and others after ponies; some made geological collections; others sketched the wonderful sunsets; but before and above all we ate and slept. We must have spent a good twelve hours asleep in our bags every day after our six weeks' sledging. And we rested. Perhaps this is not everybody's notion of a very good time, but it was good enough for us.

The Weddell seal which frequents the seas which fringe the Antarctic continent was a standby for most of our wants;

12. Bowers.

for he can at a pinch provide not only meat to eat, fuel for your fire and oil for your lamp, but also leather for your finnesko and an antidote to scurvy. As he lies out on the sea-ice, a great ungainly shape, nothing short of an actual prod will persuade him to take much notice of an Antarctic explorer. Even then he is as likely as not to yawn in your face and go to sleep again. His instincts are all to avoid the water when alarmed, for he knows his enemies the Killer whales live there: but if you drive him into the water he is transformed in the twinkling of an eye into a thing of beauty and grace, which can travel and turn with extreme celerity and which can successfully chase the fish on which he feeds.

We were lucky now in that a small bay of sea-ice, about an acre in extent, still remained within two miles of us at a corner where Barrier, sea, and land meet, called Pram Point by Scott in the *Discovery* days.

Now Pram Point during the summer months is one of the most populous seal nurseries in McMurdo Sound. In this neighbourhood the Barrier, moving slowly towards the Peninsula, buckles the sea-ice into pressure ridges. As the trough of each ridge is forced downwards, so in summer pools of sea water are formed in which the seal make their holes and among these ridges they lie and bask in the sun; the males fight their battles, the females bring forth their young: the children play and chase their tails just like kittens. Now that the sea-ice had broken up, many seals were to be found in this sheltered corner under the green and blue ice-cliffs of Crater Hill.

If you go seal killing you want a big stick, a bayonet, a flensing knife and a steel. Any big stick will do, so long as it will hit the seal a heavy blow on the nose: this stuns him and afterwards mercifully he feels no more. The bayonet knife (which should be fitted into a handle with a crosspiece to prevent the slipping of the hand down on to the blade) should be at least 14 inches long without the handle; this is used to reach the seal's heart. Our flensing knives were one foot long including the handle, the blades were seven inches long by

1¼ inches broad: some were pointed and others round and I do not know which was best. The handles should be of wood as being warmer, to hold.

Killing and cutting up seals is a gruesome but very necessary business, and the provision of suitable implements is humane as well as economic in time and labour. The skin is first cut off with the blubber attached: the meat is then cut from the skeleton, the entrails cleaned out, the liver carefully excised. The whole is then left to freeze in pieces on the snow, which are afterwards collected as rock-like lumps. The carcass can be cut up with an axe when needed and fed to the dogs. Nothing except entrails was wasted.

Lighting was literally a burning question. I do not know that any lamp was better than a tin matchbox fed with blubber, with strands of lamp wick sticking up in it, but all kinds of patterns big and small were made by proud inventors; they generally gave some light, though not a brilliant one. There were more ambitious attempts than blubber. The worst of these perhaps was produced by Oates. Somebody found some carbide and Oates immediately schemed to light the hut with acetylene. I think he was the only person who did not view the preparation with ill-concealed nervousness. However, Wilson took the situation into his tactful hands. For several days Oates and Wilson were deep in the acetylene plant scheme and then, apparently without reason, it was found that it could not be done. It was a successful piece of strategy which no woman could have bettered.

Bowers, Wilson, Atkinson and I were on Crater Hill one morning when we espied a sledge party approaching from the direction of Castle Rock. As we expected, this was the Geological party, consisting of Griffith Taylor, Wright, Debenham and Seaman Evans, home from the Western Mountains. They entirely failed to recognize in our black faces the men whom they had last seen from the ship at Glacier Tongue. I hope their story will be told by Debenham. For days their doings were the topic of conversation. Both numerically and intellectually they were an addition to our party, which now numbered sixteen. Taylor especially is

seldom at a loss for conversation and his remarks are generally original, if sometimes crude. Most of us were glad to
listen when the discussions in which he was a leading figure
raged round the blubber stove. Scott and Wilson were always
in the thick of it, and the others chimed in as their interest,
knowledge and experience led. Rash statements on questions
of fact were always dangerous, for our small community
contained so many specialists that errors were soon exposed.
At the same time there were few parts of the world that one
or other of us had not visited at least once. Later, when we
came to our own limited quarters, books of reference were
constantly in demand to settle disputes. Such books as the
Times Atlas, a good encyclopedia and even a Latin Dictionary
are invaluable to such expeditions for this purpose. To them
I would add *Who's Who*.

From odd corners we unearthed some *Contemporary
Reviews*, the *Girls' Own Paper* and the *Family Herald*, all of
ten years ago! We also found encased in ice an incomplete
copy of Stanley Weyman's *My Lady Rotha*; it was carefully
thawed out and read by everybody, and the excitement was
increased by the fact that the end of the book was missing.

'Who's going to cook?' was one of the last queries each
night, and two men would volunteer. It is not great fun
lighting an ordinary coal fire on a cold winter's morning, but
lighting the blubber fire at Hut Point when the metal frosted
your fingers and the frozen blubber had to be induced to drip
was a far more arduous task. The water was converted from
its icy state and, by that time, the stove was getting hot, in
inverse proportion to your temper. Seal liver fry and cocoa
with unlimited *Discovery* Cabin biscuits were the standard
dish for breakfast, and when it was ready a sustained cry of
'hoosh' brought the sleepers from their bags, wiping reindeer
hairs from their eyes. I think I was responsible for the greatest
breakfast failure when I fried some biscuits and sardines (we
only had one tin). Leaving the biscuits in the frying pan, the
lid of a cooker, after taking it from the fire, they went on
cooking and became as charcoal. This meal was known as
'the burnt-offering'. On 1 April Bowers prepared to make a

fool of two of us by putting chaff in our pannikins and covering the top only with seal meat. The plan turned back upon the maker, for he had not enough left to make up the deficiency, and, as I found out many weeks afterwards, surreptitiously gave up his own hoosh to the April fools and went without himself. Of such are the small incidents which afforded real amusement and even live in the memory as outstanding features of our existence.

Breakfast done, there was a general clean-up. One seized the apology for a broom which existed: day foot-gear, finnesko, hair socks, ordinary socks and puttees, took the place of fleecy sleeping-socks and fur-lined sleeping-boots: lunch cooks began to make their preparations: ice was fetched for water: a frozen chunk of red seal meat or liver was levered and chopped with an ice axe from the general store of seal meat: fids of sealskin, with the blubber attached, a good three inches of it perhaps, were brought in and placed by the stove, much as we bring in a scuttle of coal. Gradually the community scattered as duty or inclination led, leaving some members to dig away the snow-drifts which had accumulated round the door and windows during the night.

By lunch time every one had some new item of interest. Wright had found a new form of ice crystal: Scott had tested the ice off the Point and found it five inches thick: Wilson had found new seal holes off Cape Armitage, and we had hopes of finding our food and fuel nearer home: Atkinson had killed an Emperor penguin which weighed over ninety pounds, a record: and the assistant zoologist felt he would have to skin it, and did not want to do so: Meares had found an excellent place to roll stones down Arrival Heights into the sea: Debenham had a new theory to account for the Great Boulder, as a mammoth block different in structure from the surrounding geological features was called: Bowers had a scheme for returning from the Pole by the Plateau instead of the Barrier: Oates might be heard saying that he thought he could do with another chupattie. A favourite pastime was the making of knots. Could you make a clove hitch with one hand?

The afternoon was like the morning, save that the sun was now sinking behind the Western Mountains. These autumn effects were among the most beautiful sights of the world, and it was now that Wilson made the sketches for many of the water-colours which he afterwards painted at Winter Quarters. The majority were taken from the summit of Observation Hill, crouching under the lee of the rocks into which, nearly two years after, we built the Cross which now stands to commemorate his death and that of his companions. He sketched quickly with bare fingers and mittened hands, jotting down the outlines of hills and clouds, and pencilling in the colours by name. After a minute, more or less, the fingers become too cold for such work, and they must be put back into the wool and fur mitts until they are again warm enough to continue. Pencil and sketch book, a Windsor and Newton, were carried in a little blubber-stained wallet on his belt. Scott carried his sledge diaries in similar books in a similar wallet made of green Willesden canvas and fastened with a lanyard.

There was a good fug in the hut by dinner time: this was a mixed blessing. It was good for our gear: sleeping-bags, finnesko, mitts, socks were all hung up and dried, most necessary after sledging, and most important for the preservation of the skins; but it also started the most infernal drip-drip from the roof. I have spoken of the double roof of the old *Discovery* hut. This was still full of solid ice; indeed some time afterwards a large portion of it fell, but luckily the inhabitants were outside. The immediate problem was to prevent the leaks falling on ourselves, our food or our clothing and bags. And so every tin was brought into use and hung from leaky spots, while water chutes came into their own. As the stove cooled so did the drip cease, and in no prehistoric cavern did more stalactites and stalagmites grow apace.

On 16 March the last sledge party to the Barrier that season started for Corner Camp with provisions to increase the existing depot there. The party was in charge of Lieutenant Evans, and consisted of Bowers, Oates, Atkinson,

Wright, and myself, with two seamen, Crean and Forde. The journey out and back took eight days and was uneventful as sledge journeys go. Thick weather prevailed for several days, and after running down our distance to Corner Camp we waited for it to clear. We found ourselves six miles from the depot and among crevasses, which goes to show how easy it is to steer off the course under such conditions, and how creditable the navigation is when a course is kept correctly, sometimes more by instinct than by skill.

But we got our first experience of cold weather sledging which was useful. The minus thirties and forties are not very cold as we were to understand cold afterwards, but quite cold enough to start with; cold enough to teach you how to look after your footgear, handle metal and not to waste time. However, the sun was still well up during the day, and this makes all the difference, since any sun does more drying of clothes and gear than none at all. At the same time we began to realize the difficulties which attend upon spring journeys, though we could only imagine what might be the trials on a journey in mid-winter, such as we intended to essay.

It is easy to be wise after the event, but, in looking back upon the expedition as a whole, and the tragedy which was to come, mainly from the unforeseen cold of the autumn on the Barrier (such as minus forties in February) it seems that we might have grasped that these temperatures were lower than might have been expected in the middle of March quite near the open sea. Even if this had occurred to any one, and I do not think that it did, I doubt whether the next step of reasoning would have followed, namely, the possibility that the interior of the Barrier would, as actually happened, prove to be much colder than was expected at this date. On the contrary I several times heard Scott mention the possibility of the Polar Party not returning until April. At the same time it must be realized that pony transport to the foot of the Beardmore Glacier made a late start inevitable, for the blizzards our ponies had already suffered proved that spring weather on the Barrier would be intolerable to them. As a matter of fact, Scott says in his Message to the Public, 'no one in the world would have expected the temperature and surfaces which we encountered at this time of the year'.

We returned to find everything at Hut Point, including the hut, covered with frozen spray. This was the result of a blizzard of which we only felt the tail end on the Barrier. Scott wrote:

> The sea was breaking constantly and heavily on the ice foot. The spray carried right over the Point – covering all things and raining on the roof of the hut. Poor Vince's cross, some 30 feet above the water, was enveloped in it. Of course the dogs had a very poor time, and we went and released two or three, getting covered in spray during the operation – our wind clothes very wet. This is the third gale from the South since our arrival here (i.e. in 2½ weeks). Any one of these would have rendered the Bay impossible for a ship, and, therefore, it is extraordinary that we should have entirely escaped such a blow when the *Discovery* was in it in 1902.[13]

It is difficult to see long distances across open water at this time of year because the comparatively warm water throws up into the air a fog, known as frost-smoke. If there is a wind this smoke is carried over the surface of the sea, but if calm the smoke rises and forms a dense curtain. Standing on Arrival Heights, which form the nail of the finger-like Peninsula on which we now lived, we could see the four islands which lie near Cape Evans, and a black smudge in the face of the glaciers which descend from Erebus, which we knew to be the face of the steep slope above Cape Evans, afterwards named The Ramp. But, for the present, our comfortable hut might have been thousands of miles away for all the good it was to us. As soon as the wind fell calm the sea was covered by a thin layer of ice, in twenty-four hours it might be four or five inches thick, but as yet it never proved strong enough to resist the next blizzard. In March the ice to the south was safe; there was appearance of ice in

13. *Scott's Last Expedition*, vol. i, p. 207.

the two bays at the foot of Erebus' slopes in the beginning of April.

We treated newly formed ice with far too little respect. It was on 7 April that Scott asked whether any of us would like to walk northwards over the newly formed ice towards Castle Rock. We had walked about two miles, the ice heaving up and down as we went, dodging the open pools and leads to the best of our ability, when Taylor went right in. Luckily he could lever himself out without help, and returned to the hut with all speed. We prepared to cross this ice to Cape Evans the next day, but the whole of it went out in the night. On another occasion we were prepared to set out the following morning, but the ice on which we were to cross went out on the turn of the tide some five hours before we timed ourselves to start.

Scott was of the opinion that the ice in the two Bays under Erebus was firm, and prepared to essay this route. The first of these bays is formed by the junction of the Hut Point Peninsula with Erebus to the south, and by Glacier Tongue to the north. Crossing Glacier Tongue a party can descend on to the second bay beyond, the northern boundary of which is Cape Evans. The Dellbridge Islands, of which Great Razorback is in direct line between Glacier Tongue and Cape Evans, help to hold in any ice which forms here. The route had never been attempted before, but it was hoped that a way down from the Peninsula on to the frozen sea might be found at the Hutton Cliffs, an outcrop of lava rock in the irregular ice face.

A party consisting of Scott, Bowers, Taylor, and Seaman Evans with one tent, and Lieutenant Evans, Wright, Debenham, Gran and Crean with another, started for Hut Point. It was dark to the south and snowing by the time they reached the top of Ski Slope. We helped them past Third Crater. The ice from Hut Point to Glacier Tongue was impossible, and so they went on past Castle Rock and were to try and get down somewhere by the Hutton Cliffs on to some fast-ice which seemed to have held there some time, and so across Glacier

Tongue on to sea-ice which also seemed to be fast as far as Cape Evans.

After lunch Wilson and I started about 4 p.m. in half a blizzard. It was much better on the Heights and fairly clear towards Erebus, but we could not see any traces of the party on the ice.

12 April. This morning as it was beginning to get light a blizzard started, and it is blowing very hard now. The large amount of snow which has fallen will make it very thick. We are all anxious about the returning party, for Scott talked of camping on the sea-ice. The ice in Arrival Bay (just north of Hut Point) has gone out. They have sleeping-bags, food for two meals, and a full primus for each tent.

13 April. We are very anxious about the returning party, especially when all the ice north of Hut Point went out. The blizzard blew itself out this morning, and it was a great change to see White Island and the Bluff once more. Atkinson came in before lunch and told me that, looking from the Heights, the ice from Glacier Tongue to Cape Evans appeared to have gone out. This sobered our lunch. We all made our way to Second Crater afterwards, and found the ice from the Hutton Cliffs to Glacier Tongue and thence to Cape Evans was still in.

Before leaving, Scott arranged to give Véry Lights at 10 p.m. from Cape Evans on the first clear night of the next three. Tonight is the third, and the first clear night. We were out punctually, and then as we watched a flare blazed up, followed by quite a firework display. We all went wild with excitement – knowing that all was well. Meares ran in and soaked some awning with paraffin, and we lifted it as an answering flare and threw it into the air again and again, until it was burning in little bits all over the snow. The relief was great.[14]

Bowers must tell the story of the returning party:

14. My own diary.

173

We topped the ridges and headed for Erebus beyond Castle Rock. It looked a little threatening at first, but cleared a bit as we got on. It was quite interesting to be breaking new ground. Scott is a fine stepper in a sledge, and he set a fast and easy swing all the time. It was snowing and misty when we got beyond the Hutton Cliffs, but we pitched the tents for lunch before going down the slope. There was no doubt that a blizzard was coming up. It cleared during lunch, which we finished about 3.30 p.m., as it had been a long morning march.

It was just as well for us that the mist cleared, for the slope was not only crevassed in one direction, but it ended in a high ice-cliff. By working along we found a lowish place about thirty feet down from top to bottom. Over this we lowered men and sledges. It had started to blow and the drift was flying off the cliff in clouds. We put in a couple of strong male bamboos to lower the last man away, leaving the Alpine rope there to facilitate ascent (i.e. for any party returning to Hut Point with food). We then repacked the sledges and headed across the bay towards the Glacier Tongue, where we arrived after dark about 6 p.m. The young sea-ice was covered in a salt deposit which made it like pulling a sledge over treacle instead of ice, and it was very heavy going after the snow uplands. The Tongue was mostly hard blue ice, which is slipperiness itself, and crevassed every few yards. Most of these were bridged, but you were continually pushing a foot, or sometimes two, into nothingness, in the semi-darkness. None of us, however, went down to the extent of our harness.

Arrived on the other side we struck a sheltered dip, where we decided to camp for something to eat. It was after 8 p.m. and I was camping there for the night, as it seemed to me folly to venture upon a piece of untried newly frozen sea-ice in inky darkness, with a blizzard coming up behind us. Against this of course we were only five miles from Cape Evans, and though we had hardly any grub with us, not having anticipated the cliff or the saltiness of the sea-ice, and having to set out to do the journey in one day, I thought hunger in a sleeping-bag better than lying out in a blizzard on less than one foot of young ice.

After a meal we started off at 9.30 p.m. in a snowy mist in which we could see literally nothing. It had fallen calm though, and at last we could see the outline of the nearest of the Dellbridge Islands called the Great Razorback. As we neared the Little Razorback Island the snow hid everything; in fact we could hardly see the island itself when we were right under it. It was impossible to go wandering on, so we had after all to camp on the sea-ice. There was scarcely any snow to put on the valances of the tents, and the wet salt soaked the bags, and you knew that there was only about six or ten inches of precarious ice between you and the black waters beneath. Altogether I decided that I for one would lie awake in such an insecure camp.

As expected the blizzard overtook us shortly after midnight, and the shrieking of the wind among the rocks above might have been pretty unpleasant had it not assured me that we were still close to the island and not moving seaward. Needless to say, I said that I was sure the camp was as safe as a church. At daylight Taylor dived out and in until the wind from the door blew out the ice valance and the next moment the tent closed on us like an umbrella. We would never have spread it again had not some of the drift settled round us, and so we were able to secure it after an hour or two. The air was full of thick drift, and to work off some of Taylor's energy I said we might climb the island and look for Cape Evans.

The island rose up straight from the sea at a sharp angle all round, and we climbed it with difficulty. On the top we saw the reason of its name, as it was absolutely so sharp right along that you could bestride the top as though sitting in a saddle. It was too windy sitting up there to be pleasant, so we descended, having seen nothing but clouds of flying snow, and the peak of Inaccessible Island. At the bottom of the weather side we found a small ledge perfectly flat and just big enough to take two tents pitched close together. At this place the island made a wind buffer and it was practically calm though the blizzard yelled all round. I urged Captain Scott to camp on this ledge and Taylor fizzled for making for Cape Evans, so Scott decided to ensure Taylor's safety, as he put it, and we made for the ledge. Once there we had an ideal camp on good hard ground and no wind, and had we had food the blizzard might have lasted a week for aught I cared.

We were two nights there and on the morning of the 13th it took off enough for us to head for home. We saw Sunny Jim's [Simpson's] Observatory on the Hill, but still did not know how the hut had fared till we got round the cape into North Bay. There was the Winter Station all intact, however, and though North Bay had only just frozen in, it was strong enough to bear us safely. Somebody saw us and in another moment the hut poured out her little party, consisting of Sunny Jim, Ponting, Nelson, Day, Lashly, Hooper, Clissold, Dimitri and Anton. Ponting's face was a study as he ran up; he failed to recognize any of us and stopped dead with a blank look – as he admitted afterwards, he thought it was the Norwegian expedition for the space of a moment; and then we were all being greeted as heartily as if we had really done something to be proud of.

The motors had had to be shifted, and a lot of gear placed higher up the beach, but the water had never reached the hut, so all was well. Inside it looked tremendous, and we looked at our grimy selves in a glass for the first time for three months; no wonder Ponting did not recognize the ruffians. He photographed a group of us, which will amuse you some day, when it is permissible to send photos. We ate heartily and had hot baths and generally civilized ourselves. I have since concluded that the hut is the finest place in the southern hemisphere, but then I could not shake down to it at once. I hankered for a sleeping-bag out on the snow, or for the blubbery atmosphere of Hut Point. I expect the truth of the matter was that all my special pals, Bill, Cherry, Titus, and Atch, had been left behind.

We found eight ponies at Winter Quarters in the stable, Hackenschmidt having died. These with our two at Hut Point left us with ten to start the winter with. I at once looked out the other big Siberian horse that had been a pair with my late lamented (they were the only Siberian ponies, all the rest being Manchurians) and singled him out for myself, should 'the powers that be' be willing.

A party had to return to Hut Point with some provision in a day or two, so I asked to go. Captain Scott had decided to go himself, but said he would be very pleased if I would go too; so it being a fine day we left the following Monday. The two teams consisted of Captain Scott, Lashly, Day, and Dimitri with one tent and sledge, and Crean, Hooper, Nelson and myself with the other. We had it fine as far as the Glacier Tongue; and then along came the cheery old south wind in our faces; we crossed the Tongue and struggled against this till we could camp under the Hutton Cliffs where we got some shelter. All of us had our faces frost-bitten, the washing and shaving having made mine quite tender. It was a bit of a job getting up the cliff: we had to stand on top of a pile of fallen ice and hoist a 10-feet sledge on to our shoulders, at least on to the shoulders of the tall ones; this just touched the overhanging cornice. A cornice of snow is caused by continual drift over a sharp edge: it takes all sorts of fantastic shapes, but usually hangs over like this. Looking edgeways it looks as if it must fall down, but as a matter of fact is usually very tough indeed. In this case steps were cut in it with an ice axe from our extemporary ladder, and Captain Scott and I got up first. With the aid of a rope and the ladder we got the light ones up first, and hauled up the gear last of all; hanging the sledge from the top with one rope enabled the last two to struggle up it assisted by a rope round them from above. It was a cold job and more frost-bites occurred in two of our novices, one on a foot and the other on a finger.

We faced the blast again, but got it partially behind us on reaching the Heights. We camped for the night under Castle Rock on an inclined slope. It calmed down to a glorious night with a low temperature. Crean and I lay head down hill to make Nelson and Hooper – who had never sledged before – more comfortable. As a result Crean slipped half out of the tent and let in a cold stream of air under the valance for which

I was at a loss to account until the morning disclosed him thus, fast asleep of course. It takes a lot to worry Captain Scott's coxswain.

We arrived at Hut Point and had a great reception there, chiefly on account of the food we brought, particularly the sugar. We had been living on some paraffin sugar when I left before, and even this was finished. The next day we stayed there to kill seals. Cherry and I skinned one and then went for a walk round Cape Armitage. It was blowing big guns off the cape, fairly fizzing in fact. We went as far as Pram Point and then turned, coming in with it behind us. I only had a thin balaclava and my ears were nearly nipped.[15]

Meanwhile those of us who had been left at Hut Point with the ponies and dogs journeyed out one afternoon to Safety Camp to get some more bales of compressed fodder. Easter Sunday we spent in a howling blizzard, which cleared in the afternoon sufficiently to see a golden sun sinking into a sea of purple frost-smoke and drift.

I have it on record that we had tinned haddock this day for breakfast, made by Oates with great care, a biscuit and cheese hoosh for lunch, and a pemmican fry this evening, followed by cocoa with a tin of sweetened Nestlés milk in it, truly a great luxury. For the rest we mended our finnesko, and read *Bleak House*. Meares told us how the Chinese who were going to war with the Lolos (who are one of the Eighteen tribes on the borders of Thibet and China) tied the Lolo hostage to a bench, and, having cut his throat, caught the blood which dripped from it. Into this they dipped their flag, and then cut out the heart and liver, which the officers ate, while the men ate the rest!

The relief party arrived on 18 April:

> We had spent such a happy week, just the seven of us, at the *Discovery* hut that I think, glad as we were to see the men,

15. Bowers.

we would most of us have rather been left undisturbed, and I expected that it would mean that we should have to move homewards, as it turned out.

Meares is to be left in charge of the party which remains, namely Forde and Keohane of the old stagers, and Nelson, Day, Lashly and Dimitri of the new-comers. He is very amusing with the stories and is evidently afraid that the food which has just been brought in (sugar, self-raising flour, chocolate, etc.) will all be eaten up by those who have brought it. So we have dampers without butter, and a minimum of chocolate.

Tuesday and Tuesday night was one of our few still, cold days, nearly minus thirty. The sea northwards from Hut Point, whence the ice had previously all gone out, froze nearly five inches by Wednesday midday, when we got three more seal. Scott was evidently thinking that on Thursday, when we were to start, we might go by the sea-ice all the way – when suddenly with no warning it silently floated out to sea.[16]

The following two teams travelled to Cape Evans via the Hutton Cliffs on 21 April: 1st team Scott, Wilson, Atkinson, Crean; 2nd team Bowers, Oates, Cherry-Garrard, Hooper. It was blowing hard, as usual, at the Hutton Cliffs, and we got rather frost-bitten when lowering the sledges on to the sea-ice. The sun was leaving us for the next four months, but luckily the light just lasted for this operation, though not for the subsequent meal which we hastily ate under the cliffs, nor for the crossing of Glacier Tongue. Bowers wrote home:

I had the lighter team and, knowing what a flier Captain Scott is I took care to have the new sledge myself. Our weights were nothing and the difference was only in the sledge runners, but it made all the difference to us that day. Scott fairly legged it, as I expected, and we came along gaily behind him. He could not understand it when the pace began to tell more on his heavy team than on us. After lowering

16. My own diary.

down the sledges over the cliffs we recovered the rope we had left in the first place, and then struck out over the sea-ice. Then our good runners told so much that I owned up to mine being the better sledge, and offered to give them one of my team. This was declined, but after we crossed the Tongue Captain Scott said he would like to change sledges at the Little Razorback. At any time over this stretch we could have run away from his team, and once they got our sledge they started that game on us. We expected it, and never had I stepped out so hard before. We had been marching hard for nearly 12 hours and now we had two miles' spurt to do, and we should have stuck it, bad·runners and all, had we had smooth ice. As it was we struck a belt of rough ice, and in the dark we all stumbled and I went down a whack, that nearly knocked me out. This was not noticed fortunately, and still we clung on to the end of their sledge while I turned hot and cold and sick and went through the various symptoms before I got my equilibrium back, which I fortunately did while legging it at full speed. They started to go ahead soon after that though, and we could not hold our own, although we were close to the cape. I had the same thing happen again after another fall, but we stuck it round the cape and arrived only about 50 yards behind. I have never felt so done, and so was my team. Of course we need not have raced, but we did, and I would do the same thing every time. Titus produced a mug of brandy he had sharked from the ship and we all lapped it up with avidity. The other team were just about laid out, too, so I don't think there was much to be said either way.[17]

Two days later the sun appeared for the last time for four months.

Looking back I realized two things. That sledging, at any rate in summer and autumn, was a much less terrible ordeal than my imagination had painted it, and that those Hut Point days would prove some of the happiest in my life. Just enough to eat and keep us warm, no more – no frills nor

17. Bowers's letter.

trimmings: there is many a worse and more elaborate life. The necessaries of civilization were luxuries to us: and as Priestley found under circumstances compared to which our life at Hut Point was a Sunday School treat, the luxuries of civilization satisfy only those wants which they themselves create.

Chapter Six
THE FIRST WINTER

The highest object that human beings can set before themselves is not the pursuit of any such chimera as the annihilation of the unknown: it is simply the unwearied endeavour to remove its boundaries a little further from our little sphere of action.

HUXLEY

A ND SO WE came back to our comfortable hut. Whatever merit there may be in going to the Antarctic, once there you must not credit yourself for being there. To spend a year in the hut at Cape Evans because you explore is no more laudable than to spend a month at Davos because you have consumption, or to spend an English winter at the Berkeley Hotel. It is just the most comfortable thing and the easiest thing to do under the circumstances.

In our case the best thing was not at all bad, for the hut, as Arctic huts go, was as palatial as is the Ritz, as hotels go. Whatever the conditions of darkness, cold and wind, might be outside, there was comfort and warmth and good cheer within.

And there was a mass of work to be done, as well as at least two journeys of the first magnitude ahead.

When Scott first sat down at his little table at Winter Quarters to start working out a most complicated scheme of weights and averages for the Southern Journey, his thoughts were gloomy, I know. 'This is the end of the Pole,' he said to me, when he pulled us off the bergs after the sea-ice had broken up; the loss of six ponies out of the eight with which we started the Depot Journey, the increasing emaciation and weakness of the pony transport as we travelled farther on the Barrier, the arrival of the dogs after their rapid journey home, starved rakes which looked as though they were absolutely done – these were not cheerful recollections with which to start to plan a journey of eighteen hundred miles.

On the other hand, we had ten ponies left, though two or three of them were of more than doubtful quality; and it was obvious that considerable improvement could and must be made in the feeding of both ponies and dogs. With regard to the dogs the remedy was plain; their ration was too small. With regard to the ponies the question was not so simple. One of the main foods for the ponies which we had brought was compressed fodder in the shape of bales. Theoretically this fodder was excellent food value, and was made of wheat which was cut green and pressed. Whether it was really wheat or not I do not know, but there could be no two opinions about its nourishing qualities for our ponies. When fed upon it they lost weight until they were just skin and bone. Poor beasts! It was pitiful to see them.

In Oates we had a man who had forgotten as much as most men know about horses. It was no fault of his that this fodder was inadequate, nor that we had lost so many of the best ponies which we had. Oates had always been for taking the worst ponies out on the Depot Journey: travelling as far on to the Barrier as they could go, and there killing them and depoting their flesh. Now Oates took the ten remaining ponies into his capable hands. Some of them were scarecrows, especially poor Jehu, who was never expected to start at all, and ended by gallantly pulling his somewhat diminished load eight marches beyond One Ton Camp, a distance of 238 miles. Another, Christopher, was a man-killer if ever a horse was; he had to be thrown in order to attach him to the sledge; to the end he would lay out any man who was rash enough to give him the chance; once started, and it took four men to achieve this, it was impossible to halt him during the day's march, and so Oates and his three tent mates and their ponies had to go without any lunch meal for 130 miles of the Southern Journey.

Oates trained them and fed them as though they were to run in the Derby. They were exercised whenever possible throughout the winter and spring by those who were to lead them on the actual journey. Fresh and good food was found in the shape of oilcake and oats, a limited quantity of each of which had been brought and was saved for the actual Polar Journey, and everything which care and foresight could devise was done to save them discomfort. It is a grim life for animals, but in the end we were to know that up to the time of that bad blizzard almost at the Glacier Gateway, which was the finishing post of these plucky animals, they had fed all they needed, slept as well and lived as well as any, and better than most horses in ordinary life at home. 'I congratulate you, Titus,' said Wilson, as we stood under the shadow of Mount Hope, with the ponies' task accomplished, and 'I thank you,' said Scott.

Titus grunted and was pleased.

Transport difficulties for the Polar Journey were considerable, but in every other direction the outlook was bright. The men who were to do the sledging had been away from Winter Quarters for three months. They had had plenty of sledging experience, some of it none too soft. The sledges, clothing, man-food, and outfit generally were excellent, although some changes were suggested and could be put into effect. There was no obvious means, however, of effecting the improvement most desired, a satisfactory snow-shoe for the ponies.

The work already accomplished was enormous. On the Polar Journey the ponies and dogs could now travel light for the first hundred and thirty geographical miles, when, at One Ton Camp, they would for the first time take their full loads: the advantage of being able to start again with full loads when so far on your way is obvious when it is considered that the distance travelled depends upon the weight of food that can be carried. During the geological journey on the western side of the Sound, Taylor and his party had carried out much useful geological work in Dry Valley and on the Ferrar and Koettlitz Glaciers, which had been accurately plotted for the charts, and had been examined for the first time by an expert physiographer and ice specialist. The ordinary routine of scientific and meteorological observations usual with all Scott's sledging parties was observed.

Further, at Cape Evans there had been running for more than three months a scientific station, which rivalled in thoroughness and exactitude any other such station in the world. I hope that later a more detailed account may be given of this continuous series of observations, some of them demanding the most complex mechanism, and all of them watched over by enthusiastic experts. It must here suffice to say that we who on our return saw for the first time the hut and its annexes completely equipped were amazed; though perhaps the gadget which appealed most to us at first was the electric apparatus by which the cook, whose invention it was, controlled the rising of his excellent bread.

Glad as we were to find it all and to enjoy the food, bath and comfort which it offered, we had no illusions about Cape Evans itself. It is uninteresting, as only a low-lying spit of black lava covered for the most part with snow, and swept constantly by high winds and drift, can be uninteresting. The kenyte lava of which it is formed is a remarkable rock, and is found in few parts of the world: but when you have seen one bit of kenyte you have seen all. Unlike the spacious and lofty Hut Peninsula, thirteen miles to the south, it has no outstanding hills and craters; no landmarks such as Castle Rock. Unlike the broad folds of Cape Royds, six miles to the north, it has none of the rambling walks and varied lakes, in which is found most of the limited plant life which exists in these latitudes, and though a few McCormick skuas meet here, there is no nursery of penguins such as that which makes Cape Royds so attractive in summer. Nor has the Great Ice Sheet, which reached up Erebus and spread over the Ross Sea in the past, spilled over Cape Evans in its retreat a wealth of foreign granites, dolerites, porphyrys and sand-stone such as cover the otherwise dull surface round Shackleton's old Winter Quarters.

Cape Evans is a low lava flow jutting out some three thousand feet from the face of the glaciers which clothe the slopes of Erebus. It is roughly an equilateral triangle in shape, at its base some three thousand feet (%/₁₆th mile) across. This base-line, which divides the cape from the slopes of Erebus and the crevassed glaciers and giant ice-falls which clothe them, consists of a ramp with a slope of thirty degrees, and a varying height of some 100 to 150 feet. From our hut, four hundred yards away, it looks like a great embankment behind which rises the majestic volcano Erebus, with its plume of steam and smoke.

The cape itself does not rise on the average more than thirty feet, and somewhat resembles the back of a hog with several backbones. The hollows between the ridges are for the most part filled with snow and ice, while in one or two places where the accumulation of snow is great enough there are little glacierets which do not travel far before they ignominiously peter out. There are two small lakes, called Skua Lake and Island Lake respectively. There is only one hill which is almost behind the hut, and is called Wind Vane Hill, for on it were placed one of our wind vanes and certain other meteorological instruments. Into the glacieret which flowed down in the lee of this hill we drove two caves, which gave both an even low temperature and excellent insulation. One of them was therefore used for our magnetic obser-vations, and the other as an ice-house for the mutton we had brought from New Zealand.

The north side, upon which we had built our hut, slopes down by way of a rubbly beach to the sea in North Bay. We knew there was a beach for we landed upon it, but we never saw it again even in the height of summer, for the winter blizzards formed an ice foot several feet thick. The other side of the cape ends abruptly in black bastions and baby cliffs some thirty feet high. The apex of the triangle which forms as it were the cape proper is a similar kenyte bluff. The whole makes a tricky place on which to walk in the dark, for the surface is strewn with boulders of all sizes and furrowed and channelled by drifts of hard and icy snow, and quite suddenly you may find yourself prostrate upon a surface of slippery blue ice. It may be easily imagined that it is no seemly place to exercise skittish ponies or mules in a cold wind, but there is no other place when the sea-ice is unsafe.

Come and stand outside the hut door. All round you, except where the cape joins the mountain, is the sea. You are facing north with your back to the Great Ice Barrier and the Pole, with your eyes looking out of the mouth of McMurdo Sound over the Ross Sea towards New Zealand, two thousand miles of open water, packs and bergs. Look over the sea to your left. It is midday, and though the sun will not appear above the horizon he is still near enough to throw a soft yellow light over the Western Mountains. These form the coast-line thirty miles across the Sound, and as they disappear northwards are miraged up into the air and float, black islands in a lemon sky. Straight ahead of you there is nothing to be seen but black open sea, with a high light over the horizon, which you know betokens pack; this is ice blink. But as you watch there appears and disappears a little dark smudge. This puzzles you for some time, and then you realize that this is the mirage of some far mountain or of Beaufort Island, which guards the mouth of McMurdo Sound against such traffic as ever comes that way, by piling up the ice floes across the entrance.

As you still look north, in the middle distance, jutting out into the sea, is a low black line of land, with one excrescence. This is Cape Royds, with Shackleton's old hut upon it; the excrescence is High Peak, and this line marks the first land upon the eastern side of McMurdo Sound which you can see, and indeed is actually the most westerly point of Ross Island. It disappears abruptly behind a high wall, and if you let your eyes travel round towards your right front you see that the wall is a perpendicular cliff two hundred feet high of pure green and blue ice, which falls sheer into the sea, and forms, with Cape Evans, on which we stand, the bay which lies in front of our hut, and which we called North Bay. This great ice-cliff with its crevasses, towers, bastions and cornices, was a never-ending source of delight to us; it forms the snout of one of the many glaciers which slide down the slopes of Erebus: in smooth slopes and contours where the mountain

187

underneath is of regular shape: in impassable icefalls where the underlying surface is steep or broken. This particular ice stream is called the Barne Glacier, and is about two miles across. The whole background from our right front to our right rear, that is from N.E. to S.E., is occupied by our massive and volcanic neighbour, Erebus. He stands 13,500 feet high. We live beneath his shadow and have both admiration and friendship for him, sometimes perhaps tinged with respect. However, there are no signs of dangerous eruptive disturbances in modern times, and we feel pretty safe, despite the fact that the smoke which issues from his crater sometimes rises in dense clouds for many thousands of feet, and at others the trail of his plume can be measured for at least a hundred miles.

If you are not too cold standing about (it does not pay to stand about at Cape Evans) let us make our way behind the hut and up Wind Vane Hill. This is only some sixty-five feet high, yet it dominates the rest of the cape and is steep enough to require a scramble, even now when the wind is calm. Look out that you do not step on the electric wires which connect the wind-vane cups on the hill with the recording dial in the hut. These cups revolve in the wind, the revolutions being registered electrically: every four miles a signal was sent to the hut, and a pen working upon a chronograph registered one more step. There is also a meteorological screen on the summit, which has to be visited at eight o'clock each morning in all weathers.

Arrived on the top you will now be facing south, that is in the opposite direction to which you were facing before. The first thing that will strike you is that the sea, now frozen in the bays though still unfrozen in the open sound, flows in nearly to your feet. The second, that though the sea stretches back for nearly twenty miles, yet the horizon shows land or ice in every direction. For a ship this is a cul-de-sac, as Ross found seventy years ago. But as soon as you have grasped these two facts your whole attention will be riveted to the amazing sight on your left. Here are the southern slopes of Erebus; but how different from those which you have lately seen. Northwards they fell in broad calm lines to a beautiful stately cliff which edged the sea. But here – all the epithets and all the adjectives which denote chaotic immensity could not adequately tell of them. Visualize a torrent ten miles long and twenty miles broad; imagine it falling over mountainous rocks and tumbling over itself in giant waves; imagine it arrested in the twinkling of an eye, frozen and white. Countless blizzards have swept their drifts over it, but have failed to hide it. And it continues to move. As you stand in the still cold air you may sometimes hear the silence broken by the sharp reports as the cold contracts or its own weight splits it. Nature is tearing up that ice as human beings tear paper.

The sea-cliff is not so high here, and is more broken up by crevasses and caves, and more covered with snow. Some five miles along the coast the white line is broken by a bluff and black outcrop of rock; this is Turk's Head, and beyond it is the low white line of Glacier Tongue, jutting out for miles into the sea. We know, for we have already crossed it, that there is a small frozen bay of sea-ice beyond, but all we can see from Cape Evans is the base of the Hut Point Peninsula, with a rock outcrop just showing where the Hutton Cliffs lie. The Peninsula prevents us from seeing the Barrier, though the Barrier wind is constantly flowing over it, as the clouds of drift now smoking over the Cliffs bear witness. Farther to the right still, the land is clear: Castle Rock stands up like a sentinel, and beyond are Arrival Heights and the old craters we have got to know so well during our stay at Hut Point. The *Discovery* hut, which would, in any case, be invisible at fifteen miles, is round that steep rocky corner which ends the Peninsula, due south from where we stand.

There remains undescribed the quadrant which stretches to our right front from south to west. Just as we have previously seen the line of the Western Mountains disappearing to the north miraged up in the light of the midday sun, so now we see the same line of mountains running south, with many miles of sea or Barrier between us and them. On the far southern horizon, almost in transit with Hut Point, stands Minna Bluff, some ninety miles away, beyond which we have laid the One Ton Depot, and from this point, as our eyes move round to the right, we see peak after peak of these great mountain ranges – Discovery, Morning, Lister, Hooker, and the glaciers which divide them one from another. They rise almost without a break to a height of thirteen thousand feet. Between us and them is the Barrier to the south, and the sea to the north. Unless a blizzard is impending or blowing, they are clearly visible, a gigantic wall of snow and ice and rock, which bounds our view to the west, constantly varied by the ever-changing colour of the Antarctic. Beyond is the plateau.

We have not yet mentioned four islands which lie within a radius of about three miles from where we stand. The most important is a mile from the end of Cape Evans and is called Inaccessible Island, owing to the inhospitality of its steep lava side, even when the sea is frozen; we found a way up, but it is not a very interesting place. Tent Island lies farther out and to the south-west. The remaining two, which are more islets than islands, rise in front of us in South Bay. They are called Great and Little Razorback, being ribs of rock with a sharp divide in the centre. The latter of these is the refuge upon which Scott's party returning to Cape Evans pitched their camp when overtaken by a blizzard some weeks ago. All these islands are of volcanic origin and black in general colour, but I believe there is evidence to show that the lava stream which created them flowed from McMurdo Sound rather than from the more obvious craters of Erebus. Their importance in this story is the indirect help they gave in holding in sea-ice against southerly blizzards, and in forming landmarks which proved useful more than once to men who had lost their bearings in darkness and thick weather. In this respect also several icebergs which sailed in from the Ross Sea and grounded on the shallows which run between Inaccessible Island and the cape, as well as in South Bay, were most useful as well as being interesting and beautiful. For two years we watched the weathering of these great towers and bastions of ice by sea and sun and wind, and left them still lying in the same positions, but mere tumbled ruins of their former selves.

Many places in the panorama we have examined show black rock, and the cape on which we stand exposes at times more black than white. This fact always puzzles those who naturally conclude that all the Antarctic is covered with ice and snow. The explanation is simple, that winds of the great velocity which prevails in this region will not only prevent snow resting to windward of outcropping rocks and cliffs, but will even wear away the rocks themselves. The fact that these winds always blow from the south, or southerly, causes a tendency for this aspect of any projecting rock to be blown free from snow, while the north or lee side is drifted up by a marbled and extremely hard tongue of snow, which disappears into a point at a distance which depends upon the size of the rock.

Of course for the most part the land is covered to such a depth by glaciers and snow that no wind will do more than pack the snow or expose the ice beneath. At the same time, to visualize the Antarctic as a white land is a mistake, for, not only is there much rock projecting wherever mountains or rocky capes and islands rise, but the snow seldom looks white, and if carefully looked at will be found to be shaded with many colours, but chiefly with cobalt blue or rose-madder, and all the graduations of lilac and mauve which the mixture of these colours will produce. A White Day is so rare that I have recollections of going out from the hut or the tent and being impressed by the fact that the snow really looked white. When to the beautiful tints in the sky and the delicate shading on the snow are added perhaps the deep colours of the open sea, with reflections from the ice foot and ice-cliffs in it, all brilliant blues and emerald greens, then indeed a man may realize how beautiful this world can be, and how clean.

Though I may struggle with inadequate expression to show the reader that this pure Land of the South has many gifts to squander upon those who woo her, chiefest of these gifts is that of her beauty. Next, perhaps, is that of grandeur and immensity, of giant mountains and limitless spaces, which must awe the most casual, and may well terrify the least imaginative of mortals. And there is one other gift which she gives with both hands, more prosaic, but almost more desirable. That is the gift of sleep. Perhaps it is true of others as is certainly the case with me, that the more horrible the conditions in which we sleep, the more soothing and wonderful are the dreams which visit us. Some of us have slept in a hurricane of wind and a hell of drifting snow and darkness, with no roof above our heads, with no tent to help us home, with no conceivable chance that we should ever see our friends again, with no food that we could eat, and only the snow which drifted into our sleeping-bags which we could drink day after day and night after night. We slept not only soundly the greater part of these days and nights, but with a certain numbed pleasure. We wanted something sweet to eat: for preference tinned peaches in syrup! Well! That is the kind of sleep the Antarctic offers you at her worst, or nearly at her worst. And if the worst, or best, happens, and Death comes for you in the snow, he comes disguised as Sleep, and you greet him rather as a welcome friend than as a gruesome foe. She treats you thus when you are in the extremity of peril and hardship; perhaps then you can imagine what draughts of deep and healthy slumber she will give a tired sledger at the end of a long day's march in summer, when after a nice hot supper he tucks his soft dry warm furry bag round him with the light beating in through the green silk tent, the homely smell of tobacco in the air, and the only noise that of the ponies tethered outside, munching their supper in the sun.

And so it came about that during our sojourn at Cape Evans, in our comfortable warm roomy home, we took our full allotted span of sleep. Most were in their bunks by 10 p.m., sometimes with a candle and a book, not rarely with a piece of chocolate. The acetylene was turned off at 10.30, for we had a limited quantity of carbide, and soon the room was in complete darkness, save for the glow of the galley stove and where a splash of light showed the night watchman preparing his supper. Some snored loudly, but none so loud as Bowers; others talked in their sleep, the more so when some nasty experience had lately set their nerves on edge. There was always the ticking of many instruments, and sometimes the ring of a little bell: to this day I do not know what most of them meant. On a calm night no sound penetrated except, perhaps, the whine of a dog, or the occasional kick of a pony in the stable outside. Any disturbance was the night watchman's job. But on a bad blizzard night the wind, as it tore seawards over the hut, roared and howled in the ventilator let into the roof: in the more furious gusts the whole hut shook, and the pebbles picked up by the hurricane scattered themselves noisily against the woodwork of the southern wall. We did not get many nights like these the first winter; during the second we seemed to get nothing else. One ghastly blizzard blew for six weeks.

The night watchman took his last hourly observation at 7 a.m., and was free to turn in after waking the cook and making up the fire. Frequently, however, he had so much work to do that he preferred to forgo his sleep and remain up. For instance, if the weather looked threatening, he would take his pony out for exercise as soon as possible in the morning, or those lists of stores were not finished, or that fish trap had to be looked after: all kinds of things.

A sizzling on the fire and a smell of porridge and fried seal liver heralded breakfast, which was at 8 a.m. in theory and a good deal later in practice. A sleepy eye might see the meteorologist stumping out (Simpson always stumped) to change the records in his magnetic cave and visit his instruments on the Hill. Twenty minutes later he would be back, as often as not covered with drift and his wind helmet all iced up. Meanwhile, the more hardy ones were washing: that is, they rubbed themselves, all shivering, with snow, of a minus temperature, and pretended they liked it. Perhaps they were right, but we told them it was swank. I'm not sure that it wasn't! It should be explained that water was seldom possible in a land where ice is more abundant than coal.

One great danger threatened all our meals in this hut,

namely that of Cag. A Cag is an argument, sometimes well informed and always heated, upon any subject under the sun, or temporarily in our case, the moon. They ranged from the Pole to the Equator, from the Barrier to Portsmouth Hard and Plymouth Hoe. They began on the smallest of excuses, they continued through the widest field, they never ended; they were left in mid air, perhaps to be caught up again and twisted and tortured months after. What caused the cones on the Ramp; the formation of ice crystals; the names and order of the public-houses if you left the Main Gate of Portsmouth Dockyard and walked to the Unicorn Gate (if you ever reached so far); the best kinds of crampons in the Antarctic, and the best place in London for oysters; the ideal pony rug; would the wine steward at the Ritz look surprised if you asked him for a pint of bitter? Though the *Times Atlas* does not rise to public-houses nor *Chambers's Encyclopaedia* sink to behaviour at our more expensive hotels, yet they settled more of these disputes than anything else.

On the day we are discussing, though mutterings can still be heard from Nelson's cubicle, the long table has been cleared and every one is busy by 9.30. From now until supper at 7 work is done by all in some form or other, except for a short lunch interval. I do not mean for a minute that we all sit down, as a man may do in an office at home, and solidly grind away for upwards of nine hours or more. Not a bit of it. We have much work out of doors, and exercise is a consideration of the utmost importance. But when we go out, each individual quite naturally takes the opportunity to carry out such work as concerns him, whether it deals with ice or rocks, dogs or horses, meteorology or biology, tide-gauges or balloons.

When blizzards allowed, the ponies were exercised by their respective leaders between breakfast and midday, when they were fed. The exercising of animals might be a pleasant business, on the other hand it could be the deuce and all: it depended on the pony and the weather. A blubber fire was kept burning in the snug stable, which was built against the lee wall of the hut; the ponies were, therefore, quite warm, and found it chilly directly they were led outside, even if there was no wind.

The difficulties of exercising them in the dark were so great that with the best intentions in the world it was difficult to give them sufficient work for the good feeding they received. Add to this the fact that one at any rate of these variable animals was really savage, and that most of them were keen to break away if possible, and the hour of exercise was not without its thrills even on the calmest and most moonlight days. The worst days were those when it was difficult to say whether the ponies should be taken out on the sea-ice or not. It was thick weather that was to be feared, for then, if the leader once lost his bearings, it was most difficult for him to return. An overcast sky, light falling snow, perhaps a light northerly wind generally meant a blizzard, but the blizzard might not break for twenty-four hours, it might be upon you in four seconds. It was difficult to say whether the pony should miss his exercise, whether the fish trap should be raised, whether to put off your intended trip to Cape Royds. Generally the risks were taken, for, on the whole, it is better to be a little over-bold than a little over-cautious, while always there was a something inside urging you to do it just because there was a certain risk, and you hardly liked not to do it. It is so easy to be afraid of being afraid!

Let me give one instance: it must be typical of many. It was thick as it could be, no moon, no stars, light falling snow, and not even a light breeze to keep in your face to give direction. Bowers and I decided to take our ponies out, and once over the tide crack, where the working sea-ice joins the fast land-ice, we kept close under the tall cliffs of the Barne Glacier. So far all was well, and also when we struck along a small crack into the middle of the bay, where there was a thermometer screen. This we read with some difficulty by the light of a match and started back towards the hut. In about a quarter of an hour we knew we were quite lost until an iceberg which we recognized showed us that we had been walking at right angles to our course, and got us safe home.

On a clear crisp day, with the full moon to show you the ridges and cracks and sastrugi, it was most pleasant to put on your ski and wander forth with no object but that of healthy pleasure. Perhaps you would make your way round the bluff end of the cape and strike southwards. Here you may visit Nelson working with his thermometers and current meters and other instruments over a circular hole in the ice, which he keeps open from day to day by breaking out the 'biscuit' of newly formed ice. He has connected himself with the hut by telephone, and built round himself an igloo of drifted snow and the aforesaid 'biscuits', which effectually shelter him from the wind. Or you may meet Meares and Dimitri returning with the dog-teams from a visit to Hut Point. A little further on the silence is complete. But now your ear catches the metallic scratch of ski sticks on hard ice; there is someone else ski-ing over there; it may be many miles away, for sound travels in an amazing way. Every now and then there comes a sharp crack like a pistol shot; it is the ice contracting in the glaciers of Erebus, and you know that it is getting colder. Your breath smokes, forming white rime over your face, and ice in your beard; if it is very cold you may actually hear it crackle as it freezes in mid air!

These were the days which remain visibly in the mind as the most enjoyable during this first winter season. It was all so novel, these much-dreaded, and amongst us much-derided, terrors of the Long Winter Night. The atmosphere is very clear when it is not filled with snow or ice crystals, and the moonlight lay upon the land so that we could see the main outlines of the Hut Point Peninsula, and even Minna Bluff out on the Barrier ninety miles away. The ice-cliffs of Erebus showed as great dark walls, but above them the blue ice of the glaciers gleamed silvery, and the steam bowed lazily from the crater carried away in a long line, showing us that the northerly breezes prevailed up there, and were storing up trouble in the south. Sometimes a shooting star would seem to fall right into the mountain, and for the most part the Aurora flitted uneasily about in the sky.

The importance of plenty of out-door exercise was generally recognized, and our experience showed us that the happiest and healthiest members of our party during this first year were those who spent the longest period in the fresh air. As a rule we walked and worked and ski-ed alone, not I feel sure because of any individual distaste for the company of our fellows but rather because of a general inclination to spend a short period of the day without company. At least this is certainly true of the officers: I am not so sure about the men. Under the circumstances, the only time in the year that a man could be alone was in his walks abroad from Winter Quarters, for the hut, of course, was always occupied, and when sledging this sardine-like existence was continuous night and day.

There was one regular exception to this rule. Every possible evening, that is to say if it was not blowing a full blizzard, Wilson and Bowers went up the Ramp together 'to read Bertram'. Now this phrase will convey little meaning without some explanation. I have already spoken of the Ramp as the steep rubbly slope partly covered by snow and partly by ice which divided the cape on which we lived from the glaciated slopes of Erebus. After a breathless scramble up this embankment one came upon a belt of rough boulder-strewn ground from which arose at intervals conical mounds, the origin of which puzzled us for many months. At length, by the obvious means of cutting a section through one of them, it was proved that there was a solid kenyte lava block in the centre of this cone, proving that the whole was formed by the weathering of a single rock. Threading your way for some hundreds of yards through this terrain, a scramble attended by many slips and falls on a dark night, you reached the first signs of glaciation. A little farther, isolated in the ice stream, is another group of debris cones and on the largest of these we placed meteorological Screen 'B', commonly called Bertram. This screen, together with 'A' (Algernon) and 'C' (Clarence), which were in North and South Bays respectively, were erected by Bowers, who thought, rightly, that they would form an object to which men could guide their walks, and that at the same time the observations of maximum, minimum and present temperatures would be a useful check to the meteorologist when he came to compare them with those taken at the hut. As a matter of fact the book in which we used to enter these observations shows that the air temperatures out on the sea-ice vary considerably from those on the cape, and that the temperatures several hundred feet up on the slopes of Erebus are often several degrees higher than those taken at sea-level. I believe that much of the weather in this part of the world is an intensely local affair, and these screens produced useful data.

Wilson and Bowers would go up the Ramp when it was blowing and drifting fairly hard, so that although the rocks and landmarks immediately round them were visible, all beyond was blotted out. It is quite possible to walk thus among landmarks which you know at a time when it is most unwise to go out on to the sea-ice where there are no fixed points to act as a guide.

It was Wilson's pleasant conceit to keep his balaclava rolled up, so that his face was bare, on such occasions, being somewhat proud of the fact that he had not, as yet, been frost-bitten. Imagine our joy when he entered the hut one cold windy evening with two white spots on his cheeks which he vainly tried to hide behind his dogskin mitts.

The ponies' lunch came at midday, when they were given snow to drink and compressed fodder with oats or oil-cake on alternate days to eat, the proportion of which was arranged according to the work they were able to do in the present, or expected to do in the future. Our own lunch was soon after one, and a few minutes before that time Hooper's voice would be heard: 'Table please, Mr Debenham,' and all writing materials, charts, instruments and books would have to be removed. On Sunday, this table displayed a dark blue cloth, but for meals and at all other times it was covered with white oilcloth.

Lunch itself was a pleasant meatless meal, consisting of unlimited bread and butter with plenty of jam or cheese, tea or cocoa, the latter being undoubtedly a most useful drink in a cold country. Many controversies raged over the rival merits of tea and cocoa. Some of us made for ourselves buttered toast at the galley fire; I must myself confess to a weakness for Welsh Rarebit, and others followed my example on cheese days in making messes of which we were not a little proud. Scott sat at the head of the table, that is at the east end, but otherwise we all took our places haphazard from meal to meal as our conversation, or want of it, merited, or as our arrival found a vacant chair. Thus if you felt talkative you might always find a listener in Debenham; if inclined to listen yourself it was only necessary to sit near Taylor or Nelson; if, on the other hand, you just wanted to be quiet, Atkinson or Oates would, probably, give you a congenial atmosphere.

There was never any want of conversation, largely due to the fact that no conversation was expected: we most of us know the horrible blankness which comes over our minds when we realize that because we are eating we are also supposed to talk, whether we have anything to say or not. It was also due to the more primitive reason that in a company of specialists, whose travels extended over most parts of the earth, and whose subjects overlapped and interlocked at so many points, topics of conversation were not only numerous but full of possibilities of expansion. Add to this that from the nature of our work we were probably people of an inquisitive turn of mind and wanted to get to the bottom of the subjects which presented themselves, and you may expect to find, as was in fact the case, an atmosphere of pleasant and quite interesting conversation which sometimes degenerated into heated and noisy argument.

The business of eating over, pipes were lit without further formality. I mention pipes only because while we had a most bountiful supply of tobacco, the kindly present of Mr Wills, our supply of cigarettes from the same source was purposely limited and only a small quantity were landed, allowing of a ration to such members who wished. Consequently cigarettes were an article of some value, and in a land where the ordinary forms of currency are valueless they became a frequent stake to venture when making bets. Indeed, 'I bet you ten cigarettes,' or 'I bet you a dinner when we get back to London,' became the most frequent bids of the argumentative gambler, occasionally varied when the bettor was more than usually certain of the issue by the offer of a pair of socks.

By two o'clock we were dispersed once more to our various works and duties. If it was bearable outside, the hut would soon be empty save for the cook and a couple of seamen washing up the plates; otherwise everyone went out to make the most of any glimmering of daylight which still came to us from the sun below the northern horizon. And here it may be explained that whereas in England the sun rises more or less in the east, is due south at midday, and sets in the west, this is not the case in the Antarctic regions. In the latitude in which we now lived the sun is at his highest at midday in the north, at his lowest at midnight in the south. As is generally known he remains entirely above the horizon for four months of the summer (October–February) and entirely below the horizon for four months in the winter (21 April–21 August). About 27 February, the end of summer, he begins to set and rise due south at midnight; the next day he sets a little earlier and dips a little deeper. During March and April he is going deeper and deeper every day, until, by the middle of April, he is set all the time except for just a peep over the northern horizon at midday, which is his last farewell before he goes away.

The reverse process takes place from 21 August onwards. On this date the sun just peeped above the sea to the north of our hut. The next day he rose a little higher and longer, and in a few weeks he was rising well in the east and sinking behind the Western Mountains. But he did not stop there. Soon he was rising in the S.E. until in the latter days of September he never rose, for he never set; but circled round us by day and night. On Midsummer Day (21 December) at the South Pole the sun circles round for twenty-four hours without changing his altitude for one minute of a degree, but elsewhere he is always rising in the sky until midday in the north and falling from that time until midnight in the south.

Often, far too often, it was blizzing, and it was impossible to go out except into the camp to take the observations, to care for the dogs, to get ice for water or to bring in stores. Even a short excursion of a few yards had to be made with great care under such circumstances, and certainly no one went outside more than was necessary, if only because one was obliged to dig the accumulated drift from the door before it was possible to proceed. Blizzard or no blizzard, most men were back in the hut soon after four, and from then until 6.30 worked steadily at their jobs. As supper time approached some kindly-disposed person would sit down and play on the Broadwood pianola which was one of our blessings, and so it was that we came to supper with good tempers as well as keen appetites.

Soup, in which the flavour of tomatoes occurred all too frequently, followed by seal or penguin, and twice a week by New Zealand mutton, with tinned vegetables, formed the basis of our meal, and this was followed by a pudding. We drank lime juice and water which sometimes included a suspicious penguin flavour derived from the ice slopes from which our water was quarried.

During our passage out to New Zealand in the ship (or as Meares always insisted on calling her, the steamer) it was our pleasant custom to have a glass of port or a liqueur after dinner. Alas, we had this no longer: after leaving New Zealand space allowed of little wine being carried in the *Terra Nova*, even if the general medical opinion of the expedition had not considered its presence undesirable. We had, however, a few cases for special festivals, as well as some excellent liqueur brandy which was carried as medical comforts on our sledge journeys. Any officer who allowed the distribution of this luxury on nearing the end of a journey became extremely popular.

Lack of wine probably led to the suspension of a custom which had prevailed on the *Terra Nova*, namely, the drinking of the old toast of Saturday night, 'Sweethearts and wives; may our sweethearts become our wives, and our wives remain our sweethearts,' and that more appropriate (in our case) toast of Sunday, namely, 'absent friends'. We had but few married officers, though I must say most survivors of the expedition hurried to remedy this single state of affairs when they returned to civilization. Only two of them are unmarried now. Most of them will probably make a success of it, for the good Arctic explorer has most of the defects and qualities of a good husband.

On the top of the pianola, close to the head of the table, lived the gramophone; and under the one looking-glass we possessed, which hung on the bulkhead of Scott's cubicle, was a home-made box with shelves on which lay our records. It was usual to start the gramophone after dinner, and its value may be imagined. It is necessary to be cut off from civilization and all that it means to enable you to realize fully the power music has to recall the past, or the depths of meaning in it to soothe the present and give hope for the future. We had also records of good classical music, and the kindly-disposed individual who played them had his reward in the pleasant atmosphere of homeliness which made itself felt. After dinner had been cleared away, some men sat on the table occupied with books and games. Others dispersed to various jobs. In the matter of games it was noticeable that one would have its vogue and yield place to another without any apparent reason. For a few weeks it might be chess, which would then yield its place to draughts and backgammon, and again come into favour. It is a remarkable fact that, though we had playing cards with us none of our company appeared desirous to use them. In fact I cannot remember seeing a game of cards played except in the ship on the voyage from England.

With regard to books we were moderately well provided with good modern fiction, and very well provided with such authors as Thackeray, Charlotte Brontë, Bulwer-Lytton and Dickens. With all respect to the kind givers of these books, I would suggest that the literature most acceptable to us in the circumstances under which we did most of our reading, that is in Winter Quarters, was the best of the more recent novels, such as Barrie, Kipling, Merriman and Maurice Hewlett. We certainly should have taken with us as much of Shaw, Barker,

Ibsen and Wells as we could lay our hands on, for the train of ideas started by these works and the discussions to which they would have given rise would have been a godsend to us in our isolated circumstances. The one type of book in which we were rich was Arctic and Antarctic travel. We had a library of these given to us by Sir Lewis Beaumont and Sir Albert Markham which was very complete. They were extremely popular, though it is probably true that these are books which you want rather to read on your return than when you are actually experiencing a similar life. They were used extensively in discussions or lectures on such polar subjects as clothing, food rations, and the building of igloos, while we were constantly referring to them on specific points and getting useful hints, such as the use of an inner lining to our tents, and the mechanism of a blubber stove.

I have already spoken of the importance of maps and books of reference, and these should include a good encyclopedia and dictionaries, English, Latin and Greek. Oates was generally deep in Napier's *History of the Peninsular War*, and some of us found Herbert Paul's *History of Modern England* a great stand-by. Most of us managed to find room in our personal gear when sledging for some book which did not weigh much and yet would last. Scott took some Browning on the Polar Journey, though I only saw him reading it once; Wilson took *Maud* and *In Memoriam*; Bowers always had so many weights to tally and observations to record on reaching camp that I feel sure he took no reading matter. *Bleak House* was the most successful book I ever took away sledging, though a volume of poetry was useful, because it gave one something to learn by heart and repeat during the blank hours of the daily march, when the idle mind is all too apt to think of food in times of hunger, or possibly of purely imaginary grievances, which may become distorted into real foundations of discord under the abnormal strain of living for months in the unrelieved company of three other men. If your companions have much the same tastes as yourself it is best to pool your allowance of weights and take one book which will offer a wide field of thought and discussion. I have heard Scott and Wilson bless the thought which led them to take Darwin's *Origin of Species* on their first Southern Journey. Such is the object of your sledging book, but you often want the book which you read for half an hour before you go to sleep at Winter Quarters to take you into the frivolous fripperies of modern social life which you may not know and may never wish to know, but which it is often pleasant to read about, and never so much so as when its charms are so remote as to be entirely tantalizing.

Scot, who always amazed me by the amount of work he got through without any apparent effort, was essentially the driving force of the expedition: in the hut quietly organizing, working out masses of figures, taking the greatest interest in the scientific work of the station, and perhaps turning out, quite by the way, an elaborate paper on an abstruse problem in the neighbourhood; fond of his pipe and a good book, Browning, Hardy (*Tess* was one of his favourites), Galsworthy. Barrie was one of his greatest friends.

He was eager to accept suggestions if they were workable, and always keen to sift even the most unlikely theories if by any means they could be shaped to the desired end: a quick and modern brain which he applied with thoroughness to any question of practice or theory. Essentially an attractive personality, with strong likes and dislikes, he excelled in making his followers his friends by a few words of sympathy or praise: I have never known anybody, man or woman, who could be so attractive when he chose.

Sledging he went harder than any man of whom I have ever heard. Men never realized Scott until they had gone sledging with him. On our way up the Beardmore Glacier we were going at top pressure some seventeen hours out of the twenty-four, and when we turned out in the morning we felt as though we had only just turned in. By lunch time we felt that it was impossible to get through in the afternoon a similar amount of work to that which we had done in the morning. A cup of tea and two biscuits worked wonders, and the first two hours of the afternoon's march went pretty well, indeed they were the best hours' marching of the day;

but by the time we had been going some 4½ or 5 hours we were watching Scott for that glance to right and left which betokened the search for a good camping site. 'Spell oh!' Scott would cry, and then 'How's the enemy, Titus?' to Oates, who would hopefully reply that it was, say, seven o'clock. 'Oh, well, I think we'll go on a little bit more,' Scott would say. 'Come along!' It might be an hour or more before we halted and made our camp: sometimes a blizzard had its silver lining. Scott could not wait. However welcome a blizzard could be to tired bodies (I speak only of summer sledging), to Scott himself any delay was intolerable. And it is hard to realize how difficult waiting may be to one in a responsible position. It was our simple job to follow, to get up when we were roused, to pull our hardest, to do our special work as thoroughly and quickly as possible; it was Scott who had to organize distances and weights and food, as well as do the same physical work as ourselves. In sledging responsibility and physical work are combined to an extent seldom if ever found elsewhere.

His was a subtle character, full of lights and shades.

England knows Scott as a hero; she has little idea of him as a man. He was certainly the most dominating character in our not uninteresting community: indeed, there is no doubt that he would carry weight in any gathering of human beings. But few who knew him realized how shy and reserved the man was, and it was partly for this reason that he so often laid himself open to misunderstanding.

Add to this that he was sensitive, femininely sensitive, to a degree which might be considered a fault, and it will be clear that leadership to such a man may be almost a martyrdom, and that the confidence so necessary between leader and followers, which must of necessity be based upon mutual knowledge and trust, becomes in itself more difficult. It wanted an understanding man to appreciate Scott quickly; to others knowledge came with experience.

He was not a *very* strong man physically, and was in his youth a weakly child, at one time not expected to live. But he was well proportioned, with broad shoulders and a good chest, a stronger man than Wilson, weaker than Bowers or Seaman Evans. He suffered from indigestion, and told me at the top of the Beardmore that he never expected to go on during the first stage of the ascent.

Temperamentally he was a weak man, and might very easily have been an irritable autocrat. As it was he had moods and depressions which might last for weeks, and of these there is ample evidence in his diary. The man with the nerves gets things done, but sometimes he has a terrible time in doing them. He cried more easily than any man I have ever known.

What pulled Scott through was character, sheer good grain, which ran over and under and through his weaker self and clamped it together. It would be stupid to say he had all the virtues: he had, for instance, little sense of humour, and he was a bad judge of men. But you have only to read one page of what he wrote towards the end to see something of his sense of justice. For him justice was God. Indeed I think you must read all those pages; and if you have read them once, you will probably read them again. You will not need much imagination to see what manner of man he was.

And notwithstanding the immense fits of depression which attacked him, Scott was the strongest combination of a strong mind in a strong body that I have ever known. And this because he was so weak! Naturally so peevish, highly strung, irritable, depressed and moody. Practically such a conquest of himself, such vitality, such push and determination and withal in himself such personal and magnetic charm. He was naturally an idle man, he has told us so;[1] he had been a poor man, and he had a horror of leaving those dependent upon him in difficulties. You may read it over and over again in his last letters and messages.[2]

He will go down to history as the Englishman who conquered the South Pole and who died as fine a death as any man has had the honour to die. His triumphs are many – but

1. *Scott's Last Expedition*, vol. i, p. 604.
2. ibid., pp. 599, 602, 607.

the Pole was not by any means the greatest of them. Surely the greatest was that by which he conquered his weaker self, and became the strong leader whom we went to follow and came to love.

Scott had under him this year in his Main Party a total of 15 officers and 9 men. These officers may be divided into three executive officers and twelve scientific staff, but the distinction is very rough, inasmuch as a scientist such as Wilson was every bit as executive as anybody else, and the executive officers also did much scientific work. I will try here briefly to give the reader some idea of the personality and activities of these men as they work any ordinary day in the hut. It should be noticed that not all the men we had with us were brought to do sledging work. Some were chosen rather for their scientific knowledge than for their physical or other fitness for sledging. The regular sledgers in this party of officers were Scott, Wilson, Evans, Bowers, Oates (ponies), Meares (dogs), Atkinson (surgeon), Wright (physicist), Taylor (physiographer), Debenham (geologist), Gran and myself, while Day was to drive his motors as far as they would go on the Polar Journey. This leaves Simpson, who was the meteorologist and whose observations had of necessity to be continuous; Nelson, whose observations into marine biology, temperatures of sea, salinity, currents and tides came under the same heading; and Ponting, whose job was photography, and whose success in this art everybody recognizes.

However much of good I may write of Wilson, his many friends in England, those who served with him on the ship or in the hut, and most of all those who had the good fortune to sledge with him (for it is sledging which is far the greatest test) will all be dissatisfied, for I know that I cannot do justice to his value. If you knew him you could not like him: you simply had to love him. Bill was of the salt of the earth. If I were asked what quality it was before others that made him so useful, and so lovable, I think I should answer that it was because he never for one moment thought of himself. In this respect also Bowers, of whom I will speak in a moment, was most extraordinary, and in passing may I be allowed to say that this is a most necessary characteristic of a good Antarctic traveller? We had many such, officers and seamen, and the success of the expedition was in no small measure due to the general and unselfish way in which personal likes and dislikes, wishes or tastes were ungrudgingly subordinated to the common weal. Wilson and Pennell set an example of expedition first and the rest nowhere which others followed ungrudgingly: it pulled us through more than one difficulty which might have led to friction.

Wilson was a man of many parts. He was Scott's right-hand man, he was the expedition's Chief of the Scientific Staff: he was a doctor of St George's Hospital, and a zoologist specializing in vertebrates. His published work on whales, penguins and seals contained in the *Scientific Report of the Discovery Expedition* is still the best available, and makes excellent reading even to the non-scientist. On the outward journey of the *Terra Nova* he was still writing up his work for the Royal Commission on Grouse Disease, the published report of which he never lived to see. But those who knew him best will probably remember Wilson by his water-colour paintings rather than by any other form of his many-sided work.

As a boy his father sent him away on rambling holidays, the only condition being that he should return with a certain number of drawings. I have spoken of the drawings which he made when sledging or when otherwise engaged away from painting facilities, as at Hut Point. He brought back to Winter Quarters a note-book filled with such sketches of outlines and colours: of sunsets behind the Western Mountains: of lights reflected in the freezing sea or in the glass houses of the ice foot: of the steam clouds on Erebus by day and of the Aurora Australis by night. Next door to Scott he rigged up for himself a table, consisting of two venesta cases on end supporting a large drawing-board some four feet square. On this he set to work systematically to paint the effects which he had seen and noted. He painted with his paper wet, and necessarily, therefore, he worked quickly. An admirer of Ruskin, he wished to paint what he saw as truly as possible. If he failed to catch the effect he wished, he tore up the picture however beautiful the result he had obtained. There is no doubt as to the faithfulness of his colouring: the pictures recalled then and will still recall now in intimate detail the effects which we saw together. As to the accuracy of his drawing it is sufficient to say that in the *Discovery Expedition* Scott wrote of his Southern Journey:

> Wilson is the most indefatigable person. When it is fine and clear, at the end of our fatiguing days he will spend two or three hours seated in the door of the tent, sketching each detail of the splendid mountainous coast-scene to the west. His sketches are most astonishingly accurate; I have tested his proportions by actual angular measurement and found them correct.[3]

In addition to the drawings of land, pack, icebergs and Barrier, the primary object of which was scientific and geographical, Wilson has left a number of paintings of atmospheric phenomena which are not only scientifically accurate but are also exceedingly beautiful. Of such are the records of auroral displays, parhelions, paraselene, lunar halos, fog bows, iridescent clouds, refracted images of mountains and mirage generally. If you look at a picture of a parhelion by Wilson not only can you be sure that the mock suns, circles and shafts appeared in the sky as they are shown on paper, but you can also rest assured that the number of degrees between, say, the sun and the outer ring of light were in fact such as he has represented them. You can also be certain in looking at his pictures that if cirrus cloud is shown, then cirrus and not stratus cloud was in the sky: if it is not shown, then the sky was clear. It is accuracy such as this which gives an exceptional value to work viewed from a

3. Scott, *Voyage of the Discovery*, vol. ii, p. 33.

scientific standpoint. Mention should also be made of the paintings and drawings made constantly by Wilson for the various specialists on the expedition whenever they wished for colour records of their specimens; in this connexion the paintings of fish and various parasites are especially valuable.

I am not specially qualified to judge Wilson from the artistic point of view. But if you want accuracy of drawing, truth of colour, and a reproduction of the soft and delicate atmospheric effects which obtain in this part of the world, then you have them here. Whatever may be said of the painting as such, it is undeniable that an artist of this type is of inestimable value to an expedition which is doing scientific and geographical work in a little-known part of the earth.

Wilson himself set a low value on his artistic capacity. We used to discuss what Turner would have produced in a land which offered colour effects of such beauty. If we urged him to try and paint some peculiar effect and he felt that to do so was beyond his powers he made no scruple of saying so. His colour is clear, his brush-work clean: and he handled sledging subjects with the vigour of a professional who knew all there was to be known about a sledging life.

Scott and Wilson worked hand in hand to further the scientific objects of the expedition. For Scott, though no specialist in any one branch, had a most genuine love of science. 'Science – the rock foundation of all effort,' he wrote; and whether discussing ice problems with Wright, meteorology with Simpson, or geology with Taylor, he showed not only a mind which was receptive and keen to learn, but a knowledge which was quick to offer valuable suggestions. I remember Pennell condemning anything but scientific learning in dealing with the problems round us; 'no guesswork' was his argument. But he emphatically made an exception of Scott, who had an uncanny knack of hitting upon a solution. Over and over again in his diary we can read of the interest he took in pure and applied science, and it is doubtful whether this side of an expedition in high northern or southern latitudes has ever been more fortunate in their leader.

Wilson's own share in the scientific results is more obvious because he was the director of the work. But no published reports will give an adequate idea of the ability he showed in coordinating the various interests of a varied community, nor of the tact he displayed in dealing with the difficulties which arose. Above all his judgement was excellent, and Scott as well as the rest of us relied upon him to a very great extent. The value of judgement in a land where a wrong decision may mean disaster as well as loss of life is beyond all price; weather in which changes are most sudden is a case in point, also the state of sea-ice, the direction to be followed in difficult country when sledging, the best way of taking crevassed areas when they must be crossed, and all the ways by which the maximum of result may be combined with the minimum of danger in a land where Nature is sometimes almost too big an enemy to fight: all this wants judgement, and if possible experience. Wilson could supply both, for his experience was as wide as that of Scott, and I have constantly known Scott change his mind after a talk with Bill. For the rest I give quotations from Scott's diary:

'He has had a hand in almost every lecture given, and has been consulted in almost every effort which has been made towards the solution of the practical or theoretical problems of our Polar world.'[4]

Again:

Words must always fail me when I talk of Bill Wilson. I believe he really is the finest character I ever met – the closer one gets to him the more there is to admire. Every quality is so solid and dependable; cannot you imagine how that counts down here? Whatever the matter, one knows Bill will be sound, shrewdly practical, intensely loyal and quite unselfish. Add to this a wider knowledge of persons and things than is at first guessable, a quiet vein of honour and really consummate tact, and you have some idea of his values. I think he is

4. *Scott's Last Expedition*, vol. i, p. 295.

the most popular member of the party, and that is saying much.[5]

And at the end, when Scott himself lay dying, he wrote to Mrs Wilson:

'I can do no more to comfort you, than to tell you that he died as he lived, a brave, true man – the best of comrades and staunchest of friends.'[6]

Physically Scott had been a delicate boy but developed into a strong man, 5 feet 9 inches in height, 11 stone 6 lbs. in weight, with a chest measurement of 39¼ inches. Wilson was not a particularly strong man. On leaving with the *Discovery* he was but lately cured of consumption, yet he went with Scott to his farthest South, and helped to get Shackleton back alive. Shackleton owed his life to those two. Wilson was of a slimmer, more athletic build, a great walker, 5 feet 10½ inches in height, 11 stones in weight, with a chest measurement of 36 inches. He was an ideal example of my contention, which I believe can be proved many times over to be a fact, that it is not strength of body but rather strength of will which carries a man farthest where mind and body are taxed at the same time to their utmost limit. Scott was 43 years of age at his death, and Wilson 39.

Bowers was of a very different build. Aged 28, he was only 5 feet 4 inches in height while his chest measurement (which I give more as a general guide to his physique than for any other reason) was 40 inches, and his weight 12 stones. He was recommended to Scott by Sir Clements Markham, who was dining one day with Captain Wilson-Barker on the *Worcester*, on which ship Bowers was trained. Bowers was then home from India, and the talk turned to the Antarctic. Wilson-Barker turned to Sir Clements in the course of conversation and alluding to Bowers said: 'Here is a man who will be leading one of those expeditions some day.'

He lived a rough life after passing from the *Worcester* into

5. ibid., pp. 432–3.
6. *Scott's Last Expedition*, vol. i, p. 597.

the merchant service, sailing five times round the world in the *Loch Torridon*. Thence he passed into the service of the Royal Indian Marine, commanded a river gunboat on the Irrawaddy, and afterwards served on H.M.S. *Fox*, where he had considerable experience, often in open boats, preventing the gun-running which was carried on by the Afghans in the Persian Gulf.

Thence he came to us.

It is at any rate a curious fact, and it may be a significant one, that Bowers, who enjoyed a greater resistance to cold than any man on this expedition, joined it direct from one of the hottest places on the globe. My knowledge is insufficient to say whether it is possible that any trace can be found here of cause and effect, especially since the opposite seems to be the more common experience, in that such people as return from India to England generally find the English winter trying. I give the fact for what it may be worth, remarking only that the cold of an English winter is generally damp, while that of the Antarctic is dry, so far at any rate as the atmosphere is concerned. Bowers himself always professed the greatest indifference not only to cold, but also to heat, and his indifference was not that of a *poseur*, as many experiences will show.

At the same time he was temperamentally one who refused to admit difficulties. Indeed, if he did not actually welcome them he greeted them with scorn, and in scorning went far to master them. Scott believed that difficulties were made to be overcome: Bowers certainly believed that he was the man to overcome them. This self-confidence was based on a very deep and broad religious feeling, and carried conviction with it. The men swore by him both on the ship and ashore. 'He's all right,' was their judgement of his seamanship, which was admirable. 'I like being with Birdie, because I always know where I am,' was the remark made to me by an officer one evening as we pitched the tent. We had just been spending some time in picking up a depot which a less able man might well have missed.

As he was one of the two or three greatest friends of my

life I find it hard to give the reader a mental picture of Birdie Bowers which will not appear extravagant. There were times when his optimism appeared forced and formal, though I believe it was not really so: there were times when I have almost hated him for his infernal cheerfulness. To those accustomed to judge men by the standards of their fashionable and corseted drawing-rooms Bowers appeared crude. 'You couldn't kill that man if you took a pole-axe to him,' was the comment of a New Zealander at a dance at Christchurch. Such men may be at a discount in conventional life; but give me a snowy ice-floe waving about on the top of a black swell, a ship thrown aback, a sledge-party almost shattered, or one that has just upset their supper on to the floorcloth of the tent (which is much the same thing), and I will lie down and cry for Bowers to come and lead me to food and safety.

Those whom the gods love die young. The gods loved him, if indeed it be benevolent to show your favourites a clear, straight, shining path of life, with plenty of discomfort and not a little pain, but with few doubts and no fears. Browning might well have had Bowers in mind when he wrote of

One who never turned his back, but marched breast forward;
    Never doubted clouds would break;
Never dreamed, though right were worsted, wrong would
    triumph;
        Held we fall to rise, are baffled to fight better,
            Sleep to wake.

There was nothing subtle about him. He was transparently simple, straightforward and unselfish. His capacity for work was prodigious, and when his own work happened to take less than his full time he characteristically found activity in serving a scientist or exercising an animal. So he used to help to send up balloons with self-recording instruments attached to them, and track the threads which led to them when detached. He was responsible for putting up the three outlying meteorological screens and read them more often than anybody else. At times he looked after some of the dogs because at the moment there was nobody else whose proper job it happened to be, and he took a particular fancy to one of our strongest huskies called Krisravitza, which is the Russian (so I'm told) for 'most beautiful'. This fancy originated in the fact that to Kris, as the most truculent of our untamed devils, fell a large share of well-deserved punishment. A living thing in trouble be it dog or man was something to be helped. Being the smallest man in the party he schemed to have allotted to him the largest pony available both for the Depot and Polar Journeys. Their exercise, when he succeeded, was a matter for experiment, for his knowledge of horses was as limited as his love of animals was intense. He started to exercise his second pony (for the first was lost on the floe) by riding him. 'I'll soon get used to him,' he said one day when Victor had just deposited him in the tide-crack, 'to say nothing of his getting used to me,' he added in a more subdued voice.

This was open-air work, and as such more congenial than that which had to be done inside the hut. But his most important work was indoors, and he brought to it just the same restless enthusiasm which allowed no leisure for reading or relaxation.

He joined as one of the ship's officers in London. Given charge of the stores, the way in which he stowed the ship aroused the admiration of even the stevedores, especially when he fell down the main hatch one morning on to the pig-iron below, recovered consciousness in about half a minute, and continued work for the rest of the day as though nothing had happened.

As the voyage out proceeded it became obvious that his knowledge of the stores and undefeatable personality would be of great value to the shore party, and it was decided that he should land, to his great delight. He was personally responsible for all food supplies, whether for home consumption or for sledging, for all sledging stores and the distribution of weights, the loading of sledges, the consumption of coal, the issue of clothing, bosun's stores, and carpenter's stores. Incidentally the keeper of stores wanted a very exact knowledge of the cases which contained them, for the drifts of snow soon buried them as they lay in the camp outside.

As time proved his capacity Scott left one thing after another in Bowers's hands. Scott was a leader of men, and it is a good quality in such to delegate work from themselves on to those who prove their power to shoulder the burden. Undoubtedly Bowers saved Scott a great deal of work, and gave him time which he might not otherwise have been able to spare to interest himself in the scientific work of the station, greatly to its benefit, and do a good deal of useful writing. The two ways in which Bowers helped Scott most this winter were in the preparation of the plans and the working out of the weights of the Southern Journey, which shall be discussed later, and in the routine work of the station, for which he was largely responsible, and which ran so smoothly that I am unable to tell the reader how the stores were issued, or the dinner settled, by what rule the working parties for fetching ice for water and other kindred jobs about the camp were ordered. They just happened, and I don't know how. I only know that Bowers had the bunk above mine in the hut, and that when I was going to sleep he was generally standing on a chair and using his own bunk as a desk, and I conclude from the numerous lists of stores and weights which are now in my hands that these were being produced. Anyway the job was done, and the fact that we knew nothing about it goes far to prove how efficiently it was carried through.

For him difficulties simply did not exist. I have never known a more buoyant, virile nature. Scott's writings abound in references to the extraordinary value he placed upon his help, and after the share which he took in the Depot and Winter Journeys it was clear that he would probably be taken in the Polar Party, as indeed proved to be the case. No man of that party better deserved his place. 'I believe he is the hardest traveller that ever undertook a Polar Journey, as well as one of the most undaunted.'[7]

The standard is high.

Bowers gave us two of our best lectures, the first on the Evolution of Sledge Foods, at the end of which he discussed our own rations on the Depot Journey, and made suggestions which he had worked out scientifically for those of the Polar Journey. His arguments were sound enough to disarm the hostility if not to convert to his opinions at least one scientist who had come to hear him strongly of opinion that an untrained man should not discuss so complex a subject. The second lecture, on the Evolution of Polar Clothing, was also the fruit of much work. The general conclusion come to (and this was after the Winter Journey) was that our own clothing and equipment could not be bettered in any important respect, though it must be always understood that the expedition wore wind-proof clothing and not furs, except for hands and feet. When man-hauling, wind-proof, I am convinced, cannot be improved upon, but for dog-driving in cold weather I suspect that furs may be better.

The table was cleared after supper and we sat round it for these lectures three times a week. There was no compulsion about them, and the seamen only turned up for those which especially interested them, such as Meares's vivid account of his journeyings on the Eastern or Chinese borderland of Thibet. This land is inhabited by the 'Eighteen Tribes', the original inhabitants of Thibet who were driven out by the present inhabitants, and Meares told us chiefly of the Lolos who killed his companion Brook after having persuaded him that they were friendly and anxious to help him.

He had no pictures and very makeshift maps, yet he held us entranced for nearly two hours by the sheer interest of his adventures. The spirit of the wanderer is in Meares's blood: he has no happiness but in the wild places of the earth. I have

7. *Scott's Last Expedition*, vol. 1. p. 362.

never met so extreme a type. Even now he is looking forward
to getting away by himself to Hut Point, tired already of our
scant measure of civilization.[8]

Three lectures a week were too many in the opinion of the
majority. The second winter with our very reduced company
we had two a week, and I feel sure that this was an
improvement. No officer nor seaman, however, could have
had too many of Ponting's lectures, which gave us glimpses
into many lands illustrated by his own inimitable slides. Thus
we lived every now and then for a short hour in Burmah,
India or Japan, in scenes of trees and flowers and feminine
charm which were the very antithesis of our present situation,
and we were all the better for it. Ponting also illustrated the
subjects of other lectures with home-made slides of photographs taken during the autumn or from printed books. But
for the most part the lecturers were perforce content with
designs and plans, drawn on paper and pinned one on the top
of the other upon a large drawing-board propped up on the
table and torn off sheet by sheet.

From the practical point of view the most interesting
evening to us was that on which Scott produced the Plan of
the Southern Journey. The reader may ask why this was not
really prepared until the winter previous to the journey itself,
and the answer clearly is that it was impossible to arrange
more than a rough idea until the autumn sledging had taught
its lesson in food, equipment, relative reliability of dogs,
ponies and men, and until the changes and chances of our life
showed exactly what transport would be available for the
following sledging season. Thus it was with lively anticipation that we sat down on 8 May, an advisory committee as
it were, to hear and give our suggestions on the scheme
which Scott had evolved in the early weeks of the winter
after the adventures of the Depot Journey and the loss of six
ponies.

It was on just such a winter night, too, that Scott read his

8. *Scott's Last Expedition*, vol. i. p. 396.

interesting paper on the Ice Barrier and Inland Ice which will probably form the basis for all future work on these subjects. The Barrier, he maintained, is probably afloat, and covers at least five times the extent of the North Sea with an average thickness of some 400 feet, though it has only been possible to get the very roughest of levels. According to the movement of a depot laid in the *Discovery* days the Barrier moved 608 yards towards the open Ross Sea in 13½ months. It must be admitted that the inclination of the ice-sheet is not sufficient to cause this, and the old idea that the glacier streams flowing down from the Inland Plateau provide the necessary impetus is imperfect. It was Simpson's suggestion that 'the deposition of snow on the Barrier leads to an expansion due to the increase of weight'. Some admittedly vague ideas as to the extent and character of the inland ice-sheet ended a clever and convincing paper which contained a lot of good reasoning.

Simpson proved an excellent lecturer, and in meteorology and in the explanation of the many instruments with which his corner of the hut was full he possessed subjects which interested and concerned everybody. Nelson on Biological Problems and Taylor on Physiography were always interesting. 'Taylor, I dreamt of your lecture last night. How could I live so long in the world and not know something of so fascinating a subject!' Thus Scott on the morning following one of these lectures.[9] Wright on Ice Problems, Radium, and the Origin of Matter had highly technical subjects which left many of us somewhat befogged. But Atkinson on Scurvy had an audience each member of which felt that he had a personal interest in the subject under discussion. Indeed one of his hearers was to suffer the advanced stage of this dread disease within six months. Atkinson inclined to Almroth Wright's theory that scurvy is due to an acid intoxication of the blood caused by bacteria. He described the litmus-paper test which was practised on us monthly, and before and after sledge journeys. In this the blood of each individual is drawn

9. *With Scott: The Silver Lining*, Taylor, p. 240.

and various strengths of dilute sulphuric acid are added to it until it is neutralized, the healthy man showing normal 30 to 50, while the man with scorbutic signs will be normal 50 to 90 according to the stage to which he has reached. The only thing which is certain to stop scurvy is fresh vegetables: fresh meat when life is otherwise under extreme conditions will not do so, an instance being the Siege of Paris when they had plenty of horse meat. In 1795 voyages were being ruined by scurvy and Anson lost 300 out of 500 men, but in that year the first discoveries were made and lime-juice was introduced by Blaine. From this time scurvy practically disappeared from the Navy, and there was little scurvy in Nelson's days; but the reason is not clear, since, according to modern research, lime-juice only helps to prevent it. It continued in the Merchant Service, and in a decade from about 1865 some 400 cases were admitted into the Dreadnought Hospital, whereas in the decade 1887 to 1896 there were only 38 cases. We had, at Cape Evans, a salt of sodium to be used to alkalize the blood as an experiment, if necessity arose. Darkness, cold, and hard work are in Atkinson's opinion important causes of scurvy.

Nansen was an advocate of variety of diet as being anti-scorbutic, and Scott recalled a story told him by Nansen which he had never understood. It appeared that some men had eaten tins of tainted food. Some of it was slightly tainted, some of it was really bad. They rejected the really bad ones, and ate those only which were slightly tainted. 'And of course,' said Nansen, 'they should have eaten the worst.'

I have since asked Nansen about this story. He tells me that he must have been referring to the crew of the *Windward*, the ship of the Jackson-Harmsworth Expedition to Franz Josef Land in 1894–7. The crew of this ship, which was travelling to and from civilization, got scurvy, though the land party kept healthy. Of this Jackson writes:

> In the case of the crew of the *Windward* I fear that there was considerable carelessness in the use of tinned meats that were not free from taint, although tins quite gone were

rejected. . . . We [on shore] largely used fresh bear's meat, and the crew of the *Windward* were also allowed as much as they could be induced to eat. They, however, preferred tinned meat several days a week to a diet of bear's meat alone; and some of the crew had such a prejudice against bear's meat as to refuse to eat it at all.[10]

Of course tainted food should not have been eaten at all, but if it had to be eaten, then, according to Nansen, the ptomaines which cause scurvy in the earlier stages of decomposition are destroyed by the ferment which forms in the later stages. They should therefore have taken the worst tins, if any at all.

Wilson was strongly of opinion that fresh meat alone would stop scurvy: on the *Discovery* seal meat cured it. As to scurvy on Scott's *Discovery* Southern Journey, he made light of it: however, during the Winter Journey I remember Wilson stating that Shackleton several times fell in a faint as he got outside the tent, and he seems to have been seriously ill: Wilson knew that he himself had scurvy some time before the others knew it, because the discoloration of his gums did not show in front for some time. He did not think their dogs on that journey had scurvy, but ptomaine poisoning from fish which had travelled through the tropics. He was of opinion that on returning from sledge journeys on the *Discovery* they had wrongly attributed to scurvy such symptoms as rash on the body, swollen legs and ankles, which were rather the result of excessive fatigue. I may add that we had these signs on our return from the Winter Journey.

Then there were lectures on Geology by Debenham, on birds and beasts and also on Sketching by Wilson, on Surveying by Evans: but perhaps no lecture remains more vividly in my memory than that given by Oates on what *we* called 'The Mismanagement of Horses'. Of course to all of us who were relying upon the ponies for the first stage of the Southern Journey the subject was of interest as well as utility,

10. F. G. Jackson, *A Thousand Days in the Arctic*, vol. ii, pp. 380–81.

but the greater share of interest centred upon the lecturer, for it was certainly supposed that taciturn Titus could not have concealed about his person the gift of the gab, and it was as certain as it could be that the whole business was most distasteful to him. Imagine our delight when he proved to have an elaborate discourse with full notes of which no one had seen the preparation. 'I have been fortunate in securing another night,' he mentioned amidst mirth, and proceeded to give us the most interesting and able account of the minds and bodies of horses in general and ours in particular. He ended with a story of a dinner-party at which he was a guest, probably against his will. A young lady was so late that the party sat down to dinner without waiting longer. Soon she arrived covered with blushes and confusion. 'I'm sorry,' she said, 'but that horse was the limit, he . . .' 'Perhaps it was a jibber,' suggested her hostess to help her out. 'No, he was a—. I heard the cabby tell him so several times.'

Titus Oates was the most cheerful and lovable old pessimist that you could imagine. Often, after tethering and feeding our ponies at a night camp on the Barrier, we would watch the dog-teams coming up into camp. 'I'll give these dogs ten days more,' he would murmur in a voice such as some people used when they heard of a British victory. I am acquainted with so few dragoons that I do not know their general characteristics. Few of them, I imagine, would have gone about with the slouch which characterized his method of locomotion, nor would many of them have dined in a hat so shabby that it was picked off the peg and passed round as a curiosity.

He came to look after the horses, and as an officer in the Inniskillings he, no doubt, had excellent training. But his skill went far deeper than that. There was little he didn't know about horses, and the pity is that he did not choose our ponies for us in Siberia: we should have had a very different lot. In addition to his general charge of them all, Oates took as his own pony the aforesaid devil Christopher for the Southern Journey and for previous training. We shall hear much more of Christopher, who appeared to have come down to the Antarctic to initiate the well-behaved inhabitants into all the vices of civilization, but from beginning to end Oates's management of this animal might have proved a model to any governor of a lunatic asylum. His tact, patience and courage, for Christopher was a very dangerous beast, remain some of the most vivid recollections of a very gallant gentleman.

In this connexion let me add that no animals could have had more considerate and often self-sacrificing treatment than these ponies of ours. Granted that they must be used at all (and I do not mean to enter into that question) they were fed, trained, and even clothed as friends and companions rather than as beasts of burden. They were never hit, a condition to which they were clearly unaccustomed. They lived far better than they had before, and all this was done for them in spite of the conditions under which we ourselves lived. We became very fond of our beasts, but we could not be blind to their faults. The mind of a horse is a very limited concern, relying almost entirely upon memory. He rivals our politicians in that he has little real intellect. Consequently, when the pony was faced with conditions different from those to which he was accustomed, he showed but little adaptability; and when you add to this frozen harness and rugs, with all their straps and buckles and lashings, an incredible facility for eating anything within reach including his own tethering ropes and the headstalls, fringes and whatnots of his companions, together with our own scanty provisions and a general wish to do anything except the job of the moment, it must be admitted that the pony leader's lot was full of occasions for bad temper. Nevertheless leaders and ponies were on the best of terms (excepting always Christopher), which is really not surprising when you come to think that most of the leaders were sailors whose love of animals is profound.

A lean-to roof was built against the northern side of the hut, and the ends and open side were boarded up. This building when buttressed by the bricks of coal which formed our fuel, and drifted up with snow by the blizzards, formed an extremely sheltered and even warm stable. The ponies stood in stalls with their heads towards the hut and divided from it by a corridor; the bars which kept them in carried also their food boxes. They lay down very little, the ground was too cold, and Oates was of opinion that litter would not have benefited them if we had had space in the ship to bring it. The floor of their stall was formed of the gravel on which the hut was built. On any future occasion it might be worth consideration whether a flooring of wood might add to their comfort. As you walked down this narrow passage you passed a line of heads, many of which would have a nip at you in the semi-darkness, and at the far end Oates had rigged up for himself a blubber stove, more elaborate than the one we had made with the odds and ends at Hut Point, but in principle the same, in that the fids of sealskin with the blubber attached to them were placed on a grid, and the heat generated caused them to drop their oil on to ashes below which formed the fire. This fire not only warmed the stable, but melted the snow to water the ponies and heated their bran mashes. I do not wonder that this warm companionable home appealed to their minds when they were exercising in the cold, dark, windy sea-ice: they were always trying to get rid of their leader, and if successful generally went straight back to the hut. Here they would dodge their pursuers until such time as they were sick of the game, when they quietly walked into the stable of their own accord to be welcomed with triumphant squeals and kicking by their companions.

I have already spoken of their exercise. Their ration during the winter was as follows:

8 a.m. Chaff.
12 noon. Snow. Chaff and oats or oil-cake alternate days.
5 p.m. Snow. Hot bran mash with oil-cake, or boiled oats and chaff; finally a small quantity of hay.

In the spring they were got into condition on hard food all cold, and by a carefully increased scale of exercise during the latter part of which they drew sledges with very light loads.

Unfortunately I have no record as to what changes of feeding stuffs Oates would have made if it had been possible.

Certainly we should not have brought the bales of compressed fodder, which as I have already explained,[11] was theoretically green wheat cut young, but practically no manner of use as a food, though of some use perhaps as bulk. Probably he would have used hay for this purpose at Winter Quarters had our stock of it not been very limited, for hay takes up too much room on a ship when every square inch of stowage space is of value. The original weights of fodder with which we left New Zealand were: compressed chaff, 30 tons; hay, 5 tons; oil-cake, 5–6 tons; bran, 4–5 tons; and two kinds of oats, of which the white was better than the black. We wanted more bran than we had.[12] This does not exhaust our list of feeding stuffs, for one of our ponies called Snippets would eat blubber, and so far as I know it agreed with him.

We left New Zealand with nineteen ponies, seventeen of which were destined for the Main Party and two for the help of Campbell in the exploration of King Edward VII's Land. Two of these died in the big gale at sea, and we landed fifteen ponies at Cape Evans in January. Of these we lost six on the Depot Journey, while Hackenschmidt, who was a vicious beast, sickened and wasted away in our absence, for no particular reason that we could discover, until there was nothing to do but shoot him. Thus eight only out of the original seventeen Main Party ponies which started from New Zealand were left by the beginning of the winter.

I have told[13] how, during our absence on the Depot Journey, the ship had tried to land Campbell with his two ponies on King Edward VII's Land, but had been prevented from reaching it by pack ice. Coasting back in search of a landing place they found Amundsen in the Bay of Whales. Under the circumstances Campbell decided not to land his party there but to try and land on the north coast of South Victoria Land, in which he was finally successful. In the

11. See p. 182.
12. *Scott's Last Expedition*, vol. i. p. 4.
13. See pp. 131–2.

interval the ship returned to Cape Evans with the news, and since he was of opinion that his animals would be useless to him in that region he took the opportunity to swim the two ponies ashore, a distance of half a mile, for the ship could get no nearer and the sea-ice had gone. Thus we started the winter with Campbell's two ponies (Jehu and Chinaman), two ponies which had survived the Depot Journey (Nobby and James Pigg), and six ponies which had been left at Cape Evans (Snatcher, Snippets, Bones, Victor, Michael and Christopher), a total of ten.

Of these ten Christopher was the only real devil with vice, but he was a strong pony, and it was clear that he would be useful if he could be managed. Bones, Snatcher, Victor and Snippets were all useful ponies. Michael was a highly-strung nice beast, but his value was doubtful; Chinaman was more doubtful still, and it was questionable sometimes whether Jehu would be able to pull anything at all. This leaves Nobby and Jimmy Pigg, both of which were with us on the Depot Journey. Nobby was the better of the two; he was the only survivor from the sea-ice disaster, and I am not sure that his rescue did not save the situation with regard to the Pole. Jimmy Pigg was wending his way slowly back from Corner Camp at this time and so was also saved. He was a weak pony but did extremely well on the Polar Journey. It may be coincidence that these two ponies, the only ponies which had gained previous sledging experience, did better according to their strength than any of the others, but I am inclined to believe that their familiarity with the conditions on the Barrier was of great value to them, doing away with much useless worry and exhaustion.

And so it will be understood with what feelings of anxiety any cases of injury or illness to our ponies were regarded. The cases of injury were few and of small importance, thanks to the care with which they were exercised in the dark on ice which was by no means free from inequalities. Let me explain in passing that this ice is almost always covered by at least a thin layer of drifted snow and for the most part is not slippery. Every now and then there would be a great banging and crashing heard through the walls of the hut in the middle of the night. The watchman would run out, Oates put on his boots, Scott be audibly uneasy. It was generally Bones or Chinaman kicking their stalls, perhaps to keep themselves warm, but by the time the watchman had reached the stable he would be met by a line of sleepy faces blinking at him in the light of the electric torch, each saying plainly that he could not possibly have been responsible for a breach of the peace!

But antics might easily lead to accidents, and more than once a pony was found twisted up in some way in his stall, or even to have fallen to the ground. Their heads were tied on either side to the stanchions of the stall, and so if they tried to lie down complications might arise. More alarming was the one serious case of illness, preceded by a slighter case of a similar nature in another pony. Jimmy Pigg had a slight attack of colic in the middle of June, but he was feeding all right again during the evening of the same day. It was at noon, 14 July, that Bones went off his feed. This was followed by spasms of acute pain.

> Every now and again he attempted to lie down, and Oates
> eventually thought it was wiser to allow him to do so. Once
> down, his head gradually drooped until he lay at length, every
> now and then twitching very horribly with the pain, and
> from time to time raising his head and even scrambling to his
> legs when it grew intense. I don't think I ever realized before
> how pathetic a horse could be under such conditions; no
> sound escapes him, his misery can only be indicated by those
> distressing spasms and by dumb movement of the head with
> a patient expression always suggestive of appeal.[14]

Towards midnight it seemed that we were to lose him, and, apart from other considerations, we knew that unless we could keep all the surviving animals alive the risks of failure in the coming journey were much increased.

14. *Scott's Last Expedition*, vol. i, p. 352.

THE WORST JOURNEY IN THE WORLD

It was shortly after midnight when I [Scott] was told that
the animal seemed a little easier. At 2.30 I was again in the
stable and found the improvement had been maintained; the
horse still lay on its side with outstretched head, but the
spasms had ceased, its eye looked less distressed, and its ears
pricked to occasional noises. As I stood looking it suddenly
raised its head and rose without effort to its legs; then in a
moment, as though some bad dream had passed, it began to
nose at some hay and at its neighbour. Within three minutes
it had drunk a bucket of water and had started to feed.[15]

The immediate cause of the trouble was indicated by 'a
small ball of semi-fermented hay covered with mucus and
containing tape-worms; so far not very serious, but unfortunately attached to this mass was a strip of the lining of the
intestine.'[16]

The recovery of Bones was uninterrupted. Two days later
another pony went off his feed and lay down, but was soon
well again.

Considerable speculation as to the original cause of this
illness never found a satisfactory answer. Some traced it to a
want of ventilation, and it is necessary to say that both the
ponies who were ill stood next to the blubber stove; at any
rate a big ventilator was fitted and more fresh air let in.
Others traced it to the want of water, supposing that the
animals would not eat as much snow as they would have
drunk water; the easy remedy for this was to give them water
instead of snow. We also gave them more salt than they had
had before. Whatever the cause may have been we had no
more of this colic, and the improvement in their condition
until we started sledging was uninterrupted.

All the ponies were treated for worms; it was also found
that they had lice, which were eradicated after some time and
difficulty by a wash of tobacco and water. I know that Oates
wished that he had clipped the ponies at the beginning of the
winter, believing that they would have grown far better coats

15. ibid., p. 353.   16. ibid., vol. i, p. 353.

if this had been done. He also would have wished for a loose box for each pony.

No account of the ponies would be complete without mention of our Russian pony boy, Anton. He was small in height, but he was exceedingly strong and had a chest measurement of 40 inches.

I believe both Anton and Dimitri, the Russian dog driver, were brought originally to look after the ponies and dogs on their way from Siberia to New Zealand. But they proved such good fellows and so useful that we were very glad to take them on the strength of the landing party. I fear that Anton, at any rate, did not realize what he was in for. When we arrived at Cape Crozier in the ship on our voyage south, and he saw the two great peaks of Ross Island in front and the Barrier Cliff disappearing in an unbroken wall below the eastern horizon, he imagined that he had reached the South Pole, and was suitably elated. When the darkness of the winter closed down upon us, this apparently unnatural order of things so preyed upon his superstitious mind that he became seriously alarmed. Where the sea-ice joined the land in front of the hut was of course a working crack, caused by the rise and fall of the tide. Sometimes the sea-water found its way up, and Anton was convinced that the weird phosphorescent lights which danced up out of the sea were devils. In propitiation we found that he had sacrificed to them his most cherished luxury, his scanty allowance of cigarettes, which he had literally cast upon the waters in the darkness. It was natural that his thoughts should turn to the comforts of his Siberian home, and the one-legged wife whom he was going to marry there, and when it became clear that another year would be spent in the South his mind was troubled. And so he went to Oates and asked him, 'If I go away at the end of this year, will Captain Scott disinherit me?' In order to try and express his idea, for he knew little English, he had some days before been asking 'what we called it when a father died and left his son nothing'. Poor Anton!

He looked long and anxiously for the ship, and with his

kit-bag on his shoulder was amongst the first to trek across the ice to meet her. Having asked for and obtained a job of work there was no happier man on board: he never left her until she reached New Zealand. Nevertheless he was always cheerful, always working, and a most useful addition to our small community.

It is still usual to talk of people living in complete married happiness when we really mean, so Mr Bernard Shaw tells me, that they confine their quarrels to Thursday nights. If then I say that we lived this life for nearly three years, from the day when we left England until the day we returned to New Zealand, without any friction of any kind, I shall be supposed to be making a formal statement of somewhat limited truth. May I say that there is really no formality about it, and nothing but the truth. To be absolutely accurate I must admit to having seen a man in a very 'prickly' state on one occasion. That was all. It didn't last and may have been well justified for aught I know: I have forgotten what it was all about. Why we should have been more fortunate than polar travellers in general it is hard to say, but undoubtedly a very powerful reason was that we had no idle hours: there was no time to quarrel.

Before we went South people were always saying, 'You will get fed up with one another. What will you do all the dark winter?' As a matter of fact the difficulty was to get through with the work. Often after working all through a long night-watch officers carried on as a matter of course through the following day in order to clear off arrears. There was little reading or general relaxation during the day: certainly not before supper, if at all. And while no fixed hours for work were laid down, the custom was general that all hours between breakfast and supper should be so used.

Our small company was desperately keen to obtain results. The youngest and most cynical pessimist must have had cause for wonder to see a body of healthy and not unintellectual men striving thus single-mindedly to add their small quota of scientific and geographical knowledge to the sum total of the world – with no immediate prospect of its practical utility. Laymen and scientists alike were determined to attain the objects to gain which they had set forth.

And I believe that in a vague intangible way there was an ideal in front of and behind this work. It is really not desirable for men who do not believe that knowledge is of value for its own sake to take up this kind of life. The question constantly put to us in civilization was and still is: 'What is the use? Is there gold? or Is there coal?' The commercial spirit of the present day can see no good in pure science: the English manufacturer is not interested in research which will not give him a financial return within one year: the city man sees in it only so much energy wasted on unproductive work: truly they are bound to the wheel of conventional life.

Now unless a man believes that such a view is wrong he has no business to be 'down South'. Our magnetic and meteorological work may, I suppose, have a fairly immediate bearing upon commerce and shipping: otherwise I cannot imagine any branch of our labours which will do more at present than swell the central pool of unapplied knowledge. The members of this expedition believed that it was worth while to discover new land and new life, to reach the Southern Pole of the earth, to make elaborate meteorological and magnetic observations and extended geological surveys with all the other branches of research for which we were equipped. They were prepared to suffer great hardship; and some of them died for their beliefs. Without such ideals the spirit which certainly existed in our small community would have been impossible.

But if the reasons for this happy state of our domestic life were due largely to the adaptability and keenness of the members of our small community, I doubt whether the frictions which have caused other expeditions to be less comfortable than they might have been, would have been avoided in our case, had it not been for the qualities in some of our men which set a fashion of hard work without any thought of personal gain.

With all its troubles it is a good life. We came back from the Barrier, telling one another we loathed the place and nothing on earth should make us return. But now the Barrier comes back to 'us, with its clean, open life, and the smell of the cooker, and its soft sound sleep. So much of the trouble of this world is caused by memories, for we only remember half.

We have forgotten – or nearly forgotten – how the loss of a biscuit crumb left a sense of injury which lasted for a week; how the greatest friends were so much on one another's nerves that they did not speak for days for fear of quarrelling; how angry we felt when the cook ran short on the weekly bag; how sick we were after the first meals when we could eat as much as we liked; how anxious we were when a man fell ill many hundreds of miles from home, and we had a fortnight of thick weather and had to find our depots or starve. We remember the cry of *Camp Ho!* which preceded the cup of tea which gave us five more miles that evening; the good fellowship which completed our supper after safely crossing a bad patch of crevasses; the square inch of plum pudding which celebrated our Christmas Day; the chanties we sang all over the Barrier as we marched our ponies along.

We travelled for Science. Those three small embryos from Cape Crozier, that weight of fossils from Buckley Island, and that mass of material, less spectacular, but gathered just as carefully hour by hour in wind and drift, darkness and cold, were striven for in order that the world may have a little more knowledge, that it may build on what it knows instead of on what it thinks.

Some of our men were ambitious: some wanted money, others a name; some a help up the scientific ladder, others an F.R.S. Why not? But we had men who did not care a rap for money or fame. I do not believe it mattered to Wilson when he found that Amundsen had reached the Pole a few days before him – not much. Pennell would have been very bored if you had given him a knighthood. Lillie, Bowers, Priestley, Debenham, Atkinson and many others were much the same.

But there is no love lost between the class of men who go out and do such work and the authorities at home who deal with their collections. I remember a conversation in the hut during the last bad winter. Men were arguing fiercely that professionally they lost a lot by being down South, that they fell behind in current work, got out of the running and so forth. There is a lot in that. And then the talk went on to the publication of results, and the way in which they would wish them done. A said he wasn't going to hand over his work to be mucked up by such and such a body at home; B said he wasn't going to have his buried in museum bookshelves never to be seen again; C said he would jolly well publish his own results in the scientific journals. And the ears of the armchair scientists who might deal with our hard-won specimens and observations should have been warm that night.

At the time I felt a little indignant. It seemed to me that these men ought to think themselves lucky to be down South at all: there were thousands who would have liked to take their place. But now I understand quite a lot more than I did then. Science is a big thing if you can travel a Winter Journey in her cause and not regret it. I am not sure she is not bigger still if you can have dealings with scientists and continue to follow in her path.

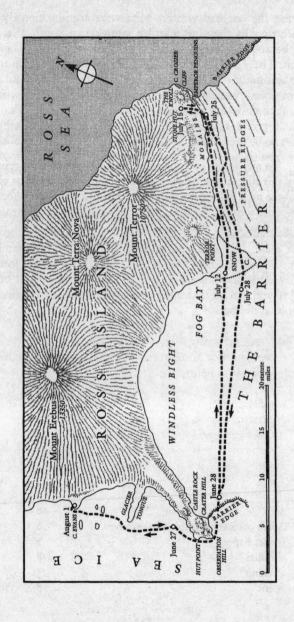

ROSS SEA

N

C. CROZIER
CLIFF
EMPEROR PENGUINS
BARRIER EDGE

THE KNOLL
STONE HUT July 15
MORAINE July 25

Mount Terra-Nova

Mount Terror
10750

PRESSURE RIDGES

ROSS ISLAND

TERROR POINT

Mount Erebus
13350

FOG BAY

SNOW
July 12 July 28

WINDLESS BIGHT

THE BARRIER

GLACIER
TONGUE

CASTLE ROCK
CRATER HILL

June 28

August 1
C. EVANS

HUT POINT
June 27
OBSERVATION HILL

BARRIER
EDGE

20 statute
miles

S E A   I C E

0   5   10   15

Chapter Seven
THE WINTER JOURNEY

Ah, but a man's reach should exceed his grasp,
Or what's a Heaven for?

R. BROWNING, *Andrea del Sarto*

To me, and to everyone who has remained here the result of this effort is the appeal it makes to our imagination, as one of the most gallant stories in Polar History. That men should wander forth in the depth of a Polar night to face the most dismal cold and the fiercest gales in darkness is something new; that they should have persisted in this effort in spite of every adversity for five full weeks is heroic. It makes a tale for our generation which I hope may not be lost in the telling.

Scott's diary, at Cape Evans

THE FOLLOWING list of the Winter Journey sledge weights (for three men) is taken from the reckoning made by Bowers before we started:

Expendible Stores	lbs.	lbs.
'Antarctic' biscuit	135	
3 Cases for same	12	
Pemmican	110	
Butter	21	
Salt	3	
Tea	4	
Oil	60	
Spare parts for primus, and matches	2	
Toilet Paper	2	
Candles	8	
Packing	5	
Spirit	8	370

Permanent Weights, etc.	lbs.	lbs.
		370
2 9-ft Sledges, 41 lbs. each	82	
1 Cooker complete	13	
2 Primus filled with oil	8	
1 Double tent complete	35	
1 Sledging shovel	3.5	
3 Reindeer sleeping-bags, 12 lbs. each	36	
3 Eider-down sleeping-bag linings, 4 lbs. each	12	
1 Alpine rope	5	
1 Bosun's bag, containing repairing materials, and		
1 Bonsa outfit, containing repairing tools	5	
3 Personal bags, each containing 15 lbs.		
spare clothing, etc.	45	
Lamp box with knives, steel, etc., for seal and		
penguin	21	
Medical and scientific box	40	
2 Ice axes, 3 lbs. each	6	
3 Man-harnesses	3	
3 Portaging harnesses	3	
Cloth for making roof and door for stone igloo	24	
Instrument box	7	
3 pairs skis and sticks (discarded afterwards)	33	
1 Pickaxe	11	
3 Crampons, 2 lbs. 3 oz. each	6.5	
2 Bamboos for measuring tide if possible,		
14 feet each	4	
2 Male bamboos	4	
1 Plank to form top of door of igloo	2	
1 Bag sennegrass	1	
6 Small female bamboo ends and		
1 Knife for cutting snow block to make igloo	4	
Packing	8	420*
		790

* This total as given in the Penguin edition of 1970.

The 'Lamp box' mentioned above contained the following:

1 Lamp for burning blubber.	1 Blubber cooker.
1 Lamp for burning spirit.	1 Blowpipe.
1 Tent candle lamp.	

The party of three men set out with a total weight of 757 lbs. to draw, the ski and sticks in the above list being left behind at the last moment.

It was impossible to load the total bulk upon one 12-ft sledge, and so two 9-ft sledges were taken, one toggled on behind the other. While this made the packing and handling of gear much easier, it nearly doubled the friction surface against which the party had to pull.

June 22. Midwinter Night

A hard night: clear, with a blue sky so deep that it looks black: the stars are steel points: the glaciers burnished silver. The snow rings and thuds to your footfall. The ice is cracking to the falling temperature and the tide crack groans as the water rises. And over all, wave upon wave, fold upon fold, there hangs the curtain of the aurora. As you watch, it fades away, and then quite suddenly a great beam flashes up and rushes to the zenith, an arch of palest green and orange, a tail of flaming gold. Again it falls, fading away into great search-light beams which rise behind the smoking crater of Mount Erebus. And again the spiritual veil is drawn –

Here at the roaring loom of Time I ply
And weave for God the garment thou seest him by.

Inside the hut are orgies. We are very merry – and indeed why not? The sun turns to come back to us tonight, and such a day comes only once a year.

After dinner we had to make speeches, but instead of making a speech Bowers brought in a wonderful Christmas tree, made of split bamboos and a ski stick, with feathers tied to the end of each branch; candles, sweets, preserved fruits, and the most absurd toys of which Bill was the owner. Titus got three things which pleased him immensely, a sponge, a whistle, and a pop-gun which went off when he pressed the butt. For the rest of the evening he went round asking whether you were sweating. 'No.' 'Yes, you are,' he said, and wiped your face with the sponge. 'If you want to please me very much you will jfall down when I shoot you,' he said to me, and then he went round shooting everybody. At intervals he blew the whistle.

He danced the Lancers with Anton, and Anton, whose dancing puts that of the Russian Ballet into the shade, continually apologized for not being able to do it well enough. Ponting gave a great lecture with slides which he had made since we arrived, many of which Meares had coloured. When one of these came up one of us would shout, 'Who coloured that,' and another would cry, 'Meares,' – then uproar. It was impossible for Ponting to speak. We had a milk punch, when Scott proposed the Eastern Party, and Clissold, the cook, proposed Good Old True Milk. Titus blew away the ball of his gun. 'I blew it into the cerulean – how doth Homer have it? – cerulean azure – hence Erebus.' As we turned in he said, 'Cherry, are you responsible for your actions?' and when I said Yes, he blew loudly on his whistle, and the last thing I remembered was that he woke up Meares to ask him whether he was fancy free.

It was a magnificent bust.

Five days later and three men, one of whom at any rate is feeling a little frightened, stand panting and sweating out in McMurdo Sound. They have two sledges, one tied behind the other, and these sledges are piled high with sleeping-bags and camping equipment, six weeks' provisions, and a venesta case full of scientific gear for pickling and preserving. In addition there is a pickaxe, ice-axes, an Alpine rope, a large piece of green Willesden canvas and a bit of board. Scott's amazed remark when he saw our sledges two hours ago, 'Bill, why are you taking all this oil?' pointing to the six cans lashed to the tray on the second sledge, had a bite in it. Our weights for such travelling are enormous – 253 lbs. a man.

It is midday but it is pitchy dark, and it is not warm.

As we rested my mind went back to a dusty, dingy office in Victoria Street some fifteen months ago. 'I want you to come,' said Wilson to me, and then, 'I want to go to Cape Crozier in the winter and work out the embryology of the Emperor penguins, but I'm not saying much about it – it might never come off.' Well! this was better than Victoria Street, where the doctors had nearly refused to let me go because I could only see the people across the road as vague blobs walking. Then Bill went and had a talk with Scott about it, and they said I might come if I was prepared to take the additional risk. At that time I would have taken anything.

After the Depot Journey, at Hut Point, walking over that beastly, slippery, sloping ice-foot which I always imagined would leave me some day in the sea, Bill asked me whether I would go with him – and who else for a third? There can have been little doubt whom we both wanted, and that evening Bowers had been asked. Of course he was made to come. And here we were. 'This winter travel is a new and bold venture,' wrote Scott in the hut that night, 'but the right men have gone to attempt it.'

I don't know. There never could have been any doubt about Bill and Birdie. Probably Lashly would have made the best third, but Bill had a prejudice against seamen for a journey like this – 'They don't take enough care of themselves, and they *will* not look after their clothes.' But Lashly was wonderful – if Scott had only taken a four-man party and Lashly to the Pole!

What is this venture? Why is the embryo of the Emperor penguin so important to Science? And why should three sane and common-sense explorers be sledging away on a winter's night to a Cape which has only been visited before in daylight, and then with very great difficulty?

The Emperor is a bird which cannot fly, lives on fish and never steps on land even to breed. It lays its eggs on the bare ice during the winter and carries out the whole process of incubation on the sea-ice, resting the egg upon its feet, pressed closely to the lower abdomen. But it is because the Emperor is probably the most primitive bird in existence that the working out of his embryology is so important. The embryo shows remains of the development of an animal in former ages and former states; it recapitulates its former lives. The embryo of an Emperor may prove the missing link between birds and the reptiles from which birds have sprung.

Only one rookery of Emperor Penguins had been found at this date, and this was on the sea-ice inside a little bay of the Barrier edge of Cape Crozier, which was guarded by miles of some of the biggest pressure in the Antarctic. Chicks had been found in September, and Wilson reckoned that the eggs must be laid in the beginning of July. And so we started just after midwinter on the weirdest bird's-nesting expedition that has ever been or ever will be.

But the sweat was freezing in our clothing and we moved on. All we could see was a black patch away to our left which was Turk's Head: when this disappeared we knew that we had passed Glacier Tongue which, unseen by us, eclipsed the rocks behind. And then we camped for lunch.

That first camp only lives in my memory because it began our education of camp work in the dark. Had we now struck the blighting temperature which we were to meet . . .

There was just enough wind to make us want to hurry: down harness, each man to a strap on the sledge – quick with the floor cloth – the bags to hold it down – now a good spread with the bamboos and the tent inner lining – hold them, Cherry, and over with the outer covering – snow on to the skirting and inside with the cook with his candle and a box of matches. . . .

That is how we tied it: that is the way we were accustomed to do it, day after day and night after night when the sun was still high or at any rate only setting, sledging on the Barrier in spring and summer and autumn; pulling our hands from our mitts when necessary – plenty of time to warm up afterwards; in the days when we took pride in getting our tea boiling within twenty minutes of throwing off our harness: when the man who wanted to work in his fur mitts was thought a bit too slow.

But now it *didn't* work. 'We shall have to go a bit slower,' said Bill, and 'we shall get more used to working in the dark.' At this time, I remember, I was still trying to wear spectacles.

We spent that night on the sea-ice, finding that we were too far in towards Castle Rock; and it was not until the following afternoon that we reached and lunched at Hut Point. I speak of day and night, though they were much the same, and later on when we found that we could not get the work into a twenty-four-hour day, we decided to carry on as though such a convention did not exist; as in actual fact it did not. We had already realized that cooking under these conditions would be a bad job, and that the usual arrangement by which one man was cook for the week would be intolerable. We settled to be cook alternately day by day. For food we brought only pemmican and biscuit and butter; for drink we had tea, and we drank hot water to turn in on.

Pulling out from Hut Point that evening we brought along our heavy loads on the two nine-foot sledges with comparative ease; it was the first, and though we did not know it then, the only bit of good pulling we were to have. Good pulling to the sledge traveller means easy pulling. Away we went round Cape Armitage and eastwards. We knew that the Barrier edge was in front of us and also that the break-up of the sea-ice had left the face of it as a low perpendicular cliff. We had therefore to find a place where the snow had formed a drift. This we came right up against and met quite suddenly a very keen wind flowing, as it always does, from the cold Barrier down to the comparatively warm sea-ice. The temperature was −47° F., and I was a fool to take my hands out of my mitts to haul on the ropes to bring the sledges up. I started away from the Barrier edge with all ten fingers frostbitten. They did not really come back until we were in the tent for our night meal, and within a few hours there were two or three large blisters, up to an inch long, on all of them. For many days those blisters hurt frightfully.

We were camped that night about half a mile in from the Barrier edge. The temperature was −56°. We had a baddish time, being very glad to get out of our shivering bags next morning (29 June). We began to suspect, as we knew only too well later, that the only good time of the twenty-four hours was breakfast, for then with reasonable luck we need not get into our sleeping-bags again for another seventeen hours.

The horror of the nineteen days it took us to travel from Cape Evans to Cape Crozier would have to be re-experienced to be appreciated; and any one would be a fool who went again: it is not possible to describe it. The weeks which followed them were comparative bliss, not because later our conditions were better – they were far worse – but because we were callous. I for one had come to that point of suffering at which I did not really care if only I could die without much pain. They talk of the heroism of the dying – they little know – it would be so easy to die, a dose of morphia, a friendly crevasse, and blissful sleep. The trouble is to go on . . .

It was the darkness that did it. I don't believe minus seventy temperatures would be bad in daylight, not comparatively bad, when you could see where you were going, where you were stepping, where the sledge straps were, the cooker, the primus, the food; could see your footsteps lately trodden deep into the soft snow that you might find your way back to the rest of your load; could see the lashings of the food bags; could read a compass without striking three or four different boxes to find one dry match; could read your watch to see if the blissful moment of getting out of your bag was come without groping in the snow all about; when it would not take you five minutes to lash up the door of the tent, and five hours to get started in the morning . . .

But in these days we were never less than four hours from the moment when Bill cried 'Time to get up' to the time when we got into our harness. It took two men to get one man into his harness, and was all they could do, for the canvas was frozen and our clothes were frozen until sometimes not even two men could bend them into the required shape.

The trouble is sweat and breath. I never knew before how much of the body's waste comes out through the pores of the skin. On the most bitter days, when we had to camp before we had done a four-hour march in order to nurse back our frozen feet, it seemed that we must be sweating. And all this sweat, instead of passing away through the porous wool of our clothing and gradually drying off us, froze and accumulated. It passed just away from our flesh and then became ice: we shook plenty of snow and ice down from inside our trousers every time we changed our foot-gear, and we could have shaken it from our vests and from between our vests and shirts, but of course we could not strip to this extent. But when we got into our sleeping-bags, if we were fortunate, we became warm enough during the night to thaw this ice: part remained in our clothes, part passed into the skins of our sleeping-bags, and soon both were sheets of armour-plate.

As for our breath – in the daytime it did nothing worse than cover the lower parts of our faces with ice and solder our balaclavas tightly to our heads. It was no good trying to get your balaclava off until you had had the primus going quite a long time, and then you could throw your breath about if you wished. The trouble really began in your sleeping-bag, for it was far too cold to keep a hole open through which to breathe. So all night long our breath froze into the skins, and our respiration became quicker and quicker as the air in our bags got fouler and fouler: it was never possible to make a match strike or burn inside our bags!

Of course we were not iced up all at once: it took several days of this kind of thing before we really got into big difficulties on this score. It was not until I got out of the tent one morning fully ready to pack the sledge that I realized the possibilities ahead. We had had our breakfast, struggled into our foot-gear, and squared up inside the tent, which was comparatively warm. Once outside, I raised my head to look round and found I could not move it back. My clothing had frozen hard as I stood – perhaps fifteen seconds. For four hours I had to pull with my head stuck up, and from that time we all took care to bend down into a pulling position before being frozen in.

By now we had realized that we must reverse the usual sledging routine and do everything slowly, wearing when possible the fur mitts which fitted over our woollen mitts, and always stopping whatever we were doing, directly we felt that any part of us was getting frozen, until the circulation was restored. Henceforward it was common for one or other of us to leave the other two to continue the camp work while he stamped about in the snow, beat his arms, or nursed some exposed part. But we could not restore the circulation of our feet like this – the only way then was to camp and get some hot water into ourselves before we took our foot-gear off. The difficulty was to know whether our feet were frozen or not, for the only thing we knew for certain was that we had lost all feeling in them. Wilson's knowledge as a doctor came in here: many a time he had to decide from our descriptions of our feet whether to camp or to go on for another hour. A wrong decision meant disaster, for if one of us had been crippled the whole party would have been placed in great difficulties. Probably we should all have died.

On 29 June the temperature was −50° all day and there was sometimes a light breeze which was inclined to frost-bite our faces and hands. Owing to the weight of our two sledges and the bad surface our pace was not more than a slow and very heavy plod: at our lunch camp Wilson had the heel and sole of one foot frost-bitten, and I had two big toes. Bowers was never worried by frost-bitten feet.

That night was very cold, the temperature falling to −66°, and it was −55° at breakfast on 30 June. We had not shipped the eider-down linings to our sleeping-bags, in order to keep them dry as long as possible. My own fur bag was too big for me, and throughout this journey was more difficult to thaw out than the other two: on the other hand, it never split, as did Bill's.

We were now getting into that cold bay which lies between the Hut Point Peninsula and Terror Point. It was known from old *Discovery* days that the Barrier winds are deflected from this area, pouring out into McMurdo Sound behind us, and into the Ross Sea at Cape Crozier in front. In consequence of the lack of high winds the surface of the snow is never swept and hardened and polished as elsewhere: it was now a mass of the hardest and smallest snow crystals, to pull through which in cold temperatures was just like pulling through sand. I have spoken elsewhere of Barrier surfaces, and how, when the cold is very great, sledge runners cannot melt the crystal points but only advance by rolling them over and over upon one another. That was the surface we met on this journey, and in soft snow the effect is accentuated. Our feet were sinking deep at every step.

And so when we tried to start on 30 June we found we could not move both sledges together. There was nothing for it but to take one on at a time and come back for the other. This has often been done in daylight when the only risks run are those of blizzards which may spring up suddenly and obliterate tracks. Now in darkness it was more complicated. From 11 a.m. to 3 p.m. there was enough light to see the big holes made by our feet, and we took on one sledge, trudged back in our tracks, and brought on the second. Bowers used to toggle and untoggle our harnesses when we changed sledges. Of course in this relay work we covered three miles in distance for every one mile forward, and even the single sledges were very hard pulling. When we lunched the temperature was −61°. After lunch the little light had gone, and we carried a naked lighted candle back with us when we went to find our second sledge. It was the weirdest kind of procession, three frozen men and a little pool of light. Generally we steered by Jupiter, and I never see him now without recalling his friendship in those days.

We were very silent, it was not very easy to talk: but sledging is always a silent business. I remember a long discussion which began just now about cold snaps – was this the normal condition of the Barrier, or was it a cold snap? – what constituted a cold snap? The discussion lasted about a week. Do things slowly, always slowly, that was the burden of Wilson's leadership: and every now and then the question, Shall we go on? and the answer Yes. 'I think we are all right as long as our appetites are good,' said Bill. Always patient, self-possessed, unruffled, he was the only man on earth, as I believe, who could have led this journey.

That day we made 3¼ miles, and travelled 10 miles to do it. The temperature was −66° when we camped, and we were already pretty badly iced up. That was the last night I lay (I had written slept) in my big reindeer bag without the lining of eider-down which we each carried. For me it was a very bad night: a succession of shivering fits which I was quite unable to stop, and which took possession of my body for many minutes at a time until I thought my back would break, such was the strain placed upon it. They talk of chattering teeth: but when your body chatters you may call yourself cold. I can only compare the strain to that which I have been unfortunate enough to see in a case of lock-jaw. One of my big toes was frost-bitten, but I do not know for how long. Wilson was fairly comfortable in his smaller bag, and Bowers was snoring loudly. The minimum temperature that night as taken under the sledge was −69°; and as taken on the sledge was −75°. That is a hundred and seven degrees of frost.

We did the same relay work on 1 July, but found the pulling harder still; and it was all that we could do to move the one sledge forward. From now onwards Wilson and I, but not to the same extent as Bowers, experienced a curious optical delusion when returning in our tracks for the second sledge. I have said that we found our way back by the light of a candle, and we found it necessary to go back in our same footprints. These holes became to our tired brains not depressions but elevations: hummocks over which we stepped, raising our feet painfully and draggingly. And then we remembered, and said what fools we were, and for a while we compelled ourselves to walk through these phantom hills. But it was no lasting good, and as the days passed we realized that we must suffer this absurdity, for we could not do anything else. But of course it took it out of us.

During these days the blisters on my fingers were very painful. Long before my hands were frost-bitten, or indeed anything but cold, which was of course a normal thing, the matter inside these big blisters, which rose all down my fingers with only a skin between them, was frozen into ice. To handle the cooking gear or the food bags was agony; to start the primus was worse; and when, one day, I was able to prick six or seven of the blisters after supper and let the liquid matter out, the relief was very great. Every night after that I treated such others as were ready in the same way until they gradually disappeared. Sometimes it was difficult not to howl.

I *did* want to howl many times every hour of these days and nights, but I invented a formula instead, which I repeated to myself continually. Especially, I remember, it came in useful when at the end of the march with my feet frost-bitten, my heart beating slowly, my vitality at its lowest ebb, my body solid with cold, I used to seize the shovel and go on digging snow on to the tent skirting while the cook inside was trying to light the primus. 'You've got it in the neck – stick it – stick it – you've got it in the neck,' was the refrain, and I wanted every little bit of encouragement it would give me: then I would find myself repeating 'Stick it – stick it – stick it – stick it,' and then 'You've got it in the neck.' One of the joys of summer sledging is that you can let your mind wander thousands of miles away for weeks and weeks. Oates used to provision his little yacht (there was a pickled herring he was going to have): I invented the compactest little revolving bookcase which was going to hold not books, but pemmican and chocolate and biscuit and cocoa and sugar, and have a cooker on the top, and was going to stand always ready to quench my hunger when I got home: and we visited restaurants and theatres and grouse moors, and we thought of a pretty girl, or girls, and. . . . But now that was all impossible. Our conditions forced themselves upon us without pause: it was not possible to think of anything else. We got no respite. I found it best to refuse to let myself think of the past or the future – to live only for the job of the moment, and to compel myself to think only how to do it most efficiently. Once you let yourself imagine . . .

This day also (1 July) we were harassed by a nasty little wind which blew in our faces. The temperature was −66°, and in such temperatures the effect of even the lightest airs is blighting, and immediately freezes any exposed part. But we all fitted the bits of wind-proof lined with fur, which we had made in the hut, across our balaclavas in front of our noses, and these were of the greatest comfort. They formed other places upon which our breath could freeze, and the lower parts of our faces were soon covered with solid sheets of ice, which was in itself an additional protection. This was a normal and not uncomfortable condition during the journey: the hair on our faces kept the ice away from the skin, and for myself I would rather have the ice than be without it, until I want to get my balaclava off to drink my hoosh. We only made 2¼ miles, and it took 8 hours.

It blew force 3 that night with a temperature of −65.2°, and there was some drift. This was pretty bad, but luckily the wind dropped to a light breeze by the time we were ready to start the next morning (2 July). The temperature was then −60°, and continued so all day, falling lower in the evening. At 4 p.m. we watched a bank of fog form over the peninsula to our left and noticed at the same time that our frozen mitts thawed out on our hands, and the outlines of the land as shown by the stars became obscured. We made 2½ miles with the usual relaying, and camped at 8 p.m. with the temperature −65°. It really was a terrible march, and parts of both my feet were frozen at lunch. After supper I pricked six or seven of the worst blisters, and the relief was considerable.

I have met with amusement people who say, 'Oh, we had minus fifty temperatures in Canada; they didn't worry *me*,' or 'I've been down to minus sixty something in Siberia.' And then you find that they had nice dry clothing, a nice night's sleep in a nice aired bed, and had just walked out after lunch for a few minutes from a nice warm hut or an overheated train. And they look back upon it as an experience to be remembered. Well! of course as an experience of cold this can only be compared to eating a vanilla ice with hot chocolate cream after an excellent dinner at Claridge's. But in our present state we began to look upon minus fifties as a luxury which we did not often get.

That evening, for the first time, we discarded our naked candle in favour of the rising moon. We had started before the moon on purpose, but as we shall see she gave us little light. However, we owed our escape from a very sticky death to her on one occasion.

It was a little later on when we were among crevasses, with Terror above us, but invisible, somewhere on our left, and the Barrier pressure on our right. We were quite lost in the darkness, and only knew that we were running downhill, the sledge almost catching our heels. There had been no light all day, clouds obscured the moon, we had not seen her since yesterday. And quite suddenly a little patch of clear sky drifted, as it were, over her face, and she showed us three paces ahead a great crevasse with just a shining icy lid not much thicker than glass. We should all have walked into it, and the sledge would certainly have followed us down. After that I felt we had a chance of pulling through: God could not be so cruel as to have saved us just to prolong our agony.

But at present we need not worry about crevasses; for we had not reached the long stretch where the moving Barrier, with the weight of many hundred miles of ice behind it, comes butting up against the slopes of Mount Terror, itself some eleven thousand feet high. Now we were still plunging ankle-deep in the mass of soft sandy snow which lies in the windless area. It seemed to have no bottom at all, and since the snow was much the same temperature as the air, our feet, as well as our bodies, got colder and colder the longer we marched: in ordinary sledging you begin to warm up after a quarter of an hour's pulling, here it was just the reverse. Even now I find myself unconsciously kicking the toes of my right foot against the heels of my left: a habit I picked up on this journey by doing it every time we halted. Well no. Not always. For there was one halt when we just lay on our backs and gazed up into the sky, where, so the others said, there was blazing the most wonderful aurora they had ever seen. I did not see it, being so near-sighted and unable to wear spectacles owing to the cold. The aurora was always before us as we travelled east, more beautiful than any seen by previous expeditions wintering in McMurdo Sound, where Erebus must have hidden the most brilliant displays. Now most of the sky was covered with swinging, swaying curtains which met in a great whirl overhead: lemon yellow, green and orange.

The minimum this night was −65°, and during 3 July it ranged between −52° and −58°. We got forward only 2½ miles, and by this time I had silently made up my mind that we had not the ghost of a chance of reaching the penguins. I am sure that Bill was having a very bad time these nights, though it was an impression rather than anything else, for he never said so. We knew we did sleep, for we heard one another snore, and also we used to have dreams and night-mares; but we had little consciousness of it, and we were now beginning to drop off when we halted on the march.

Our sleeping-bags were getting really bad by now, and already it took a long time to thaw a way down into them at night. Bill spread his in the middle, Bowers was on his right, and I was on his left. Always he insisted that I should start getting my legs into mine before *he* started: we were rapidly cooling down after our hot supper, and this was very unselfish of him. Then came seven shivering hours and first thing on getting out of sleeping-bags in the morning we stuffed our personal gear into the mouth of the bag before it could freeze: this made a plug which when removed formed a frozen hole for us to push into as a start in the evening.

We got into some strange knots when trying to persuade our limbs into our bags, and suffered terribly from cramp in consequence. We would wait and rub, but directly we tried to move again down it would come and grip our legs in a vice. We also, especially Bowers, suffered agony from cramp in the stomach. We let the primus burn on after supper now for a time – it was the only thing which kept us going – and when one who was holding the primus was seized with cramp we hastily took the lamp from him until the spasm was over. It was horrible to see Birdie's stomach cramp sometimes: he certainly got it much worse than Bill or I. I suffered a lot from heartburn, especially in my bag at nights: we were eating a great proportion of fat and this was probably the cause. Stupidly I said nothing about it for a long time. Later when Bill found out, he soon made it better with the medical case.

Birdie always lit the candle in the morning – so called, and this was an heroic business. Moisture collected on our matches if you looked at them. Partly I suppose it was bringing them from outside into a comparatively warm tent; partly from putting boxes into pockets in our clothing. Sometimes it was necessary to try four or five boxes before a match struck. The temperature of the boxes and matches was about a hundred degrees of frost, and the smallest touch of the metal on naked flesh caused a frost-bite. If you wore mitts you could scarcely feel anything – especially since the tips of our fingers were already very callous. To get the first light going in the morning was a beastly cold business, made worse by having to make sure that it was at last time to get up. Bill insisted that we must lie in our bags seven hours every night.

In civilization men are taken at their own valuation because there are so many ways of concealment, and there is so little time, perhaps even so little understanding. Not so down South. These two men went through the Winter Journey and lived: later they went through the Polar Journey and died. They were gold, pure, shining, unalloyed. Words cannot express how good their companionship was.

Through all these days, and those which were to follow, the worst I suppose in their dark severity that men have ever come through alive, no single hasty or angry word passed their lips. When, later, we were sure, so far as we can be sure of anything, that we must die, they were cheerful, and so far as I can judge their songs and cheery words were quite unforced. Nor were they ever flurried, though always as quick as the conditions would allow in moments of emergency. It is hard that often such men must go first when others far less worthy remain.

There are those who write of Polar Expeditions as though the whole thing was as easy as possible. They are trusting, I suspect, in a public who will say, 'What a fine fellow this is! we know what horrors he has endured, yet see, how little he makes of all his difficulties and hardships.' Others have gone to the opposite extreme. I do not know that there is any use in trying to make a −18° temperature appear formidable to an uninitiated reader by calling it fifty degrees of frost. I want to do neither of these things. I am not going to pretend that this was anything but a ghastly journey, made bearable and even pleasant to look back upon by the qualities of my two companions who have gone. At the same time I have no wish to make it appear more horrible than it actually was: the reader need not fear that I am trying to exaggerate.

During the night of 3 July the temperature dropped to −65°, but in the morning we wakened (we really did wake that morning) to great relief. The temperature was only −27° with the wind blowing some 15 miles an hour with steadily falling snow. It only lasted a few hours, and we knew it must be blowing a howling blizzard outside the windless area in which we lay, but it gave us time to sleep and rest, and get thoroughly thawed, and wet, and warm, inside our sleeping-bags. To me at any rate this modified blizzard was a great relief, though we all knew that our gear would be worse than ever when the cold came back. It was quite impossible to march. During the course of the day the temperature dropped to −44°: during the following night to −54°.

The soft new snow which had fallen made the surface the next day (5 July) almost impossible. We relayed as usual, and managed to do eight hours' pulling, but we got forward only 1½ miles. The temperature ranged between −55° and −61°, and there was at one time a considerable breeze, the effect of which was paralysing. There was the great circle of a halo round the moon with a vertical shaft, and mock moons. We hoped that we were rising on to the long snow cape which marks the beginning of Mount Terror. That night the temperature was −75°; at breakfast −70°; at noon nearly −77°. The day lives in my memory as that on which I found out that records are not worth making. The thermometer as swung by Bowers after lunch at 5.51 p.m. registered −77.5°, which is 109½ degrees of frost, and is I suppose as cold as any one will want to endure in darkness and iced-up gear and clothes. The lowest temperature recorded by a *Discovery* Spring Journey party was −67.7°,[1] and in those days fourteen days was a long time for a Spring Party to be away sledging, and they were in daylight. This was our tenth day out and we hoped to be away for six weeks.

Luckily we were spared wind. Our naked candle burnt steadily as we trudged back in our tracks to fetch our other sledge, but if we touched metal for a fraction of a second with naked fingers we were frost-bitten. To fasten the strap buckles over the loaded sledge was difficult: to handle the cooker, or mugs, or spoons, the primus or oil can was worse. How Bowers managed with the meteorological instruments I do not know, but the meteorological log is perfectly kept. Yet as soon as you breathed near the paper it was covered with a film of ice through which the pencil would not bite. To handle rope was always cold and in these very low temperatures dreadfully cold work. The toggling up of our harnesses to the sledge we were about to pull, the untoggling at the end of the stage, the lashing up of our sleeping-bags in the morning, the fastening of the cooker to the top of the instrument box, were bad, but not nearly so bad as the smaller lashings which were now strings of ice. One of the worst was round the weekly food bag, and those round the pemmican, tea and butter bags inside were thinner still. But

1. A thermometer which registered −77° at the Winter Quarters of H.M.S. *Alert* on 4 March 1876 is preserved by the Royal Geographical Society. I do not know whether it was screened.

the real devil was the lashing of the tent door: it was like wire, and yet had to be tied tight. If you had to get out of the tent during the seven hours spent in our sleeping-bags you must tie a string as stiff as a poker, and re-thaw your way into a bag already as hard as a board. Our paraffin was supplied at a flash point suitable to low temperatures and was only a little milky: it was very difficult to splinter bits off the butter.

The temperature that night was −75.8°, and I will not pretend that it did not convince me that Dante was right when he placed the circles of ice below the circles of fire. Still we slept sometimes, and always we lay for seven hours. Again and again Bill asked us how about going back, and always we said no. Yet there was nothing I should have liked better: I was quite sure that to dream of Cape Crozier was the wildest lunacy. That day we had advanced 1½ miles by the utmost labour, and the usual relay work. This was quite a good march – and Cape Crozier is 67 miles from Cape Evans!

More than once in my short life I have been struck by the value of the man who is blind to what appears to be a common-sense certainty: he achieves the impossible. We never spoke our thoughts: we discussed the Age of Stone which was to come, when we built our cosy warm rock hut on the slopes of Mount Terror, and ran our stove with penguin blubber, and pickled little Emperors in warmth and dryness. We were quite intelligent people, and we must all have known that we were not going to see the penguins and that it was folly to go forward. And yet with quiet persever-ance, in perfect friendship, almost with gentleness those two men led on. I just did what I was told.

It is desirable that the body should work, feed and sleep at regular hours, and this is too often forgotten when sledging. But just now we found we were unable to fit 8 hours marching and 7 hours in our sleeping-bags into a 24-hour day: the routine camp work took more than 9 hours, such were the conditions. We therefore ceased to observe the quite imaginary difference between night and day, and it was noon on Friday (7 July) before we got away. The temperature was −68° and there was a thick white fog: generally we had but the vaguest idea where we were, and we camped at 10 p.m. after managing 1¾ miles for the day. But what a relief. Instead of labouring away, our hearts were beating more naturally: it was easier to camp, we had some feeling in our hands, and our feet had not gone to sleep. Birdie swung the thermometer and found it only −55°. 'Now if we tell people that to get only 87 degrees of frost can be an enormous relief they simply won't believe us,' I remember saying. Perhaps you won't, but it was, all the same: and I wrote that night: 'There is something after all rather good in doing something never done before.' Things were looking up, you see.

Our hearts were doing very gallant work. Towards the end of the march they were getting beaten and were finding it difficult to pump the blood out to our extremities. There were few days that Wilson and I did not get some part of our feet frost-bitten. As we camped. I suspect our hearts were beating comparatively slowly and weakly. Nothing could be done until a hot drink was ready – tea for lunch, hot water for supper. Directly we started to drink then the effect was wonderful: it was, said Wilson, like putting a hot-water bottle against your heart. The beats became very rapid and strong and you felt the warmth travelling outwards and downwards. Then you got your foot-gear off – puttees (cut in half and wound round the bottom of the trousers), finnesko, saennegrass, hair socks, and two pairs of woollen socks. Then you nursed back your feet and tried to believe you were glad – a frost-bite does not hurt until it begins to thaw. Later came the blisters, and then the chunks of dead skin.

Bill was anxious. It seems that Scott had twice gone for a walk with him during the Winter, and tried to persuade him not to go, and only finally consented on condition that Bill brought us all back unharmed: we were Southern Journey men. Bill had a tremendous respect for Scott, and later when we were about to make an effort to get back home over the Barrier, and our case was very desperate, he was more anxious to leave no gear behind at Cape Crozier, even the scientific gear which could be of no use to us and of which we had plenty more at the hut. 'Scott will never forgive me if I leave gear behind,' he said. It is a good sledging principle, and the party which does not follow it, or which leaves some of its load to be fetched in later is seldom a good one: but it is a principle which can be carried to excess.

And now Bill was feeling terribly responsible for both of us. He kept on saying that he was sorry, but he had never dreamed it was going to be as bad as this. He felt that having asked us to come he was in some way chargeable with our troubles. When leaders have this kind of feeling about their men they get much better results, if the men are good: if men are bad or even moderate they will try and take advantage of what they consider to be softness.

The temperature on the night of 7 July was $-59°$.

On 8 July we found the first sign that we might be coming to an end of this soft, powdered, arrowrooty snow. It was frightfully hard pulling; but every now and then our finnesko pierced a thin crust before they sank right in. This meant a little wind, and every now and then our feet came down on a hard slippery patch under the soft snow. We were surrounded by fog which walked along with us, and far above us the moon was shining on its roof. Steering was as difficult as the pulling, and four hours of the hardest work only produced $1\frac{1}{4}$ miles in the morning, and three more hours 1 mile in the afternoon – and the temperature was $-57°$ with a breeze – horrible!

In the early morning of the next day snow began to fall and the fog was dense: when we got up we could see nothing at all anywhere. After the usual four hours to get going in the morning we settled that it was impossible to relay, for we should never be able to track ourselves back to the second sledge. It was with very great relief that we found we could move both sledges together, and I think this was mainly due to the temperature which had risen to $-36°$.

This was our fourth day of fog in addition to the normal darkness, and we knew we must be approaching the land. It would be Terror Point, and the fog is probably caused by the moist warm air coming up from the sea through the pressure cracks and crevasses; for it is supposed that the Barrier here is afloat.

I wish I could take you on to the great Ice Barrier some calm evening when the sun is just dipping in the middle of the night and show you the autumn tints on Ross Island. A last look round before turning in, a good day's march behind, enough fine fat pemmican inside you to make you happy, the homely smell of tobacco from the tent, a pleasant sense of soft fur and the deep sleep to come. And all the softest colours God has made are in the snow; on Erebus to the west, where the wind can scarcely move his cloud of smoke; and on Terror to the east, not so high, and more regular in form. How peaceful and dignified it all is.

That was what you might have seen four months ago had you been out on the Barrier plain. Low down on the extreme right or east of the land there was a black smudge of rock peeping out from great snow-drifts: that was the Knoll, and close under it were the cliffs of Cape Crozier, the Knoll looking quite low and the cliffs invisible, although they are eight hundred feet high, a sheer precipice falling to the sea.

It is at Cape Crozier that the Barrier edge, which runs for four hundred miles as an ice-cliff up to 200 feet high, meets the land. The Barrier is moving against this land at a rate which is sometimes not much less than a mile in a year. Perhaps you can imagine the chaos which it piles up: there are pressure ridges compared to which the waves of the sea are like a ploughed field. These are worst at Cape Crozier itself, but they extend all along the southern slopes of Mount Terror, running parallel with the land, and the disturbance which Cape Crozier makes is apparent at Corner Camp some forty miles back on the Barrier in the crevasses we used to find and the occasional ridges we had to cross.

In the *Discovery* days the pressure just where it hit Cape Crozier formed a small bay, and on the sea-ice frozen in this bay the men of the *Discovery* found the only Emperor penguin rookery which had ever been seen. The ice here was not blown out by the blizzards which cleared the Ross Sea, and open water or open leads were never far away. This gave the Emperors a place to lay their eggs and an opportunity to find their food. We had therefore to find our way along the pressure to the Knoll, and thence penetrate *through* the pressure to the Emperors' Bay. And we had to do it in the dark.

Terror Point, which we were approaching in the fog, is a short twenty miles from the Knoll, and ends in a long snow-tongue running out into the Barrier. The way had been travelled a good many times in *Discovery* days and in daylight, and Wilson knew there was a narrow path, free from crevasses, which skirted along between the mountain and the pressure ridges running parallel to it. But it is one thing to walk along a corridor by day, and quite another to try to do so at night, especially when there are no walls by which you can correct your course – only crevasses. Anyway, Terror Point must be somewhere close to us now, and vaguely in front of us was that strip of snow, neither Barrier nor mountain, which was our only way forward.

We began to realize, now that our eyes were more or less out of action, how much we could do with our feet and ears. The effect of walking in finnesko is much the same as walking in gloves, and you get a sense of touch which nothing else except bare feet could give you. Thus we could feel every small variation in surface, every crust through which our feet broke, every hardened patch below the soft snow. And soon we began to rely more and more upon the sound of our footsteps to tell us whether we were on crevasses or solid ground. From now onwards we were working among crevasses fairly constantly. I loathe them in full daylight when much can be done to avoid them, and when if you fall into them you can at any rate see where the sides are, which way they run and how best to scramble out; when your companions can see how to stop the sledge to which you are all attached by your harness; how most safely to hold the sledge when stopped; how, if you are dangling fifteen feet down in a chasm, to work above you to get you up to the surface again. And then our clothes were generally something like clothes. Even under the ideal conditions of good light, warmth and no wind, crevasses are beastly, whether you are pulling over a level and uniform snow surface, never knowing what moment will find you dropping into some bottomless pit, or whether you are rushing for the Alpine rope and the sledge, to help some companion who has disappeared. I dream sometimes now of bad days we had on the Beardmore and elsewhere, when men were dropping through to be caught up and hang at the full length of the harnesses and toggles many times in an hour. On the same sledge as myself on the Beardmore one man went down once head first, and another eight times to the length of his harness in 25 minutes. And always you wondered whether your harness was going to hold when the jerk came. But those days were a Sunday School treat compared to our days of blind-man's-bluff with the Emperor penguins among the crevasses of Cape Crozier.

Our troubles were greatly increased by the state of our clothes. If we had been dressed in lead we should have been able to move our arms and necks and heads more easily than we could now. If the same amount of icing had extended to our legs I believe we should still be there, standing unable to move: but happily the forks of our trousers still remained movable. To get into our canvas harness was the most absurd business. Quite in the early days of our journey we met with this difficulty, and somewhat foolishly decided not to take off our harness for lunch. The harnesses thawed in the tent, and froze back as hard as boards. Likewise our clothing was hard as boards and stuck out from our bodies in every imaginable fold and angle. To fit one board over the other required the efforts of the would-be wearer and his two companions, and the process had to be repeated for each one of us twice a day. Goodness knows how long it took; but it cannot have been less than five minutes' thumping at each man.

As we approached Terror Point in the fog we sensed that we had risen and fallen over several rises. Every now and then we felt hard slippery snow under our feet. Every now and then our feet went through crusts in the surface. And then quite suddenly, vague, indefinable, monstrous, there loomed a something ahead. I remember having a feeling as of ghosts about as we untoggled our harnesses from the sledge, tied them together, and thus roped walked upwards on that ice. The moon was showing a ghastly ragged mountainous edge above us in the fog, and as we rose we found that we were on a pressure ridge. We stopped, looked at one another, and then *bang* – right under our feet. More bangs, and creaks and groans; for that ice was moving and splitting like glass. The cracks went off all round us, and some of them ran along for hundreds of yards. Afterwards we got used to it, but at first the effect was very jumpy. From first to last during this journey we had plenty of variety and none of that monotony which is inevitable in sledging over long distances of Barrier in summer. Only the long shivering fits following close one after the other all the time we lay in our dreadful sleeping-bags, hour after hour and night after night in those temperatures – they were as monotonous as could be. Later we got frost-bitten even as we lay in our sleeping-bags. Things are getting pretty bad when you get frost-bitten in your bag.

There was only a glow where the moon was; we stood in a moonlit fog, and this was sufficient to show the edge of another ridge ahead, and yet another on our left. We were utterly bewildered. The deep booming of the ice continued, and it may be that the tide has something to do with this, though we were many miles from the ordinary coastal ice. We went back, toggled up to our sledges again and pulled in what we thought was the right direction, always with that feeling that the earth may open underneath your feet which you have in crevassed areas. But all we found were more mounds and banks of snow and ice, into which we almost ran before we saw them. We were clearly lost. It was near midnight, and I wrote, 'it may be the pressure ridges or it may be Terror, it is impossible to say, – and I should think it is impossible to move till it clears. We were steering N.E.

when we got here and returned S.W. till we seemed to be in a hollow and camped.'

The temperature had been rising from −36° at 11 a.m. and it was now −27°; snow was falling and nothing whatever could be seen. From under the tent came noises as though some giant was banging a big empty tank. All the signs were for a blizzard, and indeed we had not long finished our supper and were thawing our way little by little into our bags when the wind came away from the south. Before it started we got a glimpse of black rock, and knew we must be in the pressure ridges where they nearly join Mount Terror.

It is with great surprise that in looking up the records I find that blizzard lasted three days, the temperature and wind both rising till it was +9° and blowing force 9 on the morning of the second day (11 July). On the morning of the third day (12 July) it was blowing storm force (10). The temperature had thus risen over eighty degrees.

It was not an uncomfortable time. Wet and warm, the risen temperature allowed all our ice to turn to water, and we lay steaming and beautifully liquid, and wondered sometimes what we should be like when our gear froze up once more. But we did not do much wondering, I suspect: we slept. From that point of view these blizzards were a perfect Godsend.

We also revised our food rations. From the moment we started to prepare for this journey we were asked by Scott to try certain experiments in view of the Plateau stage of the Polar Journey the following summer. It was supposed that the Plateau stage would be the really rough part of the Polar Journey, and no one then dreamed that harder conditions could be found in the middle of the Barrier in March than on the Plateau, ten thousand feet higher, in February. In view of the extreme conditions we knew we must meet on this winter journey, far harder of course in point of weather than anything experienced on the Polar Journey, we had determined to simplify our food to the last degree. We only brought pemmican, biscuit, butter and tea; and tea is not a food, only a pleasant stimulant, and hot: the pemmican was excellent and came from Beauvais, Copenhagen.

The immediate advantage of this was that we had few food bags to handle for each meal. If the air temperature is 100 degrees of frost, then everything in the air is about 100 degrees of frost too. You have only to untie the lashing of one bag in a −70° temperature, with your feet frozen and your fingers just nursed back after getting a match to strike for the candle (you will have tried several boxes – metal), to realize this as an advantage.

The immediate and increasingly pressing disadvantage is that you have no sugar. Have you ever had a craving for sugar which never leaves you, even when asleep? It is unpleasant. As a matter of fact the craving for sweet things never seriously worried us on this journey, and there must have been some sugar in our biscuits which gave a pleasant sweetness to our midday tea or nightly hot water when broken up and soaked in it. These biscuits were specially made for us by Huntley and Palmer: their composition was worked out by Wilson and that firm's chemist, and is a secret. But they are probably the most satisfying biscuit ever made, and I doubt whether they can be improved upon. There were two kinds, called Emergency and Antarctic, but there was I think little difference between them except in the baking. A well-baked biscuit was good to eat when sledging if your supply of food was good: but if you were very hungry an underbaked one was much preferred.

By taking individually different quantities of biscuit, pemmican and butter we were able roughly to test the proportions of proteids, fats and carbohydrates wanted by the human body under such extreme circumstances. Bill was all for fat, starting with 8 oz. butter, 12 oz. pemmican and only 12 oz. biscuit a day. Bowers told me he was going for proteids, 16 oz. pemmican and 16 oz. biscuit, and suggested I should go the whole hog on carbohydrates. I did not like this, since I knew I should want more fat, but the rations were to be altered as necessary during the journey, so there was no harm in trying. So I started with 20 oz. of biscuit and 12 oz. of pemmican a day.

Bowers was all right (this was usual with him), but he did not eat all his extra pemmican. Bill could not eat all his extra butter, but was satisfied. I got hungry, certainly got more frost-bitten than the others, and wanted more fat. I also got heartburn. However, before taking more fat I increased my biscuits to 24 oz., but this did not satisfy me; I wanted fat. Bill and I now took the same diet, he giving me 4 oz. of butter which he could not eat, and I giving him 4 oz. of biscuit which did not satisfy my wants. We both therefore had 12 oz. pemmican, 16 oz. biscuit and 4 oz. butter a day, but we did not always finish our butter. This is an extremely good ration, and we had enough to eat during most of this journey. We certainly could not have faced the conditions without.

I will not say that I was entirely easy in my mind as we lay out that blizzard somewhere off Terror Point; I don't know how the others were feeling. The unearthly banging going on underneath us may have had something to do with it. But we were quite lost in the pressure and it might be the deuce and all to get out in the dark. The wind eddied and swirled quite out of its usual straightforward way, and the tent got badly snowed up: our sledge had disappeared long ago. The position was not altogether a comfortable one.

Tuesday night and Wednesday it blew up to force 10, temperature from −7° to +2°. And then it began to modify and get squally. By 3 a.m. on Thursday (13 July) the wind had nearly ceased, the temperature was falling and the stars were shining through detached clouds. We were soon getting our breakfast, which always consisted of tea, followed by pemmican. We soaked our biscuits in both. Then we set to work to dig out the sledges and tent, a big job taking several hours. At last we got started. In that jerky way in which I was still managing to jot a few sentences down each night as a record, I wrote:

'Did 7½ miles during day – seems a marvellous run – rose

and fell over several ridges of Terror – in afternoon suddenly came on huge crevasses on one of these – we were quite high on Terror – moon saved us walking in – it might have taken sledge and all.'

To do seven miles in a day, a distance which had taken us nearly a week in the past, was very heartening. The temperature was between −20° and −30° all day, and that was good too. When crossing the undulations which ran down out of the mountain into the true pressure ridges on our right we found that the wind which came down off the mountain struck along the top of the undulation, and flowing each way, caused a N.E. breeze on one side and a N.W. breeze on the other. There seemed to be wind in the sky, and the blizzard had not cleared as far away as we should have wished.

During the time through which we had come it was by burning more oil than is usually allowed for cooking that we kept going at all. After each meal was cooked we allowed the primus to burn on for a while and thus warmed up the tent. Then we could nurse back our frozen feet and do any necessary little odd jobs. More often we just sat and nodded for a few minutes, keeping one another from going too deeply to sleep. But it was running away with the oil. We started with 6 one-gallon tins (those tins Scott had criticized), and we had now used four of them. At first we said we must have at least two one-gallon tins with which to go back; but by now our estimate had come down to one full gallon tin, and two full primus lamps. Our sleeping-bags were awful. It took me, even as early in the journey as this, an hour of pushing and thumping and cramp every night to thaw out enough of mine to get into it at all. Even that was not so bad as lying in them when we got there.

Only −35° but 'a very bad night' according to my diary. We got away in good time, but it was a ghastly day and my nerves were quivering at the end, for we could not find that straight and narrow way which led between the crevasses on either hand. Time after time we found we were out of our course by the sudden fall of the ground beneath our feet – in we went and then – 'are we too far right?' – nobody knows – 'well let's try nearer in to the mountain,' and so forth!

> By hard slogging 2¾ miles this morning – then on in thick gloom which suddenly lifted and we found ourselves under a huge great mountain of pressure ridge looking black in shadow. We went on, bending to the left, when Bill fell and put his arms into a crevasse. We went over this and another, and some time after got somewhere up to the left, and both Bill and I put a foot into a crevasse. We sounded all about and everywhere was hollow, and so we ran the sledge down over it and all was well.[2]

Once we got right into the pressure and took a longish time to get out again. Bill lengthened his trace out with the Alpine rope now and often afterwards, so he found the crevasses well ahead of us and the sledge: nice for us but not so nice for Bill. Crevasses in the dark *do* put your nerves on edge.

When we started next morning (15 July) we could see on our left front and more or less on top of us the Knoll, which is a big hill whose precipitous cliffs to seaward form Cape Crozier. The sides of it sloped down towards us, and pressing against its ice-cliffs on ahead were miles and miles of great pressure ridges, along which we had travelled, and which hemmed us in. Mount Terror rose ten thousand feet high on our left, and was connected with the Knoll by a great cup-like drift of wind-polished snow. The slope of this in one place runs gently out on to the corridor along which we had sledged, and here we turned and started to pull our sledges up. There were no crevasses, only the great drift of snow, so hard that we used our crampons just as though we had been on ice, and as polished as the china sides of a giant cup which

2. My own diary.

it resembled. For three miles we slogged up, until we were only 150 yards from the moraine shelf where we were going to build our hut of rocks and snow. This moraine was above us on our left, the twin peaks of the Knoll were across the cup on our right; and here, 800 feet up the mountain side, we pitched our last camp.

We had arrived.

What should we call our hut? How soon could we get our clothes and bags dry? How would the blubber stove work? Would the penguins be there? 'It seems too good to be true, 19 days out. Surely seldom has anyone been so wet; our bags hardly possible to get into, our wind-clothes just frozen boxes. Birdie's patent balaclava is like iron – it is wonderful how our cares have vanished.'[3]

It was evening, but we were so keen to begin that we went straight up to the ridge above our camp, where the rock cropped out from the snow. We found that most of it was *in situ* but that there were plenty of boulders, some gravel, and of course any amount of the icy snow which fell away below us down to our tent, and the great pressure about a mile beyond. Between us and that pressure, as we were to find out afterwards, was a great ice-cliff. The pressure ridges, and the Great Ice Barrier beyond, were at our feet; the Ross Sea edge but some four miles away. The Emperors must be somewhere round that shoulder of the Knoll which hides Cape Crozier itself from our view.

Our scheme was to build an igloo with rock walls, banked up with snow, using a nine-foot sledge as a ridge beam, and a large sheet of green Willesden canvas as a roof. We had also brought a board to form a lintel over the door. Here with the stove, which was to be fed with blubber from the penguins, we were to have a comfortable warm home whence we would make excursions to the rookery perhaps four miles away. Perhaps we would manage to get our tent down to the rookery itself and do our scientific work there on the spot,

3. My own diary.

leaving our nice hut for a night or more. That is how we planned it.

That same night

we started to dig in under a great boulder on the top of the hill, hoping to make this a large part of one of the walls of the hut, but the rock came close underneath and stopped us. We then chose a moderately level piece of moraine about twelve feet away, and just under the level of the top of the hill, hoping that here in the lee of the ridge we might escape a good deal of the tremendous winds which we knew were common. Birdie gathered rocks from over the hill, nothing was too big for him; Bill did the banking up outside while I built the wall with the boulders. The rocks were good, the snow, however, was blown so hard as to be practically ice; a pick made little impression upon it, and the only way was to chip out big blocks gradually with the small shovel. The gravel was scanty, but good when there was any. Altogether things looked very hopeful when we turned in to the tent some 150 yards down the slope, having done about half one of the long walls.[4]

The view from eight hundred feet up the mountain was magnificent and I got my spectacles out and cleared the ice away time after time to look. To the east a great field of pressure ridges below, looking in the moonlight as if giants had been ploughing with ploughs which made furrows fifty or sixty feet deep: these ran right up to the Barrier edge, and beyond was the frozen Ross Sea, lying flat, white and peaceful as though such things as blizzards were unknown. To the north and north-east the Knoll. Behind us Mount Terror on which we stood, and over all the grey limitless Barrier seemed to cast a spell of cold immensity, vague, ponderous, a breeding-place of wind and drift and darkness. God! What a place!

4. My own diary.

There was now little moonlight or daylight, but for the next forty-eight hours we used both to their utmost, being up at all times by day and night, and often working on when there was great difficulty in seeing anything; digging by the light of the hurricane lamp. By the end of two days we had the walls built, and banked up to one or two feet from the top; we were to fit the roof cloth close before banking up the rest. The great difficulty in banking was the hardness of the snow, it being impossible to fill in the cracks between the blocks which were more like paving-stones than anything else. The door was in, being a triangular tent doorway, with flaps which we built close in to the walls, cementing it with snow and rocks. The top folded over a plank and the bottom was dug into the ground.[5]

Birdie was very disappointed that we could not finish the whole thing that day: he was nearly angry about it, but there was a lot to do yet and we were tired out. We turned out early the next morning (Tuesday 18th) to try and finish the igloo, but it was blowing too hard. When we got to the top we did some digging but it was quite impossible to get the roof on, and we had to leave it. We realized that day that it blew much harder at the top of the slope than where our tent was. It was bitterly cold up there that morning with a wind force 4–5 and a minus thirty temperature.

The oil question was worrying us quite a lot. We were now well in to the fifth of our six tins, and economizing as much as possible, often having only two hot meals a day. We had to get down to the Emperor penguins somehow and get some blubber to run the stove which had been made for us in the hut. The 19th being a calm fine day we started at 9.30, with an empty sledge, two ice-axes, Alpine rope, harnesses and skinning tools.

Wilson had made this journey through the Cape Crozier pressure ridges several times in the *Discovery* days. But then they had daylight, and they had found a practicable way close

5. My own diary.

under the cliffs which at the present moment were between us and the ridges.

As we neared the bottom of the mountain slope, farther to the north than we had previously gone, we had to be careful about crevasses, but we soon hit off the edge of the cliff and skirted along it until it petered out on the same level as the Barrier. Turning left handed we headed towards the sea-ice, knowing that there were some two miles of pressure between us and Cape Crozier itself. For about half a mile it was fair going, rounding big knobs of pressure but always managing to keep more or less on the flat and near the ice-cliff which soon rose to a very great height on our left. Bill's idea was to try and keep close under this cliff, along that same *Discovery* way which I have mentioned above. They never arrived there early enough for the eggs in those days: the chicks were hatched. Whether we should now find any Emperors, and if so whether they would have any eggs, was by no means certain.

However, we soon began to get into trouble, meeting several crevasses every few yards, and I have no doubt crossing scores of others of which we had no knowledge. Though we hugged the cliffs as close as possible we found ourselves on the top of the first pressure ridge, separated by a deep gulf from the ice-slope which we wished to reach. Then we were in a great valley between the first and second ridges: we got into huge heaps of ice pressed up in every shape on every side, crevassed in every direction: we slithered over snow-slopes and crawled along drift ridges, trying to get in towards the cliffs. And always we came up against impossible places and had to crawl back. Bill led on a length of Alpine rope fastened to the toggle of the sledge; Birdie was in his harness also fastened to the toggle, and I was in my harness fastened to the rear of the sledge, which was of great use to us both as a bridge and a ladder.

Two or three times we tried to get down the ice-slopes to the comparatively level road under the cliffs, but it was always too great a drop. In that dim light every proportion was distorted; some of the places we actually·did manage to negotiate with ice-axes and Alpine rope looked absolute precipices, and there were always crevasses at the bottom if you slipped. On the way back I did slip into one of these and was hauled out by the other two standing on the wall above me.

We then worked our way down into the hollow between the first and second large pressure ridges, and I believe on to the top of the second. The crests here rose fifty or sixty feet. After this I don't know where we went. Our best landmarks were patches of crevasses, sometimes three or four in a few footsteps. The temperatures were lowish ($-37°$), it was impossible for me to wear spectacles, and this was a tremendous difficulty to me and handicap to the party: Bill would find a crevasse and point it out; Birdie would cross; and then time after time, in trying to step over or climb over on the sledge, I put my feet right into the middle of the cracks. This day I went well in at least six times; once, when we were close to the sea, rolling into and out of one and then down a steep slope until brought up by Birdie and Bill on the rope.

We blundered along until we got into a great cul-de-sac which probably formed the end of the two ridges, where they butted on to the sea-ice. On all sides rose great walls of battered ice with steep snow-slopes in the middle, where we slithered about and blundered into crevasses. To the left rose the huge cliff of Cape Crozier, but we could not tell whether there were not two or three pressure ridges between us and it, and though we tried at least four ways, there was no possibility of getting forward.

And then we heard the Emperors calling.

Their cries came to us from the sea-ice we could not see, but which must have been a chaotic quarter of a mile away. They came echoing back from the cliffs, as we stood helpless and tantalized. We listened and realized that there was nothing for it but to return, for the little light which now came in the middle of the day was going fast, and to be caught in absolute darkness there was a horrible idea. We started back on our tracks and almost immediately I lost my footing and rolled down a slope into a crevasse. Birdie and

Bill kept their balance and I clambered back to them. The tracks were very faint and we soon began to lose them. Birdie was the best man at following tracks that I have ever known, and he found them time after time. But at last even he lost them altogether and we settled we must just go ahead. As a matter of fact, we picked them up again, and by then were out of the worst: but we were glad to see the tent.

The next morning (Thursday, 20 June) we started work on the igloo at 3 a.m. and managed to get the canvas roof on in spite of a wind which harried us all that day. Little did we think what that roof had in store for us as we packed it in with snow blocks, stretching it over our second sledge, which we put athwartships across the middle of the longer walls. The windward (south) end came right down to the ground and we tied it securely to rocks before packing it in. On the other three sides we had a good two feet or more of slack all round, and in every case we tied it to rocks by lanyards at intervals of two feet. The door was the difficulty, and for the present we left the cloth arching over the stones, forming a kind of portico. The whole was well packed in and over with slabs of hard snow, but there was no soft snow with which to fill up the gaps between the blocks. However, we felt already that nothing could drag that roof out of its packing, and subsequent events proved that we were right.

It was a bleak job for three o'clock in the morning before breakfast, and we were glad to get back to the tent and a meal, for we meant to have another go at the Emperors that day. With the first glimpse of light we were off for the rookery again.

But we now knew one or two things about that pressure which we had not known twenty-four hours ago; for instance, that there was a lot of alteration since the *Discovery* days and that probably the pressure was bigger. As a matter of fact it has been since proved by photographs that the ridges now ran out three-quarters of a mile farther into the sea than they did ten years before. We knew also that if we entered the pressure at the only place where the ice-cliffs came down to the level of the Barrier, as we did yesterday, we could neither penetrate to the rookery nor get in under the cliffs where formerly a possible way had been found. There was only one other thing to do – to go over the cliff. And this was what we proposed to try and do.

Now these ice-cliffs are some two hundred feet high, and I felt uncomfortable, especially in the dark. But as we came back the day before we had noticed at one place a break in the cliffs from which there hung a snow-drift. It *might* be possible to get down that drift.

And so, all harnessed to the sledge, with Bill on a long lead out in front and Birdie and myself checking the sledge behind, we started down the slope which ended in the cliff, which of course we could not see. We crossed a number of small crevasses, and soon we knew we must be nearly there. Twice we crept up to the edge of the cliff with no success, and then we found the slope: more, we got down it without great difficulty and it brought us out just where we wanted to be, between the land cliffs and the pressure.

Then began the most exciting climb among the pressure that you can imagine. At first very much as it was the day before – pulling ourselves and one another up ridges, slithering down slopes, tumbling into and out of crevasses and holes of all sorts, we made our way along under the cliffs which rose higher and higher above us as we neared the black lava precipices which form Cape Crozier itself. We straddled along the top of a snow ridge with a razor-backed edge, balancing the sledge between us as we wriggled: on our right was a drop of great depth with crevasses at the bottom, on our left was a smaller drop also crevassed. We crawled along, and I can tell you it was exciting work in the more than half darkness. At the end was a series of slopes full of crevasses, and finally we got right in under the rock on to moraine, and here we had to leave the sledge.

We roped up, and started to worry along under the cliffs, which had now changed from ice to rock, and rose 800 feet above us. The tumult of pressure which climbed against them showed no order here. Four hundred miles of moving ice behind it had just tossed and twisted those giant ridges until

Job himself would have lacked words to reproach their Maker. We scrambled over and under, hanging on with our axes, and cutting steps where we could not find a foothold with our crampons. And always we got towards the Emperor penguins, and it really began to look as if we were going to do it this time, when we came up against a wall of ice which a single glance told us we could never cross. One of the largest pressure ridges had been thrown, end on, against the cliff. We seemed to be stopped, when Bill found a black hole, something like a fox's earth, disappearing into the bowels of the ice. We looked at it: 'Well, here goes!' he said, and put his head in, and disappeared. Bowers likewise. It was a longish way, but quite possible to wriggle along, and presently I found myself looking out of the other side with a deep gully below me, the rock face on one hand and the ice on the other. 'Put your back against the ice and your feet against the rock and lever yourself along,' said Bill, who was already standing on firm ice at the far end in a snow pit. We cut some fifteen steps to get out of that hole. Excited by now, and thoroughly enjoying ourselves, we found the way ahead easier, until the penguins' call reached us again and we stood, three crystallized ragamuffins, above the Emperors' home. They were there all right, and we were going to reach them, but where were all the thousands of which we had heard?

We stood on an ice-foot which was really a dwarf cliff some twelve feet high, and the sea-ice, with a good many ice-blocks strewn upon it, lay below. The cliff dropped straight, with a bit of an overhang and no snow-drift. This may have been because the sea had only frozen recently; whatever the reason may have been it meant that we should have a lot of difficulty in getting up again without help. It was decided that someone must stop on the top with the Alpine rope, and clearly that one should be I, for with short sight and fogged spectacles which I could not wear I was much the least useful of the party for the job immediately ahead. Had we had the sledge we could have used it as a ladder, but of course we had left this at the beginning of the moraine miles back.

We saw the Emperors standing all together huddled under the Barrier cliff some hundreds of yards away. The little light was going fast: we were much more excited about the approach of complete darkness and the look of wind in the south than we were about our triumph. After indescribable effort and hardship we were witnessing a marvel of the natural world, and we were the first and only men who had ever done so; we had within our grasp material which might prove of the utmost importance to science; we were turning theories into facts with every observation we made, – and we had but a moment to give.

The disturbed Emperors made a tremendous row, trumpeting with their curious metallic voices. There was no doubt they had eggs, for they tried to shuffle along the ground without losing them off their feet. But when they were hustled a good many eggs were dropped and left lying on the ice, and some of these were quickly picked up by eggless Emperors who had probably been waiting a long time for the opportunity. In these poor birds the maternal side seems to have necessarily swamped the other functions of life. Such is the struggle for existence that they can only live by a glut of maternity, and it would be interesting to know whether such a life leads to happiness or satisfaction.

The men of the *Discovery* found this rookery where we now stood.[6] They made journeys in the early spring but never arrived early enough to get eggs and only found parents and chicks. They concluded that the Emperor was an impossible kind of bird who, for some reason or other, nests in the middle of the Antarctic winter with the temperature anywhere below seventy degrees of frost, and the blizzards blowing, always blowing, against his devoted back. And they found him holding his precious chick balanced upon his big feet, and pressing it maternally, or paternally (for both sexes squabble for the privilege) against a bald patch in his breast. And when at last he simply must go and eat something in the open leads near by, he just puts the child down on the

6. See Scott, *The Voyage of the Discovery*, vol. ii, pp. 5, 6, 490.

ice, and twenty chickless Emperors rush to pick it up. And they fight over it, and so tear it that sometimes it will die. And, if it can, it will crawl into any ice-crack to escape from so much kindness, and there it will freeze. Likewise many broken and addled eggs were found, and it is clear that the mortality is very great. But some survive, and summer comes; and when a big blizzard is going to blow (they know all about the weather), the parents take the children out for miles across the sea-ice, until they reach the threshold of the open sea. And there they sit until the wind comes, and the swell rises, and breaks that ice-floe off; and away they go in the blinding drift to join the main pack-ice, with a private yacht all to themselves.

You must agree that a bird like this is an interesting beast, and when, seven months ago, we rowed a boat under those great black cliffs,[7] and found a disconsolate Emperor chick still in the down, we knew definitely why the Emperor has to nest in mid-winter. For if a June egg was still without feathers in the beginning of January, the same egg laid in the summer would leave its produce without practical covering for the following winter. Thus the Emperor penguin is compelled to undertake all kinds of hardships because his children insist on developing so slowly, very much as we are tied in our human relationships for the same reason. It is of interest that such a primitive bird should have so long a childhood.

But interesting as the life history of these birds must be, we had not travelled for three weeks to see them sitting on their eggs. We wanted the embryos, and we wanted them as young as possible, and fresh and unfrozen, that specialists at home might cut them into microscopic sections and learn from the previous history of birds throughout the evolutionary ages. And so Bill and Birdie rapidly collected five eggs, which we hoped to carry safely in our fur mitts to our igloo upon Mount Terror, where we could pickle them in the alcohol we had brought for the purpose. We also wanted oil

7. See pp. 82–3.

for our blubber stove, and they killed and skinned three birds
– an Emperor weighs up to 6½ stones.

The Ross Sea was frozen over, and there were no seal in
sight. There were only 100 Emperors as compared with 2000
in 1902 and 1903. Bill reckoned that every fourth or fifth bird
had an egg, but this was only a rough estimate, for we did
not want to disturb them unnecessarily. It is a mystery why
there should have been so few birds, but it certainly looked
as though the ice had not formed very long. Were these the
first arrivals? Had a previous rookery been blown out to sea
and was this the beginning of a second attempt? Is this bay of
sea-ice becoming unsafe?

Those who previously discovered the Emperors with their
chicks saw the penguins nursing dead and frozen chicks if
they were unable to obtain a live one. They also found
decomposed eggs which they must have incubated after they
had been frozen. Now we found that these birds were so
anxious to sit on something that some of those which had no
eggs were sitting on ice! Several times Bill and Birdie picked
up eggs to find them lumps of ice, rounded and about the
right size, dirty and hard. Once a bird dropped an ice nest
egg as they watched, and again a bird returned and tucked
another into itself, immediately forsaking it for a real one,
however, when one was offered.

Meanwhile a whole procession of Emperors came round
under the cliff on which I stood. The light was already very
bad and it was well that my companions were quick in
returning: we had to do everything in a great hurry. I hauled
up the eggs in their mitts (which we fastened together round
our necks with lampwick lanyards) and then the skins, but
failed to help Bill at all. 'Pull,' he cried, from the bottom: 'I
am pulling,' I said. 'But the line's quite slack down here,' he
shouted. And when he had reached the top by climbing up
on Bowers's shoulders, and we were both pulling all we
knew Birdie's end of the rope was still slack in his hands.
Directly we put on a strain the rope cut into the ice edge and
jammed – a very common difficulty when working among
crevasses. We tried to run the rope over an ice-axe without

success, and things began to look serious when Birdie, who had been running about prospecting and had meanwhile put one leg through a crack into the sea, found a place where the cliff did not overhang. He cut steps for himself, we hauled, and at last we were all together on the top – his foot being by now surrounded by a solid mass of ice.

We legged it back as hard as we could go: five eggs in our fur mitts, Birdie with two skins tied to him and trailing behind, and myself with one. We were roped up, and climbing the ridges and getting through the holes was very difficult. In one place where there was a steep rubble and snow slope down I left the ice-axe half-way up; in another it was too dark to see our former ice-axe footsteps, and I could see nothing, and so just let myself go and trusted to luck. With infinite patience Bill said: 'Cherry, you *must* learn how to use an ice-axe.' For the rest of the trip my wind-clothes were in rags.

We found the sledge, and none too soon, and now had three eggs left, more or less whole. Both mine had burst in my mitts: the first I emptied out, the second I left in my mitt to put into the cooker; it never got there, but on the return journey I had my mitts far more easily thawed out than Birdie's (Bill had none) and I believe the grease in the egg did them good. When we got into the hollows under the ridge where we had to cross, it was too dark to do anything but feel our way. We did so over many crevasses, found the ridge and crept over it. Higher up we could see more, but to follow our tracks soon became impossible, and we plugged straight ahead and luckily found the slope down which we had come. All day it had been blowing a nasty cold wind with a temperature between −20° and 30°, which we felt a good deal. Now it began to get worse. The weather was getting thick and things did not look very nice when we started up to find our tent. Soon it was blowing force 4, and soon we missed our way entirely. We got right up above the patch of rocks which marked our igloo and only found it after a good deal of search.

I have heard tell of an English officer at the Dardanelles

who was left, blinded, in No Man's Land between the English and Turkish trenches. Moving only at night, and having no sense to tell him which were his own trenches, he was fired at by Turk and English alike as he groped his ghastly way to and from them. Thus he spent days and nights until, one night, he crawled towards the English trenches, to be fired at as usual. 'Oh God! what can I do!' someone heard him say, and he was brought in.

Such extremity of suffering cannot be measured: madness or death may give relief. But this I know: we on this journey were already beginning to think of death as a friend. As we groped our way back that night, sleepless, icy, and dog-tired in the dark and the wind and the drift, a crevasse seemed almost a friendly gift.

'Things must improve,' said Bill next day, 'I think we reached bed-rock last night.' We hadn't, by a long way.

It was like this.

We moved into the igloo for the first time, for we had to save oil by using our blubber stove if we were to have any left to travel home with, and we did not wish to cover our tent with the oily black filth which the use of blubber necessitates. The blizzard blew all night, and we were covered with drift which came in through hundreds of leaks: in this wind-swept place we had found no soft snow with which we could pack our hard snow blocks. As we flensed some rubber from one of our penguin skins the powdery drift covered everything we had.

Though uncomfortable this was nothing to worry about overmuch. Some of the drift which the blizzard was bringing would collect to leeward of our hut and the rocks below which it was built, and they could be used to make our hut more weather-proof. Then with great difficulty we got the blubber stove to start, and it spouted a blob of boiling oil into Bill's eye. For the rest of the night he lay, quite unable to stifle his groans, obviously in very great pain: he told us afterwards that he thought his eye was gone. We managed to cook a meal somehow, and Birdie got the stove going afterwards, but it was quite useless to try and warm the place. I got out and cut the green canvas outside the door, so as to get the roof cloth in under the stones, and then packed it down as well as I could with snow, and so blocked most of the drift coming in.

It is extraordinary how often angels and fools do the same thing in this life, and I have never been able to settle which we were on this journey. I never heard an angry word: once only (when this same day I could not pull Bill up the cliff out of the penguin rookery) I heard an impatient one: and these groans were the nearest approach to complaint. Most men would have howled. 'I think we reached bed-rock last night,' was strong language for Bill. 'I was incapacitated for a short time,' he says in his report to Scott.[8] Endurance was tested on this journey under unique circumstances, and always these two men with all the burden of responsibility which did not fall upon myself, displayed that quality which is perhaps the only one which may be said with certainty to make for success, self-control.

We spent the next day – it was 21 July – in collecting every scrap of soft snow we could find and packing it into the crevasses between our hard snow blocks. It was a pitifully small amount but we could see no cracks when we had finished. To counteract the lifting tendency the wind had on our roof we cut some great flat hard snow blocks and laid them on the canvas top to steady it against the sledge which formed the ridge support. We also pitched our tent outside the igloo door. Both tent and igloo were therefore eight or nine hundred feet up Terror: both were below an outcrop of rocks from which the mountain fell steeply to the Barrier behind us, and from this direction came the blizzards. In front of us the slope fell for a mile or more down to the ice-cliffs, so wind-swept that we had to wear crampons to walk upon it. Most of the tent was in the lee of the igloo, but the cap of it came over the igloo roof, while a segment of the tent itself jutted out beyond the igloo wall.

That night we took much of our gear into the tent and

8. *Scott's Last Expedition*, vol. ii, p. 42.

lighted the blubber stove. I always mistrusted that stove, and every moment I expected it to flare up and burn the tent. But the heat it gave, as it burned furiously, with the double lining of the tent to contain it, was considerable.

It did not matter, except for a routine which we never managed to keep, whether we started to thaw our way into our frozen sleeping-bags at 4 in the morning or 4 in the afternoon. I think we must have turned in during the afternoon of that Friday, leaving the cooker, our finnesko, a deal of our foot-gear, Bowers's bag of personal gear, and many other things in the tent. I expect we left the blubber stove there too, for it was quite useless at present to try and warm the igloo. The tent floor-cloth was under our sleeping-bags in the igloo.

'Things must improve,' said Bill. After all there was much for which to be thankful. I don't think anybody could have made a better igloo with the hard snow blocks and rocks which were all we had: we would get it air-tight by degrees. The blubber stove was working, and we had fuel for it: we had also found a way down to the penguins and had three complete, though frozen eggs: the two which had been in my mitts smashed when I fell about because I could not wear spectacles. Also the twilight given by the sun below the horizon at noon was getting longer.

But already we had been out twice as long in winter as the longest previous journeys in spring. The men who made those journeys had daylight where we had darkness, they had never had such low temperatures, generally nothing approaching them, and they had seldom worked in such difficult country. The nearest approach to healthy sleep we had had for nearly a month was when during blizzards the temperature allowed the warmth of our bodies to thaw some of the ice in our clothing and sleeping-bags into water. The wear and tear on our minds was very great. We were certainly weaker. We had a little more than a tin of oil to get back on, and we knew the conditions we had to face on that journey across the Barrier: even with fresh men and fresh gear it had been almost unendurable.

And so we spent half an hour or more getting into our bags. Cirrus cloud was moving across the face of the stars from the north, it looked rather hazy and thick to the south, but it is always difficult to judge weather in the dark. There was little wind and the temperature was in the minus twenties. We felt no particular uneasiness. Our tent was well dug in, and was also held down by rocks and the heavy tank off the sledge which were placed on the skirting as additional security. We felt that no power on earth could move the thick walls of our igloo, nor drag the canvas roof from the middle of the embankment into which it was packed and lashed.

'Things must improve,' said Bill.

I do not know what time it was when I woke up. It was calm, with that absolute silence which can be so soothing or so terrible as circumstances dictate. Then there came a sob of wind, and all was still again. Ten minutes and it was blowing as though the world was having a fit of hysterics. The earth was torn in pieces: the indescribable fury and roar of it all cannot be imagined.

'Bill, Bill, the tent has gone,' was the next I remember – from Bowers shouting at us again and again through the door. It is always these early morning shocks which hit one hardest: our slow minds suggested that this might mean a peculiarly lingering form of death. Journey after journey Birdie and I fought our way across the few yards which had separated the tent from the igloo door. I have never understood why so much of our gear which was in the tent remained, even in the lee of the igloo. The place where the tent had been was littered with gear, and when we came to reckon up afterwards we had everything except the bottom piece of the cooker, and the top of the outer cooker. We never saw these again. The most wonderful thing of all was that our finnesko were lying where they were left, which happened to be on the ground in the part of the tent which was under the lee of the igloo. Also Birdie's bag of personal gear was there, and a tin of sweets.

Birdie brought two tins of sweets away with him. One

we had to celebrate our arrival at the Knoll: this was the second, of which we knew nothing, and which was for Bill's birthday, the next day. We started eating them on Saturday, however, and the tin came in useful to Bill afterwards.

To get that gear in we fought against solid walls of black snow which flowed past us and tried to hurl us down the slope. Once started nothing could have stopped us. I saw Birdie knocked over once, but he clawed his way back just in time. Having passed everything we could find in to Bill, we got back into the igloo, and started to collect things together, including our very dishevelled minds.

There was no doubt that we were in the devil of a mess, and it was not altogether our fault. We had had to put our igloo more or less where we could get rocks with which to build it. Very naturally we had given both our tent and igloo all the shelter we could from the full force of the wind, and now it seemed we were in danger not because they were in the wind, but because they were not sufficiently in it. The main force of the hurricane, deflected by the ridge behind, fled over our heads and appeared to form by suction a vacuum below. Our tent had either been sucked upwards into this, or had been blown away because some of it was in the wind while some of it was not. The roof of our igloo was being wrenched upwards and then dropped back with great crashes: the drift was spouting in, not it seemed because it was blown in from outside, but because it was sucked in from within: the lee, not the weather, wall was the worst. Already everything was six or eight inches under snow.

Very soon we began to be alarmed about the igloo. For some time the heavy snow blocks we had heaved up on to the canvas roof kept it weighted down. But it seemed that they were being gradually moved off by the hurricane. The tension became well-nigh unendurable: the waiting in all that welter of noise was maddening. Minute after minute, hour after hour – those snow blocks were off now anyway, and the roof was smashed up and down – no canvas ever made could stand it indefinitely.

We got a meal that Saturday morning, our last for a very

long time as it happened. Oil being of such importance to us we tried to use the blubber stove, but after several preliminary spasms it came to pieces in our hands, some solder having melted; and a very good thing too, I thought, for it was more dangerous than useful. We finished cooking our meal on the primus. Two bits of the cooker having been blown away we had to balance it on the primus as best we could. We then settled that in view of the shortage of oil we would not have another meal for as long as possible. As a matter of fact God settled that for us.

We did all we could to stop up the places where the drift was coming in, plugging the holes with our socks, mitts and other clothing. But it was no real good. Our igloo was a vacuum which was filling itself up as soon as possible: and when snow was not coming in a fine black moraine dust took its place, covering us and everything. For twenty-four hours we waited for the roof to go: things were so bad now that we dare not unlash the door.

Many hours ago Bill had told us that if the roof went he considered that our best chance would be to roll over in our sleeping-bags until we were lying on the openings, and get frozen and drifted in.

Gradually the situation got more desperate. The distance between the taut-sucked canvas and the sledge on which it should have been resting became greater, and this must have been due to the stretching of the canvas itself and the loss of the snow blocks on the top: it was not drawing out of the walls. The crashes as it dropped and banged out again were louder. There was more snow coming through the walls, though all our loose mitts, socks and smaller clothing were stuffed into the worst places: our pyjama jackets were stuffed between the roof and the rocks over the door. The rocks were lifting and shaking here till we thought they would fall.

We talked by shouting, and long before this one of us proposed to try and get the Alpine rope lashed down over the roof from outside. But Bowers said it was an absolute impossibility in that wind. 'You could never ask men at sea to try such a thing,' he said. He was up and out of his bag continually, stopping up holes, pressing against bits of roof to try and prevent the flapping and so forth. He was magnificent.

And then it went.

Birdie was over by the door, where the canvas which was bent over the lintel board was working worse than anywhere else. Bill was practically out of his bag pressing against some part with a long stick of some kind. I don't know what I was doing but I was half out of and half in my bag.

The top of the door opened in little slits and that green Willesden canvas flapped into hundreds of little fragments in fewer seconds than it takes to read this. The uproar of it all was indescribable. Even above the savage thunder of that great wind on the mountain came the lash of the canvas as it was whipped to little tiny strips. The highest rocks which we had built into our walls fell upon us, and a sheet of drift came in.

Birdie dived for his sleeping-bag and eventually got in, together with a terrible lot of drift. Bill also – but he was better off: I was already half into mine and all right, so I turned to help Bill. 'Get into your own,' he shouted, and when I continued to try and help him, he leaned over until his mouth was against my ear. '*Please*, Cherry,' he said, and his voice was terribly anxious. I know he felt responsible: feared it was he who had brought us to this ghastly end.

The next I knew was Bowers's head across Bill's body. 'We're all right,' he yelled, and we answered in the affirmative. Despite the fact that we knew we only said so because we knew we were all wrong, this statement was helpful. Then we turned our bags over as far as possible, so that the bottom of the bag was uppermost and the flaps were more or less beneath us. And we lay and thought, and sometimes we sang.

I suppose, wrote Wilson, we were all revolving plans to get back without a tent: and the one thing we had left was the floor-cloth upon which we were actually lying. Of course we could not speak at present, but later after the blizzard had stopped we discussed the possibility of digging a hole in the snow each night and covering it over with the floor-cloth. I do not think we had any idea that we could really get back in those temperatures in our present state of ice by such means, but no one ever hinted at such a thing. Birdie and Bill sang quite a lot of songs and hymns, snatches of which reached me every now and then, and I chimed in, somewhat feebly I suspect. Of course we were getting pretty badly drifted up. 'I was resolved to keep warm,' wrote Bowers, 'and beneath my debris covering I paddled my feet and sang all the songs and hymns I knew to pass the time. I could occasionally thump Bill, and as he still moved I knew he was alive all right – what a birthday for him!' Birdie was more drifted up than we, but at times we all had to hummock ourselves up to heave the snow off our bags. By opening the flaps of our bags we could get small pinches of soft drift which we pressed together and put into our mouths to melt. When our hands warmed up again we got some more; so we did not get very thirsty. A few ribbons of canvas still remained in the wall over our heads, and these produced volleys of cracks like pistol shots hour after hour. The canvas never drew out from the walls, not an inch. The wind made just the same noise as an express train running fast through a tunnel if you have both the windows down.

I can well believe that neither of my companions gave up hope for an instant. They must have been frightened, but they were never disturbed. As for me I never had any hope at all; and when the roof went I felt that this was the end. What else could I think? We had spent days in reaching this place through the darkness in cold such as had never been experienced by human beings. We had been out for four weeks under conditions in which no man had existed previously for more than a few days, if that. During this time we had seldom slept except from sheer physical exhaustion, as men sleep on the rack; and every minute of it we had been fighting for the bed-rock necessaries of bare existence, and always in the dark. We had kept ourselves going by enormous care of our feet and hands and bodies, by burning oil, and by having plenty of hot fatty food. Now we had no tent, one tin of oil left out of six, and only part of our cooker. When we were lucky and not too cold we could almost wring water from our clothes, and directly we got out of our sleeping-bags we were frozen into solid sheets of armoured ice. In cold temperatures with all the advantages of a tent over our heads we were already taking more than an hour of fierce struggling and cramp to get into our sleeping-bags – so frozen were they and so long did it take us to thaw our way in. No! Without the tent we were dead men.

And there seemed not one chance in a million that we should ever see our tent again. We were 900 feet up on the mountain side, and the wind blew about as hard as a wind can blow straight out to sea. First there was a steep slope, so hard that a pick made little impression upon it, so slippery that if you started down in finnesko you never could stop: this ended in a great ice-cliff some hundreds of feet high, and then came miles of pressure ridges, crevassed and tumbled, in which you might as well look for a daisy as a tent: and after that the open sea. The chances, however, were that the tent had just been taken up into the air and dropped somewhere in this sea well on the way to New Zealand. Obviously the tent was gone.

Face to face with real death one does not think of the things that torment the bad people in the tracts, and fill the good people with bliss. I might have speculated on my chances of going to Heaven; but candidly I did not care. I could not have wept if I had tried. I had no wish to review the evils of my past. But the past did seem to have been a bit wasted. The road to Hell may be paved with good intentions: the road to Heaven is paved with lost opportunities.

I wanted those years over again. What fun I would have with them: what glorious fun! It was a pity. Well has the Persian said that when we come to die we, remembering that God is merciful, will gnaw our elbows with remorse for thinking of the things we have not done for fear of the Day of Judgement.

And I wanted peaches and syrup – badly. We had them at the hut, sweeter and more luscious than you can imagine.

And we have been without sugar for a month. Yes – especially the syrup.

Thus impiously I set out to die, making up my mind that I was not going to try and keep warm, that it might not take too long, and thinking I would try and get some morphia from the medical case if it got very bad. Not a bit heroic, and entirely true! Yes! comfortable, warm reader. Men do not fear death, they fear the pain of dying.

And then quite naturally and no doubt disappointingly to those who would like to read of my last agonies (for who would not give pleasure by his death?) I fell asleep. I expect the temperature was pretty high during this great blizzard, and anything near zero was very high to us. That and the snow which drifted over us made a pleasant wet kind of snipe marsh inside our sleeping-bags, and I am sure we all dozed a good bit. There was so much to worry about that there was not the least use in worrying: and we were so *very* tired. We were hungry, for the last meal we had had was in the morning of the day before, but hunger was not very pressing.

And so we lay, wet and quite fairly warm, hour after hour while the wind roared round us, blowing storm force continually and rising in the gusts to something indescribable. Storm force is force 11, and force 12 is the biggest wind which can be logged: Bowers logged it force 11, but he was always so afraid of overestimating that he was inclined to underrate. I think it was blowing a full hurricane. Sometimes awake, sometimes dozing, we had not a very uncomfortable time so far as I can remember. I knew that parties which had come to Cape Crozier in the spring had experienced blizzards which lasted eight or ten days. But this did not worry us as much as I think it did Bill: I was numb. I vaguely called to mind that Peary had survived a blizzard in the open: but wasn't that in the summer?

It was in the early morning of Saturday (22 July) that we discovered the loss of the tent. Some time during that morning we had had our last meal. The roof went about noon on Sunday and we had had no meal in the interval because our supply of oil was so low; nor could we move out of our bags except as a last necessity. By Sunday night we had been without a meal for some thirty-six hours.

The rocks which fell upon us when the roof went did no damage, and though we could not get out of our bags to move them, we could fit ourselves into them without difficulty. More serious was the drift which began to pile up all round and over us. It helped to keep us warm of course, but at the same time in these comparatively high temperatures it saturated our bags even worse than they were before. If we did not find the tent (and its recovery would be a miracle) these bags and the floor-cloth of the tent on which we were lying were all we had in that fight back across the Barrier which could, I suppose, have only had one end.

Meanwhile we had to wait. It was nearly 70 miles home and it had taken us the best part of three weeks to come. In our less miserable moments we tried to think out ways of getting back, but I do not remember very much about that time. Sunday morning faded into Sunday afternoon, – into Sunday night, – into Monday morning. Till then the blizzard had raged with monstrous fury; the winds of the world were there, and they had all gone mad. We had bad winds at Cape Evans this year, and we had far worse the next winter when the open water was at our doors. But I have never heard or felt or seen a wind like this. I wondered why it did not carry away the earth.

In the early hours of Monday there was an occasional hint of a lull. Ordinarily in a big winter blizzard, when you have lived for several days and nights with that turmoil in your ears, the lulls are more trying than the noise: 'the feel of not to feel it'.[9] I do not remember noticing that now. Seven or eight more hours passed, and though it was still blowing we could make ourselves heard to one another without great difficulty. It was two days and two nights since we had had a meal.

We decided to get out of our bags and make a search for the tent. We did so, bitterly cold and utterly miserable,

9. Keats.

though I do not think any of us showed it. In the darkness we could see very little, and no trace whatever of the tent. We returned against the wind, nursing our faces and hands, and settled that we must try and cook a meal somehow. We managed about the weirdest meal eaten north or south. We got the floor-cloth wedged under our bags, then got into our bags and drew the floor-cloth over our heads. Between us we got the primus alight somehow, and by hand we balanced the cooker on top of it, minus the two members which had been blown away. The flame flickered in the draughts. Very slowly the snow in the cooker melted, we threw in a plentiful supply of pemmican, and the smell of it was better than anything on earth. In time we got both tea and pemmican, which was full of hairs from our bags, penguin feathers, dirt and debris, but delicious. The blubber left in the cooker got burnt and gave the tea a burnt taste. None of us ever forgot that meal: I enjoyed it as much as such a meal could be enjoyed, and that burnt taste will always bring back the memory.

It was still dark and we lay down in our bags again, but soon a little glow of light began to come up, and we turned out to have a further search for the tent. Birdie went off before Bill and me. Clumsily I dragged my eider-down out of my bag on my feet, all sopping wet: it was impossible to get it back and I let it freeze: it was soon just like a rock. The sky to the south was as black and sinister as it could possibly be. It looked as though the blizzard would be on us again in a moment.

I followed Bill down the slope. We could find nothing. But, as we searched, we heard a shout somewhere below and to the right. We got on a slope, slipped, and went sliding down quite unable to stop ourselves, and came upon Birdie with the tent, the outer lining still on the bamboos. Our lives had been taken away and given back to us.

We were so thankful we said nothing.

The tent must have been gripped up into the air, shutting as it rose. The bamboos, with the inner lining lashed to them, had entangled the outer cover, and the whole went up together like a shut umbrella. This was our salvation. If it had opened in the air nothing could have prevented its destruction. As it was, with all the accumulated ice upon it, it must have weighed the best part of 100 lbs. It had been dropped about half a mile away, at the bottom of a steep slope: and it fell in a hollow, still shut up. The main force of the wind had passed over it, and there it was, with the bamboos and fastenings wrenched and strained, and the ends of two of the poles broken, but the silk untorn.

If that tent went again we were going with it. We made our way back up the slope with it, carrying it solemnly and reverently, precious as though it were something not quite of the earth. And we dug it in as tent was never dug in before; not by the igloo, but in the old place farther down where we had first arrived. And while Bill was doing this Birdie and I went back to the igloo and dug and scratched and shook away the drift inside until we had found nearly all our gear. It is wonderful how little we lost when the roof went. Most of our gear was hung on the sledge, which was part of the roof, or was packed into the holes of the hut to try and make it drift-proof, and the things must have been blown inwards into the bottom of the hut by the wind from the south and the back draught from the north. Then they were all drifted up. Of course a certain number of mitts and socks were blown away and lost, but the only important things were Bill's fur mitts, which were stuffed into a hole in the rocks of the hut. We loaded up the sledge and pushed it down the slope. I don't know how Birdie was feeling, but I felt so weak that it was the greatest labour. The blizzard looked right on top of us.

We had another meal, and we wanted it: and as the good hoosh ran down into our feet and hands, and up into our cheeks and ears and brains, we discussed what we would do next. Birdie was all for another go at the Emperor penguins. Dear Birdie, he never would admit that he was beaten – I don't know that he ever really was! 'I think he (Wilson) thought he had landed us in a bad corner and was determined to go straight home, though I was for one other tap at the Rookery. However, I had placed myself under his orders for this trip voluntarily, and so we started the next day for home.'[10] There could really be no common-sense doubt: we had to go back, and we were already very doubtful whether we should ever manage to get into our sleeping-bags in very low temperature, so ghastly had they become.

I don't know when it was, but I remember walking down that slope – I don't know why, perhaps to try and find the bottom of the cooker – and thinking that there was nothing on earth that a man under such circumstances would not give for a good warm sleep. He would give everything he possessed: he would give – how many – years of his life. One or two at any rate – perhaps five? Yes – I would give five. I remember the sastrugi, the view of the Knoll, the dim hazy black smudge of the sea far away below: the tiny bits of green canvas that twittered in the wind on the surface of the snow: the cold misery of it all, and the weakness which was biting into my heart.

For days Birdie had been urging me to use his eider-down lining – his beautiful dry bag of the finest down – which he had never slipped into his own fur bag. I had refused: I felt that I should be a beast to take it.

We packed the tank ready for a start back in the morning and turned in, utterly worn out. It was only $-12°$ that night, but my left big-toe was frost-bitten in my bag which I was trying to use without an eider-down lining, and my bag was always too big for me. It must have taken several hours to get it back, by beating one foot against the other. When we got up, as soon as we could, as we did every night, for our bags were nearly impossible, it was blowing fairly hard and looked like blizzing. We had a lot to do, two or three hours' work, packing sledges and making a depot of what we did not want, in a corner of the igloo. We left the second sledge, and a note tied to the handle of the pickaxe.

10. Bowers.

We started down the slope in a wind which was rising all the time and −15°. My job was to balance the sledge behind: I was so utterly done I don't believe I could have pulled effectively. Birdie was much the strongest of us. The strain and want of sleep was getting me in the neck, and Bill looked very bad. At the bottom we turned our faces to the Barrier, our backs to the penguins, but after doing about a mile it looked so threatening in the south that we camped in a big wind, our hands going one after the other. We had nothing but the hardest wind-swept sastrugi, and it was a long business: there was only the smallest amount of drift, and we were afraid the icy snow blocks would chafe the tent. Birdie lashed the full biscuit tin to the door to prevent its flapping, and also got what he called the tent downhaul round the cap and then tied it about himself outside his bag: if the tent went he was going too.

I was feeling as if I should crack, and accepted Birdie's eider-down. It was wonderfully self-sacrificing of him: more than I can write. I felt a brute to take it, but I was getting useless unless I got some sleep which my big bag would not allow. Bill and Birdie kept on telling me to do less: that I was doing more than my share of the work: but I think that I was getting more and more weak. Birdie kept wonderfully strong: he slept most of the night: the difficulty for him was to get into his bag without going to sleep. He kept the meteorological log untiringly, but some of these nights he had to give it up for the time because he could not keep awake. He used to fall asleep with his pannikin in his hand and let it fall: and sometimes he had the primus.

Bill's bag was getting hopeless: it was really too small for an eider-down and was splitting all over the place: great long holes. He never consciously slept for nights: he did sleep a bit, for we heard him. Except for this night, and the next when Birdie's eider-down was still fairly dry, I never consciously slept; except that I used to wake for five or six nights running with the same nightmare – that we were drifted up, and that Bill and Birdie were passing the gear into my bag, cutting it open to do so, or some other variation, – I did not know that I had been asleep at all.[11]

'We had hardly reached the pit,' wrote Bowers,

when a furious wind came on again and we had to camp. All that night the tent flapped like the noise of musketry, owing to two poles having been broken at the ends and the fit spoilt. I thought it would end matters by going altogether and lashed it down as much as I could, attaching the apex to a line round my own bag. The wind abated after 1½ days and we set out, doing five or six miles before we found ourselves among crevasses.[12]

We had plugged ahead all that day (26 July) in a terrible light, blundering in among pressure and up on to the slopes of Terror. The temperature dropped from −21° to −45°.

Several times [we] stepped into rotten-lidded crevasses in smooth wind-swept ice. We continued, however, feeling our way along by keeping always off hard ice-slopes and on the crustier deeper snow which characterizes the hollows of the pressure ridges, which I believed we had once more fouled in the dark. We had no light, and no landmarks to guide us, except vague and indistinct silhouetted slopes ahead, which were always altering and whose distance and character it was impossible to judge. We never knew whether we were approaching a steep slope at close quarters or a long slope of Terror, miles away, and eventually we travelled on by the ear, and by the feel of the snow under our feet, for both the sound and the touch told one much of the chances of crevasses or of safe going. We continued thus in the dark in the hope that we were at any rate in the right direction.[13]

11. My own diary.
12. Bowers.
13. Wilson in *Scott's Last Expedition*, vol. ii, p. 58.

And then we camped after getting into a bunch of crevasses, completely lost. Bill said, 'At any rate I think we are
well clear of the pressure.' But there were pressure pops all
night, as though someone was whacking an empty tub.

It was Birdie's picture hat which made the trouble next
day. 'What do you think of *that* for a hat, sir?' I heard him
say to Scott a few days before we started, holding it out
much as Lucille displays her latest Paris model. Scott looked
at it quietly for a time: 'I'll tell you when you come back,
Birdie,' he said. It was a complicated affair with all kinds of
nose-guards and buttons and lanyards: he thought he was
going to set it to suit the wind much as he would set the sails
of a ship. We spent a long time with our housewifes before
this and other trips, for everybody has their own ideas as to
how to alter their clothing for the best. When finished some
looked neat, like Bill: others baggy, like Scott or Seaman
Evans: others rough and ready, like Oates and Bowers: a few
perhaps more rough than ready, and I will not mention
names. Anyway Birdie's hat became improper immediately
it was well iced up.

When we got a little light in the morning we found we
were a little north of the two patches of moraine on Terror.
Though we did not know it, we were on the point where the
pressure runs up against Terror, and we could dimly see that
we were right up against something. We started to try and
clear it, but soon had an enormous ridge, blotting out the
moraine and half Terror, rising like a great hill on our right.
Bill said the only thing was to go right on and hope it would
lower; all the time, however, there was a bad feeling that we
might be putting any number of ridges between us and the
mountain. After a while we tried to cross this one, but had to
turn back for crevasses, both Bill and I putting a leg down. We
went on for about twenty minutes and found a lower place,
and turned to rise up it diagonally, and reached the top. Just
over the top Birdie went right down a crevasse, which was
about wide enough to take him. He was out of sight and out of
reach from the surface, hanging in his harness. Bill went for

his harness, I went for the bow of the sledge: Bill told me to get the Alpine rope and Birdie directed from below what we could do. We could not possibly haul him up as he was, for the sides of the crevasse were soft and he could not help himself.[14]

'My helmet was so frozen up,' wrote Bowers,

that my head was encased in a solid block of ice, and I could not look down without inclining my whole body. As a result Bill stumbled one foot into a crevasse and I landed in it with both mine [even as I shouted a warning[15]], the bridge gave way and down I went. Fortunately our sledge harness is made with a view to resisting this sort of thing, and there I hung with the bottomless pit below and the ice-crusted sides alongside, so narrow that to step over it would have been quite easy had I been able to see it. Bill said, 'What do you, want?' I asked for an Alpine rope with a bowline for my foot: and taking up first the bowline and then my harness they got me out.[16]

Meanwhile on the surface I lay over the crevasse and gave Birdie the bowline: he put it on his foot: then he raised his foot, giving me some slack: I held the rope while he raised himself on his foot, thus giving Bill some slack on the harness: Bill then held the harness, allowing Birdie to raise his foot and give me some slack again. We got him up inch by inch, our fingers getting bitten, for the temperature was $-46°$. Afterwards we often used this way of getting people out of crevasses, and it was a wonderful piece of presence of mind that it was invented, so far as I know, on the spur of the moment by a frozen man hanging in one himself.

In front of us we could see another ridge, and we did not know how many lay beyond that. Things looked pretty bad. Bill took a long lead on the Alpine rope and we got down our

14. My own diary.
15. Wilson.   16. Bowers.

present difficulty all right. This method of the leader being on a long trace in front we all agreed to be very useful. From this moment our luck changed and everything went for us to the end. When we went out on the sea-ice the whole experience was over in a few days, Hut Point was always in sight, and there was daylight. I always had the feeling that the whole series of events had been brought about by an extraordinary run of accidents, and that after a certain stage it was quite beyond our power to guide the course of them. When on the way to Cape Crozier the moon suddenly came out of the cloud to show us a great crevasse which would have taken us all with our sledge without any difficulty, I felt that we were not to go under this trip after such a deliverance. When we had lost our tent, and there was a very great balance of probability that we should never find it again, and we were lying out the blizzard in our bags, I saw that we were face to face with a long fight against cold which we could not have survived. I cannot write how helpless I believed we were to help ourselves, and how we were brought out of a very terrible series of experiences. When we started back I had a feeling that things were going to change for the better, and this day I had a distinct idea that we were to have one more bad experience and that after that we could hope for better things.

By running along the hollow we cleared the pressure ridges, and continued all day up and down, but met no crevasses. Indeed, we met no more crevasses and no more pressure. I think it was upon this day that a wonderful glow stretched over the Barrier edge from Cape Crozier: at the base it was the most vivid crimson it is possible to imagine, shading upwards through every shade of red to light green, and so into a deep blue sky. It is the most vivid red I have ever seen in the sky.[17]

It was −49° in the night and we were away early in −47°. By midday we were rising Terror Point, opening Erebus

17. My own diary.

rapidly, and got the first really light day, though the sun would not appear over the horizon for another month. I cannot describe what a relief the light was to us. We crossed the point outside our former track, and saw inside us the ridges where we had been blizzed for three days on our outward journey.

The minimum was −66° the next night and we were now back in the windless bight of Barrier with its soft snow, low temperatures, fogs and mists, and lingering settlements of the inside crusts. Saturday and Sunday, the 29th and 30th, we plugged on across this waste, iced up as usual but always with Castle Rock getting bigger. Sometimes it looked like fog or wind, but it always cleared away. We were getting weak, how weak we can only realize now, but we got in good marches, though slow – days when we did 4½, 7¼, 6¾, 6½, 7½ miles. On our outward journey we had been relaying and getting forward about 1½ miles a day at this point. The surface which we had dreaded so much was not so sandy or soft as when we had come out, and the settlements were more marked. These are caused by a crust falling under your feet. Generally the area involved is some twenty yards or so round you, and the surface falls through an air space for two or three inches with a soft 'crush' which may at first make you think there are crevasses about. In the region where we now travelled they were much more pronounced than else-where, and one day, when Bill was inside the tent lighting the primus, I put my foot into a hole that I had dug. This started a big settlement: sledge, tent and all of us dropped about a foot, and the noise of it ran away for miles and miles: we listened to it until we began to get too cold. It must have lasted a full three minutes.

In the pauses of our marching we halted in our harness, the ropes of which lay slack in the powdery snow. We stood panting with our backs against the mountainous mass of frozen gear which was our load. There was no wind, at any rate no more than light airs: our breath crackled as it froze. There was no unnecessary conversation: I don't know why our tongues never got frozen, but all my teeth, the nerves of which had been killed, split to pieces. We had been going perhaps three hours since lunch.

'How are your feet, Cherry?' from Bill.

'Very cold.'

'That's all right; so are mine.' We didn't worry to ask Birdie: he never had a frost-bitten foot from start to finish.

Half an hour later, as we marched, Bill would ask the same question. I tell him that all feeling has gone: Bill still has some feeling in one of his but the other is lost. He settled we had better camp: another ghastly night ahead.

We started to get out of our harnesses, while Bill, before doing anything else, would take the fur mitts from his hands, carefully shape any soft parts as they froze (generally, however, our mitts did not thaw on our hands), and lay them on the snow in front of him – two dark dots. His proper fur mitts were lost when the igloo roof went: these were the delicate dog-skin linings we had in addition, beautiful things to look at and to feel when new, excellent when dry to turn the screws of a theodolite, but too dainty for straps and lanyards. Just now I don't know what he could have done without them.

Working with our woollen half-mitts and mitts on our hands all the time, and our fur mitts over them when possible, we gradually got the buckles undone, and spread the green canvas floor-cloth on the snow. This was also fitted to be used as a sail, but we never could have rigged a sail on this journey. The shovel and the bamboos, with a lining, itself lined with ice, lashed to them, were packed on the top of the load and were now put on the snow until wanted. Our next job was to lift our three sleeping-bags one by one on to the floor-cloth: they covered it, bulging over the sides – those obstinate coffins which were all our life to us. . . . One of us is off by now to nurse his fingers back. The cooker was unlashed from the top of the instrument box; some parts of it were put on the bags with the primus, methylated spirit can, matches and so forth; others left to be filled with snow later. Taking a pole in each hand we three spread the bamboos over the whole. 'All right? Down!' from Bill; and we lowered them gently on to the soft snow, that they might not sink too far. The ice on the inner lining of the tent was formed mostly from the steam of the cooker. This we had been unable to beat or chip off in the past, and we were now, truth to tell, past worrying about it. The little ventilator in the top, made to let out this steam, had been tied up in order to keep in all possible heat. Then over the outer cover, and for one of us the third worst job of the day was to begin. The worst job was to get into our bags: the second or equal worst was to lie in them for six hours (we had brought it down to six): this third worst was to get the primus lighted and a meal on the way.

As cook of the day you took the broken metal framework, all that remained of our candlestick, and got yourself with difficulty into the funnel which formed the door. The enclosed space of the tent seemed much colder than the outside air: you tried three or four match-boxes and no match would strike: almost desperate, you asked for a new box to be given you from the sledge and got a light from this because it had not yet been in the warmth, so called, of the tent. The candle hung by a wire from the cap of the tent. It would be tedious to tell of the times we had getting the primus alight, and the lanyards of the weekly food bag unlashed. Probably by now the other two men have dug in the tent; squared up outside; filled and passed in the cooker; set the thermometer under the sledge and so forth. There were always one or two odd jobs which wanted doing as well: but you may be sure they came in as soon as possible when they heard the primus hissing, and saw the glow of light inside. Birdie made a bottom for the cooker out of an empty biscuit tin to take the place of the part which was blown away. On the whole this was a success, but we had to hold it steady – on Bill's sleeping-bag, for the flat frozen bags spread all over the floor space. Cooking was a longer business now. Someone whacked out the biscuit, and the cook put the ration of pemmican into the inner cooker which was by now half full of water. As opportunity offered we got out of our day, and into our night foot-gear – fleecy camel-hair stockings and fur boots. In the dim light we examined our feet for frost-bite.

I do not think it took us less than an hour to get a hot meal to our lips: pemmican followed by hot water in which we soaked our biscuits. For lunch we had tea and biscuits: for breakfast, pemmican, biscuits and tea. We could not have managed more food bags – three were bad enough, and the lashings of everything were like wire. The lashing of the tent door, however, was the worst, and it *had* to be tied tightly, especially if it was blowing. In the early days we took great pains to brush rime from the tent before packing it up, but we were long past that now.

The hoosh got down into our feet: we nursed back frost-bites: and we were all the warmer for having got our dry foot-gear on before supper. Then we started to get into our bags.

Birdie's bag fitted him beautifully, though perhaps it would have been a little small with an eider-down inside. He must have had a greater heat supply than other men; for he never had serious trouble with his feet, while ours were constantly frost-bitten: he slept, I should be afraid to say how much, longer than we did, even in these last days: it was a pleasure, lying awake practically all night, to hear his snores. He turned his bag inside out from fur to skin, and skin to fur, many times during the journey, and thus got rid of a lot of moisture which came out as snow or actual knobs of ice. When we did turn our bags the only way was to do so directly we turned out, and even then you had to be quick before the bag froze. Getting out of the tent at night it was quite a race to get back to your bag before it hardened. Of course this was in the lowest temperatures.

We could not burn our bags and we tried putting the lighted primus into them to thaw them out, but this was not very successful. Before this time, when it was very cold, we lighted the primus in the morning while we were still in our bags: and in the evening we kept it going until we were just getting or had got the mouths of our bags levered open. But returning we had no oil for such luxuries, until the last day or two.

I do not believe that any man, however sick he is, has a much worse time than we had in those bags, shaking with cold until our backs would almost break. One of the added troubles which came to us on our return was the sodden condition of our hands in our bags at night. We had to wear our mitts and half-mitts, and they were as wet as they could be: when we got up in the morning we had washer-women's hands – white, crinkled, sodden. That was an unhealthy way to start the day's work. We really wanted some bags of saennegrass for hands as well as feet; one of the blessings of that kind of bag being that you can shake the moisture from it: but we only had enough for our wretched feet.

The horrors of that return journey are blurred to my memory and I know they were blurred to my body at the time. I think this applies to all of us, for we were much weakened and callous. The day we got down to the penguins I had not cared whether I fell into a crevasse or not. We had been through a great deal since then. I know that we slept on the march; for I woke up when I bumped against Birdie, and Birdie woke when he bumped against me. I think Bill steering out in front managed to keep awake. I know we fell asleep if we waited in the comparatively warm tent when the primus was alight – with our pannikins or the primus in our hands. I know that our sleeping-bags were so full of ice that we did not worry if we spilt water or hoosh over them as they lay on the floor-cloth, when we cooked on them with our maimed cooker. They were so bad that we never rolled them up in the usual way when we got out of them in the morning: we opened their mouths as much as possible before they froze, and hoisted them more or less flat on to the sledge. All three of us helped to raise each bag, which looked rather like a squashed coffin and was probably a good deal harder. I know that if it was only −40° when we camped for the night we considered quite seriously that we were going to have a warm one, and that when we got up in the morning if the temperature was in the minus sixties we did not inquire what it was. The day's march was bliss compared to the night's rest, and both were awful. We were about as bad as men can be and do good travelling: but I never heard a word of complaint, nor, I believe, an oath, and I saw self-sacrifice standing every test.

Always we were getting nearer home: and we were doing good marches. We were going to pull through; it was only a matter of sticking this for a few more days; six, five, four . . . three perhaps now, if we were not blizzed. Our main hut was behind that ridge where the mist was always forming and blowing away; and there was Castle Rock: we might even see Observation Hill tomorrow, and the *Discovery* Hut furnished and trim was behind it, and they would have sent some dry sleeping-bags from Cape Evans to greet us there. We reckoned our troubles over at the Barrier edge, and assuredly it was not far away. 'You've got it in the neck, stick it, you've got it in the neck' – it was always running in my head.

And we *did* stick it. How good the memories of those days are. With jokes about Birdie's picture hat: with songs we remembered off the gramophone: with ready words of sympathy for frost-bitten feet: with generous smiles for poor jests; with suggestions of happy beds to come. We did not forget the Please and Thank You, which means much in such circumstances, and all the little links with decent civilization which we could still keep going. I'll swear there was still a grace about us when we staggered in. And we kept our tempers – even with God.

We *might* reach Hut Point tonight: we were burning more oil now, that one-gallon tin had lasted us well: and burning more candle too; at one time we feared they would give out. A hell of a morning we had: −57° in our present state. But it was calm, and the Barrier edge could not be much farther now. The surface was getting harder: there were a few wind-blown furrows, the crust was coming up to us. The sledge was dragging easier: we always suspected the Barrier sloped downwards hereabouts. Now the hard snow was on the surface, peeping out like great inverted basins on which we slipped, and our feet became warmer for not sinking into soft snow. Suddenly we saw a gleam of light in the line of darkness running across our course. It was the Barrier edge: we were all right now.

We ran the sledge off a snow-drift on to the sea-ice, with the same cold stream of air flowing down it which wrecked my hands five weeks ago: pushed out of this, camped and had a meal: the temperature had already risen to −43°. We could almost feel it getting warmer as we went round Cape Armitage on the last three miles. We managed to haul our sledge up the ice foot, and dug the drift away from the door. The old hut struck us as fairly warm.

Bill was convinced that we ought not to go into the warm hut at Cape Evans when we arrived there – tomorrow night! We ought to get back to warmth gradually, live in a tent outside, or in the annexe for a day or two. But I'm sure we never meant to do it. Just now Hut Point did not prejudice us in favour of such abstinence. It was just as we had left it: there was nothing sent down for us there – no sleeping-bags, nor sugar: but there was plenty of oil. Inside the hut we pitched a dry tent left there since Depot Journey days, set two primuses going in it; sat dozing on our bags; and drank cocoa without sugar so thick that next morning we were gorged with it. We were very happy, falling asleep between each mouthful, and after several hours discussed schemes of not getting into our bags at all. But someone would have to keep the primus going to prevent frost-bite, and we could not trust ourselves to keep awake. Bill and I tried to sing a part-song. Finally we sopped our way into our bags. We only stuck *them* three hours, and thankfully turned out at 3 a.m., and were ready to pack up when we heard the wind come away. It was no good, so we sat in our tent and dozed again. The wind dropped at 9.30: we were off at 11. We walked out into what seemed to us a blaze of light. It was not until the following year that I understood that a great part of such twilight as there is in the latter part of the winter was cut off from us by the mountains under which we travelled. Now, with nothing between us and the northern horizon below which lay the sun, we saw as we had not seen for months, and the iridescent clouds that day were beautiful.

We just pulled for all we were worth and did nearly two miles an hour: for two miles a baddish salt surface, then big undulating hard sastrugi and good going. We slept as we walked. We had done eight miles by 4 p.m. and were past Glacier Tongue. We lunched there.

As we began to gather our gear together to pack up for the last time, Bill said quietly, 'I want to thank you two for what you have done. I couldn't have found two better companions – and what is more I never shall.'

I am proud of that.

Antarctic exploration is seldom as bad as you imagine, seldom as bad as it sounds. But this journey had beggared our language: no words could express its horror.

We trudged on for several more hours and it grew very dark. There was a discussion as to where Cape Evans lay. We rounded it at last: it must have been ten or eleven o'clock, and it was possible that someone might see us as we pulled towards the hut. 'Spread out well,' said Bill, 'and they will be able to see that there are three men.' But we pulled along the cape, over the tide-crack, up the bank to the very door of the hut without a sound. No noise from the stable, nor the bark of a dog from the snow drifts above us. We halted and stood there trying to get ourselves and one another out of our frozen harnesses – the usual long job. The door opened – 'Good God! here is the Crozier Party,' said a voice, and disappeared.

Thus ended the worst journey in the world.

And now the reader will ask what became of the three penguins' eggs for which three human lives had been risked three hundred times a day, and three human frames strained to the utmost extremity of human endurance.

Let us leave the Antarctic for a moment and conceive ourselves in the year 1913 in the Natural History Museum in South Kensington. I had written to say that I would bring the eggs at this time. Present, myself, C.-G., the sole survivor of the three, with First or Doorstep Custodian of the Sacred Eggs. I did not take a verbatim report of his welcome; but the spirit of it may be dramatized as follows:

FIRST CUSTODIAN. Who are you? What do you want? This ain't an egg-shop. What call have you to come meddling with our eggs? Do you want me to put the police on to you? Is it the crocodile's egg you're after? I don't know nothing about no eggs. You'd best speak to Mr Brown: it's him that varnishes the eggs.

I resort to Mr Brown, who ushers me into the presence of the Chief Custodian, a man of scientific aspect, with two manners: one, affably courteous, for a Person of Importance (I guess a Naturalist Rothschild at least) with whom he is conversing, and the other, extraordinarily offensive even for an official man of science, for myself.

I announce myself with becoming modesty as the bearer of the penguins' eggs, and proffer them. The Chief Custodian takes them into custody without a word of thanks, and turns to the Person of Importance to discuss them. I wait. The temperature of my blood rises. The conversation proceeds for what seems to me a considerable period. Suddenly the Chief Custodian notices my presence and seems to resent it.

CHIEF CUSTODIAN. You needn't wait.

HEROIC EXPLORER. I should like to have a receipt for the eggs, if you please.

CHIEF CUSTODIAN. It is not necessary: it is all right. You needn't wait.

HEROIC EXPLORER. I should like to have a receipt.

But by this time the Chief Custodian's attention is again devoted wholly to the Person of Importance. Feeling that to persist in overhearing their conversation would be an indelicacy, the Heroic Explorer politely leaves the room, and establishes himself on a chair in a gloomy passage outside, where he wiles away the time by rehearsing in his imagination how he will tell off the Chief Custodian when the Person of Importance retires. But this the Person of Importance shows no sign of doing, and the Explorer's thoughts and intentions become darker and darker. As the day wears on, minor officials, passing to and from the Presence, look at him doubtfully and ask his business. The reply is always the same, 'I am waiting for a receipt for some penguins' eggs.' At last it becomes clear from the Explorer's expression that what he is really waiting for is not to take a receipt but to commit murder. Presumably this is reported to the destined victim: at all events the receipt finally comes; and the Explorer goes his way with it, feeling that he has behaved like a perfect gentleman, but so very dissatisfied with that vapid consolation that for hours he continues his imaginary rehearsals of what he would have liked to have done to that Custodian (mostly with his boots) by way of teaching him manners.

Some time after this I visited the Natural History Museum with Captain Scott's sister. After a slight preliminary skirmish in which we convinced a minor custodian that the specimens brought by the expedition from the Antarctic did not include the moths we found preying on some of them, Miss Scott expressed a wish to see the penguins' eggs. Thereupon the minor custodian flatly denied that any such eggs were in existence or in their possession. Now Miss Scott was her brother's sister; and she showed so little disposition to take this lying down that I was glad to get her away with no worse consequences than a profanely emphasized threat on my part that if we did not receive ample satisfaction in writing within twenty-four hours as to the safety of the eggs England would reverberate with the tale.

The ultimatum was effectual; and due satisfaction was forthcoming in time; but I was relieved when I learnt later on that they had been entrusted to Professor Assheton for the necessary microscopic examination. But he died before he could approach the task; and the eggs passed into the hands of Professor Cossar Ewart of Edinburgh University.

His report is as follows:

PROFESSOR COSSAR EWART'S REPORT

It was a great disappointment to Dr Wilson that no Emperor Penguin embryos were obtained during the cruise of the

Discovery. But though embryos were conspicuous by their absence in the Emperor eggs brought home by the National Antarctic Expedition, it is well to bear in mind that the naturalists on board the *Discovery* learned much about the breeding habits of the largest living member of the ancient penguin family. Amongst other things it was ascertained (1) that in the case of the Emperor, as in the King Penguin, the egg during the period of incubation rests on the upper surface of the feet protected and kept in position by a fold of skin from the lower breast; and (2) that in the case of the Emperor the whole process of incubation is carried out on sea ice during the coldest and darkest months of the antarctic winter.

After devoting much time to the study of penguins Dr Wilson came to the conclusion that Emperor embryos would throw new light on the origin and history of birds, and decided that if he again found his way to the Antarctic he would make a supreme effort to visit an Emperor rookery during the breeding season. When, and under what conditions, the Cape Crozier rookery was eventually visited and Emperor eggs secured is graphically told in *The Winter Journey*. The question now arises, Has 'the weirdest bird's-nesting expedition that has ever been made' added appreciably to our knowledge of birds?

It is admitted that birds are descended from bipedal reptiles which flourished some millions of years ago – reptiles in build not unlike the kangaroo. From Archaeopteryx of Jurassic times we know primeval birds had teeth, three fingers with claws on each hand, and a long lizard-like tail provided with nearly twenty pairs of well-formed true feathers. But unfortunately neither this lizard-tailed bird, nor yet the fossil birds found in America, throw any light on the origin of feathers. Ornithologists and others who have devoted much time to the study of birds have as a rule assumed that feathers were made out of scales, that the scales along the margin of the hand and forearm and along each side of the tail were elongated, frayed and otherwise modified to form the wing and tail quills, and that later other scales were altered to provide a coat capable of preventing loss of hĕat. But as it happens, a study of the development of feathers affords no evidence that they were made out of scales. There are neither rudiments of scales nor feathers in very young bird embryos. In the youngest of the three Emperor embryos there are, however, feather rudiments in the tail region, – the embryo was probably seven or eight days old – but in the two older embryos there are a countless number of feather rudiments, i.e. of minute pimples known as papillae.

In penguins as in many other birds there are two distinct crops of feather papillae, viz: a crop of relatively large papillae which develop into prepennae, the forerunners of true feathers (pennae), and a crop of small papillae which develop into preplumulae, the forerunners of true down feathers (plumulae).

In considering the origin of feathers we are not concerned with the true feathers (pennae), but with the nestling feathers (prepennae), and more especially with the papillae from which the prepennae are developed. What we want to know is, Do the papillae which in birds develop into the first generation of feathers correspond to the papillae which in lizards develop into scales?

The late Professor Assheton, who undertook the examination of some of the material brought home by the *Terra Nova*, made a special study of the feather papillae of the Emperor Penguin embryos from Cape Crozier. Drawings were made to indicate the number, size and time of appearance of the feather papillae, but unfortunately in the notes left by the distinguished embryologist there is no indication whether the feather papillae were regarded as modified scale papillae or new creations resulting from the appearance of special feather-forming factors in the germ-plasm.

When eventually the three Emperor Penguin embryos reached me that their feather rudiments might be compared with the feather rudiments of other birds, I noticed that in Emperor embryos the feather papillae appeared before the scale papillae. Evidence of this was especially afforded by the largest embryo, which had reached about the same stage in its development as a 16-day goose embryo.

In the largest Emperor embryo feather papillae occur all over the hind-quarters and on the legs to within a short distance of the tarsal joint. Beyond the tarsal joint even in the largest embryo no attempt had been made to produce the papillae which in older penguin embryos represent, and ultimately develop into, the scaly covering of the foot. The absence of papillae on the foot implied either that the scale papillae were fundamentally different from feather papillae or that for some reason or other the development of the papillae destined to give rise to the foot scales had been retarded. There is no evidence as far as I can ascertain that in modern lizards the scale papillae above the tarsal joint appear before the scale papillae beyond this joint.

The absence of papillae below the tarsal joint in Emperor embryos, together with the fact that in many birds each large feather papilla is accompanied by two or more very small feather papillae, led me to study the papillae of the limbs of other birds. The most striking results were obtained from the embryos of Chinese geese in which the legs are relatively longer than in penguins. In a 13-day goose embryo the whole of the skin below and for some distance above the tarsal joint is quite smooth, whereas the skin of the rest of the leg is studded with feather papillae. On the other hand, in an 18-day goose embryo in which the feather papillae of the legs have developed into filaments, each containing a fairly well-formed feather, scale papillae occur not only on the foot below and for some distance above the tarsal joint but also between the roots of the feather filaments between the tarsal and the knee joints. More important still, in a 20-day goose embryo a number of the papillae situated between the feather filaments of the leg were actually developing into scales each of which overlapped the root (calamus) of a feather just as scales overlap the foot feathers in grouse and other feather-footed birds.

As in bird embryos there is no evidence that feather papillae ever develop into scales or that scale papillae ever develop into feathers it may be assumed that feather papillae are fundamentally different from scale papillae, the difference presumably being due to the presence of special factors in the germ-plasm. Just as in armadillos hairs are found emerging from under the scales, in ancient birds as in the feet of some modern birds the coat probably consisted of both feathers and scales. But in course of time, owing perhaps to the growth of the scales being arrested, the coat of the birds, instead of consisting throughout of well-developed scales and small inconspicuous feathers, was almost entirely made up of a countless number of downy feathers, well-developed scales only persisting below the tarsal joint.

If the conclusions arrived at with the help of the Emperor Penguin embryos about the origin of feathers are justified, the worst journey in the world in the interest of science was not made in vain.

Chapter Eight
SPRING

INSIDE WAS pandemonium. Most men had gone to bed, and I have a blurred memory of men in pyjamas and dressing-gowns getting hold of me and trying to get the chunks of armour which were my clothes to leave my body. Finally they cut them off and threw them into an angular heap at the foot of my bunk. Next morning they were a sodden mass weighing 24 lbs. Bread and jam, and cocoa; showers of questions; 'You know this is the hardest journey ever made,' from Scott; a broken record of George Robey on the gramophone which started us laughing until in our weak state we found it difficult to stop. I have no doubt that I had not stood the journey as well as Wilson: my jaw had dropped when I came in, so they tell me. Then into my warm blanket bag, and I managed to keep awake just long enough to think that Paradise must feel something like this.

We slept ten thousand thousand years, were wakened to find everybody at breakfast, and passed a wonderful day, lazying about, half asleep and wholly happy, listening to the news and answering questions.

We are looked upon as beings who have come from another world. This afternoon I had a shave after soaking my face in a hot sponge, and then a bath. Lashly had already cut my hair. Bill looks very thin and we are all very blear-eyed from want of sleep. I have not much appetite, my mouth is very dry and throat sore with a troublesome hacking cough which I have had all the journey. My taste is gone. We are getting badly spoiled, but our beds are the height of all our pleasures.[1]

But this did not last long:

1. My own diary.

Another very happy day doing nothing. After falling asleep two or three times I went to bed, read *Kim*, and slept. About two hours after each meal we all want another, and after a tremendous supper last night we had another meal before turning in. I have my taste back but all our fingers are impossible, they might be so many pieces of lead except for the pins and needles feeling in them which we have also got in our feet. My toes are very bulbous and some toe-nails are coming off. My left heel is one big burst blister. Going straight out of a warm bed into a strong wind outside nearly bowled me over. I felt quite faint, and pulled myself together thinking it was all nerves: but it began to come on again and I had to make for the hut as quickly as possible. Birdie is now full of schemes for doing the trip again next year. Bill says it is too great a risk in the darkness, and he will not consider it, though he thinks that to go in August might be possible.[2]

And again a day or two later:

I came in covered with a red rash which is rather ticklish. My ankles and knees are a bit puffy, but my feet are not so painful as Bill's and Birdie's. Hands itch a bit. We must be very weak and worn out, though I think Birdie is the strongest of us. He seems to be picking up very quickly. Bill is still very worn and rather haggard. The kindness of everybody would spoil an angel.[3]

I have put these personal experiences down from my diary because they are the only contemporary record I possess. Scott's own diary at this time contains the statement:

The Crozier party returned last night after enduring for five weeks the hardest conditions on record. They looked more weather-worn than anyone I have yet seen. Their faces were scarred and wrinkled, their eyes dull, their hands

2. My own diary.　　3. ibid.

whitened and creased with the constant exposure to damp and
cold, yet the scars of frost-bite were very few . . . today after
a night's rest our travellers are very different in appearance
and mental capacity.[4]

'Atch has been lost in a blizzard,' was the news which we
got as soon as we could grasp anything. Since then he has
spent a year of war in the North Sea, seen the Dardanelles
campaign, and much fighting in France, and has been blown
up in a monitor. I doubt whether he does not reckon that
night the worst of the lot. He ought to have been blown into
hundreds of little bits, but always like some hardy indiarub-
ber ball he turns up again, a little dented, but with the same
tough elasticity which refuses to be hurt. And with the same
quiet voice he volunteers for the next, and tells you how
splendid everybody was except himself.

It was the blizzard of 4 July, when we were lying in the
windless bight on our way to Cape Crozier, and we knew it
must be blowing all round us. At any rate it was blowing at
Cape Evans, though it eased up in the afternoon, and
Atkinson and Taylor went up the Ramp to read the thermometers there. They returned without great difficulty, and
some discussion seems to have arisen as to whether it was
possible to read the two screens on the sea-ice. Atkinson said
he would go and read that in North Bay: Gran said he was
going to South Bay. They started independently at 5.30 p.m.
Gran returned an hour and a quarter afterwards. He had gone
about two hundred yards.

Atkinson had not gone much farther when he decided that
he had better give it up, so he turned and faced the wind,
steering by keeping it on his cheek. We discovered afterwards
that the wind does not blow quite in the same direction at the
end of the Cape as it does just where the hut lies. Perhaps it
was this, perhaps his left leg carried him a little farther than
his right, perhaps it was that the numbing effect of a blizzard
on a man's brain was already having its effect, certainly

4. *Scott's Last Expedition*, vol. 1, p. 361.

Atkinson does not know himself, but instead of striking the Cape which ran across his true front, he found himself by an old fish trap which he knew was 200 yards out on the sea-ice. He made a great effort to steady himself and make for the Cape, but anyone who has stood in a blizzard will understand how difficult that is. The snow was a blanket raging all round him, and it was quite dark. He walked on, and found nothing.

Everything else is vague. Hour after hour he staggered about: he got his hand badly frost-bitten: he found pressure: he fell over it: he was crawling in it, on his hands and knees. Stumbling, tumbling, tripping, buffeted by the endless lash of the wind, sprawling through miles of punishing snow, he still seems to have kept his brain working. He found an island, thought it was Inaccessible, spent ages in coasting along it, lost it, found more pressure, and crawled along it. He found another island, and the same horrible, almost senseless, search went on. Under the lee of some rocks he waited for a time. His clothing was thin though he had his wind-clothes, and, a horrible thought if this was to go on, he had boots on his feet instead of warm finnesko. Here also he kicked out a hole in a drift where he might have more chance if he were forced to lie down. For sleep is the end of men who get lost in blizzards. Though he did not know it he must now have been out more than four hours.

There was little chance for him if the blizzard continued, but hope revived when the moon showed in a partial lull. It is wonderful that he was sufficiently active to grasp the significance of this, and groping back in his brain he found he could remember the bearing of the moon from Cape Evans when he went to bed the night before. The hut must be somewhere over there: this must be Inaccessible Island! He left the island and made in that direction, but the blizzard came down again with added force and the moon was blotted out. He tried to return to the island and failed: then he stumbled on another island, perhaps the same one, and waited. Again the lull came, and again he set off, and walked and walked, until he recognized Inaccessible Island on his left. Clearly he must have been under Great Razorback Island and this is some four miles from Cape Evans. The moon still showed, and on he walked and then at last he saw a flame.

Atkinson's continued absence was not noticed at the hut until dinner was nearly over at 7.15; that is, until he had been absent about two hours. The wind at Cape Evans had dropped though it was thick all round, and no great anxiety was felt: some went out and shouted, others went north with a lantern, and Day arranged to light a paraffin flare on Wind Vane Hill. Atkinson never experienced this lull, and having seen the way blizzards will sweep down the Strait though the coastline is comparatively clear and calm, I can understand how he was in the thick of it all the time. I feel convinced that most of these blizzards are local affairs. The party which had gone north returned at 9.30 without news, and Scott became seriously alarmed. Between 9.30 and 10 six search parties started out. But time was passing and Atkinson had been away more than six hours.

The light which Atkinson had seen was a flare of tow soaked in petrol lit by Day at Cape Evans. He corrected his course and before long was under the rock upon which Day could be seen working like some lanky devil in one of Dante's hells. Atkinson shouted again and again but could not attract his attention, and finally walked almost into the hut before he was found by two men searching the Cape. 'It was all my own damned fault,' he said, 'but Scott never slanged me at all.' I really think we should all have been as merciful! Wouldn't *you*?

And that was that: but he had a beastly hand.

Theoretically the sun returned to us on 23 August. Practically there was nothing to be seen except blinding drift. But we saw his upper limb two days later. In Scott's words the daylight came 'rushing' at us. Two spring journeys were contemplated; and with preparations for the Polar Journey, and the ordinary routine work of the station, everybody had as much on his hands as he could get through.

Lieutenant Evans, Gran and Forde volunteered to go out to Corner Camp and dig out this depot as well as that of

Safety Camp. They started on 9 September and camped on the sea-ice beyond Cape Armitage that night, the minimum temperature being −45°. They dug out Safety Camp next morning, and marched on towards Corner Camp. The minimum that night was −62.3°. The next evening they made their night camp as a blizzard was coming up, the temperature at the same time being −34.5° and minimum for the night −40°. This is an extremely low temperature for a blizzard. They made a start in a very cold wind the next afternoon (12 September) and camped at 8.30 p.m. That night was bitterly cold and they found that the minimum showed −73.3° for that night. Evans reports adversely on the use of the eider-down bag and inner tent, but here none of our Winter Journey men would agree with him.[5] Most of 13 September was spent in digging out Corner Camp which they left at 5 p.m., intending to travel back to Hut Point without stopping except for meals. They marched all through that night with two halts for meals and arrived at Hut Point at 3 p.m. on 14 September, having covered a distance of 34.6 statute miles. They reached Cape Evans the following day after an absence of 6½ days.[6]

During this journey Forde got his hand badly frost-bitten which necessitated his return in the *Terra Nova* in March 1912. He owed a great deal to the skilful treatment Atkinson gave it.

Wilson was still looking grey and drawn some days, and I was not too fit, but Bowers was indefatigable. Soon after we got in from Cape Crozier he heard that Scott was going over to the Western Mountains: somehow or other he persuaded Scott to take him, and they started with Seaman Evans and Simpson on 15 September on what Scott calls 'a remarkably pleasant and instructive little spring journey',[7] and what Bowers called a jolly picnic.

This picnic started from the hut in a −40° temperature,

5. *Scott's Last Expedition*, vol. ii, p. 293.
6. ibid., pp. 291–7; written by Lieutenant Evans.
7. ibid., vol. i, p. 409.

dragging 180 lbs. per man, mainly composed of stores for the geological party of the summer. They penetrated as far north as Dunlop Island and turned back from there on 24 September, reaching Cape Evans on 29 September, marching twenty-one miles (statute) into a blizzard wind with occasional storms of drift and a temperature of −16°: and they marched a little too long; for a storm of drift came against them and they had to camp. It is never very easy pitching a tent on sea-ice because there is not very much snow on the ice: on this occasion it was only after they had detached the inner tent, which was fastened to the bamboos, that they could hold the bamboos, and then it was only inch by inch that they got the outer cover on. At 9 p.m. the drift took off though the wind was as strong as ever, and they decided to make for Cape Evans. They arrived at 1.15 a.m. after one of the most strenuous days which Scott could remember: and that meant a good deal. Simpson's face was a sight! During his absence Griffith Taylor became meteorologist-in-chief. He was a greedy scientist, and he also wielded a fluent pen. Consequently his output during the year and a half which he spent with us was large, and ranged from the results of the two excellent scientific journeys which he led in the Western Mountains, to this work during the latter half of September. He was a most valued contributor to the *South Polar Times*, and his prose and poetry both had a bite which was never equalled by any other of our amateur journalists. When his pen was still, his tongue wagged, and the arguments he led were legion. The hut was a merrier place for his presence. When the weather was good he might be seen striding over the rocks with a complete disregard of the effect on his clothes: he wore through a pair of boots quicker than anybody I have ever known, and his socks had to be mended with string. Ice movement and erosion were also of interest to him, and almost every day he spent some time in studying the slopes and huge ice-cliffs of the Barne Glacier, and other points of interest. With equal ferocity he would throw himself into his curtained bunk because he was bored, or emerge from it to take part in some argument which was troubling the table. His diary must have been almost as long as the reports he wrote for Scott of his geological explorations. He was a demon note-taker, and he had a passion for being equipped so that he could cope with any observation which might turn up. Thus Old Griff on a sledge journey might have notebooks protruding from every pocket, and hung about his person, a sundial, a prismatic compass, a sheath knife, a pair of binoculars, a geological hammer, chronometer, pedometer, camera, aneroid and other items of surveying gear, as well as his goggles and mitts. And in his hand might be an ice-axe which he used as he went along to the possible advancement of science, but the certain disorganization of his companions.

His gaunt, untamed appearance was atoned for by a halo of good-fellowship which hovered about his head. I am sure he must have been an untidy person to have in your tent: I feel equally sure that his tent-mates would have been sorry to lose him. His gear took up more room than was strictly his share, and his mind also filled up a considerable amount of space. He always bulked large, and when he returned to the Australian Government, which had lent him for the first two sledging seasons, he left a noticeable gap in our company.

From the time we returned from Cape Crozier until now Scott had been full of buck. Our return had taken a weight off his mind: the return of the daylight was stimulating to everybody: and to a man of his impatient and impetuous temperament the end of the long period of waiting was a relief. Also everything was going well. On 10 September he writes with a sigh of relief that the detailed plans for the Southern Journey are finished at last.

Every figure has been checked by Bowers, who has been an enormous help to me. If the motors are successful, we shall have no difficulty in getting to the Glacier, and if they fail, we shall still get there with any ordinary degree of good fortune. To work three units of four men from that point onwards requires no small provision, but with the proper provision it should take a good deal to stop the attainment of our object. I have tried to take every reasonable possibility of misfortune into consideration, and to so organize the parties as to be prepared to meet them. I fear to be too sanguine, yet taking everything into consideration I feel that our chances ought to be good.[8]

And again he writes:

Of hopeful signs for the future none are more remarkable than the health and spirit of our people. It would be impossible to imagine a more vigorous community, and there does not seem to be a single weak spot in the twelve good men and true who are chosen for the Southern advance. All are now experienced sledge travellers, knit together with a bond of friendship that has never been equalled under such circumstances. Thanks to these people, and more especially to Bowers and Petty Officer Evans, there is not a single detail of our equipment which is not arranged with the utmost care and in accordance with the tests of experience.[9]

Indeed Bowers had been of the very greatest use to Scott in the working out of these plans. Not only had he all the details of stores at his finger-tips, but he had studied polar clothing and polar food, was full of plans and alternative plans, and, best of all, refused to be beaten by any problem which presented itself. The actual distribution of weights between dogs, motors and ponies, and between the different ponies, was largely left in his hands. We had only to lead our ponies out on the day of the start and we were sure to find our sledges ready, each with the right load and weight. To the leader of an expedition such a man was worth his weight in gold.

But now Scott became worried and unhappy. We were running things on a fine margin of transport, and during the month before we were due to start mishap followed mishap

8. *Scott's Last Expedition*, vol. i, p. 403.
9. ibid., p. 404.

in the most disgusting way. Three men were more or less incapacitated: Forde with his frozen hand, Clissold who concussed himself by a fall from a berg, and Debenham who hurt his knee seriously when playing football. One of the ponies, Jehu, was such a crock that at one time it was decided not to take him out at all: and very bad opinions were also held of Chinaman. Another dog died of a mysterious disease. 'It is trying,' writes Scott, 'but I am past despondency. Things must take their course.'[10] And 'if this waiting were to continue it looks as though we should become a regular party of "crocks".'[11]

Then on the top of all this came a bad accident to one of the motor axles on the eve of departure.

Tonight the motors were to be taken on to the floe. The drifts made the road very uneven, and the first and best motor overrode its chain; the chain was replaced and the machine proceeded, but just short of the floe was thrust to a steep inclination by a ridge, and the chain again overrode the sprockets; this time by ill fortune Day slipped at the critical moment and without intention jammed the throttle full on. The engine brought up, but there was an ominous trickle of oil under the back axle, and investigation showed that the axle casing (aluminium) had split. The casing had been stripped and brought into the hut: we may be able to do something to it, but time presses. It all goes to show that we want more experience and workshops. I am secretly convinced that we shall not get much help from the motors, yet nothing has ever happened to them that was unavoidable. A little more care and foresight would make them splendid allies. The trouble is that if they fail, no one will ever believe this.[12]

In the meantime Meares and Dimitri ran out to Corner Camp from Hut Point twice with the two dog-teams. The first time they journeyed out and back in two days and a

10. *Scott's Last Expedition*, vol. i, p. 425.
11. ibid., p. 437.   12. ibid., p. 429.

night, returning on 15 October; and another very similar run was made before the end of the month.

The motor party was to start first, but was delayed until 24 October. They were to wait for us in latitude 80° 30′, man-hauling certain loads on if the motors broke down. The two engineers were Day and Lashly, and their two helpers, who steered by pulling on a rope in front, were Lieutenant Evans and Hooper. Scott was 'immensely eager that these tractors should succeed, even though they may not be of great help to our Southern advance. A small measure of success will be enough to show their possibilities, their ability to revolutionize polar transport.'[13]

Lashly, as the reader may know by now, was a chief stoker in the Navy, and accompanied Scott on his Plateau Journey in the *Discovery* days. The following account of the motors' chequered career is from his diary, and for permission to include here both it and the story of the adventures of the Second Return Party, an extraordinarily vivid and simple narrative, I cannot be too grateful.

After the motors had been two days on the sea-ice on their way to Hut Point Lashly writes on 26 October 1911:

> Kicked off at 9.30; engine going well, surface much better, dropped one can of petrol each and lubricating oil, lunched about two miles from Hut Point. Captain Scott and supporting party came from Cape Evans to help us over blue ice, but they were not required. Got away again after lunch but was delayed by the other sledge not being able to get along, it is beginning to dawn on me the sledges are not powerful enough for the work as it is one continual drag over this sea-ice, perhaps it will improve on the barrier, it seems we are going to be troubled with engine overheating; after we have run about three-quarters to a mile it is necessary to stop at least half an hour to cool the engine down, then we have to close up for a few minutes to allow the carbrutta to warm up or we can't get the petrol to vaporize; we are getting new experi-

13. ibid., p. 438.

ences every day. We arrived at Hut Point and proceeded to
Cape Armitage it having come on to snow pretty thickly, so
we pitched our tent and waited for the other car to come up,
she has been delayed all the afternoon and not made much
headway. At 6.30 Mr Bowers and Mr Garrard came out to us
and told us to come back to Hut Point for the night, where
we all enjoyed ourselves with a good hoosh and a nice night
with all hands.

27 October 1911

This morning being fine made our way out to the cars and
got them going after a bit of trouble, the temperature being a
bit low. I got away in good style, the surface seems to be
improving, it is better for running on but very rough and the
overheating is not overcome nor likely to be as far as I can
see. Just before arriving at the Barrier my car began to develop
some strange knocking in the engine, but with the help of the
party with us I managed to get on the Barrier, the other car
got up the slope in fine style and waited for me to come up;
as my engine is giving trouble we decided to camp, have
lunch and see what is the matter. On opening the crank
chamber we found the crank brasses broke into little pieces,
so there is nothing left to do but replace them with the spare
ones; of course this meant a cold job for Mr Day and myself,
as handling metal on the Barrier is not a thing one looks
forward to with pleasure. Anyhow we set about it after
Lieutenant Evans and Hooper had rigged up a screen to shelter
us a bit, and by 10 p.m. we were finished and ready to
proceed, but owing to a very low temperature we found it
difficult to get the engines to go, so we decided to camp for
the night.

28 October 1911

Turned out and had another go at starting which took
some little time owing again to the low temperature. We got
away but again trouble is always staring us in the face,
overheating, and the surface is so bad and the pull so heavy
and constant that it looks we are in for a rough time. We are
continually waiting for one another to come up, and every

time we stop something has to be done, my fan got jammed and delayed us some time, but have got it right again. Mr Evans had to go back for his spare gear owing to some one [not] bringing it out in mistake; he had a good tramp as we were about 15 miles out from Hut Point.

29 October 1911

Again we got away, but did not get far before the other car began to give trouble. I went back to see what was the matter, it seems the petrol is dirty due perhaps to putting in a new drum, anyhow got her up and camped for lunch. After lunch made a move, and all seemed to be going well when Mr Day's car gave out at the crank brasses the same as mine, so we shall have to see what is the next best thing to do.

30 October 1911

This morning before getting the car on the way had to reconstruct our loads as Mr Day's car is finished and no more use for further service. We have got all four of us with one car now, things seem to be going fairly well, but we are still troubled with the overheating which means to say half our time is wasted. We can see dawning on us the harness before long. We covered seven miles and camped for the night. We are now about six miles from Corner Camp.

31 October 1911

Got away with difficulty, and nearly reached Corner Camp, but the weather was unkind and forced us to camp early. One thing we have been able to bring along a good supply of pony food and most of the man food, but so far the motor sledges have proved a failure.

1 November 1911

Started away with the usual amount of agony, and soon arrived at Corner Camp where we left a note to Captain Scott explaining the cause of our breakdown. I told Mr Evans to say this sledge won't go much farther. After getting about a mile past Corner Camp my engine gave out finally, so here is an end to the motor sledges. I can't say I am sorry because I am not, and the others are, I think, of the same opinion as myself. We have had a heavy task pulling the heavy sledges up every time we stopped, which was pretty frequent, even now we have to start man-hauling we shall not be much more tired than we have already been at night when we had finished. Now comes the man-hauling part of the show, after reorganizing our sledge and taking aboard all the man food we can pull, we started with 190 lbs. per man, a strong head wind made it a bit uncomfortable for getting along, anyhow we made good about three miles and camped for the night. The surface not being very good made the travelling a bit heavy.

After three days' man-hauling.

5 November 1911

Made good about 14½ miles, if the surface would only remain as it is now we could get along pretty well. We are now thinking of the ponies being on their way, hope they will get better luck than we had with the motor sledges, but by what I can see they will have a tough time of it.

6 November 1911

Today we have worked hard and covered a good distance 12 miles, surface rough but slippery, all seems to be going pretty well, but we have generally had enough by the time comes for us to camp.

7 November 1911

We have again made good progress, but the light was very trying, sometimes we could not see at all where we were going. I tried to find some of the Cairns that were built by the Depot Party last year, came upon one this afternoon which is about 20 miles from One Ton Depot, so at the rate we have been travelling we ought to reach there some time tomorrow night. Temperature today was pretty low, but we are beginning to get hardened into it now.

8 November 1911

Made a good start, but the surface is getting softer every day and makes our legs ache; we arrived at One Ton Depot and camped. Then proceeded to dig out some of the provisions, we have to take on all the man food we can, this is a wild-looking place no doubt, have not seen anything of the ponies.

9 November 1911

Today we have started on the second stage of our journey. Our orders are to proceed one degree south of One Ton Depot and wait for the ponies and dogs to come up with us; as we have been making good distances each day, the party will hardly overtake us, but we have found today the load is much heavier to drag. We have just over 200 lbs. per man, and we have been brought up on several occasions, and to start again required a pretty good strain on the rope, anyhow we done 10½ miles, a pretty good show considering all things.

10 November 1911

Again we started off with plenty of vim, but it was jolly tough work, and it begins to tell on all of us; the surface today is covered with soft crystals which don't improve things. Tonight Hooper is pretty well done up, but he have stuck it well and I hope he will, although he could not tackle the food in the best of spirits, we know he wanted it. Mr Evans, Mr Day and myself could eat more, as we are just beginning to feel the tightening of the belt. Made good 11¼ miles and we are now building cairns all the way, one about three miles: then again at lunch and one in the afternoon and one at night. This will keep us employed.

11 November 1911

Today it has been very heavy work. The surface is very bad and we are pretty well full up, but not with food; man-hauling is no doubt the hardest work one can do, no wonder the motor sledges could not stand it. I have been thinking of the trials I witnessed of the motor engines in Wolseley's works in Birmingham, they were pretty stiff but nothing compared to the drag of a heavy load on the Barrier surface.

12 November 1911

Today have been similar to the two previous days, but the light have been bad and snow have been falling which do not improve the surface; we have been doing 10 miles a day Geographical and quite enough too as we have all had enough by time it goes Camp.

13 November 1911

The weather seems to be on the change. Should not be surprised if we don't get a blizzard before long, but of course we don't want that. Hooper seems a big fagged but he sticks it pretty well. Mr Day keeps on plodding, his only complaint is should like a little more to eat.

14 November 1911

When we started this morning Mr Evans said we had about 15 miles to go to reach the required distance. The hauling have been about the same, but the weather is somewhat finer and the blizzard gone off. We did 10 miles and camped; have not seen anything of the main party yet but shall not be surprised to see them at any time.

15 November 1911

We are camped after doing five miles where we are supposed to be [lat. 80° 32']; now we have to wait the others coming up. Mr Evans is quite proud to think we have arrived before the others caught us, but we don't expect they will be long although we have nothing to be ashamed of as our daily distance have been good. We have built a large cairn this afternoon before turning in. The weather is cold but excellent.

They waited there six days before the pony party arrived, when the Upper Barrier Depot (Mount Hooper) was left in the cairn.

Chapter Nine
THE POLAR JOURNEY

> Come, my friends,
> 'Tis not too late to seek a newer world.
> Push off, and sitting well in order smite
> The sounding furrows; for my purpose holds
> To sail beyond the sunset, and the baths
> Of all the western stars, until I die.
> It may be that the gulfs will wash us down:
> It may be we shall touch the Happy Isles,
> And see the great Achilles, whom we knew.
> Tho' much is taken, much abides; and tho'
> We are not now that strength which in old days
> Moved earth and heaven; that which we are, we are;
> One equal temper of heroic hearts,
> Made weak by time and fate, but strong in will
> To strive, to seek, to find, and not to yield.

TENNYSON, *Ulysses*

Take it all in all it is wonderful that the South Pole was reached so soon after the North Pole had been conquered. From Cape Columbia to the North Pole, straight going, is 413 geographical miles, and Peary who took on his expedition 246 dogs, covered this distance in 37 days. From Hut Point to the South Pole and back is 1532 geographical or 1766 statute miles, the distance to the top of the Beardmore Glacier alone being more than 100 miles farther than Peary had to cover to the North Pole. Scott travelled from Hut Point to the South Pole in 75 days, and to the Pole and back to his last camp in 147 days, a period of five months. A. C.-G.

(All miles are geographical unless otherwise stated.)

`I.   THE BARRIER STAGE

THE DEPARTURE from Cape Evans at 11 p.m. on 1 November is described by Griffith Taylor, who started a few days later on the second Geological Journey with his own party:

On the 31st October the pony parties started. Two weak ponies led by Atkinson and Keohane were sent off first at 4.30, and I accompanied them for about a mile. Keohane's pony rejoiced in the name of Jimmy Pigg, and he stepped out much better than his fleeter-named mate Jehu. We heard through the telephone of their safe arrival at Hut Point.

Next morning the Southern Party finished their mail, posting it in the packing case on Atkinson's bunk, and then at 11 a.m. the last party were ready for the Pole. They had packed the sledges overnight, and they took 20 lbs. personal baggage. The Owner had asked me what book he should take. He wanted something fairly filling. I recommended Tyndall's *Glaciers* – if he wouldn't find it 'coolish'. He didn't fancy this! So then I said, 'Why not take Browning, as I'm doing?' And I believe that he did so.

Wright's pony was the first harnessed to its sledge. China-man is Jehu's rival for last place, and as some compensation is easy to harness. Seaman Evans led Snatcher, who used to rush ahead and take the lead as soon as he was harnessed. Cherry had Michael, a steady goer, and Wilson led Nobby – the pony rescued from the killer whales in March. Scott led out Snippets to the sledges, and harnessed him to the foremost, with little Anton's help – only it turned out to be Bowers's sledge! However he transferred in a few minutes and marched off rapidly to the south. Christopher, as usual, behaved like a demon. First they had to trice his front leg up tight under his shoulder, then it took five minutes to throw him. The sledge was brought up and he was harnessed in while his head was held down on the floe. Finally he rose up, still on three legs, and started off galloping as well as he was able. After several violent kicks his foreleg was released, and after more watch-spring flicks with his hind legs he set off fairly steadily. Titus can't stop him when once he has started, and will have to do the fifteen miles in one lap probably!

Dear old Titus – that was my last memory of him. Imperturbable as ever; never hasty, never angry, but soothing that vicious animal, and determined to get the best out of most unpromising material in his endeavour to do his simple duty.

Bowers was last to leave. His pony, Victor, nervous but not vicious, was soon in the traces. I ran to the end of the Cape and watched the little cavalcade – already strung out into remote units – rapidly fade into the lonely white waste to southward.

That evening I had a chat with Wilson over the telephone from the Discovery Hut – my last communication with those five gallant spirits.[1]

All the ponies arrived at Hut Point by 4 p.m., just in time to escape a stiff blow. Three of them were housed with ourselves inside the hut, the rest being put into the verandah. The march showed that with their loads the speed of the different ponies varied to such an extent that individuals were soon separated by miles. 'It reminded me of a regatta or a somewhat disorganized fleet with ships of very unequal speed.'[2]

It was decided to change to night marching, and the following evening we proceeded in the following order, which was the way of our going for the present. The three slowest ponies started first, namely, Jehu with Atkinson, Chinaman with Wright, James Pigg with Keohane. This party was known as the Baltic Fleet.

Two hours later Scott's party followed; Scott with Snippets, Wilson with Nobby, and myself with Michael.

Both these parties camped for lunch in the middle of the night's march. After another hour the remaining four men

---

1. Taylor, with Scott, *The Silver Lining*, pp. 325–6.
2. *Scott's Last Expedition*, vol. i, p. 448.

set to work to get Christopher into his sledge; when he was started they harnessed in their own ponies as quickly as possible and followed, making a non-stop run right through the night's march. It was bad for men and ponies, but it was impossible to camp in the middle of the march owing to Christopher. The composition of this party was, Oates with Christopher, Bowers with Victor, Seaman Evans with Snatcher, Crean with Bones.

Each of these three parties was self-contained with tent, cooker and weekly bag, and the times of starting were so planned that the three parties arrived at the end of the march about the same time.

There was a strong head wind and low drift as we rounded Cape Armitage on our way to the Barrier and the future. Probably there were few of us who did not wonder when we should see the old familiar place again.

Scott's party camped at Safety Camp as the Baltic fleet were getting under weigh again. Soon afterwards Ponting appeared with a dog sledge and a cinematograph, – how anomalous it seemed – which

> was up in time to catch the flying rearguard which came along in fine form, Snatcher leading and being stopped every now and again – a wonderful little beast. Christopher had given the usual trouble when harnessed, but was evidently subdued by the Barrier Surface. However, it was not thought advisable to halt him, and so the party fled through in the wake of the advance guard.[3]

Immediately afterwards Scott's party packed up. 'Goodbye and good luck,' from Ponting, a wave of the hand not holding in a frisky pony and we had left the last link with the hut. 'The future is in the lap of the gods; I can think of nothing left undone to deserve success.'[4]

The general scheme was to average 10 miles (11.5 statute)

3. *Scott's Last Expedition*, vol. 1, p. 449.
4. ibid., p. 446.

a day from Hut Point to One Ton Depot with the ponies lightly laden. From One Ton to the Gateway a daily average of 13 miles (15 statute) was necessary to carry twenty-four weekly units of food for four men each to the bottom of the glacier. This was the Barrier Stage of the journey, a distance of 369 miles (425 statute) as actually run on our sledge-meter. The twenty-four weekly units of food were to carry the Polar Party and two supporting parties forward to their farthest point, and back again to the bottom of the Beardmore, where three more units were to be left in a depot.[5]

All went well this first day on the Barrier, and encouraging messages left on empty petrol drums told us that the motors were going well when they passed. But the next day we passed five petrol drums which had been dumped. This meant that there was trouble, and some 14 miles from Hut Point we learned that the big end of the No. 2 cylinder of Day's motor had broken, and half a mile beyond we found the motor itself, drifted up with snow, and looking a mournful wreck. The next day's march (Sunday, 5 November, a.m.) brought us to Corner Camp. There were a few legs down crevasses during the day but nothing to worry about.

From here we could see to the South an ominous mark in the snow which we hoped might not prove to be the second motor. It was: 'the big end of No. 1 cylinder had cracked, the machine otherwise in good order. Evidently the engines are not fitted to working in this climate, a fact that should be certainly capable of correction. One thing is proved; the system of propulsion is altogether satisfactory.'[6] And again: 'It is a disappointment. I had hoped better of the machines once they got away on the Barrier Surface.'[7]

Scott had set his heart upon the success of the motors. He had run them in Norway and Switzerland; and everything was done that care and forethought could suggest. At the

5. See pp. 363, 571–2.
6. *Scott's Last Expedition*, vol. 1, p. 453.
7. ibid., p. 452.

back of his mind, I feel sure, was the wish to abolish the cruelty which the use of ponies and dogs necessarily entails.

A small measure of success will be enough to show their possibilities, their ability to revolutionize polar transport. Seeing the machines at work today [leaving Cape Evans] and remembering that every defect so far shown is purely mechanical, it is impossible not to be convinced of their value. But the trifling mechanical defects and lack of experience show the risk of cutting out trials. A season of experiment with a small workshop at hand may be all that stands between success and failure.[8]

I do not believe that Scott built high hopes on these motors: but it was a chance to help those who followed him. Scott was always trying to do that.

Did they succeed or fail? They certainly did not help us much, the motor which travelled farthest drawing a heavy load to just beyond Corner Camp. But even so fifty statute miles is fifty miles, and that they did it at all was an enormous advance. The distance travelled included hard and soft surfaces, and we found later when the snow bridges fell in during the summer that this car had crossed safely some broad crevasses. Also they worked in temperatures down to $-30°$ Fahr. All this was to the good, for no motor-driven machine had travelled on the Barrier before. The general design seemed to be right, all that was now wanted was experience. As an experiment they were successful in the South, but Scott never knew their true possibilities; for they were the direct ancestors of the 'tanks' in France.

Night-marching had its advantages and disadvantages. The ponies were pulling in the colder part of the day and resting in the warm, which was good. Their coats dried well in the sun, and after a few days to get accustomed to the new conditions, they slept and fed in comparative comfort. On the other hand the pulling surface was undoubtedly better

8. ibid., pp. 438–9.

when the sun was high and the temperature warmer. Taking one thing with another there was no doubt that night-marching was better for ponies, but we seldom if ever tried it man-hauling.

Just now there was an amazing difference between day and night conditions. At midnight one was making short work of everything, nursing fingers after doing up harness with minus temperatures and nasty cold winds: by supper time the next morning we were sitting on our sledges writing up our diaries or meteorological logs, and even dabbling our bare toes in the snow, but not for long! Shades of darkness! How different all this was from what we had been through. My personal impression of this early summer sledging on the Barrier was one of constant wonder at its comfort. One had forgotten that a tent could be warm and a sleeping-bag dry: so deep were the contrary impressions that only actual experience was convincing.

> It is a sweltering day, the air breathless, the glare intense – one loses sight of the fact that the temperature is low [−22°], one's mind seeks comparison in hot sunlit streets and scorching pavements, yet six hours ago my thumb was frost-bitten. All the inconveniences of frozen footwear and damp clothes and sleeping-bags have vanished entirely.[9]

We could not expect to get through this windy area of Corner Camp without some bad weather. The wind-blown surface improved, the ponies took their heavier loads with ease, but as we came to our next camp it was banking up to the S.E. and the breeze freshened almost immediately. We built pony walls hurriedly and by the time we had finished supper it was blowing force 5 (a.m. 6 November, Camp 4). There was a moderate gale with some drift all day which increased to force 8 with more drift at night. It was impossible to march. The drift took off a bit the next morning, and Meares and Dimitri with the two dog-teams

9. *Scott's Last Expedition*, vol. i, p. 450.

appeared and camped astern of us. This was according to the previous plan by which the dog-teams were to start after us and catch us up, since they travelled faster than the ponies.

> The snow and drift necessitated digging out ponies again and again to keep them well sheltered from the wind. The walls made a splendid lee, but some sledges at the extremities were buried altogether, and our tent being rather close to windward of our wall got the back eddy and was continually being snowed up above the door. After noon the snow ceased except for surface drift. Snatcher knocked his section of the wall over, and Jehu did so more than ever. All ponies looked pretty miserable, as in spite of the shelter they were bunged up, eyes and all, in drift which had become ice and could not be removed without considerable difficulty.[10]

Towards evening it ceased drifting altogether, but a wind, force 4, kept up with disconcerting regularity. Eventually Atkinson's party got away at midnight. 'Castle Rock is still visible, but will be closed by the north end of White Island in the next march – then goodbye to the old landmarks for many a long day.'[11]

The next day (November 8–9)

> started at midnight and had a very pleasant march. Truly sledging in such weather is great. Mounts Discovery and Morning, which we gradually closed, looked fine in the general panorama of mountains. We are now nearly abreast the north end of the Bluff. We all came up to camp together this morning: it looked like a meet of the hounds, and Jehu ran away!!![12]

The next march was just the opposite. Wind force 5 to 6 and falling snow.

10. Bowers.   11. Bowers.   12. My own diary.

The surface was very slippery in parts and on the hard sastrugi it was a case of falling or stumbling continually. The light got so bad that one might have been walking in the clouds for all that could be discerned, and yet it was only snowing slightly. The Bluff became completely obscured, and the usual signs of a blizzard were accentuated.

At lunch camp Scott packed up and followed us. We overhauled Atkinson about 1½ hours later, he having camped, and we were not sorry, as in addition to marching against a fresh southerly breeze the light brought a tremendous strain on the eyes in following tracks.[13]

A little more than eight miles for the day's total.

We carried these depressing conditions for three more marches, that is till the morning of 13 November. The surface was wretched, the weather horrid, the snow persistent, covering everything with soft downy flakes, inch upon inch, and mile upon mile. There are glimpses of despondency in the diaries. 'If this should come as an exception, our luck will be truly awful. The camp is very silent and cheerless, signs that things are going awry.'[14] 'The weather was horrid, overcast, gloomy, snowy. One's spirits became very low.'[15] 'I expected these marches to be a little difficult, but not near so bad as today.'[16] Indefinite conditions always tried Scott most: positive disasters put him into more cheerful spirits than most. In the big gale coming South when the ship nearly sank, and when we lost one of the cherished motors through the sea-ice, his was one of the few cheerful faces I saw. Even when the ship ran aground off Cape Evans he was not despondent. But this kind of thing irked him. Bowers wrote:

The unpleasant weather and bad surface, and Chinaman's indisposition, combined to make the outlook unpleasant, and on arrival [in camp] I was not surprised to find that Scott had

13. Bowers.   14. *Scott's Last Expedition*, vol. 1, p. 463.
15. ibid., p. 462.   16. ibid., p. 461.

THE WORST JOURNEY IN THE WORLD

a grievance. He felt that in arranging the consumption of
forage his own unit had not been favoured with the same
reduction as ours, in fact accused me of putting upon his three
horses to save my own. We went through the weights in
detail after our meal, and, after a certain amount of argument,
decided to carry on as we were going. I can quite understand
his feelings, and after our experience of last year a bad day
like this makes him fear our beasts are going to fail us. The
Talent [i.e. the doctors] examined Chinaman, who begins to
show signs of wear. Poor ancient little beggar, he ought to be
a pensioner instead of finishing his days on a job of this sort.
Jehu looks pretty rocky too, but seeing that we did not expect
him to reach the Glacier Tongue, and that he has now done
more than 100 miles from Cape Evans, one really does not
know what to expect of these creatures. Certainly Titus
thinks, as he has always said, that they are the most unsuitable
scrap-heap crowd of unfit creatures that could possibly be got
together.[17]

The weather was about as poisonous as one could wish; a
fresh breeze and driving snow from the E. with an awful
surface. The recently fallen snow thickly covered the ground
with powdery stuff that the unfortunate ponies fairly wal-
lowed in. If it was only ourselves to consider I should not
mind a bit, but to see our best ponies being hit like this at the
start is most distressing. A single march like that of last night
must shorten their usefulness by days, and here we are a
fortnight out, and barely one-third of the distance to the
glacier covered, with every pony showing signs of wear.
Victor looks a lean and lanky beast compared with his
condition two weeks ago.[18]

But the ponies began to go better; and it was about this
time that Jehu was styled the Barrier Wonder, and Chinaman
the Thunderbolt. 'Our four ponies have suffered most,'
writes Bowers.

17. Bowers.   18. Bowers.

336

I don't agree with Titus that it is best to march them right through without a lunch camp. They were undoubtedly pretty tired, and worst of all did not go their feeds properly. It was a fine warm morning for them (13 Nov.); +15°, our warmest temperature hitherto. In the afternoon it came on to snow in large flakes like one would get at home. I have never seen such snow down here before; it makes the surface very bad for the sledges. The ponies' manes and rugs were covered in little knots of ice.[19]

The next march (13–14 November) was rather better, though the going was very deep and heavy, and all the ponies were showing signs of wear and tear. This was followed by a delightfully warm day, and all the animals were standing drowsily in the sunshine. We could see the land far behind us, the first sight of land we had had for many days. On 15 November we reached One Ton Depot, having travelled a hundred and thirty miles from Hut Point.

The two sledges left standing were still upright, and the tattered remain of a flag flapped over the main cairn. In a salt tin lashed to the bamboo flag-pole was a note from Lieutenant Evans to say that he had gone on with the motor party five days before, and would continue man-hauling to 80° 30'S. and await us there. 'He has done something over 30 miles in 2½ days – exceedingly good going.[20] We dug out the cairn, which we found just as we had left it except that there was a big tongue of drift, level with the top of the cairn to leeward, and running about 150 yards to N.E., showing that the prevailing wind here is S.W. Nine months before we had sprinkled some oats on the surface of the snow hoping to get a measurement of the accretion of snow during the winter. Unfortunately we were unable to find the oats again, but other evidence went to show that the snow deposit was very small. A minimum thermometer which was lashed with great care to a framework registered −73°. After the tempera-

19. Bowers.   20. *Scott's Last Expedition*, vol. 1, p. 465.

tures already experienced by us on the Barrier during the winter and spring this was surprisingly high, especially as our minimum temperatures were taken under the sledge, which means that the thermometer is shaded from radiation, while this thermometer at One Ton was left open to the sky. On the Winter Journey we found that a shaded thermometer registered −69° when an unshaded one registered −75°, a difference of 6°. All the provisions left here were found to be in excellent condition.

We then had a prolonged council of war. This meant that Scott called Bowers, and perhaps Oates, into our tent after supper was finished in the morning. Somehow these conferences were always rather serio-comic. On this occasion, as was usually the case, the question was ponies. It was decided to wait here one day and rest them, as there was ample food. The main discussion centred round the amount of forage to be taken on from here, while the state of the ponies, the amount they could pull and the distance they could go had to be taken into consideration.

Oates thinks the ponies will get through, but that they have lost condition quicker than he expected. Considering his usually pessimistic attitude this must be thought a hopeful view. Personally I am much more hopeful. I think that a good many of the beasts are actually in better form than when they started, and that there is no need to be alarmed about the remainder, always excepting the weak ones which we have always regarded with doubt. Well, we must wait and see how things go.[21]

The decision made was to take just enough food to get the ponies to the glacier, allowing for the killing of some of them before that date. It was obvious that Jehu and Chinaman could not go very much farther, and it was also necessary that ponies should be killed in order to feed the dogs. The

21. *Scott's Last Expedition*, vol. i, p. 465.

two dog-teams were carrying about a week's pony food, but they were unable to advance more than a fortnight from One Ton without killing ponies.

This decision practically meant that Scott abandoned the idea of taking ponies up the glacier. This was a great relief, for the crevassed state of the lower reaches of the glacier as described by Shackleton led us to believe that the attempt was suicidal. All the winter our brains were exercised to try and devise some method by which the ponies could be driven from behind, and by which the connexion between pony and sledge could be loosed if the pony fell into a crevasse, but I confess that there seemed little chance of this happening. From all we saw of the glacier I am convinced that there is no reasonable chance of getting ponies up it, and that dogs could only be driven down it if the way up was most carefully surveyed and kept on the return. I am sure that in this kind of uncertainty the mental strain on the leader of a party is less than that on his men. The leader knows quite well what he thinks worth while risking or not: in this case Scott probably was always of the opinion that it would not be worth while taking ponies on to the glacier. The pony leaders, however, only knew that the possibility was ahead of them. I can remember now the relief with which we heard that it was not intended that Wilson should take Nobby, the fittest of our ponies, farther than the Gateway.

Up to now Christopher had lived up to his reputation, as the following extracts from Bowers's diary will show:

Three times we downed him, and he got up and threw us about, with all four of us hanging on like grim death. He nearly had me under him once; he seems fearfully strong, but it is a pity he wastes so much good energy. . . . Christopher, as usual, was strapped on three legs and then got down on his knees. He gets more cunning each time, and if he does not succeed in biting or kicking one of us before long it won't be his fault. He finds the soft snow does not hurt his knees like sea-ice, and so plunges about on them *ad lib*. One's finnesko are so slippery that it is difficult to exert full strength on him, and to-day he bowled Oates over and got away altogether. Fortunately the lashing on his fourth leg held fast, and we were able to secure him when he rejoined the other animals. Finally he lay down, and thought he had defeated us, but we had the sledge connected up by that time, and as he got up we rushed him forward before he had time to kick over the traces. . . . Dimitri came and gave us a hand with Chris. Three of us hung on to him while the other two connected up the sledge. We had a struggle for over twenty minutes, and he managed to tread on me, but no damage done. . . . Got Chris in by a dodge. Titus did away with his back strap, and nearly had him away unaided before he realized that the hated sledge was fast to him. Unfortunately he started off just too soon, and bolted with only one trace fast. This pivoted him to starboard, and he charged the line. I expected a mix-up, but he stopped at the wall between Bones and Snatcher, and we cast off and cleared sledge before trying again. By laying the traces down the side of the sledge instead of ahead we got him off his guard again, and he was away before he knew what had occurred . . . We had a bad time with Chris again. He remembered having been bluffed before, and could not be got near the sledge at all. Three times he broke away, but fortunately he always ran back among the other ponies, and not out on to the Barrier. Finally we had to down him, and he was so tired with his recent struggles, that after one abortive attempt we got him fast and away.[22]

Meanwhile it was not so much the difficulties of sledging as the depressing blank conditions in which our march was so often made, that gave us such troubles as we had. The routine of a tent makes a lot of difference. Scott's tent was a comfortable one to live in, and I was always glad when I was told to join it, and sorry to leave. He was himself extraordinary quick, and no time was ever lost by his party in camping

22. Bowers.

or breaking camp. He was most careful, some said over-careful but I do not think so, that everything should be neat and shipshape, and there was a recognized place for every-thing. On the Depot Journey we were bidden to see that every particle of snow was beaten off our clothing and finnesko before entering the tent: if it was drifting we had to do this after entering and the snow was carefully cleared off the floor-cloth. Afterwards each tent was supplied with a small brush with which to perform this office. In addition to other obvious advantages this materially helped to keep clothing, finnesko, and sleeping-bags dry, and thus prolong the life of furs. 'After all is said and done,' said Wilson one day after supper, 'the best sledger is the man who sees what has to be done, and does it – and says nothing about it.' Scott agreed. And if you were 'sledging with the Owner' you had to keep your eyes wide open for the little things which cropped up, and do them quickly, and say nothing about them. There is nothing so irritating as the man who is always coming in and informing all and sundry that he has repaired his sledge, or built a wall, or filled the cooker, or mended his socks.

I moved into Scott's tent for the first time in the middle of the Depot Journey, and was enormously impressed by the comfort which a careful routine of this nature evoked. There was a homelike air about the tent at supper time, and, though a lunch camp in the middle of the night is always rather bleak, there was never anything slovenly. Another thing which struck me even more forcibly was the cooking. We were of course on just the same ration as the tent from which I had come. I was hungry and said so. 'Bad cooking,' said Wilson shortly; and so it was. For two or three days the sharpest edge was off my hunger. Wilson and Scott had learned many a cooking tip in the past, and, instead of the same old meal day by day, the weekly ration was so manoeuvred by a clever cook that it was seldom quite the same meal. Sometimes pemmican plain, or thicker pemmican with some arrowroot mixed with it: at others we surrendered a biscuit and a half apiece and had a dry hoôsh, i.e. biscuit fried in pemmican with a little water added, and a good big cup of cocoa to follow. Dry hooshes also saved oil. There were cocoa and tea upon which to ring the changes, or better still 'teaco' which combined the stimulating qualities of tea with the food value in cocoa. Then much could be done with the dessert-spoonful of raisins which was our daily whack. They were good soaked in the tea, but best perhaps in with the biscuits and pemmican as a dry hoosh. 'You are going far to earn my undying gratitude, Cherry,' was a satisfied remark of Scott one evening when, having saved, unbeknownst to my companions, some of their daily ration of cocoa, arrow-root, sugar and raisins, I made a 'chocolate hoosh'. But I am afraid he had indigestion next morning. There were meals when we had interesting little talks, as when I find in my diary that: 'we had a jolly lunch meal, discussing authors. Barrie, Galsworthy and others are personal friends of Scott. Some one told Max Beerbohm that he was like Captain Scott, and immediately, so Scott assured us, he grew a beard.'

But about three weeks out the topics of conversation became threadbare. From then onwards it was often that whole days passed without conversation beyond the routine Camp ho! All ready? Pack up. Spell ho. The latter after some two hours' pulling. When man-hauling we used to start pulling immediately we had the tent down, the sledge packed and our harness over our bodies and ski on our feet. After about a quarter of an hour the effects of the marching would be felt in the warming of hands and feet and the consequent thawing of our mitts and finnesko. We then halted long enough for everybody to adjust their ski and clothing: then on, perhaps for two hours or more, before we halted again.

Since it had been decided to lighten the ponies' weights, we left at least 100 lbs. of pony forage behind when we started from One Ton on the night of 16–17 November on our first 13-mile march. This was a distinct saving, and instead of 695 lbs. each with which the six stronger ponies left Corner Camp, they now pulled only 625 lbs. Jehu had only 455 lbs. and Chinaman 448 lbs. The dog-teams had 860 lbs. of pony food between them, and according to plan the two teams were to carry 1,570 lbs. from One Ton between them. These weights included the sledges, with straps and fittings, which weighed about 45 lbs.

Summer seemed long in coming for we marched into a considerable breeze and the temperature was −18°. Oates and Seaman Evans had quite a crop of frost-bites. I pointed out to Meares that his nose was gone; but he left it, saying that he had got tired of it, and it would thaw out by and by. The ponies were going better for their rest. The next day's march was over crusty snow with a layer of loose powdery snow at the top, and a temperature of −21° was chilly. Towards the end of it Scott got frightened that the ponies were not going as well as they should. Another council of war was held, and it was decided that an average of thirteen miles a day must be done at all costs, and that another sack of forage should be dumped here, putting the ponies on short rations later, if necessary. Oates agreed, but said the ponies were going better than he expected: that Jehu and Chinaman might go a week, and almost certainly would go three days. Bowers was always against this dumping. Meanwhile Scott wrote: 'It's touch and go whether we scrape up to the glacier; meanwhile we get along somehow.'[23]

As a result of one of Christopher's tantrums Bowers records that his sledge-meter was carried away this morning:

I took my sledge-meter into the tent after breakfast and rigged up a fancy lashing with raw hide thongs so as to give it the necessary play with security. A splendid parhelia exhibition was caused by the ice-crystals. Round the sun was a 22° halo [that is a halo 22° from the sun's image], with four mock suns in rainbow colours, and outside this another halo in complete rainbow colours. Above the sun were the arcs of two other circles touching these halos, and the arcs of the great all-round circle could be seen faintly on either side. Below was a dome-shaped glare of white which contained an exaggerated

23. *Scott's Last Expedition*, vol. i, p. 468.

mock sun, which was as dazzling as the sun himself. Altogether a fine example of a pretty common phenomenon down here.[24]

And the next day: 'We saw the party ahead in inverted mirage some distance above their heads.'

In the next three marches we covered our daily 13 miles, for the most part without very great difficulty. But poor Jehu was in a bad way, stopping every few hundred yards. It was a funereal business for the leaders of these crock ponies; and at this stage of the journey Atkinson, Wright and Keohane had many more difficulties than most of us, and the success of their ponies was largely due to their patience and care. Incidentally big icicles formed upon the ponies' noses during the march and Chinaman used Wright's windproof blouse as a handkerchief. During the last of these marches, that is on the morning of 21 November, we saw a massive cairn ahead, and found there the motor party, consisting of Lieutenant Evans, Day, Lashly and Hooper. The cairn was in 80° 32′, and under the name Mount Hooper formed our Upper Barrier Depot. We left there three S (summit) rations, two cases of emergency biscuits and two cases of oil, which constituted three weekly food units for the three parties which were to advance from the bottom of the Beardmore Glacier. This food was to take them back from 80° 32′ to One Ton Camp. We all camped for the night 3 miles farther on: sixteen men, five tents, ten ponies, twenty-three dogs and thirteen sledges.

The man-hauling party had been waiting for six days; and, having expected us before, were getting anxious about us. They declared that they were very hungry, and Day, who was always long and thin, looked quite gaunt. Some spare biscuits which we gave them from our tent were carried off with gratitude. The rest of us who were driving dogs or leading ponies still found our Barrier ration satisfying.

We had now been out three weeks and had travelled 192

24. Bowers.

miles, and formed a very good idea as to what the ponies could do. The crocks had done wonderfully:

> We hope Jehu will last three days; he will then be finished in any case and fed to the dogs. It is amusing to see Meares looking eagerly for the chance of a feed for his animals; he has been expecting it daily. On the other hand, Atkinson and Oates are eager to get the poor animal beyond the point at which Shackleton killed his first beast. Reports on Chinaman are very favourable, and it really looks as though the ponies are going to do what is hoped of them.[25]

From first to last Nobby, who was rescued from the floe, was the strongest pony we had, and was now drawing a heavier load than any other pony by 50 lbs. He was a well-shaped, contented kind of animal, misnamed a pony. Indeed several of our beasts were too large to fit this description. Christopher, of course, was wearing himself out quicker than most, but all of them had lost a lot of weight in spite of the fact that they had all the oats and oil-cake they could eat. Bowers writes of his pony:

> Victor, my pony, has taken to leading the line, like his opposite number last season. He is a steady goer, and as gentle as a dear old sheep. I can hardly realize the strenuous times I had with him only a month ago, when it took about four of us to get him harnessed to a sledge, and two of us every time with all our strength to keep him from bolting when in it. Even at the start of the journey he was as nearly unmanageable as any beast could be, and always liable to bolt from sheer excess of spirits. He is more sober now after three weeks of featureless Barrier, but I think I am more fond of him than ever. He has lost his rotundity, like all the other horses, and is a long-legged, angular beast, very ugly as horses go, but still I would not change him for any other.[26]

25. *Scott's Last Expedition*, vol. i, pp. 470, 471.
26. Bowers.

The ponies were fed by their leaders at the lunch and supper halts, and by Oates and Bowers during the sleep halt about four hours before we marched. Several of them developed a troublesome habit of swinging their nosebags off, some as soon as they were put on, others in their anxiety to reach the corn still left uneaten in the bottom of the bag. We had to lash their bags on to their headstalls. 'Victor got hold of his head rope yesterday, and devoured it: not because he is hungry, as he won't eat all his allowance even now.'[27]

The original intention was that Day and Hooper should return from 80° 30', but it was now decided that their unit of four should remain intact for a few days, and constitute a light man-hauling advance party to make the track.

The weather was much more pleasant and we saw the sun most days, while I note only one temperature below −20° since leaving One Ton. The ponies sank in a cruel distance some days, but we were certainly not overworking them and they had as much food as they could eat. We knew the grim part was to come, but we never realized how grim it was to be. From this Northern Barrier Depot the ponies were mostly drawing less than 500 lbs. and we had hopes of getting through to the glacier without much difficulty. All depended on the weather, and just now it was glorious, and the ponies were going steadily together. Jehu, the crockiest of the crocks, was led back along the track and shot on the evening of 24 November, having reached a point at least 15 miles beyond that where Shackleton shot his first pony. When it is considered that it was doubtful whether he could start at all this must be conceded to have been a triumph of horse-management in which both Oates and Atkinson shared, though neither so much as Jehu himself, for he must have had a good spirit to have dragged his poor body so far. 'A year's care and good feeding, three weeks' work with good treatment, a reasonable load and a good ration, and then a painless end. If anybody can call that cruel I cannot either understand it or agree with them.' Thus Bowers, who

27. ibid.

346

continues: 'The midnight sun reflected from the snow has started to burn my face and lips. I smear them with hazeline before turning in, and find it a good thing. Wearing goggles has absolutely prevented any recurrence of snow-blindness. Captain Scott says they make me see everything through rose-coloured spectacles.'

We said good-bye to Day and Hooper next morning, and they set their faces northwards and homewards.[28] Two-men parties on the Barrier are not much fun. Day had certainly done his best about the motors and they had helped us over a bad bit of initial surface. That night Scott wrote: 'Only a few more marches to feel safe in getting to our goal.'[29] At the lunch halt on 26 November, in lat. 81° 35', we left our Middle Barrier Depot, containing one week's provisions for each returning unit as at Mount Hooper, a reduction of 200 lbs. in our weights. The march that day was very trying. 'It is always rather dismal work walking over the great snow plain when sky and surface merge in one pall of dead whiteness, but it is cheering to be in such good company with everything going on steadily and well.'[30]

There was no doubt that the animals were tiring, and 'a tired animal makes a tired man, I find.'[31] The next day (28 November) was no better: 'the most dismal start imaginable. Thick as a hedge, snow falling and drifting with keen southerly wind.'[32]

Bowers notes: 'We have now run down a whole degree of latitude without a fine day, or anything but clouds, mist, and driving snow from the south.' We certainly did have some difficult marches, one of the worst effects of which was that

28. A note to Cape Evans is as follows: – MY DEAR SIMPSON. This goes with Day and Hooper now returning. We are making fair progress and the ponies doing fairly well. I hope we shall get through to the glacier without difficulty, but to make sure I am carrying the dog-teams farther than I intended at first – the teams may be late returning, unfit for further work or non-existent. . . . R. SCOTT.
29. *Scott's Last Expedition*, vol. i, p. 474.
30. ibid., p. 475.   31. ibid., p. 476.   32. ibid., p. 476.

we knew we must be making a winding course and we had to pick up our depots on the return somehow. Here is a typical bad morning from Bowers's diary:

> The first four miles of the march were utter misery for me, as Victor, either through lassitude or because he did not like having to plug into the wind, went as slow as a funeral horse. The light was so bad that wearing goggles was most necessary, and the driving snow filled them up as fast as you cleared them. I dropped a long way astern of the cavalcade, could hardly see them at times through the snow, but the fear that Victor, of all beasts, should give out was like a nightmare. I have always been used to starting later than the others by a quarter of a mile, and catching them up. At the four-mile cairn I was about fed up to the neck with it, but I said very little as everybody was so disgusted with the weather and things in general that I saw that I was not the only one in tribulation. Victor turned up trumps after that. He stepped out and led the line in his old place, and at a good swinging pace considering the surface, my temper and spirits improving at every step. In the afternoon he went splendidly again, and finished up by rolling in the snow when I had taken his harness off, a thing he has not done for ten or twelve days. It certainly does not look like exhaustion!

Indeed these days we were fighting for our marches, and Chinaman who was killed this night seemed well out of it. He reached a point less than 90 miles from the glacier, though this was small comfort to him.

Stumbling and groping our way along as we had been during the last blizzard we were totally unprepared for the sight which met us during our next march on 29 November. The great ramp of mountains which ran to the west of us, and would soon bar our way to the South, partly cleared: and right on top of us it seemed were the triple peaks of Mount Markham. After some 300 miles of bleak, monotonous Barrier it was a wonderful sight indeed. We camped at night in latitude 82° 21′ S., four miles beyond Scott's previous

Farthest South in 1902. Then they had the best of luck in clear fine weather, which Shackleton has also recorded at this stage of his southern journey.

It is curious to see how depressed all our diaries become when this bad weather obtained, and how quickly we must have cheered up whenever the sun came out. There is no doubt that a similar effect was produced upon the ponies. Truth to tell, the mental strain upon those responsible was very great in these early days, and there is little of outside interest to relieve the mind. The crystal surface which was an invisible carpet yesterday becomes a shining glorious sheet of many colours today: the irregularities which caused you so many falls are now quite clear and you step on or over them without a thought: and when there is added some of the most wonderful scenery in the world it is hard to recall in the enjoyment of the present how irritable and weary you felt only twenty hours ago. The whisper of the sledge, the hiss of the primus, the smell of the hoosh and the soft folds of your sleeping-bag: how jolly they can all be, and generally were.

> I would that I could once again
>   Around the cooker sit
> And hearken to its soft refrain
>   And feel so jolly fit.
>
> Instead of home-life's silken chains,
>   The uneventful round,
> I long to be mid snow-swept plains,
>   In harness, outward bound.
>
> With the pad, pad, pad, of fin'skoed feet,
>   With two hundred pounds per man,
> Not enough hoosh or biscuit to eat,
>   Well done, lads! Up tent! Outspan.
>   (NELSON in the *South Polar Times*)

Certainly as we skirted these mountains, range upon range, during the next two marches (30 November and 1 Decem-

ber), we felt we could have little cause for complaint. They
brought us to lat. 82° 47′ S., and here we left our last depot
on the Barrier, called the Southern Barrier Depot, with a
week's ration for each returning party as usual. 'The man
food is enough for one week for each returning unit of four
men, the next depot beyond being the Middle Barrier Depot,
73 miles north. As we ought easily to do over 100 miles a
week on the return journey, there is little likelihood of our
having to go on short commons if all goes well.'[33] And this
was what we all felt – until we found the Polar Party. This
was our twenty-seventh camp, and we had been out a month.

It was important that we should have fine clear weather
during the next few days when we should be approaching
the land. On his previous southern journey Scott had been
prevented from reaching the range of mountains which ran
along to our right by a huge chasm. This phenomenon is
known to geologists as a shear crack and is formed by the
movement of a glacier away from the land which bounds it.
In this case a mass of many hundred miles of Barrier has
moved away from the mountains, and the disturbance is
correspondingly great. Shackleton has described how he
approached the Gateway, as he named the passage between
Mount Hope and the mainland, by means of which he passed
through on to the Beardmore Glacier. As he and his companions were exploring the way they came upon an enormous chasm, 80 feet wide and 300 feet deep, which barred
their path. Moving along to the right they found a place
where the chasm was filled with snow, and here they crossed
to the land some miles ahead. At our Southern Barrier Depot
we reckoned we were some forty-four miles from this
Gateway and in three more marches we hoped to be camped
under this land.

Christopher was shot at the depot. He was the only pony
who did not die instantaneously. Perhaps Oates was not so
calm as usual, for Chris was his own horse though such a

33. Bowers.

brute. Just as Oates fired he moved, and charged into the camp with the bullet in his head. He was caught with difficulty, nearly giving Keohane a bad bite, led back and finished. We were well rid of him: while he was strong he fought, and once the Barrier had tamed him, as we were not able to do, he never pulled a fair load. He could have gone several more days, but there was not enough pony food to take all the animals forward. We began to wonder if we had done right to leave so much behind. Each pony provided at least four days' food for the dog-teams, some of them more, and there was quite a lot of fat on them – even on Jehu. This was comforting, as going to prove that their hardships were not too great. Also we put the undercut into our own hoosh, and it was very good, though we had little oil to cook it.

We had been starting later each night, in order that the transition from night to day marching might be gradual. For we intended to march by day when we started pulling up the glacier, and there were no ponies to rest when the sun was high. It may be said therefore that our next march was on 2 December.

Before we started Scott walked over to Bowers. 'I have come to a decision which will shock you.' Victor was to go at the end of the march, because pony food was running so short. Birdie wrote at the end of the day:

[He] did a splendid march and kept ahead all day, and as usual marched into camp first, pulling over 450 lbs. easily. It seemed an awful pity to have to shoot a great strong animal, and it seemed like the irony of fate to me, as I had been downed for over-provisioning the ponies with needless excess of food, and the drastic reductions had been made against my strenuous opposition up to the last. It is poor satisfaction to me to know that I was right now that my horse is dead. Good old Victor! He has always had a biscuit out of my ration, and he ate his last before the bullet sent him to his rest. Here ends my second horse in 83° S., not quite so tragically as my first when the sea-ice broke up, but none the less I feel sorry for a beast that has been my constant companion and care for so long. He has done his share in our undertaking anyhow, and may I do my share as well when I get into harness myself.

The snow has started to fall over his bleak resting-place, and it looks like a blizzard. The outlook is dark, stormy and threatening.

Indeed it had been a dismal march into a blank white wall, and the ponies were sinking badly in the snow, leaving holes full a foot deep. The temperature was +17° and the flakes of snow melted when they lay on the dark colours of the tents and our furs. After building the pony walls water was running down our windproofs.

I note 'we are doing well on pony meat and go to bed very content.' Notwithstanding the fact that we could not do more than heat the meat by throwing it into the pemmican we found it sweet and good, though tough. The man-hauling party consisted of Lieut. Evans and Lashly who had lost their motors, and Atkinson and Wright who had lost their ponies. They were really quite hungry by now, and most of us pretty well looked forward to our meals and kept a biscuit to eat in our bags if we could. The pony meat therefore came as a relief. I think we ought to have depoted more of it on the cairns. As it was, what we did not eat was given to the dogs. With some tins of extra oil and a depoted pony the Polar Party would probably have got home in safety.

On 3 December we roused out at 2.30 a.m. It was thick and snowy. As we breakfasted the blizzard started from the south-east, and was soon blowing force 9, a full gale, with heavy drift. 'The strongest wind I have known here in summer.'[34] It was impossible to start, but we turned out and made up the pony walls in heavy drift, one of them being blown down three times. By 1.30 p.m. the sun was shining, and the land was clear. We started at 2, with what we thought was Mount Hope showing up ahead, but soon great snow-clouds were banking up and in two hours we were walking in

34. *Scott's Last Expedition*, vol. 1, p. 483.

deep gloom which made it difficult to find the track made by
the man-hauling party ahead. By the time we reached the
cairn, which was always built at the end of the first four miles,
it was blowing hard from the N.N.W. of all the unlikely
quarters of the compass. Bowers and Scott were on ski.

> I put on my windproof blouse and nosed out the track for
> two miles, when we suddenly came upon the tent of the
> leading party. They had camped owing to the difficulty of
> steering a course in such thick weather. The ponies, however,
> with the wind abaft the beam were going along splendidly,
> and Scott thought it worth while to shove on. We therefore
> carried on another four miles, making ten in all, a good half
> march, before we camped. On ski it was simply ripping,
> except for the inability to see anything at all. With the wind
> behind, and the good sliding surface made by the wind-
> hardened snow, one fairly slithered along. Camping was less
> pleasant as it was blowing a gale by that time. We are all in
> our bags again now, with a good hot meal inside one, and
> blow high or blow low one might be in a worse place than a
> reindeer bag.[35]

It was all right for the people on ski (and this in itself gave
us a certain sense of grievance), but things had not been so
easy with the ponies, who were sinking very deeply in places,
while we ourselves were sinking well over our ankles. This
day we began to cross the great undulations in the Barrier,
with the crests some mile apart, which here mark the
approach to the land. We had built the walls to the north of
the ponies on camping, because the wind was from that
direction, but by breakfast on 4 December it was blowing a
thick blizzard from the south-east. We began to feel bewildered by these extraordinary weather changes, and not a little
exasperated too. Again we could not march, and again we
had to dig out the sledges and ponies, and to move them all
round to the other side of the walls which we had partly to

---

35. Bowers.

rebuild. 'Oh for the simple man-hauling life!' was our thought, and 'poor helpless beasts – this is no country for live stock.' By this time we could not see the neighbouring tents for the drift. The situation was not improved by the fact that our tent doors, the tents having been pitched for the strong north wind then blowing, were now facing the blizzard, and sheets of snow entered with each individual. The man-hauling party came up just before the worst of the blizzard started. The dogs alone were comfortable, buried deep beneath the drifted snow. The sailors began to debate who was the Jonah. They said he was the cameras. The great blizzard was brewing all about us.

But at midday as though a curtain was rolled back, the thick fog cleared off, while at the same time the wind fell calm, and a great mountain appeared almost on the top of us. Far away to the south-east we could distinguish, by looking very carefully, a break in the level Barrier horizon – a new mountain which we reckoned must be at least in latitude 86° and very high. Towards it the ranges stretched away, peak upon peak, range upon range, as far as the eye could see.

> The mountains surpassed anything I have ever seen: beside the least of these giants Ben Nevis would be a mere mound, and yet they are so immense as to dwarf each other. They are intersected at every turn with mighty glaciers and ice-falls and eternally ice-filled valleys that defy description. So clear was everything that every rock seemed to stand out, and the effect of the sun as he came round (between us and the mountains) was to make the scene still more beautiful.[36]

Altogether we marched eleven miles this day, and camped right in front of the Gateway, which we reckoned to be some thirteen miles away. We saw no crevasses but crossed ten or twelve very large undulations, and estimated that the dips between them were twelve to fifteen feet. Mount Hope was bigger than we expected, and beyond it, stretching out into

36. Bowers.

the Barrier as far as we could see, was a great white line of jagged edges, the chaos of pressure which this vast glacier makes as it flows into the comparatively stationary ice of the Barrier.

My own pony Michael was shot after we came into camp. He was as attractive a little beast as we had. His light weight helped him on soft surfaces, but his small hoofs let him in farther than most and I notice in Scott's diary that on 19 November the ponies were sinking halfway to the hock, and Michael once or twice almost to the hock itself. A highly strung, spirited animal his off days took the form of fidgets, during which he would be constantly trying to stop and eat snow, and then rush forward to catch up the other ponies. Life was a constant source of wonder to him, and no movement in the camp escaped his notice. Before we had been long on the Barrier he developed mischievous habits and became a rope eater and gnawer of other ponies' fringes, as we called the coloured tassels we hung over their eyes to ward off snow-blindness. However, he was by no means the only culprit, and he lost his own fringe to Nobby quite early in the proceedings. It was not that he was hungry, for he never quite finished his own feed. At any rate he enjoyed the few weeks before he died, pricking up his ears and getting quite excited when anything happened, and the arrival of the dog-teams each morning after he had been tethered sent him to bed with much to dream of. And I must say his master dreamed pretty regularly too. Michael was killed right in front of the Gateway on 4 December, just before the big blizzard, which, though we did not know it, was on the point of breaking upon us, and he was untying his cloth and chewing up everything he could reach to the last.

It was decided after we camped, and he had his feed already on: Meares reported that he had no more food for the dogs. He walked away, and rolled in the snow on the way down, not having done so when we got in. He was just like a naughty child all the way, and pulled all out. He has been a good friend, and has a good record, 82° 23′S. He was a bit done today: the blizzard had knocked him. Gallant little Michael![37]

As we got into our bags the mountain tops were fuzzy with drift. We wanted one clear day to get across the chasm: one short march and the ponies' task was done. Their food was nearly finished. Scott wrote that night: 'We are practically through with the first stage of our journey.'[38]

Tuesday, 5 December. Camp 30. Noon. We awoke this morning to a raging howling blizzard. The blows we have had hitherto have lacked the very fine powdering snow, that especial feature of the blizzard. Today we have it fully developed. After a minute or two in the open one is covered from head to foot. The temperature is high, so that what falls or drives against one sticks. The ponies – heads, tails, legs and all parts not protected by their rugs – are covered with ice; the animals are standing deep in snow, the sledges are almost covered, and huge drifts above the tents. We have had breakfast, rebuilt the walls, and are now again in our bags. One cannot see the next tent, let alone the land. What on earth does such weather mean at this time of year? It is more than our share of ill-fortune, I think, but the luck may turn yet . . .

11 p.m. It has blown hard all day with quite the greatest snowfall I remember. The drifts about the tents are simply huge. The temperature was +27° this forenoon, and rose to +31° in the afternoon, at which time the snow melted as it fell on anything but the snow, and, as a consequence, there are pools of water on everything, the tents are wet through, also the wind-clothes, night-boots, etc.; water drips from the tent poles and door, lies on the floor-cloth, soaks the sleeping-bags, and makes everything pretty wretched. If a cold snap follows before we have had time to dry our things, we shall be mighty uncomfortable. Yet after all it would be humorous

37. My own diary.
38. *Scott's Last Expedition*, vol. i, p. 486.

enough if it were not for the seriousness of delay – we can't afford that, and it's real hard luck that it should come at such a time. The wind shows signs of easing down, but the temperature does not fall and the snow is as wet as ever, not promising signs of abatement.

Wednesday, 6 December. Camp 30. Noon. Miserable, utterly miserable. We have camped in the 'Slough of Despond'. The tempest rages with unabated violence. The temperature has gone to +33°; everything in the tent is soaking. People returning from the outside look exactly as though they had been in a heavy shower of rain. They drip pools on the floor-cloth. The snow is steadily climbing higher about walls, ponies, tents and sledges. The ponies look utterly desolate. Oh! But this is too crushing, and we are only 12 miles from the glacier. A hopeless feeling descends on one and is hard to fight off. What immense patience is needed for such occasions![39]

Bowers describes the situation as follows:

It is blowing a blizzard such as one might expect to be driven at us by all the powers of darkness. It may be interesting to describe it, as it is my first experience of a really warm blizzard, and I hope to be troubled by cold ones only, or at least moderate ones only, in future as regards temperature.

When I swung the thermometer this morning I looked and looked again, but unmistakably the temperature was +33° F., above freezing point (out of the sun's direct rays) for the first time since we came down here. What this means nobody can conceive. We try to treat it as a huge joke, but our wretched condition might be amusing to read of later. We are wet through, our tents are wet, our bags which are our life to us and the objects of our greatest care, are wet; the poor ponies are soaked and shivering far more than they would be ordinarily in a temperature fifty degrees lower. Our sledges – the parts that are dug out – are wet, our food is wet,

39. *Scott's Last Expedition*, vol. 1, pp. 486–9.

everything on and around and about us is the same – wet as ourselves and our cold, clammy clothes. Water trickles down the tent poles and only forms icicles in contact with the snow floor. The warmth of our bodies has formed a snow bath in the floor for each of us to lie in. This is a nice little catchwater for stray streams to run into before they freeze. This they cannot do while a warm human lies there, so they remain liquid and the accommodating bag mops them up. When we go out to do the duties of life, fill the cooker, etc., for the next meal, dig out or feed the ponies, or anything else, we are bunged up with snow. Not the driving, sandlike snow we are used to, but great slushy flakes that run down in water immediately and stream off you. The drifts are tremendous, the rest of the show is indescribable. I feel most for the unfortunate animals and am thankful that poor old Victor is spared this. I mended a pair of half mitts today, and we are having two meals instead of three. This idleness when one is simply jumping to go on is bad enough for most, but must be worse for Captain Scott. I feel glad that he has Dr Bill (Wilson) in his tent; there is something always so reassuring about Bill, he comes out best in adversity.[40]

Thursday, 7 December. Camp 30. The storm continues and the situation is now serious. One small feed remains for the ponies after today, so that we must either march tomorrow or sacrifice the animals. That is not the worst; with the help of the dogs we could go on, without doubt. The serious part is that we have this morning started our Summit rations – that is to say, the food calculated from the Glacier Depot has been begun. The first supporting party can only go on a fortnight from this date and so forth.[41]

This day was just as warm, and wetter – much wetter. The temperature was +35.5°, and our bags were like sponges. The huge drifts had covered everything, including most of

40. Bowers.
41. *Scott's Last Expedition*, vol. i, p. 489.

the tent, the pony walls and sledges. At intervals we dug our way out and dug up the wretched ponies, and got them on to the top again.

> Henceforward our full ration will be 16 oz. biscuit, 12 oz. pemmican, 2 oz. butter, 0.57 oz. cocoa, 3.0 oz. sugar and 0.86 oz. tea. This is the Summit ration, total 34.43 oz., with a little onion powder and salt. I am all for this: Seaman Evans and others are much regretting the loss of chocolate, raisins and cereals. For the first week up the glacier we are to go one biscuit short to provision Meares on the way back. The motors depoted too much and Meares has been brought on far farther than his orders were originally bringing him. Originally he was to be back at Hut Point on 10 December. The dogs, however, are getting all the horse that is good for them, and are very fit. He has to average 24 miles a day going back. Michael is well out of this: we are now eating him. He was in excellent condition and tastes very good, though tough.[42]

By this time there was little sleep left for us as we lay in our sleeping-bags. Three days generally see these blizzards out, and we hoped much from Friday, 8 December. But when we breakfasted at 10 a.m. (we were getting into day-marching routine) wind and snow were monotonously the same. The temperature rose to +34.3°. These temperatures and those recorded by Meares on his way home must be a record for the interior of the Barrier. So far as we were concerned it did not matter now whether it was +40° or +34°. Things did look really gloomy that morning.

But at noon there came a gleam of comfort. The wind dropped, and immediately we were out plunging about, always up to our knees in soft downy snow, and often much farther. First we shifted our tents, digging them up with the greatest care that the shovel might not tear them. The valances were encased in solid ice from the water which had

---

42. My own diary.

run down. Then we started to find our sledges which were about four feet down: they were dragged out, and everything on them was wringing wet. There was a gleam of sunshine, which soon gave place to snow and gloom, but we started to make experiments in haulage. Four men on ski managed to move a sledge with four others sitting upon it. Nobby was led out, but sank to his belly. As for the drifts I saw Oates standing behind one, and only his head appeared, and this was all loose snow.

> We are all sitting round now after some tea – it is much better than getting into the bags. I can hardly think that the ponies can pull on, but Titus thinks they can pull tomorrow; all the food is finished, and what they have had today was only what they would not eat out of their last feed yesterday. It is a terrible end – driven to death on no more food, to be then cut up, poor devils. I have swopped the *Little Minister* with Silas Wright for *Dante's Inferno*![43]

The steady patter of the falling snow upon the tents was depressing as we turned in, but the temperature was below freezing.

The next morning (Saturday, 9 December) we turned out to a cloudy snowy day at 5.30 a.m. By 8.30 we had hauled the sledges some way out of the camp and started to lead out the ponies. 'The horses could hardly move, sank up to their bellies, and finally lay down. They had to be driven, lashed on. It was a grim business.'[44]

My impressions of that day are of groping our way, for Bowers and I were pulling a light sledge ahead to make the track, through a vague white wall. First a confused crowd of men behind us gathered round the leading pony sledge, pushing it forward, the poor beast barely able to struggle out of the holes it made as it plunged forward. The others were

43. ibid.   44. ibid.

induced to follow, and after a start had been made the regular man-hauling party went back to fetch their load. There was not one man there who would willingly have caused pain to a living thing. But what else was to be done – we could not leave our pony depot in that bog. Hour after hour we plugged on: and we dare not halt for lunch, we knew we could never start again. After crossing many waves huge pressure ridges suddenly showed themselves all round, and we got on to a steep rise with the coastal chasm on our right hand appearing as a great dip full of enormous pressure. Scott was naturally worried about crevasses, and though we knew there was a way through, the finding of it in the gloom was most difficult. For two hours we zig-zagged about, getting forward it is true, but much bewildered, and once at any rate almost bogged. Scott joined us, and we took off our ski so as to find the crevasses, and if possible a hard way through. Every step we sank about fifteen inches, and often above our knees. Meanwhile Snatcher was saving the situation in snow-shoes, and led the line of ponies. Snippets nearly fell back into a big crevasse, into which his hind quarters fell: but they managed to unharness him, and scramble him out.

I do not know how long we had been going when Scott decided to follow the chasm. We found a big dip with hard ice underneath, and it was probably here that we made the crossing: we could now see the ring of pressure behind us. Almost it was decided to make the depot here, but the ponies still plugged on in the most plucky way, though they had to be driven. Scott settled to go as far as they could be induced to march, and they did wonderfully. We had never thought that they would go a mile: but painfully they marched for eleven hours without a long halt, and covered a distance which we then estimated at seven miles. But our sledge-meters were useless being clogged with the soft snow, and we afterwards came to believe the distance was not so great: probably not more than five. When we had reached a point some two miles from the top of the snow divide which fills the Gateway we camped, thankful to rest, but more thankful still that we need drive those weary ponies no more. Their rest was near. It was a horrid business, and the place was known as Shambles Camp.

Oates came up to Scott as he stood in the shadow of Mount Hope. 'Well! I congratulate you, Titus,' said Wilson.

'And *I* thank you, Titus,' said Scott.

And that was the end of the Barrier Stage.

Chapter Ten
THE POLAR JOURNEY
(Continued)

The Southern Journey involves the most important object of the Expedition. . . . One cannot afford to be blind to the situation: the scientific public, as well as the more general public, will gauge the result of the scientific work of the Expedition largely in accordance with the success or failure of the main object. With success all roads will be made easy, all work will receive its proper consideration. With failure even the most brilliant work may be neglected and forgotten, at least for a time.

SCOTT

II. THE BEARDMORE GLACIER

THE PONIES had dragged twenty-four weekly units of food for four men to some five miles from the bottom of the glacier, but we were late. For some days we had been eating the Summit ration, that is the food which should not have been touched until the Glacier Depot had been laid, and we were still a day's run from the place where this was to be done: it was of course the result of the blizzard which no one could have expected in December, usually one of the two most settled months. Still more serious was the deep snow which lay like down upon the surface, and into which we sank commonly to our knees, our sledges digging themselves in until the crosspieces were ploughing through the drift. Shackleton had fine weather, and found blue ice in the bottom reaches of the glacier, and Scott lamented what was unquestionably bad luck.

It was noon of 10 December before we had made the readjustments necessary for man-hauling. We left here pony meat for man and dog food, three ten-foot sledges, one twelve-foot sledge, and a good many oddments of clothing and pony gear. We started with three four-man teams, each pulling for these first few miles about 500 lbs., as follows: (I) Scott, Wilson, Oates, Seaman Evans: (II) Lieut. Evans, Atkinson, Wright, Lashly: (III) Bowers, Cherry-Garrard, Crean, Keohane. The team numbered (II) had been man-hauling together some days, and two members of it, Lieut. Evans and Lashly, had already been man-hauling since the breakdown of the second motor at Corner Camp; it was certainly not so fit as the other two. In addition to these three sledges the two dog-teams, which had been doing splendid work, were carrying 600 lbs. of our weight as well as the provisions for the Lower Glacier Depot, weighing 200 lbs. It began to look as if Amundsen had chosen the right form of transport.

The Gateway is a gap in the mountains, a side door, as it were, to the great tumbled glacier. By lunch we were on the top of the divide, but it took six hours of the hardest hauling to cover the mile which formed the rise. As long as possible we stuck to ski, but we reached a point at which we could not move the sledges on ski: once we had taken them off we were up to our knees, and the sledges were ploughing the snow which would not support them. But our gear was drying in the bright sunshine, our bags were spread out at every opportunity, and the great jagged cliffs of red granite were welcome to the eyes after 425 statute miles of snow. The Gateway is filled by a giant snowdrift which has been formed between Mount Hope on our left and the mainland on our right. From Shackleton's book we gathered that the Beardmore was a very bad glacier indeed. Once on the top of the divide we lunched, and we descended in the evening, camping at midnight on the edge of the glacier, which we found, as we had feared, covered with soft snow which was so deep as to give no indication whatever of the hard ice which Shackleton found here. 'We camped in considerable drift and a blizzard wind, which is still blowing, and I hope will go on, for every hour it is sweeping away inches of this soft powdery snow into which we have been sinking all day.'[1]

1. My own diary.

Before setting out on 11 December we rigged up the Lower Glacier Depot, three weekly Summit units of provisions, two cases of emergency biscuit which was the ration for three weekly units, and two cans of oil. These provisions were calculated to carry the three returning parties as far as the Southern Barrier Depot. We also left one can of spirit, used for lighting the primus, one bottle of medical brandy and certain spare and personal gear not required. On the sledges themselves we stowed eighteen weekly Summit units, besides the three ready bags containing the ration for the current week, and the complement of biscuit, for this was ten cases in addition to the three boxes of biscuit which the three parties were using. Then there were eighteen cans of oil, with two cans of lighting spirit and a little additional Christmas fare which Bowers had packed. Every unit of food was worked out for four men for one week.

During this time of deep snow the sledge-meters would not work and we were compelled to estimate the distance marched each day.

It has been a tremendous slog, but I think a most hopeful day. Before starting it took us about two hours to make the depot and then we got straight into the midst of the big pressure. The dogs, with ten cases of biscuit, came behind and pulled very well. We soon caught sight of a big boulder, and Bill and I roped up and went over to it. It was a block of very coarse granite, nearly gneiss, with large crystals of quartz in it, rusty outside and quite pinkish when chipped, and with veins of quartz running through it. It was a vast thing to be carried along on the ice, and looked very typical of the rock round. Instead of keeping under the great cliff where Shackleton made his depot, we steered for Mount Kyffin, that is towards the middle of the glacier, until lunch, when we had probably done about two or three miles. There was a crevasse wherever we went, but we managed to pull on ski and had no one down, and the deep snow saved the dogs.[2]

2. ibid.

The dog-teams were certainly running very big risks that morning. They turned back after lunch, having been brought on far longer than had been originally intended, for, as I have said, they were to have been back at Hut Point before now, and their provision allowance would not allow of further advance. Perhaps we rather overestimated the dogs' capacities when Bowers wrote: 'The dogs are wonderfully fit and will rush Meares and Dimitri back like the wind. I expect he will be nearly back by Christmas, as they will do about thirty miles a day.' But Meares told us when we got back to the hut that the dogs had by no means had an easy journey home. Now, however, 'with a whirl and a rush they were off on the homeward trial. I could not see them (being snow-blind), but heard the familiar orders as the last of our animal transports left us.'[3]

Our difficulties during the next four days were increased by the snow-blindness of half the men. The evening we reached the glacier Bowers wrote:

I am afraid I am going to pay dearly for not wearing goggles yesterday when piloting the ponies. My right eye has gone bung, and my left one is pretty dicky. If I am in for a dose of snow glare it will take three or four days to leave me, and I am in the ditch this time. It is painful to look at this paper, and my eyes are fairly burning as if some one had thrown sand into them.

And then:

I have missed my journal for four days, having been enduring the pains of hell with my eyes as well as doing the most back-breaking work I have ever come up against . . . I was blind as a bat, and so was Keohane in my team. Cherry pulled alongside me, with Crean and Keohane behind. By sticking plaster over my glasses except one small central spot I shut off most light and could see the points of my ski, but

3. Bowers.

366

the glasses were always fogged with perspiration and my eyes kept on streaming water which cannot be wiped off on the march as a ski stick is held in each hand; and so heavy were our weights [we had now taken on the weights which had been on the dog sledges] that if any of the pair slacked a hand even, the sledge stopped. It was all we could do to keep the sledge moving for short spells of a few hundred yards, the whole concern sinking so deeply into the soft snow as to form a snow-plough. The starting was worse than pulling as it required from ten to fifteen desperate jerks on the harness to move the sledge at all.

Many others were also snow-blind, caused partly by the strain of the last march of the ponies, partly by not having realized that now that we were day-marching the sun was more powerful and more precautions should be taken. The cocaine and zinc sulphate tablets which we had were excellent, but we also found that our tea leaves, which had been boiled twice and would otherwise have been thrown away, relieved the pain if tied into some cotton and kept pressed against the eyes. The tannic acid in the tea acted as an astringent. A snow-blind man can see practically nothing anyhow and so he is not much worse off if a handkerchief is tied over his eyes.

'*Beardmore Glacier*. Just a tiny note to be taken back by the dogs. Things are not so rosy as they might be, but we keep our spirits up and say the luck must turn. This is only to tell you that I find I can keep up with the rest as well as of old.'[4]

Then for the first time we were with our full loads of 800 lbs. a sledge. Even Bowers asked Scott whether he was going to try it without relaying. That night Scott's diary runs:

It was a very anxious business when we started after lunch, about 4.30. Could we pull our full loads or not? My own

4. Scott.

party got away first, and, to my joy, I found we could make fairly good headway. Every now and again the sledge sank in a soft patch, which brought us up, but we learned to treat such occasions with patience. We got sideways to the sledge and hauled it out, Evans (P.O.) getting out of his ski to get better purchase. The great thing is to keep the sledge moving, and for an hour or more there were dozens of critical moments when it all but stopped, and not a few when it brought up altogether. The latter were very trying and tiring.[5]

Altogether it was an encouraging day and we reckoned we had made seven miles. Generally it was not Scott's team which made the heaviest weather these days but on 12 December they were in greater difficulties than any of us. It was indeed a gruelling day, for the surface was worse than ever and many men were snow blind. After five hours' work in the morning we were about half a mile forward. We were in a sea of pressure, the waves coming at us from our starboard bow, the distance between the crests not being very great. We could not have advanced at all had it not been for our ski: 'on foot one sinks to the knees, and if pulling on a sledge to half-way between knee and thigh.'[6]

On 13 December,

the sledges sank in over twelve inches, and all the gear, as well as the thwartship pieces, were acting as breaks. The tugs and heaves we enjoyed, and the number of times we had to get out of our ski to upright the sledge, were trifles compared with the strenuous exertion of every muscle and nerve to keep the wretched drag from stopping when once under weigh; and then it would stick, and all the starting operations had to be gone through afresh. We did perhaps half a mile in the forenoon. Anticipating a better surface in the afternoon we got a shock. Teddy [Evans] led off half an hour earlier to pilot a way, and Captain Scott tried some fake with his spare

5. *Scott's Last Expedition*, vol. i, p. 497.
6. ibid., p. 499.

runners [he lashed them under the sledge to prevent the cross-pieces ploughing the snow] that involved about an hour's work. We had to continually turn our runners up to scrape the ice off them, for in these temperatures they are liable to get warm and melt the snow on them, and that freezes into knobs of ice which act like sandpaper or spikes on a pair of skates. We bust off second full of hope having done so well in the forenoon, but pride goeth [before a fall]. We stuck ten yards from the camp, and nine hours later found us little more than half a mile on. I have never seen a sledge sink so. I have never pulled so hard, or so nearly crushed my inside into my backbone by the everlasting jerking with all my strength on the canvas band round my unfortunate tummy. We were all in the same however.

I saw Teddy struggling ahead and Scott astern, but we were the worst off as the leading team had topped the rise and I was too blind to pick out a better trail. We fairly played ourselves out that time, and finally had to give it up and relay. Halving the load we went forward about a mile with it, and, leaving that lot, went back for the remainder. So done were my team that we could do little more than pull the half loads. Teddy's team did the same, and though Scott's did not, we camped practically the same time, having gone over our distance three times. Mount Kyffin was still ahead of us to the left: we seemed as if we can never come up with it. Tomorrow Scott decided that if we could not move our full loads we would start relaying systematically. It was a most depressing outlook after such a day of strenuous labour.[7]

We got soaked with perspiration these days, though generally pulling in vest, pants, and windproof trousers only. Directly we stopped we cooled quickly. Two skuas appeared at lunch, attracted probably by the pony flesh below, but it was a long way from the sea for them to come. On Thursday 14 December, Scott wrote: 'Indigestion and the soggy condition of my clothes kept me awake for some time last night,

7. Bowers.

and the exceptional exercise gives bad attacks of cramp. Our lips are getting raw and blistered. The eyes of the party are improving, I am glad to say. We are just starting our march with no very hopeful outlook.'

But we slogged along with much better results.

Once into the middle of the glacier we had been steering more or less for the Cloudmaker and by supper today were well past Mount Kyffin and were about 2000 feet up after an estimated run of 11 or 12 statute miles. But the most cheering sign was that the blue ice was gradually coming nearer the surface; at lunch it was two feet down, and at our supper camp only one foot. In pitching our tent Crean broke into a crevasse which ran about a foot in front of the door and there was another at Scott's door. We threw an empty oil can down and it echoed for a terribly long time.[8]

We spent the morning of 15 December crossing a maze of crevasses though they were well bridged; I believe all these lower reaches of the glacier are badly crevassed, but the thick snow and our ski kept us from tumbling in. There was a great deal of competition between the teams which was perhaps unavoidable but probably a pity. This day Bowers's diary records, 'Did a splendid bust off on ski, leaving Scott in the lurch, and eventually overhauling the party which had left some time before us. All the morning we kept up a steady, even swing which was quite a pleasure.' But the same day Scott wrote, 'Evans' is now decidedly the slowest unit, though Bowers' is not much faster. We keep up and overhaul either without difficulty.' Bowers's team considered themselves quite good, but both teams were satisfied of their own superiority; as a matter of fact Scott's was the faster, as it should have been for it was certainly the heavier of the two.

It was a very bad light all day, but after lunch it began to get worse, and by 5 o'clock it was snowing hard and we could

8. My own diary.

see nothing. We went on for nearly an hour, steering by the wind and any glimpse of sastrugi, and then, very reluctantly, Scott camped. It looks better now. The surface is much harder and more wind-swept, and as a rule the ice is only six inches underneath. We are beginning to talk about Christmas. We get very thirsty these days in the warm temperatures: we shall feel it farther up when the cold gets into our open pores and sunburnt hands and cracked lips. I am plastering some skin on mine tonight. Our routine now is: turn out 5.30, lunch 1, and camp at 7, and we get a short 8 hours' sleep, but we are so dead tired we could sleep half into the next day: we get about 9½ hours' march. Tea at lunch a positive godsend. We are raising the land to the south well, and are about 2500 feet up, latitude about 84° 8'S.[9]

The next day, 16 December, Bowers wrote:

We have had a really enjoyable day's march, except the latter end of the afternoon. At the outset in the forenoon my sledge was a bit in the lurch, and Scott drew steadily away from us. I knew I could ordinarily hold my own with him, but for the first two hours we dropped till we were several hundred yards astern; try as I would to rally up my team we could gain nothing. On examining the runners however we soon discovered the cause by the presence of a thin film of ice. After that we ran easily. The thing one must avoid doing is to touch them with the hand or mitt, as anything damp will make ice on them. We usually turn the sledge on its side and scrape one runner at a time with the back of our knives so as to avoid any chance of cutting or chipping them. In the afternoon either the tea or the butter we had at lunch made us so strong that we fairly overran the other team.[10]

We must push on all we can, for we are now 6 days behind Shackleton, all due to that wretched storm. So far, since we got among the disturbances we have not seen such alarming

9. My own diary.   10. Bowers.

crevasses as I had expected; certainly dogs could have come up as far as this.[11]

At lunch we could see big pressure ahead having done first over five miles. Soon after lunch, having gone down a bit, we rose among very rough stuff. We plugged on until 4.30, when ski became quite impossible, and we put them on the sledges and started on foot. We immediately began putting legs down: one step would be on blue ice and the next two feet into snow: very hard going. The pressure ahead seemed to stretch right into a big glacier next the Keltie Glacier to the east, and so we altered course for a small bluff point about two-thirds of the way along the base of the Cloudmaker. We were to camp at 6, but did not do so until about 6.30, the last 1½ hours in big pressure, crossing big and smaller waves, and hundreds of crevasses which one of us generally found. We are now camped in very big pressure, and with difficulty we found a patch big enough to pitch the tent free from crevasses. We are pretty well past the Keltie Glacier which is a vast tumbled mass: there is a long line of ice falls ahead, and I think there is a hard day ahead of us tomorrow among that pressure which must be enormous. We can't go farther inshore here, being under the north end of the Cloudmaker, and a fine mountain it is, rising precipitously above us.[12]

Sunday, 17 December. Nearly 11 Miles. Temp. 12.5°. 3500 feet. We have had an exciting day – this morning was just like the scenic railway at Earls Court. We got straight on to the big pressure waves, and headed for the humpy rock at the base of the Cloudmaker. It was a hard plug up the waves, very often standing pulls, and all that we could do for a course was a very varied direction. Going down the other side was the exciting part: all we could do was to set the sledge straight, hang on to the straps, give her a little push and rush down the slope, which was sometimes so sheer that the sledge

11. *Scott's Last Expedition*, vol. 1, p. 506.
12. My own diary.

was in the air. Sometimes there was no chance to brake the sledge, and we all had to get on to the top, and we rushed down with the wind whistling in our ears. After three hours of this it levelled out again a bit, and we took the top of a wave, and ran south along it on blue ice: enormous pressure to our right, largely I think caused by the Keltie Glacier. Then we ascended a rise, snowy and crevassed, and camped after doing just under five miles, with big pressure ahead.[13]

In the afternoon we had a hard surface. Scott started off at a great speed, Teddy [Evans] and I following. There was something wrong with my team or my sledge, as we had a desperate job to keep up at first. We did keep up all right, but were heartily glad when after about 2½ hours Scott stopped for a spell. I rearranged our harness, putting Cherry and myself on the long span again, which we had temporarily discarded in the morning. We were both winded and felt wronged. The rearrangement was a success however, and the remainder of the march was a pleasure instead of a desperate struggle. It finished up on fields of blue rippled ice with sharp knife edges, and snow patches few and far between. We are all camped on a small snow patch in the middle of a pale blue rippled sea, about 3600 feet above sea level and past the Cloudmaker, which means that we are half-way up the Glacier.[14]

We had done 12½ miles (statute).

The Beardmore Glacier is twice as large as the Malaspina in Alaska, which was the largest known glacier until Shackleton discovered the Beardmore. Those who knew the Ferrar Glacier professed to find the Beardmore unattractive, but to me at any rate it was grand. Its very vastness, however, tends to dwarf its surroundings, and great tributary glaciers and tumbled ice-falls, which anywhere else would have aroused admiration, were almost unnoticed in a stream which stretched in places forty miles from bank to bank. It was only

13. ibid.   14. Bowers.

when the theodolite was levelled that we realized how vast
were the mountains which surrounded us: one of which we
reckoned to be well over twenty thousand feet in height, and
many of the others must have approached that measurement.
Lieutenant Evans and Bowers were surveying whenever the
opportunity offered, whilst Wilson sat on the sledge on his
sleeping-bag, and sketched.

Before leaving on the morning of 18 December we bagged
off three half-weekly units and made a depot marked by a
red flag on a bamboo which was stuck into a small mound.
Unfortunately it began to snow in the night and no bearings
were taken until the following morning when only the base
of the mountains on the west side was visible. We knew we
might have difficulty in picking up this depot again, and
certainly we all did.

It was thick, with low stratus clouds in the morning, and
snow was falling in large crystals. Our socks and finnesko,
hung out to dry, were covered with most beautiful feathery
crystals. In the warm weather one gets fairly saturated with
perspiration on the march, and foot-gear is always wet, except
the outside covering which is as a rule more or less frozen
according to existing temperature. On camping at night I shift
to night foot-gear as soon as ever the tent is pitched, and
generally slip on my wind-proof blouse, as one cools down
like smoke after the exertion of man-hauling a heavy sledge
for hours. At lunch camp one's feet often get pretty cold, but
this goes off as soon as some hot tea gets into the system. As
a rule, even when snowing, one's socks, etc., will dry if there
is a bit of a breeze. They are always frozen stiff in the morning
and can best be thawed out by bundling the lot [under one's]
jersey during breakfast. They can then be put on tolerably
warm even if wet.

We started off on a hard rippled blue surface like a sea
frozen intact while the wind was playing on it. It soon got
worse and we had to have one and sometimes two hands back
to keep the sledge from skidding. Of course it was easy
enough stuff to pull on, but the ground was very uneven, and

sledges constantly capsized. It did not improve the runners either. There were few crevasses.

All day we went on in dull cloudy weather with hardly any land visible, and the glacier to be seen only for a short distance. In the afternoon the clouds lifted somewhat and showed us the Adam Mountains. The surface was better for the sledges but worse for us, as there were countless cracks and small crevasses, into which we constantly trod, barking our shins. As the afternoon sun came round the perspiration fairly streamed down, and it was impossible to keep goggles clear. The surface was so slippery and uneven that it was difficult to keep one's foothold. However we did 12½ miles, and felt that we had really done a good day's work when we camped. It was not clear enough to survey in the evening, so I took the sledge-meter in hand and worked at it half the night to repair Christopher's damage.[15] I ended up by making a fixing of which I was very proud, but did not dare to look at the time, so I don't know how much sleep I missed.

There is no doubt that Scott knows where to aim for in a glacier, as it was just here that Shackleton had two or three of his worst days' work, in such a maze of crevasses that he said that often a slip meant death for the whole party. He avoids the sides of the glacier and goes nowhere near the snow: he often heads straight for apparent chaos and somehow, when we appear to have reached a cul-de-sac, we find it an open road.[16]

However, we all found the trouble on our way back.

On our right we have now a pretty good view of the Adam, Marshall and Wild Mountains, and their very curious horizontal stratification. Wright has found, amongst bits of wind-blown débris, an undoubted bit of sandstone and a bit of black basalt. We must get to know more of the geology before leaving the glacier finally.[17]

15. See p. 343.   16. Bowers.
17. *Scott's Last Expedition*, vol. 1, p. 509.

December 19, +7°. Total height 5800 feet. Things are certainly looking up, seeing that we have risen 1100 feet, and marched 17 to 18 statute miles during the day, whereas Shackleton's last march was 13 statute. It was still thick when we turned out at 5.45, but it soon cleared with a fresh southerly wind, and we could see Buckley Island and the land at the head of the glacier just rising. We started late for Birdie wanted to get our sledge-meter dished up: it has been quite a job today getting it on, but it rode well this afternoon. We started over the same crevassed stuff, but soon got on to blue ice, and for two hours had a most pleasant pull, and then up a steepish rise sometimes on blue ice and sometimes on snow. After the pleasantest morning we have had, we completed 8½ miles.

Angles and observations were taken at lunch, and quite a lot of work was done. There is a general getting squared up with gear, for we know that those going on will not have many more days of warm temperatures. At one time today I think Scott meant trying the right hand of the island or nunatak, but as we rose this was obviously impossible, for there is a huge mass of pressure coming down there. From here the Dominion Range also looks as if it were a nunatak. Some of these mountains, which don't look very big, are huge (since the six thousand feet which we have risen have to be added on to them), and many of them are very grand indeed. The Mill Glacier is a vast thing, with big pressure across it. There also seems to be a big series of ice-falls between Buckley Island and the Dominion Range, for the centre of which Scott is going tomorrow. A pretty hard plug this afternoon, but no disturbance, and gradually we have left the bare ice, and are mostly travelling on *névé*. Much of the ice is white. I have been writing down angles and times for Birdie, and writing this in the intervals. Scott's heel is troubling him again. ['I have bad bruises on knee and thigh'],[18] and generally there has been a run on the medical cases for chafes, and minor ailments. There is now a keen southerly

18. ibid., vol. i, p. 510.

wind blowing. It gets a little colder each day, and we are already beginning to feel it on our sunburnt faces and hands.[19]

Of the crevasses met in the morning Bowers wrote:

So far nobody has dropped down the length of his harness, as I did on the Cape Crozier journey. On this blue ice they are pretty conspicuous, and as they are mostly snow-bridged one is well advised to step over any line of snow. With my short legs this was strenuous work, especially as the weight of the sledge would often stop me with a jerk just before my leading foot quite cleared a crevasse, and the next minute one would be struggling out so as to keep the sledge on the move. It is fatal to stop the sledge as nobody waits for stragglers, and you have to pick up your lost ground by strenuous hurry. Of course some one often gets so far down a hole that it is necessary to stop and help him out.

December 20. Today has been a great march – over two miles an hour, and on the whole rising a lot. Soon after starting we got onto the most beautiful icy surface, smooth except for cracks and only patches of snow, most of which we could avoid. We came along at a great rate.

The most interesting thing to see was that the Mill Glacier is not, as was supposed, a tributary, but probably is an outlet falling from this glacier, and a great size. However it was soon covered up with dense black cloud, and there were billows of cloud behind us and below.

At lunch Birdie made the disastrous discovery that the registering dial of his sledge-meter was off. A screw had shaken out on the bumpy ice, and the clockwork had fallen off. This is serious for it means that one of the three returning parties will have to go without, and their navigation will be much more difficult. Birdie is very upset, especially after all the trouble he has taken with it, and the hours which he has sat up. After lunch he and Bill walked back near two miles in

19. My own diary.

the tracks, but could not see it. It was then getting very thick, coming over from the north.[20]

It appeared to be blizzing down the glacier, though clear to the south. The northerly wind drove up a back-draught of snow, and very soon fogged us completely. However we found our way back to camp by the crampon tracks on the blue ice and then packed up to leave.[21]

We started, making a course to hit the east side of the island where there seems to be the only break in the ice-falls which stretch right across. The weather lifted, and we are now camped with the island just to our right, the long strata of coal showing plainly in it, and just in front of us is this steep bit up through the falls. We have done nearly 23 statute miles today, pulling 160 lbs. a man.

This evening has been rather a shock. As I was getting my finnesko on to the top of my ski beyond the tent Scott came up to me, and said that he was afraid he had rather a blow for me. Of course I knew what he was going to say, but could hardly grasp that I was going back – tomorrow night. The returning party is to be Atch, Silas, Keohane and self.

Scott was very put about, said he had been thinking a lot about it but had come to the conclusion that the seamen with their special knowledge, would be needed: to rebuild the sledge, I suppose. Wilson told me it was a toss-up whether Titus or I should go on: that being so I think Titus will help him more than I can. I said all I could think of – he seemed so cut up about it, saying 'I think somehow, it is specially hard on you.' I said I hoped I had not disappointed him, and he caught hold of me and said 'No – no – No,' so if that is the case all is well. He told me that at the bottom of the glacier he was hardly expecting to go on himself: I don't know what the trouble is, but his foot is troubling him, and also, I think, indigestion.[22]

20. My own diary.   21. Bowers.
22. My own diary.

Scott just says in his diary, 'I dreaded this necessity of choosing – nothing could be more heartrending.' And then he goes on to sum up the situation, 'I calculated our programme to start from 85° 10' with 12 units of food and eight men. We ought to be in this position tomorrow night, less one day's food. After all our harassing trouble one cannot but be satisfied with such a prospect.'[23]

December 21. Upper Glacier Depot. Started off with a nippy S.Wly. wind in our faces, but bright sunshine. One's nose and lips being chapped and much skinned with alternate heat and cold, a breeze in the face is absolute agony until you warm up. This does not take long, however, when pulling a sledge, so after the first quarter of an hour more or less one is comfortable unless the wind is very strong.

We made towards the only place where it seemed possible to cross the mass of pressure ice caused by the junction of the plateau with the glacier, and congested between the nunatak [Buckley Island] and the Dominion Range. Scott had considered at one time going up to westward of the nunatak, but this appeared more chaotic than the other side. We made for a slope close to the end of the island or nunatak, where Shackleton must have got up also; it is obviously the only place when you look at it from a commanding rise. We did not go quite so close to the land as Shackleton did, and therefore, as had been the case with us all the way up the glacier, found less difficulties than he met with. Scott is quite wonderful in his selections of route, as we have escaped excessive dangers and difficulties all along. In this case we had fairly good going, but got into a perfect mass of crevasses into which we all continually fell; mostly one foot, but often two, and occasionally we went down altogether, some to the length of their harness to be hauled out with the Alpine rope. Most of them could be seen by the strip of snow on the blue ice. They were often too wide to jump though, and the only thing was to plant your feet on the bridge and try not to tread

23. *Scott's Last Expedition*, vol. i, pp. 511–12.

heavily. As a rule the centre of a bridged crevasse is the safest place, the rotten places are at the edges. We had to go over dozens by hopping right on to the ice. It is a bit of a jar when it gives way under you, but the friendly harness is made to trust one's life to. The Lord only knows how deep these vast chasms go down, they seem to extend into blue black nothingness thousands of feet below.

Before reaching the rise we had to go up and down many steep slopes, and on the one side the sledges were overrunning us, and on the other it fairly took the juice out of you to reach the top. We saw the stratification on the nunatak which Shackleton supposed to be coal: there was also much sandstone and red granite. I should like to have scratched round these rocks: we may get a chance on our return journey. As we topped each rise we found another one beyond it, and so on.

About noon some clouds settled in a fog round us, and being fairly in a trough of crevasses we could not get on. Fortunately we found a snow patch to pitch the tents on, but even there were crevasses under us. However, we enjoyed a hearty lunch, and I improved the shining hour by preparing my rations for the Upper Glacier Depot.

At 3 p.m. it cleared, and Mount Darwin, a nunatak to the S.W. of the others, could be seen. This we made for, and some two miles on exchanged blue ice for the new snow which was much harder pulling. Scott was fairly wound up, and he went on and on. Every rise topped seemed to fire him with a desire to top the next, and every rise had another beyond and above it. We camped at 8 p.m., all pretty weary, having come up nearly 1500 feet, and done over eleven miles in a S.W. direction. We were south of Mount Darwin in 85° 7′ S., and our corrected altitude proved to be 7000 feet above the Barrier. I worked up till a very late hour getting the depot stores ready, and also weighing out and arranging allowances for the returning party, and arranging the stores and distribution of weights of the two parties going on. The temperature was down to zero today, the lowest it has been for some time this summer weather.[24]

24. Bowers.

There is a very mournful air tonight – those going on and those turning back. Bill came in while I was cooking, to say good-bye. He told me he fully expected to come back with the next party: that he could see Scott was going to take on the strongest fellows, perhaps three seamen. It would be a great disappointment if Bill did not go on.[25]

We gave away any gear which we could spare to those going on, and I find the following in my diary:

'I have been trying to give away my spare gear where it may be most acceptable: finnesko to Birdie, pyjama trousers to Bill, and a bag of baccy for Bill to give Scott on Christmas Day, some baccy to Titus, jaeger socks and half my scarf to Crean, and a bit of handkerchief to Birdie. Very tired tonight.'

Scott wrote: 'We are struggling on, considering all things against odds. The weather is a constant anxiety, otherwise arrangements are working exactly as planned.

'Here we are practically on the summit and up to date in the provision line. We ought to get through.'[26]

25. My own diary.
26. *Scott's Last Expedition*, vol. i, p. 513.

Chapter Eleven
THE POLAR JOURNEY
(Continued)

People, perhaps, still exist who believe that it is of no importance to explore the unknown polar regions. This, of course, shows ignorance. It is hardly necessary to mention here of what scientific importance it is that these regions should be thoroughly explored. The history of the human race is a continual struggle from darkness towards light. It is, therefore, to no purpose to discuss the use of knowledge; no man wants to know, and when he ceases to do so, he is no longer man.

NANSEN

III.   THE PLATEAU FROM MOUNT DARWIN
TO LAT. 87° 32′ S.

First Sledge	Second Sledge
SCOTT	LIEUT. EVANS
WILSON	BOWERS
OATES	LASHLY
SEAMAN EVANS	CREAN

FOR THE FIRST week on the plateau Bowers wrote a full diary, which I give below. After 28 December there are little more than fragmentary notes until 19 January, the day the party started to return from the Pole. From then until 25 January, he wrote fully; nothing after that until 29 January, followed by more fragments to 'February 3rd (I suppose)'. That is the last entry he made.

But this is not surprising, even in a man of Bowers's energy. The time a man can give to writing under such conditions is limited, and Bowers had a great deal of it to do before he could think of a diary – the meteorological log; sights for position as well as rating sights for time; and all the routine work of weights, provisions and depots. He wrote no diary at the Pole, but he made a very full meteorological report while there in addition to working out sights. The wonder is that he kept a diary at all.

From Bowers's Diary

December 22. *Midsummer Day.* We have had a brilliant day with a temperature about zero and no wind, altogether charming conditions. I rigged up the Upper Glacier Depot after breakfast. We depoted two half-weekly units for return of the two parties, also all crampons and glacier gear, such as ice-axes, crowbar, spare Alpine rope, etc., personal gear, medical, and in fact everything we could dispense with. I left my old finnesko, wind trousers and some other spare gear in a bag for going back.

The two advance parties' weights amounted to 190 lbs. per man. They consisted of the permanent weights, twelve weeks' food and oil, spare sledge runners, etc. We said good-bye and sent back messages and photo films with the First Returning Party, which consisted of Atch, Cherry, Silas and Keohane. It was quite touching saying farewell to our good pals – they wished us luck, and Cherry, Atch and Silas quite overwhelmed me.

We went forward, the Owner's team as before consisting of Dr Bill, Titus and [Seaman] Evans, and [Lieut.] Teddy Evans and Lashly coming over to my sledge and tent to join up with Crean and myself. We all left the depot cairn marked with two spare 10-feet sledge runners and a large black flag on one. Our morning march was not so long as usual owing to making up the depot, but we did five miles uphill, hauling our heavier loads more easily than the lighter ones yesterday. A fall in the temperature had improved the surface. We had also sandpapered our runners after the tearing up they had had on the glacier; this made a tremendous difference. The afternoon march brought our total up to 10.6 miles for the day on a S.W. course.

We are steering S.W. with a view to avoiding ice-falls which Shackleton met with. We came across very few crevasses; the few found were as broad as a street, and crossing them the whole party, sledge and all, would be on the bridge at once. They only gave way at the edges, and we did nothing worse than put our feet through now and then. The surface is all snow now, névé and hard sastrugi, which seem to point to a strong prevalent S.S.E. wind here.

We are well clear of the land now, and it is a beautiful evening. I have just taken six photographs of the Dominion Range. We can see many new mountains. Our position by observation is 86° 13′ 29″ S., 161° 54′ 45″ E., variation being 175° 45′.

December 23. Turned out at usual time, 5.45 a.m. I am cook this week in our tent. After breakfast built two cairns to mark spot and shoved off at quarter to eight.

We started up a big slope on a S.W. course to avoid the pressure which lay across our track to the southward. It was a pretty useful slog up the rise, at one time it seemed as if we would never top the slope. We stopped for five minutes to look around after 2½ hours' hard plugging and about 1½ hours later reached the top, from which we could see the distant mountains which have so recently been our companions. They are beginning to look pretty magnificent. The top of the great pressure ridge was running roughly S.E. and N.W.: it was one of a succession of ridges which probably cover an area of fifty or sixty square miles. In this neighbourhood Shackleton met them almost to 86½° south. At the top of the ridge were vast crevasses into which we could have dropped the *Terra Nova* easily. The bridges were firm, however, except at the sides, though we had frequent stumbles into the conservatory roof, so to speak. The sledges were rushed over them without mishap. We had to head farther west to clear disturbances, and at one time were going W.N.W.

At lunch camp we had gone 8½ miles, and in the afternoon we completed fifteen on a S.W. course over improved ground. Our routine is to actually haul our sledges for nine hours a day; five in the morning, 7.15 a.m. till 1 p.m.; and four in the afternoon, 2.30 p.m.–6.30 p.m. We turn out at 5.45 a.m. just now. The loads are still pretty heavy, but the surface is remarkably good considering all things. One gets pretty weary towards the end of the day; all my muscles have had their turn at being [stiffened] up. These hills are giving my back ones a reminder, but they will ache less tomorrow and finally cease to do so, as is the case with legs, etc., which had their turn first.

December 24. *Christmas Eve.* We started off heading due south this morning, as we are many miles to the westward of Shackleton's course and should if anywhere be clear of the ice-falls and pressure. Of course no mortals having been here, one can only conjecture; as a matter of fact, we found later in the day that we were not clear by any means, and had to do a bit of dodging about to avoid disturbances, as well as mount vast ridges with the tops of them a chaos of crevasses. The tops are pretty hard ice-snow, over which the sledges run easily; it is quite a holiday after slogging up the slopes on the softer surface with our heavy loads, which amount to over 190 lbs. per man.

We mark our night camp by two cairns and our lunch camp by single ones. It is doubtful, however, among these ridges, if we will ever pick them up again, and it does not really matter, as we have excellent land for the Upper Glacier Depot. We completed fourteen miles and turned in as usual pretty tired.

December 25. *Christmas Day.* A strange and strenuous Christmas for me, with plenty of snow to look at and very little ease. The breeze that had blown in our faces all yesterday blew more freshly today, with surface drift. It fairly nipped one's nose and face starting off – until one got warmed up. We had to pull in wind blouses, as though one's body kept warm enough on the march the arms got numbed with the penetrating wind no matter how vigorously they were swung. Another thing is that one cannot stop the team on the march to get clothes on and off, so it is better to go the whole hog and be too hot than cause delays. We had the addition of a little pony meat for breakfast to celebrate the day. I am the cook for our tent this week.

We steered south again and struck our friends the crevasses

and climbed ridges again. About the middle of the morning we were all falling in continually, but Lashly in my team had the worst drop. He fell to the length of his harness and the trace. I was glad that having noticed his rope rather worn, I had given him a new one a few days before. He jerked Crean and me off our feet backwards, and Crean's harness being jammed under the sledge, which was half across an eight-feet bridge, he could do nothing. I was a little afraid of sledge and all going down, but fortunately the crevasse ran diagonally. We could not see Lashly, for a great overhanging piece of ice was over him. Teddy Evans and I cleared Crean and we all three got Lashly up with the Alpine rope cut into the snow sides which overhung the hole. We then got the sledge into safety.

Today is Lashly's birthday; he is married and has a family; is 44 years of age, and due for his pension from the service. He is as strong as most and is an undefeated old sportsman. Being a chief stoker, R.N., his original job was charge of one of the ill-fated motor sledges.

The following is Lashly's own account:

Christmas Day and a good one. We have done 15 miles over a very changing surface. First of all it was very much crevassed and pretty rotten; we were often in difficulties as to which way we should tackle it. I had the misfortune to drop clean through, but was stopped with a jerk when at the end of my harness. It was not of course a very nice sensation, especially on Christmas Day and being my birthday as well. While spinning round in space like I was it took me a few seconds to gather together my thoughts and see what kind of a place I was in. It certainly was not a fairy's place. When I had collected myself I heard some one calling from above, 'Are you all right, Lashly?' I was all right it is true, but I did not care to be dangling in the air on a piece of rope, especially when I looked round and saw what kind of a place it was. It seemed about 50 feet deep and 8 feet wide, and 120 feet long. This information I had ample time to gain while dangling there. I could measure the width with my ski sticks, as I had them on my wrists. It seemed a long time before I saw the rope come down alongside me with a bowline in it for me to put my foot in and get dragged out. It was not a job I should care to have to go through often, as by being in the crevasse I had got cold and a bit frost-bitten on the hands and face, which made it more difficult for me to help myself. Anyhow Mr Evans, Bowers and Crean hauled me out and Crean wished me many happy returns of the day, and of course I thanked him politely and the others laughed, but all were pleased I was not hurt bar a bit of a shake. It was funny although they called to the other team to stop they did not hear, but went trudging on and did not know until they looked round just in time to see me arrive on top again. They then waited for us to come up with them. The Captain asked if I was all right and could go on again, which I could honestly say 'Yes' to, and at night when we stopped for dinner I felt I could do two dinners in. Anyhow we had a pretty good tuck-in. Dinner consisted of pemmican, biscuits, chocolate éclair, pony meat, plum pudding and crystallized ginger and four caramels each. We none of us could hardly move.[1]

We had done over eight miles at lunch. I had managed to scrape together from the Barrier rations enough extra food to allow us a stick of chocolate each for lunch, with two spoonfuls of raisins each in our tea. In the afternoon we got clear of crevasses pretty soon, but towards the end of the afternoon Captain Scott got fairly wound up and went on and on. The breeze died down and my breath kept fogging my glasses, and our windproofs got oppressively warm and altogether things were pretty rotten. At last he stopped and we found we had done 14¾ miles. He said, 'What about fifteen miles for Christmas Day?' so we gladly went on – anything definite is better than indefinite trudging.

We had a great feed which I had kept hidden and out of the official weights since our departure from Winter Quarters. It consisted of a good fat hoosh with pony meat and ground

1. Lashly's diary.

biscuit; a chocolate hoosh made of water, cocoa, sugar, biscuit, raisins, and thickened with a spoonful of arrowroot. (This is the most satisfying stuff imaginable.) Then came $2\frac{1}{2}$ square inches of plum-duff each, and a good mug of cocoa washed down the whole. In addition to this we had four caramels each and four squares of crystallized ginger. I positively could not eat all mine, and turned in feeling as if I had made a beast of myself. I wrote up my journal – in fact I should have liked somebody to put me to bed.

December 26. We have seen many new ranges of mountains extending to the S.E. of the Dominion Range. They are very distant, however, and must evidently be the top of those bounding the Barrier. They could only be seen from the tops of the ridges as waves up which we are continually mounting. Our height yesterday morning by hypsometer was 8000 feet. This is our last hypsometer record, as I had the misfortune to break the thermometer. The hypsometer was one of my chief delights, and nobody could have been more disgusted than myself at its breaking. However, we have the aneroid to check the height. We are going gradually up and up. As one would expect, a considerable amount of lassitude was felt over breakfast after our feed last night. The last thing on earth I wanted to do was to ship the harness round my poor tummy when we started. As usual a stiff breeze from the south and a temperature of $-7°$ blew in our faces. Strange to say, however, we don't get frost-bitten. I suppose it is the open-air life.

I could not tell if I had a frost-bite on my face now, as it is all scales, so are my lips and nose. A considerable amount of red hair is endeavouring to cover up matters. We crossed several ridges, and after the effects of over-feeding had worn off did a pretty good march of thirteen miles.

[No more Christmas Days, so no more big hooshes.[2]]

December 27. There is something the matter with our sledge or our team, as we have an awful slog to keep up with

2. Lashly's diary.

the others. I asked Dr Bill and he said their sledge ran very easily. Ours is nothing but a desperate drag with constant rallies to keep up. We certainly manage to do so, but I am sure we cannot keep this up for long. We are all pretty well done up tonight after doing 13.3 miles.

Our salvation is on the summits of the ridges, where hard névé and sastrugi obtain, and we skip over this slippery stuff and make up lost ground easily. In soft snow the other team draw steadily ahead, and it is fairly heart-breaking to know you are putting your life out hour after hour while they go along with little apparent effort.

December 28. The last few days have been absolutely cloudless, with unbroken sunshine for twenty-four hours. It sounds very nice, but the temperature never comes above zero and what Shackleton called 'the pitiless increasing wind' of the great plateau continues to blow at all times from the south. It never ceases, and all night it whistles round the tents, all day it blows in our faces. Sometimes it is S.S.E., or S.E. to S., and sometimes even S. to W., but always southerly, chiefly accompanied by low drift which at night forms quite a deposit round the sledges. We expected this wind, so we must not growl at getting it. It will be great fun sailing the sledges back before it. As far as weather is concerned we have had remarkably fine days up here on this limitless snow plain. I should like to know what there is beneath us – mountains and valleys simply levelled off to the top with ice? We constantly come across disturbances which I can only imagine are caused by the peaks of ice-covered mountains, and no doubt some of the ice-falls and crevasses are accountable to the same source. Our coming west has not cleared them, as we have seen more disturbances to the west, many miles away. However, they are getting less and less, and are now nothing but featureless rises with apparently no crevasses. Our first two hours' pulling today . . .

From Lashly's Diary

December 29, 1911. A nasty head wind all day and low drift which accumulates in patches and makes it the deuce of a job to get along. We have got to put in long days to do the distance.

December 30, 1911. Sledges going heavy, surface and wind the same as yesterday. We depoted our ski tonight, that is the party returning *tomorrow*, when we march in the forenoon and camp to change our sledge runners into 10 feet. Done 11 miles but a bit stiff.

December 31, 1911. After doing 7 miles we camped and done the sledges which took us until 11 p.m., and we had to dig out to get them done by then, made a depot and saw the old year out and the new year in. We all wondered where we should be next New Year. It was so still and quiet; the weather was dull and overcast all night, in fact we have not seen much of the sun lately; it would be so nice if we could sometimes get a glimpse of it, the sun is always cheering.

January 1912. *New Year's Day*. We pushed on as usual, but were rather late getting away, 9.10 – something unusual for us to be as late. The temperature and wind is still very troublesome. We are now ahead of Shackleton's dates and have passed the 87th parallel, so it is only 180 miles to the Pole.

January 2, 1912. The dragging is still very heavy and we seem to be always climbing higher. We are now over 10,000 feet above sea level. It makes it bad as we don't get enough heat in our food and the tea is not strong enough to run out of the pot. Everything gets cold so quickly, the water boils at about 196° F.

Scott's own diary of this first fortnight on the plateau shows the immense shove of the man: he was getting every inch out of the miles, every ounce out of his companions. Also he was in a hurry, he always was. That blizzard which had delayed him just before the Gateway, and the resulting surfaces which had delayed him in the lower reaches of the glacier! One can feel the averages running through his brain:

so many miles today: so many more tomorrow. When shall we come to an end of this pressure? Can we go straight or must we go more west? And then the great undulating waves with troughs eight miles wide, and the buried mountains, causing whirlpools in the ice – how immense, and how annoying. The monotonous march: the necessity to keep the mind concentrated to steer amongst disturbances: the relief of a steady plod when the disturbances cease for a time: then more pressure and more crevasses. Always slog on, slog on. Always a fraction of a mile more. . . . On 30 December he writes, 'We have caught up Shackleton's dates.'[3]

They made wonderful marches, averaging nearly fifteen statute miles (13 geog.) a day for the whole-day marches until the Second Return Party turned back on 4 January. Scott writes on 26 December, 'It seems astonishing to be disappointed with a march of 15 (statute) miles when I had contemplated doing little more than 10 with full loads.'[4]

The Last Returning Party came back with the news that Scott must reach the Pole with the greatest ease. This seemed almost a certainty: and yet it was, as we know now, a false impression. Scott's plans were based on Shackleton's averages over the same country. The blizzard came and put him badly behind: but despite this he caught Shackleton up. No doubt the general idea then was that Scott was going to have a much easier time than he had expected. We certainly did not realize then, and I do not think Scott himself had any notion of, the price which had been paid.

Of the three teams of four men each which started from the bottom of the Beardmore, Scott's team was a very long way the strongest: it was the team which, with one addition, went to the Pole. Lieutenant Evans's team had mostly done a lot of man-hauling already: it was hungry and I think a bit stale. Bowers's team was fresh and managed to keep up for the most part, but it was very done at the end of the day. Scott's own team went along with comparative ease. From

3. *Scott's Last Expedition*, vol. i, p. 525.
4. ibid., p. 521.

the top of the glacier two teams went on during the last fortnight of which we have been speaking. The first of them was Scott's unit complete, just as it had pulled up the glacier. The second team consisted, I believe, of the men whom Scott considered to be the strongest; two from Evans's team, and two from Bowers's. All Scott's team were fresh to the extent that they had done no man-hauling until we started up the glacier. But two of the other team, Lieutenant Evans and Lashly, had been man-hauling since the breakdown of the second motor on 1 November. They had man-hauled four hundred statute miles farther than the rest. Indeed Lashly's man-hauling journey from Corner Camp to beyond 87° 32′ S., and back, is one of the great feats of polar travelling.

Surely and not very slowly, Scott's team began to wear down the other team. They were going easily when the others were making heavy weather and were sometimes far behind. During the fortnight they rose, according to the corrected observations, from 7151 feet (Upper Glacier Depot) to 9392 feet above sea level (Three Degree Depot). The rarefied air of the Plateau with its cold winds and lower temperatures, just now about −10° to −12° at night and −3° during the day, were having their effect on the second team, as well as the forced marches. This is quite clear from Scott's diary, and from the other diaries also. What did not appear until after the Last Returning Party had turned homewards was that the first team was getting worn out too. This team which had gone so strong up the glacier, which had done those amazingly good marches on the plateau, broke up unexpectedly and in some respects rapidly from the 88th parallel onwards.

Seaman Evans was the first man to crack. He was the heaviest, largest, most muscular man we had, and that was probably one of the main reasons: for his allowance of food was the same as the others. But one mishap which contributed to his collapse seems to have happened during this first fortnight on the plateau. On 31 December the 12-feet sledges were turned into 10-feet ones by stripping off the old scratched runners which had come up the glacier and shipping new 10-feet ones which had been brought for the purpose. This job was done by the seamen, and Evans appears to have had some accident to his hand, which is mentioned several times afterwards.

Meanwhile Scott had to decide whom he was going to take on with him to the Pole, – for it was becoming clear that in all probability he *would* reach the Pole: 'What castles one builds now hopefully that the Pole is ours,' he wrote the day after the supporting party left him. The final advance to the Pole was, according to plan, to have been made by four men. We were organized in four-man units: our rations were made up for four men for a week: our tents held four men: our cookers held four mugs, four pannikins and four spoons. Four days before the Supporting Party turned, Scott ordered the second sledge of four men to depot their ski. It is clear, I suppose, that at this time he meant the Polar Party to consist of four men. I think there can be no doubt that he meant one of those men to be himself: 'for your own ear also, I am exceedingly fit and can go with the best of them,' he wrote from the top of the glacier.[5]

He changed his mind and went forward a party of five: Scott, Wilson, Bowers, Oates and Seaman Evans. I am sure he wished to take as many men as possible to the Pole. He sent three men back: Lieutenant Evans in charge, and two seamen, Lashly and Crean. It is the vivid story of those three men, who turned on 4 January in latitude 87° 32', which is told by Lashly in the next chapter. Scott wrote home: 'A last note from a hopeful position. I think it's going to be all right. We have a fine party going forward and arrangements are all going well.'[6]

Ten months afterwards we found their bodies.

5. *Scott's Last Expedition*, vol. i, p. 513.
6. ibid., p. 529.

Chapter Twelve
THE POLAR JOURNEY
(Continued)

THE DEVIL. And these are the creatures in whom you discover
what you call a Life Force!

DON JUAN. Yes; for now comes the most surprising part of
the whole business.

THE STATUE. What's that?

DON JUAN. Why, that you can make any of these cowards
brave by simply putting an idea into his head.

THE STATUE. Stuff! As an old soldier I admit the cowardice:
it's as universal as sea sickness, and matters just as little.
But that about putting an idea into a man's head is stuff
and nonsense. In a battle all you need to make you fight is
a little hot blood and the knowledge that it's more dangerous to lose than to win.

DON JUAN. That is perhaps why battles are so useless. But
men never really overcome fear until they imagine they are
fighting to further a universal purpose – fighting for an
idea, as they call it.

BERNARD SHAW, *Man and Superman*

IV. RETURNING PARTIES

TWO DOG TEAMS (Meares and Dimitri) turned back
from the bottom of the Beardmore Glacier on 11
December 1911. They reached Hut Point on 4 January 1912.

First Supporting Party (Atkinson, Cherry-Garrard,
Wright, Keohane) turned back in lat. 85° 15′ on 22 December
1911. They reached Hut Point 26 January 1912.

Last Supporting Party (Lieut. Evans, Lashly, Crean)
turned back in lat. 87° 32′ on 4 January 1912. They reached
Hut Point 22 February 1912.

Of the three teams which started up the Beardmore Glacier
the first to return, a fortnight after starting the Summit

Rations, was known as the First Supporting Party: the second to return, a month after starting the Summit Rations, was known as the Last Supporting Party. Of the two dog-teams under Meares, which had already turned homewards at the bottom of the glacier after having been brought forward farther than had been intended, I will speak later.[1]

I am going to say very little about the First Return Party, which consisted of Atkinson, Wright, Keohane and myself. Atkinson was in command, and before we left Scott told him to bring the dog-teams out to meet the Polar Party if, as seemed likely, Meares returned home. Atkinson is a naval surgeon and you will find this party referred to in Lashly's diary as 'the Doctor's'.

> It was a sad job saying good-bye. It was thick, snowing and drifting clouds when we started back after making the depot, and the last we saw of them as we swung the sledge north was a black dot just disappearing over the next ridge and a big white pressure wave ahead of them. . . . Scott said some nice things when we said good-bye. Anyway he has only to average seven miles a day to get to the Pole on full rations – it's practically a cert for him. I do hope he takes Bill and Birdie. The view over the ice-falls and pressure by the Mill Glacier from the top of the ice-falls is one of the finest things I have ever seen. Atch is doing us proud.[2]

No five hundred mile journey down the Beardmore and across the Barrier can be uneventful, even in midsummer. We had the same dreary drag, the same thick weather, fears and anxieties which other parties have had. A touch of the same dysentery and sickness: the same tumbles and crevasses: the same Christmas comforts, a layer of plum pudding at the bottom of our cocoa, and some rocks collected from a moraine under the Cloudmaker: the same groping for tracks: the same cairns lost and found, the same snow-blindness and

1. See pp. 396, 397, 424–7.
2. My own diary, 22 December 1911.

weariness, nightmares, food dreams. . . . Why repeat? Comparatively speaking it was a very little journey: and yet the distance from Cape Evans to the top of the Beardmore Glacier and back is 1164 statute miles. Scott's Southern Journey of 1902–3 was 950 statute miles.

One day only is worth recalling. We got into the same big pressure above the Cloudmaker which both the other parties experienced. But where the other two parties made east to get out of it, we went west at Wright's suggestion: west was right. The day really lives in my memory because of the troubles of Keohane. He fell into crevasses to the full length of his harness eight times in twenty-five minutes. Little wonder he looked a bit dazed. And Atkinson went down into one chasm head foremost: the worst crevasse fall I've ever seen. But luckily the shoulder straps of his harness stood the strain and we pulled him up little the worse.

All three parties off the plateau owed a good deal to Meares, who, on his return with the two dog-teams, built up the cairns which had been obliterated by the big blizzard of 5–8 December. The ponies' walls were drifted level with the surface, and Meares himself had an anxious time finding his way home. The dog tracks also helped us a good deal: the dogs were sinking deeply and making heavy weather of it.

At the Barrier Depots we found rather despondent notes from Meares about his progress. To the Southern Barrier Depot he had uncomfortably high temperatures and a very soft surface, and found the cairns drifted up and hard to see. At the Middle Barrier Depot we found a note from him dated 20 December. 'Thick weather and blizzards had delayed him, and once he had got right off the tracks and had been out from his camp hunting for them. They were quite well: a little eye strain from searching for cairns. He was taking a little butter from each bag [of the three depoted weekly units], and with this would have enough to the next depot on short rations.'[3] At the Upper Glacier Depot [Mount

3. My own diary.

Hooper] the news from Meares was dated Christmas Eve, in the evening:

> The dogs were going slowly but steadily in very soft stuff, especially his last two days. He was running short of food, having only biscuit crumbs, tea, some cornflour, and half a cup of pemmican. He was therefore taking fifty biscuits, and a day's provisions for two men from each of our units. He had killed one American dog some camps back: if he killed more he was going to kill Krisravitza who he said was the fattest and laziest. We shall take on thirty biscuits short.[4]

Meares was to have turned homewards with the two dog-teams in lat. 81° 15'. Scott took him on to approximately 83° 35'. The dogs had the ponies on which to feed: to make up the deficiency of man-food we went one biscuit a day short when going up the Beardmore: but the dogs went back slower than was estimated and his provisions were insufficient. It was evident that the dog-teams would arrive too late and be too done to take out the food which had still to be sledged to One Ton for the three parties returning from the plateau. It was uncertain whether a man-hauling party with such of this food as they could drag would arrive at the depot before us.[5] We might have to travel the 130 geographical miles from One Ton to Hut Point on the little food which was already at that depot and we were saving food by going on short rations to meet this contingency if it arose. Judge therefore our joy when we reached One Ton in the evening of 15 January to find three of the five XS rations which were necessary for the three parties. A man-hauling party consisting of Day, Nelson, Hooper and Clissold had brought out this food; they left a note saying the crevasses near Corner Camp were bad and open. Day and Hooper had reached Cape Evans from the Barrier[6] on 21 December: they started out again on this depot-laying trip on 26 December.

It is common experience for men who have been hungry

to be ill after reaching plenty of food. Atkinson was not at all well during our journey in to Hut Point, which we reached without difficulty on 26 January.

When I was looking for data concerning the return of the Last Supporting Party of which no account has been published, I wrote to Lashly and asked him to meet and tell me all he could remember. He was very willing, and added that somewhere or other he had a diary which he had written: perhaps it might be of use? I asked him to send it me, and was sent some dirty thumbed sheets of paper. And this is what I read:

3 January 1912

Very heavy going today. This will be our last night together, as we are to return tomorrow after going on in the forenoon with the party chosen for the Pole, that is Capt. Scott, Dr Wilson, Capt. Oates, Lieut. Bowers and Taff Evans. The Captain said he was satisfied we were all in good condition, fit to do the journey, but only so many could go on, so it was his wish Mr Evans, Crean and myself should return. He was quite aware we should have a very stiff job, but we told him we did not mind that, providing he thought they could reach the Pole with the assistance we had been able to give them. The first time I have heard we were having mules coming down to assist us next year. I was offering to remain at Hut Point, to be there if any help was needed, but the Captain said it was his and also Capt. Oates's wish if the mules arrived I was to take charge of and look after them until their return; but if they did not arrive there was no reason why I should not come to Hut Point and wait their return. We had a long talk with the owner [Scott] in our tent about things in general and he seemed pretty confident of success. He seemed a bit afraid of us getting hung up, but as he said we had a splendid navigator, who he was sure he could trust to pull us through. He also thanked us all heartily for the way we had assisted in the Journey and he should be sorry when we parted. We are of course taking the mail, but what a time before we get back to send it. We are nearly as far as

Shackleton was on his Journey. I shall not write more tonight, it is too cold.

4 January 1912

We accompanied the Pole party for about five miles and everything seemed to be going pretty well and Capt. Scott said they felt confident they could pull the load quite well, so there was no more need for us to go on farther; so we stopped and did all the talking we could in a short time. We wished them every success and a safe return, and asked each one if there was anything we could do for them when we got back, but they were all satisfied they had left nothing undone, so the time came for the last handshake and good-bye. I think we all felt it very much. They then wished us a speedy return and safe, and then they moved off. We gave them three cheers, and watched them for a while until we began to feel cold. Then we turned and started for home. We soon lost sight of each other. We travelled a long time so as to make the best of it while the weather was suitable, as we have to keep up a good pace on the food allowance. It won't do to lay up much. One thing since we left Mt. Darwin, we have had weather we could travel in, although we have not seen the sun much of late. We did 13 miles as near as we can guess by the cairns we have passed. We have not got a sledge meter so shall have to go by guess all the way home.

[Owing to the loss of a sledge meter on the Beardmore Glacier one of the three parties had to return without one. A sledge meter gives the navigator his dead reckoning, indicating the miles travelled, like the log of a ship. To be deprived of it in a wilderness of snow without landmarks adds enormously to the difficulties and anxieties of a sledge party.]

5 January 1912

We were up and off this morning, the weather being fine but the surface is about the same, the temperature keeps low. We have got to change our pulling billets. Crean has become snow-blind today through being leader, so I shall have the job tomorrow, as Mr Evans seems to get blind rather quickly, so if I lead and he directs me from behind we ought to get along pretty well. I hope my eyes will keep alright. We made good 17 miles and camped.

6 January 1912

We are making good progress on the surface we have to contend with. We picked up the 3 Degree Depot soon after noon, which puts us up to time. We took our provision for a week. We have got to reach Mt. Darwin Depot, a distance of 120 miles, with 7 days' provisions. We picked up our ski and camped for the night. We have been wondering if the others have got the same wind as us. If so it is right in their face, whereas it is at our back, a treat to what it is facing it. Crean's eyes are pretty bad tonight. Snow-blindness is an awful complaint, and no one I can assure you looks forward with pleasure when it begins to attack.

7 January 1912

We have had a very good day as far as travelling goes, the wind has been behind us and is a great help to us. We have been on ski all day for the first time. It seems a good change to footing it, the one thing day after day gets on one's nerves. Crean's eyes are a bit better today, but far from being well. The temperature is pretty low, which don't improve the surface for hauling, but we seem to be getting along pretty well. We have no sledge meter so we have to go by guess. Mr Evans says we done 17½ miles, but I say 16½. I am not going to over-estimate our day's run, as I am taking charge of the biscuit so that we don't over-step the mark. This we have all agreed to so that we should exactly know how we stand, from day to day. I am still leading, not very nice as the light is bad. We caught a glimpse of the land to the east of us, but could only have been a mirage.

8 January 1912

On turning out this morning we found it was blowing a bliz so it was almost a case of having to remain in camp, but on second thoughts we thought it best to kick off as we can't afford to lay up on account of food, so thought it best to push on. I wonder if the Pole Party have experienced this. If so they could not travel as it would be in their face, where we have got it at our back. We have lost the outward bound track, so have decided to make a straight line to Mt. Darwin, which will be on Shackleton's course according to his and Wild's Diary.

[Each of the three parties which went forward up the Beardmore Glacier carried extracts from the above diaries. Wild was Shackleton's right-hand man in his Southern Journey in 1908.]

9 January 1912

Travelling is very difficult, bad light and still blizzing; it would have been impossible to keep in touch with the cairns in this weather. I am giving 12 miles tonight. The weather have moderated a bit and looks a bit more promising. Can see land at times.

10 January 1912

The light is still very bad, with a good deal of drift, but we must push on as we are a long way from our depot, but we hope to reach it before our provisions run out. I am keeping a good eye on them. Crean's eyes have got alright again now.

11 January 1912

Things are a bit better today. Could see the land alright and where to steer for. It is so nice to have something to look at, but I am thinking we shall all have our work cut out to reach the depot before our provisions run short. I am deducting a small portion of each meal so that we shall not have to go without altogether if we don't bring up at the proper time. Have done about 14 miles.

12 January 1912

The day has been full of adventure. At first we got into some very rough stuff, with plenty of crevasses. Had to get rid of the ski and put our thinking cap on, as we had not got under way long before we were at the top of some ice-fall; these probably are what Shackleton spoke of. We could see it meant a descent of 600/700 feet, or make a big circuit, which meant a lot of time and a big delay, and this we can't afford just now, so we decided on the descent into the valley. This proved a difficult task, as we had no crampons, having left them at Mt Darwin Depot; but we managed after a time by getting hold of the sledge each side and allowing her to run into a big lump of pressure which was we knew a risky thing to do. It took us up to lunch time to reach the valley, where we camped for lunch, where we all felt greatly relieved, having accomplished the thing safely, no damage to ourselves or the sledge, but we lost one of Crean's ski sticks. Some of the crevasses we crossed were 100 to 200 feet wide, but well bridged in the centre, but the edges were very dangerous indeed. This is where the snow and ice begin to roll down the glacier. After starting on our way again we found we had to climb the hill. Things don't look very nice ahead again tonight. We don't seem to be more than a day's run from the depot, but it will surprise me if we reach it by tomorrow night; if not we shall have to go on short rations, as our supply is nearly run out, and we have not lost any time, but we knew on starting we had to average 15½ miles per day to reach it in time.

13 January 1912

This has been a very bad day for us, what with ice-falls and crevasses. We feel all full up tonight. The strain is tremendous some days. We are camped, but not at the depot, but we hope to pick it up some time tomorrow. We shall be glad to get off the Summit, as the temperature is very low. We expected the party would have reached the Pole yesterday, providing they had anything of luck.

[Scott reached the Pole on January 17.]

14 January 1912

Sunday, we reached the Mt. Darwin Depot at 2 p.m. and camped for lunch. We had just enough now for our meal; this is cutting it a bit fine. We have now taken our 3½ days' allowance, which has got to take us another 57 miles to the Cloudmaker Depot. This we shall do if we all keep as fit as we seem just now. We left a note at the depot to inform the Captain of our safe arrival, wishing them the best of a journey home. We are quite cheerful here tonight, after having put things right at the depot, where we found the sugar exposed to the sun; it had commenced to melt, but we put everything alright before we left, and picked up our crampons and got away as soon as we could. We know there is not much time to spare. We are now beginning to descend rapidly. Tonight it is quite warm, and our tea and food is warmer. Things are going pretty favourable. We are looking forward to making good runs down the glacier. We have had some very heavy dragging lately [up] the sharp rises we found on the outward journey. After a sharp rise we found a long gradual run down, two and three miles in length. We noticed this on our outward journey and remarked on it, but coming back the long uphill drag we found out was pretty heavy work.

15 January 1912

Had a good run today but the ice was very rough and very much crevassed, but with crampons on we made splendid progress. We did not like to stop, but we thought it would not be advisable to overdo our strength as it is a long way to go yet.

16 January 1912

We made good headway again today, but tonight we camped in some very rough ice and pressure ridges. We are under the impression we are slightly out of our proper course, but Mr Evans thinks we can't be very far out either way, and Crean and I are of the same opinion according to the marks on the land. Anyhow we hope to get out of it in the morning and make the Cloudmaker Depot by night. We shall then feel safe, but the weather don't look over promising again tonight, I am thinking. So far we have not had to stop for weather. We have wondered if the Pole Party have been as lucky with the weather as we have. They ought by now to be homeward bound. We have more chance now of writing as the temperature is much better down here. Tonight we have been discussing how the dogs got home, and also the progress made by the Doctor's [Atkinson] Party. They ought to be nearing home. We have thought of the time it will take us to reach it at the rate we are getting along now

17 January 1912

We have today experienced what we none of us ever wants to be out lot again. I cannot describe the maze we got into and the hairbreadth escapes we have had to pass through today. This day we shall remember all our lives. The more we tried to get clear the worse the pressure got; at times it seemed almost impossible for us to get along, and when we had got over the places it was more than we could face to try and retreat; so we struggled on for hours to try and free ourselves, but everything seemed against us. I was leading with a long trace so that I could get across some of the ridges when we thought it possible to get the sledge over without being dashed down into the fathomless pits each side of us which were too numerous to think of. Often and often we saw openings where it was possible to drop the biggest ship afloat in and loose her. This is what we have travelled over all day. It has been a great strain on us all, and Mr Evans is rather down and thinks he has led us into such a hole, but as we have told him it is no fault of his, as it is impossible for anyone coming down the glacier to see what is ahead of them, so we must be thankful that we are so far safe. Tonight we seem to be in a better place. We have camped not being able to reach the depot, which we are certain is not far off. Don't want many days like this.

18 January 1912

We started off all in good spirits trusting we should be able to reach the depot all in good time, but we had not got far before we came into pressure far worse than we were in yesterday. My God! what a day this have been for us all. I cannot describe what we really have today come through, no one could believe that we came through with safety, if we had only had a camera we could have obtained some photographs that would have surprised anyone living. We travelled all day with very little food, as we are a day and a half overdue, but when we got clear, I can say 'clear' now because I am dotting down this at the depot where we have arrived. I had managed to keep behind just a small amount of biscuit and a drop of tea to liven us up to try and reach the depot, which we reached at 11 p.m. after one of the most trying days of my life. Shall have reason to never forget the 17 and 18 of January 1912. Tonight Mr Evans is complaining of his eyes, more trouble ahead!

19 January 1912

After putting the depot in order and rearranging things, we kicked off again for D. [Lower Glacier] Depot. Mr Evans's eyes were very bad on starting this morning, but we made a pretty good start. I picked some rock today which I intend to try and get back with, as it is the only chance we have had of getting any up to the present, and it seemed a funny thing: the rock I got some pieces of looked as if someone before me had been chipping some off. I wonder if it was the Doctor's party, but we could not see any trace of their sledge, but we could account for that, as it was all blue ice and not likely to leave any marks behind. After travelling for some distance we got on the same ridge as we ran along on the outward Journey and passed what we took to be the Doctor's Xmas Camp. We had not gone far past before we got into soft snow, so we decided to camp for lunch. Mr Evans's eyes being very bad indeed, we are travelling now on our own. I am leading and telling him the course I am steering, that is the different marks on the mountains, but we shall keep on this ridge for some distance yet. After lunch today we did not proceed far before we decided to camp, the surface being so bad and Mr Evans's eyes so bad, we thought it would do us all good to have a rest. Last night we left a note for Capt. Scott, but did not say much about our difficulties just above the Cloudmaker, as it would be better to tell him when we see him.

20 January 1912

We did not get away very smart today, but as we found the surface very soft, we decided to go on ski. Mr Evans is still suffering with his eyes and badly, after getting his ski on we tied him on to the trace so that he could help to drag a bit, when we were troubling about the ridges we came over on our outward Journey, but strange to say we never encountered any ridges at all and the surface, although very soft, was the best I have ever sledged over ever since I have been at it. We fancied on our left or to the west we saw what we took to be the ridges what we seem to have missed altogether, although Mr Evans have been blind and could not see anything at all we have made splendid progress and covered at least 20 miles, as near as we can guess. We passed today one of the Doctor's homeward bound camps, and kept on their track for some time, but finally lost it. We are camped tonight and we all feel confident we shall, if the weather remains good, reach the depot tomorrow night.

21 January 1912

Sunday: We started off as usual, again on ski, the weather again being favourable. Mr Evans's eyes is still bad, but improving. It will be a good job when they are better. I picked up our outward bound course soon after we started this morning and asked Mr Evans if I should try and keep it, as it will save him the trouble of directing me, and another thing we came out without going through any crevasses and I have noticed a good many crevasses today what seems to be very dangerous ones, and on two occasions where our sledges [on the outward journey] had gone over, two of the crevasses had fallen through. We accomplished the journey from the Cloudmaker to this depot in three days. We all feel quite proud of our performance. Mr Evans is a lot better tonight and old Tom is giving us a song while he is covering up the tent with snow. We have rearranged the depot and left our usual note for Capt. Scott, wishing them a speedy return. Tomorrow we hope to see and reach the Barrier, and be clear of the Beardmore for ever. We none of us minds the struggle we have been through to attain the amount of success so far reached. It is all for the good of science, as Crean says. We reached the depot at 6.45 p.m.

22 January 1912

We made a good start this morning and Mr Evans's eyes is got pretty well alright again, so things looks a bit brighter. After starting we soon got round the corner from the Granite Pillars to between the mainland and Mt. Hope, on rising up on the slope between the mountain and the mainland, as soon as we sighted the Barrier, Crean let go one huge yell enough to frighten the ponies out of their graves of snow, and no more Beardmore for me after this. When we began to descend on to the Barrier it only required one of us to drag the sledge down to within a mile of the pony and sledge depot, after exchanging our sledge as arranged, picking up a small amount of pony meat, and fitted up bamboo for mast so that we shall be able to fix up a sail when favourable, we proceeded on our way to cross the Barrier. We have now 360 miles to travel geographically to get to Hut Point. Mr Evans complained to me while outside the tent that he had a stiffness at the back of his legs behind the knees. I asked him what he thought it was, and he said could not account for it, so if he don't soon get rid of it I am to have a look and see if anything is the matter with him, as I know from what I have seen and been told before the symptoms of scurvy is pains and swelling behind the knee round the ankle and loosening of the teeth, ulcerated gums. Tonight I watched to see his gums, and I am convinced he is on the point of something anyhow, and this I have spoken to Crean about, but he don't seem to realize it. But I have asked him to wait developments for a time. It seems we are in for more trouble now, but let's hope for the best.

23 January 1912

We got away pretty well and did a good journey, having covered about 14 miles over a fairly good surface. We have passed the Blizzard Camp and glad of it too, again today we saw in several places where the bridges on the crevasses had fallen through. A good job they none of them fell through when we were going over them as the width would have taken all through with them, and in every case where they had fallen through was where we had gone over, as the mark of the sledge was very distinct in each case. Mr Evans seems better today.

24 January 1912

Did a good run today over a good surface. The weather have been very warm, not much to write tonight as everything is going well.

25 January 1912

Started off in very thick weather, the temperature is very high and the snow is wet and clogging all day on our ski, which made dragging heavy, and towards evening it got worse. After lunch we got a good breeze for an hour, when it changed to a blizzard and almost rained. We saw the depot ahead sometimes, so we tried to reach it as we thought we might be in for another few days like we had near the land on our outward journey. Anyhow we reached it after a tremendous struggle owing to the wet and bad light. I took off my ski and carried them on my shoulder to finish up the last half a mile. The blizzard died down after we had camped and turned in for the night. Looked at the thermometer which showed 34.

26 January 1912

This have been a most wonderful day for surface. This morning when we started the thermometer stood at 34, much too high for sledging. We were on ski or we might have been on stilts for the amount of snow clogging on our ski, don't know how we should have got on without our ski, as the snow was so very soft we sank right in when we tried to go on foot, but we were fortunate to get the wind behind us and able to make use of the sail. We made a very good day of it, did 13 miles: 8 of this after lunch. I did not feel well outside the tent this morning. I came over quite giddy and faint, but it passed off quickly and have felt no more of it all day.

27 January 1912

We had a good run today with the sail up. It only required one of us to keep it straight, no need whatever to pull, but it was very hot, anyone could take off all their clothes and march. It is really too hot for this part of the world, but I daresay we shall soon get it a bit colder. Did 14½ miles, it is nice to be able to see the tracks and cairns of our outward journey. We feel satisfied when we have done a good day and in good time. Mr Evans is now suffering from looseness of the bowels. Crean had a touch of it a few days ago, but he is quite alright again.

28 January 1912

Today it have been a very heavy drag. The snow is still very soft and the sun very hot, it fairly scorches anyone's face. We are almost black now and our hair is long and getting white through being exposed to the light, it gets bleached. I am glad to say it is cooler tonight, generally. We got over 12½ miles again today. Mr Evans is still very loose in his bowels. This, of course, hinders us, as we have had to stop several times. Only another few more Sundays and we hope to be safely housed at Hut Point, or Cape Evans. We have now been out 97 days.

29 January 1912

Another good day was helped by the sail all day. One man could again manage for about two hours. The weather is still very warm, plus 20 again. Did 16½ miles, only 14 to the next depot. Mr Evans is still suffering from the same complaint: have come to the conclusion to stop his pemmican, as I feel that it have got something to do with him being out of sorts.

Anyhow we are going to try it. Gave him a little brandy and he is taking some chalk and opium pills to try and stop it. His legs are getting worse and we are quite certain he is suffering from scurvy, at least he is turning black and blue and several other colours as well.

30 January 1912

Very bad light but fair wind, picked up the depot this evening. Did the 14 miles quite in good time, after taking our food we found a shortage of oil and have taken what we think will take us to the next depot. There seems to have been some leakage in the one can, but how we could not account for that we have left a note telling Capt. Scott how we found it, but they will have sufficient to carry them on to the next depot, but we all know the amount of oil allowed on the Journey is enough, but if any waste takes place it means extra precautions in the handling of it. Mr Evans is still without pemmican and seems to have somewhat recovered from the looseness, but things are not by a long way with him as they should be. Only two more depots now to pick up.

31 January 1912

Another very good run today but the light being very bad we had to continually stop and steer by compass. This a difficult task, especially as there was no wind to help keep on the course, but it have cleared again tonight, the temperature is plus 20 in the day and 10 at night just now. Did 13 miles. Mr Evans is allowed a little pemmican as the work is hard and it wants a little warm food to put life into anyone in this part of the world.

1 February 1912

We had a very fine day but a very heavy pull, but we did 13 miles. Mr Evans and myself have been out 100 days today. I have had to change my shirt again. This is the last clean side I have got. I have been wearing two shirts and each side will now have done duty next the skin, as I have changed round each month, and I have certainly found the benefit of it, and on the point we all three agree. Mr Evans is still gradually worse: it is no good closing our eyes to the fact. We must push on as we have a long way to go yet.

2 February 1912

A very bad light again today: could not make much progress, only did 11 miles, but we must think ourselves lucky we have not had to lay up and get delayed, but we have had the wind and more behind us, otherwise we should have had to stop. Mr Evans is no better but seems to be in great pain, but he keeps quite cheerful we are pleased to say.

3 February 1912

This morning we were forced to put Mr Evans on his ski and strap him on, as he could not lift his legs. I looked at them again and found they are rapidly getting worse, things are looking serious on his part, but we have been trying to pump him up he will get through alright, but he begins to think different himself, but if we get to One Ton and can get a change of food it may relieve him. He is a brick, there is plenty of pluck: one cannot but admire such pluck. The light have been dreadful all day and I seemed to have got a bit depressed at times, not being able to see anything to know where I was on the course or not and not getting a word from Mr Evans. I deliberately went off the course to see if anyone was taking notice but to my surprise I was quickly told I was off the course. This I thought, but wanted to know if he was looking out, which he was. It came on to bliz after we camped, we ought to reach Mt. Hooper tomorrow night.

4 February 1912

Started in splendid weather, but the surface was bad and dragging was very heavy, but it improved as the day went on, and we arrived at the depot at 7.40 p.m. We are now 180 miles from Hut Point, and this Sunday night we hope to be only two more Sundays on the Barrier. No improvement in Mr Evans, much worse. We have taken out our food and left nearly all the pemmican as we don't require it on account of none of us caring for it, therefore we are leaving it behind for the others. They may require it. We have left our note and wished them every success on their way, but we have decided it is best not to say anything about Mr Evans being ill or suffering from scurvy. This old cairn have stood the weather and is still a huge thing.

5 February 1912

Had a very fine day and a good light all day, which makes things much more cheerful. Did not get away before 9 o'clock but we did 11½ miles, it is gradually getting colder. Mr Evans is still getting worse, today he is suffering from looseness in the bowels: shall have to stop his pemmican.

6 February 1912

Another fine day but sun was very hot and caused us to sweat a good deal, but we don't mind as we are pretty used to such changes. We shall soon be looking for land ahead, which will be Mt. Discovery or Mt. Erebus, we have 155 miles to go to Hut Point: done alright again 13½ miles, we do wonderfully well especially as Mr Evans have got to go very slowly first off after stopping until he gets the stiffness out of his legs, but he is suffering a good deal and in silence, he never complains, but he don't get much sleep. We shall all be glad when we arrive at One Ton, where there is a change of food for us all. The pemmican is too much, especially when the weather is warm.

7 February 1912

A very fine day but heavy going. We are bringing the land in sight. The day have been simply lovely, did 12 miles. No better luck with our patient, he gets along without a murmur. We have got to help him in and out of the tent, but we have consulted on the matter and he is determined to go to the last, which we know is not far off, as it is difficult for him to stand, but he is the essence of a brick to keep it up, but we shall have to drag him on the sledge when he can't go any further.

8 February 1912

Today have been very favourable and fine, we had a good breeze and set sail after lunch. If we get a good day tomorrow we hope to reach One Ton. Mr Evans have passed a good deal of blood today, which makes things look a lot worse. I have to do nearly everything for him now.

9 February 1912

A very fine day and quite warm. Reached the depot at 5.5 p.m. and we all had a good feed of oatmeal. Oh, what a God-send to get a change of food! We have taken enough food for 9 days, which if we still keep up our present rate of progress it ought to take us in to Hut Point. We cannot take too heavy a load, as there is only the two of us pulling now, and this our last port of call before we reach Hut Point, but things are not looking any too favourable for us, as our leader is gradually getting lower every day. It is almost impossible for him to get along, and we are still 120 miles from Hut Point.

10 February 1912

We did a good march, in very thick weather. Tonight we are camped and I am sorry to say Mr Evans is in a very bad state. If this is scurvy I am sorry for anyone it attacks. We shall do our utmost to get him back alive, although he is so ill, he is very cheerful, which is very good and tries to do anything to help us along. We are thinking the food, now we have got a change, may improve things. I am very pleased to say Crean and myself are in the best of health, which we are thankful for.

11 February 1912

Today we built a cairn and left all our gear we could do without, as it is impossible for us to drag the load now, and Mr Evans we think is doing well as long as he can keep on his legs. We have had a very bad light all day, and tonight we have a bliz on us, so we had to camp early. Our day's run has been 11 miles. We are now about 99 miles from our base.

12 February 1912

We did not get away until 10 o'clock on account of bad weather, but after we put Mr Evans on his ski he went on slowly. It is against our wish to have to send him on a little in advance, but it is best as we shall have to drag him out of this we are certain. He has fainted on two or three occasions, but after a drop of brandy he has been able to proceed, but it is very awkward, especially as the temperature is so low. We are afraid of his getting frost-bitten. Our progress is very slow, the light is very bad, and it is seldom we see the land.

13 February 1912

We got away in good time, but progress was slow, and Mr Evans could not go, and we consulted awhile and came to the conclusion it would be best to put him on the sledge, otherwise he may not pull through, so we stopped and camped, and decided to drop everything we can possibly do without, so we have only got our sleeping bags, cooker, and what little food and oil we have left. Our load is not much, but Mr Evans on the sledge makes it pretty heavy work for us both, but he says he is comfortable now. This morning he wished us to leave him, but this we could not think of. We shall stand by him to the end one way or other, so we are the masters today. He has got to do as we wish and we hope to pull him through. This morning when we depoted all our gear I changed my socks and got my foot badly frostbitten, and the only way was to fetch it round. So although Mr Evans was so bad he proposed to stuff it on his stomach to try and get it right again. I did not like to risk such a thing as he is certainly very weak, but we tried it, and it succeeded in bringing it round, thanks to his thoughtfulness, and I shall never forget the kindness bestowed on me at a critical time in our travels, but I think we could go to any length of trouble to assist one another; in such time and such a place we must trust in a higher power to pull us through. When we pack up now and have to move off we have to get everything ready before we attempt to move the tent, as it is impossible for our leader now to stand, therefore it is necessary to get him ready before we start. We then pull the sledge alongside his bag and lift him on to it and strap him on. It is a painful piece of work and he takes it pretty well, but we can't help hurting him, as it is very awkward to lift him, the snow being soft and the light so bad, but he don't complain. The only thing we hear him grind his teeth.

14 February 1912

Another good start after the usual preparation, we have not got much to pack, but it takes us some time to get our invalid ready, the surface is very bad and our progress is very slow, but we have proposed to go longer hours and try to cover the distance, that is if we can stick it ourselves.

15 February 1912

We started in fine weather this morning, but it soon came over thick and progress became slow. We had to continually consult the compass, as we have had no wind to assist us, but after awhile the sun peeped out and the wind sprang up and we were able to set sail, which helped us put in a good march.

16 February 1912

Today it have been a very heavy drag all day, and the light is very bad, but we had the pleasure of seeing Castle Rock and Observation Hill. We uncovered Mr Evans to let him have a look and we have reduced our ration now to one half as it is impossible for us to reach Hut Point under four days, that is if everything goes favourable with us.

17 February 1912

Today it has been thick, this morning soon after we started we saw what we thought was the dog tent [the two dog-teams going out to meet the Polar Party], a thing we had been looking for to try and get relief, but when we came up to it we found it was only a piece of biscuit box stuck on an old camp for a guide. It shows how deceiving the things here are. I can tell you our hopes were raised, but on reaching it they dropped again considerably. We were able to-see the land occasionally, and during one of the breaks this afternoon we spotted the motor. Oh, what joy! We again uncovered Mr Evans to let him have a look and after trudging for another three hours we brought up alongside it and camped for the night. We are now only a little over 30 miles from Hut Point: if we could only see the dogs approaching us, but they, we think, may have passed us while the weather have been thick. Mr Evans is getting worse every day, we are almost afraid to sleep at night as he seems very weak. If the temperature goes much lower it will be a job to keep him warm. We have found some biscuits here at the motor but nothing else, but that will assist greatly on our way. The slogging have been heavy all day. We are pretty tired tonight. I don't think we have got the go in us we had, but we must try and push on.

18 February 1912

I started to move Mr Evans this morning, but he completely collapsed and fainted away. Crean was very upset and almost cried, but I told him it was no good to create a scene but put up a bold front and try to assist. I really think he thought Mr Evans had gone, but we managed to pull him through. We used the last drop of brandy. After awhile we got him on the sledge and proceeded as usual, but finding the surface very bad and we are unable to make less than a mile an hour, we stopped and decided to camp. We told Mr Evans of our plans, which were: Crean should proceed, it being a splendid day, on foot to Hut Point to obtain relief if possible. This we had agreed to between ourselves. I offered to do the Journey and Crean remain behind, but Tom said he would much rather I stayed with the invalid and look after him, so I thought it best I should remain, and these plans were agreed to by all of us, so after we camped the next thing was the food problem. We had about a day's provisions with extra biscuit taken from the motor, and a little extra oil taken from the same place, so we gave Crean what he thought he could manage to accomplish the Journey of 30 miles geographical on, which was a little chocolate and biscuits. We put him up a little drink, but he would not carry it. What a pity we did not have some ski, but we dumped them to save weight. So Crean sailed away in splendid weather for a try to bring relief. I was in a bit of a sweat all day and remained up to watch the weather till long after midnight. I was afraid of the weather, but it kept clear and I thought he might have reached or got within easy distance of Hut Point; but there was the possibility of his dropping down a crevasse, but that we had to leave to chance, but none the more it was anxious moments as if it comes on to drift the weather is very treacherous in these parts. After Crean left I left Mr Evans and proceeded to Corner Camp which was about a mile away, to see if there was any provisions left there that would be of use to us. I found a little butter, a little cheese, and a little treacle that had been brought there for the ponies. I also went back to the motor and got a little more oil while the weather was fine. I also got a large piece of burbery and tied on a long bamboo and stuck up a big flag on our sledge so that anyone could not pass our way without seeing us or our flag. I found a note left at Corner Camp by Mr Day saying there was a lot of very bad crevasses between there and the sea ice, especially off White Island. This put me in a bit of a fix, as I, of course, at once thought of Crean. He being on foot was more likely to go down than he would had he been on ski. I did not tell Mr Evans anything about the crevasses, as I certainly thought it would be best kept from him I just told him the note was there and all was well.

19 February 1912

Today Mr Evans seems a bit better and more cheerful, the rest will do him good and assist in getting a little strength. We have been wondering when relief will reach us, but we cannot expect it for at least a day or two yet at the earliest. It was very thick this morning and also very cold. The temperature is dropping rapidly. Our tent was all covered in frost rime today, a sure sign of colder weather. It was very thick this morning but cleared as the day advanced, but we could not see Hut Point. I wonder if poor old Tom reached alright. We have very little food now except biscuit, but oil is better.

We have ½ gallon and if relief don't come for some time we shall be able to have hot water when all other things are gone. I have thought out a plan for the future, in case of no relief coming, but of course we took all things into consideration in case of failure, but we must hope for the best. Of course I know it is no use thinking of Mr Evans being able to move any further as he can't stand at all, the only thing is, we may have missed the dogs, if so there is still a chance of some one being at Hut Point. I am cold now and cannot write more tonight. We lose the sun at midnight now. If all had went well we should have been home by now.

20 February 1912

Tuesday not a nice day. A low drift all the morning and increased to a blizzard at times. Have had to remain in the tent all day to try and keep warm. Have not got much food except biscuits. Mr Evans is about the same but quite cheerful. We have had whole journey over and over: it have passed these three days away. We have wondered how they are getting on behind us; we have worked it out and they ought to be on the Barrier now, with anything of luck. We have been gambling on the condition of the ice and the possibility of the open water at Hut Point at any time now, and also about what news of home, although home is one of the foremost thoughts we hardly ever mention it, only what we are going to have to eat when we do arrive there. I think we have got everything that is good down on our list. Of course New Zealand have got to be answerable for a good deal: plenty of apples we are going to have and some nice home-made cake, not too rich, as we think we can eat more. I wonder if the mules will have arrived, as I am to look after them till Capt. Oates returns, as Anton will be gone home, or at least going soon. We shall have to hurry up as the ship is to leave again on the 2nd of March, as it is not safe to remain longer in these regions. I am now too cold to write, and I don't seem settled at all and the weather is still pretty bad outside, so we are not going to look for anything to come along tonight. 'Hark!' from us both. 'Yes, it is the dogs near.

Relief at last. Who is there?' I did not stay to think more before I was outside the tent. 'Yes, sir, it is alright.' The Doctor and Dimitri. 'How did you see us?' 'The flag Lash,' says Dimitri. The Doctor, 'How is Mr Evans?' 'Alright, but low.' But this had a good effect on him. After the first few minutes we got their tent pitched and the food they brought us I was soon on the way preparing a meal for us all, but Mr Evans cannot have pemmican, but the Doctor have brought everything that will do him good, some onions to boil and several other things. Dimitri brought along a good lump of cake: we are in clover. Tonight after the Doctor had examined my patient and we got through a good deal of talk about everything we could think of, especially home news and the return parties and the ship and those in her. We were sorry to hear she had not been able to get very near, and that the mules had arrived, and I don't know what, we now settled down for a good night. It seems to me we are in a new world, a weight is off my mind and I can once more see a bright spot in the sky for us all, the gloom is now removed. The bliz is bad outside, and Doctor and Dimitri is gone and turned in, so will [I] once more, but sleep is out of the question.

21 February 1912

The day have been very bad and we are obliged to remain until it clears. We are going to move off as soon as it clears, the day have been very cold, so we have had to remain in our bags, but things are alright and we have got plenty to eat now. We have all retired for the night as the bliz is still raging outside.

22 February 1912

The wind went down about 9 p.m., so we began to move and were ready to kick off at 10, and proposed to do the journey in two stages. It was fearfully heavy going for the poor dogs, we arranged so that Mr Evans was on Dimitri's sledge and Doctor and myself was on the other. We have done about half the journey and are now camped for a rest for the dogs and ourselves. We had a stiff 16 miles: the Doctor and myself, we took turns in riding on the sledge and walking and running to keep up to the dogs. Sometimes we sank in up to the knees, but we struggled through it. My legs is the most powerful part of me now, but I am tired and shall be glad when it is over. I must lie down now, as we are starting again soon for Hut Point, but the surface is getting better as we have passed White Island and can see so plainly the land. Castle Rock and good old Erebus look so stately with the smoke rolling out. It is so clear and calm and peaceful. What a change in our surroundings of a few days ago and also our prospects. Doctor and Dimitri have done everything they could for us.

22 February 1912

We started off after a rest for the dogs and reached here at Hut Point at 1 p.m. where we can rest in peace for a time. Dimitri and Crean are going to Cape Evans: the ship is nowhere in sight. Have had to get some seal meat and ice and prepare a meal. Mr Evans is alright and asleep. We are looking for a mail now. How funny we should always be looking for something else, now we are safe.

[End of Lashly's Diary]

Crean has told me the story of his walk as follows:

He started at 10 on Sunday morning and 'the surface was good, very good surface indeed', and he went about sixteen miles before he stopped. Good clear weather. He had three biscuits and two sticks of chocolate. He stopped about five minutes, sitting on the snow, and ate two biscuits and the chocolate, and put one biscuit back in his pocket. He was quite warm and not sleepy.

He carried on just the same and passed Safety Camp on his right some five hours later, and thinks it was about twelve-thirty on Monday morning that he reached the edge of the Barrier, tired, getting cold in the back and the weather coming on thick. It was bright behind him but it was coming over the Bluff, and White Island was obscured though he

could still see Cape Armitage and Castle Rock. He slipped a
lot on the sea-ice, having several falls on to his back and it
was getting thicker all the time. At the Barrier edge there
was a light wind, now it was blowing a strong wind, drifting
and snowing. He made for the Gap and could not get up at
first. To avoid taking a lot out of himself he started to go
round Cape Armitage; but soon felt slush coming through
his finnesko (he had no crampons) and made back for the
Gap. He climbed up to the left of the Gap and climbed along
the side of Observation Hill to avoid the slippery ice. When
he got to the top it was still clear enough to see vaguely the
outline of Hut Point, but he could see no sledges nor dogs.
He sat down under the lee of Observation Hill, and finished
his biscuit with a bit of ice: 'I was very dry,' – slid down the
side of Observation Hill and thought at this time there was
open water below, for he had no goggles on the march and
his eyes were strained. But on getting near the ice-foot he
found it was polished sea-ice and made his way round to the
hut under the ice-foot. When he got close he saw the dogs
and sledges on the sea-ice, and it was now blowing very hard
with drift. He walked in and found the Doctor and Dimitri
inside. 'He gave me a tot first, and then a feed of porridge –
but I couldn't keep it down: that's the first time in my life
that ever it happened, and it was the brandy that did it.'

Chapter Thirteen
SUSPENSE

All the past we leave behind;
We debouch upon a newer, mightier world, varied world;
Fresh and strong the world we seize, world of labour and the
    march,
Pioneers! O pioneers!

We detachments steady throwing,
Down the edges, through the passes, up the mountains steep,
Conquering, holding, daring, venturing, as we go, the
    unknown ways,
Pioneers! O pioneers!

WALT WHITMAN

Let us come back to Cape Evans after the return of the
First Supporting Party.

Hitherto our ways had always been happy: for the most
part they had been pleasant. Scott was going to reach the
Pole, probably without great difficulty, for when we left him
on the edge of the plateau he had only to average seven miles
a day to go there on full rations. We ourselves had averaged
14.2 geographical miles a day on our way home to One Ton
Depot, and there seemed no reason to suppose that the other
two parties would not do likewise, and the food was not
only sufficient but abundant if such marches were made.
Thus we were content as we wandered over the cape, or sat
upon some rock warmed by the sun and watched the
penguins bathing in the lake which had formed in the sea-ice
between us and Inaccessible Island. All round us were the
cries of the skua gulls as they squabbled among themselves,
and we heard the swish of their wings as they swooped down
upon a man who wandered too near their nests. Out upon
the sea-ice, which was soggy and dangerous, lay several seal,
and the bubblings and whistlings and gurglings which came

from their throats chimed musically in contrast to the hoarse aak, aak, of the Adélie penguins: the tide crack was sighing and groaning all the time: it was very restful after the Barrier silence.

Meanwhile the *Terra Nova* had been seen in the distance, but the state of the sea-ice prevented her approach. It was not until 4 February that communication was opened with her and we got our welcome mails and news of the world during the last year. We heard that Campbell's party had been picked up at Cape Adare and landed at Evans Coves. We started unloading on 9 February, and this work was continued until 14 February: there was about three miles of ice between the ship and the shore and we were doing more than twenty miles a day. In the case of men who had been sledging much, and who might be wanted to sledge again, this was a mistake. Latterly the ice began to break up, and the ship left on the 15th to pick up the Geological Party on the western side of McMurdo Sound. But she met great obstacles, and her record near the coasts this year is one of continual fights against pack-ice, while the winds experienced as the season advanced were very strong. On 13 January the fast ice at the mouth of McMurdo Sound extended as far as the southern end of the Bird Peninsula: ten days later they found fast ice extending for thirty miles from the head of Granite Harbour. Later in the season the most determined efforts were made again and again to penetrate into Evans Coves in order to pick up Campbell and his men, until the ice was freezing all round them, and many times the propeller was brought up dead against blocks of ice.

The expedition was originally formed for two years from the date of leaving England. But before the ship left after landing us at Cape Evans in January 1911 the possibility of a third year was considered, and certain requests for additional transport and orders for stores were sent home. Thus it came about that the ship now landed not only new sledges and sledging stores but also fourteen dogs from Kamchatka and seven mules, with their food and equipment. The dogs were big and fat, but the only ones which proved of much service for sledging were Snowy, a nice white dog, and Bullett. It was Oates's idea that mules might prove a better form of transport on the Barrier than ponies. Scott therefore wrote to Sir Douglas Haig, then C.-in-C. in India, that if he failed to reach the Pole in the summer of 1911-12,

it is my intention to make a second attempt in the following season provided fresh transport can be brought down: the circumstances making it necessary to plan to sacrifice the transport animals used in any attempt.

Before directing more ponies to be sent down I have thoroughly discussed the situation with Captain Oates, and he has suggested that mules would be better than ponies for our work and that trained Indian Transport Mules would be ideal. It is evident already that our ponies have not a uniform walking pace and that in other small ways they will be troublesome to us although they are handy little beasts.

The Indian Government not only sent seven mules but when they arrived we found that they had been most carefully trained and equipped. In India they were in the charge of Lieutenant George Pulleyn, and the care and thought which had been spent upon them could not have been exceeded: the equipment was also extremely good and well adapted to the conditions, while most of the improvements made by us as a result of a year's experience were already foreseen and provided. The mules themselves, by name Lal Khan, Gulab, Begum, Ranee, Abdullah, Pyaree and Khan Sahib, were beautiful animals.

Atkinson would soon have to start on his travels again. Before we left Scott at the top of the Beardmore he gave him orders to take the two dog-teams South in the event of Meares having to return home, as seemed likely. This was not meant in any way to be a relief journey. Scott said that he was not relying upon the dogs; and that in view of the sledging in the following year, the dogs were not to be risked. Although it was settled that some members of the expedition would stay, while others returned to New Zealand, Scott and several of his companions had left undecided until the last moment the question of whether they would themselves remain in the South for another year. In the event of Scott deciding to return home the dog-teams might make the difference between catching or missing the ship. I had discussed this question with Wilson more than once, and he was of the opinion that the business affairs of the expedition demanded Scott's return if possible: Wilson himself inclined to the view that he himself would stay if Scott stayed, and return if Scott returned. I think that Oates meant to return, and am sure that Bowers meant to stay: indeed he welcomed the idea of one more year in a way which I do not think was equalled by any other member of the expedition. For the most part we felt that we had joined up for two years, but that if there was to be a third year we would rather see the thing through than return home.

I hope I have made it clear that the primary object of this journey with the dog-team was to hurry Scott and his companions home so that they might be in time to catch the ship if possible, before she was compelled by the close of the season to leave McMurdo Sound. Another thing which made Scott anxious to communicate with the ship if possible before the season forced her to leave the Sound was his desire to send back news. From many remarks which he made, and also from the discussions in the hut during the winter, it was obvious that he considered it was of the first importance that the news of reaching the Pole, if it should be reached, be communicated to the world without the delay of another year. Of course he would also wish to send news of the safe return of his party to wives and relations as soon as possible. It is necessary to emphasize the fact that the dog-teams were intended to hasten the return of the Polar Party, but that they were never meant to form a relief journey.

But now Atkinson was left in a rather difficult position. I note in my diary, after we had reached the hut, that 'Scott was to have sent back instructions for the dog party with us, but these have, it would seem, been forgotten'; but it may be that Scott considered that he had given these instructions in a conversation he had with Atkinson at the top of the Beardmore Glacier, when Scott said, 'with the depot [of dog-food] which has been laid come as far as you can.'

According to the plans for the Polar Journey the food necessary to bring the three advance parties of man-haulers back from One Ton Depot to Hut Point was to be taken out to One Ton during the absence of these parties. This food consisted of five weekly units of what were known as XS rations. It was also arranged that if possible a depot of dog-biscuits should be taken out at the same time: this was the depot referred to above by Scott. In the event of the return of the dog-teams in the first half of December, which was the original plan, the five units of food and the dog-biscuit would have been run out by them to One Ton. If the dog-teams did not return in time to do this a man-hauling party from Cape Evans was to take out three of the five units of food.

It has been shown that the dog-teams were taken farther on the Polar Journey than was originally intended,[1] indeed they were taken from 81° 15', where they were to have turned back, as far as 83° 35'. Nor were they able to make the return journey in the fast time which had been expected of them, and the dog-drivers were running very short of food and were compelled to encroach to some extent upon the supplies left to provide for the wants of those who were following in their tracks.[2] The dog-teams did not arrive back at Cape Evans until 4 January.[3]

Meanwhile a man-hauling party from Cape Evans, consisting of Day, Nelson, Clissold and Hooper, had already, according to plan, taken out three of the five XS rations for the returning parties. The weights of the man-hauling party did not allow for the transport of the remaining two XS

---

1. See pp. 366, 397.   2. See pp. 396–7.
3. The dog-teams arrived at *Hut Point* on 4 January, and at *Cape Evans* on 5 January. The dog-teams arrived approximately 3 weeks later than originally intended by Scott, and 17 days later than Scott's latest date, which was 19 December.

rations, nor for any of the dog-food. Thus it was that when Atkinson came to make his plans to go South with the dogs he found that there was no dog-food south of Corner Camp, and that the rations for the return of the Polar Party from One Ton Depot had still to be taken out. That is to say, the depot of dog-food spoken of by Scott did not exist. There was, however, enough food already at One Ton to allow the Polar Party to come in on reduced rations. This meant that what the dog-teams could do was limited, and was much less than it might have been had it been possible to take out the depot of dog-food to One Ton. Also the man-food for the Polar Party had to be added to the weights taken by the dogs.

To estimate even approximately at what date a party will reach a given point after a journey of this length when the weather conditions are always uncertain and the number of travelling days unknown, was a most difficult task. The only guide was the average marches per diem made by our own return party, and the average of the second return party if it should return before the dog party set out. A week one way or the other was certainly not a large margin. A couple of blizzards might make this much difference.

In the plan of the Southern Journey Scott, working on Shackleton's averages, mentions 27 March as a possible date of return to Hut Point, allowing seven days in from One Ton. Whilst on the outward journey I heard Scott discuss the possibility of returning in April; and the Polar Party had enough food to allow them to do this on full rations.

Atkinson and Dimitri with the two dog-teams left Cape Evans for Hut Point on 13 February because the sea-ice, which was our only means of communication between these places, and so to the Barrier, was beginning to break up. Atkinson intended to leave Hut Point for the Barrier in about a week's time. At 3.30 a.m. on 19 February Crean arrived with the astounding news that Lieutenant Evans, still alive but at his last gasp, was lying out near Corner Camp, and that Lashly was nursing him; that the Last Supporting Party had consisted of three men only, a possibility which had never been considered; and that they had left Scott, travelling rapidly and making good averages, only 148 geographical miles from the Pole. Scott was so well advanced that it seemed that he would be home much earlier than had been anticipated.

A blizzard which had been threatening on the Barrier, and actually blowing at Hut Point, during Crean's solitary journey, but which had lulled as he arrived, now broke with full force, and nothing could be done for Evans until it took off sufficiently for the dog-teams to travel. But in the meantime Crean urgently wanted food and rest and warmth. As these were supplied to him Atkinson learned bit by bit the story of the saving of Evans's life, told so graphically in Lashly's diary which is given in the preceeding chapter, and pieced together the details of Crean's solitary walk of thirty-five statute miles. This effort was made, it should be remembered, at the end of a journey of three and a half months, and over ground rendered especially perilous by crevasses, from which a man travelling alone had no chance of rescue in case of accident. Crean was walking for eighteen hours, and it was lucky for him, as also for his companions, that the blizzard which broke half an hour after his arrival did not come a little sooner, for no power on earth could have saved him then, and the news of Evans's plight would not have been brought.

The blizzard raged all that day, and the next night and morning, and nothing could be done. But during the afternoon of the 20th the conditions improved, and at 4.30 p.m. Atkinson and Dimitri started with the two dog-teams, though it was still blowing hard and very thick. They travelled, with one rest for the dogs, until 4.30 p.m. the next day, but had a very hazy idea where they were most of the time, owing to the vile weather: once at any rate they seem to have got right in under White Island. When they camped the second time they thought they were in the neighbourhood of Lashly's tent, and in a temporary clearance they saw the flag which Lashly had put up on the sledge. Evans was still alive, and Atkinson was able to give him immediately the fresh vegetables, fruit, and seal meat which his body wanted.

Atkinson has never been able to express adequately the admiration he feels for Lashly's care and nursing.

All that night and the next day the blizzard continued and made a start impossible, and it was not until 3 a.m. on the morning of the 22nd that they could start for Hut Point, Evans being carried in his sleeping-bag on the sledge. Lashly has told how they got home.

At Cape Evans we knew nothing of these events, which had made reorganization inevitable. It was clear that Atkinson, being the only doctor available, would have to stay with Evans, who was very seriously ill: indeed Atkinson told me that another day, or at the most two, would have finished him. In fact he says that when he first saw him he thought he must die. It was a considerable surprise then when Dimitri with Crean and one dog-team reached Cape Evans about midday on 23 February with a note from Atkinson, who said that he thought he had better stay with Lieutenant Evans and that someone else should take out the dogs. He suggested that Wright or myself should take them. This was our first intimation that the dogs had not already gone South.

Wright and I started for Hut Point by 2 p.m. the same day and on our arrival it was decided by Atkinson that I was to take out the dogs. Owing to the early departure of our meteorologist, Simpson, Wright, who had special qualifications for this important work, was to remain at Cape Evans. Dimitri having rested his dog-team overnight at Cape Evans arrived at Hut Point on the morning of the 24th.

Now the daily distance which every 4-man party had to average from Hut Point to its turning-point and back to Hut Point, so as to be on full rations all the way, was only 8.4 geographical miles. From Hut Point to the latitude in which he was last seen, 87° 32' S., Scott had averaged more than ten geographical miles a day.

Taking into consideration the advanced latitude, 87° 32' S., at which the Second Return Party had left Scott, and the extremely good daily averages these two parties had marched on the plateau up to this point, namely 12.3 geographical miles a day; seeing also that the First Return Party had averaged 14.2 geographical miles on their return from 85° 3′ S. to One Ton Depot; and the Second Return Party had averaged 11.2 geographical miles on their return from 87° 32′ S. to the same place, although one of the three men was seriously ill; it was supposed that all the previous estimates made for the return of the Polar Party were too late, and that the opportunity to reach One Ton Camp before them had been lost. Meanwhile the full rations for their return over the 140 miles (statute) from One Ton to Hut Point were still at Hut Point.

My orders were given me by Atkinson, and were verbal, as follows.

1. To take 24 days' food for the two men, and 21 days' food for the two dog-teams, together with the food for the Polar Party.

2. To travel to One Ton Depot as fast as possible and leave the food there.

3. If Scott had not arrived at One Ton Depot before me I was to judge what to do.

4. That Scott was not in any way dependent on the dogs for his return.

5. That Scott had given particular instructions that the dogs were not to be risked in view of the sledging plans for next season.

Since it had proved impossible to take the depot of dog-food, together with the full Polar Party rations, to One Ton before this; considering the unforeseen circumstances which had arisen; and seeing that this journey of the dog-teams was not indispensable, being simply meant to bring the last party home more speedily, I do not believe that better instructions could have been given than these of Atkinson.

I was eager to start as soon as the team which had come back from Cape Evans was rested, but a blizzard prevented this. On the morning of the 25th it was thick as a hedge, but it cleared enough to pack sledges in the afternoon, and when we turned into our bags we could see Observation Hill. We started at 2 a.m. that night.

I confess I had my misgivings. I had never driven one dog, let alone a team of them; I knew nothing of navigation; and One Ton was a hundred and thirty miles away, out in the middle of the Barrier and away from landmarks. And so as we pushed our way out through the wind and drift that night I felt there was a good deal to be hoped for, rather than to be expected. But we got along very well, Dimitri driving his team in front, as he did most of this journey, and picking up marks very helpfully with his sharp eyes. In the low temperatures we met, the glasses which I must wear are almost impossible, because of fogging. We took three boxes of dog-biscuit from Safety Camp and another three boxes from a point sixteen miles from Hut Point. Here we rested the dogs for a few hours, and started again at 6 p.m. All day the light was appalling, and the wind strong, but to my great relief we found Corner Camp after four hours' more travelling, the flag showing plainly, though the cairn itself was invisible when a hundred yards away. This was the last place where there was any dog-food on the route, and the dogs got a good feed after doing thirty-four miles (statute) for the day's run. This was more than we had hoped: the only disquieting fact was that both the sledge-meters which we had were working wrong: the better of the two seemed however to be marking the total mileage fairly correctly at present, though the hands which indicated more detailed information were quite at sea. We had no minimum thermometer, but the present temperature was $-4°$.

February 27. Mount Terror has proved our friend today, for the slope just above the Knoll has remained clear when everything else was covered, and we have steered by that – behind us. It seemed, when we started in low drift, that we should pick up nothing, but by good luck, or good I don't know what, we have got everything: first the motor, then pony walls at 10 miles, where we stopped and had a cup of tea. I wanted to do 15 miles, but we have done 18½ miles on the best running surface I have ever seen. After lunch we got a cairn which we could not see twenty yards away after we had reached it, but which we could see for a long way on the southern horizon, against a thin strip of blue sky. We camped just in time to get the tent pitched before a line of drift we saw coming out of the sky hit us. It is now blowing a mild blizzard and drifting. Forty-eight miles in two days is more than I expected: may our luck continue. Dogs pulling very fit and not done up.

February 28. I had my first upset just after starting, the sledge capsizing on a great sastrugus like the Ramp. Dimitri was a long way ahead and all behind was very thick. I had to unload the sledge for I could not right it alone. Just as I righted it the team took charge. I missed the driving-stick but got on to the sledge with no hope of stopping them, and I was carried a mile to the south, leaving four boxes of dog-food, the weekly bag, cooker, and tent poles on the ground. The team stopped when they reached Dimitri's team, and by then the gear was out of sight. We went back for it, and made good 16¾ miles for the day on a splendid surface. The sun went down at 11.15 (10.15 A.T.), miraged quite flat on top. After he had gone down a great bonfire seemed to blaze out from the horizon. Now −22° and we use a candle for the first time.

February 29. *Bluff Depot.* If anybody had told me we could reach Bluff Depot, nearly ninety miles, in four days, I would not have believed it. We have had a good clear day with much mirage. Dogs a bit tired.[4]

The next three days' run took us to One Ton. On the day we left Bluff Depot, which had been made a little more than a year ago, when certain of the ponies were sent home on the Depot Journey,[5] but which no longer contained any provisions, we travelled 12 miles; there was a good light and it was as warm as could be expected in March. The next day (2 March) we did 9 miles after a cold and sleepless night, −24° and a mild blizzard from N.W. and quite thick. On the night of 3 March we reached One Ton, heading into a strongish

4. My own diary.   5. See pp. 116–17.

wind with a temperature of $-24°$. These were the first two days on which we had cold weather, but it was nothing to worry about for us, and was certainly not colder than one could ordinarily have expected at this time of year.

Arrived at One Ton my first feeling was one of relief that the Polar Party had not been to the Depot and that therefore we had got their provisions out in time. The question of what we were to do in the immediate future was settled for us; for four days out of the six during which we were at One Ton the weather made travelling southwards, that is against the wind, either entirely impossible or such that the chance of seeing another party at any distance was nil. On the two remaining days I could have run a day farther South and back again, with the possibility of missing the party on the way. I decided to remain at the Depot where we were certain to meet.

On the day after we arrived at One Ton (4 March) Dimitri came to me and said that the dogs ought to be given more food, since they were getting done and were losing their coats: they had, of course, done a great deal of sledging already this year. Dimitri had long experience of dog-driving and I had none. I thought and I still think he was right. I increased the dog ration therefore, and this left us with thirteen more days' dog-food, including that for 4 March.

The weather was bad when we were at One Ton, for when it was blowing the temperature often remained comparatively low, and when it was not blowing it dropped considerably, and I find readings in my diary of $-34°$ and $-37°$ at 8 p.m. Having no minimum thermometer we did not know the night temperatures. On the other hand I find an entry: 'Today is the first real good one we have had, only about $-10°$ and the sun shining, – and we have shifted the tent, dried our bags and gear a lot, and been pottering about all day.' At this time, however, when we were at One Ton I looked upon these conditions as being a temporary cold snap: there was no reason then to suppose these were normal March conditions in the middle of the Barrier, where no one had ever been at this time of year. I believe now they are normal: on the other hand, in our meteorological report Simpson argues that they were abnormal for the Barrier at this time of year.[6]

Since there was no depot of dog-food at One Ton it was not possible to go farther South (except for the one day mentioned above) without killing dogs. My orders on this point were perfectly explicit; I saw no reason for disobeying them, and indeed it appeared that we had been wrong to hurry out so soon, before the time that Scott had reckoned that he would return, and that the Polar Party would really come in at the time Scott had calculated before starting rather than at the time we had reckoned from the data brought back by the Last Return Party.

From the particulars already given it will be seen that I had no reason to suspect that the Polar Party could be in want of food. The Polar Party of five men had according to our rations plenty of food either on their sledge or in the depots. In addition they had a lot of pony meat depoted at Middle Glacier Depot and onwards from there. Though we did not know it, the death of Evans at the foot of the Beardmore Glacier provided an additional amount of food for the four men who were then left. The full amount of oil for this food had been left in the depots; but we know now what we did not know then, that some of it had evaporated. These matters are discussed in greater detail in the account of the return of the Polar Party and after.[7]

Thus I felt little anxiety for the Polar Party. But I was getting anxious about my companion. Soon after arrival at One Ton it was clear that Dimitri was feeling the cold. He complained of his head; then his right arm and side were affected; and from this time onwards he found that he could do less and less with his right side. Still I did not worry much about it, and my decision as to our movements was not

6. *British Antarctic Expedition, 1910–1913*, "Meteorology", by G. C. Simpson, vol. i, pp. 28–30.
7. See pp. 568–75.

affected by this complication. I decided to allow eight days' food for our return, which meant that we must start on 10 March.

> *March* 10. Pretty cold night: −33° when we turned out at 8 a.m. Getting our gear together, and the dogs more or less into order after six days was cold work, and we started in minus thirties and a head wind. The dogs were mad, − stark, staring lunatics. Dimitri's team wrecked my sledge-meter, and I left it lying on the ground a mile from One Ton. All we could do was to hang on to the sledge and let them go: there wasn't a chance to go back, turn them or steer them. Dimitri broke his driving-stick: my team fought as they went: once I was dragged with my foot pinned under my driving stick, which was itself jammed in the grummet: several times I only managed to catch on anywhere: this went on for six or seven miles, and then they got better.[8]

Our remaining sledge-meter was quite unreliable, but following our outward tracks (for it became thick and overcast), and judging by our old camping sites, we reckoned that we had done an excellent run of 23 to 24 miles (statute) for the day. The temperature when we camped was only −14°. However it became much colder in the night, and when we turned out it was so thick that I decided we must wait. At 2 p.m. on 11 March there was one small patch of blue sky showing, and we started to steer by this: soon it was blowing a mild blizzard, and we stopped after doing what I reckoned was eight miles, steering by trying to keep the wind on my ear: but I think we were turning circles much of the time. It blew hard and was very cold during the night, and we turned out on the morning of 12 March to a blizzard with a temperature of −33°: this gradually took off, and at 10 a.m. Dimitri said he could see the Bluff, and we were right into the land, and therefore the pressure. This was startling, but later it cleared enough to reassure me, though Dimitri

8. My own diary.

was so certain that during the first part of our run that day I steered east a lot. We did 25 to 30 miles this day in drift and a temperature of $-28°$.

By now I was becoming really alarmed and anxious about Dimitri, who seemed to be getting much worse, and to be able to do less and less. Sitting on a sledge the next day with a head wind and the temperature $-30°$ was cold. The land was clear when we turned out and I could see that we must be far outside our course, but almost immediately it became foggy. We made in towards the land a good deal, and made a good run, but owing to the sledge-meter being useless and the bad weather generally during the last few days, I had a very hazy idea indeed where we were when we camped, having been steering for some time by the faint gleam of the sun through the mist. Just after camping Dimitri suddenly pointed to a black spot which seemed to wave to and fro: we decided that it was the flag of the derelict motor near Corner Camp which up to that time I thought was ten to fifteen miles away: this was a great relief, and we debated packing up again and going to it, but decided to stay where we were.

It was fairly clear on the morning of 14 March, which was lucky, for it was now obvious that we were miles from Corner Camp and much too near the land. The flag we had seen must have been a miraged piece of pressure, and it was providential that we had not made for it, and found worse trouble than we actually experienced. Try all I could that morning, my team, which was leading, insisted on edging westwards. At last I saw what I thought was a cairn, but found out just in time that it was a haycock or mound of ice formed by pressure: by its side was a large open crevasse, of which about fifty yards of snow-bridge had fallen in. For several miles we knew that we were crossing big crevasses by the hollow sound, and it was with considerable relief that I sighted the motor and then Corner Camp some two or three miles to the east of us. 'Dimitri had left his Alpine rope there, and also I should have liked to have brought in Evans' sledge, but it would have meant about five miles extra, and I left it. I hope Scott, finding no note, will not think we are lost.'[9]

Dimitri seemed to be getting worse, and we pushed on until we camped that night only fifteen miles from Hut Point. My main anxiety was whether the sea-ice between us and Hut Point was in, because I felt that the job of getting the teams up on to the Peninsula and along it and down the other side would be almost more than we could do: there was an ominous open-water sky ahead.

On 15 March we were held up all day by a strong blizzard. But by 8 a.m. the next morning we could see just the outline of White Island. I was very anxious, for Dimitri said that he had nearly fainted, and I felt that we must get on somehow, and chance the sea-ice being in. He stayed inside the tent as long as possible, and my spirits rose as the land began to clear all round while I was packing up both sledges. From Safety Camp the mirage at the edge of the Barrier was alarming, but as we approached the edge to my very great relief I found that the sea-ice was still in, and that what we had taken for frost smoke was only drift over Cape Armitage.

Pushing into the drift round the corner I found Atkinson on the sea-ice, and Keohane in the hut behind. In a few minutes we had the gist of one another's news. The ship had made attempt after attempt to reach Campbell and his five men, but they had not been taken off from Evans Coves when she finally left McMurdo Sound on 4 March; she would make another effort on her way to New Zealand. Evans was better and was being taken home. Meanwhile there were four of us at Hut Point and we could not communicate with our companions at Cape Evans until the Sound froze over, for the open sea was washing the feet of Vince's Cross.

We were not unduly alarmed about the Polar Party at present, but began to make arrangements for further sledging if

9. ibid.

necessary. It was useless to think of taking the dogs again for they were thoroughly done. The mules and the new dogs were at Cape Evans. 'In four or five days Atkinson wishes to start South again to see what we can do man-hauling, if the Polar Party is not in. I agree with him that to try and go west to meet Campbell is useless just now. If we can go north, they can come south, and to put two parties there on the new sea-ice is to double the risk.'

March 17. A blizzard day but only about force 5–6. I think they will have been able to travel all right on the Barrier. Atkinson thinks of starting on the 22nd: my view is that allowing three weeks and four days for the Summit, and ten days for being hung up by weather, we can give them five weeks after the Last Return Party (i.e. to 26 March) to get in, having been quite safe and sound all the way. We feel anxious now, but I do not think there is need for alarm till then, and they might get in well after that, and be all right.

Now our only real chance of finding them, if we go out, is from here to ten miles south of Corner Camp. After that we shall do all we can, but it would be no good, because there is no very definite route. Therefore I would start out on 27 March, when we would travel that part with most chance of meeting them there if they have any trouble. I have put this to Atkinson and will willingly do what he decides. I am feeling pretty done up, and have rested. The prospect of what will be a hard journey, feeling as I do, is rather bad. I don't think there is really cause for alarm.

March 18 *and* 19. We are very anxious, though the Pole Party could not be in yet. Also I am very done, and more so than I first thought: I am afraid it is a bit doubtful whether I can get out again yet, but today I feel better and have been for a short walk. I am taking all the rest I can.

March 20. Last night a very strong blizzard blew, wind force 9 and big snowfall and drift. This morning the doors and windows are all drifted up, and we could hardly get out: a lot of snow had got inside the hut also: I was feeling rotten, and thought that to go out and clear the window and door would do me good. This I did, but came back in a big squall, passing Atkinson as I came in. Then I felt myself going faint, and remember pushing the door to get in if possible. I knew no more until I came to on the floor just inside the door, having broken some tendons in my right hand in falling.[10]

Two days afterwards the dogs sang at breakfast-time: they often did this when a party was approaching, even when it was still far away, and they had done so when Crean came in on his walk from Corner Camp. We were cheered by the noise. But no party arrived, and the singing of the dogs was explained later by some seal appearing on the new ice in Arrival Bay. Atkinson decided to go out on to the Barrier man-hauling with Keohane on the 26th. It was obvious that I could not go with them: he told me afterwards that when I came in with the dog-teams he was sure I could not go out again.

March 25. The wind came away yesterday evening, first S.W. and then S.E. but not bad, though very thick. It was a surprise to find we could see the Western Mountains this morning, and I believe it has been a good day on the Barrier, though it is still blowing with low drift this evening. We are now on the days when I expect the Polar Party in: pray God I may be right. Atkinson and I look at one another, and he looks, and I feel, quite haggard with anxiety. He says he does not think they have scurvy. We both, I think, feel quite comfortable, in comparison, about Campbell: he only wants to exercise care, and his great care was almost a byword on the ship. They are fresh and they have plenty of seal.[11] He discussed with Pennell both the possibility of shipwreck and that of the ship being unable to get to him, and for this reason landed an extra month's rations as a depot; also he contemplated the idea of living on seal. He knows of the Butter Point

10. My own diary.
11. As a matter of fact this was not the case.

Depot, and knows that a party has been sledging in that neighbourhood: though he does not know of the depots they left at Cape Roberts and Cape Bernacchi, they are right out on the Points and Taylor says he could not miss them on his way down the coast.[12]

This day Atkinson thought he saw Campbell's party coming in, and the next day Keohane and Dimitri came in great excitement and said they could see them, and we were out on the Point and on the sea-ice in the drift for quite a long time.

Last night we had turned in about two hours when five or six knocks were hit on the little window over our heads. Atkinson shouted 'Hullo!' and cried, 'Cherry, they're in.' Keohane said, 'Who's cook?' Some one lit a candle and left it in the far corner of the hut to give them light, and we all rushed out. But there was no one there. It was the nearest approach to ghost work that I have ever heard, and it must have been a dog which sleeps in that window. He must have shaken himself, hitting the window with his tail. Atkinson thought he heard footsteps![13]

On Wednesday, 27 March, Atkinson started out on to the Barrier with one companion, Keohane. During the whole of this trip the temperatures were low, and both men obtained but little sleep, finding of course that a tent occupied by two men only is a very cold place. The first two days they made nine miles each day, on 29 March they pushed on in thick weather for eleven miles, when the weather cleared enough to show them that they had got into the White Island pressure. On 30 March they reached a point south of Corner Camp, when

taking into consideration the weather, and temperatures, and the time of the year, and the hopelessness of finding the party

12. My own diary.   13. ibid.

except at any definite point like a depot, I decided to return from here. We depoted the major portion of a week's provisions to enable them to communicate with Hut Point in case they should reach this point. At this date in my own mind I was morally certain that the party had perished, and in fact on 29 March Captain Scott, 11 miles south of One Ton Depot made the last entry in his diary.[14]

They arrived back on 1 April. Yesterday evening at 6.30 p.m. Atkinson and Keohane arrived. It was pretty thick here and blowing too, but they had had a fair day on the Barrier. They had been out to Corner Camp and eight miles farther. Their bags were bad, their clothes very bad after six days: they must have had minus forties constantly. It is a moral certainty that to go farther south would serve no purpose, and for two men would be a useless risk. They did quite right to come back. They are much in want of sleep, poor devils, and I do hope Atkinson will allow himself to rest: he looks as though he might knock up. Keohane did well, and is very fit. They came in over fifteen miles yesterday, and have brought in the sledge of the Second Return Party, the one they took out being very heavy pulling. They had no day on which they could not travel. Here it has been blowing and drifting half the time he has been absent,

and a few days later,

We have got to face it now. The Pole Party will not in all probability ever get back. And there is no more that we can do. The next step must be to get to Cape Evans as soon as it is possible. There are fresh men there: at any rate fresh compared to us.[15]

Atkinson was the senior officer left, and unless Campbell and his party came in, the command of the Main Party

14. Atkinson in *Scott's Last Expedition*, vol. II, p. 309.
15. My own diary.

devolved upon him. It was not a position which any one could envy even if he had been fresh and fit. Amidst all his anxieties and responsibilities he looked after me with the greatest patience and care. I was so weak that sometimes I could only keep on my legs with difficulty: the glands of my throat were swollen so that I could hardly speak or swallow: my heart was strained and I had considerable pain. At such a time I was only a nuisance, but nothing could have exceeded his kindness and his skill with the few drugs which we possessed.

Again and again in these days someone would see one or other of the missing parties coming in. It always proved to be mirage, a seal or pressure or I do not know what, but never could we quite persuade ourselves that these excitements might not have something in them, and every time hope sprang up anew. Meanwhile the matter of serious importance was the state of the ice in the bays between us and Cape Evans: we *must* get help. All the ice in the middle of the Sound was swept out by the winds of 30 March to 2 April, and on the following day Atkinson climbed Arrival Heights to see how the remaining ice looked.

> The ice in the two bays to Cape Evans is quite new – formed this morning, I suppose, with the rest that is in the Sound. There are open leads between Glacier Tongue and Cape Evans, inside the line joining the ends of the two. There is a big berg in between Glacier Tongue and the islands, and also a flat one off Cape Evans.[16]

We had some good freezing days after this, and on 5 April 'we tried the ice this afternoon. It is naturally slushy and salt, but some hundred yards from the old ice it is six inches thick: probably it averages about this thickness all over the Sound.'[17] Then we had a hard blizzard, on the fourth day of which it was possible to get up the Heights again and see for some distance. As far as could be judged the ice in the two

16. ibid.   17. ibid.

bays had remained firm: these bays are those formed on either side of Glacier Tongue, by the Hut Point Peninsula on the south, and by Cape Evans and the islands on the north.

On 10 April Atkinson, Keohane and Dimitri started for Cape Evans, meaning to travel along the Peninsula to the Hutton Cliffs, and thence to cross the sea-ice in these bays, if it proved to be practicable. The amount of daylight was now very restricted, and the sun would disappear for the winter a week hence. Arrived at the Hutton Cliffs, where it was blowing as usual, they lost no time in lowering themselves and their sledge on to the sea-ice, and were then pleasantly surprised to find how slippery it was.

> We set sail before a strong following breeze and, all sitting on the sledge, had reached the Glacier Tongue in twenty minutes. We clambered over the Tongue, and, our luck and the breeze still holding, we reached Cape Evans, completing the last seven miles, all sitting on the sledge, in an hour.
>
> There I called together all the members and explained the situation, telling them what had been done, and what I then proposed to do; also asking them for their advice in this trying time. The opinion was almost unanimous that all that was possible had been already done. Owing to the lateness of the year, and the likelihood of our being unable to make our way up the coast to Campbell, one or two members suggested that another journey might be made to Corner Camp. Knowing the conditions which had lately prevailed on the Barrier, I took it upon myself to decide the uselessness of this.[18]

All was well at Cape Evans. Winds and temperatures had both been high, the latter being in marked contrast to the low temperatures we had experienced at Hut Point, which averaged as much as 15° lower than those that were recorded in the previous year. The seven mules were well, but three of the new dogs had died: we were always being troubled by that mysterious disease.

18. Atkinson in *Scott's Last Expedition*, vol. ii, p. 31.

Before she left for New Zealand the following members of our company joined the ship: Simpson, who had to return to his work in India,[19] Griffith Taylor, who had been lent to us by the Australian Government for only one year; Ponting, whose photographic work was done; Day, whose work with the motors was done; Meares, who was recalled by family affairs; Forde, whose hand had never recovered from the effects of frost-bite during the spring; Clissold, who fell off a berg and concussed himself; and Anton, whose work with the ponies was done. Lieutenant Evans was invalided home.

Archer had been landed to take Clissold's place as cook; another seaman, Williamson, was landed to take Forde's place, and of our sledging companions he was the only fresh man. Wright was probably the most fit after him, and otherwise we had no one who, under ordinary circumstances, would have been considered fit to go out sledging again this season, especially at a time when the sun was just leaving us for the winter. We were sledged out.

The next few days were occupied in making preparations for a further sledge journey, and on 13 April a party started to return to Hut Point by the Hutton Cliffs. Atkinson, Wright, Keohane and Williamson were to try and sledge up the western coast to help Campbell: Gran and Dimitri were to stay with me at Hut Point. The surface of the sea-ice was now extremely slushy and bad for pulling; the ice had begun to extrude its salt. A blizzard started in their faces, and they ran for shelter to the lee of Little Razorback Island. The weather clearing they pushed on to the Glacier Tongue, and camped there for the night somewhat frost-bitten. Some difficulty was experienced the next morning in climbing the ice-cliff on the Peninsula, but Atkinson, using his knife as a purchase, and the sledge held at arm's-length by four men as a ladder, succeeded eventually in getting a foothold.

Meanwhile I was left alone at Hut Point, where blizzards

19. Scott had written that Simpson was certain to stay for another year. But the news of illness in the Meteorological Office in India caused him to return to India.

raged periodically with the usual creakings and groanings of the old hut. Foolishly I accompanied my companions, when they started for Cape Evans, as far as the bottom of Ski Slope. When I left them I found I could not keep my feet on the slippery snow and ice patches, and I had several nasty falls, in one of which I gave my shoulder a twist. It was this shaking combined with the rather desperate conditions which caused a more acute state of illness and sickness than I had experienced for some time. Some of those days I remained alone at Hut Point I was too weak to do more than crawl on my hands and knees about the hut. I had to get blubber from the door to feed the fire, and chop up seal-meat to eat, to cook, and to tend the dogs, some of whom were loose, while most of them were tied in the verandah, or between the hut door and Vince's Cross. The hut was bitterly cold with only one man in it: had there not been some morphia among the stores brought down from Cape Evans I do not know what I should have done.

The dogs realized that they could take liberties which they would not have dared to do in different circumstances. They whined and growled, and squabbled amongst themselves all the time, day and night. Seven or eight times one day I crawled across the floor to try and lay my hands upon one dog who was the ringleader. I was sure it was Dyk, but never detected him in the act, and though I thrashed him with difficulty as a speculation, the result was not encouraging. I would willingly have killed the lot of them just then, I am ashamed to say. I lay in my sleeping-bag with the floor of the hut falling from me, or its walls disappearing in the distance and coming back: and roused myself at intervals to feed blubber to the stove. I felt as though I had been delivered out of hell when the relief party arrived on the night of 14 April. I had been alone four days, and I think a few more days would have sent me off my head. Not the least welcome of the things they had brought me were my letters, copies of the *Weekly Times*, a pair of felt shoes and a comb!

Atkinson's plan was to start on 7 April over the old sea-ice which lay to the south and south-west of us: he was to take with him Wright, Keohane and Williamson, and they wanted to reach Butter Point, and thence to sledge up the western coast. If the sea-ice was in, and Campbell was sledging down upon it, they hoped to meet him and might be of the greatest assistance to him. Even if they did not meet him they could mark more obviously certain depots, of which he had no knowledge, left by our own geological parties on the route he must follow. As I have already mentioned, these were on Cape Roberts, off Granite Harbour, and on Cape Bernacchi, north of New Harbour: there was also a depot at Butter Point, but Campbell already knew of this. They could also leave instructions to this effect at points where he would be likely to see them. There was no question that there was grave risk in this journey. Not only was the winter approaching, and the daylight limited, but the sea-ice over which they must march was most dangerous. Sea-ice is always forming and being blown out to sea, or just floating away on the tide at this time of year. The amount of old ice which had remained during the summer was certain to be limited: the new ice was thin and might take them out with it at any time. However, what could be done had to be done.

Before they left certain signals by means of rockets and Véry lights were arranged, to be sent up by us at Hut Point if Campbell arrived: signals had also been arranged between Hut Point and Cape Evans in view of certain events. We did not have, but I think we ought to have had, some form of portable heliograph for communications between Hut Point and Cape Evans when the sun was up, and some kind of lamp signal apparatus to use during the winter.

They started at 10.30 a.m. on Wednesday, 17 April. The sun was now only just peeping over the northern horizon at midday, and would disappear entirely in six more days, though of course there was a long twilight as yet. For fresh men on old sea-ice it would not have been an easy venture: for worn-out men on a coast where the ice was probably freezing and blowing out at odd times it was very brave.

They had hard pulling their first two days, and the

minimum temperature for the corresponding nights was
$-43°$ and $-45°$. Consequently they soon began to be iced up.
On the other hand they found old sea-ice and made good
some 25 miles, camping on the evening of the 18th about
four miles from the Eskers. Next morning they had to
venture upon newly frozen ice, and a blizzard wind was
blowing. They crossed the four miles from their night camp
to the Eskers, glad enough to reach land the other side
without the ice going to sea with them. They then turned
towards the Butter Point Depot, but were compelled to camp
owing to the blizzard which came on with full force. The rise
in temperature to zero caused a general thaw of sleeping-bags
and clothing which dried but little when the sun had no
power. On the following morning they reached the Butter
Point Depot, which they found with difficulty, for there was
no flag standing. Even as they struck their camp they saw the
ice to the north of them breaking up and going out to sea.
There was nothing to do but to turn back, for neither could
they go north to Campbell nor could Campbell come south
to them. Wright now told Atkinson how much he had been
opposed to this journey all along: 'he had come on this trip
fully believing that there was every possibility of the party
being lost, but had never demurred and never offered a
contrary opinion, and one cannot be thankful enough to such
men.'[20] They made up the Butter Point Depot, marked it as
well as they could in case Campbell should arrive there, and
left two weeks' provisions for him. They could do no more.

They got back to the Eskers that same day and anxiously
awaited the twilight of the morning to reveal the state of the
new sea-ice which they had crossed on their outward journey.
To their joy some of it remained and they started to do the
four miles between them and the old sea-ice. For two miles
they ran with the sail set: then they had a hard pull, and some
Emperor penguins whom they could see led them to suppose
that there was open water ahead. But they got through all
right, and did ten miles for the day. On Monday 22, 'blizzard

20. Atkinson in *Scott's Last Expedition*, vol. ii, p. 314.

in morning, so started late, and made for end of Pinnacled Ice. We found our little bay of sea-ice all gone out. Luckily there was a sort of ice-foot around the Pinnacled Ice and we completed seven miles and got through.'[21]

> *Tuesday, 23 April.* Atkinson and his party got in about 7 p.m. after a long pull all day in very bad weather. They are just in the state of a party which has been out on a very cold spring journey: clothes and sleeping-bags very wet, sweaters, pyjama coats and so forth full of snow. Atkinson looks quite done up, his cheeks are fallen in and his throat shows thin. Wright is also a good deal done up, and the whole party has evidently had little sleep. They have had a difficult and dangerous trip, and it is a good thing they are in, and they are fortunate to have had no mishaps, for the sea-ice is constantly going out over there, and when they were on it they never knew that they might not find themselves cut off from the shore. Big leads were constantly opening, even in ice over a foot thick and with little wind. But even if the ice had been in I do not believe that they could have gone many days.[22]

That same day the sun appeared for the last time for four months.

April 28 seemed to be a quite good day when we awoke, and Wright, Keohane and Gran started back for Cape Evans before 10 a.m. We could then see the outline of Inaccessible Island, and the ice in the Sound looked fairly firm. So they determined to go by the way of the sea-ice under Castle Rock instead of going along the Peninsula to the Hutton Cliffs. Soon after they started it came up thick, and by 11.30 it was blowing a mild blizzard with a low temperature. We felt considerable anxiety, especially when a full blizzard set in with a temperature down to −31°, and we could not see how the ice was standing it. Two days later it cleared, and that night a flare was lit at Cape Evans at a pre-arranged time, by

---

21. Atkinson's diary.   22. My own diary.

which signal we knew that they had arrived safely. We heard afterwards that when it came up thick they decided to follow the land which was the only thing that they could see. They soon found that the ice was not nearly so good as was supposed: there were open pools of water, and some of the ice was moving up and down with their weight as they crossed it: Gran put his foot in. Then Wright went ahead with the Alpine rope, the ice being blue, the pulling easy, and the wind force 4–5. As far as Turtleback Island the ice was newly frozen, but after that they knew they were on oldish ice. They were lost on Cape Evans in the blizzard for some time, but eventually found the hut safely. One of the lessons of this expedition is that too little care was taken in travelling on sea-ice.

Atkinson, Dimitri and I left for Cape Evans with the two dog-teams on 1 May. Directly we started it was evident that the surface was very bad: even the ice near Hut Point, which had been frozen for a long time, was hard pulling for the dogs, and when after less than a mile we got on to ice which had frozen quite lately the sledges were running on snow which in turn lay on salt sleet. It seemed a long time before we got abreast of Castle Rock, following close along the land for the weather was very thick: when we started we could just see the outline of Inaccessible Island, but by now the horizon was lost in the dusk and haze. We decided to push on to Turtleback Island and go over Glacier Tongue in order to get on to the older ice as soon as possible. The dogs began to get very done: Manuki Noogis, who had been harnessed in as leader (for Rabchick had deserted in the night), gave in completely, lay down and refused to be persuaded to go on: we had to cast him off and hope that he would follow. After a time Turtleback Island was visible in the gloom, but it was all we could do, pushing and pulling the sledges to help the dogs, to get them so far. We were now on the older ice: our way was easier and we reached Cape Evans without further incident. We found Rabchick on arrival, but no Manuki Noogis, who never reappeared.

As we neared the Cape Atkinson turned to me: 'Would

you go for Campbell or the Polar Party next year?' he said. 'Campbell,' I answered: just then it seemed to me unthinkable that we should leave live men to search for those who were dead.

Chapter Fourteen
THE LAST WINTER

Ordinary people snuggle up to God as a lost leveret in a
freezing wilderness might snuggle up to a Siberian tiger. . . .

H. G. WELLS

(I) 5 men dead

SCOTT   OATES
WILSON   SEAMAN EVANS
BOWERS

(II) 9 men gone home

LIEUT. EVANS   DAY
SIMPSON   FORDE
MEARES   CLISSOLD
TAYLOR   ANTON
PONTING

(III) 2 men landed

ARCHER   WILLIAMSON

(IV) 13 men at Cape Evans
for third year

ATKINSON   LASHLY
CHERRY-   CREAN
    GARRARD   KEOHANE
WRIGHT   DIMITRI
DEBENHAM   HOOPER
GRAN   WILLIAMSON
NELSON   ARCHER

A QUITE disproportionately small part of *Scott's Last Expedition* was given to Atkinson's account of the last and worst year any of us survivors spent: some one should have compelled him to write, for he will not do so if he can help it. The problems which presented themselves were unique in the history of Arctic travel, the weather conditions which had to be faced during this last winter were such as had never been met in McMurdo Sound. The sledging personnel had lately undergone journeys, in one case no less than four journeys, of major importance, until they were absolutely worn out. The successful issue of the party was a triumph of good management and good fellowship. The saving clause was that as regards hut, food, heat, clothing and the domestic life generally we were splendidly found. To the north of us, some hundreds of miles away, Campbell's party of six men must be fighting for their lives against these same conditions, or worse – unless indeed they had already perished on their way south. We knew they must be in desperate plight, but probably they were alive: the point in their favour was that they were fresh men. To the south of us, anywhere between us and the Pole, were five men. We knew *they* must be dead.

The immediate problem which presented itself was how best to use the resources which were left to us. Our numbers were much reduced. Nine men had gone home before any hint of tragedy reached them. Two men had been landed from the ship. We were thirteen men for this last year. Of these thirteen it was almost certain that Debenham would be unable to go out sledging again owing to an injury to his knee: Archer had come to cook and not to sledge: and it was also doubtful about myself. As a matter of fact our sledging numbers for the last summer totalled eleven, five officers and six men.

We were well provided with transport, having the seven mules sent down by the Indian Government, which were excellent animals, as well as our original two dog-teams: the additional dogs brought down by the ship were with two exceptions of no real sledging value. Our dog-teams had, however, already travelled some 1500 miles on the Barrier alone, not counting the work they had done between Hut Point and Cape Evans; and, though we did not realize it at this time, they were sick of it and never worked again with that dash which we had come to expect of them.

The first thing which we settled about the winter which lay ahead of us was that, so far as possible, everything should go on as usual. The scientific work must of course be continued, and there were the dogs and mules to be looked after: a night-watch to be kept and the meteorological observations and auroral notes to be taken. Owing to our reduced numbers we should need the help of the seamen for this purpose. We were also to bring out another volume of the *South Polar Times* on Mid-winter Day. The importance of not allowing any sense of depression to become a part of the atmosphere of our life was clear to all. This was all the more necessary when, as we shall see, the constant blizzards confined us week after week to our hut. Even when we did get a fine day we were almost entirely confined to the rocky cape for our exercise and walks. When there was sea-ice it was most unsafe.

Atkinson was in command: in addition, he and Dimitri took over the care of the dogs. Many of these, both those which had been out sledging and those just arrived, were in a very poor state, and a dog hospital was soon built. At this date we had 24 dogs left from the last year, and 11 dogs brought down recently by the ship: three of the new dogs had already died. Lashly was in charge of the seven mules, which were allotted to seven men for exercise: Nelson was to continue his marine biological work: Wright was to be meteorologist as well as chemist and physicist: Gran was in charge of stores, and would help Wright in the meteorological observations: Debenham was geologist and photographer. I was ordered to take a long rest, but could do the zoological work, the *South Polar Times*, and keep the Official Account of the Expedition from day to day. Crean was in charge of sledging stores and equipment. Archer was cook. Hooper, our domestic, took over in addition the working of the acetylene plant. There was plenty of work for our other two seamen, Keohane and Williamson, in the daily life of the camp and in preparations for the sledging season to come.

The blizzard which threatened us all the way from Hut Point on 1 May broke soon after we got in. The ice in North Bay, which had been frozen for some time, was taken out on the first day of this blizzard, with the exception of a small strip running close along the shore. The rest followed the next afternoon, when the wind was still rising, and blew in the gusts up to 89 miles an hour. The curious thing was that all this time the air had been quite clear.

This was the second day of the blizzard. The wind continued in violence as the night wore on, and it began to snow, becoming very thick. From 3 a.m. to 4 a.m. the wind was so strong that there was a continuous rattle of sand and stones up against the wall of the hut. The greater part of the time the anemometer head was choked by the drifting snow, and Debenham, whose night-watch it was, had a bad time in clearing it at 4 a.m. During the period when it was working it registered a gust of over 91 miles an hour. While it was not working there came a gust which woke most people up, and which was a far more powerful one, making a regular hail of stones against the wall. The next morning the wind was found to be averaging 104 miles an hour when the anemometer on the hill was checked for three minutes. Later it was averaging 78 miles an hour. This blizzard continued to rage all this day and the next, but on 6 May, which was one of those clear beautiful days when it is hard to believe that it can ever blow again, we could see something of the damage to the sea-ice. The centre of the Sound was clear of ice, and the open water stretched to the S.W. of us as far back as Tent Island. We were to have many worse blizzards during this winter, but this particular blow was important because it came at a critical time in the freezing over of the sea, and, once it had been dispersed, the winds of the future never allowed the ice to form again sufficiently thick to withstand the wind forces which obtained.

Thus I find in my diary of 8 May:

> Up to the present we have never considered the possibility
> of the sea in this neighbourhood, and the Sound out to the
> west of us, not freezing over permanently in the winter. But
> here there is still open water, and it seems quite possible that
> there may not be any permanent freezing this year, at any rate
> to the north of Inaccessible Island and this cape. Though
> North Bay is now frozen over, the ice in it was blown away
> during the night, and, having been blown back again, is now
> only joined to the ice-foot by newly frozen ice.

During this winter the ice formed in North Bay was constantly moving away from the ice-foot, quite independently of wind. I watched it carefully as far as it was possible to do so in the dark. Sometimes at any rate the southern side of the sea-ice moved out not only northwards from the land, but also slightly westwards from the glacier face. To the north-east the ice was sometimes pressed closely up against the glacier. It seemed that the whole sheet was subject to a screw movement, the origin of which was somewhere out by Inaccessible Island. The result was that we often had a series of leads of newly frozen ice stretching out for some forty yards to an older piece of ice, each lead being of a different age. It was an interesting study in the formation of sea-ice, covered at times by very beautiful ice-flowers. But it was dangerous for the dogs, who sometimes did not realize that these leads were not strong enough to bear them. Vaida went in one day, but managed to scramble out on the far side. He was induced to return to the land with difficulty, just before the whole sheet of ice upon which he stood floated out to sea. Noogis, Dimitri's good leader, wandered away several times during the winter: once at any rate he seems to have been carried off on a piece of ice, and to have managed to swim to land, for when he arrived in camp his coat was full of icy slush: finally he disappeared altogether, all search for him was in vain, and we never found out what had happened.

Vaida was a short-tempered strong animal, who must have about doubled his weight since we came in from One Ton, and he became quite a house-dog this winter, waiting at the door to be patted by men as they went out, and coming in sometimes during the night-watch. But he did not like to be turned out in the morning, and for my part I did not like the job, for he could prove very nasty. We allowed a good many of the dogs to be loose this year, and sometimes, when standing quietly upon a rock on the cape, three or four of the dogs passed like shadows in the darkness, busily hunting the ice-foot for seals: this was the trouble of giving them their freedom, and I regret to say we found many carcasses of seal and Emperor penguins. There was one new dog, Lion, who accompanied me sometimes to the top of the Ramp to see how the ice lay out in the Sound. He seemed as interested in it as I was, and while I was using night-glasses would sit and gaze out over the sea which according to its age lay white or black at our feet. Of course we had a dog called Peary, and another one called Cooke. Peary was killed on the Barrier because he would not pull. Cooke, however, was still with us, and seemed to have been ostracized by his fellows, a position which in some lop-sided way he enjoyed. Loose dogs chased him at sight, and when Cooke appeared, and others were about, a regular steeplechase started. He also came up the Ramp with me one day: half-way up he suddenly turned and fled for the hut as hard as he could go: three other dogs came round the rocks in full chase, and they all gave the impression of thoroughly enjoying themselves.

The question of what ought to be done for the best during the coming sledging season must have been in the minds of all of us. Which of the two missing parties were we to try and find? A winter journey to relieve Campbell and his five men was out of the question. I doubt the possibility of such a journey to Evans Coves with fit men: to us at any rate it was unthinkable. Also if we could do the double journey up and down, Campbell could certainly do the single journey down. Add to this that there was every sign of open water under the Western Mountains, though this did not influence us much when the decision was made. The problem as it presented itself to us was much as follows:

Campbell's Party *might* have been picked up by the *Terra Nova*. Pennell meant to have another try to reach him on his way north, and it was probable that the ship would not be able to communicate again with Cape Evans owing to ice: on the other hand it was likely that the ship had *not* been able to relieve him. It also seemed that he could not have travelled down the coast at this time, owing to the state of the sea-ice. The danger to him and his men was primarily during the winter: every day after the winter his danger was lessened. If we started in the end of October to relieve Campbell, estimating the probable date of arrival of the ship, we judged that we could reach him only five or six weeks before the ship relieved him. All the same Campbell and his men might be alive, and, having lived through the winter, the arrival of help might make the difference between life and death.

On the other hand we knew that the Polar Party must be dead. They might be anywhere between Hut Point and the Pole, drifted over by snow, or lying at the bottom of a crevasse, which seemed the most likely thing to have happened. From the Upper Glacier Depot in 85° 5' S. to the Pole, that is the whole distance of the Plateau Journey, we did not know the courses they had steered nor the position of their depots, for Lieutenant Evans, who brought back the Last Return Party, was invalided home and neither of the seamen who remained of this party knew the courses.

After the experience of both the supporting parties on their way down the Beardmore Glacier, when we all got into frightfully crevassed areas, it was the general opinion that the Polar Party must have fallen down a crevasse; the weight of five men, as compared with the four men and three men of the other return parties, supported this theory. Lashly was inclined to think they had had scurvy. The true solution never once occurred to us, for they had full rations for a very much longer period of time than, according to their averages to 87° 32', they were likely to be out.

The first object of the expedition had been the Pole. If some record was not found, their success or failure would for ever remain uncertain. Was it due not only to the men and their relatives, but also to the expedition, to ascertain their fate if possible?

The chance of finding the remains of the Southern Party did not seem very great. At the same time Scott was strict about leaving notes at depots, and it seemed likely that he would have left some record at the Upper Glacier Depot before starting to descend the Beardmore Glacier: it would be interesting to know whether he did so. If we went south we must be prepared to reach this depot: farther than that, I have explained, we could not track him. On the other hand, if we went south prepared to go to the Upper Glacier Depot, the number of sledging men necessary, in view of the fact that we had no depots, would not allow of our sending a second party to relieve Campbell.

It was with all this in our minds that we sat down one

evening in the hut to decide what was to be done. The problem was a hard one. On the one hand we might go south, fail entirely to find any trace of the Polar Party, and while we were fruitlessly travelling all the summer Campbell's men might die for want of help. On the other hand we might go north, to find that Campbell's men were safe, and as a consequence the fate of the Polar Party and the result of their efforts might remain for ever unknown. Were we to foresake men who might be alive to look for those whom we knew were dead?

These were the points put by Atkinson to the meeting of the whole party. He expressed his own conviction that we should go south, and then each member was asked what he thought. No one was for going north: one member only did not vote for going south, and he preferred not to give an opinion. Considering the complexity of the question, I was surprised by this unanimity. We prepared for another Southern Journey.

It is impossible to express and almost impossible to imagine how difficult it was to make this decision. Then we knew nothing: now we know all. And nothing is harder than to realize in the light of facts the doubts which others have experienced in the fog of uncertainty.

Our winter routine worked very smoothly. Inside the hut we had a good deal more room than we needed, but this allowed of certain work being done in its shelter which would otherwise have had to be done outside. For instance we cut a hole through the floor of the dark-room, and sledged in some heavy boulders of kenyte lava: these were frozen solidly into the rock upon which the hut was built by the simple method of pouring hot water over them, and the pedestal so formed was used by Wright for his pendulum observations. I was able to skin a number of birds in the hut; which, incidentally, was a very much colder place in consequence of the reduction in our numbers.

The wind was most turbulent during this winter. The mean velocity of the wind, in miles per hour, for the month of May was 24.6 m.p.h.; for June 30.9 m.p.h.; and for July

29.5 m.p.h. The percentage of hours when the wind was blowing over fresh gale strength (42 m.p.h. on the Beaufort scale) for the month of May was 24.5, for June 35, and for July 33 per cent of the whole.

These figures speak for themselves: after May we lived surrounded by an atmosphere of raging winds and blinding drift, and the sea at our door was never allowed to freeze permanently.

After the blizzard in the beginning of May which I have already described, the ice round the point of Cape Evans and that in North Bay formed to a considerable thickness. We put a thermometer screen out upon it, and Atkinson started a fish-trap through a hole in it. There was a good deal of competition over this trap: the seamen started a rival one, which was to have been a very large affair, though it narrowed down to a less ambitious business before it was finished. There was a sound of cheering one morning, and Crean came in triumph from his fish-trap with a catch of 25. Atkinson's last catch had numbered one, but the seals had found his fishing-holes: a new hole caught fish until a seal found it. One of these fish, a Tremasome, had a parasitic growth over the dorsal sheath. External parasites are not common in the Antarctic, and this was an interesting find.

On 1 June Dimitri and Hooper went with a team of nine dogs to and from Hut Point, to see if they could find Noogis, the dog which had left us on our return on 1 May. There was plenty of food for him to pick up there. No trace of him could be found. The party reported a bad running surface, no pressure in the ice, as was the case the former year, but a large open working crack running from Great Razorback to Tent Island. There were big snowdrifts at Hut Point, as indeed was already the case at Cape Evans. During the first days of June we got down into the minus thirties, and our spirits rose as the thermometer dropped: we wanted permanent sea-ice.

Saturday, 8 June. The weather changes since the night before last have been, luckily for us, uncommon. Thursday evening a strong northerly wind started with some drift, and this increased during the night until it blew over forty miles an hour, the temperature being −22°. A strong wind from the north is rare, and generally is the prelude of a blizzard. This northerly wind fell towards morning, and the day was calm and clear, the temperature falling until it was −33° at 4 p.m. The barometer had been abnormally low during the day, being only 28.24 at noon. Then at 8 p.m. with the temperature at −36°, this blizzard broke, and at the same time there was a big upward jump of the barometer, which seemed to mark the beginning of the blizzard much more than the thermometer, which did not rise much. The wind during the night was very high, blowing 72 and 66 miles an hour, for hours at a time, and has not yet shown any sign of diminishing. Now, after lunch, the hut is straining and creaking, while a shower of stones rattles at intervals against it: the drift is generally very heavy.

Sunday, 9 June. The temperature has been higher, about zero, during the day, and the blizzard shows no signs of falling yet. The gusts are still of a very high velocity. A large quantity of ice to the north seems to have gone out: at any rate our narrow strip along the front, which is so valuable to us, will probably be permanent now.

Monday, 10 June. A most turbulent day. It is very hard to settle down to do anything, read or write, with such a turmoil outside, the hut shaking until we begin to wonder how long it will stand such winds. Most of the time the wind is averaging about sixty miles an hour, but the gusts are far greater, and at times it seems that something must go. Just before lunch I was racking my brains to write an Editorial for the *South Polar Times*, and had congratulated ourselves on having the sea-ice which is still in North Bay. As we were having lunch Nelson came in and said, 'The thermometers have gone!' All the ice in North Bay has gone. The part immediately next to the shore, which has now been in so long, and which was over two feet thick, we had considered sure to stay. On it has gone out the North Bay thermometer screen with its instruments, which was placed 400 yards out, the fish-trap, some shovels and a sledge with a crowbar. The gusts were exceptionally strong at lunch, and the ice must have gone out very quickly. There was no sign of it afterwards, though it was not drifting much and we could see some distance. To lose this ice in North Bay is a great disappointment, for it means so much to us here whether we have ice or water at our doors. We are now pretty well confined to the cape both for our own exercise and that of the mules, and in the dark it is very rough walking. But if the ice in South Bay were to follow, it would be a calamity, cutting us off entirely from the south and all sledging next year. Let us hope we shall be spared this.

This blizzard lasted for eight days, up till then the longest blizzard we had experienced:

It died as it had lived, blowing hard to the last, averaging 68 miles an hour from the south, and then 56 miles an hour from the north, finally back to the south, and so to calm. To sit here with no noise of wind whistling in the ventilator, calm and starlight outside, and North Bay freezing over once more, is a very great relief.[1]

It is noteworthy that this clearance of the ice, as also that in the beginning of May, coincided roughly with the maximum declination of the moon, and therefore with a run of spring tides.

It would be tedious to give any detailed account of the winds and drift which followed, night and day. There were few days which did not produce their blizzard, but in contrast the hours of bright starlight were very beautiful.

Walking home over the cape in the darkness this afternoon I saw an eruption of Erebus which, compared with anything we have seen here before, was very big. It looked as though a great mass of flame shot up some thousands of feet into the

1. My own diary.

461

air, and, as suddenly as it rose, fell again, rising again to about half the height, and then disappearing. There was then a great column of steam rising from the crater, and probably, so Debenham asserts, it was not a flame which appeared, but the reflection from a big bubble breaking in the crater. Afterwards the smoke cloud stretched away southwards, and we could not see the end of it.[2]

Blizzard followed blizzard, and at the beginning of July we had four days which were the thickest I have ever seen. Generally when you go out into a blizzard the drift is blown from your face and clothes, and though you cannot see your stretched-out hand, especially on a dark winter day, the wind prevents you being smothered. The wind also prevents the land, tents, hut and cases from being covered. But during this blizzard the drift drove at you in such blankets of snow, that your person was immediately blotted out, your face covered and your eyes plugged up. Gran lost himself for some time on the hill when taking the 8 a.m. observations, and Wright had difficulty in getting back from the magnetic cave. Men had narrow escapes of losing themselves, though they were but a few feet from the hut.

When this blizzard cleared the camp was buried, and even on unobstructed surfaces the snowdrifts averaged four feet of additional depth. Two enormous drifts ran down to the sea from either end of the hut. I do not think we ever found some of our stores again, but the larger part we carried up to the higher ground behind us where they remained fairly clear. About this time I began to notice large sheets of anchor ice off the end of Cape Evans, that is to say, ice forming and remaining on the bottom of the open sea. Now also the open water was extending round the cape into the South Bay behind us: but it was too dark to get any reliable idea of the distribution of ice in the Sound. We were afraid that we were cut off from Hut Point, but I do not believe that this was the case; though the open water must have stretched many miles

2. ibid.

to the south in the middle of the Sound. The days when it was clear enough even to potter about outside the hut were exceptional. God was very angry.

> *Sunday, 14 July.* A blizzard during the night, and after breakfast it was drifting a lot. While we were having service some of the men went over the camp to get ice for water. The sea-ice had been blown out of North Bay, and the men supposed that the sea was open, and would look black, but Crean tells me that they nearly walked over the ice-foot, and, when it cleared later, we saw the sea as white as the ice-foot itself. A strip of ice which was lying out in the Bay last night must have been brought in by the tide, even against a wind of some forty miles an hour. This shows what an influence the tides and currents have in comparison with the winds, for just at this time we are having very big tides. It was blowing and drifting all the morning, and the tide was flowing in, pressing the ice in under the ice-foot to such an extent that later it remained there, though the tide was ebbing and a strong southerly was blowing.[3]

Incidentally the bergs which were grounded in our neighbourhood were shifted and broken about considerably by these high winds: also the meteorological screen placed on the Ramp the year before was broken from its upright, which had snapped in the middle, and must have been taken up into the air and so out to sea, for there was no trace of it to be found: Wright lost two doors placed over the entrance to the magnetic cave: when he lifted them they were taken out of his hands by the wind, and disappeared into the air and were never seen again.

So ready was the sea to freeze that there can be little doubt that it already contained large numbers of ice crystals, and time and again I have stood upon the ice-foot watching the tongues of the winds licking up the waters as they roared their way out to sea. Then, with no warning, there would

3. ibid.

come, suddenly and completely, a lull. And there would be a film of ice, covering the surface of the sea, come so quickly that all you could say was that it was not there before and it was there now. And then down would come the wind again and it was gone. Once when the winter had gone and daylight had returned I stood upon the end of the cape, the air all calm around me, and there, half-a-mile away, a full blizzard was blowing: the islands, and even the berg between Inaccessible Island and the cape, were totally obscured in the thickest drift: the top of the drift, which was very distinct, thinned to show dimly the crest of Inaccessible Island: Turk's Head was visible and Erebus quite clear. In fact I was just on the edge of a thick blizzard, blowing down the Strait, the side showing as a perpendicular wall about 500 feet high and travelling, I should say, about 40 miles an hour. A roar came out from it of the wind and waves.

The weather conditions were extraordinarily local, as another experience will show. Atkinson and Dimitri were off to Hut Point with the dogs, carrying biscuit and pemmican for the coming Search Journey: I went with them some way, and then left them to place a flag upon the end of Glacier Tongue for surveying purposes. It was clear and bright, and it was easy to get a sketch of the bearings of the islands from this position, which showed how great a portion of the Tongue must have broken off in the autumn of 1911. I anticipated a pleasant walk home, but was somewhat alarmed when heavy wind and drift came down from the direction of the Hutton Cliffs. Wearing spectacles, and being unable to see without them, I managed to steer with difficulty by the sun which still showed dimly through the drift. It was amazing suddenly to walk out of the wall of drift into light airs at Little Razorback Island. One minute it was blowing and drifting hard and I could see almost nothing, the next it was calm, save for little whirlwinds of snow formed by eddies of air drawn in from the north. In another three hundred yards the wind was blowing from the north. On this day Atkinson found wind force 8 and temperature $-17°$

at Hut Point: at Cape Evans the temperature was zero and men were sitting on the rocks and smoking in the sun. Many instances might be given to show how local our weather conditions often were.

There was a morning some time in the middle of the winter when we awoke to one of our usual tearing blizzards. We had had some days of calm, and the ice had frozen sufficiently for the fish-trap to be lowered again. But that it would not stand much of this wind was obvious, and after breakfast Atkinson stuck out his jaw and said he wasn't going to lose another trap for any dash blizzard. He and Keohane sallied forth on to the ice, lost to our sight immediately in the darkness and drift. They got it, but arrived on the cape in quite a different place, and we were glad to see them back. Soon afterwards the ice blew out.

Much credit is due to the mule leaders that they were able to exercise their animals without hurt. Cape Evans in the dark, strewn with great boulders, with the open sea at your feet, is no easy place to manage a very high-spirited and excitable mule, just out of a warm stable, especially if this is his first outing for several days and the wind is blowing fresh, and you are not sure if your face is frost-bitten, and you are quite sure that your hands are. But the exercise was carried out without mishap. The mules themselves were most anxious to go out, and when Pyaree developed a housemaid's knee and was kept in, she revenged herself upon her more fortunate companions by biting each one hard as it passed her head on its way to and from the door. Gulab was the biggest handful, and Williamson managed him with skill: some of them, especially Lal Khan, were very playful, running round and round their leaders and stopping to paw the ground: Khan Sahib, on the other hand, was bored, yawning continually: it was suggested that he was suffering from polar ennui! Altogether they reflected the greatest credit upon Lashly, who groomed them every day and took the greatest care of them. They were subject to the most violent fits of jealousy, being much disturbed if a rival got undue

465

attention. The dog Vaida, however, was good friends with them all, going down the line and rubbing noses with them in their stalls.

The food of the mules was based upon that given by Oates to the ponies the year before, and the results were successful.

The accommodation given to the dogs in the *Terra Nova* on the way south is open to criticism. As the reader may remember, they were chained on the top of the deck cargo on the main deck, and of course had a horrible time during the gale, and any subsequent bad weather, which did not however last very long. But it was quite impossible to put them anywhere else, for every square inch between decks was so packed that even our personal belongings for more than two years were reduced to one small uniform case. Any seaman will easily understand that to build houses or shelters on deck over and above what we had already was out of the question. As a matter of fact I doubt whether the dogs had a worse time than we during that gale. In good weather at sea, and at all times in the pack, they were comfortable enough. But future explorers might consider whether they can give their dogs more shelter during the winter than we were able to do. Amundsen, whose Winter Quarters were on the Barrier itself, and who experienced lower temperatures and very much less wind than was our lot at Cape Evans, had his dogs in tents, and let them run loose in the camp during the day. Tents would have gone in the winds we experienced, and I have explained that we had no snow in which we could make houses, as was done by Amundsen in the Barrier.

Our more peaceable dogs were allowed to run loose, especially during this last winter, at the beginning of which we also built a dog hospital. We should have liked to loose them all, but if we did so they immediately flew at one another's throats. We might perhaps have let them loose if we had first taken the precaution Amundsen took, and muzzled all of them before doing so. The sport of fighting, so his dogs discovered, lost all its charm when they found they could not taste blood, and they gave it up, and ran about unmuzzled and happy. But the slaughter among the seals and penguins would have been horrible with us, and many dogs might have been carried away on the breaking sea-ice. The tied-up ones lay under the lee of a line of cases, each in his own hole. They curled up quite snugly buried in the snow-drift when blizzards were blowing, and lay exactly in the same way when sledging on the Barrier, the first duty of the dog-driver after pitching his own tent being to dig holes for each of his dogs. It may be that these conditions are more natural to them than any other, and that they are warmer when covered by the drifted snow than they would be in any unwarmed shelter: but this I doubt. At any rate they throve exceedingly under these rigorous conditions, soon becoming fat and healthy after the hardest sledge journeys, and their sledging record is a very fine one. We could not have built them a hut; as it was, we left our magnetic hut, a far smaller affair, in New Zealand, for there was no room to stow it on the ship. I would not advise housing dogs in a hut built with a lean-to roof as an annexe to the main living-hut, but this would be one way of doing it if you are prepared to stand the noise and smell.

The dog-biscuits, provided by Spratt, weighed 8 oz. each, and their sledging ration was 1½ lbs. a day, given to them after they reached the night camp. We made seal pemmican for them and tried this when sledging, as an occasional variation on biscuit, but they did not thrive on this diet. The oil in the biscuits caused purgation, as also did the pemmican: the fat was partly undigested and the excreta were eaten. The ponies also ate their excreta at times. Certain dogs were confirmed leather eaters, and we carried chains for them: on camping, these dogs were taken out of their canvas and raw-hide harnesses, and attached to the sledge by the chains, care being taken that they could not get at the food on the sledge. When sledging, Amundsen gave his dogs pemmican but I do not know what else: he also fed dog to dog: I do not know whether we could have fed dog to dog, for ours were Siberian dogs, which, I am told, will not eat one another. At Amundsen's winter quarters he gave them seal's flesh and blubber one day, and dried fish the next.[4] On the long voyage south in the *Fram*, he fed his dogs on dried fish, and three times a week gave them a porridge of dried fish, tallow, and maize meal boiled together.[5] At Cape Evans or at Hut Point our dogs were given plenty of biscuit some evenings, and plenty of fresh frozen seal at other times.

Our worst trouble with the dogs came from far away – probably from Asia. There are references in Scott's diary to four dogs as attacked by a mysterious disease during our first year in the South: one of these dogs died within two minutes. We lost many more dogs the last year, and Atkinson has given me the following memorandum upon the parasite, a nematode worm, which was discovered later to be the cause of the trouble:

> *Filaria immitis.* A certain proportion of the dogs became infected with this nematode, and it was the cause of their death, mainly in the second year. It was present at the time the expedition started (1910) all down the Pacific side of Asia and Papua, and there was an examination microscopically of all dogs imported at this time into New Zealand. The secondary host is the mosquito *Culex*.
>
> The symptoms varied. The onset was usually with intense pain, during which the animal yelled and groaned: this was cardiac in origin and referable to the presence of the mature form in the beast. There was marked haematuria, and the animals were anaemic from actual loss of haemoglobins. In nearly all cases there was paralysis affecting the hindquarters during the later stages, which tended to spread upwards and finally ended in death.
>
> The probable place of infection was Vladisvostok before the dogs were put on board ship and deported to New Zealand. The only method of coping with the disease is

4. See Amundsen, *The South Pole*, vol. i, p. 264.
5. ibid., vol. i, p. 119.

prevention of infection in infected areas. It is probable that the mosquitoes would not bite after the dog's coat had been rubbed with paraffin: or mosquito netting might be placed over the kennels, especially at night time. The larval forms were found microscopically in the blood, and one mature form in the heart.

We were too careful about killing animals. I have explained how Campbell's party was landed at Evans Coves. Some of the party wanted to kill some seals on the off chance of the ship not turning up to relieve them. This was before they were in any way alarmed. But it was decided that life might be taken unnecessarily if they did this – and that winter this party nearly died of starvation. And yet this country has allowed penguins to be killed by the million every year for Commerce and a farthing's worth of blubber.

We never killed unless it was necessary, and what we had to kill was used to the utmost both for food and for the scientific work in hand. The first Emperor penguin we ever saw at Cape Evans was captured after an exciting chase outside the hut in the middle of a blizzard. He kept us busy for days: the zoologist got a museum skin, showing some variation from the usual coloration, a skeleton, and some useful observation on the digestive glands: the parasitologist got a new tape-worm: we all had a change of diet. Many a pheasant has died for less.

There were plenty of Weddell seal round us this winter, but they kept out of the wind and in the water for the most part. The sea is the warm place of the Antarctic, for the temperature never falls below about 29° Fahr., and a seal which has been lying out on the ice in a minus thirty temperature, and perhaps some wind, must feel, as he slips into the sea, much the same sensations as occur to us when we walk out of a cold English winter day into a heated conservatory. On the other hand, a seaman went out into North Bay to bathe from a boat, in the full sun of a mid-summer day, and he was out almost as soon as he was in.

One of the most beautiful sights of this winter was to see the seals, outlined in phosphorescent light, swimming and hunting in the dark water.

We had lectures, but not as many as during the previous winter when they became rather excessive: and we included outside subjects. We read in many a polar book of the depressions and trials of the long polar night; but thanks to gramophones, pianolas, variety of food, and some study of the needs both of mind and body, we suffered very little from the first year's months of darkness. There is quite a store of novelty in living in the dark: most of us I think thoroughly enjoyed it. But a second winter, with some of your best friends dead, and others in great difficulties, perhaps dying, when all is unknown and every one is sledged to a standstill, and blizzards blow all day and all night, is a ghastly experience. This year there was not one of our company who did not welcome the return of the sun with thankfulness: all the more so since he came back to a land of blizzards and made many of our difficulties more easy to tackle. Those who got little outside exercise were more affected by the darkness than others. This last year, of course, the difficulties of getting sufficient outdoor exercise were much increased. Variety is important to the man who travels in polar regions: at all events those who went away on sledging expeditions stood the life more successfully than those whose duties tied them to the neighbourhood of the hut.

Other things being equal, the men with the greatest store of nervous energy came best through this expedition. Having more imagination, they have a worse time than their more phlegmatic companions; but they get things done. And when the worst came to the worst, their strength of mind triumphed over their weakness of body. If you want a good polar traveller get a man without too much muscle, with good physical tone, and let his mind be on wires – of steel. And if you can't get both, sacrifice physique and bank on will.

NOTE

A lecture given at this time by Wright on Barrier Surfaces is especially interesting with relation to the Winter Journey and the tragedy of the Polar Party. The general tend of friction set up by a sledge-runner upon snow of ordinary temperature may be called true *sliding* friction: it is probable that the runners melt to an infinitesimal degree the millions of crystal points over which they glide: the sledge is running upon water. Crystals in such temperatures are larger and softer than those encountered in low temperatures. It is now that halos may be seen in the snow, almost reaching to your feet as you pull, and moving forward with you: we steered sometimes by keeping these halos at a certain angle to us. My experience is that the best pulling surface is at an air temperature of about +17° Fahr.: Wright's experience is that below +5° during summer temperatures on the Barrier the surface is fairly good, that between +5° and +15° less good, and between +15° and +25° best. The worst is from +25° upwards, the worst of all being round about freezing point.

As the temperature became high the amount of ice melted by this sliding friction was excessive. It was then that we found ice forming upon the runners, often in almost microscopic amounts, but nevertheless causing the sledges to drag seriously. Thus on the Beardmore we took enormous care to keep our runners free from ice, by scraping them at every halt with the back of our knives. This ice is perhaps formed when the runners sink into the snow to an unusual depth, at which the temperature of the snow is sufficiently low to freeze the water previously formed by friction or radiation from the sun on to a dark runner.

In very low temperatures the snow crystals become very small and very hard, so hard that they will scratch the runners. The friction set up by runners in such temperatures may be known as *rolling* friction, and the effect, as experienced by us during the Winter Journey and elsewhere, is much like pulling a sledge over sand. This rolling friction is that of snow crystal against snow crystal.

If the barometer is rising you get flat crystals on the ice, if it is falling you get mirage and a blizzard. When you get mirage the air is actually coming out of the Barrier. Thus far Wright's lecture.

Since we returned I have had a talk with Nansen about the sledge-runners which he recommends to the future explorer. The ideal sledge-runner combines lightness and strength. He tells me that he would always have metal runners in high temperatures in which they will run better than wood. In cold temperatures wood is necessary. Metal is stronger than wood with the same weight. He has never used, but he suggests the possible use of, aluminium or magnesium for the metal. And he would also have wooden runners with metal runners attached, to be used alternately, if needed.

The Discovery Expedition used German silver, and it failed: Nansen suggests that the failure was due to the fact that these runners were fitted at home. The effect of this is that the wood shrinks and the German silver is not quite flat: the fitting should be done on the spot. Nansen did this himself on the *Fram*, and the result was excellent. [I believe that these *Discovery* runners were not a continuous strip of metal but were built up in strips, which tore at the points of junction.] Before it is fitted, German silver should be heated red hot and allowed to cool. This makes it more ductile, like lead, and therefore less springy: the metal should be as thin as possible.

As runners melt the crystals and so run on water, metal is unsuitable for cold snow. For low temperatures, therefore, Nansen would have wooden runners under the metal, the metal being taken off when cold conditions obtained. He would choose such wood as is the best conductor of heat. He tried birch wood in the first crossing of Greenland, but would not recommend it as being too easily broken. In the use of oak, ash, maple, and doubtless also hickory, for runners, the rings of growth of the tree should be as far apart as possible: that is to say, they should be fast growing. Ash with narrow rings breaks. There is ash and ash: American ash is no good for this purpose; some Norwegian ash is useful, and some not. Our own sledges with ash runners varied enormously. The runners of a sledge should curve slightly, the centre being nearest to the snow. The runners of ski should curve also slightly, in this case upwards in the centre, i.e. from the snow. This is done by the way the wood is cut. Wood always dries with the curve from the heart towards the outside of the tree.

During our last year we had six new Norwegian sledges twelve feet long, brought down by the ship, with tapered runners of hickory which were $3\frac{3}{4}$ inches broad in the fore part and $2\frac{1}{4}$ inches only at the stern. I believe that this was an idea of Scott, who considered that the broad runner in front would press down a path for the tapered part which followed, the total area of friction being much less. We took one of them into South Bay one morning and tried it against an ordinary sledge, putting 490 lbs. on each of them. The surface included fairly soft as well as harder and more rubbly going. There was no difference of opinion that the sledge with the tapered runners pulled easier, and later we used these sledges on the Barrier with great success.

If some instrument could be devised to test sledges in this way it would be of very great service. No team of men can make an exact estimate of the run of their own sledge, let alone the sledge which your pony or your dogs are pulling. Yet sledges vary enormously, and it would be an excellent thing for a leader to be able to test his sledges before buying them, and also to be able to pick out the best for his more important sledge journeys. I believe it can be done by attaching some kind of balance between the sledge and the men pulling it.

Other points mentioned by Nansen are as follows:

Tarred ski are good: the snow does not stick so much. [This probably refers to the Norwegian compound known as Fahrt.] But he does not recommend tarred runners for sledges. Having had experience of a tent of Chinese silk which would go into his pocket but was very cold, he recommends a double tent, the inner lining being detached so that ice could be taken from both coverings. He suggests the possibility of a woollen lining being warmer than cotton or silk or linen. I am, however, of opinion that wool would collect more moisture from the cooker, and it certainly would be far more difficult to shake off the ice. For four men he would have two two-men sleeping-bags and a central pole coming down between them, and the floor-cloth made in one piece with the tent. For three men a three-man sleeping-bag: *e.g.* for such a journey as our Winter Journey. He would not brush rime, formed upon the tent by the steam from the cooker and breath, from the inside of tent before striking camp. The more of it the warmer. He considers that two- or three-men sleeping-bags are infinitely warmer than single bags: objections of discomfort are overcome, for you are so tired you go to sleep anyway. I would, however, recommend the explorer to read Scott's remarks upon the same subject before making up his mind.[6]

6. Scott, *Voyage of the Discovery*, vol. i, pp. 480–87.

Chapter Fifteen
ANOTHER SPRING

> O to dream, O to awake and wander
> There, and with delight to take and render,
> Through the trance of silence,
> Quiet breath;
> Lo! for there among the flowers and grasses,
> Only the mightier movement sounds and passes;
> Only winds and rivers,
> Life and death.

THE FLOWERS were of snow, the rivers of ice, and if Stevenson had been to the Antarctic he would have made them so.

God sent His daylight to scatter the nightmares of the darkness. I can remember now the joy of an August day when the sun looked over the rim of the Barne Glacier, and my shadow lay clear-cut upon the snow. It was wonderful what a friendly thing that ice-slope became. We put the first trace upon the sunshine recorder; there was talk of expeditions to Cape Royds and Hut Point, and survey parties; and we ate our luncheons by the daylight which shone through the newly cleared window.

The coming Search Journey was organized to reach the Upper Glacier Depot, and the plans were modelled upon the Polar Journey of the year before. But now we had no extensive depots on the Barrier. It was intended that the dogs should run two trips out to Corner Camp during this spring. It was hoped that two parties of four men each might be able to ascend the Beardmore, one of them remaining about half-way up and doing geological and other scientific work while the other went up to the top.

In our inmost thoughts we were full of doubts and fears.

I had a long talk with Lashly, who asked me what I candidly thought had happened to the Southern Party. I told him a crevasse. He says he does not think so: he thinks it is scurvy. Talking about crevasses he says that, on the return of the Second Return Party, they came right over the ice-falls south of Mount Darwin, – descending about 2000 feet into a great valley, down which they travelled towards the west, and so to the Upper Glacier Depot. I believe Scott told Evans (Lieut.) that he meant to come back this same way.

Then the stuff they got into above the Cloudmaker must have been horrible. 'Why, there are places there you could put St Paul's into, and that's no exaggeration, neither,' and they spent two nights in it. All the way down to the Gateway he says there were crevasses, great big fellows thirty feet across, which we of the First Return Party had crossed both going and coming back and which we never saw. But then much of the snow had gone and they were visible. Lieut. Evans was very badly snowblind most of the time. Then outside the Gateway, on the Barrier, they crossed many crevasses, and some had fallen in where we had passed over them.

This makes one think. Is the state of affairs in which we found the glacier an extraordinary one, the snow being a special phenomenon due to that great blizzard and snowfall? Are we going to find blue ice this year where we found thick soft snow last? Well! I have got a regular bad needle again, just as I have had before. But somehow the needle has always worked off when we get right into it. What a blessing it is that things are seldom as bad in the reality as you expect they are going to be in your imagination: though I must say the Winter Journey was worse even than I had imagined. I remember that this time last year the thought of the Beardmore was very terrible: but the reality was never very bad.

Lashly thinks it would be practically impossible for five men to disappear down a crevasse. Where three men got through (and he said it would be impossible to get worse stuff than they came through), five men would be still better off. This is not my view, however. I think that the extra weight of one man might make all the difference in crossing a big crevasse: and if several men fell through one of those great bridges when sledge and men were all on it, I do not think the bridge would hold the sledge.[1]

Several trips were made to Cape Royds over the Barne Glacier, and then by portaging over the rocks to Shackleton's old hut. The sea was open here, except for small niches of ice, and the hut and the cape were comparatively free from drifts; probably the open water had swallowed the drifting snow. Not so Hut Point, which was surrounded by huge drifts: the verandah which we had built up as a stable was filled from floor to roof: there was no ice-foot to be seen, only a long snow-slope from the door to the sea-level. The hut itself, when we had dug our way into it, was clear. We took down stores for the Search Journey, and brought back with us the only surviving sledge-meter.

These instruments, which indicate by a clock-work arrangement the distance travelled in miles and yards, are actuated by a wheel which runs behind the sledge. They are of the greatest possible use, especially when sledging out of sight of land on the Barrier or Plateau, and we bitterly regretted that we had no more. They do not have an easy time on a glacier, and we lost the mechanism of one of our three Polar Journey meters when on the Beardmore. Dog-driving is hard on them; and pony-driving when the ponies are like Christopher plays the very deuce. Anyway we found we had only one left for this year, and this was more or less a dud. It was mended so far as possible but was never really reliable, and latterly was useless. A lot of trouble was taken by Lashly to make another with a bicycle wheel from one of our experimental trucks, the revolutions of which were marked on a counter which was almost exactly similar to one of our anemometer registers. A bicycle wheel of course stood much higher than our proper sledge-meters, and a difficulty rose in fixing it to the sledge so as to prevent its

1. My own diary.

wobbling and at the same time allow it the necessary amount of play.

Meanwhile the mules were being brought on in condition. With daylight and improved weather they were exercised with loaded sledges on the sea-ice which still remained in South Bay. They went like lambs, and were evidently used to the work. Gulab was a troublesome little animal: he had no objection to pulling a sledge, but was just ultra-timid. Again and again he was got into position for having his traces hitched on, and each time some little thing, the flapping of a mitt, the touch of the trace, or the feel of the bow of the sledge, frightened him and he was off, and the same performance had to be repeated. Once harnessed he was very good. The breast harness sent down for them by the Indian Government was used: it was excellent; though Oates, I believe, had an idea that collars were better. However, we had not got the collars. The mules themselves looked very fit and strong: our only doubt was whether their small hoofs would sink into soft snow even farther than the ponies had done.

No record of this expedition would be complete without some mention of the cases of fire which occurred. The first was in the lazarette of the ship on the voyage to Cape Town: it was caused by an overturned lamp and easily extinguished. The second was during our first winter in the Antarctic, when there was a fire in the motor shed, which was formed by full petrol cases built up round the motors, and roofed with a tarpaulin. This threatened to be more serious, but was also put out without much difficulty. The third and fourth cases were during the winter which had just passed, and were both inside Winter Quarters.

Wright wanted a lamp to heat a shed which he was building out of cases and tarpaulins for certain of his work. He brought a lamp (not a primus) into the hut, and tried to make it work. He spent some time in the morning on this, and after lunch Nelson joined him. The lamp was fitted with an indicator to show the pressure obtained by pumping. Nelson was pumping, kneeling at the end of the table next the bulkhead which divided the officers' and men's quarters:

his head was level with the lamp, and the indicator was not showing a high pressure. Wright was standing close by. Suddenly the lamp burst, a rent three inches long appearing in the join where the bottom of the oil reservoir is fitted to the rest of the bowl. Twenty places were alight immediately, clothing, bedding, papers and patches of burning oil were all over the table and floor. Luckily everybody was in the hut, for it was blowing a blizzard and minus twenty outside. They were very quick, and every outbreak was stopped.

On 5 September it was blowing as if it would rip your wind-clothes off you. We were bagging pemmican in the hut when someone said, 'Can you smell burning?' At first we could not see anything wrong, and Gran said it must be some brown paper he had burnt; but after three or four minutes, looking upwards, we saw that the top of the chimney piping was red hot where it went out through the roof, as was also a large ventilator trap which entered the flue at this point. We put salt down from outside, and the fire seemed to die down, but shortly afterwards the ventilator trap fell on to the table, leaving a cake of burning soot exposed. This luckily did not fall, and we raked it down into buckets. About a quarter of an hour afterwards all the chimney started blazing again, the flames shooting up into the blizzard outside. We got this out by pushing snow in at the top, and holding baths and buckets below to catch the débris. We then did what we ought to have done at the beginning of the winter – took the piping down and cleaned it all out.

Our last fire was a little business. Debenham and I were at Hut Point. I noticed that the place was full of smoke, which was quite usual with a blubber fire, but afterwards we found that the old hut was alight between the two roofs. The inner roof was too shaky to allow one to walk on it, and so, at Debenham's suggestion, we bent a tube which was lying about and syphoned some water up with complete success. Our more usual fire extinguishers were Minimax, and they left nothing to be desired: indeed, all they left were the acid stains on the material touched.

From such grim considerations it is a pleasure to turn to

the out-of-door life we now lead. Emperor penguins began to visit us in companies up to forty in number: probably they were birds whose maternal or paternal instincts had been thwarted at Cape Crozier and had now taken to a vagrant life. They suffered, I am afraid, from the loose dogs, and on one occasion Debenham was out on the sea-ice with a team of those dogs of ours which were useless for serious sledging. He had taken them in hand and formed a team which was very creditable to him, if not to themselves. On this occasion he had managed with great difficulty to restrain them from joining a company of Emperors. The dogs were frantic, the Emperors undisturbed. Unable to go himself, one dog called Little Ginger unselfishly bit through the harness which restrained two of his companions, and Debenham, helplessly holding the straining sledge, could only witness the slaughter which followed.

The first skua gull arrived on 24 October, and we knew they would soon breed on any level gravel or rock free from snow; and we should see the Antarctic petrels again, and perhaps a rare snowy petrel; and the first whales would be finding their way into McMurdo Sound. Also the Wedells, the common coastal seals of the Antarctic, were now, in the beginning of October, leaving the open water and lying out on the ice. They were nearly all females, and getting ready to give birth to their young.

The Weddell seal is black on top, and splashed with silver in other places. He measures up to 10 feet from nose to tail, eats fish, is corpulent and hulking. He sometimes carries four inches of blubber. On the ice he is one of the most sluggish of God's creatures, he sleeps continually, digests huge meals, and grunts, gurgles, pipes, trills and whistles in the most engaging way. In the sea he is transformed into one of the most elastic and lithe of beasts, catching his fish and swallowing them whole. As you stand over his blow-hole his head appears, and he snorts at you with surprise but no fear, opening and shutting his nostrils the while as he takes in a supply of fresh air. It is clear that they travel for many miles beneath the ice, and I expect they find their way from air-hole to air-hole by listening to the noise made by other seals. Some of the air-holes are exit and entrance holes as well, and I found at least one seal which appeared to have died owing to its opening freezing up. They may be heard at times grinding these holes open with their teeth (Ponting took some patient cinematographs showing the process of sawing the openings to these wells) and their teeth are naturally much worn by the time they become old. Wilson states that they are liable to kidney trouble: their skin is often irritable, which may be due to the drying salt from the sea; and I have seen one seal which was covered with a suppurating rash. Their spleens are sometimes enormously enlarged when they first come out of the sea on to the ice, which is interesting because no one seems to know much about spleens. Speculation was caused amongst us by the fact that some of these air-holes had as it were a trap-door above them. One day I was on the ice-foot at Cape Evans at a time when North Bay was frozen over with about an inch or more of ice. A seal suddenly poked his nose up through this ice to get air, and when he disappeared a slab which had been raised by his head fell back into this trap position. Clearly this was the origin of the door.

Weddell seals and the Hut Point life are inextricably mixed up in my recollections of October. Atkinson, Debenham, Dimitri and I went down to Hut Point on the 12th, with the two dog-teams. We were to run two depots out onto the Barrier, and Debenham, whose leg prevented his further sledging, was to do geological work and a plane table survey. Those of us who had borne the brunt of the travelling of the two previous sledge seasons were sick of sledging. For my part I confess I viewed the whole proceedings with distaste, and I have no doubt the others did too; but the job had to be done if possible, and there was no good in saying we were sick of it. From beginning to end of this year men not only laboured willingly, but put their hearts and souls into the work. To have to do another three months' journey seemed bad enough, and to leave our comfortable Winter Quarters three weeks before we started on that journey was an additional irritation. We ran down in surface drift: it was thick to the south, the wind bit our faces and hands; we could see nothing by the time we got in, and the snow was falling heavily. The stable was full of beastly snow, the hut was cold and cheerless, and there was no blubber for the stove. And if we had only taken the ship and gone home when the period for which we had joined was passed, we might have been in London for the last six months!

But then the snow stopped, the wind went down, and the mountain tops appeared in all their glorious beauty. We were in the middle of a perfect summer afternoon, with a warm sun beating on the rocks as we walked round to Pram Point. There were many seals here already, and it was clear that the place would form a jolly nursery this year, for there must have been a lot of movement on the Barrier and the sea-ice was seamed with pressure ridges up to twenty feet in height. The hollows were buckled until the sea water came up and formed frozen ponds which would thaw later into lovely baths. Sheltered from the wind the children could chase their ridiculous tails to their hearts' content: their mothers would lie and sleep, awakening every now and then to scratch themselves with their long finger-nails. Not quite yet, but they were not far away: Lappy, one of our dogs who always looked more like a spaniel than anything else, heard one under the ice and started to burrow down to him.

Nearly three weeks later I paid several more visits to this delightful place. It was thick with seals, big seals and little seals, hairy seals and woolly seals: every day added appreciably to the number of babies, and to the baaings and bleatings which made the place sound like a great sheepfold. In every case where I approached, the mothers opened their mouths and bellowed at me to keep away, but they did not come for me though I actually stroked one baby. Often when the mother bellowed the little one would also open his mouth, producing just the ghost of a bellow: not because he seemed afraid of us, but rather because he thought it was the right thing to do: as indeed it probably was. One old cow was marked with hoops all round her body, like an advertisement of Michelin tyres: only the hoops were but an inch apart from one another, and seemed to be formed by darker and longer bands of hair: probably something to do with the summer moult. Two cows, which scrambled out of the same hole one after the other, were fighting, the hinder one biting the other savagely as she made an ungainly entrance. The first was not in calf, the aggressor, however, was: this may have had something to do with it. They were both much cut about and bleeding.

A seal is never so pretty as when he is a baby. With his grey woolly coat, which he keeps for a fortnight, his comparatively long flippers and tail, and his big dark eyes, he looks very clean and pussy-like. I watched one running round and round after his tail, putting his flipper under his head as a pillow, and scratching himself, seemingly as happy as possible: yet it was pretty cold with some wind.

Little is known of the lighter side of a Weddell's life. It seems probable that their courtship is a ponderous affair. About 26 October Atkinson found an embryo of about a fortnight old, which is an interesting stage, and this was preserved with many others we found, but all of them were too old to be of any real value. I think there is a good deal of variation in the size of the calves at birth. There is certainly much difference between the care of individual mothers, some of which are most concerned when you approach, while others take little notice or lop away from you, leaving their calf to look after itself, or to find another mother. Sometimes they are none too careful not to roll or lie on their calves.

One afternoon I drove a bull seal towards a cow with a calf. The cow went for him bald-headed, with open mouth, bellowing and most disturbed. The bull defended himself as best he might but absolutely refused to take the offensive. The calf imitated his mother as best he could.

Meanwhile Atkinson and Dimitri took some mule-fodder and dog-biscuit to a point twelve miles south of Corner Camp. They started on 14 October with the two dog-teams and found a most terrible surface on the Barrier, the sledges sometimes sinking as far as the 'fore-and-afters'; the minimum temperatures the first two nights were $-39°$ and $-25°$; strong blizzard at Corner Camp; a lie-up for a day and a half, before they could push on in wind and drift and lay the depot. The dogs ran back from Corner Camp to Hut Point on 19 October, a distance of thirty miles. Three miles from Corner Camp three dogs of Atkinson's team fell into a crevasse, one of them falling right down to the length of his harness. The rest of the team, however, pulled on, and dragged the three dogs out as they went. Atkinson lost his driving-stick, which was left standing in the snow and served to mark a place to be avoided. Altogether a rather lucky escape: two men out alone with two dog-teams are somewhat helpless in case of emergency.

On 25 October Dimitri and I started to take a further depot out to Corner Camp with the two dog-teams, pulling about 600 lbs. each. We found a much better surface than that experienced by Atkinson; in places really smooth and hard. 'It is good to be out again in such weather, and it has been a very pleasant day.' The minimum was only $-24°$ that night, and we reached Corner Camp on the afternoon of the next day, following the old tracks where possible, and halting occasionally to hunt when we lost them. 'Here we made the depot and the dogs had a rest of $3\frac{1}{2}$ hours, and two biscuits. It was quaint to see them waiting for more food, for they knew they had not had their full whack.'[2]

There was plenty of evidence that the Barrier had moved a long way during the last year. It had buckled up the sea-ice at Pram Point; there were at least three new and well-marked undulations before reaching Corner Camp; and the camp itself had moved visibly, judged by the bearings and sketches we possessed. I believe the annual movement had not been less than half a mile.

Corner Camp is a well-known trap for blizzards on the line of their exit at Cape Crozier, and it was clouding up, the barometer falling, and the temperature rising rapidly.

2. My own diary.

So we decided to come back some way, and have in the end come right back to the Biscuit Depot, since it looked very threatening to the east. Here the temperature is lower ($-15°$) and it is clearing. Ross Island has been largely obscured, but the clouds are opening on Terror. We had a very good run and the dogs pulled splendidly, making light work of it: 29 miles for the day, half of it with loaded sledges! Lappy's feet are bleeding a good bit, owing to the snow balling in between his toes where the hair is unusually long. Bullet, who is fat and did not pull, celebrated his arrival in camp by going for Bielchik who had pulled splendidly all day! There is much mirage, and Observation Hill and Castle Rock are reversed.[3]

We reached Hut Point the next day. Lappy's feet were still bad, and Dimitri wrapped him in his windproof blouse and strapped him on to the sledge. All went well until we got on to the sea-ice, when Lappy escaped and arrived an easy first.

Dog-driving is the devil! Before I started, my language would not have shamed a Sunday School, and now – if it were not Sunday I would tell you more about it. It takes all kinds to make a world and a dog-team. We had aristocrats like Osman, and Bolsheviks like Krisravitza, and lunatics like Hol-hol. The present-day employer of labour might stand amazed when he saw a crowd of prospective workmen go mad with joy at the sight of their driver approaching them with a harness in his hands. The most ardent trade unionist might boil with rage at the sight of eleven or thirteen huskies dragging a heavy load, including their idle master, over the floe with every appearance of intense joy. But truth to tell there were signs that they were getting rather sick of it, and within a few days we were to learn that dogs can chuck their paws in as well as many another. They had their king, of course: Osman was that. They combined readily and with immense effect against any companion who did not pull his weight, or against one who pulled too much. Dyk was unpopular among them, for when the team of which he was

3. ibid.

a member was halted he constantly whined and tugged at his harness in his eagerness to go on: this did not allow the rest of the team to rest, and they were justifiably resentful. Sometimes a team got a down upon a dog without our being able to discover their doggy reason. In any case we had to watch carefully to prevent them carrying out their intentions, their method of punishment always being the same and ending, if unchecked, in what they probably called justice, and we called murder.

I have referred to the crusts on the Barrier, where the snow lies in layers with an air-space, perhaps a quarter of an inch, or more, between them. These will subside as you pass over them, giving the inexperienced polar traveller some nasty moments until he learns that they are not crevasses. But the dogs thought they were rabbits, and pounced, time after time. There was a little dog called Mukaka, who got dragged under the sledge in one of the mad penguin rushes the dog-teams made when we were landing stores from the *Terra Nova*: his back was hurt and afterwards he died.

> He is paired with a fat, lazy and very greedy black dog, Noogis by name, and in every march this sprightly little Mukaka will once or twice notice that Noogis is not pulling and will jump over the trace, bite Noogis like a snap, and be back again in his own place before the fat dog knows what has happened.[4]

Then there was Stareek (which is the Russian for old man, starouka being old woman). 'He is quite a ridiculous "old man", and quite the nicest, quietest, cleverest old dog I have ever come across. He looks in face as though he knew all the wickedness of all the world and all its cares, and as if he were bored to death by them.'[5] He was the leader of Wilson's team on the Depot Journey, but decided that he was not going out again. Thereafter when he thought there was no one looking

4. Wilson's Journal, *Scott's Last Expedition*, vol. i. p. 616.
5. ibid.

he walked naturally; but if he saw you looking at him he immediately had a frost-bitten paw, limped painfully over the snow, and looked so pitiful that only brutes like us could think of putting him to pull a sledge. We tried but he refused to work, and his final victory was complete.

One more story: Dimitri is telling us how a 'funny old Stareek' at Sydney came and objected to his treatment of the dogs (which were more than half wolves and would eat you without provocation).

'He says to me, "You not whip" – I say, "What ho!" He go and fetch Mr Meares – he try put me in choky. Then he go to Anton – give Anton cigarette and match – he say – "How old that horse?" pointing to Hackenschmidt – Anton say, very young – he not believe – he go try see Hackenschmidt's teeth – and old Starouka too – and Hackenschmidt he draw back and he rush forward and bite old Stareek twice, and he fall backwards over case – and ole woman pick him up. He very white beard which went so – I not see him again.'

Chapter Sixteen
THE SEARCH JOURNEY

Sleep after toyle, port after stormie seas,
Ease after warre, death after life, does greatly please.

SPENSER, *The Faerie Queen*

From my own diary

October 28. Hut Point. A beautiful day. We finished digging
out the stable for the mules this morning and brought in some
blubber this afternoon. The Bluff has its cap on, but otherwise
the sky is nearly clear: there is a little cumulus between White
Island and the Bluff, the first I have seen this year on the
Barrier. It is most noticeable how much snow has disappeared
off the rocks and shingle here.

October 29. Hut Point. The mule party, under Wright,
consisting of Gran, Nelson, Crean, Hooper, Williamson,
Keohane and Lashly, left Cape Evans at 10.30 and arrived
here at 5 p.m. after a good march in perfect weather. They
leave Debenham and Archer at the hut, and I am afraid it will
be dull work for them the next three months. Archer turned
out early and made some cakes which they have brought with
them. They camped for lunch seven miles from Cape Evans.

This is the start of the Search Journey. Everything which
forethought can do has been done, and to a point twelve miles
south of Corner Camp the mules will be travelling light
owing to the depots which have been laid. The barometer
has been falling the last few days and is now low, while the
Bluff is overcast. Yet it does not look like a blizzard to come.
Two Adélie penguins, the first, came to Cape Evans yesterday, and a skua was seen there on the 24th: so summer is
really here.

October 30. Hut Point. It is now 8 p.m., and the mules are
just off, looking very fit, keeping well together, and giving
no trouble at the start. Their leaders turned in this afternoon,
and tonight begins the new routine of night marching, just

the same as last year. It did look thick on the Barrier this afternoon, and it was quite a question whether it was advisable for them to start. But it is rolling away now, being apparently only fog, which is now disappearing before some wind, or perhaps because the sun is losing its power. I think they will have a good march.

November 2, 5 a.m. Biscuit Depot. Atkinson, Dimitri and I, with two dog-teams, left Hut Point last night at 8.30. We have had a coldish night's run, −21° when we left after lunch, −17° now. The surface was very heavy for the dogs, there being a soft coating of snow over everything since we last came this way, due no doubt to the foggy days we have been having lately. The sledge-meter makes it nearly 16 miles.

The mule party has two days' start on us, and their programme is to do twelve miles a day to One Ton Depot. Their tracks are fairly clear, but there has been some drift from the east since they passed. We picked up our cairns well. We are pretty wet, having been running nearly all the way.

November 3. Early morning. 14½ miles. We are here at Corner Camp, but not without a struggle. We left the Biscuit Depot at 6.30 p.m. yesterday, and it is now 4 a.m. The last six miles took us four hours, which is very bad going for dogs, and we have all been running most of the way. The surface was very bad, crusty and also soft: it was blowing with some low drift, and overcast and snowing. We followed the drifted-up mule tracks with difficulty and are lucky to have got so far. The temperature has been a constant zero.

There is a note here from Wright about the mules, which left here last night. They only saw two small crevasses on the way, but Khan Sahib got into the tide-crack at the edge of the Barrier, and had to be hauled out with a rope. The mules are going fast over the first part of the day, but show a tendency to stop towards the end: they keep well together except Khan Sahib, who is a slower mule than the others. It is now blowing with some drift, but nothing bad, and beyond the Bluff it seems to be clear. We are all pretty tired.

November 4. *Early morning*. Well! this has been a disappointing day, but we must hope that all will turn out well. We turned out at 2 a.m. yesterday and then it was clearing all round, a mild blizzard having been blowing since we camped. We started at five in some wind and low drift. It was good travelling weather, and except for the first three miles the surface has been fair to good, and the last part very good. Yet the dogs could not manage their load, which according to programme should go up a further 150 lbs. each team here at Dimitri Depot. One of our dogs, Kusoi, gave out, but we managed to get him along tied to the stern of the sledge, because the team behind tried to get at him and he realized he had better mend his ways. We camped for lunch when Tresor also was pretty well done. We were then on a very good surface, but were often pushing the sledge to get it along. The mule party were gone when we started again, and probably did not see us. We came on to the depot, but we cannot hope to get along far on bad surfaces if we cannot get along on good ones. The note left by Wright states that their sledge-meter has proved useless, and this leaves all three parties of us with only one, which is not very reliable now.

So it has been decided that the dogs must return from 80° 30', or 81° at the farthest, and instead of four mules, as was intended, going on from there, five must go on instead. The dogs can therefore now leave behind much of their own weights and take on the mules' weights instead. And this is the part where the mules' weights are so heavy. Perhaps the new scheme is the best, but it puts everything on the mules from 80° 30': if they will do it all is well: if they won't we have nothing to fall back on.

Midnight, November 4–5. It has been blowing and drifting all day. We turned out again at midday on the 4th, and re-made the depot with what we were to leave owing to the new programme. This is all rather sad, but it can't be helped. It was then blowing a summer blizzard, and we were getting frost-bitten when we started, following the mule tracks. There were plenty of cairns for us to pick up, and with the lighter loads and a very good surface we came along much better. Lunching at eight miles we arrived just as the mule party had finished their hoosh preparatory to starting, and it has been decided that the mules are not to go on tonight, but we will all start marching together tomorrow.

The news from this party is on the whole good, not the least good being that the sledge-meter is working again, though not very reliably. They are marching well, and at a great pace, except for Khan Sahib. Gulab, however, is terribly chafed both by his collar and by his breast harness, both of which have been tried. He has a great raw place where this fits on one side, and is chafed, but not so badly, on the other side. Lal Khan is pulling well, but is eating very little. Pyaree is doing very well, but has some difficulty in lifting her leg when in soft snow. Abdullah seems to be considered the best mule at present. On the whole good hearing.

Wright's sleeping-bag is bad, letting in light through cracks in a good many places. But he makes very little of it and does not seem to be cold – saying it is good ventilation. The mule cloths, which have a rough lining to their outside canvas, are collecting a lot of snow, and all the mules are matted with cakes of snow. They are terrible rope-eaters, cloth-eaters, anything to eat, though they are not hungry. And they have even learnt to pull their picketing buckles undone, and go walking about the camp. Indeed Nelson says that the only time when Khan Sahib does not cast himself adrift is when he is ready to start on the march.

November 6. Early morning. We had a really good lie-in yesterday, and after the hard slogging with the dogs during the last few days I for one was very glad of it. We came on behind, and in sight of the mules this last march, and the change in the dogs was wonderful. Where it had been a job to urge them on over quite as good a surface yesterday, today for some time we could not get off the sledge except for short runs: although we had taken 312 lbs. weight off the mules and loaded it on to the dogs.

We had a most glorious night for marching, and it is now bright sunlight, and the animals' fur is quite warm where the sun strikes it. We have just had a bit of a fight over the dog-food, Vaida going for Dyk, and now the others are somewhat excited, and there are constant growlings and murmurings.

The camp makes more of a mark than last year, for the mules are dark while the ponies were white or grey, and the cloths are brown instead of light green. The consequence is that the camp shows up from a long distance off. We are building cairns at regular distances, and there should be no difficulty in keeping on the course in fair weather at any rate. Now in the land of big sastrugi. Erebus is beginning to look small, but we could see an unusually big smoke from the crater all day.

November 7. Early morning. Not an easy day. It was −9° and overcast when we turned out, and the wind was then dying down, but it had been blowing up to force 5, with surface drift during the day. We started in a bad light and the surface, which was the usual hard surface common here, with big sastrugi, was covered by a thin layer of crystals which were then falling. This naturally made it very much harder pulling: we with the dogs have been running nearly all the twelve miles, and I for one am tired. At lunch Atkinson thought he saw a tent away to our right, – the very thought of it came as a shock, – but it proved to be a false alarm. We have been keeping a sharp look-out for the gear which was left about this part by the Last Return Party, but have seen no sign of it.

It is now −14°, but the sun is shining brightly in a clear sky, and it feels beautifully warm. It seems a very regular thing for the sky to cloud over as the sun gets low towards nightfall – and directly the sun begins to rise again the clouds disappear in a most wonderful way.

November 8. Early morning. Last night's twelve miles was quite cold for the time of year, being −23° at lunch and now −18°. But it is calm, with bright sun, and this temperature feels warm. However, there are some frost-bites as a result, both Nelson and Hooper having swollen faces. The same powder and crystals have been on the surface, but we have carried the good Bluff surface so far, being now four miles beyond Bluff Depot. This is fortunate, and to the best of my recollection we were already getting on to a soft surface at this point last summer. If so there must have been more wind here this year than last, which, according to the winter we have had, seems probable.

We made up the Bluff Depot after lunch, putting up a new flag and building up the cairn, leaving two cases of dog-biscuit for the returning dog-teams. It is curious that the drift to leeward of the cairn, that is N.N.E., was quite soft, the snow all round and the drifts on either side being hard – exceptionally hard in fact. Why this drift should remain soft when a drift in the same place is usually hard is difficult to explain. All is happy in the mule camp. They have given Lal a drink of water and he has started to eat, which is good news. Some of the mules seem snow-blind, and they are now all wearing their blinkers. I have just heard that Gran swung the thermometer at four this morning and found it −29°. Nelson's face is a sight – his nose a mere swollen lump, frost-bitten cheeks, and his goggles have frosted him where the rims touched his face. Poor Marie!

November 9. Early morning. Twelve more miles to the good, and we must consider ourselves fortunate in still carrying on the same good surface, which is almost if not quite as good as that of yesterday. This is the only time I have ever seen a hard surface here, not more than fifteen miles from One Ton, and it looks as if there had been much higher winds. The sastrugi, which have been facing S.W., are now beginning to run a little more westerly. I believe this to be quite a different wind circulation from Ross Island, which as a whole gets its wind from the Bluff. The Bluff is, I believe, the dividing line, though big general blizzards sweep over the whole, irrespective of local areas of circulation. This was amply corroborated by our journey out here last autumn. Well, this is better than then – just round here we had a full blizzard and −33°.

November 10. Early morning. A perfect night for marching, but about −20° and chilly for waiting about. The mules are going well, but Lal Khan is thinning down a lot: Abdullah and Khan Sahib are also off their feed. Their original allow-ance of 11 lbs. oats and oil cake has been reduced to 9 lbs., and they are not eating this. The dogs took another 300 lbs. off them today, and pulled it very well. The surface has been splendidly hard, which is most surprising. Wright does not think that there has been an abnormal deposition of snow the last winter; he says it is about $1\frac{1}{2}$ feet, which is much the same as last year. The mules are generally not sinking in more than two inches, but in places, especially latterly, they have been in five or six. This is the first we have had this year of crusts, and some of them today have been exceptionally big: two at lunch must have lasted several seconds. The dogs seem to think the devil is after them when one of these goes off, and put on a terrific spurt. It is interesting to watch them snuffing in the hoof-marks of the mules, where there is evidently some scent left. In these temperatures they are always kicking their legs about at the halts. As the sun gained power this morning a thick fog came up very suddenly. I believe this is a sign of good weather.

November 11. Early morning. One Ton Depot. Wright got a latitude sight yesterday putting us six miles from One Ton, and our sledge-meter shows $5\frac{3}{4}$, and here we are. More frost-bite this morning, and it was pretty cold starting in a fair wind and $-7°$ temperature. We have continued this really splendid surface, and now the sastrugi are pointing a little more to the south of S.W. While there are not such big mounds, the surface does not yet show any signs of getting bad. There were the most beautiful cloud-effects as we came along – a deep black to the west, shading into long lines of grey and lemon yellow round the sun, with a vertical shaft through them, and a bright orange horizon. Now there is a brilliant parhelion. Given sun, two days here are never alike. Whatever the monotony of the Barrier may be, there is endless variety in the sky, and I do not believe that anywhere in the world such beautiful colours are to be seen.

I had a fair panic as we came up to the depot. I did not see that one body of the ponies had gone head of the others and camped, but ahead of the travelling ponies was the depot, looking very black, and I thought that there was a tent. It would be too terrible to find that, though one knew that we had done all that we could, if we had done something different we could have saved them.

And then we find that the provisions we left here for them in the tank are soaked with paraffin. How this has happened is a mystery, but I think that the oil in the XS tin, which was very full, must have forced its way out in a sudden rise of temperature in a winter blizzard, and though the tin was not touching the tank, it has found its way in.

Altogether things seemed rather dismal, but a visit to the mules is cheering, for they seem very fit as a whole and their leaders are cheerful. There are three sacks of oats here – had we known it would have saved a lot of weight – but we didn't, and we have plenty with what we have brought, so they will be of little use to us. There is no compressed fodder, which would have been very useful, for the animals which are refusing the oats would probably eat it.

Gulab has a very bad chafe, but he is otherwise fit – and it does not seem possible in this life to kill a mule because of chafing. It is a great deal to know that he does not seem to be hurt by it, and pulls away gallantly. Crean says he had to run a mile this morning with Rani. Marie says he is inventing some new ways of walking, one step forward and one hop back, in order to keep warm when leading Khan Sahib. Up to date we cannot say that the Fates have been unkind to us.

November 12. Early morning. Lunch 2.30 a.m. I am afraid our sledge-meters do not agree over this morning's march. The programme is to do thirteen miles a day if possible from here: that is 7½ before lunch and 5½ afterwards. We could see two cairns of last year on our right as we came along. We have got on to a softer surface now, and there is bad news of Lal Khan, and it will depend on this after-lunch march whether he must be shot this evening or not. It was intended to shoot a mule two marches from One Ton, but till just lately it had not been thought that it must be Lal Khan. He is getting very slow, and came into camp with Khan Sahib: the trouble of course is that he will not eat: he has hardly eaten, they say, a day's ration since he left Hut Point, and he can't work on nothing. It is now −16°, with a slight southerly wind.

Nearly midday. 11–12 miles south of One Ton. We have found them – to say it has been a ghastly day cannot express it – it is too bad for words. The tent was there, about half-a-mile to the west of our course, and close to a drifted-up cairn of last year. It was covered with snow and looked just like a cairn, only an extra gathering of snow showing where the ventilator was, and so we found the door.

It was drifted up some 2–3 feet to windward. Just by the side two pairs of ski sticks, or the topmost half of them, appeared over the snow, and a bamboo which proved to be the mast of the sledge.

Their story I am not going to try and put down. They got to this point on 21 March, and on the 29th all was over.

Nor will I try and put down what there was in that tent. Scott lay in the centre, Bill on his left, with his head towards the door, and Birdie on his right, lying with his feet towards the door.

Bill especially had died very quietly with his hands folded over his chest. Birdie also quietly.

Oates's death was a very fine one. We go on tomorrow to try and find his body. He was glad that his regiment would be proud of him.

They reached the Pole a month after Amundsen.

We have everything – records, diaries, etc. They have among other things several rolls of photographs, a meteorological log kept up to 13 March, considering all things, a great many geological specimens. *And they have stuck to everything.* It is magnificent that men in such case should go on pulling everything that they have died to gain. I think they realized their coming end a long time before. By Scott's head was tobacco: there is also a bag of tea.

Atkinson gathered everyone together and read to them the account of Oates's death given in Scott's diary: Scott expressly states that he wished it known. His (Scott's) last words are:

'For God's sake take care of our people.'

Then Atkinson read the lesson from the Burial Service from Corinthians. Perhaps it has never been read in a more magnificent cathedral and under more impressive circumstances – for it is a grave which kings must envy. Then some prayers from the Burial Service: and there with the floor-cloth under them and the tent above we buried them in their sleeping-bags – and surely their work has not been in vain.[1]

That scene can never leave my memory. We with the dogs had seen Wright turn away from the course by himself and the mule party swerve right-handed ahead of us. He had seen what he thought was a cairn, and then something looking black by its side. A vague kind of wonder gradually gave way to a real alarm. We came up to them all halted. Wright came across to us. 'It is the tent.' I do not know how he knew. Just a waste of snow: to our right the remains of one of last year's cairns, a mere mound: and then three feet of bamboo sticking quite alone out of the snow: and then another mound, of snow, perhaps a trifle more pointed. We walked up to it. I do not think we quite realized – not for very long – but someone reached up to a projection of snow, and brushed it away. The green flap of the ventilator of the tent appeared, and we knew that the door was below.

Two of us entered, through the funnel of the outer tent, and through the bamboos on which was stretched the lining of the inner tent. There was some snow – not much – between the two linings. But inside we could see nothing – the snow had drifted out the light. There was nothing to do but to dig the tent out. Soon we could see the outlines. There were three men here.

Bowers and Wilson were sleeping in their bags. Scott had thrown back the flaps of his bag at the end. His left hand was stretched over Wilson, his lifelong friend. Beneath the head of his bag, between the bag and the floor-cloth, was the green wallet in which he carried his diary. The brown books of diary were inside: and on the floor-cloth were some letters.

Everything was tidy. The tent had been pitched as well as ever, with the door facing down the sastrugi, the bamboos with a good spread, the tent itself taut and ship-shape. There was no snow inside the inner lining. There were some loose pannikins from the cooker, the ordinary tent gear, the

1. My own diary.

497

personal belongings and a few more letters and records – personal and scientific. Near Scott was a lamp formed from a tin and some lamp wick off a finnesko. It had been used to burn the little methylated spirit which remained. I think that Scott had used it to help him to write up to the end. I feel sure that he had died last – and once I had thought that he would not go so far as some of the others. We never realized how strong that man was, mentally and physically, until now.

We sorted out the gear, records, papers, diaries, spare clothing, letters, chronometers, finnesko, socks, a flag. There was even a book which I had lent Bill for the journey – and he had brought it back. Somehow we learnt that Amundsen had been to the Pole, and that they too had been to the Pole, and both items of news seemed to be of no importance whatever. There was a letter there from Amundsen to King Haakon. There were the personal chatty little notes we had left for them on the Beardmore – how much more important to us than all the royal letters in the world.

We dug down the bamboo which had brought us to this place. It led to the sledge, many feet down, and had been rigged there as a mast. And on the sledge were some more odds and ends – a piece of paper from the biscuit box: Bowers's meteorological log: and the geological specimens, thirty pounds of them, all of the first importance. Drifted over also were the harnesses, ski and ski-sticks.

Hour after hour, so it seemed to me, Atkinson sat in our tent and read. The finder was to read the diary and then it was to be brought home – these were Scott's instructions written on the cover. But Atkinson said he was only going to read sufficient to know what had happened – and after that they were brought home unopened and unread. When he had the outline we all gathered together and he read to us the Message to the Public, and the account of Oates's death, which Scott had expressly wished to be known.

We never moved them. We took the bamboos of the tent away, and the tent itself covered them. And over them we built the cairn.

I do not know how long we were there, but when all was finished, and the chapter of Corinthians had been read, it was midnight of some day. The sun was dipping low above the Pole, the Barrier was almost in shadow. And the sky was blazing – sheets and sheets of iridescent clouds. The cairn and Cross stood dark against a glory of burnished gold.

Copy of Note left at the Cairn over the Bodies

12 November, 1912.
Lat. 79° 50′ S.

This Cross and Cairn are erected over the bodies of Capt. Scott, C.V.O., R.N.; Dr E. A. Wilson, M.B., B.A. Cantab.: Lt. H. R. Bowers, Royal Indian Marines. A slight token to perpetuate their gallant and successful attempt to reach the Pole. This they did on the 17th January 1912 after the Norwegian expedition had already done so. Inclement weather and lack of fuel was the cause of their death.

Also to commemorate their two gallant comrades, Capt. L. E. G. Oates of the Inniskilling Dragoons, who walked to his death in a blizzard to save his comrades, about 18 miles south of this position; also of Seaman Edgar Evans, who died at the foot of the Beardmore Glacier.

The Lord gave and the Lord taketh away. Blessed be the name of the Lord.

Relief Expedition.
(Signed by all members of the party.)

My diary goes on:

Midnight, November 12–13. I cannot think that anything which could be done to give these three great men – for great they were – a fitting grave has been left undone.

A great cairn has been built over them, a mark which must last for many years. That we can make anything that will be permanent on this Barrier is impossible, but as far as a lasting mark can be made it has been done. On this a cross has been fixed, made out of ski. On either side are the two sledges, fixed upright and dug in.

The whole is very simple and most impressive.

On a bamboo standing by itself is left the record which I have copied into this book, and which has been signed by us all.

We shall leave some provisions here, and go on lightly laden to see if we can find Titus Oates's body: and so give it what burial we can.

We start in about an hour, and I for one shall be glad to leave this place.

I am very very sorry that this question of the shortage of oil has arisen. We in the First Return Party were most careful with our measurement – having a ruler of Wright's and a piece of bamboo with which we did it: measuring the total height of oil in each case, and then dividing up the stick accordingly with the ruler: and we were *always* careful to take *a little less than we were entitled to*, which was stated to me, and stated by Birdie in his depot notes, to be one-third of everything in the depot.

How the shortage arose is a mystery. And they eleven miles from One Ton and plenty!

Titus did not show his foot till about three days before he died. The foot was then a great size, and almost every night it would be frost-bitten again. Then the last day at lunch he said he could go on no more – but they said he must: he wanted them to leave him behind in his bag. That night he turned in, hoping never to wake: but he woke, and then he asked their advice: they said they must all go on together. A thick blizzard was blowing, and he said, after a bit, 'Well, I am just going outside, and I may be some time.' They searched for him but could not find him.

They had a terrible time from 80° 30′ on to their last camp. There Bill was very bad, and Birdie and the Owner had to do the camping.

And then, eleven miles from plenty, they had *nine days of blizzard, and that was the end.*

They had a good spread on their tent, and their ski-sticks were standing, but their ski were drifted up on the ground.

The tent was in excellent condition – only down some of the poles there were some chafes.

They had been trying a spirit lamp when all the oil was gone.

At 88° or so they were getting temperatures from −20° to −30°. At 82°, 10,000 feet lower, it was regularly down to −47° in the night-time, and −30° during the day: for no explainable reason.

Bill's and Birdie's feet got bad – the Owner's feet got bad last.

It is all too horrible – I am almost afraid to go to sleep now.

November 13. *Early morning.* We came on just under seven miles with a very cold moist wind hurting our faces all the way. We have left most of the provisions to pick up again. We purpose going on thirteen miles tomorrow and search for Oates's body, and then turn back and get the provisions back to Hut Point and see what can be done over in the west to get up that coast.

We hope to get two mules back to Hut Point. If possible, we want to communicate with Cape Evans.

Atkinson has been quite splendid in this very trying time.

November 14. *Early morning.* It has been a miserable march. We had to wait some time after hoosh to let the mules get ahead. Then we went on in a cold raw fog and some head wind, with constant frost-bites. The surface has been very bad all day for the thirteen miles: if we had been walking in arrowroot it would have been much like this was. At lunch the temperature was −14.7°.

Then on when it was drifting with the wind in our faces and in a bad light. What we took to be the mule party ahead proved to be the old pony walls 26 miles from One Ton. There was here a bit of sacking on the cairn, and Oates's bag. Inside the bag was the theodolite, and his finnesko and socks. One of the finnesko was slit down the front as far as the leather beckets, evidently to get his bad foot into it. This was fifteen miles from the last camp, and I suppose they had brought on his bag for three or four miles in case they might find him still alive. Half-a-mile from our last camp there was a very large and quite unmistakable undulation, one-quarter to one-third of a mile from crest to crest: the pony walls behind us disappeared almost as soon as we started to go down, and reappeared again on the other side. There were, I feel sure, other rolls, but this was the largest. We have seen no sign of Oates's body.

About half an hour ago it started to blow a blizzard, and it is now thick, but the wind is not strong. The mules, which came along well considering the surface, are off their feed, and this may be the reason.

Dimitri saw the Cairn with the Cross more than eight miles away this morning, and in a good light it would be seen from much farther off.

November 15. Early morning. We built a cairn to mark the spot near which Oates walked out to his death, and we placed a cross on it. Lashed to the cross is a record, as follows:

> Hereabouts died a very gallant gentleman, Captain L. E. G. Oates of the Inniskilling Dragoons. In March 1912, returning from the Pole, he walked willingly to his death in a blizzard to try and save his comrades, beset by hardship. This note is left by the Relief Expedition. 1912.

This was signed by Atkinson and myself.

We saw the cairn for a long way in a bad light as we came back today.

The original plan with which we started from Cape Evans was, if the Party was found where we could still bear out sufficiently to the eastward to have a good chance of missing the pressure caused by the Beardmore, to go on and do what we could to survey the land south of the Beardmore: for this was the original plan of Captain Scott for this year's sledging. But as things are I do not think there can be much doubt that we are doing right in losing no time in going over to the west of McMurdo Sound to see whether we can go up to Evans Coves, and help Campbell and his party.

We brought on Oates's bag. The theodolite was inside.

A thickish blizzard blew all day yesterday, but it was clear and there was only surface drift when we turned out for the night march. Then again as we came along, the sky became overcast – all except over the land, which remains clear these nights when everything else is obscured. We noticed the same thing last year. Now the wind, which had largely dropped, has started again and it is drifting. We have had wind and drift on four out of the last five days.

November 16. *Early morning.* When we were ready to start with the dogs it was blowing a thick blizzard, but the mules had already started some time, when it was not thick. We had to wait until nearly 4 a.m. before we could start, and came along following tracks. It is very warm and the surface is covered with loose snow, but the slide in it seems good. We found the mules here at the Cairn and Cross, having been able to find their way partly by the old tracks.

I have been trying to draw the grave. Of all the fine monuments in the world none seems to me more fitting; and it is also most impressive.

November 17. *Early morning.* I think we are all going crazy together – at any rate things are pretty difficult. The latest scheme is to try and find a way over the plateau to Evans Coves, trying to strike the top of a glacier and go down it. There can be no good in it: if ever men did it, they would arrive about the time the ship arrived there too, and their labour would be in vain. If they got there and the ship did not arrive, there is another party stranded. They would have to wait till February 15 or 20 to see if the ship was coming, and then there would be no travelling back over the plateau: even if we could do it those men there could not.

It was almost oppressively hot yesterday – but I'll never grumble about heat again. It has now cleared a lot and we came along on the cairns easily – but on a very soft downy surface, and the travelling has not been fast. We bring with us the Southern Party's gear. The sledge, which was the 10-foot which they brought on from the bottom of the glacier, has been left.

November 18. *Early morning.* I am thankful to say that the plateau journey idea has been given up.

Once more we have come along in thick, snowy weather. If we had not men on ski to steer we could never keep much of a course, but Wright is steering us very straight, keeping a check on the course by watching the man behind, and so far we have been picking up all the cairns. This morning we passed the pony walls made on 10 November. And yet they were nearly level with the ground; so they are not much of a mark. Yank has just had a disagreement with Kusoi – for Kusoi objected to his trying to get at the meat on the sledge. The mules have been sinking in a long way, and are marching very slowly. Pyaree eats the tea-leaves after meals: Rani and Abdullah divide a rope between them at the halts; and they have eaten the best part of a trace since our last camp. These animals eat anything but their proper food, and this some of them will hardly touch.

It cleared a bit for our second march, and we have done our 13 miles, but it was very slow travelling. Now it is drifting as much as ever. Yank, that redoubtable puller, has just eaten himself loose for the third time since hoosh. This time I had to go down to the pony walls to get him.

We have had onions for the first time tonight in our hoosh – they are most excellent. Also we have been having some Nestlés condensed milk from One Ton Depot – which I do not want to see again, the depot I mean. Peary must know what he is about, taking milk as a ration: the sweetness is a great thing, but it would be heavy: we have been having it with temperature down to −14°, when it was quite manageable, but I don't know what it would be like in colder temperatures.

November 19. *Early morning.* We have done our 13 miles today and have got on to a much better surface. By what we and others have seen before, it seems that last winter must have generally been an exceptional one. There have been many parties out here: we have never before seen this windswept surface, on which it is often too slippery to walk comfortably. I do not know what temperatures the *Discovery* had in April, but it was much colder last April than it was the year before. And then nothing had been experienced down here to compare with the winds last winter.

There was a high wind and a lot of drift yesterday during the day, and now it is blowing and drifting as usual. During the last nine days there has only been one, the day we found the tent, when it has not been drifting during all or part of the day. It is all right for travelling north, but we should be having very uncomfortable marches if we were marching the other way.

November 20. *Early morning.* Today we have seemed to be walking in circles through space. Wright, by dint of having a man behind to give him a fixed point to steer upon, has steered us quite straight, and we have picked up every cairn. The pony party camped for lunch by two cairns, but they never knew the two cairns were there until a piece of paper blew away and had to be fetched: and it was caught against one of the cairns. They left a flag there to guide us, and though we saw and brought along the flag, we never saw the cairns. The temperature is −22.5°, and it is now blowing a full blizzard. All this snow has hitherto been lying on the ground and making a very soft surface, for though the wind has always been blowing it has never been very strong. This snow and wind, which have now persisted for nine out of the last ten days, make most dispiriting marches; for there is nothing to see, and finding tracks or steering is a constant strain. We are certainly lucky to have been able to march as we have.

Notes on Mules. The most ardent admirer of mules could not say that they were a success. The question is whether they might be made so. There was really only one thing against them but that is a very important one – they would not eat on the Barrier. From the time they went away to the day they returned (those that did return, poor things) they starved themselves, and yet they pulled biggish loads for 30 days.

If they would have eaten they would have been a huge success. They travelled faster than the ponies and, with one exception, kept together better than the ponies. If both were eating their ration it is questionable whether a good mule or a good pony is to be preferred. Our mules were of the best, and they were beautifully trained and equipped by the Indian Government: yet on 13 November, a fortnight from the start, Wright records, 'mules are a poor substitute for ponies. Not many will see Hut Point again, I think. Doubt if any would have got much farther than this if surfaces had been as bad this year as last.'[2]

Though they would not eat oats, compressed fodder and oil-cake, they were quite willing to eat all kinds of other things. If we could have arrived at the mule equivalent to a vegetarian diet they might have pulled to the Beardmore without stopping. The nearest to this diet at which we could arrive was saennegrass, tea-leaves, tobacco ash and rope – all of which were eaten with gusto. But supplies were very limited. They ate dog-biscuit as long as they thought we were not looking – but as soon as they realized they were meant to eat it they went on hunger-strike again. But during halts at cairns Rani and Pyaree would stand solemnly chewing the same piece of rope from different ends. Abdullah always led the line, and followed Wright's ski tracks faithfully, so that if another man was ahead and Wright turned aside Abdullah always turned too. It was quite a manoeuvre for Wright to read the sledge-meter at the back of the sledge. As for Begum: 'Got Begum out of a soft patch by rolling her over.'[3]

On the whole the mules failed to adapt themselves to this life, and as such must at present be considered to be a failure for Antarctic work. Certainly those of our ponies which had the best chance to adapt themselves went farthest,

2. Wright's diary.   3. ibid.

such as Nobby and Jimmy Pigg, both of whom had experience of Barrier sledging before they started on the Polar Journey.

November 21. Early morning. It has cleared at last, the disturbance rolling away to the east during our first march. The surface was very bad and the mules were not going well. At this time last year many of the ponies were still quite difficult to make stand just before starting. But these mules start off now most dolefully. I am afraid they will not all get back to Hut Point.

Two and a half miles after lunch, i.e. just over forty miles from the depot, we turned out to the eastward and found the gear left by the Second Return Party, when Evans was so ill. The theodolite, which belonged to Evans, is I believe there, but though we dug all round we were unable to find it. The ski were all upright, drifted to within six inches of the shoes. Most of the gear was clothing, which we have left, with the skis, in the tank. We brought on a roll of Birdie's photographs, taken on the plateau, and three geological specimens: deep-seated rocks I think. This was all of importance that there was there.

The N Ration, which we have now come to, consists of about 40 oz. of food. At present, doing the work we are doing, and with these high temperatures, $-23°$ when we started, for instance, and $-17°$ now, the men do not want it. For what it was intended for, hard man-hauling, it would probably be an excellent ration, and very satisfying.

November 22. Early morning. We could not have had a more perfect night to march. Yesterday at 4 p.m., holding the thermometer in the sun, the spirit rose to 30°: it was almost too warm in the tent. The cairns show very plainly – in such weather navigation of this kind would be dead easy. But they are already being eaten away and toppling. The pony walls are drifted level – huge drifts, quite hard, running up to windward and down to lee.

The dogs are getting more hungry, and want to get at the mules, which makes them go better. They went very well today, but too fast once, for we had a general mix-up: Bieliglass under the sledge and the rest all tangled up and ready for a fight at the first chance. How one of the front pair of dogs got under the sledge is a mystery.

Among the Polar Party's gear is a letter to the King of Norway. It was left by the Norwegians for Scott to take back. It is wrapped in a piece of thin windcloth with one dark check line in it. Coarser and rougher and, I should say, heavier than our Mandelbergs.

November 23. Early morning. We were to make Dimitri Depot this morning, but we came on in a fog, and the mule party camped after running down the distance. Wright came back and said, 'If we have passed it, it's over there' – and as he pointed the depot showed – not more than 200 yards away. So that is all right. We, the dog party, go on in advance tomorrow, so that no time may be lost, and if the ice is still good, Atkinson will get over to Cape Evans.

November 24. Early morning. A glut of foot-walloping in soft snow and breaking crusts. We have done between 17 and 18 miles today. We saw no crevasses, and have marked the course well, building up the cairns and leaving two flags – so the mule party should be all right. The dogs were going well behind the ponies, but directly we went ahead they seemed to lose heart. I think they are tired of the Barrier: a cairn now awakens little interest: they know it is only a mark and it does not mean a camp: they are all well fed, and fairly fat and in good condition. With a large number of dogs I suppose one team can go ahead when it is going well – changing places with another – each keeping the others going. But I do not think that these dogs now will do much more; but they have already done as much as any dogs of which we have any record.

The land is clearing gradually. I have never seen such contrasts of black rock and white snow, and White Island was capped with great ranges of black cumulus, over which rose the pure white peaks of the Royal Society Range in a blue sky. The Barrier itself was quite a deep grey, making a beautiful picture. And now Observation Hill and Castle Rock are in front. I don't suppose I shall ever see this view again: but it is associated with many memories of returning to home and plenty after some long and hard journeys: in some ways I feel sorry – but I have seen it often enough.

November 25. Early morning. We came in 24 miles with our loads, to find the best possible news – Campbell's Party, all well, are at Cape Evans. They arrived here on 6 November, starting from Evans Coves on 30 September. What a relief it is, and how different things seem now! It is the first real bit of good news since February last – it seems an age. We mean to get over the sea-ice, if possible, as soon as we can, and then we shall hear their story.

November 26. Early morning. Starting from Hut Point about 6.45 p.m. last evening, we came through by about 9 p.m., and sat up talking and hearing all the splendid news till past 2 a.m. this morning.

All the Northern Party look very fat and fit, and they are most cheerful about the time they have had, and make light of all the anxious days they must have spent and their hard times.

I cannot write all their story. When the ship was battling with the pack to try and get in to them they had open water in Terra Nova Bay to the horizon, as seen from 200 feet high. They prepared for the winter, digging their hut into a big snowdrift a mile from where they were landed. They thought that the ship had been wrecked – or that everyone had been taken off from here, and that then the ship had been blown north by a succession of furious gales which they had and could not get back. They never considered seriously the possibility of sledging down the coast before the winter. They got settled in and were very warm – so warm that in August they did away with one door, of which they had three, of biscuit boxes and sacking.

Their stove was the bottom of an oil tin, and they cooked by dripping blubber on to seal bones, which became soaked with the blubber, and Campbell tells me they cooked almost as quickly as a primus. Of course they were filthy. Their main difficulty was dysentery and ptomaine poisoning.

Their stories of the winter are most amusing – of 'Placing the Plug, or Sports in the Antarctic'; of lectures; of how dirty they were; of their books, of which they had four, including *David Copperfield*. They had a spare tent, which was lucky, for the bamboos of one of theirs were blown in during a big wind, and the men inside it crept along the piedmont on hands and knees to the igloo and slept two in a bag. How the seal seemed as if they would give out, and they were on half rations and very hungry: and they were thinking they would have to come down in the winter, when they got two seals: of the fish they got from the stomach of a seal – 'the best feed they had' – the blubber they have eaten.

But they were buried deep in the snow and quite warm. Big winds all the time from the W.S.W., cold winds off the plateau – in the igloo they could hear almost nothing outside – how they just had a biscuit a day at times, sugar on Sundays, etc.

And so all is well in this direction, and we have done right in going south, and we have at least succeeded in getting all records. I suppose any news is better than no news.

Evening. The Pole Party photos of themselves at the Pole and at the Norwegian cairn (a Norwegian tent, post and two flags) are very good indeed – one film is unused, one used on these two subjects: taken with Birdie's camera. All the party look fit and well, and their clothes are not iced up. It was calm at the time: the surface looks rather soft.

Atkinson and Campbell have gone to Hut Point with one dog-team, and we are all to forgather here. The ice still seems good from here to Hut Point: all else open water as far as can be seen.

A steady southerly wind has been blowing here for three days now. The mules should get into Hut Point today.

It is the happiest day for nearly a year – almost the only happy one.

Chapter Seventeen
THE POLAR JOURNEY
(Continued)

DON JUAN: This creature Man, who in his own selfish affairs is a coward to the backbone, will fight for an idea like a hero. He may be abject as a citizen; but he is dangerous as a fanatic. He can only be enslaved while he is spiritually weak enough to listen to reason. I tell you, gentlemen, if you can show a man a piece of what he now calls God's work to do, and what he will later on call by many new names, you can make him entirely reckless of the consequences to himself personally . . .

DON JUAN: Every idea for which Man will die will be a Catholic idea. When the Spaniard learns at last that he is no better than the Saracen, and his prophet no better than Mahomet, he will arise, more Catholic than ever, and die on a barricade across the filthy slum he starves in, for universal liberty and equality.

THE STATUE: Bosh!

DON JUAN: What you call bosh is the only thing men dare die for. Later on, Liberty will not be Catholic enough: men will die for human perfection, to which they will sacrifice all their liberty gladly.

BERNARD SHAW, *Man and Superman*

V. THE POLE AND AFTER

The Polar Party	Depots
SCOTT	One Ton [79° 29′]
WILSON	Upper Barrier or Mount Hooper [80° 32′]
BOWERS	Middle Barrier [81° 35′]
OATES	Lower Barrier [82° 47′]
Seaman EVANS	Shambles Camp [N. of Gateway]
	Lower Glacier [S. of Gateway]
	Middle Glacier [Cloudmaker]

Upper Glacier [Mt. Darwin]
Three Degree [86° 56′]
1½ Degree [88° 29′]
Last Depot [89° 32′]

SCOTT RETURNED from the *Discovery* Expedition impressed by the value of youth in polar work; but the five who went forward from 87° 32′ were all grown men, chosen from a body which was largely recruited on a basis of youth. Four of them were men who were accustomed to take responsibility and to lead others. Four of them had wide sledging experience and were accustomed to cold temperatures. They were none of them likely to get flurried in emergency, to panic under any circumstances, or to wear themselves out by loss of nervous control. Scott and Wilson were the most highly strung of the party: I believe that the anxiety which Scott suffered served as a stimulus against mental monotony rather than as a drain upon his energy. Scott was 43, Wilson 39, Evans 37, Oates 32, and Bowers 28 years old. Bowers was exceptionally old for his age.

In the event of one man crocking a five-man party may be better able to cope with the situation, but with this doubtful exception Scott had nothing to gain and a good deal to lose by taking an extra man to the Pole. That he did so means, I think, that he considered his position a very good one at this time. He was anxious to take as many men with him as possible. I have an impression that he wanted the army represented as well as the navy. Be that as it may, he took five men: he decided to take the extra man at the last moment, and in doing so he added one more link to a chain. But he was content; and four days after the Last Return Party left them, as he lay out a blizzard, quite warm in his sleeping-bag though the midday temperature was −20°, he wrote a long diary praising his companions very highly indeed 'so our five people are perhaps as happily selected as it is possible to imagine.'[1] He speaks of Seaman Evans as being a giant

1. *Scott's Last Expedition*, vol. i, p. 536.

worker with a really remarkable headpiece. There is no mention of the party feeling the cold, though they were now at the greatest height of their journey; the food satisfied them thoroughly. There is no shadow of trouble here: only Evans has got a nasty cut on his hand!

There were more disadvantages in this five-man party than you might think. There was 5½ weeks' food for four men: five men would eat this in about four weeks. In addition to the extra risk of breakdown, there was a certain amount of discomfort involved, for everything was arranged for four men as I have already explained; the tent was a four-man tent, and an inner lining had been lashed to the bamboos making it smaller still: when stretched out for the night the sleeping-bags of the two outside men must have been partly off the floor-cloth, and probably on the snow: their bags must have been touching the inner tent and collecting the rime which was formed there: cooking for five took about half an hour longer in the day than cooking for four – half an hour off your sleep, or half an hour off your march? I do not believe that five men on the lid of a crevasse are as safe as four. Wilson writes that the stow of the sledge with five sleeping-bags was pretty high: this makes it top-heavy and liable to capsize in rough country.

But what would have paralysed anybody except Bowers was the fact that they had only four pairs of ski between the five of them. To slog along on foot, in soft snow, in the middle of four men pulling rhythmically on ski, must have been tiring and even painful; and Birdie's legs were very short. No steady swing for him, and little chance of getting his mind off the job in hand. Scott could never have meant to take on five men when he told his supporting team to leave their ski behind, only four days before he reorganized.

'May I be there!' wrote Wilson of the men chosen to travel the ice-cap to the Pole. 'About this time next year may I be there or thereabouts! With so many young bloods in the heyday of youth and strength beyond my own I feel there will be a most difficult task in making choice towards the end.' 'I should like to have Bill to hold my hand when we get to the Pole,' said Scott.

Wilson *was* there and his diary is that of an artist, watching the clouds and mountains, of a scientist observing ice and rock and snow, of a doctor, and above all of a man with good judgement. You will understand that the thing which really interested him in this journey was the acquisition of knowledge. It is a restrained, and for the most part a simple, record of facts. There is seldom any comment, and when there is you feel that, for this very reason, it carries more weight. Just about this time: 'December 24. Very promising, thoroughly enjoyed the afternoon march': 'Christmas Day, and a real good and happy one with a very long march': 'January 1, 1912. We had only 6 hours' sleep last night by a mistake, but I had mine solid in one piece, actually waking in exactly the same position as I fell asleep in 6 hours before – never moved': 'January 2. We were surprised today by seeing a Skua gull flying over us – evidently hungry but not weak. Its droppings, however, were clear mucus, nothing in them at all. It appeared in the afternoon and disappeared again about ½ hour after.' And then on 3 January: 'Last night Scott told us what the plans were for the South Pole. Scott, Oates, Bowers, Petty Officer Evans and I are to go to the Pole. Teddie Evans is to return from here tomorrow with Crean and Lashly. Scott finished his week's cooking tonight and I begin mine tomorrow.' Just that.

The next day Bowers wrote:

I had my farewell breakfast in the tent with Teddy Evans, Crean and Lashly. After so little sleep the previous night I rather dreaded the march. We gave our various notes, messages and letters to the returning party and started off. They accompanied us for about a mile before returning, to see that all was going well. Our party were on ski with the exception of myself: I first made fast to the central span, but afterwards connected up to the toggle of the sledge, pulling in the centre between the inner ends of Captain Scott's and Dr Wilson's traces. This was found to be the best place, as I had to go my own step.

Teddy and party gave us three cheers, and Crean was half in tears. They have a feather-weight sledge to go back with of course, and ought to run down their distance easily.[2] We found we could manage our load easily, and did 6.3 miles before lunch, completing 12.5 by 7.15 p.m. Our marching hours are nine per day. It is a long slog with a well-loaded sledge, and more tiring for me than the others, as I have no ski. However, as long as I can do my share all day and keep fit it does not matter much one way or the other.

We had our first northerly wind on the plateau today, and a deposit of snow crystals made the surface like sand latterly on the march. The sledge dragged like lead. In the evening it fell calm, and although the temperature was $-16°$ it was positively pleasant to stand about outside the tent and bask in the sun's rays. It was our first calm since we reached the summit too. Our socks and other damp articles which we hung out to dry at night become immediately covered with long feathery crystals exactly like plumes. Socks, mitts and finnesko dry splendidly up here during the night. We have little trouble with them compared with spring and winter journeys. I generally spread my bag out in the sun during the $1\frac{1}{2}$ hours of lunch time, which gives the reindeer hair a chance to get rid of the damage done by the deposit of breath and any perspiration during the night.[3]

Plenty of sun, heavy surfaces, iridescent clouds . . . the worst windcut sastrugi I have seen, covered with bunches of crystals like gorse . . . ice blink all round . . . hairy faces and mouths dreadfully iced up on the march . . . hot and sweaty days' work, but sometimes cold hands in the loops of the ski sticks . . . windy streaky cirrus in every direction, all thin

2. It is to be noticed that every return party, including the Polar Party, was supposed by their companions to be going to have a very much easier time than, as a matter of fact, they had. A. C.-G.
3. Bowers.

and filmy and scrappy . . . horizon clouds all being wafted about. . . . These are some of the impressions here and there in Wilson's diary during the first ten days of the party's solitary march. On the whole he is enjoying himself, I think.

You should read Scott's diary yourself and form your own opinions, but I think that after the Last Return Party left him there is a load off his mind. The thing had worked so far, it was up to *them* now: that great mass of figures and weights and averages, those years of preparation, those months of anxiety – no one of them had been in vain. They were up to date in distance, and there was a very good amount of food, probably more than was necessary to see them to the Pole and off the plateau on full rations. Best thought of all perhaps, the motors with their uncertainties, the ponies with their suffering, the glacier with its possibilities of disaster, all were behind: and the two main supporting parties were safely on their way home. Here with him was a fine party, tested and strong, and only 148 miles from the Pole.

I can see them, working with a business-like air, with no fuss and no unnecessary talk, each man knowing his job and doing it: pitching the tent: finishing the camp work and sitting round on their sleeping-bags while their meal was cooked: warming their hands on their mugs: saving a biscuit to eat when they woke in the night: packing the sledge with a good neat stow: marching with a solid swing – we have seen them do it so often, and they did it jolly well.

And the conditions did not seem so bad.

Tonight it is flat calm; the sun so warm that in spite of the temperature we can stand about outside in the greatest comfort. It is amusing to stand thus and remember the constant horrors of our situation as they were painted for us: the sun is melting the snow on the ski, etc. The plateau is now very flat, but we are still ascending slowly. The sastrugi are getting more confused, predominant from the S.E. I wonder what is in store for us. At present everything seems to be going with extraordinary smoothness. . . . We feel the cold very little, the great comfort of our situation is the excellent drying effect of the sun. . . .Our food continues to amply satisfy. What luck to have hit on such an excellent ration. We really are an excellently found party . . . we lie so very comfortably, warmly clothed in our comfortable bags, within our double-walled tent.[4]

Then something happened.

While Scott was writing the sentences you have just read, he reached the summit of the plateau and started, ever so slightly, to go downhill. The list of corrected altitudes given by Simpson in his meteorological report are of great interest: Cape Evans 0, Shambles Camp 170, Upper Glacier Depot 7151, Three Degree Depot 9392, One and a Half Degree Depot 9862, South Pole 9072 feet above sea-level.[5]

What happened is not quite clear, but there is no doubt that the surface became very bad, that the party began to feel the cold, and that before long Evans especially began to crock. The immediate trouble was bad surfaces. I will try and show why these surfaces should have been met in what was, you must remember, now a land which no man had travelled before.

Scott laid his One and a Half Degree Depot (i.e. 1½° or 90 miles from the Pole) on 10 January. That day they started to go down, but for several days before that the plateau had been pretty flat. Time after time in the diaries you find crystals – crystals – crystals: crystals falling through the air, crystals bearding the sastrugi, crystals lying loose upon the snow. Sandy crystals, upon which the sun shines and which made pulling a terrible effort: when the sky clouds over they get along much better. The clouds form and disperse without visible reason. And generally the wind is in their faces.

Wright tells me that there is certain evidence in the records which may explain these crystals. Halos are caused by crystals and nearly all those logged from the bottom of the Beardmore to the Pole and back were on this stretch of country,

4. *Scott's Last Expedition*, vol. i, pp. 530–34.
5. Simpson, *B.A.E., 1910–1913*, 'Meteorology', vol. i, p. 291.

where the land was falling. Bowers mentions that the crystals did not appear in all directions, which goes to show that the air was not always rising, but sometimes was falling and therefore not depositing its moisture. There is no doubt that the surfaces met were very variable, and it may be that the snow lay in waves. Bowers mentions big undulations for thirty miles before the Pole, and other inequalities may have been there which were not visible. There is sometimes evidence that these crystals were formed on the windward side of these waves, and carried over by a strong wind and deposited on the lee side.

It is common knowledge that as you rise in the atmosphere so the pressure decreases: in fact, it is usual to measure your height by reading the barometer. Now the air on this last stretch to the Pole was rising, for the wind was from the south, and, as we have seen, the plateau here was sloping down towards the Pole. The air, driven uphill by this southerly wind, was forced to rise. As it rose it expanded, because the pressure was less. Air which has expanded without any heat being given to it from outside, that is in a heat-proof vessel, is said to expand by adiabatic expansion. Such air tends first to become saturated, and then to precipitate its moisture. These conditions were approximately fulfilled on the plateau, where the air expanded as it rose, but could get little or no heat from outside. The air therefore precipitated its moisture in the form of crystals.

Owing to the rapid changes in surfaces (on one occasion they depoted their ski because they were in a sea of sastrugi, and had to walk back for them because the snow became level and soft again) Scott guessed that the coastal mountains could not be far away, and we now know that the actual distance was only 130 miles. About the same time Scott mentions that he had been afraid that they were weakening their pulling, but he was reassured by getting a patch of good surface and finding the sledge coming as easily as of old. On the night of 12 January, eight days after leaving the Last Return Party, he writes:

At camping tonight every one was chilled and we guessed a cold snap, but to our surprise the actual temperature was higher than last night, when we could dawdle in the sun. It is most unaccountable why we should suddenly feel the cold in this manner: partly the exhaustion of the march, but partly some damp quality in the air, I think. Little Bowers is wonderful; in spite of my protest he *would* take sights after we had camped tonight, after marching in the soft snow all day when we have been comparatively restful on ski.[6]

On 14 January, Wilson wrote: 'A very cold grey thick day with a persistent breeze from the S.S.E. which we all felt considerably, but temperature was only $-18°$ at lunch and $-15°$ in the evening. Now just over 40 miles from the Pole.' Scott wrote the same day: 'Again we noticed the cold; at lunch today all our feet were cold but this was mainly due to the bad state of our finnesko. I put some grease under the bare skin and found it made all the difference. Oates seems to be feeling the cold and fatigue more than the rest of us, but we are all very fit.' And on 15 January, lunch: 'We were all pretty done at camping.'[7] And Wilson: 'We made a depot [The Last Depot] of provisions at lunch time and went on for our last lap with nine days' provision. We went much more easily in the afternoon, and on till 7.30 p.m. The surface was a funny mixture of smooth snow and sudden patches of sastrugi, and we occasionally appear to be on a very gradual down gradient and on a slope down from the west to east.' In the light of what happened afterwards I believe that the party was not as fit at this time as might have been expected ten days before, and that this was partly the reason why they felt the cold and found the pulling so hard. The immediate test was the bad surface, and this was the result of the crystals which covered the ground.

6. *Scott's Last Expedition*, vol. i, p. 540.
7. ibid., pp. 541–2.

Simpson had worked out[8] that there is an almost constant pressure gradient driving the air on the plateau northwards parallel to the 146° E. meridian, and parallel also to the probable edge of the plateau. The mean velocity for the months of this December and January was about 11 miles an hour. During this plateau journey Scott logged wind force 5 and over on 23 occasions, and this wind was in their faces from the Beardmore to the Pole, and at their backs as they returned. A low temperature when it is calm is paradise compared to a higher temperature with a wind, and it is this constant pitiless wind, combined with the altitude and low temperatures, which has made travelling on the Antarctic plateau so difficult.

While the mean velocity of wind during the two midsummer months seems to be fairly constant, there is a very rapid fall of temperature in January. The mean actual temperature found on the plateau this year in December was −8.6°, the minimum observed being −19.3°. Simpson remarks that 'it must be accounted as one of the wonders of the Antarctic that it contains a vast area of the earth's surface where the mean temperature during the warmest month is more than 8° below the Fahrenheit zero, and when throughout the month the highest temperature was only +5.5° F.'[9] But the mean temperature on the plateau dropped 10° in January to −18.7°, the minimum observed being −29.7°. These temperatures have to be combined with the wind force described above to imagine the conditions of the march. In the light of Scott's previous plateau journey and Shackleton's Polar Journey this wind was always expected by our advance parties. But there can be no doubt that the temperature falls as solar radiation decreases more rapidly than was generally supposed. Scott probably expected neither such a rapid fall of temperature, nor the very bad surfaces, though he knew that the plateau would mean a trying time, and indeed it was

8. Simpson, *B.A.E., 1910–1913*, 'Meteorology', vol. i, pp. 144–6.
9. ibid., p. 41.

supposed that it would be much the hardest part of the journey.

On the night of 15 January, Scott wrote 'it ought to be a certain thing now, and the only appalling possibility the sight of the Norwegian flag forestalling ours.'[10] They were 27 miles from the Pole.

The story of the next three days is taken from Wilson's diary:

January 16. We got away at 8 a.m. and made 7.5 miles by 1.15, lunched, and then in 5.3 miles came on a black flag and the Norwegians' sledge, ski, and dog tracks running about N.E. and S.W. both ways. The flag was of black bunting tied with string to a fore-and-after which had evidently been taken off a finished-up sledge. The age of the tracks was hard to guess but probably a couple of weeks – or three or more. The flag was fairly well frayed at the edges. We camped here and examined the tracks and discussed things. The surface was fairly good in the forenoon, −23° temperature, and all the afternoon we were coming downhill with again a rise to the W., and a fall and a scoop to the east where the Norwegians came up, evidently by another glacier.

January 17. We camped on the Pole itself at 6.30 p.m. this evening. In the morning we were up at 5 a.m. and got away on Amundsen's tracks going S.S.W. for three hours, passing two small snow cairns, and then, finding the tracks too much snowed up to follow, we made our own bee-line for the Pole: camped for lunch at 12.30 and off again from 3 to 6.30 p.m. It blew from force 4 to 6 all day in our teeth with temperature −22°, the coldest march I ever remember. It was difficult to keep one's hands from freezing in double woollen and fur mitts. Oates, Evans, and Bowers all have pretty severe frost-bitten noses and cheeks, and we had to camp early for lunch on account of Evans's hands. It was a very bitter day. Sun was out now and again, and observations taken at lunch, and before and after supper, and at night, at 7 p.m. and at 2 a.m.

10. *Scott's Last Expedition*, vol. i, p. 543.

by our time. The weather was not clear, the air was full of crystals driving towards us as we came south, and making the horizon grey and thick and hazy. We could see no sign of cairn or flag, and from Amundsen's direction of tracks this morning he has probably hit a point about 3 miles off. We hope for clear weather tomorrow, but in any case are all agreed that he can claim prior right to the Pole itself. He has beaten us in so far as he made a race of it. We have done what we came for all the same and as our programme was made out. From his tracks we think there were only 2 men, on ski, with plenty of dogs on rather low diet. They seem to have had an oval tent. We sleep one night at the Pole and have had a double hoosh with some last bits of chocolate, and X's cigarettes have been much appreciated by Scott and Oates and Evans. A tiring day: now turning into a somewhat starchy frozen bag. Tomorrow we start for home and shall do our utmost to get back in time to send the news to the ship.

January 18. Sights were taken in the night, and at about 5 a.m. we turned out and marched from this night camp about 3¾ miles back in a S.E.ly direction to a spot which we judged from last night's sights to be the Pole. Here we lunched camp: built a cairn: took photos: flew the Queen Mother's Union Jack and all our own flags. We call this the Pole, though as a matter of fact we went ½ mile farther on in a S. easterly direction after taking further sights to the actual final spot, and here we left the Union Jack flying. During the forenoon we passed the Norwegians' last southerly camp: they called it Polheim and left a small tent with Norwegian and *Fram* flags flying, and a considerable amount of gear in the tent: half reindeer sleeping-bags, sleeping-socks, reinskin trousers 2 pair, a sextant, and artif[icial] horizon, a hypsometer with all the thermoms broken, etc. I took away the spirit-lamp of it, which I have wanted for sterilizing and making disinfectant lotions of snow. There were also letters there: one from Amundsen to King Haakon, with a request that Scott should send it to him. There was also a list of the five men who made up their party, but no news as to what they had done. I made some sketches here, but it was blowing very cold, −22°.

Birdie took some photos. We found no sledge there though they said there was one: it may have been buried in a drift. The tent was a funny little thing for 2 men, pegged out with white line and tent-pegs of yellow wood. I took some strips of blue-grey silk off the tent seams: it was perished. The Norskies had got to the Pole on 16 December, and were here from 15th to 17th. At our lunch South Pole Camp we saw a sledge-runner with a black flag about ½ mile away blowing from it. Scott sent me on ski to fetch it, and I found a note tied to it showing that this was the Norskies' actual final Pole position. I was given the flag and the note with Amundsen's signature, and I got a piece of the sledge-runner as well. The small chart of our wanderings shows best how all these things lie. After lunch we made 6.2 miles from the Pole Camp to the north again, and here we are camped for the night.[11]

The following remarks on the South Pole area were written by Bowers in the meteorological log, apparently on 17 and 18 January:

Within 120 miles of the South Pole the sastrugi crossed seem to indicate belts of certain prevalent winds. These were definitely S.E.ly up to about Lat. 78° 30′ S., where the summit was passed and we started to go definitely downhill toward the Pole. An indefinite area was then crossed S.E.ly, S.ly and S.W.ly sastrugi. Later, in about 79° 30′ S., those from the S.S.W. predominated. At this point also the surface of the ice-cap became affected by undulations running more or less at right angles to our course. These resolved themselves into immense waves some miles in extent,[12] with a uniform surface both in hollow and crust. The whole surface was carpeted with a deposit of ice-crystals which, while we were there, fell sometimes in the form of minute spicules and sometimes in plates. These caused an almost continuous display of parhelia.

11. Wilson.
12. Evidently meaning some miles from crest to crest.

The flags left a month previously by the Norwegian expedition were practically undamaged and so could not have been exposed to very heavy wind during that time. Their sledging and ski tracks, where marked, were raised slightly, also the dogs' footprints. In the neighbourhood of their South Pole Camp the drifts were S.W.ly, but there was one S.S.E. drift to leeward of tent. They had pitched their tent to allow for S.W.ly wind. For walking on foot the ground was all pretty soft, and on digging down the crystalline structure of the snow was found to alter very little, and there were no layers of crust such as are found on the Barrier. The snow seems so lightly put together as not to cohere, and makes very little water for its bulk when melted. The constant and varied motion of cirrus, and the forming and motion of radiant points, shows that in the upper atmosphere at this time of the year there is little or no tranquillity.[13]

That is the bare bones of what was without any possible doubt a great shock. Consider! These men had been out 2½ months and were 800 miles from home. The glacier had been a heavy grind: the plateau certainly not worse, probably better, than was expected, as far as that place where the Last Return Party left them. But then, in addition to a high altitude, a head wind, and a temperature which averaged −18.7°, came this shower of ice-crystals, turning the surface to sand, especially when the sun was out. They were living in cirrus clouds, and the extraordinary state seems to have obtained that the surface of the snow was colder when the sun was shining than when clouds checked the radiation from it. They began to descend. Things began to go not quite right: they felt the cold, especially Oates and Evans: Evans's hands also were wrong – ever since the seamen made that new sledge. The making of that sledge must have been fiercely cold work: one of the hardest jobs they did. I am not sure that enough notice has been taken of that.

And then:

13. Bowers, *Polar Meteorological Log*.

The Norwegians have forestalled us and are first at the Pole. It is a terrible disappointment, and I am very sorry for my loyal companions. Many thoughts come and much discussion have we had. Tomorrow we must march on to the Pole and then hasten home with all the speed we can compass. All the day-dreams must go; it will be a wearisome return.

The Pole. Yes, but under very different circumstances from those expected . . . companions labouring on with cold feet and hands. . . . Evans had such cold hands we camped for lunch . . . the wind is blowing hard, T. −21°, and there is that curious damp, cold feeling in the air which chills one to the bone in no time. . . . Great God! this is an awful place . . .[14]

This is not a cry of despair. It is an ejaculation provoked by the ghastly facts. Even now in January the temperature near the South Pole is about 24° lower than it is during the corresponding month of the year (July) near the North Pole[15] and if it is like this in mid-summer, what is it like in mid-winter? At the same time it was, with the exception of the sandy surfaces, what they had looked for, and every detail of organization was working out as well as if not better than had been expected.

Bowers was so busy with the meteorological log and sights which were taken in terribly difficult circumstances that he kept no diary until they started back. Then he wrote on seven consecutive days, as follows:

January 19. A splendid clear morning with a fine S.W. wind blowing. During breakfast time I sewed a flap attachment on to the hood of my green hat so as to prevent the wind from blowing down my neck on the march. We got up the mast and sail on the sledge and headed north, picking up Amundsen's cairn and our outgoing tracks shortly afterwards. Along

14. *Scott's Last Expedition*, vol. i, pp. 543–4.
15. Simpson, *B.A.E., 1910–1913*, 'Meteorology', vol. i, p. 40.

these we travelled till we struck the other cairn and finally the black flag where we had made our 58th outward camp. We then with much relief left all traces of the Norwegians behind us, and headed on our own track till lunch camp, when we had covered eight miles.

In the afternoon we passed No. 2 cairn of the British route, and fairly slithered along before a fresh breeze. It was heavy travelling for me, not being on ski, but one does not mind being tired if a good march is made. We did sixteen [miles] altogether for the day, and so should pick up our Last Depot tomorrow afternoon. The weather became fairly thick soon afternoon, and at the end of the afternoon there was considerable drift, with a mist caused by ice-crystals, and parhelion.

January 20. Good sailing breeze again this morning. It is a great pleasure to have one's back to the wind instead of having to face it. It came on thicker later, but we sighted the Last Depot soon after 1 p.m. and reached it at 1.45 p.m. The red flag on the bamboo pole was blowing out merrily to welcome us back from the Pole, with its supply of necessaries of life below. We are absolutely dependent upon our depots to get off the plateau alive, and so welcome the lonely little cairns gladly. At this one, called the Last Depot, we picked up four days' food, a can of oil, some methylated spirit (for lighting purposes) and some personal gear we had left there. The bamboo was bent on to the floor-cloth as a yard for our sail instead of a broken sledge-runner of Amundsen's which we had found at the Pole and made a temporary yard of.

As we had marched extra long in the forenoon in order to reach the depot, our afternoon march was shorter than usual. The wind increased to a moderate gale with heavy gusts and considerable drift. We should have had a bad time had we been facing it. After an hour I had to shift my harness aft so as to control the motions of the sledge. Unfortunately the surface got very sandy latterly, but we finished up with 16.1 miles to our credit and camped in a stiff breeze, which resolved itself into a blizzard a few hours later. I was glad we had our depot safe.

January 21. Wind increased to force 8 during night with

heavy drift. In the morning it was blizzing like blazes and marching was out of the question. The wind would have been of great assistance to us, but the drift was so thick that steering a course would have been next to impossible. We decided to await developments and get under weigh as soon as it showed any signs of clearing. Fortunately it was shortlived, and instead of lasting the regulation two days it eased up in the afternoon, and 3.45 found us off with our sail full. It was good running on ski but soft plodding for me on foot. I shall be jolly glad to pick up my dear old ski. They are nearly 200 miles away yet, however. The breeze fell altogether latterly and I shifted up into my old place as middle number of the five. Our distance completed was 5.5 miles, when camp was made again. Our old cairns are of great assistance to us, also the tracks, which are obliterated in places by heavy drift and hard sastrugi, but can be followed easily.

January 22. We came across Evans's sheepskin boots this morning. They were almost covered up after their long spell since they fell off the sledge [on 11 January]. The breeze was fair from the S.S.W. but got lighter and lighter. At lunch camp we had completed 8.2 miles. In the afternoon the breeze fell altogether, and the surface, acted on by the sun, became perfect sawdust. The light sledge pulled by five men came along like a drag without a particle of slide or give. We were all glad to camp soon after 7 p.m. I think we were all pretty tired out. We did altogether 19.5 miles for the day. We are only thirty miles from the 1½ Degree Depot, and should reach it in two marches with any luck. [The minimum temperature this night was −30° (uncorrected).]

January 23. Started off with a bit of a breeze which helped us a little [temperature −28°]. After the first two hours it increased to force 4, S.S.W., and filling the sail we sped along merrily, doing 8¾ miles before lunch. In the afternoon it was even stronger, and I had to go back to the sledge and act as guide and brakesman. We had to lower the sail a bit, but even then she ran like a bird.

We are picking up our old cairns famously. Evans got his nose frost-bitten, not an unusual thing with him, but as we were all getting pretty cold latterly we stopped at a quarter to seven, having done 16½ miles. We camped with considerable difficulty owing to the force of the wind.[16]

The same night Scott wrote:

We came along at a great pace, and should have got within an easy march of our [One and a Half Degree] Depot had not Wilson suddenly discovered that Evans's nose was frost-bitten – it was white and hard. We thought it best to camp at 6.45. Got the tent up with some difficulty, and now pretty cosy after good hoosh.

There is no doubt Evans is a good deal run down – his fingers are badly blistered and his nose is rather seriously congested with frequent frost-bites. He is very much annoyed with himself, which is not a good sign. I think Wilson, Bowers and I are as fit as possible under the circumstances. Oates gets cold feet. One way and another I shall be glad to get off the summit! . . . The weather seems to be breaking up.[17]

Bowers resumes the tale:

January 24. Evans has got his fingers all blistered with frost-bites, otherwise we are all well, but thinning, and in spite of our good rations get hungrier daily. I sometimes spend much thought on the march with plans for making a pig of myself on the first opportunity. As that will be after a further march of 700 miles they are a bit premature.

It was blowing a gale when we started and it increased in force. Finally with the sail half down, one man detached tracking ahead and Titus and I breaking back, we could not always keep the sledge from overrunning. The blizzard got worse till, having done only seven miles, we had to camp soon after twelve o'clock. We had a most difficult job

16. Bowers.
17. *Scott's Last Expedition*, vol. i, pp. 550–51.

camping, and it has been blowing like blazes all the afternoon. I think it is moderating now, 9 p.m. We are only seven miles from our depot and this delay is exasperating.[18]

[Scott wrote: 'This is the second full gale since we left the Pole. I don't like the look of it. Is the weather breaking up? If so, God help us, with the tremendous summit journey and scant food. Wilson and Bowers are my stand-by. I don't like the easy way in which Oates and Evans get frost-bitten.][19]

January 25. It was no use turning out at our usual time (5.45 a.m.), as the blizzard was as furious as ever; we therefore decided on a late breakfast and no lunch unless able to march. We have only three days' food with us and shall be in Queer Street if we miss the depot. Our bags are getting steadily wetter, so are our clothes. It shows a tendency to clear off now (breakfast time) so, D. V., we may march after all. I am in tribulation as regards meals now as we have run out of salt, one of my favourite commodities. It is owing to Atkinson's party taking back an extra tin by mistake from the Upper Glacier Depot. Fortunately we have some depoted there, so I will only have to endure another two weeks without it.

10 p.m. – We have got in a march after all, thank the Lord. Assisted by the wind we made an excellent rundown to our One and a Half Degree Depot, where the big red flag was blowing out like fury with the breeze, in clouds of driving drift. Here we picked up 1¼ cans of oil and one week's food for five men, together with some personal gear depoted. We left the bamboo and flag on the cairn. I was much relieved to pick up the depot: now we only have one other source of anxiety on this endless snow summit, viz. the Three Degree Depot in latitude 86° 56′ S.

In the afternoon we did 5.2 miles. It was a miserable march, blizzard all the time and our sledge either sticking in sastrugi or overrunning the traces. We had to lower the

18. Bowers.
19. *Scott's Last Expedition*, vol. 1, p. 552.

sail half down, and Titus and I hung on to her. It was most strenuous work, as well as much colder than pulling ahead. Most of the time we had to brake back with all our strength to keep the sledge from overrunning. Bill got a bad go of snow glare from following the track without goggles on.

This day last year we started the Depot Journey. I did not think so short a time would turn me into an old hand at polar travelling, neither did I imagine at the time that I would be returning from the Pole itself.[20]

Wilson was very subject to these attacks of snow blindness, and also to headaches before blizzards. I have an idea that his anxiety to sketch whenever opportunity offered, and his willingness to take off his goggles to search for tracks and cairns had something to do with it. This attack was very typical.

I wrote this at lunch and in the evening had a bad attack of snow blindness.

Blizzard in afternoon. We only got in a forenoon march. Couldn't see enough of the tracks to follow at all. My eyes didn't begin to trouble me till tomorrow [yesterday], though it was the strain of tracking and the very cold drift which we had today that gave me this attack of snow glare.

Marched on foot in the afternoon as my eyes were too bad to go on ski. We had a lot of drift and wind and very cold. Had $ZuSO_4$ and cocaine in my eyes at night and didn't get to sleep at all for the pain – dozed for about an hour in the morning only.

Marched on foot again all day as I couldn't see my way on ski at all. Birdie used my ski. Eyes still very painful and watering. Tired out by the evening, had a splendid night's sleep, and though very painful across forehead tonight they are much better.[21]

20. Bowers.   21. Wilson.

The surface was awful: in his diary of the day after they left the Pole (19 January) Wilson wrote an account of it.

> We had a splendid wind right behind us most of the afternoon and went well until about 6 p.m. when the sun came out and we had an awful grind until 7.30 when we camped. The sun comes out on sandy drifts, all on the move in the wind, and temp. −20°, and gives us an absolutely awful surface with no glide at all for ski and sledge, and just like fine sand. The weather all day has been more or less overcast with white broken alto-stratus, and for 3 degrees above the horizon there is a grey belt looking like a blizzard of drift, but this in reality is caused by a constant fall of minute snow crystals, very minute. Sometimes instead of crystal plates the fall is of minute agglomerate spicules like tiny sea-urchins. The plates glitter in the sun as though of some size, but you can only just see them as pin-points of your burberry. So the spicule collections are only just visible. Our hands are never warm enough in camp to do any neat work now. The weather is always uncomfortably cold and windy, about −23°, but after lunch today I got a bit of drawing done.[22]

All the joy had gone from their sledging. They were hungry, they were cold, the pulling was heavy, and two of them were not fit. As long ago as 14 January Scott wrote that Oates was feeling the cold and fatigue more than the others[23] and again he refers to the matter on 20 January.[24] On 19 January Wilson wrote: 'We get our hairy faces and mouths dreadfully iced up on the march, and often one's hands very cold indeed holding ski-sticks. Evans, who cut his knuckle some days ago at the last depot, has a lot of pus in it tonight.' January 20: 'Evans has got 4 or 5 of his finger-tips badly blistered by the cold. Titus also his nose and cheeks – al[so] Evans and Bowers.' January 28: 'Evans has a number of badly blistered finger-ends which he got at the Pole. Titus'

22. Wilson.   23. *Scott's Last Expedition*, vol. 1, p. 541.
24. ibid., p. 549.

big toe is turning blue-black.' January 31: 'Evans' finger-nails all coming off, very raw and sore.' February 4: 'Evans is feeling the cold a lot, always getting frost-bitten. Titus' toes are blackening, and his nose and cheeks are dead yellow. Dressing Evans' fingers every other day with boric vaseline: they are quite sweet still.' February 5: 'Evans' fingers suppurating. Nose very bad [hard] and rotten-looking.'[25]

Scott was getting alarmed about Evans, who 'has dislodged two finger-nails tonight; his hands are really bad, and, to my surprise, he shows signs of losing heart over it. He hasn't been cheerful since the accident.'[26] 'The party is not improving in condition, especially Evans, who is becoming rather dull and incapable.' 'Evans' nose is almost as bad as his fingers. He is a good deal crocked up.'[27]

Bowers's diary, quoted above, finished on 25 January, on which day they picked up their One and a Half Degree Depot. 'I shall sleep much better with our provision bag full again,' wrote Scott that night. 'Bowers got another rating sight tonight – it was wonderful how he managed to observe in such a horribly cold wind.' They marched 16 miles the next day, but got off the outward track, which was crooked. On 27 January they did 14 miles on a 'very bad surface of deep-cut sastrugi all day, until late in the afternoon when we began to get out of them.'[28] 'By Jove, this is tremendous labour,' said Scott.

They were getting into the better surfaces again: 15.7 miles for 28 January, 'a fine day and a good march on very decent surface.'[29] On 29 January Bowers wrote his last full day's diary:

> Our record march today. With a good breeze and improving surface we were soon in among the double tracks where the supporting party left us. Then we picked up the memorable camp where I transferred to the advance party. How glad I was to change over. The camp was much drifted up and

25. Wilson.   26. *Scott's Last Expedition*, vol. i, p. 557.
27. ibid., pp. 560, 561.   28. Wilson.   29. ibid.

immense sastrugi were everywhere, S.S.E. in direction and
S.E. We did 10.4 miles before lunch. I was breaking back on
sledge and controlling; it was beastly cold and my hands were
perished. In the afternoon I put on my dogskin mitts and was
far more comfortable. A stiff breeze with drift continues:
temperature −25°. Thank God our days of having to face it
are over. We completed 19.5 miles [22 statute] this evening,
and so are only 29 miles from our precious [Three Degree]
Depot. It will be bad luck indeed if we do not get there in a
march and a half anyhow.[30]

Nineteen miles again on 30 January, but during the previous
day's march Wilson had strained a tendon in his leg. 'I got a
nasty bruise on the Tib[ialis] ant[icus] which gave me great
pain all the afternoon.' 'My left leg exceedingly painful all
day, so I gave Birdie my ski and hobbled alongside the sledge
on foot. The whole of the Tibialis anticus is swollen and
tight, and full of teno synovitis, and the skin red and
oedematous over the shin. But we made a very fine march
with the help of a brisk breeze.' January 31:

Again walking by the sledge with swollen leg but not
nearly so painful. We had 5.8 miles to go to reach our Three
Degree Depot. Picked this up with a week's provision and a
line from Evans, and then for lunch an extra biscuit each,
making 4 for lunch, and 1/10 whack of butter extra as well.
Afternoon we passed cairn where Birdie's ski had been left.
These we picked up and came on till 7.30 p.m. when the
wind which had been very light all day dropped, and with
temp. −20° it felt delightfully warm and sunny and clear. We
have 1/10 extra pemmican in the hoosh now also. My leg
pretty swollen again tonight.[31]

They travelled 13.5 miles that day, and 15.7 on the next. 'My
leg much more comfortable, gave me no pain, and I was able

30. Bowers.   31. Wilson.

to pull all day, holding on to the sledge. Still some oedema. We came down a hundred feet or so today on a fairly steep gradient.'[32]

They were now approaching the crevassed surfaces and the ice-falls which mark the entrance to the Beardmore Glacier, and 2 February was marked by another accident, this time to Scott.

> On a very slippery surface I came an awful 'purler' on my shoulder. It is horribly sore tonight and another sick person added to our tent – three out of five injured, and the most troublesome surfaces to come. We shall be lucky if we get through without serious injury. Wilson's leg is better, but might easily get bad again, and Evans' fingers. . . . We have managed to get off 17 miles. The extra food is certainly helping us, but we are getting pretty hungry. The weather is already a trifle warmer, the altitude lower and only 80 miles or so to Mount Darwin. It is time we were off the summit – Pray God another four days will see us pretty well clear of it. Our bags are getting very wet and we ought to have more sleep.[33]

They had been spending some time in finding the old tracks. But they had a good landfall for the depot at the top of the glacier and on 3 February they decided to push on due north, and to worry no more for the present about tracks and cairns. They did 16 miles that day. Wilson's diary runs:

> Sunny and breezy again. Came down a series of slopes, and finished the day going up one. Enormous deep-cut sastrugi and drifts and shiny egg-shell surface. Wind all S.E.E.ly. Today at about 11 p.m. we got our first sight again of mountain peaks on our eastern horizon. . . . We crossed the outmost line of crevassed ridge top today, the first on our return.
>
> *February 4.* 18 miles. Clear cloudless blue sky, surface drift.

32. ibid.
33. *Scott's Last Expedition*, vol. i, p. 559.

During forenoon we came down gradual descent including 2 or 3 irregular terrace slopes, on crest of one of which were a good many crevasses. Southernmost were just big enough for Scott and Evans to fall in to their waists, and very deceptively covered up. They ran east and west. Those nearer the crest were the ordinary broad street-like crevasses, well lidded. In the afternoon we again came to a crest, before descending, with street crevasses, and one we crossed had a huge hole where the lid had fallen in, big enough for a horse and cart to go down. We have a great number of mountain tops on our right and south of our beam as we go due north now. We are now camped just below a great crevassed mound, on a mountain top evidently.

February 5. 18.2 miles. We had a difficult day, getting in amongst a frightful chaos of broad chasm-like crevasses. We kept too far east and had to wind in and out amongst them and cross a multitude of bridges. We then bore west a bit and got on better all the afternoon and got round a good deal of the upper disturbances of the falls here.

[Scott wrote: 'We are camped in a very disturbed region, but the wind has fallen very light here, and our camp is comfortable for the first time for many weeks.'[34]]

February 6. 15 miles. We again had a forenoon of trying to cut corners. Got in amongst great chasms running E. and W. and had to come out again. We then again kept west and downhill over tremendous sastrugi, with a slight breeze, very cold. In afternoon, continued bearing more and more towards Mount Darwin: we got round one of the main lines of ice-fall and looked back up to it. . . . Very cold march: many crevasses: I walking by the sledge on foot found a good many: the others all on ski.

February 7. 15.5 miles. Clear day again and we made a tedious march in the forenoon along a flat or two, and down a long slope: and then in the afternoon we had a very fresh breeze, and very fast run down long slopes covered with big sastrugi. It was a strenuous job steering and checking behind

34. ibid., p. 561.

by the sledge. We reached the Upper Glacier Depot by 7.30 p.m. and found everything right.[35]

This was the end of the plateau: the beginning of the glacier. Their hard time should be over so far as the weather was concerned. Wilson notes how fine the land looked as they approached it: 'The colour of the Dominion Range rock is in the main all brown madder or dark reddish chocolate, but there are numerous bands of yellow rock scattered amongst it. I think it is composed of dolerite and sandstone as on the W. side.'[36]

The condition of the party was of course giving anxiety: how much it is impossible to say. A good deal was to be hoped from the warm weather ahead. Scott and Bowers were probably the fittest men. Scott's shoulder soon mended and 'Bowers is splendid, full of energy and bustle all the time.'[37] Wilson was feeling the cold more than either of them now. His leg was not yet well enough to wear ski. Oates had suffered from a cold foot for some time. Evans, however, was the only man whom Scott seems to have been worried about. 'His cuts and wounds suppurate, his nose looks very bad, and altogether he shows considerable signs of being played out.' . . . 'Well, we have come through our seven weeks' ice-cap journey and most of us are fit, but I think another week might have had a very bad effect on P.O. Evans, who is going steadily down-hill.'[38] They had all been having extra food which had helped them much, though they complained of hunger and want of sleep. Directly they got into the warmer weather on the glacier their food satisfied them, 'but we must march to keep on the full ration, and we want rest, yet we shall pull through all right, D.V. We are by no means worn out.'[39]

There are no germs in the Antarctic, save for a few isolated

35. Wilson.   36. ibid.
37. *Scott's Last Expedition*, vol. i, p. 561.
38. ibid., pp. 562, 563.   39. ibid., p. 566.

specimens which almost certainly come down from civilization in the upper air currents. You can sleep all night in a wet bag and clothing, and sledge all day in a mail of ice, and you will not catch a cold nor get any aches. You can get deficiency diseases, like scurvy, for inland this is a deficiency country, without vitamins. You can also get poisoned if you allow your food to remain thawed out too long, and if you do not cover the provisions in a depot with enough snow the sun will get at them, even though the air temperature is far below freezing. But it is not easy to become diseased.

On the other hand, once something does go wrong it is the deuce and all to get it right: especially cuts. And the isolation of the polar traveller may place him in most difficult circumstances. There are no ambulances and hospitals, and a man on a sledge is a very serious weight. Practically any man who undertakes big polar journeys must face the possibility of having to commit suicide to save his companions, and the difficulty of this must not be over-rated, for it is in some ways more desirable to die than to live, if things are bad enough: we got to that stage on the Winter Journey. I remember discussing this question with Bowers, who had a scheme of doing himself in with a pick-axe if necessity arose, though how he could have accomplished it I don't know: or, as he said, there might be a crevasse and at any rate there was the medical case. I was horrified at the time: I had never faced the thing out with myself like that.

They left the Upper Glacier Depot under Mount Darwin on 8 February. This day they collected the most important of those geological specimens to which, at Wilson's special request, they clung to the end, and which were mostly collected by him. Mount Darwin and Buckley Island, which are really the tops of high mountains, stick out of the ice at the top of the glacier, and the course ran near to both of them, but not actually up against them. Shackleton found coal on Buckley Island, and it was clear that the place was of great geological importance, for it was one of the only places in the Antarctic where fossils could be found, so far as we knew. The ice-falls stretched away as far as you could see towards the mountains which bound the glacier on either side, and as you looked upwards towards Buckley Island they were like a long breaking wave. One of the great difficulties about the Beardmore was that you saw the ice-falls as you went up, and avoided them, but coming down you knew nothing of their whereabouts until you fell into the middle of pressure and crevasses, and then it was almost impossible to say whether you should go right or left to get out.

Evans was unable to pull this day, and was detached from the sledge, but this was not necessarily a very serious sign: Shackleton on his return journey was not able to pull at this place. Wilson wrote as follows:

February 8, *Mt. Buckley Cliffs.* A very busy day. We had a very cold forenoon march, blowing like blazes from the S. Birdie detached and went on ski to Mt. Darwin and collected some dolerite, the only rock he could see on the Nunatak, which was the nearest. We got into a sort of crusted surface where the snow broke through nearly to our knees and the sledge-runner also. I thought at first we were all on a thinly bridged crevasse. We then came on east a bit, and gradually got worse and worse going over an ice-fall, having great trouble to prevent sledge taking charge, but eventually got down and then made N.W. or N. into the land, and camped right by the moraine under the great sandstone cliffs of Mt. Buckley, out of the wind and quite warm again: it was a wonderful change. After lunch we all geologized on till supper, and I was very late turning in, examining the moraine after supper. Socks, all strewn over the rocks, dried splendidly. Magnificent Beacon sandstone cliffs. Masses of limestone in the moraine, and dolerite crags in various places. Coal seams at all heights in the sandstone cliffs, and lumps of weathered coal with fossil vegetable. Had a regular field-day and got some splendid things in the short time.

February 9, *Moraine visit.* We made our way along down the moraine, and at the end of Mt. Buckley [I] unhitched and had half an hour over the rocks and again got some good things written up in sketch-book. We then left the moraine and made a very good march on rough blue ice all day with very small and scarce scraps of névé, on one of which we camped for the night with a rather overcast foggy sky, which cleared to bright sun in the night. We are all thoroughly enjoying temps of +10° or thereabouts now, with no wind instead of the summit winds which are incessant with temp. −20°.

February 10. ?16m. We made a very good forenoon march from 10 to 2.45 towards the Cloudmaker. Weather overcast gradually obscured everything in snowfall fog, starting with crystals of large size. . . . We had to camp after 2½ hours' afternoon march as it got too thick to see anything and we were going downhill on blue ice . . .[40]

The next day in bad lights and on a bad surface they fell into the same pressure which both the other returning parties experienced. Like them they were in the middle of it before they realized.

Then came the fatal decision to steer east. We went on for 6 hours, hoping to do a good distance, which I suppose we did, but for the last hour or two we pressed on into a regular trap. Getting on to a good surface we did not reduce our lunch meal, and thought all going well, but half an hour after lunch we got into worst ice mess I have ever been in. For three hours we plunged on on ski, first thinking we were too much to the right, then too much to the left; meanwhile the disturbance got worse and my spirits received a very rude shock. There were times when it seemed almost impossible to find a way out of the awful turmoil in which we found ourselves.

. . . The turmoil changed in character, irregular crevassed surface giving way to huge chasms, closely packed and most difficult to cross. It was very heavy work, but we had grown

40. Wilson.

desperate. We won through at 10 p.m., and I write after 12 hours on the march . . .[41]

Wilson continues the story:

February 12. We had a good night just outside the ice-falls and disturbances, and a small breakfast of tea, thin hoosh and biscuit, and began the forenoon by a decent bit of travelling on rubbly blue ice in crampons: then plunged into an ice-fall and wandered about in it for hours and hours.

February 13. We had one biscuit and some tea after a night's sleep on very hard and irregular blue ice amongst the ice-fall crevasses. No snow on the tent, only ski, etc. Got away at 10 a.m. and by 2 p.m. found the depot, having had a good march over hard rough blue ice. Only ½ hour in the disturbance of yesterday. The weather was very thick, snowing and overcast, could only just see the points of bearing for depot. However, we got there, tired and hungry, and camped and had hoosh and tea and 3 biscuits each. Then away again with our three and a half days' food from this red flag depot and off down by the Cloudmaker moraine. We travelled about 4 hours on hard blue ice, and I was allowed to geologize the last hour down the two outer lines of boulders. The outer one all dolerite and quartz rocks, the inner all dolerite and sandstone. . . . We camped on the inner line of boulders, weather clearing all the afternoon.[42]

Meanwhile both Wilson and Bowers had been badly snow-blind, though Wilson does not mention it in his diary; and this night Scott says Evans had no power to assist with camping work. A good march followed on 14 February, but

there is no getting away from the fact that we are not pulling strong. Probably none of us: Wilson's leg still troubles him and he doesn't like to trust himself on ski; but the worse case

41. *Scott's Last Expedition*, vol. i, p. 567.
42. Wilson.

is Evans, who is giving us serious anxiety. This morning he suddenly disclosed a huge blister on his foot. It delayed us on the march, when he had to have his crampon readjusted. Sometimes I feel he is going from bad to worse, but I trust he will pick up again when we come to steady work on ski like this afternoon. He is hungry and so is Wilson. We can't risk opening out our food again, and as cook at present I am serving something under full allowance. We are inclined to get slack and slow with our camping arrangement, and small delays increase. I have talked of the matter tonight and hope for improvement. We cannot do distance without the hours.[43]

There was something wrong with this party: more wrong, I mean, than was justified by the tremendous journey they had already experienced. Except for the blizzard at the bottom of the Beardmore and the surfaces near the Pole it had been little worse than they expected. Evans, however, who was considered by Scott to be the strongest man of the party, had already collapsed, and it is admitted that the rest of the party was becoming far from strong. There seems to be an unknown factor here somewhere.

Wilson's diary continues:

February 15. 13¾ *m. geog.* I got on ski again first time since damaging my leg and was on them all day for 9 hours. It was a bit painful and swelled by the evening, and every night I put on snow poultice. We are not yet abreast of Mt. Kyffin, and much discussion how far we are from the Lower Glacier Depot, probably 18 to 20 m.: and we have to reduce food again, only one biscuit tonight with a thin hoosh of pemmican. Tomorrow we have to make one day's food which remains last over the two. The weather became heavily overcast during the afternoon and then began to snow, and though we got in our 4 hours' march it was with difficulty, and we only made a bit over 5 miles. However, we are nearer the depot tonight.

43 *Scott's Last Expedition*, vol. i, pp. 570–71.

February 16. 12½ *m. geog.* Got a good start in fair weather after one biscuit and a thin breakfast, and made 7½ m. in the forenoon. Again the weather became overcast and we lunched almost at our old bearing on Kyffin of lunch Dec. 15. All the afternoon the weather became thick and thicker and after 3½ hours Evans collapsed, sick and giddy, and unable to walk even by the sledge on ski, so we camped. Can see no land at all anywhere, but we must be getting pretty near the Pillar Rock. Evans' collapse has much to do with the fact that he has never been sick in his life and is now helpless with his hands frost-bitten. We had thin meals for lunch and supper.

February 17. The weather cleared and we got away for a clear run to the depot and had gone a good part of the way when Evans found his ski shoes coming off. He was allowed to readjust and continue to pull, but it happened again, and then again, so he was told to unhitch, get them right, and follow on and catch us up. He lagged far behind till lunch, and when we camped we had lunch, and then went back for him as he had not come up. He had fallen and had his hands frost-bitten, and we then returned for the sledge, and brought it, and fetched him in on it as he was rapidly losing the use of his legs. He was comatose when we got him into the tent, and he died without recovering consciousness that night about 10 p.m. We had a short rest for an hour or two in our bags that night, then had a meal and came on through the pressure ridges about 4 miles farther down and reached our Lower Glacier Depot. Here we camped at last, had a good meal and slept a good night's rest which we badly needed. Our depot was all right.[44]

A very terrible day. . . . On discussing the symptoms we think he began to get weaker just before we reached the Pole, and that his downward path was accelerated first by the shock of his frost-bitten fingers, and later by falls during rough travelling on the glacier, further by his loss of all confidence in himself. Wilson thinks it certain he must have injured his

44. Wilson.

brain by a fall. It is a terrible thing to lose a companion in this way, but calm reflection shows that there could not have been a better ending to the terrible anxieties of the past week. Discussion of the situation at lunch yesterday shows us what a desperate pass we were in with a sick man on our hands at such a distance from home.[45]

45. *Scott's Last Expedition*, vol. i, p. 573.

Chapter Eighteen
THE POLAR JOURNEY
(*Continued*)

> This happy breed of men, this little world,
> This precious stone set in the silver sea,
> Which serves it in the office of a wall, . . .
> This blessed plot, this earth, this realm, this England,
> This nurse, this teeming womb of royal kings, . . .
> This land of such dear souls, this dear, dear land.

SHAKESPEARE

VI.   FARTHEST SOUTH

STEVENSON has written of a traveller whose wife slumbered by his side what time his spirit re-adventured forth in memory of days gone by. He was quite happy about it, and I suppose his travels had been peaceful, for days and nights such as these men spent coming down the Beardmore will give you nightmare after nightmare, and wake you shrieking – years after.

Of course they were shaken and weakened. But the conditions they had faced, and the time they had been out, do not in my opinion account entirely for their weakness nor for Evans's collapse, which may have had something to do with the fact that he was the biggest, heaviest and most muscular man in the party. I do not believe that this is a life for such men, who are expected to pull their weight and to support and drive a larger machine than their companions, and at the same time to eat no extra food. If, as seems likely, the ration these men were eating was not enough to support the work they were doing, then it is clear that the heaviest man will feel the deficiency sooner and more severely than others who are smaller than he. Evans must have had a most terrible time: I think it is clear from the diaries that he had suffered very greatly without complaint. At home he would have been nursed in bed: here he must march (he was pulling the day he died) until he was crawling on his frost-bitten hands and knees in the snow – horrible: most horrible perhaps for those who found him so, and sat in the tent and watched him die. I am told that simple concussion does not kill as suddenly as this: probably some clot had moved in his brain.

For one reason and another they took very nearly as long to come down the glacier with a featherweight sledge as we had taken to go up it with full loads. Seven days' food were allowed from the Upper to the Lower Glacier Depot. Bowers told me that he thought this was running it fine. But the two supporting parties got through all right, though they both tumbled into the horrible pressure above the Cloudmaker. The Last Return Party took 7½ days: the Polar Party 10 days: the latter had been 25½ days longer on the plateau than the former. Owing to their slow progress down the glacier the Polar Party went on short rations for the first and last time until they camped on 19 March: with the exception of these days they had either their full, or more than their full ration until that date.

Until they reached the Barrier on their return journey the weather can be described neither as abnormal nor as unexpected. There were 300 statute miles (260 geo.) to be covered to One Ton Depot, and 150 statute miles (130 geo.) more from One Ton to Hut Point. They had just picked up one week's food for five men: between the Beardmore and One Ton were three more depots each with one week's food for five men. They were four men: their way was across the main body of the Barrier out of sight of land, and away from any immediate influence of the comparatively warm sea ahead of them. Nothing was known of the weather conditions in the middle of the Barrier at this time of year, and no one suspected that March conditions there were very cold. Shackleton turned homeward on 10 January: reached his Bluff Depot on 23 February, and Hut Point on 28 February.

Wilson's diary continues:

February 18. We had only five hours' sleep. We had butter and biscuit and tea when we woke up at 2 p.m., then came over the Gap entrance to the pony-slaughter camp, visiting a rock moraine of Mt. Hope on the way.

February 19. Late in getting away after making up new 10-foot sledge and digging out pony meat. We made 5½ m. on a very heavy surface indeed.[1]

This bad surface is the feature of their first homeward marches on the Barrier. From now onwards they complain always of the terrible surfaces, but a certain amount of the heavy pulling must be ascribed to their own weakness. In the low temperatures which occurred later bad surfaces were to be expected: but now the temperatures were not really low, about zero to −17°: fine clear days for the most part and, a thing to be noticed, little wind. They wanted wind, which would probably be behind them from the south. 'Oh! for a little wind,' Scott writes. 'E. Evans evidently had plenty.' He was already very anxious.

> If this goes on we shall have a bad time, but I sincerely trust it is only the result of this windless area close to the coast and that, as we are making steadily outwards, we shall shortly escape it. It is perhaps premature [19 Feb.] to be anxious about covering distance. In all other respects things are improving. We have our sleeping-bags spread on the sledge and they are drying, but, above all, we have our full measure of food again. Tonight we had a sort of stew fry of pemmican and horseflesh, and voted it the best hoosh we had ever had on a sledge journey. The absence of poor Evans is a help to the commissariat, but if he had been here in a fit state we might have got along faster. I wonder what is in store for us, with some little alarm at the lateness of the season.

And on 20 February, when they made 7 miles, 'At present our sledge and ski leave deeply ploughed tracks which can be

1. Wilson.

seen winding for miles behind. It is distressing, but as usual trials are forgotten when we camp, and good food is our lot. Pray God we get better travelling as we are not so fit as we were, and the season is advancing apace.' And on 21 February, 'We never won a march of 8½ miles with greater difficulty, but we can't go on like this.'[2]

A breeze suddenly came away from S.S.E., force 4 to 6, at 11 a.m. on 22 February, and they hoisted the sail on the sledge they had just picked up. They immediately lost the tracks they were following, and failed to find the cairns and camp remains which they should have picked up if they had been on the right course, which was difficult here owing to the thick weather we had on the outward march. Bowers was sure they were too near the land and they steered out, but still failed to pick up the line on which their depots and their lives depended. Scott was convinced they were outside, not inside the line. The next morning Bowers took a round of angles, and they came to the conclusion, on slender evidence, that they were still too near the land. They had an unhappy march still off the tracks, 'but just as we decided to lunch, Bowers' wonderful sharp eyes detected an old double lunch cairn, the theodolite telescope confirmed it, and our spirits rose accordingly.'[3] Then Wilson had another 'bad attack of snow-glare: could hardly keep a chink of eye open in goggles to see the course. Fat pony hoosh.'[4] This day they reached the Lower Barrier Depot.

They were in evil case, but they would have been all right, these men, if the cold had not come down upon them, a bolt quite literally from the blue of a clear sky: unexpected, unforetold and fatal. The cold itself was not so tremendous until you realize that they had been out four months, that they had fought their way up the biggest glacier in the world in feet of soft snow, that they had spent seven weeks under plateau conditions or rarefied air, big winds and low temperatures, and they had watched one of their companions die –

2. *Scott's Last Expedition*, vol. i, pp. 575–6.
3. ibid., p. 577.   4. Wilson.

not in a bed, in a hospital or ambulance, nor suddenly, but slowly, night by night and day by day, with his hands frostbitten and his brain going, until they must have wondered, each man in his heart, whether in such case a human being could be left to die, that four men might live. He died a natural death and they went out on to the Barrier.

Given such conditions as were expected, and the conditions for which preparation had been made, they would have come home alive and well. Some may say the weather was abnormal: there is some evidence that it was. The fact remains that the temperature dropped into the minus thirties by day and the minus forties by night. The fact also remains that there was a great lack of southerly winds, and in consequence the air near the surface was not being mixed: excessive radiation took place, and a layer of cold air formed near the ground. Crystals also formed on the surface of the snow and the wind was not enough to sweep them away. As the temperature dropped so the surface for the runners of the sledges became worse, as I explained elsewhere.[5] They were pulling as it were through sand.

In the face of the difficulties which beset them their marches were magnificent: 11½ miles on 25 February and again on the following day: 12.2 miles on 27 February, and 11½ miles again on 28 and 29 February. If they could have kept this up they would have come through without a doubt. But I think it was about now that they suspected, and then were sure, that they could not pull through. Scott's diary, written at lunch, 2 March, is as follows:

Misfortunes rarely come singly. We marched to the [Middle Barrier] depot fairly easily yesterday afternoon, and since that have suffered three distinct blows which have placed us in a bad position. First, we found a shortage of oil; with most rigid economy it can scarce carry us to the next depot on this surface [71 miles away]. Second, Titus Oates disclosed his feet, the toes showing very bad indeed, evidently bitten

5. See note at end of Chapter 14.

by the late temperatures. The third blow came in the night, when the wind, which we had hailed with some joy, brought dark overcast weather. It fell below −40° in the night, and this morning it took 1½ hours to get our foot-gear on, but we got away before eight. We lost cairn and tracks together and made as steady as we could N. by W., but have seen nothing. Worse was to come – the surface is simply awful. In spite of strong wind and full sail we have only done 5½ miles. We are in *very* Queer Street, since there is no doubt we cannot do the extra marches and feel the cold horribly.[6]

They did nearly ten miles that day, but on 3 March they had a terrible time. 'God help us,' wrote Scott, 'we can't keep up this pulling, that is certain. Amongst ourselves we are unendingly cheerful, but what each man feels in his heart I can only guess. Putting on foot-gear in the morning is getting slower and slower, therefore every day more dangerous.'

The following extracts are taken from Scott's diary.

March 4. Lunch. We are in a very tight place indeed, but none of us despondent *yet*, or at least we preserve every semblance of good cheer, but one's heart sinks as the sledge stops dead at some sastrugi behind which the surface sand lies thickly heaped. For the moment the temperature is in the −20° – an improvement which makes us much more comfortable, but a colder snap is bound to come again soon. I fear that Oates at least will weather such an event very poorly. Providence to our aid! We can expect little from man now except the possibility of extra food at the next depot. It will be real bad if we get there and find the same shortage of oil. Shall we get there? Such a short distance it would have appeared to us on the summit! I don't know what I should do if Wilson and Bowers weren't so determinedly cheerful over things.

Monday, March 5. Lunch. Regret to say going from bad to worse. We got a slant of wind yesterday afternoon, and going

6. *Scott's Last Expedition*, vol. i, pp. 582, 583.

on 5 hours we converted our wretched morning run of 3½ miles into something over 9. We went to bed on a cup of cocoa and pemmican solid with the chill off. . . . The result is telling on all, but mainly on Oates, whose feet are in a wretched condition. One swelled up tremendously last night and he is very lame this morning. We started march on tea and pemmican as last night – we pretend to prefer the pemmican this way. Marched for 5 hours this morning over a slightly better surface covered with high moundy sastrugi. Sledge capsized twice; we pulled on foot, covering 5½ miles. We are two pony marches and 4 miles from our depot. Our fuel dreadfully low and the poor Soldier nearly done. It is pathetic enough because we can do nothing for him; more hot food might do a little, but only a little, I fear. We none of us expected these terribly low temperatures, and of the rest of us, Wilson is feeling them most; mainly, I fear, from his self-sacrificing devotion in doctoring Oates' feet. We cannot help each other, each has enough to do to take care of himself. We get cold on the march when the trudging is heavy, and the wind pierces our worn garments. The others, all of them, are unendingly cheerful when in the tent. We mean to see the game through with a proper spirit, but it's tough work to be pulling harder than we ever pulled in our lives for long hours, and to feel that the progress is so slow. One can only say 'God help us!' and plod on our weary way, cold and very miserable, though outwardly cheerful. We talk of all sorts of subjects in the tent, not much of food now, since we decided to take the risk of running a full ration. We simply couldn't go hungry at this time.

Tuesday, March 6. Lunch. We did a little better with help of wind yesterday afternoon, finishing 9½ miles for the day, and 27 miles from depot. But this morning things have been awful. It was warm in the night and for the first time during the journey I overslept myself by more than an hour; then we were slow with foot-gear; then, pulling with all our might (for our lives) we could scarcely advance at a rate of a mile an hour; then it grew thick and three times we had to get out of harness to search for tracks. The result is something less than

3½ miles for the forenoon. The sun is shining now and wind gone. Poor Oates is unable to pull, sits on the sledge when we are track-searching – he is wonderfully plucky, as his feet must be giving him great pain. He makes no complaint, but his spirits only come up in spurts now, and he grows more silent in the tent. We are making a spirit lamp to try and replace the primus when our oil is exhausted. . . .

Wednesday, March 7. A little worse, I fear. One of Oates' feet *very* bad this morning; he is wonderfully brave. We still talk of what we will do together at home.

We only made 6½ miles yesterday. This morning in 4½ hours we did just over 4 miles. We are 16 miles from our depot. If we only find the correct proportion of food there and this surface continues, we may get to the next depot [Mt. Hooper, 72 miles farther] but not to One Ton Camp. We hope against hope that the dogs have been to Mt. Hooper; then we might pull through. If there is a shortage of oil we can have little hope. One feels that for poor Oates the crisis is near, but none of us are improving, though we are wonderfully fit considering the really excessive work we are doing. We are only kept going by good food. No wind this morning till a chill northerly air came ahead. Sun bright and cairns showing up well. I should like to keep the track to the end.

Thursday, March 8. *Lunch.* Worse and worse in morning; poor Oates' left foot can never last out, and time over foot-gear something awful. Have to wait in night foot-gear for nearly an hour before I start changing, and then am generally first to be ready. Wilson's feet giving trouble now, but this mainly because he gives so much help to others. We did 4½ miles this morning and are now 8½ miles from the depot – a ridiculously small distance to feel in difficulties, yet on this surface we know we cannot equal half our marches, and that for that effort we expend nearly double the energy. The great question is: What shall we find at the depot? If the dogs have visited it we may get along a good distance, but if there is another short allowance of fuel, God help us indeed. We are in a very bad way, I fear, in any case.

Saturday, March 10. Things steadily downhill. Oates' foot

worse. He has rare pluck and must know that he can never get through. He asked Wilson if he had a chance this morning, and of course Bill had to say he didn't know. In point of fact he has none. Apart from him, if he went under now, I doubt whether we could get through. With great care we might have a dog's chance, but no more. The weather conditions are awful, and our gear gest steadily more icy and difficult to manage . . .

Yesterday we marched up the depot, Mt. Hooper. Cold comfort. Shortage on our allowance all round. I don't know that any one is to blame. The dogs which would have been our salvation have evidently failed. Meares had a bad trip home I suppose.

This morning it was calm when we breakfasted, but the wind came from the W.N.W. as we broke camp. It rapidly grew in strength. After travelling for half an hour I saw that none of us could go on facing such conditions. We were forced to camp and are spending the rest of the day in a comfortless blizzard camp, wind quite foul.

Sunday, March 11. Titus Oates is very near the end, one feels. What we or he will do, God only knows. We discussed the matter after breakfast; he is a brave fine fellow and understands the situation, but he practically asked for advice. Nothing could be said but to urge him to march as long as he could. One satisfactory result to the discussion: I practically ordered Wilson to hand over the means of ending our troubles to us, so that any one of us may know how to do so. Wilson had no choice between doing so and our ransacking the medicine case. We have 30 opium tabloids apiece and he is left with a tube of morphine. So far the tragical side of our story.

The sky completely overcast when we started this morning. We could see nothing, lost the tracks, and doubtless have been swaying a good deal since – 3.1 miles for the forenoon – terribly heavy dragging – expected it. Know that 6 miles is about the limit of our endurance now, if we get no help from wind or surfaces. We have 7 days' food and should be about 55 miles from One Ton Camp tonight, $6 \times 7 = 42$, leaving us 13 miles short of our distance, even if things get no worse. Meanwhile the season rapidly advances.

Monday, March 12. We did 6.9 miles yesterday, under our necessary average. Things are left much the same, Oates not pulling much, and now with hands as well as feet pretty well useless. We did 4 miles this morning in 4 hours 20 min. – we may hope for 3 this afternoon, $7 \times 6 = 42$. We shall be 47 miles from the depot. I doubt if we can possibly do it. The surface remains awful, the cold intense, and our physical condition running down. God help us! Not a breath of favourable wind for more than a week, and apparently liable to head winds at any moment.

Wednesday, March 14. No doubt about the going downhill, but everything going wrong for us. Yesterday we woke to a strong northerly wind with temp. $-37°$. Couldn't face it, so remained in camp til 2, then did 5¼ miles. Wanted to march later, but party feeling the cold badly as the breeze (N.) never took off entirely, and as the sun sank the temp. fell. Long time getting supper in dark.

This morning started with southerly breeze, set sail and passed another cairn at good speed; half-way, however, the wind shifted to W. by S. or W.S.W., blew through our wind-clothes and into our mitts. Poor Wilson horribly cold, could [not] get off ski for some time. Bowers and I practically made camp, and when we got into the tent at last we were all deadly cold. Then temp. now midday down $-43°$ and the wind strong. We *must* go on, but now the making of every camp must be more difficult and dangerous. It must be near the end, but a pretty merciful end. Poor Oates got it again in the foot. I shudder to think what it will be like tomorrow. It is only with greatest pains rest of us keep off frost-bites. No idea there could be temperatures like this at this time of year with such winds. Truly awful outside the tent. Must fight it out to the last biscuit; but can't reduce rations.

Friday, March 16, *or Saturday,* 17. Lost track of dates, but think the last correct. Tragedy all along the line. At lunch, the day before yesterday, poor Titus Oates said he couldn't go on; he proposed we should leave him in his sleeping-bag. That we could not do, and we induced him to come on, on the afternoon march. In spite of its awful nature for him he struggled on and we made a few miles. At night he was worse and we knew the end had come.

Should this be found I want these facts recorded. Oates' last thoughts were of his mother, but immediately before he took pride in thinking that his regiment would be pleased with the bold way in which he met his death. We can testify to his bravery. He has borne intense suffering for weeks without complaint, and to the very last was able and willing to discuss outside subjects. He did not – would not – give up hope till the very end. He was a brave soul. This was the end. He slept through the night before last, hoping not to wake; but he woke in the morning – yesterday. It was blowing a blizzard. He said, 'I am just going outside and may be some time.' He went out into the blizzard and we have not seen him since.

I take this opportunity of saying that we have stuck to our sick companions to the last. In case of Edgar Evans, when absolutely out of food and he lay insensible, the safety of the remainder seemed to demand his abandonment, but Providence mercifully removed him at this critical moment. He died a natural death, and we did not leave him till two hours after his death. We knew that poor Oates was walking to his death, but though we tried to dissuade him, we knew it was the act of a brave man and an English gentleman. We all hope to meet the end with a similar spirit, and assuredly the end is not far.

I can only write at lunch and then only occasionally. The cold is intense, $-40°$ at midday. My companions are unendingly cheerful, but we are all on the verge of serious frost-bites, and though we constantly talk of fetching through I don't think any one of us believes it in his heart.

We are cold on the march now, and at all times except meals. Yesterday we had to lay up for a blizzard and today we move dreadfully slowly. We are at No. 14 Pony Camp, only two pony marches from One Ton Depot. We leave here our theodolite, a camera, and Oates' sleeping-bags. Diaries, etc., and geological specimens carried at Wilson's special request, will be found with us or on our sledge.

Sunday, March 18. Today, lunch, we are 21 miles from the depot. Ill fortune presses, but better may come. We have had more wind and drift from ahead yesterday; had to stop marching; wind N.W., force 4, temp. −35°. No human being could face it, and we are worn out *nearly*.

My right foot has gone, nearly all the toes – two days ago I was proud possessor of best feet. . . . Bowers takes first place in condition, but there is not much to choose after all. The others are still confident of getting through – or pretend to be – I don't know! We have the last *half* fill of oil in our primus and a very small quantity of spirit – this alone between us and thirst. The wind is fair for the moment, and that is perhaps a fact to help. The mileage would have seemed ridiculously small on our outward journey.

Monday, March 19. *Lunch*. We camped with difficulty last night and were dreadfully cold till after our supper of cold pemmican and biscuit and a half pannikin of cocoa cooked over the spirit. Then, contrary to expectation, we got warm and all slept well. Today we started in the usual dragging manner. Sledge dreadfully heavy. We are 15½ miles from the depot and ought to get there in three days. What progress! We have two days' food but barely a day's fuel. All our feet are getting bad – Wilson's best, my right foot worse, left all right. There is no chance to nurse one's feet till we can get hot food into us. Amputation is the least I can hope for now, but will the trouble spread? That is the serious question. The weather doesn't give us a chance – the wind from N. to N.W. and −40° temp. today.

Wednesday, March 21. Got within 11 miles of depot Monday night; had to lay up all yesterday in severe blizzard. Today forlorn hope, Wilson and Bowers going to depot for fuel.

22 *and* 23. Blizzard bad as ever – Wilson and Bowers unable to start – tomorrow last chance – no fuel and only one

or two of food left – must be near the end. Have decided it shall be natural – we shall march for the depot with or without our effects and die in our tracks.

Thursday, March 29. Since the 21st we have had a continuous gale from W.S.W. and S.W. We had fuel to make two cups of tea apiece and bare food for two days on the 20th. Every day we have been ready to start for our depot 11 *miles* away, but outside the door of the tent it remains a scene of whirling drift. I do not think we can hope for any better things now. We shall stick it out to the end, but we are getting weaker, of course, and the end cannot be far.

It seems a pity, but I do not think I can write more.

R. SCOTT

Last entry. For God's sake, look after our people.

The following extracts are from letters written by Scott:

To Mrs E. A. Wilson

MY DEAR MRS WILSON. If this letter reaches you, Bill and I will have gone out together. We are very near it now and I should like you to know how splendid he was at the end – everlastingly cheerful and ready to sacrifice himself for others, never a word of blame to me for leading him into this mess. He is not suffering, luckily, at least only minor discomforts.

His eyes have a comfortable blue look of hope and his mind is peaceful with the satisfaction of his faith in regarding himself as part of the great scheme of the Almighty. I can do no more to comfort you than to tell you that he died as he lived, a brave, true man – the best of comrades and staunchest of friends.

My whole heart goes out to you in pity. Yours,

R. SCOTT

To Mrs Bowers

MY DEAR MRS BOWERS. I am afraid this will reach you after one of the heaviest blows of your life.

I write when we are very near the end of our journey, and I am finishing it in company with two gallant, noble gentlemen. One of these is your son. He had come to be one of my closest and soundest friends, and I appreciate his wonderful upright nature, his ability and energy. As the troubles have thickened his dauntless spirit ever shone brighter and he has remained cheerful, hopeful and indomitable to the end . . .

To Sir J. M. Barrie

MY DEAR BARRIE. We are pegging out in a very comfortless spot. Hoping this letter may be found and sent to you, I write a word of farewell . . . Good-bye. I am not at all afraid of the end, but sad to miss many a humble pleasure which I had planned for the future on our long marches. I may not have proved a great explorer, but we have done the greatest march ever made and come very near to great success. Good-bye, my dear friend. Yours ever,

R. SCOTT

We are in a desperate state, feet frozen, etc. No fuel and a long way from food, but it would do your heart good to be in our tent, to hear our songs and the cheery conversation as to what we will do when we get to Hut Point.

Later. We are very near the end, but have not and will not lose our good cheer. We have four days of storm in our tent and nowhere's food or fuel. We did intend to finish ourselves when things proved like this, but we have decided to die naturally in the tracks.[7]

The following extracts are from letters written to other friends:

. . . I want to tell you that I was *not* too old for this job. It was the younger men that went under first. . . . After all we are setting a good example to our countrymen, if not by getting into a tight place, by facing it like men when we were there. We could have come through had we neglected the sick.

7. *Scott's Last Expedition*, vol. i, pp. 584–99.

Wilson, the best fellow that ever stepped, has sacrificed himself again and again to the sick men of the party . . .

. . . Our journey has been the biggest on record, and nothing but the most exceptional hard luck at the end would have caused us to fail to return.

What lots and lots I could tell you of this journey. How much better has it been than lounging in too great comfort at home.

MESSAGE TO THE PUBLIC

The causes of the disaster are not due to faulty organization, but to misfortune in all risks which had to be undertaken.

1. The loss of pony transport in March 1911 obliged me to start later than I had intended, and obliged the limits of stuff transported to be narrowed.

2. The weather throughout the outward journey, and especially the long gale in 83° S., stopped us.

3. The soft snow in lower reaches of glacier again reduced pace.

We fought these untoward events with a will and conquered, but it cut into our provision reserve.

Every detail of our food supplies, clothing and depots made on the interior ice-sheet and over that long stretch of 700 miles to the Pole and back, worked to perfection. The advance party would have returned to the glacier in fine form and with surplus of food, but for the astonishing failure of the man whom we had least expected to fail. Edgar Evans was thought the strongest man of the party.

The Beardmore Glacier is not difficult in fine weather, but on our return we did not get a single completely fine day; this with a sick companion enormously increased our anxieties.

As I have said elsewhere, we got into frightfully rough ice and Edgar Evans received a concussion of the brain – he died a natural death, but left us a shaken party with the season unduly advanced.

But all the facts above enumerated were as nothing to the surprise which awaited us on the Barrier. I maintain that our arrangements for returning were quite adequate, and that no one in the world would have expected the temperatures and surfaces which we encountered at this time of the year. On the summit in lat. 85°–86° we had −20°, −30°. On the Barrier in lat. 82°, 10,000 feet lower, we had −30° in the day, −47° at night pretty regularly, with continuous head-wind during our day marches. It is clear that these circumstances come on very suddenly, and our wreck is certainly due to this sudden advent of severe weather, which does not seem to have any satisfactory cause. I do not think human beings ever came through such a month as we have come through, and we should have got through in spite of the weather but for the sickening of a second companion, Captain Oates, and a shortage of fuel in our depots for which I cannot account, and finally, but for the storm which has fallen on us within 11 miles of the depot at which we hoped to secure our final supplies. Surely misfortune could scarcely have exceeded this last blow. We arrived within 11 miles of our old One Ton Camp with fuel for one last meal and food for two days. For four days we have been unable to leave the tent – the gale howling about us. We are weak, writing is difficult, but for my own sake I do not regret this journey, which has shown that Englishmen can endure hardships, help one another, and meet death with as great a fortitude as ever in the past. We took risks, we knew we took them; things have come out against us, and therefore we have no cause for complaint, but bow to the will of Providence, determined still to do our best to the last. But if we have been willing to give our lives to this enterprise, which is for the honour of our country, I appeal to our countrymen to see that those who depend on us are properly cared for.

Had we lived, I should have had a tale to tell of the hardihood, endurance, and courage of my companions which would have stirred the heart of every Englishman. These rough notes and our dead bodies must tell the tale, but surely, surely a great rich country like ours will see that those who are dependent on us are properly provided for. R. SCOTT.[8]

8. *Scott's Last Expedition*, vol. i, pp. 605–7.

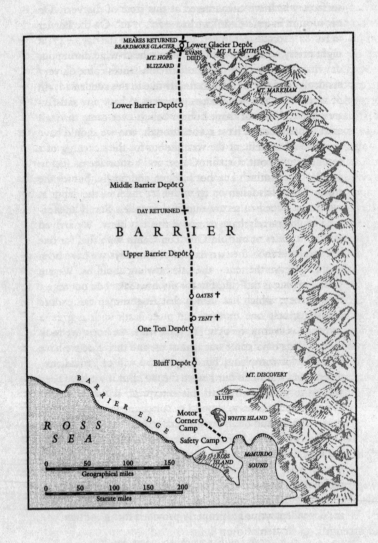

MEARES RETURNED
BEARDMORE GLACIER ○ Lower Glacier Depôt
MT. HOPE EVANS *MT. F. L. SMITH*
DIED
BLIZZARD

MT. MARKHAM

Lower Barrier Depôt ○

Middle Barrier Depôt ○

DAY RETURNED ✝

B A R R I E R

Upper Barrier Depôt ○

○ *OATES* ✝

○ *TENT* ✝

One Ton Depôt ○

Bluff Depôt ○

MT. DISCOVERY

B
A
R
R
I
E
R   *BLUFF*   *WHITE ISLAND*

E
D
G
E   Motor
    Corner
R O S S   Camp ○
        Safety Camp
S E A   *ROSS*   *McMURDO*
                ISLAND *SOUND*

0   50   100   150
|————————————————————————|
Geographical miles

0   50   100   150   200
|————————————————————————————|
Statute miles

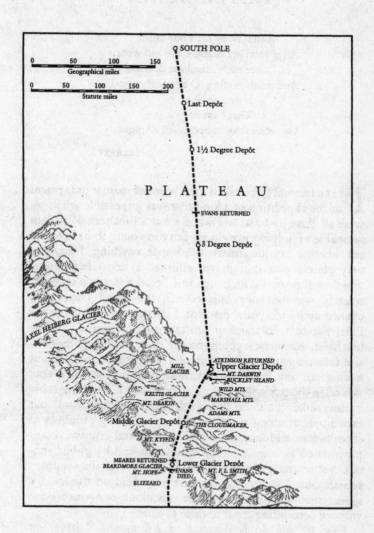

SOUTH POLE

0   50   100   150
Geographical miles

0   50   100   150   200
Statute miles

Last Depôt

1½ Degree Depôt

P L A T E A U

EVANS RETURNED

3 Degree Depôt

AXEL HEIBERG GLACIER

MILL
GLACIER

ATKINSON RETURNED
Upper Glacier Depôt
MT. DARWIN
BUCKLEY ISLAND
WILD MTS.

KELTIE GLACIER
MT. DEAKIN

MARSHALL MTS.

ADAMS MTS.

Middle Glacier Depôt

THE CLOUDMAKER

MT. KYFFIN

MEARES RETURNED
BEARDMORE GLACIER
MT. HOPE

Lower Glacier Depôt
EVANS
DIED

MT. F. L. SMITH

BLIZZARD

Chapter Nineteen
NEVER AGAIN

And now in age I bud again,
After so many deaths I live and write;
I once more smell the dew and rain,
And relish versing. O my onely light,
It cannot be
That I am he
On whom thy tempests fell all night.

HERBERT

I SHALL inevitably be asked for a word of mature judgement of the expedition of a kind that was impossible when we were all close up to it, and when I was a subaltern of 24, not incapable of judging my elders, but too young to have found out whether my judgement was worth anything. I now see very plainly that though we achieved a first-rate tragedy, which will never be forgotten just because it was a tragedy, tragedy was not our business. In the broad perspective opened up by ten years' distance, I see not one journey to the Pole, but two, in startling contrast one to another. On the one hand, Amundsen going straight there, getting there first, and returning without the loss of a single man, and without having put any greater strain on himself and his men than was all in the day's work of polar exploration. Nothing more business-like could be imagined. On the other hand, our expedition, running appalling risks, performing prodigies of superhuman endurance, achieving immortal renown, commemorated in august cathedral sermons and by public statues, yet reaching the Pole only to find our terrible journey superfluous, and leaving our best men dead on the ice. To ignore such a contrast would be ridiculous: to write a book without accounting for it a waste of time.

First let me do full justice to Amundsen. I have not attempted to disguise how we felt towards him when, after leading us to believe that he had equipped the *Fram* for an Arctic journey, and sailed for the north, he suddenly made his dash for the south. Nothing makes a more unpleasant impression than a feint. But when Scott reached the Pole only to find that Amundsen had been there a month before him, his distress was not that of a schoolboy who has lost a race. I have described what it had cost Scott and his four companions to get to the Pole, and what they had still to suffer in returning until death stopped them. Much of that risk and racking toil had been undertaken that men might learn what the world is like at the spot where the sun does not decline in the heavens, where a man loses his orbit and turns like a joint on a spit, and where his face, however he turns, is always to the North. The moment Scott saw the Norwegian tent he knew that he had nothing to tell that was not already known. His achievement was a mere precaution against Amundsen perishing on his way back; and that risk was no greater than his own. The Polar Journey was literally laid waste: that was the shock that staggered them. Well might Bowers be glad to see the last of Norskies' tracks as their homeward paths diverged.

All this heartsickness has passed away now; and the future explorer will not concern himself with it. He will ask, what was the secret of Amundsen's slick success? What is the moral of our troubles and losses? I will take Amundsen's success first. Undoubtedly the very remarkable qualities of the man himself had a good deal to do with it. There is a sort of sagacity that constitutes the specific genius of the explorer; and Amundsen proved his possession of this by his guess that there was terra firma in the Bay of Whales as solid as on Ross Island. Then there is the quality of big leadership which is shown by daring to take a big chance. Amundsen took a very big one indeed when he turned from the route to the Pole explored and ascertained by Scott and Shackleton and determined to find a second pass over the mountains from the Barrier to the plateau. As it happened, he succeeded, and established his route as the best way to the Pole until a better is discovered. But he might easily have failed and perished in the attempt; and the combination of reasoning and daring that nerved him to make it can hardly be overrated. All these things helped him. Yet any rather conservative whaling captain might have refused to make Scott's experiment with motor transport, ponies and man-hauling, and stuck to the dogs; and to the use of ski in running those dogs; and it was this quite commonplace choice that sent Amundsen so gaily to the Pole and back: with no abnormal strain on men or dogs, and no great hardship either. He never pulled a mile from start to finish.

The very ease of the exploit makes it impossible to infer from it that Amundsen's expedition was more highly endowed in personal qualities than ours. We did not suffer from too little brains or daring: we may have suffered from too much. We were primarily a great scientific expedition, with the Pole as our bait for public support, though it was not more important than any other acre of the plateau. We followed in the steps of a polar expedition which brought back more results than any of its fore-runners: Scott's *Discovery* voyage. We had the largest and most efficient scientific staff that ever left England. We were discursive. We were full of intellectual interests and curiosities of all kinds. We took on the work of two or three expeditions.

It is obvious that there are disadvantages in such a division of energy. Scott wanted to reach the Pole: a dangerous and laborious exploit, but a practicable one. Wilson wanted to obtain the egg of the Emperor penguin: a horribly dangerous and inhumanly exhausting feat which is none the less impracticable because the three men who achieved it survived by a miracle. These two feats had to be piled one on top of the other. What with the Depot Journey and others, in addition to these two, we were sledged out by the end of our second sledging season, and our worst year was still to come. We, the survivors, went in search of the dead when there was a possibly living party waiting in the ice somewhere for us to succour them. That turned out all right, because when we got back, we found Campbell's party self-extricated and waiting for us, alive and well. But suppose they also had perished, what would have been said of us?

The practical man of the world has plenty of criticism of the way things were done. He says dogs should have been taken; but he does not show how they could have been got up and down the Beardmore. He is scandalized because 30 lbs. of geological specimens were deliberately added to the weight of the sledge that was dragging the life out of the men who had to haul it; but he does not realize that it is the friction surfaces of the snow on the runners which mattered and not the dead weight, which in this case was almost negligible. Nor does he know that these same specimens dated a continent and may elucidate the whole history of plant life. He will admit that we were all very wonderful, very heroic, very beautiful and devoted: that our exploits gave a glamour to our expedition that Amundsen's cannot claim; but he has no patience with us, and declares that Amundsen was perfectly right in refusing to allow science to use up the forces of his men, or to interfere for a moment with his single business of getting to the Pole and back again. No doubt he was; but we were not out for a single business: we were out for everything we could add to the world's store of knowledge about the Antarctic.

Of course the whole business simply bristles with 'ifs': If Scott had taken dogs and succeeded in getting them up the Beardmore; if we had not lost those ponies on the Depot Journey: if the dogs had not been taken so far and the One Ton Depot had been laid: if a pony and some extra oil had been depoted on the Barrier: if a four-man party had been taken to the Pole: if I had disobeyed my instructions and gone on from One Ton, killing dogs as necessary: or even if I had just gone on a few miles and left some food and fuel under a flag upon a cairn: if they had been first at the Pole: if it had been any other season but that. . . . But always the bare fact remains that Scott could not have travelled from McMurdo Sound to the Pole faster than he did except with dogs; all the king's horses and all the king's men could not have done it. Why, then, says the practical man, did we go to McMurdo Sound instead of to the Bay of Whales? Because we gained that continuity of scientific observation which is so important in this work: and because the Sound was the starting-point for continuing the exploration of the only ascertained route to the Pole, via the Beardmore Glacier.

I am afraid it was all inevitable: we were as wise as anyone can be before the event. I admit that we, scrupulously economical of our pemmican, were terribly prodigal of our man-power. But we had to be: the draft, whatever it may have been on the whole, was not excessive at any given point; and anyhow we just had to use every man to take every opportunity. There is so much to do, and the opportunities for doing it are so rare. Generally speaking, I don't see how we could have done differently, but I don't want to see it done again; I don't want it to be necessary to do it again. I want to see this country tackle the job, and send enough men to do one thing at a time. They do it in Canada: why not in England too?

But we wasted our man-power in one way which could have been avoided. I have described how every emergency was met by calling for volunteers, and how the volunteers were always forthcoming. Unfortunately volunteering was relied on not only for emergencies, but for a good deal of everyday work that should have been organized as routine; and the inevitable result was that the willing horses were overworked. It was a point of honour not to ca' canny. Men were allowed to do too much, and were told afterwards that they had done too much; and that is not discipline. They should not have been allowed to do too much. Until our last year we never insisted on a regular routine.

Money was scarce: probably Scott could not have obtained the funds for the expedition if its objective had not been the Pole. There was no lack of the things which could be bought across the counter from big business houses – all landing, sledging and scientific equipment was first-class – but one of the first and most important items, the ship, would have sent Columbus on strike, and nearly sent us to the bottom of the sea.

People talk of the niggardly equipment of Columbus when he sailed west from the Canaries to try a short-cut to an inhabited continent of magnificent empires, as he thought; but his three ships were, relatively to the resources of that time, much better than the one old tramp in which we sailed for a desert of ice in which the evening and morning are the year and not the day, and in which not even polar bears and reindeers can live. Amundsen had the *Fram*, built for polar exploration *ad hoc*. Scott had the *Discovery*. But when one thinks of these *Nimrod*s and *Terra Nova*s, picked up second-hand in the wooden-ship market, and faked up for the transport of ponies, dogs, motors, and all the impedimenta of a polar expedition, to say nothing of the men who have to try and do scientific work inside them, one feels disposed to clamour for a Polar Factory Act making it a crime to ship men for the ice in vessels more fit to ply between London Bridge and Ramsgate.

And then the begging that is necessary to obtain even this equipment. Shackleton hanging round the doors of rich men! Scott writing begging letters for months together! Is the country not ashamed?

Modern civilized States should make up their minds to the endowment of research, which includes exploration; and as all States benefit alike by the scientific side of it there is plenty of scope for international arrangement, especially in a region where the mere grabbing of territory is meaningless, and no Foreign Office can trace the frontier between King Edward's Plateau and King Haakon's. The Antarctic continent is still mostly unexplored; but enough is known of it to put any settlement by ordinary pioneer emigration, pilgrim fathers and the like, out of the question. Ross Island is not a place for a settlement: it is a place for an elaborately equipped scientific station, with a staff in residence for a year at a time. Our stay of three years was far too much: another year would have driven the best of us mad. Of the five main journeys which fell to my lot, one, the Winter Journey, should not have been undertaken at all with our equipment; and two others, the Dog Journey and the Search Journey, had better have been done by fresh men. It is no use repeating that Englishmen will respond to every call and stick it to the death: they will (some of them); but they have to pay the price all the same; and the price in my case was an overdraft on my vital capital which I shall never quite pay off, and in the case of five bigger, stronger, more seasoned men, death. The establishment of such stations and of such a service cannot be done by individual heroes and enthusiasts cadging for cheques from rich men and grants from private scientific societies: it is a business, like the Nares Arctic expedition, for public organization.

I do not suppose that in these days of aviation the next visit to the Pole will be made by men on foot dragging sledges, or by men on sledges dragged by dogs, mules or ponies; nor will depots be laid in that way. The pack will not, I hope, be broken through by any old coal-burning ship that can be picked up in the second-hand market. Specially built ships, and enough of them; specially engined tractors and aeroplanes; specially trained men and plenty of them, will all be needed if the work is to be done in any sort of humane and civilized fashion; and Cabinet ministers and voters alike must learn to value knowledge that is not baited by suffering and death. My own bolt is shot; I do not suppose I shall ever go south again before I go west; but if I do it will be under proper and reasonable conditions. I may not come back a hero; but I shall come back none the worse; for I repeat, the Antarctic, in moderation as to length of stay, and with such accommodation as is now easily within the means of modern civilized Powers, is not half as bad a place for public service as the worst military stations on the equator. I hope that by the time Scott comes home – for he is coming home: the Barrier is moving, and not a trace of our funeral cairn was found by Shackleton's men in 1916 – the hardships that wasted his life will be only a horror of the past, and his *via dolorosa* a highway as practicable as Piccadilly.

And now let me come down to tin tacks. No matter how well the thing is done in future, its organizers will want to know at first all we can tell them about oil, about cold, and about food. First, as to oil.

Scott complains of a shortage of oil at several of his last depots. There is no doubt that this shortage was due to the perishing of the leather washers of the tins which contained the paraffin oil. All these tins had been subjected to the warmth of the sun in summer and the autumn temperatures, which were unexpectedly cold. In his *Voyage of the Discovery* Scott wrote as follows of the tins in which they drew their oil when sledging:

> Each tin had a small cork bung, which was a decided weakness; paraffin *creeps* in the most annoying manner, and a good deal of oil was wasted in this way, especially when the sledges were travelling over rough ground and were shaken or, as frequently happened, capsized. It was impossible to make these bungs quite tight, however closely they were jammed down, so that in spite of a trifling extra weight a much better fitting would have been a metallic screwed bung. To find on opening a fresh tin of oil that it was only three-parts full was very distressing, and of course meant that the cooker had to be used with still greater care.[1]

Amundsen wrote of his paraffin: 'We kept it in the usual cans but they proved too weak; not that we lost any paraffin, but Bjaaland had to be constantly soldering to keep them tight.'[2]

Our own tins were furnished with the metallic screwed stoppers which Scott recommended. There was no trouble reported[3] until we came up to One Ton Camp when on the Search Journey. Here was the depot of food and oil which I had laid in the previous autumn for the Polar Party, stowed in a canvas 'tank' which was buried beneath seven feet of snow; the oil was placed on the top of the snow, in order

1. Scott, *Voyage of the Discovery*, vol. i, p. 449.
2. Amundsen, *The South Pole*, vol. ii, p. 19.
3. Lashly's diary records that the Second Return Party found a shortage of oil at the Middle Barrier Depot (see p. 410).

that the red tins might prove an additional mark for the depot. When we dug out the tank the food inside was almost uneatable owing to the quantity of paraffin which had found its way down through seven feet of snow during the winter and spring.

We then found the Polar Party and learned of the shortage of oil. After our return to Cape Evans someone was digging about the camp and came across a wooden case containing eight one-gallon tins of paraffin. These had been placed there in September 1911, to be landed at Cape Crozier by the *Terra Nova* when she came down. The ship could not take them: they were snowed up during the winter, lost and forgotten, until dug up fifteen months afterwards. Three tins were full, three empty, one a third full and one two-thirds full.

There can be no doubt that the oil, which was specially volatile, tended to vaporize and escape through the stoppers, and that this process was accelerated by the perishing, and I suggest also the hardening and shrinking, of the leather washers. Another expedition will have to be very careful on this point: they might reduce the risk by burying the oil.

The second point about which something must be said is the unexpected cold met by Scott on the Barrier, which was the immediate cause of the disaster.

No one in the world would have expected the temperatures and surfaces which we encountered at this time of the year. . . . It is clear that these circumstances come on very suddenly, and our wreck is certainly due to this sudden advent of severe weather, which does not seem to have any satisfactory cause.[4]

They came down the glacier in plus temperatures: nor was there anything abnormal for more than a week after they got on to the Barrier. Then there came a big drop to a $-37°$ minimum on the night of 26 February. It is significant that the sun began to dip below the southern horizon at midnight

4. Scott, 'Message to the Public'.

about this time. 'There is no doubt the middle of the Barrier is a pretty awful locality,' wrote Scott.

Simpson, in his meteorological report, has little doubt that the temperatures met by the Polar Party were abnormal. The records 'clearly bring to light the possibility of great cold at an extremely early period in the year within a comparatively few miles of an open sea where the temperatures were over 40 degrees higher.' 'It is quite impossible to believe that normally there is a difference of nearly 40 degrees in March between McMurdo Sound and the South of the Barrier.' The temperatures recorded by other sledge parties in March 1912 and those recorded at Cape Evans form additional evidence, in Simpson's opinion, that the temperatures experienced by Scott were not such as might be expected during normal autumn weather.

Simpson's explanation is based upon the observations made in McMurdo Sound by sending up balloons with self-recording instruments attached. These showed that very rapid radiation takes place from the snow surface in winter, which cools the air in the immediate neighbourhood: a cold layer of air is thus formed near the ground, which may be many degrees colder than the air above it. It becomes, as it were, colder than it ought to be. This, however, can only happen during an absence of wind: when a wind blows the cold layer is swept away, the air is mixed and the temperature rises.

The absence of wind from the south noted by Scott was, in Simpson's opinion, the cause of the low temperatures met by Scott: the temperature was reduced ten degrees below normal at Cape Evans, and perhaps twenty degrees where Scott was.[5]

The third question is that of food. It is this point which is most important to future explorers. It is a fact that the Polar Party failed to make their distance because they became

5. A full discussion of these and other Antarctic temperatures is to be found in the scientific reports of the British Antarctic Expedition, 1910–13, 'Meteorology', vol. i, chap. ii, by G. C. Simpson.

weak, and that they became weak although they were eating their full ration or more than their full ration of food, save for a few days when they went short on the way down the Beardmore Glacier. The first man to weaken was the biggest and heaviest man in the expedition: 'the man whom we had least expected to fail'.

The rations were of two kinds. The Barrier (B) ration was that which was used on the Barrier during the outward journey towards the Pole. The Summit (S) ration was the result of our experiments on the Winter Journey. I expect it is the best ration which has been used to date, and consisted of biscuits 16, pemmican 12, butter 2, cocoa 0.57, sugar 3 and tea 0.86 ounces; total 34.43 ounces daily per man.

The twelve men who went forward started this S ration at the foot of the Beardmore, and it was this ration which was left in all depots to see them home. It was much more satisfying than the Barrier ration, and men could not have eaten so much when leading ponies or driving dogs in the early stages of summer Barrier sledging: but man-hauling is a different business altogether from leading ponies or driving dogs.

It is calculated that the body requires certain proportions of fat, carbohydrates and proteins to do certain work under certain conditions: but just what the absolute quantities are is not ascertained. The work of the Polar Party was laborious: the temperatures (the most important of the conditions) varied from comparative warmth up and down the glacier to an average of about $-20°$ in the rarefied air of the plateau. The temperatures met by them on their return over the Barrier were not really low for more than a week, and then there came quite commonly minus thirties during the day with a further drop to minus forties at night, when for a time the sun was below the horizon. These temperatures, which are not very terrible to men who are fresh and whose clothing is new, were ghastly to these men who had striven night and day almost ceaselessly for four months on, as I maintain, insufficient food. Did these temperatures kill them?

Undoubtedly the low temperatures caused their death, inasmuch as they would have lived had the temperatures remained high. But Evans would not have lived: he died before the low temperatures occurred. What killed Evans? And why did the other men weaken as they did, though they were eating full rations and more? Weaken so much that in the end they starved to death?

I have always had a doubt whether the weather conditions were sufficient to cause the tragedy. These men on full rations were supposed to be eating food of sufficient value to enable them to do the work they were doing, under the conditions which they actually met until the end of February, without loss of strength. They had more than their full rations, but the conditions in March were much worse than they imagined to be possible: when three survivors out of the five pitched their Last Camp they were in a terrible state. After the war I found that Atkinson had come to wonder much as I, but he had gone farther, for he had the values of our rations worked out by a chemical expert according to the latest knowledge and standards. I may add that, being in command after Scott's death, he increased the ration for the next year's sledging, so I suppose he had already come to the conclusion that the previous ration was not sufficient. The following are some of the data for which I am indebted to him: the whole subject will be investigated by him and the results published in a more detailed form.

According to the most modern standards the food requirements for laborious work at a temperature of zero Fahr. (which is a fair Barrier average temperature to take) are 7714 calories to produce 10,069 foot-tons of work. The actual Barrier ration which we used would generate 4003 calories, equivalent to 5331 foot-tons of work. Similar requirements for laborious work at −10° Fahr. (which is a high average plateau temperature) are 8500 calories to produce 11,094 foot-tons of work. The actual Summit ration would generate 4889 calories, equivalent to 6608 foot-tons of work. These requirements are calculated for total absorption of all food-stuffs:

but in practice, by visual proof, this does not take place: this is especially noticeable in the case of fats, a quantity of which were digested neither by men, ponies, nor dogs.

Several things go to prove that our ration was not enough. In the first case we were probably not as fit as we seemed after long sledge journeys. There is no doubt that when sledging men developed an automaticity of certain muscles at the expense of other muscles: for instance, a sledge could be hauled all day at the expense of the arms, and we had little power to lift weights at the end of several months of sledging. In relation to this I would add that, when the relief ship arrived in February 1912, four of us were at Cape Evans, but just arrived from three months of the Polar Journey. The land party, we four among them, were turned on to sledge stores ashore. This in practice meant twenty miles every day dragging a sledge; a good deal of 'humping' heavy cases, from five o'clock in the morning to very late at night; with uncertain meals and no rests. I can remember now how hard that work was to myself and, I expect, to those others who had been away sledging. The ship's party sledged only every other day 'because they were not used to it'. This was extremely bad organization, and in view of the possibility that some of the men might be required for further sledging in the autumn, just silly.

Again, there is the experience of the man-hauling parties of the Polar Journey. There was, you may remember, a man-hauling party on the way to the Beardmore Glacier. They travelled with a light sledge but they lost weight on the Barrier ration. It is significant that they picked up condition when they started the Summit ration, especially Lashly.

The Polar Party and the two remaining parties, who were on the Summit ration from the foot of the Beardmore until the end of their journeys, weakened, in Atkinson's opinion, more than they should have done had their ration been sufficient. The First Return Party covered approximately 1100 statute miles. At the end of their journey their pulling muscles were all right, but Atkinson, who led the party, considers that they were at least 70 per cent weaker in other muscles. They all lost a great deal of weight, though they had the best conditions of the three returning parties, and the temperatures met by them averaged well over zero.

The Second Return Party faced much worse conditions. They were only three men, and one of the three was so sick that for 120 miles he could not pull and for 90 miles he had to be dragged on the sledge. The average temperature approximated zero. They were extremely exhausted.

Scott makes constant reference to the increasing hunger of the Polar Party: it is clear that the food did not compensate for the conditions which were met in increasing severity. Yet they were eating rather more than their full ration a considerable part of the time. It has to be considered that the temperatures met by them averaged far below $-10°$: that they did not absorb all their food: that increased heat was wanted not only for energy to do extra work caused by bad surfaces and contrary winds, but also to heat their bodies, and to thaw out their clothing and sleeping-bags.

I believe it to be clear that the rations used by us most not only be increased by future expeditions, but coordinated in different proportions of fats, proteins and carbohydrates. Taking into consideration the fact that our bodies were not digesting the amount of fats we had provided, Atkinson suggests that it is useless to increase the fats at the expense of the protein and carbohydrates. He recommends that fats should total about 5 ounces daily. The digestion of carbohydrates is easy and complete, and though that of protein is more complicated there are plenty of the necessary digestive ferments. The ration should be increased by equal amounts of protein and carbohydrates: both should be provided in as dry and pure a form as possible.

There is no censure attached to this criticism. Our ration was probably the best which has been used: but more is known now than was known then. We are all out to try and get these things for the future.[6]

6. Modern research suggests that the presence or absence of certain vitamins makes a difference, and it may be a very great difference, in the ability of

Campbell reached Hut Point only five days after we left it with the dog-teams. A characteristic note left to greet us on our return regretted they were too late to take part in the Search Journey. If I had lived through ten months such as those men had just endured, wild horses would not have dragged me out sledging again. But they were keen to get some useful work done in the time which remained until the ship arrived.

We had the Polar records: Campbell and his men, unaided, had not only survived their terrible winter, but had sledged down the coast after it. We ourselves, faced by a difficult alternative, had fallen on our feet. We never hoped for more than this: we seldom hoped for so much.

I wanted a series of Adélie penguin embryos from the rookery at Cape Royds, but had not expected an opportunity of getting them because I was away sledging during the summer months. Now the chance had come. Atkinson wanted to work on parasites at the same place, and others to survey. But the real job was an ascent of Erebus, the active volcano which rose from our doors to some 13,400 feet in height. A party of Shackleton's men under Professor David went up it in March, and managed to haul a sledge up to 5800 feet, from which point they had to portage their gear. A year before this, Debenham, with the help of a telescope, selected a route by which they could haul a sledge up to 9000

---

any individual to profit by the food supplied to him. If this be so, this factor must have had great influence upon the fate of the Polar Party, whose diet was seriously deficient in, if not absolutely free from vitamins. The importance of this deficiency to the future explorer can hardly be exaggerated, and I suggest that no future Antarctic sledge party can ever set out to travel inland again without food which contains these vitamins. It is to be noticed that, although the Medical Research Council's authoritative publication on the true value of these accessory substances was not available when we went South in 1910, yet Atkinson insisted that fresh onions, which had been brought down by the ship, be added to our ration for the Search Journey. Compare recent work of Professor Leonard Hill on the value of ultra-violet rays in compensating for lack of vitamins. A. C.-G.

feet. There proved to be no great difficulty about it; it was just a matter of legs and breath.

They were a cheery company, part-singing in the evenings and working hard all day. It was an uneventful trip, Debenham said, and very harmonious: the best trip he had down there. Both Debenham and Dickason suffered from mountain sickness, however, and they were the two smokers! The clearness of the air was marked. At 5000 feet they could plainly see Mount Melbourne and Cape Jones, between two and three hundred miles away, and several uncharted mountains over to the west, but they were unable to plot them accurately because they could get direction rays from one point only. The Sound itself was covered by cloud most of the time, but Beaufort Island and Franklin Island were clear. Unlike David's party, they could see no signs whatever of volcanic action on Mount Bird, which is almost entirely covered with ice on which it was to be expected that some mark might be left. At 9000 feet Terror looked very imposing, but Mount Bird and Terra Nova were insignificant and uninteresting. The valley between the old crater and the slopes of the second crater greatly impressed them, and they found a fine little crevassed glacier in it. Both Priestley and Debenham are of opinion that it is possible to get to Terror by this valley, and that there are no crevassed areas or impossible slopes on the way. All the same it would probably be more sensible to go from Cape Crozier.

At a point about 9000 feet up, Priestley, Gran, Abbott and Hooper started to make the ascent to the active crater on 10 December. They packed the tent, poles, bags, inner cooker and cooking gear, with four days' provisions, and reached the second crater at about 11,500 feet, to be hung up by cloud all the next day. At these altitudes the temperature varied between −10° and −30°, though at sea-level simultaneously they were round about freezing-point. By 1 a.m. on the 12th the conditions were good − clear, with a southerly wind blowing the steam away from the summit. The party got away as soon as possible and reached the lip of the active crater in a few hours. Looking down they were unable to see the bottom, for it was full of steam: the sides sloped at a steep angle for some 500 feet, when they became sheer precipices: the opening appeared to be about 14,000 paces round. The top is mostly pumice, but there is also a lot of kenyte, much the same as at sea-level: the old crater was mostly kenyte, proving that this is the oldest rock of the island: felspar crystals must be continually thrown out, for they were lying about on the top of the snow; I have one nearly 3½ inches long.

Two men went back to the camp, for one had a frost-bitten foot. This left Priestley and Gran, who tried to boil the hypsometer but failed owing to the wind, which was variable and enveloped them from time to time in steam and sulphur vapour. They left a record on a cairn and started to return. But when they had got 500 feet down Priestley found that he had left a tin of exposed films on the top instead of the record. Gran said he would go back and change it. He had reached the top when there was a loud explosion: large blocks of pumice were hurled out with a big smoke cloud; probably a big bubble had burst. Gran was in the middle of it, heard it gurgle before it burst, saw 'blocks of pumiceous lava, in shape like the halves of volcanic bombs, and with bunches of long, drawn-out, hair-like shreds of glass in their interior.'[7] This was Pélé's hair. Gran was a bit sick from sulphur dioxide fumes afterwards. They reached Cape Royds on the 16th, the very successful trip taking fifteen days.

Meanwhile Shackleton's old hut was very pleasant at this time of year: in winter it was a bit too draughty. With bright sunlight, a lop on the sea which splashed and gurgled under the ice-foot, the beautiful mountains all round us, and the penguins nesting at our door, this was better than the Beardmore Glacier, where we had expected to be at this date. What then must it have been to the six men who were just returned from the very Gate of Hell? And the food:

7. *Scott's Last Expedition*, vol. ii, p. 356.

Truly Shackleton's men must have fed like turkey-cocks from all the delicacies here: boiled chicken, kidneys, mushrooms, ginger, Garibaldi biscuits, soups of all kinds: it is a splendid change. Best of all are the fresh-buttered skua's eggs which we make for breakfast. In fact, life is bearable with all that has been unknown so long at last cleared up, and our anxieties for Campbell's party laid at rest.[8]

For three weeks I worked among the Adélie penguins at Cape Royds, and obtained a complete series of their embryos. It was always Wilson's idea that embryology was the next job of a vertebral zoologist down south. I have already explained that the penguin is an interesting link in the evolutionary chain, and the object of getting this embryo is to find out where the penguins come in.[9] Whether or no they are more primitive than other non-flying birds, such as the apteryx, the ostrich, the rhea and the moa, which last is only just extinct, is an open question. But wingless birds are still hanging on to the promontories of the southern continents, where there is less rivalry than in the highly populated land areas of the north. It may be that penguins are descended from ancestors who lived in the northern hemisphere in a winged condition (even now you may sometimes see them try to fly), and that they have been driven towards the south.

If penguins are primitive, it is rational to infer that the most primitive penguin is farthest south. These are the two Antarcticists, the Emperor and the Adélie. The latter appears to be the more numerous and successful of the two, and for this reason we are inclined to search among the Emperors as being among the most primitive penguins, if not the most primitive of birds now living: hence the Winter Journey. I was glad to get, in addition, this series of Adélie penguins' embryos, feeling somewhat like a giant who had wandered

8. My own diary.   9. See pp. 238–9.

on to the wrong planet, and who was distinctly in the way of its true inhabitants.

We returned too late to see the eggs laid, and therefore it was impossible to tell how old the embryos were. My hopes rose, however, when I saw some eggless nests with penguins sitting upon them, but later I found that these were used as bachelor quarters by birds whose wives were sitting near. I tried taking eggs from nests and was delighted to find that new eggs appeared: these I carefully marked, and it was not until I opened one two days later to find inside an embryo at least two weeks old, that I realized that penguins added baby-snatching to their other immoralities. Some of those from whom I took eggs sat upon stones of a similar size and shape with every appearance of content: one sat upon the half of the red tin of a Dutch cheese. They are not very intelligent.

All the world loves a penguin: I think it is because in many respects they are like ourselves, and in some respects what we should like to be. Had we but half their physical courage none could stand against us. Had we a hundredth part of their maternal instinct we should have to kill our children by the thousand. Their little bodies are so full of curiosity that they have no room for fear. They like mountaineering, and joy-riding on ice-floes: they even like to drill.

One day there had been a blizzard, and lying open to the view of all was a deserted nest, a pile of coveted stones. All the surrounding rookery made their way to and fro, each husband acquiring merit, for, after each journey, he gave his wife a stone. This was the plebeian way of doing things; but my friend who stood, ever so unconcerned, upon a rock knew a trick worth two of that: he and his wife who sat so cosily upon the other side.

The victim was a third penguin. He was without a mate, but this was an opportunity to get one. With all the speed his little legs could compass he ran to and fro, taking stones from the deserted nest, laying them beneath a rock, and hurrying back for more. On that same rock was my friend. When the victim came up with his stone he had his back turned. But as soon as the stone was laid and the other gone for more, he jumped down, seized it with his beak, ran round, gave it to his wife and was back on the rock (with his back turned) before you could say Killer Whale. Every now and then he looked over his shoulder, to see where the next stone might be.

I watched this for twenty minutes. All that time, and I do not know for how long before, that wretched bird was bringing stone after stone. And there were no stones there. Once he looked puzzled, looked up and swore at the back of my friend on his rock, but immediately he came back, and he never seemed to think he had better stop. It was getting cold and I went away: he was coming for another.

The life of an Adélie penguin is one of the most unchristian and successful in the world. The penguin which went in for being a true believer would never stand the ghost of a chance. Watch them go to bathe. Some fifty or sixty agitated birds are gathered upon the ice-foot, peering over the edge, telling one another how nice it will be, and what a good dinner they are going to have. But this is all swank: they are really worried by a horrid suspicion that a sea-leopard is waiting to eat the first to dive. The really noble bird, according to our theories, would say, 'I will go first and if I am killed I shall at any rate have died unselfishly, sacrificing my life for my companions'; and in time all the most noble birds would be dead. What they really do is to try and persuade a companion of weaker mind to plunge: failing this, they hastily pass a conscription act and push him over. And then – bang, helter-skelter, in go all the rest.

They take turns in sitting on their eggs, and after many days the fathers may be seen waddling down towards the sea with their shirt fronts muddied, their long trick done. It may be a fortnight before they return, well-fed, clean, pleased with life, and with a grim determination to relieve their wives, to do their job. Sometimes they are met by others going to bathe. They stop and pass the time of day. Well! Perhaps it would be more pleasant, and what does a day or two matter anyhow. They turn; clean and dirty alike are off to the seaside again. This is when they say, 'The women are splendid.'

Life is too strenuous for them to have any use for the virtues of brotherly love, good works, charity and benevolence. When they mate the best thief wins: when they nest the best pair of thieves hatch out their eggs. In a long unbroken stream, which stretches down below the sea-ice horizon, they march in from the open sea. Some are walking on their human feet: others tobogganing upon their shiny white breasts. After their long walk they must have a sleep, and then the gentlemen make their way into the already crowded rookery to find them wives. But first a suitor must find, or steal, a pebble, for such are the penguin jewels: they are of lava, black, russet or grey, with almond-shaped crystals bedded in them. They are rare and of all sizes, but that which is most valued is the size of a pigeon's egg. Armed with one of these he courts his maid, laying it at her feet. If accepted he steals still more stones: she guards them jealously, taking in the meantime any safe opportunity to pick others from under her nearest neighbours. Any penguin which is unable to fight and steal successfully fails to make a good high nest, or loses it when made. Then comes a blizzard, and after that a thaw: for it thaws sometimes right down by the sea-shore where the Adélies have their nurseries. The eggs of the strong and wicked hatch out, but those of the weak are addled. You must have a jolly good pile of stones to hatch eggs after a blizzard like that in December 1911, when the rookeries were completely snow-covered: nests, eggs, parents and all.

Once hatched the chicks grow quickly from pretty grey atoms of down to black lumps of stomach topped by a small and quite inadequate head. They are two or more weeks old, and they leave their parents, or their parents leave them, I do not know which. If socialism be the nationalization of the means of production and distribution, then they are socialists. They divide into parents and children. The adult community comes up from the open sea, bringing food inside them: they are full of half-digested shrimps. But not for their own children: these, if not already dead, are lost in a crowd of hungry tottering infants which besiege each food-provider as he arrives. But not all of them can get food, though all of them are hungry. Some have already been behindhand too long: they have not managed to secure food for days, and they are weak and cold and very weary.

As we stood there and watched this race for food we were gradually possessed with the idea that the chicks looked upon each adult coming up full-bellied from the shore as not a parent only, but a food-supply. The parents were labouring under a totally different idea, and intended either to find their own infants and feed them, or else to assimilate their already partially digested catch themselves. The more robust of the young thus worried an adult until, because of his importunity, he was fed. But with the less robust a much more pathetic ending was the rule. A chick that had fallen behind in this literal race for life, starving and weak, and getting daily weaker because it could not run fast enough to insist on being fed, again and again ran off pursuing with the rest. Again and again it stumbled and fell, persistently whining out its hunger in a shrill and melancholy pipe, till at last the race was given up. Forced thus by sheer exhaustion to stop and rest, it had no chance of getting food. Each hurrying parent with its little following of hungry chicks, intent on one thing only, rushed quickly by, and the starveling dropped behind to gather strength for one more effort. Again it fails, a robuster bird has forced the pace, and again success is wanting to the runt. Sleepily it stands there, with half-shut eyes, in a torpor resulting from exhaustion, cold, and hunger, wondering perhaps what all the bustle round it means, a little dirty, dishevelled dot, in the race for life a failure, deserted by its parents, who have hunted vainly for their own offspring round the nest in which they hatched it, but from which it may by now have wandered half a mile. And so it stands, lost to everything around, till a skua in its beat drops down beside

it, and with a few strong, vicious pecks puts an end to the
failing life.[10]

There is a great deal to be said for this kind of treatment.
The Adélie penguin has a hard life: the Emperor penguin a
horrible one. Why not kill off the unfit right away, before
they have had time to breed, almost before they have had
time to eat? Life is a stern business in any case: why pretend
that it is anything else? Or that any but the best can survive
at all? And in consequence, I challenge you to find a more
jolly, happy, healthy lot of old gentlemen in the world. We
must admire them: if only because they are so much nicer
than ourselves! But it is grim: Nature is an uncompromising
nurse.

Nature was going to give us a bad time too if we were not
relieved, and on 17 January, as there were still no signs of the
ship, it was decided to prepare for another winter. We were
to go on rations; to cook with oil, for nearly all the coal was
gone; to kill and store up seal. On 18 January we started our
preparations, digging a cave to store more meat, and so forth.
I went off seal hunting after breakfast, and having killed and
cut up two, came back across the Cape at midday. All the
men were out working in the camp. There was nothing to be
seen in the Sound, and then, quite suddenly, the bows of the
ship came out from behind the end of the Barne Glacier, two
or three miles away. We watched her cautious approach with
immense relief.

'Are you all well,' through a megaphone from the bridge.
'The Polar Party died on their return from the Pole: we
have their records.' A pause and then a boat.

Evans, who had been to England and made a good
recovery from scurvy, was in command: with him were
Pennell, Rennick, Bruce, Lillie and Drake. They reported
having had a very big gale indeed on their way home last
year.

We got some apples off the ship, 'beauties, I want nothing

10. Wilson, *Nat. Ant. Exp., 1901–1904*, 'Zoology', part ii, pp. 44–5.

better. . . . Pennell is first-class, as always. . . .' 'One notices among the ship's men a rather unnatural way of talking: not so much in special instances, but as a whole, contact with civilization gives it an affected sound: I notice it in both officers and men.'[11]

January 19. *On board the Terra Nova.* After 28 hours' loading we left the old hut for good and all at 4 p.m. this afternoon. It has been a bit of a rush and little sleep last night. It is quite wonderful now to be travelling a day's journey in an hour: we went to Cape Royds in about that time and took off geological and zoological specimens. I should like to sit up and sketch all these views, which would have meant long travelling without the ship, but I feel very tired. The mail is almost too good for words. Now, with the latest waltz on the gramophone, beer for dinner and apples and fresh vegetables to eat, life is more bearable than it has been for many a long weary week and month. I leave Cape Evans with no regret: I never want to see the place again. The pleasant memories are all swallowed up in the bad ones.[12]

Before the ship arrived it was decided among us to urge the erection of a cross on Observation Hill to the memory of the Polar Party. On the arrival of the ship the carpenter immediately set to work to make a great cross of jarrah wood. There was some discussion as to the inscription, it being urged that there should be some quotation from the Bible because 'the women think a lot of these things'. But I was glad to see the concluding line of Tennyson's 'Ulysses' adopted: 'To strive, to seek, to find, and not to yield.'

The open water stretched about a mile and a half south of Tent Island, and here we left the ship to sledge the cross to Hut Point at 8 a.m. on 20 January. The party consisted of Atkinson, Wright, Lashly, Crean, Debenham, Keohane and Davies, the ship's carpenter and myself.

11. My own diary.   12. ibid.

Evening. Hut Point. We had a most unpleasant experience coming in. We struck wind and drift just about a mile from Hut Point: then we saw there was a small thaw pool off the Point, and came out to give it a wide berth. Atkinson put his feet down into water: we turned sharp out, and then Crean went right in up to his arms, and we realized that the ice was not more than three or four inches of slush. I managed to give him a hand out without the ice giving, and we went on floundering about. Then Crean went right in again, and the sledge nearly went too: we pulled the sledge, and the sledge pulled him out. Except for some more soft patches that was all, but it was quite enough. I think we got out of it most fortunately.

Crean got some dry clothes here, and the cross has had a coat of white paint and is drying. We went up Observation Hill and have found a good spot right on the top, and have already dug a hole which will, with the rock alongside, give us three feet. From there we can see that this year's old ice is in a terrible state, open water and open water slush all over near the land – I have never seen anything like it here. Off Cape Armitage and at the Pram Point pressure it is extra bad. I only hope we can find a safe way back.

You would not think Crean had had such a pair of duckings to hear him talking so merrily tonight . . .

I really do think the cross is going to look fine.[13]

Observation Hill was clearly the place for it, it knew them all so well. Three of them were *Discovery* men who lived three years under its shadow: they had seen it time after time as they came back from hard journeys on the Barrier: Observation Hill and Castle Rock were the two which always welcomed them in. It commanded McMurdo Sound on one side, where they had lived: and the Barrier on the other, where they had died. No more fitting pedestal, a pedestal which in itself is nearly 1000 feet high, could have been found.

13. ibid.

Tuesday, January 22. Rousing out at 6 a.m. we got the large piece of the cross up Observation Hill by 11 a.m. It was a heavy job, and the ice was looking very bad all round, and I for one was glad when we had got it up by 5 o'clock or so. It is really magnificent, and will be a permanent memorial which could be seen from the ship nine miles off with a naked eye. It stands nine feet out of the rocks, and many feet into the ground, and I do not believe it will ever move. When it was up, facing out over the Barrier, we gave three cheers and one more.

We got back to the ship all right and coasted up the Western Mountains to Granite Harbour; a wonderfully interesting trip to those of us who had only seen these mountains from a distance. Gran went off to pick up a depot of geological specimens. Lillie did a trawl.

This was an absorbing business, though it was only one of a long and important series made during the voyages of the *Terra Nova*. Here were all kinds of sponges, siliceous, glass rope, tubular, and they were generally covered with mucus. Some fed on diatoms so minute that they can only be collected by centrifuge: some have gastric juices to dissolve the siliceous skeletons of the diatoms on which they feed: they anchor themselves in the mud and pass water in and out of their bodies: sometimes the current is stimulated by cilia. There were colonies of Gorgonacea, which share their food unselfishly; and corals and marine degenerate worms, which started to live in little cells like coral, but have gone down in the world. And there were starfishes, sea-urchins, brittle-stars, feather-stars and sea-cucumbers. The sea-urchins are formed of hexagonal plates, the centre of each of which is a ball, upon which a spine works on a ball and socket joint. These spines are used for protection, and when large they can be used for locomotion. But the real means of locomotion are five double rows of water-tube feet, working by suction, by which they withdraw the water inside a receptacle in the shell, thereby forming a vacuum; starfishes do the same. We found a species of sea-urchin which had such large spines that they practically formed bars; the spines were twice as long as the sea-urchin and shaped just like oars, being even fluted. A lobster grows by discarding his suit, hiding and getting another, growing meanwhile. A snail or an oyster retains his original shell, and adds to it in layers all the way down, increasing one edge. But our sea-urchin grows by an increment of calcareous matter all round the outside of each plate. As the animal grows the plates get bigger.

There was a sea-cucumber which nurses its young, having a brood cavity which is really formed out of the mouth: this is a peculiarity of a new Antarctic genus found first on the *Discovery*. It has the most complex watertubes, which it uses as legs, and a few limy rods in its soft skin instead of the bony calcareous plates of sea-urchins and starfish. After them came the feather-stars, a relic of the old crinoids which used to flourish in the carboniferous period, examples of which can be found in the Derbyshire limestone; and there were thousands of brittle-stars, like beautiful wheels of which the hubs and spokes remained, but not the circumstances. These spokes or legs are muscular, sensory and locomotive. They differ from the starfishes in that they have no digestive glands in their legs and from the feather-stars in that they do not use their legs to waft food into their mouths. Once upon a time they had a stalk and were anchored to a rock, and there are still very old rare stalked echinoderms living in the sea. This apparently geological thing was found by Wyville Thomson in 1868 still living in the seas to the north of Scotland, and this find started the *Challenger* Expedition for deep-sea soundings in 1872. But the *Challenger* brought back little in this line. Most of the species we found were peculiar to the Antarctic.

There were Polychaete worms by the hundred, showing the protrusible mouth, which is shoved into the mud and then brought back into the body, and the bristles on the highly developed projections which act as legs, by which they get about the mud. These beasts have apparently given rise to the Arthropods. In a modified and later form they had taken to living in a tube, both for protection and because they found that they could not go through the mud, which had become too viscous for them. So they stand up in a tube and collect the sediment which is falling by means of tentacles. They spread from one locality to another by going through a plankton embryonic stage in their youth. They may be compared to the mason worms, which also build tubes.

But as Lillie squatted on the poop surrounded by an inner ring of jars and tangled masses of the catch, and an outer ring of curious scientists, pseudo-scientists and seamen, no find pleased him so much as the frequent discovery of pieces of *Cephalodiscus rarus*, of which even now there are but some four jars full in the world. It is as interesting as it is uncommon, for its ancestor was a link between the vertebrates and invertebrates, though no one knows what it was like. It has been a vertebrate and gone back, and now has the signs of a notochord in early life, and it also has gills. First found on the Graham's Land side of the Antarctic continent, it has only recently been discovered in the Ross Sea, and occurs nowhere else in the world so far as is known.

We left Granite Harbour in the early morning of 23 January, and started to make our way out. Our next job was to pick up the geological specimens at Evans Coves, where Campbell and his men had wintered in the igloo, and also to leave a depot there for future explorers. We met very heavy pack, having to return at least twelve miles and try another way.

The sea has been freezing out here, which seems an extraordinary thing at this time of year. There was a thin layer of ice over the water between the floes this morning, and I feel sure that most of these big level floes, of which we have seen several, are the remains of ice which has frozen comparatively recently.[14]

14. My own diary.

The propeller had a bad time, constantly catching up on ice. At length we were some thirty miles north of Cape Bird making roughly towards Franklin Island. That night we made good progress in fairly open water, and we passed Franklin Island during the day. But the outlook was so bad in the evening (24 January) that we stopped and banked fires.

We lay just where we stopped until at 5 a.m. on January 25, when the ice eased up sufficiently for us to get along, and we started to make the same slow progress – slow ahead, stop (to the engine-room) – bump and grind for a bit – then slow astern, stop – slow ahead again, and so on, until at 7 p.m., after one real big bump which brought the dinner some inches off the table, Cheetham brought us out into open water.[15]

Mount Nansen rose sheer and massive ahead of us with a table top, and at 3 a.m. on 26 January we were passing the dark brown granite headland of the northern foothills. We were soon made fast to a stretch of some 500 yards of thick sea-ice, upon which the wind had not left a particle of snow, and before us the foothills formed that opening which Campbell had well named Hell's Gate.

I wish I had seen that igloo: with its black and blubber and beastliness. Those who saw it came back with faces of amazement and admiration. We left a depot at the head of the bay, marked with a bamboo and a flag, and then we turned homewards, counting the weeks, and days, and then the hours. In the early hours of 27 January we left the pack. On 29 January we were off Cape Adare, 'head sea, and wind, and fog, very ticklish work groping along hardly seeing the ship's length. Then it lifts and there is a fair horizon. Everybody pretty sea-sick, including most of the seamen from Cape Evans. All of us feeling rotten.'[16] Very thick that night, and difficult going. At midday (lat. 69° 50′ S.) a partial clearance showed a berg right ahead. By night it was blowing a full

15. ibid.   16. ibid.

gale, and it was not too easy to keep in our bunks. Our object was now to make east in order to allow for the westerlies later on. We passed a very large number of bergs, varied every now and then by growlers. On 1 February, latitude 64° 15′ S. and longitude 159° 15′ E., we coasted along one side of a berg which was twenty-one geographical miles long; the only other side of which we got a good view stretched away until lost below the horizon. In latitude 62° 10′ S. and longitude 158° 15′ E. we had

a real bad day: head wind from early morning, and simply crowds of bergs all round. At 8 a.m. we had to wedge in between a berg and a long line of pack before we could find a way through. Then thick fog came down. At 9.45 a.m. I went out of the ward-room door, and almost knocked my head against a great berg which was just not touching the ship on the starboard side. There was a heavy cross-swell, and the sea sounded cold as it dashed against the ice. After crossing the deck it was just possible to see in the fog that there was a great Barrier berg just away on the port side.

We groped round the starboard berg to find others beyond. Our friend on the opposite side was continuous and apparently without end. It was soon clear that we were in a narrow alley-way – between one very large berg and a number of others. It took an hour and a quarter of groping to leave the big berg behind. At 4 p.m., six hours later, we were still just feeling our way along. And we had hopes of being out of the ice in this latitude!

The *Terra Nova* is a wood barque, built in 1884 by A. Stephen & Sons, Dundee; tonnage 764 gross and 400 net; measuring 187′ × 31′ × 19′; compound engines with two cylinders of 140 nominal horse-power; registered at St Johns, Newfoundland. She is therefore not by any means small as polar ships go, but Pennell and his men worked her short-handed, with bergs and growlers all round them, generally with a big sea running and often in darkness or fog. On this occasion we were spared many of the most ordinary dangers.

It was summer. Our voyage was an easy one. There was twilight most of the night: there were plenty of men on board, and heaps of coal. Imagine then what kind of time Pennell and his ship's company had in late autumn, after remaining in the south until only a bare ration of coal was left for steaming, until the sea was freezing round them and the propeller brought up dead as they tried to force their way through it. Pennell was a very sober person in his statements, yet he described the gale through which the *Terra Nova* passed on her way to New Zealand in March 1912 as seeming to blow the ship from the top of one wave to the top of the next; and the nights were dark, and the bergs were all round them. They never tried to lay a meal in those days, they just ate what they could hold in their hands. He confessed to me that one hour he did begin to wonder what was going to happen next: others told me that he seemed to enjoy every minute of it all.

Owing to press contracts and the necessity of preventing leakage of news the *Terra Nova* had to remain at sea for twenty-four hours after a cable had been sent to England. Also it was of the first importance that the relatives should be informed of the facts before the newspapers published them.

And so at 2.30 a.m. on 10 February we crept like a phantom ship into the little harbour of Oamaru on the east coast of New Zealand. With what mixed feelings we smelt the old familiar woods and grassy slopes, and saw the shadowy outlines of human homes. With untiring persistence the little lighthouse blinked out the message, 'What ship's that?' 'What ship's that?' They were obviously puzzled and disturbed at getting no answer. A boat was lowered and Pennell and Atkinson were rowed ashore and landed. The seamen had strict orders to answer no questions. After a little the boat returned, and Crean announced: 'We was chased, sorr, but they got nothing out of us.'

We put out to sea.

When morning broke we could see the land in the distance – greenness, trees, every now and then a cottage. We began to feel impatient. We unpacked the shore-going clothes with their creases three years old which had been sent out from home, tried them on – and they felt unpleasantly tight. We put on our boots, and they were positively agony. We shaved off our beards! There was a hiatus. There was nothing to do but sail up and down the coast and, if possible, avoid coastwise craft.

In the evening the little ship which runs daily from Akaroa to Lyttelton put out to sea on her way and ranged close alongside. 'Are all well?' 'Where's Captain Scott?' 'Did you reach the Pole?' Rather unsatisfactory answers and away they went. Our first glimpse, however, of civilised life.

At dawn the next morning, with white ensign at half-mast, we crept through Lyttelton Heads. Always we looked for trees, people and houses. How different it was from the day we left and yet how much the same: as though we had dreamed some horrible nightmare and could scarcely believe we were not dreaming still.

The Harbour-master came out in the tug and with him Atkinson and Pennell. 'Come down here a minute,' said Atkinson to me, and 'It's made a tremendous impression, I had no idea it would make so much,' he said. And indeed we had been too long away, and the whole thing was so personal to us, and our perceptions had been blunted: we never realized. We landed to find the Empire – almost the civilized world – in mourning. It was as though they had lost great friends.

To a sensitive pre-war world the knowledge of these men's deaths came as a great shock: and now, although the world has almost lost the sense of tragedy, it appeals to their pity and their pride. The disaster may well be the first thing which Scott's name recalls to your mind (as though an event occurred in the life of Columbus which caused you to forget that he discovered America); but Scott's reputation is not founded upon the conquest of the South Pole. He came to a new continent, found out how to travel there, and gave knowledge of it to the world: he discovered the Antarctic, and founded a school. He is the last of the great geographical explorers: it is useless to try and light a fire when everything has been burned; and he is probably the last old-fashioned polar explorer, for, as I believe, the future of such exploration is in the air, but not yet. And he was strong: we never realized until we found him lying there dead how strong, mentally and physically, that man was.

In both his polar expeditions he was helped, to an extent which will never be appreciated, by Wilson: in the last expedition by Bowers. I believe that there has never been a finer sledge party than these three men, who combined in themselves initiative, endurance and high ideals to an extra-ordinary degree. And they could organize: they did organize the Polar Journey and their organization seemed to have failed. Did it fail? Scott said No. 'The causes of this disaster are not due to faulty organization, but to misfortune in all risks which had to be undertaken.' Nine times out of ten, says the meteorologist, he would have come through: but he stuck the tenth. 'We took risks, we knew we took them; things have come out against us, and therefore we have no cause for complaint.' No better epitaph has been written.

He decided to use the only route towards the Pole of which the world had any knowledge, that is to go up the Beardmore Glacier, then the only discovered way up through the mountains which divide the polar plateau from the Great Ice Barrier: probably it is the only possible passage for those who travel from McMurdo Sound. The alternative was to winter on the Barrier, as Amundsen did, so many hundred miles away from the coast-line that, in travelling south, the chaos caused in the ice plain by the Beardmore in its outward flow would be avoided. To do so meant the abandonment of a great part of the scientific programme, and Scott was not a man to go south just to reach the Pole. Amundsen knew that Scott was going to McMurdo Sound when he decided to winter in the Bay of Whales: otherwise he might have gone to McMurdo Sound. Probably no man would have refused the knowledge which had already been gained.

I have said that there are those who say that Scott should have relied on ski and dogs. If you read Shackleton's account of his discovery and passage of the Beardmore Glacier you will not be prejudiced in favour of dogs: and as a matter of fact, though we found a much better way up than Shackleton, I do not believe it possible to take dogs up and down, and over the ice disturbances at the junction with the plateau, unless there is ample time to survey a route, if then. 'Dogs could certainly have come up as far as this,' I heard Scott say somewhere under the Cloudmaker, approximately half-way up the glacier, but the best thing you could do with the dogs in pressure such as we all experienced on our way down would be to drop them into the nearest chasm. If you can avoid such messes well and good: if not, you must not rely on dogs, and the people who talk of these things have no knowledge.

If Scott was going up the Beardmore he was probably right not to take dogs: actually he relied on ponies to the foot of the glacier and man-haulage on from that point. Because he relied on ponies he was not able to start before November: the experience of the Depot Journey showed that ponies could not stand the weather conditions before that date. But he could have started earlier if he had taken dogs, in place of ponies, to the foot of the glacier. This would have gained him a few days in his race against the Autumn conditions when returning.

Such tragedies inevitably raise the question, 'Is it worth it?' What is worth what? Is life worth risking for a feat, or losing for your country? To face a thing because it was a feat, and only a feat, was not very attractive to Scott: it had to contain an additional object – knowledge. A feat had even less attraction for Wilson, and it is a most noteworthy thing in the diaries which are contained in this book, that he made no comment when he found that the Norwegians were first at the Pole: it is as though he felt that it did not really matter, as indeed it probably did not.

It is most desirable that someone should tackle these and kindred questions about polar life. There is a wealth of matter in polar psychology: there are unique factors here, especially the complete isolation, and four months' darkness every year.

Even in Mesopotamia a long-suffering nation insisted at last that adequate arrangements must be made to nurse and evacuate the sick and wounded. But at the Poles a man must make up his mind that he may be rotting of scurvy (as Evans was) or living for ten months on half-rations of seal and full rations of ptomaine poisoning (as Campbell and his men were) but no help can reach him from the outside world for a year, if then. There is no chance of a 'cushy' wound: if you break your leg on the Beardmore you must consider the most expedient way of committing suicide, both for your own sake and that of your companions.

Both sexually and socially the polar explorer must make up his mind to be starved. To what extent can hard work, or what may be called dramatic imagination, provide a substitute? Compare our thoughts on the march; our food dreams at night; the primitive way in which the loss of a crumb of biscuit may give a lasting sense of grievance. Night after night I bought big buns and chocolate at a stall on the island platform at Hatfield station, but always woke before I got a mouthful to my lips; some companions who were not so highly strung were more fortunate, and ate their phantom meals.

And the darkness, accompanied it may be almost continually by howling blizzards which prevent you seeing your hand before your face. Life in such surroundings is both mentally and physically cramped; open-air exercise is restricted and in blizzards quite impossible, and you realize how much you lose by your inability to see the world about you when you are out-of-doors. I am told that when confronted by a lunatic or one who under the influence of some great grief or shock contemplates suicide, you should take that man out-of-doors and walk him about: Nature will do the rest. To normal people like ourselves living under abnormal circumstances Nature could do much to lift our thoughts out of the rut of everyday affairs, but she loses much of her healing power when she cannot be seen, but only felt, and when that feeling is intensely uncomfortable.

Somehow in judging polar life you must discount compulsory endurance; and find out what a man can shirk, remembering always that it is a sledging life which is the hardest test. It is because it is so much easier to shirk in civilization that it is difficult to get a standard of what your average man can do. It does not really matter much whether your man whose work lies in or round the hut shirks a bit or not, just as it does not matter much in civilization: it is just rather a waste of opportunity. But there's precious little shirking in Barrier sledging: a week finds most of us out.

There are many questions which ought to be studied. The effect upon men of going from heat to cold, such as Bowers coming to us from the Persian Gulf: or vice versa of Simpson returning from the Antarctic to India; differences of dry and damp cold; what is a comfortable temperature in the Antarctic and what is it compared to a comfortable temperature in England, the question of women in these temperatures. . . .? The man with the nerves goes farthest. What is the ratio between nervous and physical energy? What is vitality? Why do some things terrify you at one time and not at others? What is this early morning courage? What is the influence of imagination? How far can a man draw on his capital? Whence came Bowers's great heat supply? And my own white beard? and X's blue eyes: for he started from England with brown ones and his mother refused to own him when he came back? Growth and colour change in hair and skin?

There are many reasons which send men to the Poles, and the Intellectual Force uses them all. But the desire for knowledge for its own sake is the one which really counts and there is no field for the collection of knowledge which at the present time can be compared to the Antarctic.

Exploration is the physical expression of the Intellectual Passion.

And I tell you, if you have the desire for knowledge and the power to give it physical expression, go out and explore. If you are a brave man you will do nothing: if you are fearful you may do much, for none but cowards have need to prove their bravery. Some will tell you that you are mad, and nearly all will say, 'What is the use?' For we are a nation of shopkeepers, and no shopkeeper will look at research which does not promise him a financial return within a year. And so you will sledge nearly alone, but those with whom you sledge will not be shopkeepers: that is worth a good deal. If you march your Winter Journeys you will have your reward, so long as all you want is a penguin's egg.

Glossary

Blizzard: An Antarctic blizzard is a high southerly wind generally accompanied by clouds of drifting snow, partly falling from above, partly picked up from the surface. In the daylight of summer a tent cannot be seen a few yards off: in the darkness of winter it is easy to be lost within a few feet of a hut. There is no doubt that a blizzard has a bewildering and numbing effect upon the brain of anyone exposed to it.

Brash: Small ice fragments from a floe which is breaking up.

Cloud: The commonest form of cloud, and also that typical of blizzard conditions, was a uniform pall stretching all over the sky without distinction. This was logged by us as *stratus*. *Cumulus* clouds are the woolly billows, flat below and rounded on top, which are formed by local ascending currents of air. They were rare in the south and only formed over open water or mountains. *Cirrus* are the 'mare's tails' and similar wispy clouds which float high in the atmosphere. These and their allied forms were common. Generally speaking, the clouds were due to stratification of the air into layers rather than to ascending currents.

Crusts: Layers of snow in a snow-field with air space between them.

Finnesko: Boots made entirely of fur, soles and all.

Frost Smoke: Condensed water vapour which forms a mist over open sea in cold weather.

Ice-foot: Fringes of ice which skirt many parts of the Antarctic shores: many of them have been formed by sea-spray.

Nunatak: An island of land in a snow-field. Buckley Island is the top of a mountain sticking out of the top of the Beardmore Glacier.

Piedmont: Stretches of ancient ice which remain along the Antarctic coasts.

Pram: A Norwegian skiff, with a spoon bow.

Saennegrass: A kind of Norwegian hay used as packing in finnesko.

Sastrugi are the furrows or irregularities formed on a snow plain by the wind. They may be a foot or more deep and as hard and as slippery as ice: they may be quite soft: they may appear as great inverted pudding bowls: they may be hard knots covered with soft powdery snow.

Sledging Distances: All miles are geographical miles unless otherwise stated. 1 statute or English mile = 0.87 geographical mile: 1 geographical mile = 1.15 statute miles.

Tank: A canvas 'hold-all' strapped to the sledge to contain food bags.

Tide Crack: A working crack between the land ice and the sea ice which rises and falls with the tide.

Wind: Wind forces are logged according to the Beaufort scale, which is as follows:

No.	Description	Mean velocity in miles per hour
0	Calm	0
1	Light air	1
2	Light breeze	4
3	Gentle breeze	9
4	Moderate breeze	14
5	Fresh breeze	20
6	Strong breeze	26
7	Moderate gale	33
8	Fresh gale	42
9	Strong gale	51
10	Whole gale	62
11	Storm	75
12	Hurricane	92

Index

Abbott, George P., xx, 577

Adam Mountains, 375

Adare, Cape, 423, 590

Adélie penguin. *See* Penguin, Adélie

Albatross, capture of, 38

Alexandra, Queen, 522

Amundsen, Roald, telegram to Scott 40; arrives in Bay of Whales, 131; character, 137–8; letter to King of Norway, 508; forestalls Scott at Pole, 522; reason of success, 563–4

Antarctic Adventure (Priestley), xxvi

Anton (pony boy), 229, 444

Aptenodytes forsteri. See Penguin, Emperor

Archer, W. W., 444, 453, 488

Arethusa. See Portuguese man-of-war

Armitage, Cape, 111, 586

Arrival Heights, 100, 189

Atkinson, Edward L., and dog-food depot, xxxi; on the *Terra Nova* 3; character, 4; on South Trinidad, 18–20; accident to foot, 113; lecture on scurvy, 219–20; lost in blizzard, 314–5; Barrier Journey, 334; in command of First Return Party, 394; meets Lashly and Evans, 418; difficulties during Scott's absence, 425–6; attempts to find Scott, 439–40; in command of Main Party, 441; journey to Hutton Cliffs, 443; sledge journey, 446; fish-

trap, 459; spring journey, 483; reads Burial Service over Scott, 496–7; on diet, 574, 575 n.; lands in New Zealand, 592

Atmosphere, observations on, 33–4

Aurora borealis, 250

Balloon Bight, 133

Barne Glacier, 188, 317, 417

Barré, Cendron and Imbert, xx

Barrie, Sir J. M., visits Cherry-Garrard, xxii; Scott's letter to, 557

Barrier, the, first arrival at, 82; Scott's paper on, 219; snow surface, 245; Wright's lecture, 471; movement, 484

Beardmore Glacier, journey across, 363–81

Beaufort Island, 577

Bernacchi, Cape, 446

Biology, marine, *Terra Nova* observations, 6–7, 587 ff

Bird, Mt., 577

—Peninsula, 423

Biscuit Depot, 484

Blacksand Beach, 102

Blizzards, 115–6, 462–3

Bluff Depot, 116, 122, 432

Bowers, Lieut. H. R., on ice-floe with Cherry-Garrard, xiv; on *Terra Nova*, 3; character and personality, 4, 212–3, 214–5; at South Trinidad, 16–17; on Depot Journey, 108–9; on Winter Journey, 239; trip to Western Mountains, 316;

601